(R)evolutionizing Political Communication through Social Media

Tomaž Deželan
University of Ljubljana, Slovenia

Igor Vobič
University of Ljubljana, Slovenia

A volume in the Advances in Public Policy and Administration (APPA) Book Series

Information Science REFERENCE
An Imprint of IGI Global

Published in the United States of America by
Information Science Reference (an imprint of IGI Global)
701 E. Chocolate Avenue
Hershey PA, USA 17033
Tel: 717-533-8845
Fax: 717-533-8661
E-mail: cust@igi-global.com
Web site: http://www.igi-global.com

Library of Congress Cataloging-in-Publication Data

Names: Dezelan, Tomaz, editor. | Vobic, Igor, 1982- editor.
Title: (R)evolutionizing political communication through social media / Tomaz Dezelan and Igor Vobic, editors.
Other titles: Evolutionizing political communications through social media
Description: Hershey : Information Science Reference, 2016. | Includes bibliographical references and index.
Identifiers: LCCN 2015046889| ISBN 9781466698796 (hardcover) | ISBN 9781466698802 (ebook)
Subjects: LCSH: Social media--Political aspects. | Political participation. | Communication in politics.
Classification: LCC HM741 .R48 2016 | DDC 302.23/1--dc23 LC record available at http://lccn.loc.gov/2015046889

This book is published in the IGI Global book series Advances in Public Policy and Administration (APPA) (ISSN: Pending; eISSN: Pending)

British Cataloguing in Publication Data
A Cataloguing in Publication record for this book is available from the British Library.

All work contributed to this book is new, previously-unpublished material. The views expressed in this book are those of the authors, but not necessarily of the publisher.

For electronic access to this publication, please contact: eresources@igi-global.com.

Advances in Public Policy and Administration (APPA) Book Series

ISSN: Pending
EISSN: Pending

Mission

Proper management of the public sphere is necessary in order to maintain order in modern society. Research developments in the field of public policy and administration can assist in uncovering the latest tools, practices, and methodologies for governing societies around the world.

The **Advances in Public Policy and Administration (APPA) Book Series** aims to publish scholarly publications focused on topics pertaining to the governance of the public domain. APPA's focus on timely topics relating to government, public funding, politics, public safety, policy, and law enforcement is particularly relevant to academicians, government officials, and upper-level students seeking the most up-to-date research in their field.

Coverage

- Government
- Law enforcement
- Political Economy
- Politics
- Public Administration
- Public Funding
- Public Policy
- Resource allocation
- Urban Planning

IGI Global is currently accepting manuscripts for publication within this series. To submit a proposal for a volume in this series, please contact our Acquisition Editors at Acquisitions@igi-global.com or visit: http://www.igi-global.com/publish/.

The Advances in Public Policy and Administration (APPA) Book Series (ISSN Pending) is published by IGI Global, 701 E. Chocolate Avenue, Hershey, PA 17033-1240, USA, www.igi-global.com. This series is composed of titles available for purchase individually; each title is edited to be contextually exclusive from any other title within the series. For pricing and ordering information please visit http://www.igi-global.com/book-series/advances-public-policy-administration/97862. Postmaster: Send all address changes to above address.

Titles in this Series

For a list of additional titles in this series, please visit: www.igi-global.com

Handbook of Research on Transitional Justice and Peace Building in Turbulent Regions
Fredy Cante (Universidad del Rosario, Colombia) and Hartmut Quehl (Felsberg Institute, Germany)
Information Science Reference • copyright 2016 • 559pp • H/C (ISBN: 9781466696754) • US $295.00 (our price)

Managing Big Data Integration in the Public Sector
Anil Aggarwal (University of Baltimore, USA)
Information Science Reference • copyright 2016 • 337pp • H/C (ISBN: 9781466696495) • US $205.00 (our price)

Management and Participation in the Public Sphere
Mika Markus Merviö (Kibi International University, Japan)
Information Science Reference • copyright 2015 • 399pp • H/C (ISBN: 9781466685536) • US $200.00 (our price)

Teaching Research Methods in Public Administration
Richard W. Schwester (City University of New York, USA)
Information Science Reference • copyright 2015 • 313pp • H/C (ISBN: 9781466681163) • US $185.00 (our price)

Emergency Management and Disaster Response Utilizing Public-Private Partnerships
Marvine Paula Hamner (LeaTech, LLC, USA) S. Shane Stovall (True North Emergency Management, USA) Doaa M. Taha (GMI, Ltd, USA) and Salah C. Brahimi (GMI, Ltd, USA)
Information Science Reference • copyright 2015 • 345pp • H/C (ISBN: 9781466681590) • US $200.00 (our price)

ICT Adoption and Application in the Malaysian Public Sector
Abdul Raufu Ambali (Universiti Teknologi MARA, Malaysia & Kwara State University Malete, Nigeria) and Ahmad Naqiyuddin Bakar (Universiti Teknologi MARA, Malaysia)
Information Science Reference • copyright 2015 • 316pp • H/C (ISBN: 9781466665798) • US $195.00 (our price)

Human Rights and the Impact of ICT in the Public Sphere Participation, Democracy, and Political Autonomy
Christina M. Akrivopoulou (Hellenic Open University, Greece) and N. Garipidis (Aristotle University of Thessaloniki, Greece)
Information Science Reference • copyright 2014 • 371pp • H/C (ISBN: 9781466662483) • US $185.00 (our price)

Chaos and Complexity Theory in World Politics
Şefika Şule Erçetin (Hacettepe University, Turkey) and Santo Banerjee (University Putra Malaysia, Malaysia)
Information Science Reference • copyright 2014 • 374pp • H/C (ISBN: 9781466660700) • US $210.00 (our price)

IGI GLOBAL
DISSEMINATOR OF KNOWLEDGE
www.igi-global.com

701 E. Chocolate Ave., Hershey, PA 17033
Order online at www.igi-global.com or call 717-533-8845 x100
To place a standing order for titles released in this series, contact: cust@igi-global.com
Mon-Fri 8:00 am - 5:00 pm (est) or fax 24 hours a day 717-533-8661

List of Reviewers

Table of Contents

Section 3
Strategic Communication of Political Actors on Micro-Blogging Outlets and its Ability to Empower Democracy

Section 4
Utilization of Facebook as a Strategic Election Campaign Tool

Detailed Table of Contents

A wide body of evidence shows that the American electorate has become more politically polarized in recent years. There are a wide variety of explanations for this trend, including selective exposure to ideological news sources. This trend corresponds with the increased use of social media for political discussion. There are competing theories regarding whether the spread social media exacerbates or attenuates polarization in the evaluation of political and social groups. The purpose of this chapter is to evaluate these competing claims. This topic is explored using multivariate regression analysis and individual level data from the 2012 American National Election Time Series Study. The findings suggest that social media use actually attenuates rather than drives polarization.

Based on Habermas' public sphere theory, this chapter examined netizens' opinion expression about the "Snowden affair" on two microblogging websites, Twitter and its Chinese counterpart, Sina Weibo. The results indicated that on Sina Weibo, netizens were more likely to express their opinion and particularly show their attitude towards Snowden. However, their voice was quite homogenous, mostly supporting him. On Twitter, netizens had diverse attitudes towards Snowden, and the news reports on Twitter covered far more topics. However, Twitter users prefer forwarding news to directly expressing their own opinion. And the US government did not have active engagement on Twitter. Thus, in both democratic and authoritarian contexts, microblogging has some important elements of public sphere, although it might not be absolute. We cannot ignore the communicative power of microblogging to promote cooperation and mutual understanding, which is significant in the democratic process and civil society in both China and the US.

The daily interaction between political parties and voters is a driving force in election campaigns and can influence their outcomes. The theory of campaign intensity holds that the timing of message delivery in an election campaign is a key component of the strategies used by political actors. However, this theory also warns political actors to be cautious about the timing of different types of messages sent during the election campaign. Our objective is to examine the intensity and types of messages Slovenian political actors communicated through Twitter during different stages in the 2014 national election campaign. Our study conducts a content analysis of 7,113 tweets posted during the last four weeks of the official election campaign. It includes 17 official accounts of Slovenian parties, party leaders, and influential party twitterians. The results indicated that the stage of the campaign and the differences between established and fringe political parties significantly influenced the intensity of Twitter communications during the study period. The results also revealed that the political actors tweeted different types of political messages (e.g., to inform and to persuade voters) during different stages of the campaign.

This chapter deals with the political advertising strategies used on Facebook during the elections campaigns for the European Parliament in 2009 and 2014. It explores and examines the posts of 11 political parties and comments they received during the last two weeks before the elections. The focus of the chapter is on possible interactions among citizens and politicians or citizens themselves that would support the idea that online deliberation could function as an improvement over other types of campaigning dialogues and the ways in which individuals used Facebook. The chapter explores possible similarities and differences in campaigning of political parties with the same national and ideological background, if any. It also makes a comparison between the campaigns in 2009 and 2014.

Presidential campaigns today are increasingly integrating social media such as Facebook as an efficient tool to communicate with the public and organize their supporters. In a bid to explore how the Facebook is used by the politicians during election campaigns, this chapter explored official Facebook posts by two presidential candidates ahead of the 2012 US presidential election. The findings suggest Facebook

Preface

(R)EVOLVING POLITICAL COMMUNICATION, (R)EVOLVING SOCIAL MEDIA

Developments in technological communication have always played an important role in the way political actors communicate with citizens, other holders of social power, and among themselves. Whether it is a matter of utility or image selling, in the last two decades, the convergence of political and media logics by political parties has been increasingly articulated online because of social differentiation and the transformations in communication. This move online has had various and contradictory implications for political life, which reflect a shift in the overall style of political communication to an aggressive, continuous, and individualized mode. The move has strengthened what Alfred Hermida would call the "ambient" character of the awareness of political actors, the mass media, and the public, which implies the restructuring of power relations and the increasing centralization of power. By bringing together theoretical and empirical explorations in different political contexts and traditions, this edited volume reveals the complexities of societal, cultural, organizational, and individual articulations of contemporary technology in the connections between politics and communication with respect to social media and their global and local trajectories.

Many critical communication scholars, most notably Raymond Williams, have indicated that despite their revolutionary and emancipatory potential for changing social communication, throughout history technological innovations have been subordinated to the interests of holders of political and economic power and their attempts to preserve their privileges and certain course of social progress. Nevertheless, in the last century or so, political actors have differed in their motivations for the early adoption of new technologies, such as radio, television, and the Internet, as well as their implementations in routine representations of political power and actions. Technological innovations may have been introduced when technologically reductionist perceptions prevailed that the job could be done "cheaper and faster" and achieve predictable and positive outcomes. However, the reasons for the introduction of technological innovations tend to be much more prosaic, resting on the symbolic significance of adopting new technologies. A variety of actors want to prove that they are modern, relevant, up-to-date, and in line with their competition. Although this hypothesis has been widely confirmed in political actors that gain a foothold in cyberspace across different contexts, the jury is still out with regard to social media.

This bandwagon effect came under severe criticism in the case of marginal political actors who devised a clear rationale for their appropriation of new technologies. Because of their inferior resource capacity and very limited exposure in traditional media outlets, this type of political actor began to perceive information and communication technologies not as a mere technological utility but as a "game-changer." The manner and intensity of using new technologies are the basis of the equalization theory, which encapsulates the effects of the utopian wave of discussions on the impact of information and communication technologies in the political process. This wave examined ambitions for direct democracy, new opportunities for empowerment, the revitalization of democracy, participatory politics, the activation of an increasingly disaffected electorate, and a new, equanimous platform for political competition among political actors. Hence, the utopians claimed that the move online would challenge existing power structures and introduce a distinct type of political engagement that sharply differed from traditional activities.

Contrary to utopian aspirations, a second wave of skeptical cyber-realists has voiced doubts about the revolutionary effects of the move online on the political process and put forward the concept of "politics as usual" coined by Michael Margolis and David Resnick. They probably have made the strongest case for the normalization hypothesis by rejecting revolutionary conduct in politics and stressing that the Internet tends to reflect and reinforce behavioral patterns in the real world. This "no-change" scenario simply reflects the view that politics online are an extension of offline politics. According to normalization theorists, the utopian hopes of a new politics that would emerge in the computer era and revitalize citizenship and democracy have been shattered by ordinary politics and commercial activity, which have invaded and captured cyberspace. A sophisticated political economy has begun to dominate political, economic, social, and recreational life on the Internet. Despite the evidence of the validity of this line of thought, the emergence of social media calls for a re-examination of its relevance, preferably from a transnational comparative perspective.

Social media comprise interrelated, omnipresent, and "always-on" communication environments, thus creating different kinds of connections for actors in the political arena. Studies conducted in different countries have demonstrated the emergence of social media as ambient communication spaces where politicians and their parties are in continuous, asynchronous dialogue with their political competitors, the media, and the electorate. In this sense, various agents engage in networked co-constructions of the political arena where political actors seek power through a diverse and apparently shared communication space. From a historical perspective, the societal conditions that would allow the entry into and participation within the political sphere have never fully materialized because of the unequal access to the media, which is affected by ownership and decision-making, the uneven distribution of communication competences, and the hegemony of the opinions and positions of the powerful. Although many scholarly findings have indicated the revolutionary potential of social media, there is emerging evidence of their normalization as tools for both narrow political struggles and new evolutionary paths of political communication towards an inclusive, multi-layered, and multi-directional social phenomenon.

When we first discussed the idea of putting together a volume on the (r)evolutionary potentials of social media for political communication, we were met with a crossfire of questions: In considering the possibilities and constraints of dynamic and shared engagement in communication, can we speak about the dominant modes of political communication on social media in general? How have social media affected political communication and to what extent are the existing offline power positions mirrored in this ambient communication environment? What are the communalities and particularities of articulations between social, politics, and media across societies? Keeping in mind the challenges of setting boundaries between the different political roles of actors engaged in social media, how does they affect the prevailing modes of governmental communication, public relations, journalism, and entertainment? As the editors of this book, we have aimed to include authors from various political contexts and traditions in order to develop a volume that would explore the contingent connections between political communication and social media as they are developed or broken in particular political and social contexts and as they are manifested in different ways across the globe.

Instead of attempting to answer the questions posed above, the studies included in this volume confirm that they are relevant across various empirical contexts and analytical perspectives. In this sense, by drawing on different theoretical concepts, adopting various methods, and focusing on a broad range of research problems, the studies included here indicate various relations of dominance and subordination in connoting, symbolizing, and evoking the prevailing context-related conceptions of political communication that shape the online character of contemporary political life. More precisely, the book is structured according to four perspectives on the complex world of (r)evolutionary changes in political communication through social media: complex (re)articulations of political life; grassroots social movements, institutionalized politics, and mediatized political communication; strategic communication of mainstream political actors on micro-blogging outlets; and utilization of Facebook as a strategic election campaign tool.

COMPLEX (RE)ARTICULATIONS OF POLITICAL LIFE

The perspective of the authors in the first section of the volume is the broadest because they tackle broad aspects of political life and their articulation through social media. The chapters in this section encompass different approaches to the political dynamics tied to the emancipatory possibilities of social media technology and the particular linkages forged between social structures and agents. These complex connections in political life, which are articulated through social media as market-driven communication technologies, appear to be formed between the participatory promises of bringing people together both meaningfully and equally, enabling them to exchange opinions and act for the particular purposes and larger realities of the coercive character of contemporary surveillance societies. In this context, social media emerge as always-active communication environments where the capacities of political actions are limited by the interests and actions of political and corporate power holders. The chapters in this section indicate that vibrant spheres provide grounds for the reproduction of historically persistent processes of preserving social order and retaining established relations in political life. They also describe political and cultural contexts frameworks for the formation of particular spaces of public reasoning, cooperation, and identity formation, which are without precedence in the history of political communication.

By placing their analyses in the political context of the United States, in the first chapter, Ramona Sue McNeal and Justin W. Holmes evaluate competing claims about whether the proliferation of social media exacerbates or attenuates polarization in the political evaluations of the electorate. Contrary to the authors' initial expectations, they found that social media use appears to attenuate rather than exacerbate polarization. Although the evidence suggests that consistent ideologies have been developed with extreme stances on issues, negative attitudes towards cooperation, and dislike of political opponents, the hollowing out of the political middle, and the rise of a confrontational style of politics, McNeal and Holmes argue that social media use appears to have emerged as a modest corrective of these phenomena.

In the second chapter, Shaohai Jiang discusses whether microblogs embody basic characteristics of the Habermasian public sphere and analyses opinions about the "Snowden affair" expressed on the social networking site Twitter and its Chinese counterpart Sina Weibo. By focusing on the case of Edward Snowden, the former CIA employee who leaked classified data on the surveillance technologies and practices of the National Security Agency, the author suggests that these similar social media networks in different political contexts are public spaces that offer wide-reaching possibilities for information diffusion and gathering as well as opinion exchange and debate. However, their limitations as integral parts of what resembles Yochai Benkler's notion of the networked public sphere seem to be shaped by the inclusive and exclusive agencies of the political establishment online, which appear appearing more explicit in China and more implicit in the United States .

Pantelis Vatikiotis critically reconsiders the role of social media, particularly Twitter, Facebook, and Tumblr, in the mobilization and transformative capacities of contemporary protest movements. His study focuses on the "Arab Spring" in late 2010, the Occupy Movements that exposed and countered the logics of global financial capitalism in 2011, and movements against the established political and economic order throughout Europe in the present decade. The author concludes that contemporary social movements and their mediated activities are multifaceted in character and suggests that in order to grasp the complexities of the interplay between social and media activism, it is necessary to probe the dialectical relationship between structures and agents, by critically (re)considering mechanisms and contradictions in the interweaving of contentious social (media) practices.

GRASSROOTS SOCIAL MOVEMENTS, INSTITUTIONALIZED POLITICS, AND MEDIATIZED POLITICAL COMMUNICATION

The second section includes studies conducted from the perspective of the dynamic relationships between grassroots social movements and institutionalized politics in the context of social media communication. These dynamics are considered with respect to the complex process of the institutionalization of initially loose political groupings that communicate particular issues and propagate social change through social and mainstream media. The dynamics are explored in the often conflictual mediat(iz)ed relationships of social movements with the political powerhouses that form governments or institutionalized political oppositions. The chapters in this section consider the articulations between interrelated social movements and the troubles they face. These articulations are manifested in the discrepancies between online communications in both social media and offline actions, conflicts with institutionalized politics, temptations to take coercive measures against the attempts of movements to mobilize citizens through social media, and the prospects of concrete political effects. They are also manifest in tensions between political ideals, flattened hierarchies, inclusive decision-making on the one hand and political pragmatism during the process of institutionalization of movements on the other hand. Hence, social media do not simply move in and revolutionize the dynamics of grassroots social movements, institutionalized politics, and mediat(iz)ed political communication, but they appear as an additional public arenas for the contestation of political ideas, developments, visibility, the mobilization of social groups, and spaces for (re) articulations of established power relations.

In the fourth chapter, Lazaro M. Bacallao-Pino examines the radical online political communication of a grassroots movement that emerged on and spread through social media. This author focuses on the university student movement #YoSoy132 during the general election campaign in Mexico in 2012. By investigating the interrelationships between online communication and offline collective action,

Bacallao-Pino reveals the difficulties of transiting political momentum from social media to the streets while identifying the potential of opening up the alternative communication spaces that are necessary for democratizing social relationships and fostering social change.

Helin Alagöz Gessler explores the implications of social media for the relations between the government and the political engagement of citizens in Turkey by focusing on the protests and movements in Gezi Park. This chapter also examines the Turkish government's response, the "Twitter ban" in the attempt to preserve the status quo. In this context, the author, on the one hand, argues that Twitter makes an important contribution to inclusive political processes because it diversifies the notion of political communication. On the other hand, Gessler suggests that the Turkish political establishment took coercive actions to limit online public communication in order to protect its authority against potential citizen unrest.

Marta Pérez Escolar investigates the political communication by the leftist political party, Podemos, which emerged from the 15M movement on social media. The party aims to rearrange the power divide in Spain. Escolar focuses on the party's activities on social media two months before the European Parliamentary Elections in 2014. Her findings suggest that the social media activities of Podemos can be regarded as heterogeneous and pluralistic, resting on the idea of the "wisdom crowd." Although the party represents itself as democratically inclusive, it neglects the pragmatic character of the contemporary struggles of institutionalized politics.

STRATEGIC COMMUNICATION OF POLITICAL ACTORS ON MICRO-BLOGGING OUTLETS AND ITS ABILITY TO EMPOWER DEMOCRACY

The social media outlets collectively described as Web 2.0 increasingly have influenced the way individuals communicate and facilitate their involvement in observing, commenting, filtering, and distributing different social actions. The expansion of social media also has contributed to the significant modernization of political communication because new outlets allow for direct communication to and with wide audiences, thus bypassing the mass media and their influence on the communication of political messages to voters. For example, Twitter allow the instant dissemination of short messages from variety of sources and provides a platform that permits the ad hoc formation of public discussions and the rapid emergence of politically engaged publics. Political actors try to capitalize on the new opportunities Twitter offers, some by devising new campaign strategies, such as informing, mobilizing, fundraising, and persuading. Others take advantage of Twitter because in political battles no one wants to be portrayed as out-of-date. However, this may have a profound effect on the quality of political discussion, also due to its peculiar awareness system. The following chapters tackle questions related to the nature of political communication, the use of Twitter a channel of strategic communication, the rationale for the presence of Twitter, as well as the influence of Twitter on political communication in the public sphere.

In their chapter on political communication and Twitter in Greece, Stamatis Poulakidakos and Anastasia Veneti explore the political communication literature to examine the revisited "bandwagon" hypothesis and discuss potential enhancements of the political process because of technological advancements in an idiosyncratic political context. In their quest to answer the question of whether the increased use of information and communication technology has revitalized Greek democracy by fostering political participation and conversation, the authors focus on the potential of microblogging to animate political communication and provide a new repertoire of political action. Because Twitter appears to circumvent the biased mainstream media, particularly in environments, such as Greece, where Twitter has a rapidly growing audience, Poulakidakos and Veneti conduct content and thematic analyses of the tweets by two main political parties (New Democracy and Syriza). In the context of this heated political environment, which is marked by the increasing polarization of the public sphere, the authors seek to determine whether Twitter positively contributes to public discussions, promotes the exchange of rational argumentation about the crisis, and serves as a new, immaterial public space. The authors' answers to these questions are in line with the normalization hypothesis put forward by Margolis and Resnick (2000). Not much has changed in the old ways of communicating politics in Greece; neither the politicians nor the public exploit the potential of Twitter, instead maintaining perpetual parallel monologues. The prevailing modality of tweeting is broadcasting rather than responding or engaging in conversation, and personalized postings are virtually absent. In addition to identifying the propagandistic methods of communication used by the rivals of the main party, the authors conclude that technological innovation is only a precondition for a revolutionizing shift in political discourse and inevitably rests on the willingness and the capacity of its main carriers (i.e., political parties) to achieve a complete change.

In the following chapter, Maria Francesca Murru acknowledges that Twitter is not only one of many communication tools but also a communicative event that drives political actors to be represented through a new form of storytelling comprised of infographics, visual resources, and metrics. Focusing on its distinct architecture, Maria Francesca Murru analyzes the performative role of Twitter hashtags in the politicization of Europe in the 2014 European Parliamentary (EP) elections. Recognizing Twitter as a manifestation of the public sphere, the author analyzes the Italian EP election debate on Twitter and observes the negotiation of meaning within the specific grammar of the micro-blogging platform and its connection to the ongoing politicization of the European Union (EU) within and across national politics. Aiming to contribute to the accumulated knowledge about the social and political value of Twitter, Murru attempts to explore and explain the relationships that connect Twitter to the wide-ranging discursive practices through which topics of common interest are framed and made visible. In order to address the hashtags as triggers of affiliative and value-laden spaces of discourse whereby meanings and stances can be negotiated, the author utilizes an ethnographic approach to study the dynamics of affiliation, which resides in the mutual implications of the content and context of events on Twitter. Murro's analysis of hashtags—linguistic markers that call for affiliation and open a space of shared attention—reveals that Twitter effectively acted as a forum of the public sphere because it offered a polyphonic stage for the competitive claims-making process that brought Europe into the arena of public debate. This process has illuminated the connections that link Twitter to other forums of the public sphere because it incorporated already existing content, symbols, and facts in its streams of affiliation, and it utilized Twitter as a sounding board rather than an autonomous public sphericule.

In chapter 9, Alem Maksuti and Tomaž Deželan observe the dynamics of the political communication of political actors that compete in a primary electoral race rather than in a second-order electoral arena. As a social media outlet revered by politicians, journalists, and opinion makers, Twitter offered an excellent opportunity to observe the intensity and innovation in the use of Twitter by Slovenian political powerhouses in an important electoral battle. The study builds on the accumulated evidence that confirms Twitter as an integrative element in Slovenian party campaign strategies. It was used in political interactions with journalists and opinion makers, and it constituted a "hit-or-miss" political battlefield because of its inadequate professionalization. Maksuti and Deželan examine the intensity of campaigning on Twitter to investigate its centrality in contemporary election campaigns conducted in Slovenia. The authors also revisit the campaign intensity hypothesis of political communication, message timing, the tactic dimension, as well as the relevance of the copycat theory of party web campaigning. By conducting a content analysis of the tweets posted by the relevant political actors during the 2014 national election campaign, the authors reaffirm the claim that it is primarily up to political actors to embrace the full potential of technological innovation. They also affirm that they have utilized these tools conservatively and selectively. The study also clearly demonstrates that the Twitter strategies used by Slovenian political parties are drawn from mainstream toolboxes (e.g., TV), acknowledging the principles related to campaign intensity and recency. The authors contend that Twitter campaigning in Slovenia is bound to theories of effective campaign strategies and fundamental theories of political psychology and voting behaviour. Thus, campaigning on this outlet is one of the most central and strategically effective arenas of communicating political messages.

UTILIZATION OF FACEBOOK AS A STRATEGIC ELECTION CAMPAIGN TOOL

The users of social media encompass almost a third of humankind. With more than a billion active users, Facebook has the largest share of the political communication market. The failure to take advantage of this opportunity would be suicidal for political actors. Similar to the advent of the Internet, more relevant than the question of going on Web 2.0 is the dilemma of what to do with it. The use of this tool does not require in-depth literacy. The preferences of voters indicate that politicians frequently mimic their presence on Web 2.0 and experiment with its unprecedented potential. However, certain actors, either those suffering from structural deficiencies in the offline world (revolution hypothesis) or those with structural advantages offline but want to maintain an edge online as well (normalization hypothesis) have taken an active role in exploiting the potential of social media rather than just jumping on-board. These actors have attempted to use Facebook as a strategic tool of political communication and have utilized it to inform, engage, mobilize, interact, as well as agenda building and strategic visual planning. The chapters in the last section of this volume examine how and to the degree to which these strategies have materialized during key electoral races.

Focusing on comparatively under-explored social media outlet in the political communication literature, Lucia Vesnic-Alujevic investigates aspects of political communication on Facebook in case of second-order EP elections, which attract modest attention of voters and media from their introduction in 1979. Focusing on a market comprising nearly 200 million users, Vesnić-Alujević draws on the concept of deliberative democracy to explore citizens' interactions with politicians and their support of political deliberation. In her evaluation of the potential of Facebook as a tool in election campaigns, especially its utilization in political communication, the author concentrates on the uses of Facebook in the EP campaigns of 2009 and 2014. She identifies the most active actors, the dominant modes of communication, and the interaction between political actors and their audience. By analyzing Facebook posts, she identifies the increased professionalism of the political communication in 2014, which had far less informative content, more engaging material, and clearer strategies of targeting specific groups. She argues that Facebook has become a mainstream electoral campaign medium, with abundant audiovisual content and hyperlinks. However, because it lacks mobilizing and interactive content, Facebook is still a medium for informing rather than persuading voters. Vesnic-Alujevic concludes that Facebook still plays the role of a complementary campaign tool, and even though there is great potential for deliberation and interaction through Facebook, this outlet has not been exploited adequately by political parties. There is an absence of rational discussion leading to political deliberation and virtually no interaction between political parties and sympathizers. Vesnic-Alujevic's perspective on the limits of technological advancements and the dangers of technological determinism is similar to that of Poulakidakos and Veneti as well as many others in this volume.

In a similar study of electoral dynamics across the ocean, Ashik Shafi and Fred Vultee analyze the Facebook posts of presidential candidates in the 2012 federal election in the United States. The authors examine the Facebook posts of Mitt Romney and Barack Obama during the election campaign. They analyze the content and rhetorical features of these posts to identify the strategies of using the Facebook social media outlet it to reach both the mass media and the public instantly, thus making it a tool for agenda building. Shafi and Vultee are primarily interested in whether politicians fully exploit Facebook to influence the public and the mass media on an unprecedented scale. Their findings suggest that Facebook was used as a platform to organize like-minded voters. Similar to Vesnic-Alujevic's findings on the EP elections, Facebook was used to demonstrate political presence and inform voters rather than engage in political discussions. The authors also argue that the candidates used Facebook to convey personality, appeal to the audience, engage in cyber-rallying, and organize supporters. Based on their findings, Shafik and Vultee suggest that Facebook was utilized as a strategic public relations tool rather than an information source. Thus, they failed to detect efforts by Obama and Romney to use this social media outlet to influence agenda building.

Camelia Cmeciu demonstrates another use of Facebook as a strategic campaign tool. By focusing on the visual self-presentation of candidates on Facebook during the 2014 EP elections in Romania, Cmeciu explores the presence of the winning and losing Romanian candidates who stood for the 2014 EP elections. By taking into account the relevance of Facebook's photo imagery, the author acknowledges the visual nature of contemporary elections and the potential of images to frame politicians as social actors that perform different actions. Cmeciu also investigates politicians' timelines on Facebook's to gather evidence of their strategic use of visual discourse. In addition to levels of strategic visual planning, Cmeciu analyzes the Facebook timelines of Romanian political actors to identify the predominant themes and master frames. This visual framing analysis indicates that the winning politicians tended to be promoted visually as political leaders surrounded by an impressive campaign entourage, whereas the losers were framed as populist campaigners in the midst of large audiences or as compassionate candidates interacting with individuals. Cmeciu also identifies the prevalence of hybrid messages that focused on national contexts instead of the EU political arena, which showed candidates surrounded by national-level supporters and themes instead of those pertaining to Europe. By arguing that online visibility does not trigger the offline mobilization of voters, Cmeciu reiterates an assertion expressed throughout the chapters presented in this volume: Social media have not revolutionized political communication and not revitalized democracy.

Section 1

Complex (Re)Articulations of Political Life

Chapter 1
Social Media, Participation, and Attitudes:
Does Social Media Drive Polarization?

Justin W. Holmes
University of Northern Iowa, USA

Ramona Sue McNeal
University of Northern Iowa, USA

ABSTRACT

A wide body of evidence shows that the American electorate has become more politically polarized in recent years. There are a wide variety of explanations for this trend, including selective exposure to ideological news sources. This trend corresponds with the increased use of social media for political discussion. There are competing theories regarding whether the spread social media exacerbates or attenuates polarization in the evaluation of political and social groups. The purpose of this chapter is to evaluate these competing claims. This topic is explored using multivariate regression analysis and individual level data from the 2012 American National Election Time Series Study. The findings suggest that social media use actually attenuates rather than drives polarization.

INTRODUCTION

Over the last several decades, there has been an apparent increase in political polarization in the United States. A variety of evidence suggests that both elites and citizens have developed more consistent ideologies, extreme issue stances, negative attitudes towards cooperation, and dislike toward political opponents that indicate a hollowing out of the political middle, and the rise of a new, more extreme and confrontational style of politics. This trend in increased political polarization in the United States has given rise to speculation among politics scientists regarding the impetus for this change. Much of the popular and scholarly concern with polarization stems from the potential consequences of increased division in American politics (Fiorina, Abrams & Pope, 2010). At the elite level, the main concern is that increased distance between the parties will lead to increased gridlock and an inability to reach

DOI: 10.4018/978-1-4666-9879-6.ch001

consensus on legislation. The system of checks and balances in the United States creates a legislative process with a number of veto points, which requires compromise to govern. Increasingly polarized parties are unwilling to compromise with each other, leading to high stakes fights over policy, and increased threats of government shutdown. In this view, polarized parties and their disinclination to bargain lead to dysfunction because of a mismatch within the U.S. political system (Mann & Ornstein, 2012). On the other hand, party divergence may actually foster representation by drawing clearly lines between candidates and parties, which allows citizens a clearer choice. Further, polarization enhances party discipline, which may make it more likely that winning parties are able to enact their platform (Layman, Casey & Horowitz, 2006).

At the public level, the consequences of polarization are somewhat more mixed. On the negative side, it is possible that increased polarization leads to increasing citizen cynicism and distrust of government (Layman et al., 2006). Increasing polarization also seems to decrease citizen's feelings of political efficacy, particularly for moderates (Hetherington, 2007), which has the potential to limit participation. Lastly, public polarization has led to increased hostility and outright discrimination among citizens based on political views (Iyengar & Westwood, 2014). On the other hand, a considerable body of literature demonstrates that polarization actually fosters participation. As the parties have moved apart, voter turnout has actually increased (Hetherington, 2007). Those who are polarized by their media choices are also more apt to participate (Prior, 2007; Stroud, 2012). In recent elections, the size of the engaged public, which tends to be quite polarized, has grown dramatically. The engaged public is highly motivated to participate, and features high levels of voter turnout, volunteering, political discussion, political donation, and other behaviors generally lauded in a representative democracy (Abramowitz, 2010).

The object of this chapter is to explore the role of social media in contributing to political polarization. Attributes of social media, particularly the ability it gives users to surround themselves with information they already agree with, and filter out information they disagree with, suggests that it is a likely contributor to political polarization. In examining this question, this chapter will utilize 2012 presidential election data to explore the impact of using social network sites to gather election data on political polarization. Despite predictions that social media may help contribute to the rise in political polarization among the American electorate, the findings of this study provide strong evidence across a variety of measures that using social media as a source of political information appears to decrease polarization.

DEFINING POLARIZATION

While polarization has been a topic of both popular and academic discussion for a number of years, there is not a single agreed upon definition. There are some common elements that all polarization definitions contain. "Polarization is both a state and a process. Polarization as a state refers to the extent to which opinions on an issue are opposed in relation to some theoretical maximum. Polarization as a process refers to the increase in such opposition over time", (DiMaggio, Evans, & Bryson, 1996, p. 693). Critically, for polarization to have occurred there must be a large gap between the opinions of two groups. Frequently, the comparison is between Democrats and Republicans, but others have examined polarization by region (Bishop, 2008), Red States vs Blue States (Fiorina, Abrams & Pope 2010), social class (Brewer & Stonecash, 2007), and authoritarian vs. non-authoritarian personalities (Hetherington & Weiler, 2009).

A variety of indicators have been employed to measure polarization including the relationship between party and ideology, ideological consistency across issues, feelings about the other side, approval of elected officials and attitudes towards compromise (Dimock, Kiley, Keeter, & Doherty, 2014). A major difficulty, however, is a lack of clear standards for declaring groups polarized. When conceiving of polarization as a process, the measure is straightforward. Polarization is indicated by a gap between groups that is increasing over time. Measuring polarization as a state, however, lacks a clear standard. Clearly, there is a range of groups who disagree with each other, but there is no agreed upon cut point for declaring the groups polarized. In the strictest sense, polarization should show a bimodal distribution of opinion with a large number of people taking extreme opinions, and a small number of moderates. Others contend that the bimodal distribution is not essential to demonstrate that polarization exists, merely that, when comparing two groups, there is sufficient divergence in their opinions (Hetherington, 2009).

There is also disagreement on whether or not the public as a whole is truly polarized. There is a strong consensus, that elites are polarized. Whereas, through the 1970s, there were moderates in both parties, and even liberal Republicans and conservative Democrats, a gradual partisan realignment occurred so that today we have two parties that are internally ideologically consistent and increasingly distant from each other (Mann & Ornstein, 2012). In contrast, there is less agreement that citizens either are currently polarized, or are more polarized than they were in the past. Dimaggio et al. (1996) presented one of the first scholarly studies of contemporary polarization. They found no evidence of process polarization, but arguably there was a large divide on many issues during this period which might indicate a polarized public, just one that has consistently had a strong degree of polarization.

Fiorina et al. (2010), on the other hand, argues that there is little public polarization. They argue that there is little evidence that Americans are more polarized than they were in the past, or that the bulk of Americans hold attitudes that are particularly divided. They point to evidence that, for many issues, public opinion is still roughly bell curve shaped, with a majority taking moderate positions and that at the state level, red states and blue states are not that different from one another. What we perceive as polarization is just the increased visibility of a small number of partisan extremists (Fiorina et al., 2010).

There are a number of issues that call this lack of polarization into question. Much of this analysis compares so called red states and blue states (ones that vote for Republican and Democratic presidential candidates respectively), though as a unit of analysis, all states are heterogeneous. In other places, Fiorina et al. (2010) seem to set very low standards for what constitutes agreement. For example, they contend that most Americans take moderate, rather than extreme views on abortion. While it is true that the public is less black and white on this issue than one might expect, Fiorina et al. (2010) oversell the argument that the public is moderation on the issue by lumping in all responses other than "abortion should never be legal" and "abortion should always be legal" into the moderate category. This masks rampant disagreement, as people who believe abortion should only be legal in cases of rape and incest and people who believe that abortion should always be legal in the first two trimesters, but not the third, as having moderate opinions (Fiornina et al., 2010). Across a number of issues, this same pattern pops up, masking considerable disagreement.

In contrast, other research demonstrates that Americans are not only strongly divided politically, but have moved further apart. Abramowitz's research has been among the most prominent that finds considerable evidence of polarization (Abramowitz & Saunders, 2008; Abramowitz, 2010). This research finds that there are large gaps between American citizens on a wide variety of issues, both by party, and in comparing secular and religious voters. While few of these issues may show a bimodal distribution of opinion, Abramowitz argues that is too high of a standard, and masks the fact that over the last 30 years, the distributions have flattened considerably, with moderates disappearing and extreme positions growing. This is particularly true among engaged citizens, who are not just Fiorina's ideological outliers, but constitute a large chunk of the American public (Abramowitz, 2010).

Further research has found similar trends towards greater polarization in the public. Gallup has presidential approval data starting with the Eisenhower administration. This data illustrates that Presidents George W. Bush and Barack Obama have dramatically bigger gaps in approval between partisans than any other American presidents both at the beginning of their presidencies, and into their second terms (Jones, 2014). Iyengar, Sood, and Lelkes (2012) contend that polarization is better conceived of as feelings about opposing parties rather than policy positions. Apart from difference in policy or ideology, Democrats and Republicans have come to greatly dislike each other over the last 50 years, to a degree that it crosses the line from dislike into loathing. They demonstrate through a series of experiments that strong partisans will discriminate against their opponents in ways that are more extreme than people are willing to discriminate by race (Iyengar &Westwood, 2014). Finally, a recent study from the Pew Research Center for the People and the Press demonstrates that in the last 20 years, there has been a high level of polarization across a wide variety of indicators. From 1994 to 2014, twice as many Americans have ideologically consistent positions across a variety of issues, dislike of members of the other party has nearly tripled among partisans, people report having a larger number of friends who share their political ideology, and both sides are dramatically less willing to compromise (Dimock et al., 2014). Taken together, the evidence strongly suggests that, particularly in recent years, the American public has become much more politically divided.

SOURCES OF POLARIZATION

There are several possible sources of increased polarization in the American public, ranging from geography, to cues from partisan leaders, to media consumption habits, including social media use. It is difficult to disentangle the relative contributions of these sources, but it is likely that all have a hand in polarization. Geographic location is one potential avenue for polarization. There have always been a variety of geographic divisions in American public opinion, including the North versus the South, and cities versus suburbs versus rural areas. There is compelling evidence that in the last several decades, these divisions have become stronger. Bishop (2008) presents evidence that people have largely sorted themselves into communities and neighborhoods that are more ideologically consistent. This is not necessarily consciously based on political belief, but on a variety of lifestyle factors such as tax rates, school quality, cultural opportunities, and religion, which correlate with political belief. When people find themselves immersed in a community with strong political positions, they tend to eventually adopt them as well (Bishop, 2008).

A second cause that has received considerable attention is that citizens are mirroring partisan elites in their polarization. It is nearly a unanimous view among political scientists that elites are dramatically more polarized than they were in the past, and evidence suggests that some citizens have picked up on these cues and have become more polarized as well. Zaller (1992) presented some of the first clear evidence of mainstreaming and polarization effects of elite influence on public opinion, showing that elite divergence on an issue typically came before public divergence on that issue.

Current research demonstrates that, beyond Zaller's (1992) finding that polarization could be transmitted from elites to the public on individual issues, there is evidence that this transmission also happens for ideology on the whole. Levendusky (2009) traces the rise of greater alignment of the public's partisanship and ideology, and finds that there is strong evidence for an elite based model. Partisan elected officials and other influential became more ideologically distinct, and the public followed. Individuals in recent years have not been likely to change their parties. Instead, people who identify as Republicans have taken cues from the national leadership and become more consistently conservative, and those who identify as Democrats have become more consistently Liberal. Classen and Highton (2009) find similar evidence, but argue that it is only applicable to those who are more politically engaged and aware of the parties' positions. This is consistent with Abramowitz's finding that it is primarily the engaged public that has become more polarized, not those who largely sit out the political process (Abramowitz, 2010; Abramowitz & Saunders, 2008).

A final potential source of public polarization is changes in media consumption patterns. There have been radical changes in the way that people get news and other information over the last several decades. We have largely moved from a broadcasting model, characterized by large audiences, homogeneity of content, and an ideal of objectivity in news, to a world where people have much greater choice over what information they are exposed to. Technologies such as cable and satellite television and the Internet provide citizens with an unprecedented level of access to information. This allows for a much greater ability for selective exposure to content. In addition, during this same period, there has been a large increase in the availability of explicitly partisan news, both on cable and the Internet. These conditions present new opportunities for citizens to engage with media that doesn't challenge their beliefs, which presents a possible avenue towards increased polarization. The media explanation is especially compelling because this change in the media landscape has largely coincided with this period of increased polarization.

NEW MEDIA AND SELECTIVE EXPOSURE

Research on selective exposure to media content has a long history, although early findings were decidedly mixed. Early work was grounded in cognitive dissonance theory, which holds that people will largely try to expose themselves to information which confirms rather than challenges their beliefs as a way of avoiding psychic discomfort (Cotton, 1985). The first wave of this research in the 1950's and early1960's found only limited support for the idea that the desire to avoid cognitive dissonance drove people's media choices (Sears & Freedman, 1967). Research in the 80's, however, was much more favorable to the theory (Cotton, 1985). It is likely that people's ability to be selective about media choices was greatly hampered during the first wave of research, whereas the second wave of research took place at the beginning of widespread cable availability, which would enable greater selectivity.

Contemporary research on politics and the media is near universal in the recognition that selective exposure is fairly commonplace. From a consumer standpoint, increased control over content is excellent. It allows media consumers to better match content to their preferences. Unfortunately, for politics, there is a potential downside to increased choice: cyberbalkanization (Mossberger, Tolbert & McNeal, 2007). It is widely assumed that exposure to a wide variety of ideas is central to democratic citizenship (Mutz, 2002). For example, in a face to face setting, exposure to a diversity of people and opinions produces a pro social "bridging social capital", whereas exposure to a homogeneous group results instead in a "bonding" social capital that fails to provide much in the way of benefit to society (Putnam, 2000). Cyberbalkanization is the dark side of choice, where media users are able to fine tune their media selections to the exclusion of any information that they might find disagreeable. This has the potential to undercut an important need of democratic citizens. Negroponte (1995) was among the first to predict the technological foundations of cyberbalkinization, with his concept of the "Daily Me" a daily online newspaper which catered towards the reader's preferences. Cass Sunstein raised concerns that a news delivery mechanism like the "Daily Me" would lead to people ignoring viewpoints they disagreed with, and ultimately resulting in polarization (Sunstein, 2002). While this concept of the "Daily Me" was theoretical at the time, it does set the stage for much of the empirical research that followed, and a variety of contemporary online resources seem to fit into this mold.

One of the first consistent findings in this literature was that the ability to choose from a greater amount of content tended to limit the consumption of political information among those who were not high in political interest. Baum and Kernel (1999) found that viewership of presidential addresses was near universal among households that lacked access to cable television, but quite low among houses that had cable. In those cases, only the politically interested tuned in. The Internet expands opportunities to opt out of politics altogether, and it is evident that those who are less politically interested use the Internet to disengage from politics altogether. Those whose favorite type of programming is entertainment are very unlikely to watch news or political coverage, whereas those who prefer news to entertainment are able to use the increased access to information provided by the Internet to immerse themselves more deeply in political content (Prior, 2007). Similarly, when presented with increased amounts of content to choose from, the most politically interested consumed all the political news made available to them, whereas the least politically interested consumed almost none (Holmes, 2009).

A second consistent finding is that at least some people use the increased amount of available content to selectively expose themselves to ideologically consistent information. Iyengar and Hahn (2009) find that when given the opportunity to choose, Republican's tend to prefer to get news from identifiably conservative sources, whereas Democrats prefer to get news from identifiably liberal sources. This relationship is strengthened in individuals who are both partisans and politically engaged. One mechanism for this behavior appears to be a desire to acquire additional information to reinforce preexisting attitudes (Garret, 2009). A second possible driver of this selectivity is perceptions of media bias. Liberals and Conservatives trust different sources to be unbiased, and they therefore select sources that they perceive to be the most accurate (Stroud, 2012). Selective exposure itself is only a concern if it leads to negative outcomes. If ideologues only consume ideology congruent information but it doesn't change their attitudes in some fashion, then there is little reason for concern. With a few important exceptions, the bulk of the research on the effects of selective exposure on opinion finds that increased access to partisan media sources does contribute to polarization.

In many ways, the broadcast era of communication is a historical anomaly. Prior to the rise of broadcast media such as radio and television, media sources were fairly heterogeneous in their political viewpoints. This seemed to drive a polarization in public opinion. The rise of broadcast media limited opportunities for selective exposure, and decreased polarization in the public (Campante & Hojman, 2013). This is similar to Zaller's (1992) mainstreaming effect for political elites. As broadcasting gives way to high choice media outlets, this raises the potential for greater polarization. Prior's comparison of broadcast media and cable finds that, at least among users who are interested in news, increased chances for selective exposure drive polarization (Prior, 2007). Stroud finds similar effects for specific media outlets such as Fox News and MSNBC (Stroud, 2012). While it may seem counterintuitive to expect much opinion change among ideologues, Levendusky finds that selective exposure pushes moderate ideologues to take more extreme positions, leading to increases in overall levels of polarization (Levendusky, 2013). Additionally, selective exposure activates partisan attitudes and allows them to have more influence over political behavior (Knoblach-Westerwick, 2012).

At least one study calls into question this theoretical relationship between selectivity and polarization. The expected connection between media content and polarization is that ideologically consistent information should lead to polarization, whereas exposure to a diversity of information should moderate attitudes somewhat. Arceneaux and Johnson, however, do not find this expected result. Instead, their research indicates that exposing ideologues to information that challenges their beliefs does not cause them to moderate, but to increase their commitment to their initial position (Arceneaux & Johnson, 2013).

SOCIAL MEDIA AND POLARIZATION

Social media represents a new communication technology that has been rapidly adopted, and has the potential to shape people's political beliefs as well. Services such as Facebook and Twitter represent the potential realization of Sunstein's "Daily Me." Users only see content from "friends" whom they have selected, and sources that they have "liked." Further, Facebook does not show you the totality of posts from your friends and liked sources. Instead, they employ an algorithm that chooses to show users a subset of available posts that it believes will give users the information they find most interesting (Facebook, 2014). Ultimately, one's social media experience is highly curated and tailored to the user's preferences. It is a slightly disorienting experience to see someone else's Facebook or Twitter feeds, as aesthetically they are similar to one's own, but the content is potentially entirely different.

This raises the possibility that social media, at least for some users, social media could lead to increased polarization. The user interfaces for both Facebook and Twitter potentially allow politically engaged ideological users to limit the flow of information in their social media outlets to information sources that they already agree with. The question is- to what extent do people engage in this sort of ideological use? It is possible that some users will use social media to create a "Daily Me" that serves up a steady stream of ideologically comfortable information. On the other hand, it is also possible that most users' social media experiences are not so tightly controlled. In this case, social media might function more like Mutz's cross cutting face to face social networks, which increase exposure to different ideas, and ultimately lead to a degree of tolerance of different viewpoints (Mutz, 2013).

The Pew Internet and American Life Project has conducted some of the most comprehensive research on how people use social media for political purposes. They have several findings that are relevant to expectations about social media and polarization. First, only a relatively small number of users seem to make an effort to eliminate political content they disagree with. Only 16% of liberals and 8% of conservatives had ever unfriended someone for posting political content they disagreed with. Conversely, 24% of self-identified "very liberal" users and 25% of "very conservative users" had friended someone because they shared political views. As far as perceptions of agreement, most users find that their friends post a mix of political content that they agree and disagree with (Rainie & Smith, 2012). Within the context of Canadian elections, similar patterns have emerged on Twitter. An analysis of individuals' networks showed that some users clustered ideologically, while other users engaged in cross ideological discourse. There seemed to be little effect on attitudes one way or the other from these interactions (Gruzd & Roy, 2014).

To date, there have only been a handful of studies of the impact of social media on polarization. Castletrione finds that, contrary to expectations of cyberbalkanization, Facebook seems to provide a mix of purposeful and incidental exposure to political information that attenuates polarization (Castletrione, 2014). Similarly, Lee et al find that high levels of social media use result in higher levels of network heterogeneity. These heterogeneous networks exposure high social media users to more diverse points of view, therefore attenuating rather than exacerbating polarization (Lee et al., 2014). What is missing from both of these analyses is the potential difference of experience based on political ideology and partisanship. Those who are not ideological or particularly politically engaged seem unlikely candidates for creating a homogenous social network, whereas ideologues and partisans are. This leaves open an important avenue of inquiry: do social networks allow ideologues to further polarize themselves? The literature suggests the following hypothesis in exploring this question:

Hypothesis: ideologues that use social media will have more polarized evaluations of political and social groups than ideologues that do not use social media, or non-ideologues.

While several studies argue that social media attenuate polarization, we do not expect that to be true for all social media users. We expect, consistent with the literature on social media exposure, ideologues will be more likely to utilize the features of social networks that allow one to be selectively exposed to information rather than to have heterogeneous networks that expose them to varied points of view. Consistent with Mutz's (2002) findings, we expect that those with limited diversity of their networks will be less likely to exhibit tolerance of diverse groups. Ideologues should have more polarized views of a variety of political and social groups, and ideologues who use social media should exhibit even greater levels of polarization.

EMPIRICAL MODEL: DATA AND METHODS

Data

In examining the question of whether individuals with strong ideological leanings, who use social media, will have more polarized opinions, this chapter will utilize the *American National Election Studies (ANES) 2012 Time Series Study*. This survey is based on U.S. citizens ages 18 or older and utilizes a dual-mode design taken at two different points during the 2012 presidential election. During the pre-election period 2,054 respondents were interviewed faced-to-face (September 8-November 5, 2012) while 3,860 respondents took the survey online (October 11-November 6, 2012). During the post-election period, 1,929 respondents were interviewed face-to-face (November 7-January 13, 2013) and 3,581 respondents took the survey online during the period from November 29 to January 24, 2013 (ANES, 2014). There are both and advantages and disadvantages associated with the dataset used in this study. The main independent variables and the majority of the control variables were collected during the pre-election period while the dependents were collected during the post-election period of this time series. This assists in establishing time order. One disadvantage associated with utilizing a dataset collected by others (secondary data analysis) for our purposes is that the data set includes only limited measures of social media usage, though the variables included are sufficient to test our hypothesis. Overall, we found the questions collected in the *ANES 2012 Time Series Study* to be well suited for this research project.

Methods

The main independent variables consist of political ideology, social network site (SNS) usage to gather information on the 2012 presidential election and their interaction effect. For political ideology, respondents were asked to place themselves on a 7-point scale ranging from extremely liberal through moderate to extremely conservative. Social network site usage was coded 1 if the respondent typically visited SNS such as Twitter and Facebook to learn about the 2012 presidential election and 0 otherwise.

It is expected that the main effect of ideology will be significant, as ideology plays an important role in shaping feelings towards a variety of groups. A significant interaction between ideology and social media use would modify and steepen the slope of the ideology coefficient for those who are social media users. This steeper slope means that, compared to nonsocial media users, social media users at the extreme ends of the ideological spectrum have more polarized evaluations of the target groups. This is consistent with the finding that partisan news media polarizes by increasing the distance between the views of people who are already strong ideologues (Levendusky, 2013). Social network site usage might on its own help to increase polarization. Research finds that when likeminded individuals hear arguments through group discussion that supports their position, they are more likely to develop polarizing positions (Isenberg, 1986).

For this study, OLS regression is used because the dependent variables approximate a continuous variable. The dependent variables measure respondent opinions of six groups or organizations that liberals and conservatives are expected to have strong and opposing viewpoints of. These groups consist of liberals, conservatives, the Tea Party, the federal government, feminists and unions. For each measure (feeling thermometer) the respondent is asked to score the political actor or group on a scale from 0 to 100 where higher scores indicate a more favorable opinion. Control variables include family income measure on a 28-point scale where 1 indicated that family income for the year 2011 before taxes ranges from $0 to $5,000 and 28 signifies a family income of $250,000 or more. Education indicates the highest level of education obtainment and is measured using a 16-point scale, ranging from less than first grade to a doctorate degree. Measures of education and income were included for several reasons. The first is that research (Hetherington, 2001; Claassen & Highton, 2009) find greater levels of polarization among the American public but not uniformly across demographical groups. Groups showing greater levels of polarization are primarily those with a greater level of political knowledge including those who are more affluent and have higher levels education attainment. In addition, studies (National Telecommunications and Information Administration [NTIA], 2014) find that individuals who are more affluent as well as those with greater levels of educational attainment are more likely to have Internet access including access to Internet services that are more convenient and faster such as broadband.

In the United States, as in many countries, there is a "digital divide" or inequalities in Internet access and usage. This can impact the possible influence of SNS on polarization in two ways. The first is that some individuals will be less likely to visit SNS such as Twitter and Facebook because of limited Internet access. The second effect is less obvious but just as important. Research (Selwyn, 2004) finds that when Internet access is more accessible and quicker it can encourages greater usage of the Internet and the development Internet skills. Among these skills is "information literacy" or the ability to determine which information to obtain from the Internet for specific tasks (Mossberger, Tolbert & Stansbury, 2003). These findings suggests that some individuals who visit SNS may experience less of a polarization effect because they are less likely to distinguish which online sources best match their personal viewpoints. Those with higher levels of income and education, however, should be among those more likely to become polarized because of greater political knowledge as well as have the Internet skills to identify websites that meet their needs.

Political interests is measured using the question, "How often do you pay attention to politics and elections?" Responses are coded on a 5-point scale where 1 indicates always and category 5 signifies a response of never. It is expected that individuals with greater political interests would be more likely to seek out greater political information. *Age* is measured in years, and *Gender* is measured using a binary variable coded 1 for male and 0 for female. The literature provides little help in predicting the impact of age on polarization. Although older individuals among those least likely to have Internet access (NTIA, 2014), they are among those most likely to be engaged politically (McAtee, & Wolak, 2011; Leighley & Nagler, 1992). Although it is expected that older individuals might search out additional political information on the web, they are also less likely to have the information literacy skills to find SNS that might best match their political views. They could be exposed to a variety of political viewpoints, lessen the effect of polarization. This trend is rapidly changing. Even though social network activities are still dominated by those between the ages of 18 and 29, this activity continues to grow and expand among older members of the electorate (Pew Internet & American Life Project, 2013a). Like age, the relationship between gender and polarization is not entirely clear. Gender is not among the demographic factors related to the Internet access or usage (NTIA, 2014). Nevertheless, there has been a long term "gender gap" between men and women in terms of party preference. Although women have been fairly consistent in their preference for the Democratic Party, men have increasingly moved to the Republican Party. Research (Kaufman & Petrocik, 1999) suggests that the differences are based on men being more conservative, in general, then women on social issues. This suggests that if there is a polarizing effect of SNS, we might expect an enlargement of the gender gap.

To control for race and ethnicity, dummy variables were included for African Americans, Others, and Latinos with non-Hispanic Whites as the reference group. The (NTIA, 2014) finds that Asian Americans and non-Hispanic Whites are more likely to have broadband Internet access at home suggesting the likelihood of greater information literacy. In addition, research (McAtee & Wolak, 2011; Leighley & Nagler, 1992) finds that non-Hispanic whites are more likely to be politically involved. This suggests that non-Hispanic whites may be among those more likely to become polarized as well as have the Internet skills to identify which political SNS will bests match their political views. A measure of party identification was included where respondents were asked to place themselves on a 7-point scale ranging from strong Democrat through moderate to strong Republican. Research (Stroud, 2008; Garrett, 2009) has found that individuals with greater levels of party attachment are better at deciphering partisan cues and should be better at identifying SNS and other news sources that better match their viewpoints.

Because individual favorability of government or government actors can be influence by judgment of them including perception of their ability to solve problems (Ulbig, 2002), a measure was included for individual perception of their economy wellbeing. Economic wellbeing is measured using the question, "Will you be better off 1 year from now?" Responses are coded on a 5-point scale where 1 indicates much better and category 5 signifies a response of much worse. Finally, SNS are not the only source of political information. To control for the influence of our media sources we included controls for Internet news, television, radio and newspapers. For each media sources, respondents were asked during a typical week, how many days did they use this media sources for news and political information. The responses were measured on a scale from 0 to 7 days.

FINDINGS AND DISCUSSION

In Tables 1 and 2, the dependent variables were coded so that higher scores are associated with greater approval for a particular political actor or group. Since the dependent variables approach a continuous variable, models are estimated using OLS regression. Table 1 presents the findings for the feeling thermometers towards conservatives, liberals and the Tea Party while Table 2 presents the findings the federal government, unions and feminists. Taken together, the findings from both tables lend support to the argument that ideologues that use social media will have less polarized evaluations of political and social groups than ideologues that do not use social media.

For 4 of the 6 dependent variables, the interaction term for political ideology and whether the respondent typically visited SNS such as Twitter and Facebook to learn about the 2012 presidential election was significant and positive. The meaning of the interaction term is dependent on the sign of the coefficient of ideology. If the signs of the interaction term are the same as the signs of the main effect of ideology, this indicates that social media increases the effect of ideology on the evaluation of the target

Table 1. Feeling Thermometers

	Conservative		Liberal		Tea Party	
Variables	**β (se)**	**p>|z|**	**β (se)**	**p>|z|**	**β (se)**	**p>|z|**
Media						
Social Network Site	**- 5.16(2.12)**	**.015**	**-3.37(1.81)**	**.063**	**4.15(2.12)**	**.051**
Internet News	**-.380(.118)**	**.001**	**-.374(.118)**	**.002**	**-.447(.138)**	**.001**
Radio	**.356(.121)**	**.003**	-.153(.120)	.201	**.712(.141)**	**.000**
Television	**.561(.137)**	**.000**	.218(.137)	.111	**.442(.161)**	**.006**
Newspaper	-.034(.121)	.782	.102(.121)	.400	**-.461(.141)**	**.001**
Individual Level Variables						
Age	**.066(.022)**	**.002**	.021(.022)	.343	-.028(.026)	.274
Male	**-3.57(.596)**	**.000**	**-1.86(.595)**	**.002**	**-2.02(.698)**	**.004**
Latino	**2.08(.882)**	**.018**	**1.89(.881)**	**.032**	1.54(1.04)	.137
Black	**3.34(.941)**	**.000**	**2.49(.940)**	**.008**	**-4.18(1.10)**	**.000**
Other	- 1.30(1.25)	.300	-.137(1.25)	.913	1.57(1.47)	.285
Education	**-.285(.138)**	**.039**	**.521(.138)**	**.000**	**-.826(.163)**	**.000**
Income	-.038(.040)	.349	-055(.040)	.175	**-.151(.047)**	**.001**
Party ID	**3.09(.191)**	**.000**	**-3.91(.191)**	**.000**	**4.03(.225)**	**.000**
Ideology	**7.30(.304)**	**.000**	**-8.41(.303)**	**.000**	**6.26(.357)**	**.000**
Ideology*SNS	.614(.415)	.139	**1.28(.414)**	**.002**	-.724(.487)	.137
Political Interest	.018(.323)	.955	**-.572(.322)**	**.076**	.450(.377)	.233
Financial Wellness	-.043(.251)	.862	**-1.63(.250)**	**.000**	**1.49(.293)**	**.000**
Constant **Adjusted R2**	**10.78(2.68)** .4182	**.000**	**95.91(2.69)** .4933	**.000** **.000**	**113.31(2.77)** .3739	**.020** **.000**
N	4287		4275		4243	

Sources: *American National Election Studies (ANES) 2012 Time Series Study.* OLS regression estimates with standard errors in parentheses. Reported probabilities are based on two-tailed tests. Statistically significant coefficients at .10 or less in bold.

Table 2. Feeling Thermometers

	Federal Government		Feminists		Unions	
Variables	**β (se)**	p>lzl	**β (se)**	p>lzl	**β (se)**	p>lzl
Media						
Social Network Site	**- 4.17(1.98)**	**.035**	-2.44(2.02)	.227	**-7.20(2.20)**	**.001**
Internet News	**-.667(.129)**	**.000**	**-.490(.132)**	**.000**	**-.712(.143)**	**.000**
Radio	**.371(.132)**	**.005**	-.152(.134)	.258	**-.261(.146)**	**.074**
Television	**.620(.150)**	**.000**	**.366(.153)**	**.017**	**.410(.166)**	**.014**
Newspaper	.098(.132)	.460	-.008(.135)	.953	**.324(.147)**	**.028**
Individual Level Variables						
Age	.008(.024)	.721	**.147(.024)**	**.000**	-.031(.026)	.233
Male	**-1.61(.650)**	**.014**	**-5.81(.664)**	**.000**	**-1.64(.721)**	**.023**
Latino	**10.03(.962)**	**.000**	**2.61(.985)**	**.008**	1.15(1.07)	.283
Black	**12.19(1.03)**	**.000**	**2.41(1.05)**	**.022**	**8.60(1.14)**	**.000**
Other	.940(1.37)	.491	-.625(1.39)	.654	-3.32(1.51)	.832
Education	**-.272(.151)**	**.071**	**.697(.154)**	**.000**	-.106(.167)	.527
Income	**-.116(.044)**	**.009**	-.010(.045)	.821	**-.111(.049)**	**.023**
Party ID	**-2.49(.209)**	**.000**	**-1.88(.214)**	**.000**	**-3.74(.232)**	**.000**
Ideology	**-2.02(.331)**	**.000**	**-4.84(.341)**	**.000**	**-4.20(.367)**	**.000**
Ideology*SNS	**1.87(.453)**	**.000**	**1.28(.463)**	**.006**	**2.09(.503)**	**.000**
Political Interest	**1.12(.351)**	**.001**	-.376(.359)	.294	-.123(.389)	.751
Financial Wellness	**-2.56(.274)**	**.000**	**-1.21(.280)**	**.000**	**-1.29(.303)**	**.000**
Constant **Adjusted R2**	**63.41(2.92)** .2597	.000 .000	**69.38(2.99)** .2239	**.000** **.000**	**88.23(3.24)** .2818	**.000** **.000**
N	4297		4274		4292	

Sources: *American National Election Studies (ANES) 2012 Time Series Study.* OLS regression estimates with standard errors in parentheses. Reported probabilities are based on two-tailed tests. Statistically significant coefficients at .10 or less in bold.

group. If, on the other hand, the signs are opposites, then the affect of ideology is attenuated, which decreases polarization. For all four of our significant interactions, the sign on ideology is negative (the more conservative you are, the less you like the group), but the interaction is positive. This suggests that taking part in social networking activities helped to limit the polarized individuals with strong ideological leanings. The four groups or political actors for which there was a positive and significant interaction effect were the federal government, unions, feminists and liberals. The two groups for which the interaction term was not significant were conservatives and the Tea Party. The groups for which social networking interactions appear to increase polarization are ones that most likely would garner positive responses from liberal individuals but negative scores from conservative respondents. Ulbig (2002) provides a possible explanation. His research finds that perception of political actors to influence perception of government in general. Because the U.S. currently has a Democratic president, individuals with a conservative ideological leaning may have a more negative perception of government and other political actors in general, but, through information found on social networks, their perceptions became slightly less negative.

The findings for political ideology and party identification were significant and in the expected direction. Republican identifiers and more political conservative individuals were more likely to give the Tea Party and conservatives a higher score while giving the federal government, unions, feminists and liberals lower scores on the feeling thermometers. Although findings for visiting a social network site to learn about the 2012 presidential election were generally significant, there is less consistency in the direction of the relationship for each dependent variable. While using social network sites for finding information on the presidential election was associated with higher scores for the Tea Party, it was not associated with changes in scores for feminists. For all other groups, social network visits was associated with lower thermometer scores. The differences in direction and relative importance of certain actors or political groups might be attributed to their relative importance and media coverage during the 2012 presidential election. One of our earliest theories to describe the linkage between politics and the media, deliberative democracy, describes media as a catalyst or energy source for political conversation. In essence, the media provides individuals with information to use during discussion (Tarde, 1899; Dewey, 1927). The media emphasized some of the political actors explored in this research more than others. This might have impacted their relative importance in discussions on the various social network sites.

Previous research did not provide a clear picture regarding the relationship between age and polarization. The findings from this study suggest that the relationship might be fairly weak. There were only two models (feminists and conservatives) for which there was a significant relationship between age and polarization. In both cases, older individuals were more likely to have a more positive perception of the political actor or group. Although previous research was unable to predict a clear relationship between age and polarization, it was expected that there would be a direct relationship between gender and polarization. Based on the gender gap, it was expected that men would have more positive views of conservative groups and institutions compared to women. However, regardless of the group or political actor, men were more likely to rate them lower than women. This suggests that men may have a greater propensity to rate groups more stringently then women. Individuals with higher levels of income and educational attainment were predicted to be among the groups more likely to show a greater level of polarization based on expected higher levels of political knowledge and information literacy. The findings supported this prediction for educations. Individuals with higher levels of education were more likely to rank conservative groups lower on thermometer scale while ranking liberal groups higher. The findings were less consistent for income. The relationship between polarization and income was not significant for feminists, conservatives and liberals while negative and statistically significant for unions, the federal government and the Tea Party.

The findings for economic wellbeing are significant and in the expected direction. Individuals who believed that they would be better off financially a year in the future were more likely to rate liberal groups higher and conservative groups lower. This follows from Ulbig (2002) and the fact that there is currently a Democratic president. Political interest, on the other hand, was not found to have a strong relationship with polarization. Political interest was only found to be statistically significant in two models (the federal government and liberals). Each news source (whether traditional or online) were found to be statistically significant in at least some models. The difference among media forms and their relationship to polarization may be dependent on how easily an individual can select information that supports their beliefs using a particular medium. The only source of news to be statistically significant across all 6 models was online news which is expected to be the easiest to tailor to one's interests and political predispositions (Sunstein, 2002).

Finally race/ethnicity was found to be an important predictor of polarization with African Americans more likely to rank all groups and political actors higher on the feeling thermometers then non-Hispanic whites with the exception of the Tea Party. In addition, Hispanics were more likely to rank all groups higher than non-Hispanic whites with the exception of the Tea Party and unions. This is inconsistent with predictions that non-Hispanic whites would be among the groups more likely to show a greater level of polarization based on expected higher levels of political participation and information literacy. Mossberger et al. (2003) provide some findings that might help explain this outcome. They found that both African American and Hispanics were more likely than non-Hispanic whites to have positive attitudes toward the Internet. They concluded that difference in Internet usage based on race/ethnicity was actually the result of other factors such as income and education. Once these factors are controlled for, there is little difference in Internet usage based on race/ethnicity. Furthermore, studies show that for some forms of social media, such as Pinterest, there is greater usage by African-Americans and Hispanic than non-Hispanic whites (Pew Internet & American Life Project, 2013b).

FUTURE RESEARCH DIRECTIONS

In examining the question of whether individuals with strong ideological leanings, who use social media, will have more polarized opinions, this chapter relied on data collected by another entity. There are advantages and disadvantages associated with all forms of data analysis. One disadvantage associated with secondary data analysis is that the data was collected for a specific purpose and may not be ideally suited for other research. We were fortunate in that this dataset was well suited for this study. It was also fortunate that the dataset was a time-series that collected data prior and after the 2012 presidential election from the same set of respondents with measurements for the dependent variables being collected in the post-election study and the main independent variables collected in the pre-election study. This allowed for the establishment of time order. Nevertheless, both sets were related to the 2012 elections. It is possible that there were events uniquely related to the 2012 precedential election that might influence the outcome of this study. Further studies are necessary to help validate our findings. For example, this survey was conducted during a presidential election which is more likely to garner significant media coverage. Additonal research should be conducted during a midterm election, when there is typically less media coverage, to see if social media usage has a greater or lesser impact on polarization.

In addition, this study did not directly measure the content of anyone's social media networks. Due to limitations of data (and the near impossibility of actually measuring and characterizing the contents), we have to make assumptions about what kind of information people are being exposed to on social media. At best, we have to infer that respondents are not as likely to ideologically censor their choices on Facebook and Twitter based on proxies for political knowledge and information literacy. This is a fairly common difficulty in non-experimental studies of media and opinion. While it forces us to speculate on the mechanisms underlying the effects we observe, it should undermine our results. Additional research, where respondents are questioned about the exact media sources used and social media sites visited would help improve upon this study.

CONCLUSION

This chapter began with the question, "Are ideologues that use social media will have more polarized evaluations of political and social groups than ideologues that do not use social media, or non-ideologues?" Contrary to our initial expectations, it appears that, in fact, social media use seems to attenuate rather than exacerbate polarization. While evidence suggests that both elites and citizens have developed more consistent ideologies, extreme issue stances, negative attitudes towards cooperation, and dislike toward political opponents that indicate a hollowing out of the political middle, and the rise of a new, more extreme and confrontational style of politics, social media use seems to serve as a modest corrective to this trend. Of course, most other forces seem to be pushing the public in the direction of more, rather than less polarization. Although there is consistent evidence that both the electorate and elites are becoming more polarized, there is not a consensus whether this trend will result in negative or positive impact on political participation in the United States. Predictions on the potential impact of increased polarization are mixed. Some argue that polarization will lead to decreased turnouts through increasing citizen cynicism and distrust of government (Layman et al., 2006) or decreasing citizen's feelings of political efficacy (Hetherington, 2007). On the other hand, a considerable body of literature demonstrates that polarization actually fosters participation. As the parties have moved apart, voter turnout has actually increased (Hetherington, 2007).

Just as there are no clear cut answers on how polarization may impact the political process, there is also disagreement on why there is a trend toward increased polarization in the U.S. Among the possible contributing factors are advances in telecommunication technology such as the Internet. The findings in our research were not consistent across all models in these studies. There was some indication that the impact of social network sites on views of various groups and institutions may be mediated by personal judgments of actors associated with these groups and institutions. Among the first to predict that the Internet could give rise to increased polarization was Negroponte (1995) who argued that people would use the Internet in such a way that it would allow them to consume news and other content in the form of "the daily me," a serving of information in quasi newspaper form perfectly tailored to one's interests and political predispositions. It appears, however, that while it is possible to use Twitter or Face book as a way of achieving Sunstein's "daily me" a large number of users are not. Instead, social media appears to be more like Mutz's cross cutting social networks, or Putnam's bridging social Capital, which promote a degree of tolerance of opposing viewpoints, rather than polarization due to exposure to a wide variety of points of view. This is consistent with the findings on people's "unfriending" habits, where a solid majority of even the most ideologically extreme respondents are not unfriending people they disagree with, but instead seem to be at least aware of political disagreement among their friends (Rainie & Smith, 2012). Unlike news, where there is solid evidence that people seek out ideologically consistent viewpoints (e.g. Stroud 2012), social media functions differently, perhaps driven by different motivations for use. When using a news site, there is a strong information seeking motive, and this would seem to foster selective exposure. By contrast, social media is used differently (hence the name). Rather than pure information seeking, there is a much stronger social component. Much like Putnam's work on social capital in non political groups, for many users, any exposure to politics in social media is incidental, rather than purposeful. A typical SNS user comes to Facebook, for example, to connect with friends both past and present, and occasionally picks up political information. They may come to learn that their friends don't agree with them politically, but recognize that disagreement isn't a deal breaker, hence fostering some attenuation of dislike for people we disagree with.

REFERENCES

Abramowitz, A. (2010). *The disappearing center: Engaged citizens, polarization, and American democracy*. New Haven, CT: Yale University Press.

Abramowitz, A., & Saunders, K. (2008). Is polarization a myth? *The Journal of Politics*, *70*(2), 542–555. doi:10.1017/S0022381608080493

American National Election Studies. (2014). User's guide and codebook for the ANES 2012 time series study. Ann Arbor, MI: The University of Michigan and Stanford University

Arceneaux, K., & Johnson, M. (2013). *Changing minds or changing channels: Partisan news in an age of choice*. Chicago: University of Chicago Press. doi:10.7208/chicago/9780226047447.001.0001

Baum, M. A., & Kernell, S. (1999). Has cable ended the golden age of presidential television? *The American Political Science Review*, *93*(1), 99–114. doi:10.2307/2585763

Bishop, B. (2008). *The big sort*. Boston: Houghton Mifflin.

Campante, F., & Hojman, J. (2013). Media polarization: Evidence from the introduction of broadcast TV in the United States. *Journal of Public Economics*, *100*, 79–92. doi:10.1016/j.jpubeco.2013.02.006

Castletrione, I. (2014). Facebook and political Information in Italy and the UK: An antidote against political fragmentation and polarization. *Online Journal of Communication and Media Technologies*, *4*(1), 27–49.

Claassen, B., & Highton, B. (2009). Policy polarization among party elites and the significance of political awareness in the mass public. *Political Research Quarterly*, *62*(3), 538–551. doi:10.1177/1065912908322415

Cotton, J. (1985). Cognitive dissonance in selective exposure. In D. Zillman & J. Bryant (Eds.), *Selective Exposure to Communication* (pp. 11–34). Hillsdale, NJ: Lawrence Erlbaum Associates.

Dewey, J. (1927). *The Public and its problems*. New York: Holt.

Dimaggio, P., Evans, J., & Bryson, B. (1996). Have Americans' social attitudes become more polarized? *American Journal of Sociology*, *102*(3), 690–755. doi:10.1086/230995

Dimmock, M., Kiley, J., Keeter, S., & Doherty, C. (2014). *Political polarization in the American public*. Retrieved July 27, 2014 from http://www.people-press.org/files/2014/06/6-12-2014-Political-Polarization-Release.pdf

Facebook. (2014). *How news feed works*. Retrieved October 4, 2014 from https://www.facebook.com/help/327131014036297/

Fiorina, M., Abrams, S., & Pope, J. (2010). *Culture war?: The myth of a polarized America* (3rd ed.). New York: Longman.

Garrett, R. (2009). Echo chambers online?: Politically motivated selective exposure among Internet users. *Journal of Computer-Mediated Communication*, *14*(2), 265–285. doi:10.1111/j.1083-6101.2009.01440.x

Hetherington, M. (2001). Resurgent mass partisanship: The role of elite mass polarization. *The American Political Science Review*, *95*(3), 619–631. doi:10.1017/S0003055401003045

Hetherington, M. (2007). Turned off or turned on? How polarization affects political engagement. In Red and Blue Nation? Consequences and Correction of America's Polarized Politics (vol. 2, pp. 1-53). Washington, DC: Brookings Institution Press.

Hetherington, M., & Weiler, J. (2009). *Authoritarianism and polarization in American politics*. New York: Cambridge University Press. doi:10.1017/CBO9780511802331

Holmes, J. (2009). *21st century media effects: Choice, predispositions, and their impact on agenda setting and priming*. (Doctoral Dissertation). University of Minnesota. Retrieved from http://purl.umn.edu/58353

Isenberg, D. (1986). Group polarization: A critical review and meta-analysis. *Journal of Personality and Social Psychology*, *50*(6), 1141–1151. doi:10.1037/0022-3514.50.6.1141

Iyengar, S., & Hahn, K. (2009). Red media, blue media: Evidence of ideological selectivity in media use. *Journal of Communication*, *59*(1), 19–39. doi:10.1111/j.1460-2466.2008.01402.x

Iyengar, S., Sood, G., & Lelkes, Y. (2012). Affect not ideology: A social identity perspective on polarization. *Public Opinion Quarterly*, *76*(3), 411–435. doi:10.1093/poq/nfs038

Iyengar, S., & Westwood, S. (2014). Fear and loathing across party lines: New evidence on group polarization. *American Journal of Political Science*. doi:10.1111/ajps.12152

Jones, J. (2014). *Obama's fifth year job approval ratings among most polarized*. Retrieved September 27, 2014 from http://www.gallup.com/poll/167006/obama-fifth-year-job-approval-ratings-among-polarized.aspx

Kaufman, K., & Petrocik, J. (1999). The changing politics of American men: Understanding the sources of the gender gap. *American Journal of Political Science*, *43*(3), 864–887. doi:10.2307/2991838

Knoblach-Westerwick, S. (2012). Selective exposure and reinforcement of attitudes and partisanship before a presidential election. *Journal of Communication*, *62*(4), 628–642. doi:10.1111/j.1460-2466.2012.01651.x

Layman, G., Carsey, T., & Horowitz, J. (2006). Party polarization in American politics: Characteristics, causes, and consequences. *Annual Review of Political Science*, *9*(1), 83–110. doi:10.1146/annurev.polisci.9.070204.105138

Lee, J., Choi, J., Kim, C., & Kim, Y. (2014). Social media, network heterogeneity, and opinion polarization. *Journal of Communication*, *64*(4), 702–722. doi:10.1111/jcom.12077

Leighley, J., & Nagler, J. (1992). Socioeconomic class bias in turn out, 1964-1988: The voters remain the same. *The American Political Science Review*, *86*(3), 725–736. doi:10.2307/1964134

Levendusky, M. (2009). *The partisan sort: How liberals became Democrats and conservatives became Republicans*. Chicago: University of Chicago Press. doi:10.7208/chicago/9780226473673.001.0001

Levendusky, M. (2013). Why do partisan media polarize viewers? *American Journal of Political Science*, *57*(3), 611–623. doi:10.1111/ajps.12008

Mann, T., & Orenstein, N. (2012). *It's even worse than it looks: How the American constitutional system collided with the new politics of extremism.* New York: Basic Books.

McAtee, A., & Wolak, J. (2011). Why people decide to participate in state politics. *Political Research Quarterly, 64*(1), 45–58. doi:10.1177/1065912909343581

Mossberger, K., Tolbert, C., & McNeal, R. (2007). *Digital citizenship: the Internet, society and participation.* Cambridge, MA: MIT Press.

Mossberger, K., Tolbert, C., & Stansbury, M. (2003). *Virtual inequality: beyond the digital divide.* Washington, DC: Georgetown Press.

Mutz, D. (2002). Cross cutting social networks: Testing democratic theory in practice. *The American Political Science Review, 96*(1), 111–126. doi:10.1017/S0003055402004264

National Telecommunications and Information Administration. (2014). *Exploring the digital nation: Embracing the mobile internet.* Retrieved from http://www.ntia.doc.gov/files/ntia/publications/exploring_the_digital_nation_embracing_the_mobile_internet_10162014.pdf

Negroponte, N. (1995). *Being Digital.* New York: Knopf.

Pew Internet & American Life Project. (2013a). *72% of Online Adults are Social Networking Site Users.* Retrieved March 10, 2014, from http://www.pewinternet.org/files/oldmedia/Files/Reports/2013/PIP_Social_networking_sites_update_PDF.pdf

Pew Internet & American Life Project. (2013b). *Teens, Social Media, and Privacy.* Retrieved March 10, 2014, from http://www.pewinternet.org/2013/05/21/teens-social-media-and-privacy

Prior, M. (2007). *Post broadcast democracy.* New York: Cambridge University Press. doi:10.1017/CBO9781139878425

Putnam, R. (2000). *Bowling alone: The collapse and revival of American community.* New York: Simon & Schuster. doi:10.1145/358916.361990

Rainie, L., & Smith, A. (2012). *Social networking sites and politics.* Retrieved September 12, 2014 from http://www.pewinternet.org/files/old-media//Files/Reports/2012/PIP_SNS_and_politics.pdf

Sears, D., & Freedman, J. (1967). Selective exposure to information: A critical review. *Public Opinion Quarterly, 31*(2), 194–213. doi:10.1086/267513

Selwyn, N. (2004). Reconsidering political and popular understandings of the digital divide. *New Media & Society, 6*(3), 341–362. doi:10.1177/1461444804042519

Stoker, L., & Jennings, K. (2008). Of time and the development of partisan polarization. *American Journal of Political Science, 52*(3), 619–635. doi:10.1111/j.1540-5907.2008.00333.x

Stroud, N. (2008). Media use and political predispositions: Revisiting the concept of selective exposure. *Political Behavior, 30*(3), 341–366. doi:10.1007/s11109-007-9050-9

Stroud, N. (2012). *Niche news: The politics of news choice.* New York: Oxford University Press.

Sunstein, C. (2002). *Republic.com.* Princeton, NJ: Princeton University Press.

Tarde, G. (1989). Opinion and conversation. (J. Ruth, Trans.). Paris: Presses Universitaires de France. (Original work published 1899).

Ulbig, S. (2002). Policies, procedures, and people: Sources of support for government. *Social Science Quarterly*, *83*(3), 789–809. doi:10.1111/1540-6237.00115

Zaller, J. (1992). *The nature and origins of mass opinion.* New York: Cambridge University Press. doi:10.1017/CBO9780511818691

ADDITIONAL READING

Baldassarri, D., & Gelman, A. (2008). Partisans without constraint: Political polarization and trends in American public opinion. *American Journal of Sociology*, *114*(2), 484–486. doi:10.1086/590649 PMID:24932012

Bimber, B. (2014). Digital media in the Obama campaigns of 2008 and 2012: Adaptation to the personal political communication environment. *Journal of Information Technology & Politics*, *11*(2), 130–150. doi:10.1080/19331681.2014.895691

Bimber, B., & Davis, R. (2003). *Campaigning online: The Internet in the U.S. elections.* New York: Oxford University Press.

Brewer, M. (2005). The rise in partisanship and the expansion of partisan conflict with the American electorate. *Political Research Quarterly*, *58*(2), 219–229. doi:10.1177/106591290505800203

Carlisle, J., & Patton, R. (2013). Is social media changing how we understand political engagement? An analysis of Facebook and the 2008 presidential election. *Political Research Quarterly*, *66*(3), 883–895. doi:10.1177/1065912913482758

Chaffee, S., & Schleuder, J. (1986). Measurement and effects of attention to media news. *Human Communication Research*, *13*(3), 373–399. doi:10.1177/009365086013003006

Fernandes, J., Giurcanu, M., Bowers, K., & Neely, J. (2010). The Writing on the wall: A content analysis of college students' Facebook groups for the 2008 presidential election. *Mass Communication & Society*, *13*(5), 653–675. doi:10.1080/15205436.2010.516865

Fiorina, M., Abrams, S., & Pope, J. (2008). Polarization in the American public: Misconceptions and misreadings. *The Journal of Politics*, *70*(2), 556–560. doi:10.1017/S002238160808050X

Gruzd, A., & Roy, J. (2014). Investigating political polarization on Twitter: A Canadian perspective. *Policy & Internet*, *6*(1), 28–45. doi:10.1002/1944-2866.POI354

Hargittai, E., & Hinnant, A. (2008). Digital inequalities: Differences in young adults' use of the Internet. *Communication Research*, *35*(5), 602–621. doi:10.1177/0093650208321782

Hetherington, M. (2009). Review article: Putting polarization in perspective. *British Journal of Political Science*, *39*(2), 413–448. doi:10.1017/S0007123408000501

Huckfeldt, R., & Sprague, J. (1991). Discussant effects on vote choice: Intimacy, structure, and interdependence. *The Journal of Politics*, *53*(1), 122–158. doi:10.2307/2131724

Hussey, L. (2012). Polarized politics and citizen disengagement: The role of belief systems. *American Politics Research*, *20*(10), 1–31.

Jones, D. (2010). Partisan polarization and congressional accountability in house elections. *American Journal of Political Science*, *54*(2), 323–337. doi:10.1111/j.1540-5907.2010.00433.x

Layman, G., & Carsey, T. (2002). Party polarization and conflict extension in the American electorate. *American Journal of Political Science*, *46*(4), 786–802. doi:10.2307/3088434

Levendusky, M. (2010). Clearer cues, more consistent voters: A benefit of elite polarization. *Political Behavior*, *32*(1), 111–131. doi:10.1007/s11109-009-9094-0

Levy, F., & Murnane, R. (1996). With what skills are computers a complement? *The American Economic Review*, *86*(2), 258–262.

Macafee, T. (2013). Some of these things are not like the others: Examining motivations and political predispositions among political Facebook activity. *Computers in Human Behavior*, *29*(6), 2766–2775. doi:10.1016/j.chb.2013.07.019

Malhotra, N. (2008). Partisan polarization and blame attribution in a federal system: The case of Hurricane Katrina. *Publius*, *38*(4), 651–670. doi:10.1093/publius/pjn018

Muhlberger, P. (2004). Access, skill, and motivation in online political discussion: Testing cyberrealism. In P. Shane (Ed.), *Democracy online: The prospects for political renewal through the Internet* (pp. 225–237). New York: Routledge.

Robertson, S., Vatrapu, R., & Medina, R. (2010). Off the wall political discourse: Facebook use in the 2008 U.S. presidential election. *Information Polity*, *15*(1/2), 11–31.

Stonecash, J., & Mariani, M. (2000). Republican gains in the House in the 1994 elections: Class polarization in American politics. *Political Science Quarterly*, *115*(1), 93–113. doi:10.2307/2658035

Sunstein, C. (2009). *Going to extremes: How like minds unite and divide*. New York: Oxford University Press.

Theriault, S. (2008). *Party polarization in Congress*. NY: Columbia University Press. doi:10.1017/CBO9780511790652

Tsfati, Y., Stroud, N., & Chotiner, A. (2014). Exposure to ideological news and perceived opinion climate: Testing the media effects component of spiral of silence in a fragmented medial landscape. *The International Journal of Press/Politics*, *19*(3), 3–23. doi:10.1177/1940161213508206

KEY TERMS AND DEFINITIONS

Bimodal Distribution: A distribution of opinion where most opinions cluster in two distant groups rather than around the median as in a normal distribution. This is a sign of polarization, as it shows many people with extreme opinions and a relatively small number in the middle.

Cyberbalkanization: Deliberate efforts to focus on online communication that confirms your pre-existing beliefs, and to avoid information that challenges them.

Information Literacy: The ability to determine which information found on the Internet is appropriate for a specific task.

Mainstreaming: The convergence of public opinion around a single position when elites also adopt a single position.

Network Heterogeneity: The degree to which a user's social media connections represent a wide variety of opinions and positions rather than a narrow cluster of likeminded ones.

Polarization: The divergence of political attitudes to extreme ideological positions at the expense of moderates. Polarization often also includes a rise in animosity between ideological camps.

Selective Exposure: Deliberate efforts to expose oneself to particular information or information sources.

Social Media: Electronic communication sources that allow users to network with friends to share a wide variety of content.

Chapter 2
"Microblog, A Public Sphere?": An Examination of Opinion Expression about "Snowden Affair" on Twitter and Sina Weibo

Shaohai Jiang
Texas A&M University, USA

ABSTRACT

Based on Habermas' public sphere theory, this chapter examined netizens' opinion expression about the "Snowden affair" on two microblogging websites, Twitter and its Chinese counterpart, Sina Weibo. The results indicated that on Sina Weibo, netizens were more likely to express their opinion and particularly show their attitude towards Snowden. However, their voice was quite homogenous, mostly supporting him. On Twitter, netizens had diverse attitudes towards Snowden, and the news reports on Twitter covered far more topics. However, Twitter users prefer forwarding news to directly expressing their own opinion. And the US government did not have active engagement on Twitter. Thus, in both democratic and authoritarian contexts, microblogging has some important elements of public sphere, although it might not be absolute. We cannot ignore the communicative power of microblogging to promote cooperation and mutual understanding, which is significant in the democratic process and civil society in both China and the US.

INTRODUCTION

Social networking sites have obtained considerable academic attention for their potential to promote civic engagement and political participation, including opinion expression by common citizens (Tumasjan, Sprenger, Sandner, & Welpe, 2011). Compared with traditional media, such as newspaper and television, which involve inevitable delays, social media can be updated constantly and timely and require less money and physical effort (Best & Krueger, 2005). Netizens on social media can consume the online version of offline content timely and also generate original content that might facilitate new political engagement. Such political participation takes many forms, such as forwarding political news, sharing

DOI: 10.4018/978-1-4666-9879-6.ch002

opinions toward current events, expressing disappointment with governments and even participating in online collective actions to fight against certain public policy (Di Gennaro & Dutton, 2006). Thus, it is the use of social media as the source of political news that greatly increases the diversity and openness of information. Due to the flood of up-to-the-second news on social media, people are readily exposed to political and social issues every day and therefore have more opportunity and motivation to express their opinions. In addition, the interactive nature of social media may amplify the political expression (Kushin & Yamamoto, 2010). People can share their voice with minimal cost, and at the same time their viewpoints may be instantly transmitted to global audiences and trigger new comment and further deliberation (Lupia & Sin, 2003). Although many scholars point out the promising potential of social media to facilitate broad political discussion and participation, such debates on the influence of social media on politics and what it really means to democracy have never been stopped. Scholars who are pessimistic about the political uses of the Internet emphasize that its virtual public sphere still mirrors the existing social structure in offline context (Margolis & Resnick, 2000). Social and political elites always talk amongst themselves. The gap between them and the common citizens has never been bridged unless those political professionals want it to be. However, the reality is that such new bridges just exist within actors in the political networks while they may not extend beyond it to engage the public.

Considering the mixed result of how social media could promote political engagement, this chapter specifically focused on one type of political participation, which is opinion expression and one social networking site, which is the microblogging. Also, there is a lack of understanding of such democratic power of social media from a cross-cultural perspective. Thus, based on Habermas' public sphere theory, this chapter explored netizens' opinion expression about one important political and international issue, the "Snowden affair", on two microblogging websites, Twitter and its Chinese counterpart, Sina Weibo. Through this analysis, it is interesting to see whether similar or different trends would emerge regarding public spheres on Twitter and Sina Weibo. To this end, this study examined the voice on these two microblog platforms regarding "Snowden affair", including the dominant topic or theme, the frequency of each theme, what population or sector generated more voice, and the attitude towards Snowden. In doing so, this chapter aims to contribute to the discourse on how the social media can be considered a networked public sphere, and how this cyberspace would affect political participation.

POLITICAL MICROBLOGGING: TWITTER VS. SINA WEIBO

Among all social media, microblogging has a particularly democratic power to facilitate public opinion due to its open and widely-connected structure. Dissimilar to other social media, such as Facebook, the microblogging is not restricted in in-network audiences. Instead, postings on the microblog can be readily seen by all the users globally, creating a platform for easy responses and comments in a vibrant online context for public discourse (Kim, 2011).

Twitter is the first and for now the most popular online microblog service around the world (Parmelee & Bichard, 2011). Everyday 140 million active Twitter users globally contribute over 340 million tweets. More than 1.6 billion search queries have been made on Twitter each day (Twitter, 2012). Although there is no accurate statistic showing how many tweets are actually read by the public, it is still convincing that Twitter serves as a significant center for connecting people from all over the world to participate in collective actions, discussing public issues and disseminating news. On Twitter, every user can have followers, who will see the users' tweets and status updates. Also, users are able to follow whoever they like. It is very convenient to reply and comment on other's postings. Many celebrities actively use Twitter as an outlet to promote themselves. Media and opinion leaders also make good use of this platform to release their voices about public issues. Government officials, such as Barack Obama, the president of the US, and David Cameron, the prime minister of the UK, are involved in tweeting with common citizens. In United States, Barack Obama's historic wins in 2008 and 2012 presidential elections have demonstrated the significance of Twitter in political campaigns. For example, about 10 million tweets were generated during the first presidential debate in 2012 and on Election Day, 20 million total postings were using #election2012 hashtag. This most tweeted event marks a new era in the history of US political election. Another statistics showed that a stunning 327,453 election tweets per minute made the 2012 election "the Twitter election" (Zhang, Seltzer, & Bichard, 2013). In addition to the political campaign, Twitter, as a great mobilizing platform for civic engagement, has demonstrated its effect on different issues and in different countries. Through the spontaneous, real-time online communication, netizens are connected with each other on diverse political or social events, such as the Arab Spring in Middle East, the Orange Revolution in Ukraine, and the Networked protests in Greece. These and other important online revolutions become hot topics in this digital era. Although Twitter has been regarded as a democratic weapon in many western countries, it has been blocked since 2009 in China. The majority of Chinese citizens thus have no access to it any more. In order to meet the increasing needs for social networking and opinion expression, Sina, a Chinese cooperate first launched its own microblog, Sina Weibo, in 2009.

Since its launch, Sina Weibo quickly reached 100 million registered users in its first year of operation, and has attracted over 500 million users in four years' time. But it took Twitter almost four years to reach its first 100 million registered users and six years for the milestone of 500 million users. It is thus clear that Sina Weibo grew faster than Twitter. The year 2011 was an important year to Sina Weibo, as it surpassed Twitter's popularity based on the number of registered users. In 2010, an average of 16 million new accounts registered on Sina Weibo every month resulted in a 300% increase in total registered users (Zhang, 2012). In addition, Sina Weibo has borrowed different functions from other social networking sites into its interface. For example, Sina Weibo offers the function of group discussion, which is quite similar to the Bullet Board System (BBS). Users can also "like" a posting, which is the same as that in Facebook. As a real multi-media platform, Sina Weibo allows people to post different types of files, including words, pictures, videos, flash, music, online voting and so on. Such flexibility and diversity increase the interactivity of the microblog service. In addition to these technical differences, Sina Weibo has some unique characteristics. First, despite the same 140-character limit, 140 Chinese characters can express more details than English. The rough Chinese to English ratio would be around 1.57 (Neubig & Duh, 2013). Thus, this word limitation serves as a suitable requirement for users to succinctly express themselves, rather than an obstacle that may stop effectively conveying ideas. Second, China has a series of strict Internet censorship programs. The "Great Firewall of China" (GFW) blocks the access to many foreign Web sites such as Google, Facebook and Twitter; the network and search filtering system which contains a list of blacklisted keywords prevents Chinese netizens from obtaining information of certain "sensitive" topics. And China's censorship regime relies heavily on domestic companies to police their own content under penalty of fines, shutdown and criminal liability (Bamman, O'Connor, & Smith, 2012). For example, Sina Weibo has a team of people specifically working for scrutinizing information and pictures. If the content is unwanted, it will be deleted within a short period of time. Despite the control of Internet content, due to the huge amount of information and voice on Sina Weibo, running such a big domestic portal is expensive and difficult to check all the postings. The number of Internet users in China increased to 564 million by the end of 2012 and about 42% of Chinese citizens have access to the Internet (Tong & Zuo, 2014). Compared with Chinese traditional media that are banned from reporting topics like mass incidents, Sina Weibo enjoys relatively more autonomy. Thus, many scholars have addressed Sina Weibo's potential for protests and social and legal mobilization, including studying its role in certain events such as the high-speed train crash in Wenzhou and the protests in Wukan (Svensson, 2014). To many western Twitter users, it may be difficult to understand the power of the only 140 Chinese characters, which becomes almost the only outlet for sounding out their voices about politics and sensitive events in a one-party state. However, another line of research attributed the popularity of Sina Weibo under the one-party system and censorship to the state's attempt to adopt microblogs as a new tool of governance. The online deliberation and consultation between the party-state and Chinese civil society still follow a top-down mode of interaction. And the rapid development of microblogs in China does not mark any major shifts in the party-state's Internet strategy (Noesselt, 2014).Therefore, microblogging in China is at an interesting position between Internet censorship and public discourse (Chan, Wu, Hao, Xi, & Jin, 2012). Whether it is an online sphere for citizen's discussion and opinion expression on political and social issues is still a question that needs further investigation.

PUBLIC SPHERE

Public opinion has obtained considerable scholarly attention. The meaning of "public" is tightly related to democratic ideals that advocate for citizen participation in public affairs (Papacharissi, 2002). Dahlgren (2005) defined the public sphere as "a constellation of communicative spaces within society, which permits the circulation of information, ideas, debates, ideally in an unfettered manner". To further understand the public sphere, Jurgen Habermas is most prominent for his discussion of this concept. Habermas has conceptualized the "public sphere" as "a realm of our social life in which something approaching public opinion can be formed" and devoted his life to the "inter-subjective communicative processes" (Calhoun, 1993).

The main feature of public sphere emerged in the early capitalism as a specific domain between state and society. According to Habermas (1991), citizens constitute a public body when they are given an opportunity to confer in an unrestricted manner, which guarantees the freedom of assembly, speech and publishing their opinions. Thus, all the citizens have equal access to the public sphere, which serves as the mediator between society and state. As the participants of the public sphere reach consensus through critical discussion, their decisions then ideally would be implemented in society by the state. Habermas called this a "bourgeois public sphere", which emerged at the end of the 17th century, with the deregulation and the abolishment of the licensing system in Britain. According to the description by Habermas (1991), "the bourgeois public sphere may be conceived above all as the sphere of private people come together as a public; they soon claimed the public sphere regulated from above against the public authorities themselves, to engage them in a debate over the general rules governing relations in the basically privatized but publicly relevant sphere of commodity exchange and social labor". Pamphlets, solons and coffee shops all created good environment for the expansion of literary public sphere, from which the political public sphere. Readers started to read and debate as a public, and social elites came to consider themselves as the public and thus transformed the public authority into more concrete practice. Therefore, the rational-critical discussion on political issues constitutes the main feature of an institutionalized public sphere (Habermas, 1991). As Webster (2011) summarized, Habermas have created "an ideal arena which is independent of government while also being autonomous of economic interests, which is dedicated to open-ended discussion and debates, the proceedings of which are open to entry and accessible to scrutiny by the citizenry".

However, the reality is far more complicated than that in Habermas' mind. For example, the public sphere takes many forms and has multiple levels. According to Keane (1995), there are mainly three sub-levels of public sphere: the micro-, meso- and macro-public spheres. Although these three levels all involve the rational-critical discussions, they have different features. The micro-public sphere reflects bottom-up, small-scale locales, where citizens create their identities as a counterbalance to top-down power that regulates public life on a local level. Micro-public spheres like discussion circles, church communities, and publishing houses are spaces where citizens could criticize the dominant concept and model of daily life and provide alternative examples to refute such opinions. The meso-public spheres are those spaces of controversy about power that encompass millions of people watching, listening, or reading across vast distances (Keane, 1995). This level of the public sphere is argued to mainly exist within the nation-state, but might also extend its boundary to audiences with a shared understanding of the sphere, like a common understanding of language. Large circulation newspapers such as Le Monde and radio and television channel like BBC are examples of media outlets that could be argued to belong to the meso-public spheres, knowing they extend their influence across geographical and cultural borders to those understanding French and English, respectively. Besides the meso-public sphere, there are macro-public spheres of global or regional magnitude, fueled by multi-national companies like Time-Warner and Reuters. But perhaps one of the most important developments within this level of public spheres is the introduction of the Internet, a network that stimulates the growth of macro-public spheres. It represents a politically constructed space that has no immediate connection to physical territory, showing how public life presently is undergoing a significant process of deterritorialization (Keane, 1995).

In addition to the different levels of public sphere, this concept should not be narrow-minded to think of it the widest possible representation of viewpoints and sound from all the public and grassroots, as Habermas addressed. Instead, we should incorporate not only ordinary citizens and NGOs, but also some privileged sectors, such as politicians, government institutions, well-resourced companies, experts, and mainstream media. In contrast with Habermas' never-realized ideal of horizontal public deliberation between "equal citizens", mass media play a significant role between citizens and the state. In the 20th century, the traditional public sphere has been dominated by the mass media. Media have added many private factors into the public sphere, which began to serve private powers (Habermas, 2006). For example, Rupert Murdoch's media kingdom exerted strong influence on political life; media empire Silvio Berlusconi became Italian prime minister. Citizens in the "control" of mass media gradually become passive participants in the conversation and passive consumers of information received. Also, many powerful figures turn into the opinion leaders that can influence other common citizens. Under such circumstance, the opinion is led mainly or even completely by those opinion leaders, making common people's discussion of public issues meaningless and no more than confirming and disseminating the existing ideas. Common people's role in contributing to the public opinion has thus been greatly weakened.

In fact, Habermas has received various criticisms since his book was translated into English in 1989. Some critics claimed it to be somewhat idealized (Fraser, 1990; Papacharissi, 2002). The symbol of democracy has been undemocratically organized throughout history, by excluding groups like women or those of lower social status, as was also acknowledged by Habermas himself. Adding upon this, Fraser (1990) augmented for the existence of multiple public spheres, formed by those who are excluded by some spheres and included in others, and where a public realm or government, who represents all these different expressions, never truly has existed. Verstraeten (1996) emphasized the term "media determinism", a subset of technological determinism, which mentioned that the mass media has strong impacts on the society. Due to its capacity of overcoming the constraint of time and space, mass media can create radically structural changes in the society. As a result, the public sphere is not the same as Habermas used to describe. As a matter of fact, Habermas himself has realized the role of television in the public sphere. To him, the social transformations in his country, Germany, was actually realized in a televisional way of communication (Habermas, 1992).

In conclusion, the public sphere is tightly connected with people's rational-critical opinion expression on political issues, the democratic government and an open and informative media. Habermas himself realized the importance of television on the public sphere. However, with the advent of Internet and particularly the social media, the conceptualization of public sphere in the traditional context should be reexamined.

ONLINE PUBLIC SPHERE

Habermas (2006) highlights the role of a self-regulating media system that is independent from its social context. Deliberate politics happen when anonymous audiences provide feedback between the informed social elites and the responsive civil society. Thus, media and politicians are further seen as critical factors in the political public sphere. However, for the greater public, there is limited or no access for them to approach mass media and politicians. This dilemma of self-expression and information dissemination has been changed with the emergence of the Internet which is an addition to the seemingly unapproachable traditional media. It is a new and effective technology that strengthens the role of the public in the political and social arena (Papacharissi, 2002). The Internet not only accelerates the gathering and spread of information online, but also provides the power to bring people together for the common topics or issues, without the obstacles of geography and economic inequalities. Therefore, in this digital era, non-mainstream sources could have the chance to challenge the dominant public sphere of mainstream sectors. This can be illustrated by the rise of NGOs, the increase of citizen media, and the presence of advocacy voices by common citizens (Dahlgren, 2005; Downey & Fenton, 2003). In this respect, the Web 2.0 applications have the ability to empower ordinary netizens and serve as a key element for the possible proliferation of online public sphere.

A couple of scholars consider the cyberspace as a new public sphere, where people easily join groups and speak out their voices on public issues. This satisfies their sense of self-fulfillment and personal development and therefore enhances democracy (Gans, 2011; Jones, 1997; Papacharissi, 2002). Dahlgren (2005) also supported the notion of an online public sphere, though he contended that the Internet is playing a minor role for political purposes and thus can only be considered as the public sphere to a small degree. Democratic deliberation is still overshadowed by consumerism, entertainment and non-political discussions online. Traditional media on both national and international levels are constrained by different sorts of censorship and limitations set by concentrations of ownership and market forces. Thus, it is difficult or even impossible to find genuine access to the larger population, weakening the media's role as the public sphere. However, the transparency protocols of the Internet, in principle, can be considered as global and interactive with reduced entry barriers, making the information easier to produce and transmit to people with different background.

However, there are also many critiques on whether the Internet can be considered as an idealized public sphere. Dean (2003) contends that it is the significant saying of the public sphere "everyone is included" that makes this public sphere problematic. We have to distinguish the differences of everyone, including the ignorant, the ill-informed and the unauthorized. Poell (2009) also fights against the statement of the Internet as a public sphere. He has examined some social media, such as blog and forum, and find out that most content on these platforms are not rational, critical, or even logical, making it difficult to meet the standards of the public sphere proposed by Habermas. Other scholars even skeptically stated that the criteria of the public sphere cannot be realized on the Internet. Online debates are not absolutely free from limitations. Instead, they are more or less influenced by factors such as family members, friends, markets, and governments. Thus, the concept of the online public sphere is vague.

SNOWDEN AFFAIR

Edward Snowden, a former CIA employee, and a former NSA contractor disclosed up to 200,000 classified documents of the PRISM surveillance program to the Guardian and the Washington Post. After releasing those secret files to the media, Snowden was charged for his espionage and became a fugitive by the US government. He then applied for his political asylum in 21 countries. On June 6, 2013 Snowden arrived in Hong Kong as his first stop for the prevention of arrest, and is now living in Russia under temporary asylum.

On the US government's side, there are three main reasons for the PRISM program. First, the surveillance does not target US citizens. Second, this program has been approved and supervised by the central government. Third, the most important reason is to fight against terrorism. On the US citizen's side, however, a lot of controversies emerged regarding whether Snowden is a hero or a traitor. On the one hand, many citizens point out that Snowden has greatly done harm to the national security and should be considered as a rebel. On the other hand, the violence of personal privacy disclosed has been viewed as an evil in many US citizens' eyes and thus they actively support Snowden and regard him as a patriot. According to the survey by the Gallup Organization, 53% of respondents objected to the surveillance program while 47% of them thought that the PRISM program was positive and effective.

At the international level, the Snowden affair has changed the US-China dialogue on cybersecurity issue to some extent. The US has long been applying pressure on China for its cyber activities. Many US companies have complained about network intrusions and data theft for years and claimed that the Chinese military was behind the systematic hacking of US business and military operations (Paul, 2013). However, the revelation of the PRISM program made it more difficult for the United States to confront China in talks over the alleged cyber theft of trade secrets. In addition to cybersecurity problem between US and China, the White House criticized China over its decision to allow Snowden to leave Hong Kong, a special administrative region of China. Although the Chinese government stated that to let Snowden leave Hong Kong was just a technical decision made by a Hong Kong immigration official, Jay Carney, a White House spokesman, considered it to be a deliberate choice made by the central government to release the fugitive, and that "this decision unquestionably has a negative impact on the US-China relationship" (Geoff, 2013). However, on China's side, the People's Daily, the top state newspaper praised Snowden for "tearing off Washington's sanctimonious mask" and rejected accusations that Beijing had facilitated Snowden's departure from Hong Kong. A commentary in the Global Times, owned by the People's Daily, even directly attacked the US for cornering "a young idealist who has exposed the sinister scandals of the US government" (Miriam & Jonathan, 2013). Considering the different reactions to the Snowden affair, it is essential and necessary to analyze the voices from American and Chinese netizens on Twitter and Sina Weibo.

METHODOLOGY

This chapter used content analysis to examine how the Snowden affair was discussed on both Twitter and Sina Weibo. The main challenge, based on exploring microblogging infrastructure, is identifying a selection of tweets to study, as there in theory are potentially hundreds of millions of posts eligible for analysis. In this study, the Daily Top 10 tweets from both Sina Weibo and Twitter were selected for analysis. The concept of "top 10" represented the most widely discussed and spread postings each day, based on the number of comments and retweets. The time period was from June 10, 2013 to June 30, 2013 when numerous media reports started to reveal mass surveillance of foreign nationals as well as US citizens. Another significant reason is that this time period is approximately when Snowden stayed in Hong Kong as his first stop for prevention from extradition. Both Sina Weibo and Twitter users in this period have generated far more tweets on the Snowden affair than ever before. Assisted with a Twitter analytical API "Topsy Pro" and a Sina Weibo analytical API "Data Weibo", the key word "Snowden" and its Chinese translation "斯诺登" were used to select the top 10 postings each day, which thus consists of a 420-posting sample, including 210 postings in Twitter and 210 in Sina Weibo.

From the selection, all the 420 postings came from verified users. Both Sina Weibo and Twitter offer a verification system for user profiles, including individual users, media, governments and non-governmental organizations. Basic requirements for having the profile verified, include a real name rather than alias as user-name, a brief job description and employment details, as well as a brief user description. After verifying and approving the application, Sina Weibo and Twitter both add a logo "V" after the username. It is acceptable and reasonable that all the daily top 10 postings were generated by verified users only. First, verification of individual users is meant to provide trustworthiness of information, and combat speculations and rumors within the microblog infrastructure. Second, previous research has demonstrated that the most widely spread postings are those from verified accounts (L. Yu, Asur, & Huberman, 2011). In fact, a small number of verified users who play active roles like influentials, dominate the connectivity in a social structure of microblogging (Wang, She, & Chen, 2014). The importance of verified accounts seems more obvious on Sina Weibo. One piece of evidence showed that the online activities have fallen by as much as 70% as those influential verified users abandon Weibo (Malcolm, 2014). The change of original content created by the verified accounts can well predict the tendency of the whole population in microblogging. Thus, forwarding tweets of verified accounts is a conspicuous feature of microblogging.

The coding book created was inspired by Gibbs' concept-driven and data-driven coding (Gibbs, 2008). The coding categories were generated from a pilot study of part of postings and a review of previous scholarly journals. The coding protocol was revised several times before the final version was constructed for content analysis. Thus, the final coding book includes the content of postings, frequency of postings, sources of postings, and attitude towards Snowden.

The most important part in the coding scheme was the content of postings, in other words, the main content characteristics. It was measured in terms of three main themes, namely providing information, expressing opinion and posting speculations about the Snowden affair. Posts that mainly provide *information and news*, contain items like the time and place of the Snowden affair, stories of Snowden, interviews about people involved in this issue, both rescue and arrest efforts to Snowden; press conference reports; reference to media reports; official reports of the development of this affair, and so forth. *Opinions* regarding the Snowden affair include items like critiques and support of Snowden, reflections on Chinese and US government, including political systems, and the value of human rights, comments on media coverage; critique and support of the individual's information privacy and so forth. Posts containing *speculations* on a variety of issues cover cause and result of surveillances, the future of Snowden, the possible countries for his political asylum; analysis of different reactions from related countries and so forth.

The frequency of postings was measured by the number of mentions of the three themes by week during the selected period. The source of postings was measured by what sector created that tweet. There were four sources included in this coding scheme, including media, opinion leader, government official and non-governmental organization (NGO). Last, the attitude towards Snowden affair was considered in terms of support, neutral and oppose.

RESULTS

As seen in Figure 1, information and news dominated as the major theme in Twitter, with 65.7% of the analyzed posts belonging to this category. Opinions also had a relatively dominant position in Twitter, with 27.1% of analyzed tweets related to discussions on a variety of topics. The speculation accounted to only 7.1% while on Sina Weibo, the result was somewhat dissimilar where the categories of Information and news, and Opinion almost shared the same percentage of selected postings, with 45.2% and 44.3% respectively. Even the speculation, the smallest part, occupied 10.5%, higher than that in Twitter. Thus, it seems that netizens on Sina Weibo were more willing to voice themselves and particularly showed their attitude towards political issues. This result coincided with previous studies of Sina Weibo. Xiao (2011) reported that microblogging in China was mainly used to express emotion, share opinion and record daily life. Yu (2011) indicated that over 25% of the most significant public opinion events in 2010 began on microblogs. Therefore, Sina Weibo becomes a platform for opinions and an important driver in the ongoing social change in China. This result demonstrates that the Chinese government allows for some degree of public discussion on Sina Weibo (Jiang, 2010). They also consider Sina Weibo as a powerful tool for Chinese society to supervise the authorities and to organize collective resistance (Noesselt, 2014), and as a catalyst for social and political transformation (Qiang, 2011). The turn towards a more responsive way of governing by the Chinese party-state indicates the adaptability of authoritarian one-party-states in the digital era.

The news-oriented nature of Twitter could also be reflected by the exact content of such news. Twitter took form as a channel for diverse content during the three-week period. This content included interviews with National Security Agency (NSA), US governmental officials, the Wikileaks, voices from different countries, such as UK, Russia, Hong Kong and so on. Another main stream of news on Twitter covered the talks and actions by Snowden himself, especially on and after June 17 when Snowden gave a Q&A session online. However, on Sina Weibo, the news coverage was much narrower than that on Twitter. The majority of news was related to Hong Kong, which was his first stop for prevention from extradition.

Figure 1. Three dominant themes

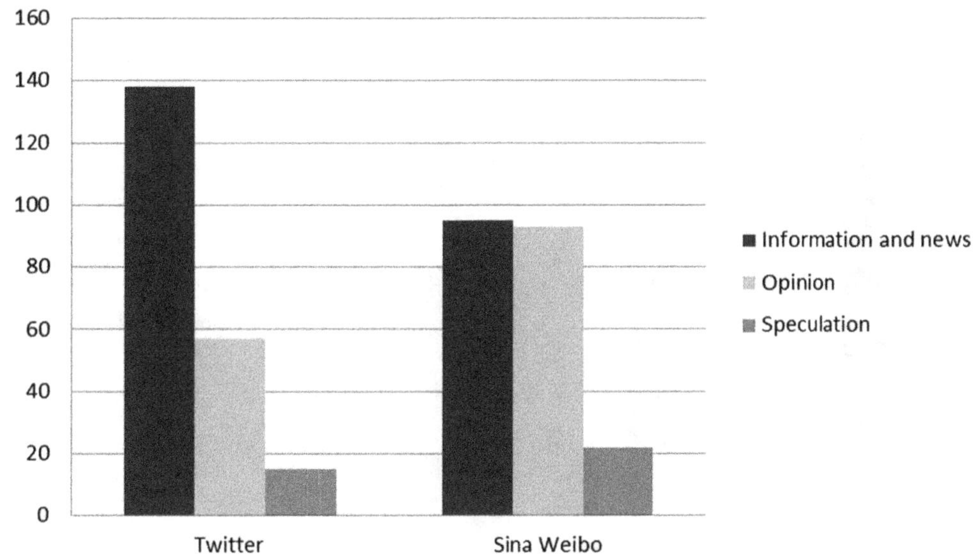

Thus, content on Sina Weibo mainly focused on interviews with Hong Kong governmental officials, scholars in Hong Kong universities, demonstrations by Hong Kong citizens and so on. The Chinese and US governments' voices have seldom been largely covered on Sina Weibo.

When the three major themes were portrayed collectively according to their date of posting, as in Figure 2 and Figure 3, the nuances between the themes of Information and news, and Opinion became clearer. On Twitter, posts containing information and news overall remained dominant throughout three weeks, while opinions regarding the affair grew as the week progressed. However, on Sina Weibo, the difference between news and opinion was constantly small. On both platforms, the category of speculation increased to a peak in the second week, when Snowden arrived at Hong Kong and people were not sure of his next decision. The difference between Twitter and Sina Weibo reflected in these two charts clearly illustrated that Sina Weibo had greater potential to involve audiences to participate in online discussion and deliberation. Civic engagement becomes available through such a popular Internet application, in China, which has long been considered as an authoritarian country. Although the Internet censorship still exists, Sina Weibo starts to challenge the state and other social authorities by allowing users to engage in controversial activities and inappropriate speech about political issues. According to a study conducted by Shanghai Jiaotong University, online public opinion events on Sina Weibo concentrated on government and political officials, followed by celebrities and enterprises. Chinese microblogging thus starts to have a salient feature of undermining social authority (Jia & Fanxu, 2014).

An analysis of any online public sphere should strive to include as many layers of the online community in question as possible. On a basic level, the public sphere is believed to be in negotiation with the state, so representatives from state agencies should be considered if possible. The mass media, serving as channels for negotiation between state and public, should also be included. On the other side of the negotiations table we find the public, so citizen-voices can be included as well. However, the public's voice is hard to spread out and they are always led by opinion leaders, thus the opinion leaders and media

Figure 2. Frequency of all themes, by week, on Twitter

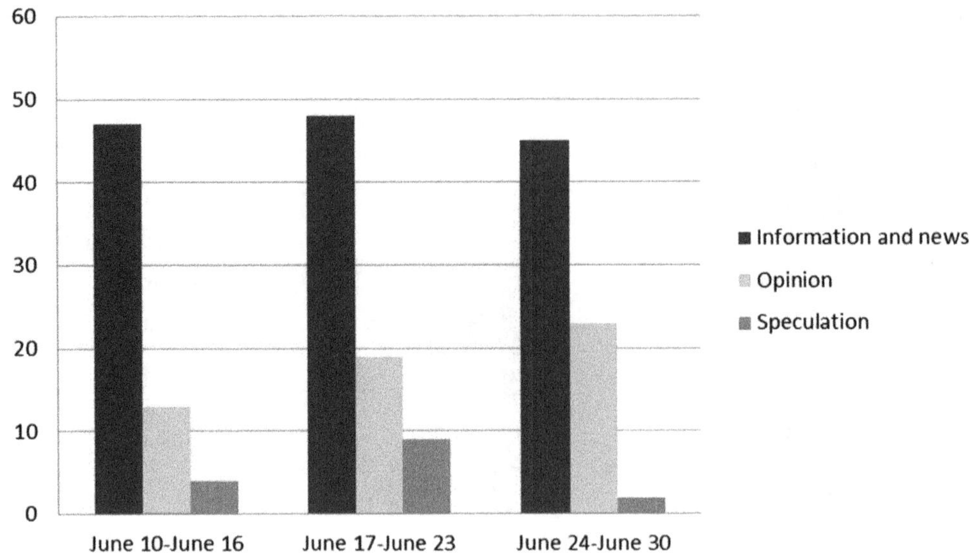

Figure 3. Frequency of all themes, by week, on Sina Weibo

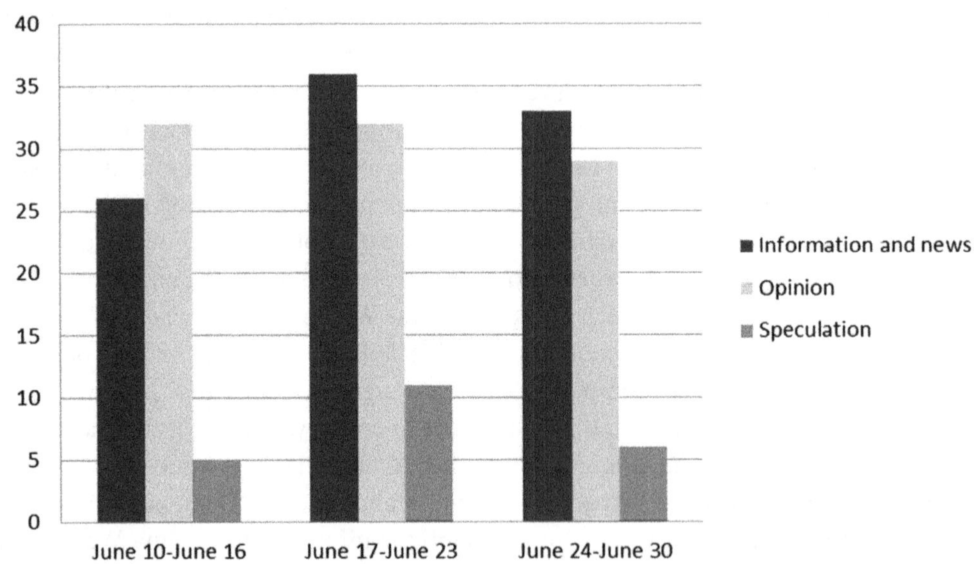

professionals were included in this analysis. At last, as the expression of public sentiment, civil society can form valuable pressure groups in negotiations between state and society. Thus non-governmental organization is also very significant in the selection.

On Sina Weibo, when considering the source of postings selected, the results in Figure 4 showed that the majority of postings came from opinion leaders, followed by media or media professionals. The government and non-governmental organizations had a weaker voice regarding the Snowden Affairs. On Twitter, as shown in Figure 5, the media are far more active in posting news, expressing opinions

Figure 4. Number of tweets by different population, on Sina Weibo

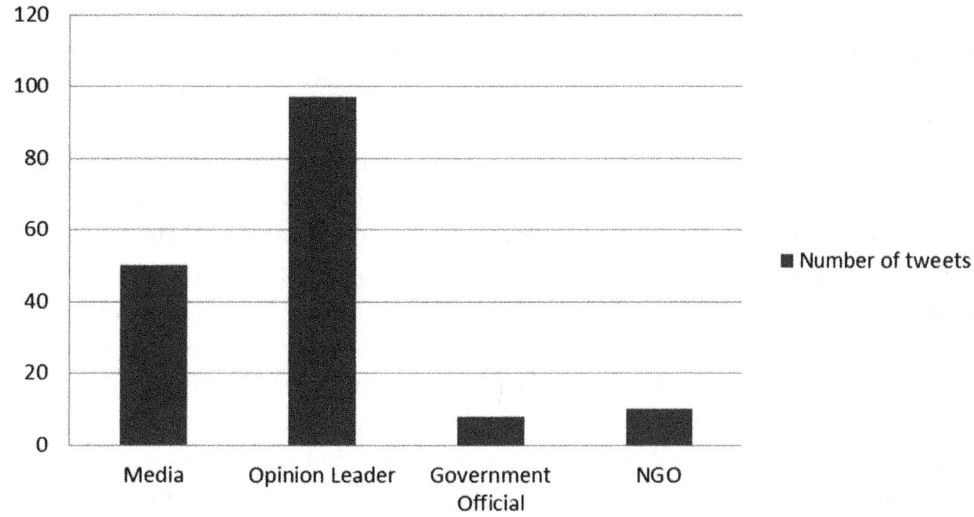

Figure 5. Number of tweets by different population, on Twitter

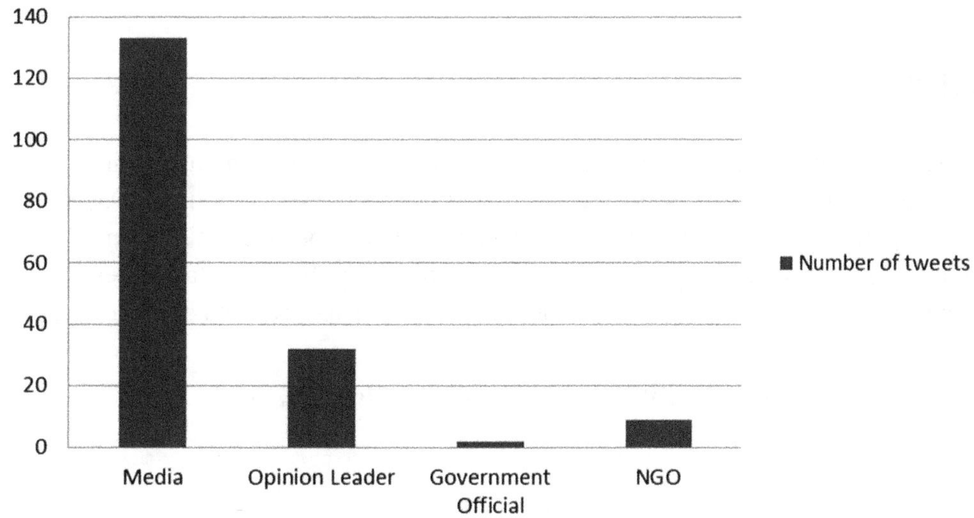

and analyzing the issue. Opinion leaders are less involved in the online discussion. Similar to Weibo, the voice from government and non-governmental organizations can rarely be heard on Twitter. However, government and government officials are more active in Sina Weibo. One possible reason is that the Chinese central government has encouraged all the departments and ministries to adopt Weibo to communicate with citizens (Liu & Zhou, 2011). The result that voice on Sina Weibo was dominated by opinion leaders in fact was consistent with several previous studies. In a study examining 286 public events and identified the presence of opinion leaders in 120 of them. In a survey that investigated which new media platform opinion leaders prefer, half of them adopt Sina Weibo to voice themselves (Lu & Qiu, 2013). Thus, Sina Weibo serves as a new arena for opinion leaders, as new authorities, to influence online discussion on social and political issues.

The last research agenda of this project concerns about people's attitude towards Snowden on Twitter and Sina Weibo. Results indicated that users on Twitter had diverse opinions on the Snowden affair. As shown in the Figure 6, on Twitter, the supportive and opposed attitudes towards the Snowden affair were almost even, with neutral views slightly lower. However, on Sina Weibo, the large majority of netizens held a supportive or neutral opinion about the Snowden affair. Only 11.4% of Sina Weibo users held a negative viewpoint of Snowden. Another difference between these two platforms came from netizens' opinions towards governments. Twitter users who support Snowden publicly criticize the US government's surveillance behavior on common citizens. However, on Sina Weibo, the criticisms have been made towards both US and Chinese governments. Netizens who were supportive of Snowden made many negative comments on the US government while those with neutral views towards Snowden and the US government mostly criticized the Chinese government for Internet censorship, disrespect of human rights and the prohibition of freedom of speech in offline settings. Another interesting point on Sina Weibo was that many postings were considered as neutral views, because such content was just entertainment. This result was consistent with a large number of studies which identified entertainment as a dominant feature of Chinese Internet. This trend continues on Sina Weibo. According to Sina Weibo's ranking, among the top 50 microbloggers, only five are not entertainment stars. This analysis also illustrated another aspect of Sina Weibo, with the obvious entertainment nature, where postings about the Snowden affair has far more entertainment content, such as jokes, pictures and videos, than on Twitter.

DISCUSSION

The current study is one of the first comparative studies to investigate whether Twitter and its Chinese counterpart, Sina Weibo, can be considered as a true public sphere. Colhoun (1993) defined a public sphere as successful when it provides discussion and discourse about societal concerns that are rational and influential. A public sphere for Habermas, is a democratic political culture where people can have critical debates and can reason freely outside the state's supervision. Results of this chapter showed that

Figure 6. Compare Twitter and Sina Weibo: Opionion towards Snowden

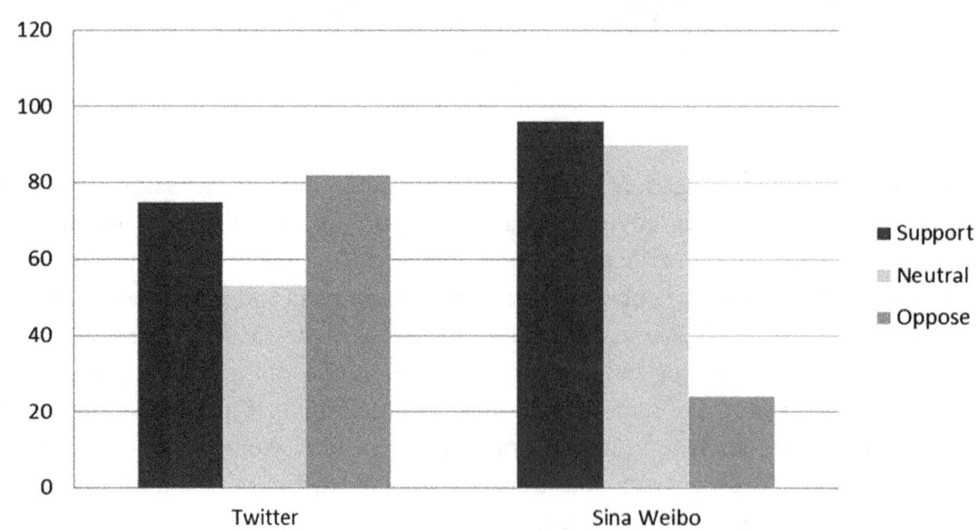

both Twitter and Sina Weibo had several important elements of a public sphere, although they might not be absolute and ideal ones. This finding is also consistent with previous studies claiming that there is no clear-cut division between democracy and authoritarianism (Luciani, 1988).

On Sina Weibo, there are huge amounts of sources for information, and discussions on a variety of topics of public concerns have demonstrated Sina Weibo's lasting and powerful influence in negotiations of power. Chinese netizens have voiced their opinions regarding the Snowden affair, a political issue. In such a one-party country, there are very few opportunities for Chinese common citizens to formally make their voice heard by the government, and it is even impossible to further influence government's public policy making. However, online political discussion becomes one of very few platforms available to netizens to talk about politics and government-related events. Opinion leaders play a significant role in promoting online discussions. They come from different backgrounds, including but not limited to political officials, business managers, university professors, lawyers, journalists and celebrities. Netizens are then motivated to forward and give comments on this political issue. The Chinese government itself does not dominate and lead the discussion. Instead, it actively encourages incorporating the Internet and microblogging into their daily work, and starts to get involved in such interactive communication methods with netizens. Although some democratic features have been reflected on Sina Weibo, it inevitably has an authoritarian root. For example, regarding the Snowden affair, the majority of netizens support Snowden while only a very limited number of negative voices can be heard. We have no idea of whether this is a result of Internet censorship. However, to become a true public sphere, the issue of how to overcome the government's censorship remains a big concern. Right now, all kinds of media in China, including the microblogs, cannot be immune to the strict government control and regulations. Such censorship systems might weaken people's willingness to express opinions on these political issues. Another factor that results in this highly homogeneous idea is that opinion leaders, a small group of elites, become dominant on Sina Weibo. Although they have dissimilar social backgrounds, they actually form alliances, connected by political stances, cultural values, business interests and friendship. These opinion leaders forward and comment on each other's messages or jointly fight against opposing views. Led by those elites, netizens' online discussion might be problematic and misleading, which in turn negatively influences the development of civil society and democracy in China.

Similarly, Twitter has tremendous strengths as well as negative attributes in the sense that it favors the concept of a "public". Twitter users have diverse attitudes towards Snowden, from being supportive, neutral, to oppositional. News reports on Twitter cover far more topics and their sources come from national and international news agencies. However, Twitter has obvious deficiency in several aspects. For example, we can seldom see Twitter users' direct opinions about Snowden. Instead, netizens on Twitter prefer forwarding news article to giving their own comments and opinions. On Twitter, the government's posting is even more sparse than that on Sina Weibo. The government's voice is an indispensable part of society -without their opinions, we cannot obtain a comprehensive idea of what different sectors are thinking about and thus it becomes difficult to form a participatory domain for diverse voices.

Mass media generally consider the public as being a passive audience that can read, listen and watch, but it is much less likely to directly participate. A public sphere should become an arena where the public can obtain information, share ideas, and even contest information. Interaction should flow between the media, opinion leaders and audiences of various sizes. Although some postings are left with no reposting and no comment, other posts can travel with great speed across network, being rapidly shared and heavily debated. Sina Weibo, an Internet application within an authoritarian country, is starting to develop basic elements of the public sphere, although it suffers from Internet censorship and content homogeneity. However, Sina Weibo has the great potential to help diffuse private opinions in a public space, where private opinions can find their way into a space of general public discourse. It can do this to a greater extent than within the traditional media channels, which largely remain subdued to an array of content regulating directives. On the other hand, although the finding of this current study showed that Western netizens seldom express direct opinions about the Snowden affair and the US government had little active engagement on Twitter, we cannot deny that Twitter has the power to help promote civic engagement by grassroots as well as high elites. As Ito noted in the book "Networked publics" (Varnelis, 2012), Twitter is a networked public space incorporating "networked publics" simultaneously bottom-up, top-down and side-by-side. Twitter publics are interconnected through fluid conversations, making Twitter an integral part of the networked public sphere (Benkler, 2006). With the growing popularity of microblogging in our daily life, we can reasonably perceive it as a relatively effective public sphere, although it might not be absolute.

In summary, by analyzing Twitter and Sina Weibo in relation to conceptual frames regarding the public sphere, microblogging applications have been identified as a potential public space with wide-reaching possibilities for interaction. They could be of importance for public deliberation and debate in both democratic and authoritarian countries. In reflection of Sina Weibo and Twitter on the Snowden affair, there are hopes for being optimistic as microblogs offer easy-to-use functions, with which information can be shared and commented readily. Also, due to the massive and still growing popularity, we have the great potential to be heard by even more people all around the world. On microblogging, netizens can express an array of views in the online discussion. Twitter users have more diverse attitudes towards Snowden, while netizens on Sina Weibo openly express their political opinion to support Snowden and criticize censorship and government officials.

From international broadcasting to satellite TV, and then to the Internet today, all the previous so-called "new media" have been politically labeled as harbingers of freedom and democracy. Although debates have never stopped in the discussion of whether mass media create and promote the public sphere, the communicative power from media, particular one of the most recent formats, the microblog, cannot be ignored. Such communicative power of microblogs comes from thousands of millions of discussion topics and public opinion that are housed within. These can promote cooperation and mutual understanding, which are significant in the democratic process and civil society in both China and the US.

REFERENCES

Bamman, D., O'Connor, B., & Smith, N. (2012). Censorship and deletion practices in Chinese social media. *First Monday*, *17*(3). doi:10.5210/fm.v17i3.3943

Benkler, Y. (2006). *The wealth of networks: How social production transforms markets and freedom*. Yale University Press.

Best, S. J., & Krueger, B. S. (2005). Analyzing the representativeness of Internet political participation. *Political Behavior*, *27*(2), 183–216. doi:10.1007/s11109-005-3242-y

Calhoun, C. (1993). Civil society and the public sphere. *Public Culture*, *5*(2), 267–267. doi:10.1215/08992363-5-2-267

Chan, M., Wu, X., Hao, Y., Xi, R., & Jin, T. (2012). Microblogging, online expression, and political efficacy among young Chinese citizens: The moderating role of information and entertainment needs in the use of Weibo. *Cyberpsychology, Behavior, and Social Networking*, *15*(7), 345–349. doi:10.1089/cyber.2012.0109 PMID:22780993

Dahlgren, P. (2005). The Internet, public spheres, and political communication: Dispersion and deliberation. *Political Communication*, *22*(2), 147–162. doi:10.1080/10584600590933160

Dean, J. (2003). Why the net is not a public sphere. *Constellations (Oxford, England)*, *10*(1), 95–112. doi:10.1111/1467-8675.00315

Di Gennaro, C., & Dutton, W. (2006). The Internet and the public: Online and offline political participation in the United Kingdom. *Parliamentary Affairs*, *59*(2), 299–313. doi:10.1093/pa/gsl004

Downey, J., & Fenton, N. (2003). New media, counter publicity and the public sphere. *New Media & Society*, *5*(2), 185–202. doi:10.1177/1461444803005002003

Fraser, N. (1990). Rethinking the public sphere: A contribution to the critique of actually existing democracy. *Social Text*, (25/26): 56–80. doi:10.2307/466240

Gans, H. J. (2011). Multiperspectival news revisited: Journalism and representative democracy. *Journalism*, *12*(1), 3–13. doi:10.1177/1464884910385289

Geoff, D. (2013). *US attacks China as Snowden stays free*. Retrieved from http://www.ft.com/cms/s/0/3861666e-dcbc-11e2-b52b-00144feab7de.html#axzz3PcyOgTbN

Gibbs, G. R. (2008). Analysing qualitative data. *Sage (Atlanta, Ga.)*.

Habermas, J. (1991). *The structural transformation of the public sphere: An inquiry into a category of bourgeois society*. MIT press.

Habermas, J. (1992). Further reflections on the public sphere. *Habermas and the Public Sphere, 422*.

Habermas, J. (2006). Political communication in media society: Does democracy still enjoy an epistemic dimension? the impact of normative theory on empirical research. *Communication Theory*, *16*(4), 411–426. doi:10.1111/j.1468-2885.2006.00280.x

Jia, L., & Fanxu, Z. (2014). Microblogging and Grassroots Surveillance in China. *China. International Journal (Toronto, Ont.)*, *12*(3), 55–71.

Jiang, M. (2010). Spaces of authoritarian deliberation: Online public deliberation in China. In The Search for Deliberative Democracy in China, (pp. 261-287). Academic Press.

Jones, S. G. (1997). The Internet and its social landscape. *Virtual Culture: Identity and Communication in Cybersociety*, 7-35.

Keane, J. (1995). Structural transformations of the public sphere. *Communication Review*, *1*(1), 1–22. doi:10.1080/10714429509388247

Kim, Y. (2011). The contribution of social network sites to exposure to political difference: The relationships among SNSs, online political messaging, and exposure to cross-cutting perspectives. *Computers in Human Behavior, 27*(2), 971–977. doi:10.1016/j.chb.2010.12.001

Kushin, M. J., & Yamamoto, M. (2010). Did social media really matter? College students' use of online media and political decision making in the 2008 election. *Mass Communication & Society, 13*(5), 608–630. doi:10.1080/15205436.2010.516863

Liu, Y., & Zhou, Y. (2011). *Social media in China: Rising Weibo in government.* Paper presented at the Digital Ecosystems and Technologies Conference (DEST). doi:10.1109/DEST.2011.5936628

Lu, J., & Qiu, Y. (2013). Microblogging and Social Change in China. *Asian Perspective, 37*(3), 305–331.

Luciani, G. (1988). Economic foundations of democracy and authoritarianism: The Arab world in comparative perspective. *Arab Studies Quarterly*, 457–475.

Lupia, A., & Sin, G. (2003). Which public goods are endangered?: How evolving communication technologies affect the logic of collective action. *Public Choice, 117*(3-4), 315–331. doi:10.1023/B:PUCH.0000003735.07840.c7

Malcolm, M. (2014). *China kills off discussion on Weibo after internet crackdown.* Retrieved from http://www.telegraph.co.uk/news/worldnews/asia/china/10608245/China-kills-off-discussion-on-Weibo-after-internet-crackdown.html

Margolis, M., & Resnick, D. (2000). *Politics as Usual: The Cyberspace Revolution* (Vol. 6). Sage Publications.

Miriam, E., & Jonathan, K. (2013). *Edward Snowden never crossed border into Russia, says foreign minister.* Retrieved from http://www.theguardian.com/world/2013/jun/25/edward-snowden-never-crossed-russia-border

Neubig, G., & Duh, K. (2013). *How Much Is Said in a Tweet? A Multilingual, Information-theoretic Perspective.* Paper presented at the AAAI Spring Symposium: Analyzing Microtext.

Noesselt, N. (2014). Microblogs and the Adaptation of the Chinese Party-State's Governance Strategy. *Governance: An International Journal of Policy, Administration and Institutions, 27*(3), 449–468. doi:10.1111/gove.12045

Papacharissi, Z. (2002). The virtual sphere The internet as a public sphere. *New Media & Society, 4*(1), 9–27. doi:10.1177/14614440222226244

Parmelee, J. H., & Bichard, S. L. (2011). *Politics and the Twitter revolution: How tweets influence the relationship between political leaders and the public.* Lexington Books.

Paul, E. (2013). *Snowden affair blunts U.S. push for China to curb cyber theft.* Retrieved from http://www.reuters.com/article/2013/07/09/us-usa-china-cyber-idUSBRE96713220130709

Poell, T. (2009). Conceptualizing forums and blogs as public spheres. Digital Material, 239-251.

Qiang, X. (2011). The battle for the Chinese Internet. *Journal of Democracy, 22*(2), 47–61. doi:10.1353/jod.2011.0020

Svensson, M. (2014). Voice, power and connectivity in China's microblogosphere: Digital divides on SinaWeibo. *China Information*, *28*(2), 168–188. doi:10.1177/0920203X14540082

Tong, J., & Zuo, L. (2014). Weibo communication and government legitimacy in China: A computer-assisted analysis of Weibo messages on two 'mass incidents'. *Information Communication and Society*, *17*(1), 66–85. doi:10.1080/1369118X.2013.839730

Tumasjan, A., Sprenger, T. O., Sandner, P. G., & Welpe, I. M. (2011). Election Forecasts With Twitter How 140 Characters Reflect the Political Landscape. *Social Science Computer Review*, *29*(4), 402–418. doi:10.1177/0894439310386557

Varnelis, K. (2012). *Networked publics*. The MIT Press.

Verstraeten, H. (1996). The Media and the Transformation of the Public Sphere A Contribution for a Critical Political Economy of the Public Sphere. *European Journal of Communication*, *11*(3), 347–370. doi:10.1177/0267323196011003004

Wang, N., She, J., & Chen, J. (2014). *How big vs dominate chinese microblog: a comparison of verified and unverified users on sina weibo*. Paper presented at the 2014 ACM Conference on Web Science. doi:10.1145/2615569.2615683

Webster, F. (2011). Information and democracy: the weakening of social democracy. *Media Perspectives for the 21st Century*, 21-40.

Xiao, M. (2011). *Research Report on Chinese Microbloggers' Behavior in 2010*. Beijing: Social Sciences Academic Press.

Yu, G. (2011). *Zhongguo shehui yuqing niandu baogao 2011* [Chinese Society Public Opinion, Annual Report 2011]. Beijing: People's Daily Press.

Yu, L., Asur, S., & Huberman, B. A. (2011). *What trends in Chinese social media*. arXiv preprint arXiv:1107.3522

Zhang, W., Seltzer, T., & Bichard, S. L. (2013). Two Sides of the Coin Assessing the Influence of Social Network Site Use During the 2012 US Presidential Campaign. *Social Science Computer Review*, *31*(5), 542–551. doi:10.1177/0894439313489962

Chapter 3
Social Media Activism:
A Contested Field

Pantelis Vatikiotis
Izmir University of Economics, Turkey

ABSTRACT

This chapter critically evaluates the role of social networking platforms (Facebook, Twitter and Tumblr) in contemporary protest movements (Arab Spring, European Movements and Occupy Movement), pointing out continuities and discontinuities of the new wave of contention. From this perspective, it evaluates the societal conditions of different contexts, the interplay between different media formats during the relevant episodes of contention, and the diversity of social actors engaged in these practices that have accordingly influenced the emergence and the prospects of the protests.

INTRODUCTION

The chapter draws on the wave of protests that emerged in 2011 across different parts of the world – in the Middle East, North Africa, the United States, and Europe – and reflects on theoretical approaches that have been developed in reference to the interplay between social and media activism. The uprisings of 2011 have shifted the focus of research agenda towards the relation between media and social change. In this context, there is a growing interest in analyzing new media practices generated within social movements and the implications of this synergy. For media sociologists, and not only, this has been a particular challenge. It is not the first time that 'new' media uses and experiences convey participatory, democratic imageries. The attempt to interpret recent, various mobilizations and protest movements requires comparison and contrast. There are several similarities among these practices, on the grounds of which the emergence of a new, mediated, global wave of protest movements has been acknowledged by many studies. However, the present study questions this perspective, pointing out the differences among the 2011 movements and their practices across the different sociopolitical contexts.

The use of social media in the last decade's wave of contention has rejuvenated the rhetoric on the emancipatory potentials of technology and new media. Several scholars and analysts have welcomed a new era of social media revolution, while skeptical ones have raised critical voices questioning the role

DOI: 10.4018/978-1-4666-9879-6.ch003

of social media in triggering social changes. Techno-optimistic accounts of new technologies evaluate the power of social networking sites as liberating (Shirky, 2008; 2011), labeling recent mobilizations Twitter/Facebook/wiki/2.0 revolutions (Tapscott, 2011; Ghonin, 2012), while techno-pessimistic approaches point out the shortcomings of the use of new technologies, in terms of accommodating "feel-good online activism that has zero political or social impact" (Morozov, 2011), and building weak, instead of strong, social ties (Gladwell, 2010). What both approaches have in common though is that they adopt a determinist perspective, understanding social media as adequate or inadequate agents of social change. Less deterministic approaches emphasize more complex practices developed in the interplay between social movements and media, from different perspectives – in relation to the emergence either of "multitude" (Hardt & Negri, 2012), or "networked social movements" (Castells, 2012), or the "choreography of the assembly" (Gerbaudo, 2012) or "connective action"(Bennett & Segerberg, 2013). These approaches are critically reviewed here, pointing out the strengths and shortcomings of their analyses.

Subsequently, the chapter addresses and compares recent protest movements in the contexts of their implementation, taking into account their simultaneous upsurge as well as the development of social struggles over the long haul. On this basis, it argues the following theses: a) the consideration of protest movements as part of the same cycle of contention is rather simplistic since it underestimates the specific societal conditions (antagonisms in economic, political and ideological structures of each society); b) most approaches overestimate the role of social media in the development of protests, neglecting the contribution of other media formats (mainstream and alternative ones) and their overall interactions. On these grounds, the chapter casts light on a range of contradictions that are identified when it comes to address structural parameters and the wider mediascape. In view of that, it proposes the employment of research frameworks that advance broad and in-depth comparison of the movements' repertoire of actions. In this regard, it also discusses emerging trends and research opportunities for the study of social media activism.

BACKGROUND: SOCIAL MOVEMENTS AND NEW MEDIA

The discussion about the interaction between social movements and media practices has been mostly addressed in fragmented terms, either on the lens of social movement studies or media studies. Early social movement theories focused on the instrumental role of communications/media, as a tool to mobilize resources – 'resource mobilization theory'. The constructivist approach of 'new social movements' theory perceives the formation of collective identity as a dynamic and reflexive process – "identization" (Melluci, 1996); nevertheless, it only addresses indirectly the importance of communication in the interactions between social actors and their environment. Despite their limitations in researching how social movements intertwine with media, social movement media studies have contributed significantly to the investigation of the organizational structures of social movements, their "repertoires of contention" (Tilly, 1978), and the routines and values of collective social actors (della Porta & Diani, 2006). Moreover, these studies have evaluated the development of social movements in time, in terms of "cycles of contention" (Tarrow, 1994), or "cultural epochs of contention" (McAdam & Sewell, 2001). These aspects are still relevant when researching contemporary mobilizations in a systematic way, in relation to the political, economic and social context of their materialization and the complex relations between social movements and media.

The employment of communication and media technologies by social movement actors has a long history. Several scholars have worked on the wide realm of activist media practices (including posters, community radio, popular music, street theatre, video projects and so forth), evaluating them as tools of resistance, conveyors of a popular oppositional culture, contributors to the democratization of communication/political practice, arenas for the development of alternative to mainstream modes of media organization, and locus of empowerment for those engaged in the process (see Vatikiotis, 2005). Hence, various terms have been employed to describe these aspects – "radical media" (Downing, 1984), "participatory media" (Huesca, 1995; Servaes, 1999), "community media" (Hollander & Stappers, 1992; Rennie, 2006), "social movement media" (Downing, 2008), "alternative media" (Atton, 2002; Couldry & Curran, 2003), and "citizens' media" (Rodriguez, 2001). This prolific research field has evaluated various aspects of engagement of diverse social actors with/in decentralized media practices. However, the focus of most studies is limited, leaving out of the spectrum the role of mass media and their interactions with alternative media.

In the last decades, the convergence of networked media and information technologies has emphatically provided the ground for evaluating further forms of engagement in civic and political life across the intersection of social movements and digital media practices. The early electronic democratic projects (mid-1980s in the United States, early-1990s in Europe) also included bottom-up initiatives, making possible for the citizens to participate directly in the political process. They were "perceived by the social actors initiating or participating in them as a means of reviving and reinvigorating democratic politics" (Tsagarousianou, 1998: 168).

Moreover, the employment of internet tools and the creation of alternative informational websites by activist groups in the late 90s and early 2000s enabled the formation of transnational activist networks. Such networks facilitated a new kind of publicness where citizens renegotiate their political engagement - communicating global activism (Bennett, 2003), providing the organizational software for media activism (Downing, 2003), and constituting a new terrain for collective political action on the whole (Rheingold 2002). Prominent case studies figure in here. The Zapatista movement of the indigenous people of Chiapas in Mexico (see Cleaver, 1998; Olesen, 2004) got a transnational character when their messages were diffused through the Internet to an emerging global audience. Moreover, the Battle of Seattle in 1999 has been an emblematic example of the employment of information and communication technologies in the social movement tactics and actions against the World Trade Organization (WTO) summit (see Smith, 2001; Eagleton-Pierce, 2001). It started with the Carnival Against Capital demonstration in June 1999, bringing together diverse social actors throughout the world (anarchists, environmentalists, feminists, anti-capitalists, and labor groups), and led to the infamous transnational protest in December 1999 against the neoliberal, globalization order. The role of mailing-lists, irc-chats and online forums in the processes of organization and mobilization of the movement was central (Kavada, 2005; Juris, 2005). The so-called "anti/alter-globalization movement" (Walgrave & van Aelst, 2004) or "global justice movement" (della Porta, 2007) was soon spread across the world. The creation of the alternative informational website Indymedia provided coverage of the events in activists' own terms ("Don't hate the media. Become the media"), spread alternative information, mobilized social actors and set a precedent in collective production of content within an alternative culture. The use of new technologies by activist groups, promoting the creation of loose transnational networks and enriching the repertoires of oppositional action, was associated to an increasing extent with terrorist activity in the name of a new global war on terror, intensified since 9/11. This had as a result the growth of political activism through the Internet. In the late 2002 and early 2003 global movements emerged against Iraq war; several political, advocacy groups (MoveOn, Answer, United for Peace and Justice) communicated anti-war information and organized anti-war activities (15/2/2003, public demonstration around the world calling for peace). "The global internet, then, is creating the base and the basis for an unparalleled world wide anti-war/pro-peace and social justice movement during a time of terrorism, war, and intense political struggle" (Kahn & Kellner, 2004, p. 88).

Furthermore, in the last years there is a rising employment of social networking sites in massive protest movements developed in various countries across the world, against neoliberal capitalist policies, the financial crisis, and/or in favor of accountable and democratic political systems. The uprisings of 2011 are the reference point; still, preliminary forms of networked activism facilitated by the use of internet and mobile media have taken place earlier as well, strengthening the communication strategies of political activists and coordinating respective collective actions. During the 'Ukrainian Orange Revolution' in November 2004, hundreds of thousands of people demonstrated for eleven nights in response to the presidential electoral fraud, using effectively the internet and its convergence with mobile phones to coordinate large scale protests (Goldstein, 2007). Also, during the 2008 candlelight (Ghotbul) protest in Seoul (initially against U.S. beef imports, and later opposing the privatization of public sectors), "real time connections and interactions between online and protest sites mediated by debate bulletin boards, chatting rooms, sms messages and especially live streaming" had a central role (Dongwon, 2010, p. 93). Finally, in the numerous demonstrations that took place in Iceland in late 2008 and early 2008 against the financial crisis the web played an important role in the dissemination of information about people's reaction to the governmental practices in the rest of the world.

The first uprisings led by social media took place in Moldova and Iran in 2009, known as 'Twitter revolutions'; though it was mainly mainstream newspapers that labeled them as such (Christiansen, 2009). In April 2009 thousands of young people protested in Chisinau against Moldova's communist leadership, using mainly social message networking (Twitter) as a tool to gather the crowd and propel the events around the world (Barry, 2009). Two months later, street protests took place in Iranian cities (Tehran, Isfahan, Shiraz) after the presidential elections. Despite the media blackout imposed by the Iranian government on social media (Twitter and YouTube), global tweets and amateur images and videos of the police brutality in the Iranian streets continued to flow at an astonishing rate (Christiansen, 2009; Sabety, 2010). The 2011' wave of uprisings has been characterized by the central role of social networking platforms in the development of the relevant protest movements. The so-called Arab Spring emerged in Tunisia and Egypt, late 2010/early 2011, and then spread to other countries of the Middle East and North Africa (MENA region) – Libya, Yemen, Syria, and Bahrain (Shihade et. al., 2012; Wolfsfeld et. al., 2013). People protested against the authoritarian regimes asking for democratic political changes. In spring of the same year, South Europe and specially Spain, Portugal and Greece, experienced a wave of protests in a number of their big cities (Perugorría & Tejerina, 2013; Baumgarten, 2013; Simiti, 2014). Protests were held against austerity measures imposed by transnational governmental bodies (European Union, European Central Bank, International Monetary Fund) and corrupted national governments. In September, on the other side of the Atlantic the Occupy Movement started with the encampment in New York (Occupy Wall Street) (Chomsky, 2012; Langman, 2013); soon after more protest camps were set in other cities across the United States as well as around the world (United Kingdom, Australia) where social actors stated their resistance to neo-liberal imaginaries and practices. Since 2011 further uprisings have shaken Turkey (2013), Brazil (2013 and 2014) and Hong Kong (2014).

The chapter, based on secondary sources and relevant studies, draws on the 2011 wave of contention, evaluates the context of their implementation with its multiple dimensions and critically reviews the role of social and other media in their emergence and development.

ANALYSIS AND REFLECTIONS

A major area of inquiry about the 2011 wave of protests concerns the extent to which they should be considered as part of the same wave of contention. Is there any common framework for this wave of mobilizations, in the same way the global justice movement provided one in the name of fighting neo-liberal globalization, linking diverse protests and practices across different parts of the world (Seattle, Porto Alegre, Prague, Gothenburg, Genoa, and Florence among others)?

Theoretical Reflections

Several studies of the last wave of contention, from the MENA region to Europe and the United States, have elaborated on the diverse aspects of, and prospects for, social media activism, in terms of enhancing the communication perspectives, networking or 'choreographing' the movements, and even introducing another type of social action.

Hardt and Negri (2012) trace the potentiality of new principles declared by the protest movements of 2011 as the basis of the constitution of another type of society. These movements provide an ideal type of the new political subject(s) and the social imaginary they convey - the "communing". Their social struggles (against repressive regimes, austerity measures, and the finance tyranny) are singular ones (orientated towards local conditions), but plural ones upon their communication perspective. The movements share a series of characteristics: a strategy - encampment; an internal organization - multitude; and, a vision - the common. In this regard, the authors highlight the unforeseen opportunity for the powers that constitute the "commoner" and the actions of "commoning".

From a different perspective, in Castells' (2012) account of Egyptian uprising, Indignados and Occupy Movement the subject is the network. All three of these social movements are perfect examples of online networks. Such movements present a number of common characteristics (ibid, p. 221-228): they are networked in multiple forms; a hybrid of cyberspace and urban space ("the space of autonomy") is the new spatial form of these movements; they are global and local at the same time, largely spontaneous in their origin, rival, highly self-reflective, non-violent, and rarely programmatic. From this point of view, the author sheds light on the values, dynamics and the prospects of these movements for social transformation, identifying new paths of social change in our times.

In his analysis of activist use of social media in the popular movements of 2011, Gerbaudo (2012), evaluates social media in terms of preparing the terrain, or setting the scene, for people coming together in public space; what he calls the construction of a "choreography of assembly". According to the author, social media played a significant role in facilitating the gathering of participants and generating an emotional tension towards participation in all the cases he researches (Egyptian uprising, Indignados in Spain, and the Occupy Movement). From this perspective, Gerbaudo critically assesses the concept of 'horizontality', found in several analyses of contemporary activism, including Castells' account of 'network' as well as Negri's and Hardt's (2000; 2005) 'swarm' and 'multitude'. "[F]ar from inaugurating a situation of absolute 'leaderlessness', social media have in fact facilitated the rise of complex and 'liquid' (Bauman, 2000) or 'soft' forms of leadership which exploit the interactive and participatory character of the new communication technologies" (Gerbaudo, 2012, Introduction, Section 4, para. 3).

Drawing on the decisive role of communication in the organizational structure, Bennett and Segerberg (2013) evaluate the protest movements of 2011 in terms of digitally enabled action networks which entail more personalized forms of collective action. In this pattern technology platforms and applications take the role of established political organizations. "[C]onventional organizations play a less central role than social technologies in relatively self-organizing networks such as the indignados of Spain, the Arab Spring uprisings, or the 'occupy' protests that spread from Wall Street around the world" (Bennett & Segerberg, 2013, p. 754). From this perspective, the authors point out the role of digital media as organizing agents, introducing thus another mode of action making, what they call "the logic of connective action" that is based on 'sharing'. In this account, the authors evaluate further contributions to the diffusion of action frames, including personal ones produced by spontaneous crowds.

These approaches provide valuable insights into the complex practices developed along the interplay between social movements and social media practices. However, even though they acknowledge issues that have to do with the context of the development of these movements and in some cases the role of other media formats within social movements, they do not probe into them.

Protest Movements of 2011: Similarities

Indeed, there are some elements that are common in, or link, the mobilizations of 2011. First, the popular nature of the movements; "[c]ontemporary protest culture is sustained by a narrative of popular reunion, which revolves around a recomposition or 'fusion' of individuals in a collective subject with majoritarian ambitions" (Gerbaudo, 2012, Introduction, Section 4, para. 5). Dissenting groups of people, of different social, economic, political, and cultural backgrounds, beyond traditional ideological, social identifications, joined, some of them for the first time, massively these movements, declaring their demands in a compelling way.

Second, in addition to the traditional forms of contention, that of street demonstrations, another form of protesting figures prominently in the repertoire of actions of these movements – the occupation of main squares, and the setting of protests camps. These practices advanced the spatio-temporal presence of collective action. They facilitated activities which sustained the mobilizations, and promoted processes that advanced the formation of collective identities. Moreover, by gathering, performing in, and using the public space activists demanded the "democratization of public space" (Leontidou, 2010, p. 1196).

Third, these occupied spaces functioned as 'laboratories' where elements of the democratic practice are mixed, remixed, developed and tested. In gatherings, meetings, general assemblies, and methods of collective decision making, activists experiment with the exercise of participatory and discursive practices, pushing forward the ideal of direct democracy. Using Keane's words (1998: 171), "[t]hey focus upon the present, wherein they practice the future social changes they seek, and their organizational means are therefore valued as ends in themselves".

Fourth, these protest movements share a similar "repertoire of communication" (Mattoni, 2013). The role of social networking platforms (Facebook, Twitter, Tumblr) along with the use of mobile phones and portable devices has been, to different degrees, vital in the mobilization and organization of the uprisings. Social media were popular platforms for communication and interaction among Internet users before the protest waves of 2011, and easier to use than previous internet applications. This made them the platform of choice to diverse users, some of whom were engaged for the first time in activist practices. Moreover, social media have allowed for more fragmented, individual, political activities to be pursued, practiced in the private realm (Papacharissi, 2010), though they cannot replace collective protest action realized in the public realm (Fuchs, 2014).

Finally, what characterizes the evolvement of these movements is their snowball inspiration. Several examples of affiliation, solidarity, and similar frames are registered in the struggles of 2011' protest movements. "In the first mass demonstration in Cairo's Tahrir Square on January 25, 2011, thousands shouted 'Tunisia is the solution,' ... When Spain's indignados started campaigning in the main squares of cities around the country in May 2011, they proclaimed that 'Iceland is the solution'" (Castells, 2012, p. 20). Protesters in Spain "raised banners chants of 'Shhh ... the Greeks are sleeping' with reference to the crushing debt crisis and severe austerity measures facing the country. This idea swiftly traveled to Greece where Facebook networks agreed to set alarm clocks at the same time to 'wake up' and demonstrate. Banners in Athens proclaimed: 'We've awakened! What time is it? Time for them to leave!'" (Bennett & Segerberg, 2013, p. 746). Also, the initial call for action in the United States on July 13th was asking American people to have their 'Tahrir moment'.

In all cases, two important parameters have to be taken into consideration when discussing social media activism in terms of highly dispersed circumstances and a rapidly accelerating hybrid media environment. These parameters are: the context in which the movements were developed and the role of different media formats in the mobilizations.

Differences I: Structural Aspects

This section reflects on the specific contexts in which the uprisings took place and highlights the differences among contemporary protest movements, drawing on structural aspects, dislocations and histories of contention in each case. As a result, it challenges the very assumption of viewing contemporary protest movements as part of a "new international cycle of contention" (Tejerina et. al., 2013).

In the case of Arab Spring social demands have a national character. They are against economic, political and social repression, and the local dictatorships. The protestors are asking for political reforms and pro-democratic changes to take place in their countries – Tunisia, Egypt, Libya, and Syria among others. Any account of the uprisings can hardly dismiss the decisive role of their context. Reflecting on the Arab uprisings, Castells (2012, p. 94) interestingly mentions: "These various movements emerged from causes specific to each country, and evolved according to the conditions of their contexts and to the idiosyncrasies of each revolt". The dominant framework of analysis of the events in the Arab world has been subjected to a western-centric perspective and its biases – eurocentrism, modernity and orientalism. In the editorial, '*The season of revolution: the Arab Spring and European mobilizations*', of a special issue in the *Interface* journal, Shihade et. al. (2012, p. 1) identify this problematic pattern. "The concept of season is embedded in a long history of Orientalizing the region, as if what happened in the history of Arab people before 2011 did not qualify for an acknowledgment of the energies, struggles, and the fighting for a better life they have been waging against western colonialism, intrusions, and unjust local governments for over 100 years". The uprisings in the Arab world did not occur into the void. There has been significant opposition to the Arab Nationalist-Socialist-bureaucratic regimes of the late 50s and 60s and opposition to oversecularism due to the gradual raise of political Islam in the Middle East. Especially, since the collapse of the Soviet Union and the Eastern block, these regimes have been anachronistic, and there have been several instances when they were challenged, including ad hoc opposition practices such as the annual protests against the rise of bread price (controled by the state) particularly in North Africa, women's disobedience actions in Saudi Arabia for their right to drive (Vatikiotis & Yörük, 2013), and a series of strikes and labour protests, sit-ins in Egypt in front of the parliament in the mid to late 2000s (Gerbaudo, 2012).

The Arab Spring was an inspiration for the European movements. "Perhaps the most significant influence was the occupation of Tahrir Square, which prompted European activists to take the practice of occupation (most often reserved for squatted social centers) into the public squares and into direct contact with other citizens, drawing in large number of people who had not mobilized before" (Shihade et. al., 2012, p. 5). Still, the social demands are different here; they have both an international character – against global (IMF) and regional (EU) capitalism, the economic crisis and the politics of austerity, and a national character – against political corruption and the national elites. According to Donatella della Porta (2012) the new wave of protest that swept Europe has continuities and discontinuities with the past, and the global justice movement in particular. "[W]hile both waves of protest talk a cosmopolitan language, claiming global rights and blaming global financial capital, the global justice movement moved from the transnational to the national (and the local), while the new wave took the reverse root" (ibid: 274). The transnational activism of the global justice movement provided a valuable source for new action forms and practices to be developed in national levels. Yet, the buildup of European mobilizations has also been in direct communication with strong pre-existing repertoires of action in a national level. The long tradition and the social capital of activist movements that preceded European mobilizations are indicative here. A number of dynamic protests took place a few years before the protests of 2011 – civil disobedience actions in Spain on March 13th 2004 (Gerbaudo, 2012), the violent confrontations in the streets of Athens in December 2008 after the shooting of a 15-year old boy by a policeman (Vatikiotis, 2011) and, in more traditional form, union-led demonstrations in Portugal (Baumgarten, 2011), general strikes in Greece (Psimitis, 2011), and university students' strikes in Spain (Perugorría & Tejerina, 2013).

The development of the Occupy Movement has been prominently a critique of the neo-liberal global capitalism, its imaginaries and practices, as well as of the representative democracy and its political elites. It has identified itself as a popular movement representing the 99% of the population, putting poverty and systemic inequality back on the political agenda (Stelter, 2011). People in the United States have accumulated unsustainable debts, inflicted higher workloads, and entertained illusions created by the housing bubble (Chomsky, 2012: Chapter 3, Section 1, para. 8). Moreover, the dominance of neoliberal ideology has destructed the sense of public space in American society. Thus, "[t]he call to 'occupy' chosen by activists was premised precisely on this sense of a crisis of public space, and on the conviction that in order to create a public space anew there was no other way than by physically 'occupying' it" (Gerbaudo, 2012: Chapter 4, Section 2, para. 2). Still, the protest camps of the Occupy Movement "each emerged out of particular places, contexts and histories of contestation" (Kidd, 2012) and linked to earlier protest movements (Graeber, 2013). In addition to the mass protests of the Seattle anti-WTO demonstrations and the protests against the U.S. invasion of Iraq in 2002 and 2003, hundreds of groups in the United States have been engaged in counter-hegemonic practices and urban struggles (over living wages, job security, affordable housing, welfare, quality education, healthcare, transportation, and immigrant rights), employing several tactical repertoires (direct action, lobbying and legislative action, alternative knowledge production and alternative economic and social practices) (Leitner et. al., 2008, cited in Kidd 2012). Furthermore, a long-standing 'reclaim the streets' subculture has long thrived in arts and culture movements in the United States (Duncombe, 1997).

Differences II: Social Media, They 'Never Walk Alone'

This section addresses the wider mediascape with regard to contemporary protest movements, highlighting the roles of diverse media formats. From this perspective, it questions the very determinant role of social media practices in the relevant activist practices. Social media have definitely contributed to the mobilization and/or organization of the uprisings of 2011 in different ways and stages. In Egypt, social media were initially employed by a minority of 'media-savvy youth'. In Spain, social media were widely used both before and after the turning point of the 15th of May (15M) protests. While, in the United States social media were broadly used only once the 'Occupy Wall Street' movement had become literally visible in the public space. In all these cases, the evaluation of the role of social media needs to be more balanced.

In the Arab world, mass media have always been a means of repression, the major vertical ideological apparatus of state oppression. This aspect registers significant differences in relation to the western mediascapes and has also implications for the respective evaluation of social media as a tool of emancipation. Several accounts have overestimated the role of social media in the Arab uprisings. The low levels of internet access rates in most of these countries (Fuchs, 2014) do not support such an analysis. Moreover, repressive internet uses (shut down of Internet and mobile phone networks) did not disrupt the protest movements; most of the participants were mobilized through other communication/media practices. Moreover, several studies have acknowledged the role of interpersonal communication and social networks (friends, families, schools workplaces; see Wilson & Dunn, 2011) and the role of mass media (the case of Al-Jazeera in the Egyptian movement) in mobilizing large sectors of population, beyond the young internet-connected middle class (Cottle, 2011), and supporting protest movements. Last but not least, WikiLeaks' reports on corruption in a number of Arab regimes, as well as hackers' operations ('Anonymous' group) against government sites adds considerably to the list of other media formats that were utilized in the movements (Vatikiotis & Yörük, 2013).

The role of social media, Facebook and Twitter, in European movements was important both in terms of initiating the mobilizations and sustaining the occupations. For example, it was the group of debate and action *'Democracia Real Ya!' (Real Democracy Now!)* that launched on its Facebook page the call for action in the streets of Spain on May 15, setting off a self-mediated movement. As a member of the network that created Democracia Real Ya points out (quoted in Castells, 2012: 116), "[t]he capacity of mass self-communication and self organization online has allowed people to overcome a media block". Twitter also played a significant role, creating fora for discussion (on the topics/hashtags #15M, #Indignados, #spanishrevolution) among activists, bloggers, and journalists. "In using social networking sites like Facebook and Twitter activists constructed resonant emotional conversations across the internet and managed to harness a widespread collective indignation transforming it into a political passion driving collective action in public space" (Gerbaudo, 2012, Chapter 3, Section 7, para. 1). In addition, a wide range of communication practices – web forums, blogs, collaborative documents, pedagogical materials, analogic versions of digital forms, cartoons, mainstream and alternative radio phone-ins, citizen photography (Flickr), videoclips, live streaming, aggregators, and link recommendation sites – contributed to the 15-M campaign (Postill, 2011). Finally, "the disclosure of WikiLeaks documents showing Spanish government officials to be less than forthright, and Stéphane Hessel's book Time for Outrage! (Indignez-vous!) also collaborated in inflaming Spanish passions" (Perugorría & Tejerina, 2013, p. 428). Nevertheless, social networking platforms facilitated the cross-national diffusion of frames, slogans and pictures, echoing messages and calls, especially among the European movements.

As it concerns the role of media in the case of the Occupy Movement, the intersection of different formats is prolific too. The original call was launched by the Canadian magazine Adbusters, an alternative news media (through its website, also creating #OccupyWallStreet hashtag and designing a poster), asking people to demonstrate on September 17th. Initially, the campaign failed to mobilize a large number of participants. Only once the movement became visible in its occupation of the Zuccotti Park, did it begin receiving attention on both mainstream (much of the dominant reporting focused on incidents of violence) and social media. Thus, social media did not actually prepare the terrain for the protests; they "only acquired importance during the phase of sustainment of the movement, being used to create a sense of solidarity between people on the ground and people following events from a distance" (Gerbaudo, 2012: Chapter 4, Section 1, para. 1). It was the social media platform Tumblr, and its page 'We are the 99%', where people shared pictures and voiced their anger, that first helped in generating and then expanding the Occupy Movement. The more popular social media platforms Twitter and Facebook were disregarded by the organizers during the first call and followed later on, producing a wide range of movement's self-representation, which they were then able to circulate to a great scope and scale. Occupy activities were also available 24/7 through the web stream, and independent and alternative media platforms then re-assembled the reports and stories for audiences off the web. Finally, activists themselves created seld-produced magazines about the camps, echoing in this way the long-lasting tradition of zines (Duncombe, 1997; Atton, 2002).

FUTURE RESEARCH DIRECTIONS

The 2011' wave of contention has also brought to the fore the need for the development of comparative frameworks of analysis when researching social media activism. These comparative frameworks have to be employed both 'vertically' and 'horizontally'.

The vertical analysis, drawing on the interaction between social actors/movements and conventional (social, cultural, political and economic) patterns, will probe cross-temporally into transformative events/moments, mobilizations/performances and activities/practices of contention, including their repertoire of communication in a specific context, evaluating thus continuities and discontinuities in the social movement milieu. "As Gitlin shows in his research on the Students for a Democratic Societies in the 1960s and 1970s, adopting a diachronic perspective is important to see the 'grammar of interaction' (Gitlin, 1980, p. 22) at work, which explains 'the terms with which [movement and media] would recognize and work on the other' over time" (Mattoni & Trerè, 2014, p. 256).

The horizontal analysis, focusing on the interactions of different media formats during the same episode of contention, will elaborate cross-spatially on the connections between multiple technologies, actors, and their practices, pointing out similarities and differences among "movements' climactic and virtually simultaneous periods of upsurge". "It is the ensemble of [media] formats which, collectively, media researchers need to address. The landmark study by Annabelle Sreberny and Ali Mohammadi of Iran's movement media against the Shah in the 1970s - *Small Media, Big Revolution* - illustrates in its breadth of media formats analyzed, the research model to follow" (Downing, 2013, p. 17).

Further questions are raised about the role of the specific protest movements and their uses of media in the long run, beyond the protest peak moments of occupying squares. To what extent did they facilitate the creation of oppositional public sphere(s), advancing political participation in their respective contexts? Did these movements have any transformative potential – empowerment of citizens, creation of tangible post-spontaneous political formations, development of antagonistic practices (like non-monetary local exchange systems, direct producers-consumers networks, and self-organized projects)? And, when it comes to the use of social media and their 'liberating' prospects, a more balance account is needed, taking into consideration reactionary uses by anti-democratic groups/movements, as well as the ways states use new technologies (monitoring and surveillance) for exercising control, coercion and domination.

CONCLUSION

In order to grasp the complexity of the interplay between social and media activism it is necessary to probe into the dialectical relationship between 'structures' and 'agents', critically evaluating challenges, opportunities, asymmetries, and contradictions in the weaving of contentious mediated practices. The societal contexts of development of the various mobilizations and protests point to how movements relate to power structures of the societies, reflecting antagonisms in the economic, political and ideological realms. These conditions disclose the realities, opportunities and risks of social movements' practices, including their media uses. Social movements are vibrant 'organisms' that interact with societies at different levels and time frames, affected also by pre-existing action repertoires and collective imaginations. And, in contemporary struggles social actors interact strongly with different types of media in multiple ways. This multifaceted relationship between social movements and media has been a particular challenge, asking for the relevant fields of study to speak to each other and research this relationship in an all encompassing way. Therefore, the employment of comparative frameworks of analysis is needed in order to evaluate the various dimensions of media intertwining with activist practices in both temporal and spatial terms across differing contexts. To conclude, social media activism is a highly contested field, incorporating diverse factors that influence the emergence and the prospects of contemporary protest movements, amplifying or limiting their potential – (de)generating the formation of political consciousness.

REFERENCES

Atton, A. (2002). *Alternative media*. London: Sage.

Barry, E. (2009, April 8). Protests in Moldova explode, with help of twitter. *The New York Times*, p. A1.

Bauman, Z. (2000). *Liquid modernity*. Cambridge, MA: Polity Press.

Baumgarten, B. (2013). Geração à Rasca and beyond: Mobilizations in Portugal after 12 March 201. *Current Sociology*, *61*(4), 457–473. doi:10.1177/0011392113479745

Bennett, W. L. (2003). Communicating global activism: Strengths and vulnerabilities of networked politics. *Information Communication and Society*, *6*(2), 143–168. doi:10.1080/1369118032000093860a

Bennett, W. L., & Segerberg, A. (2012). The logic of connective action. *Information Communication and Society*, *15*(5), 739–768. doi:10.1080/1369118X.2012.670661

Castells, M. (2012). *Networks of outrage and hope: Social movements in the internet age*. Cambridge: Polity.

Chomsky, N. (2012). *Occupy*. Retrieved from Amazon.com

Christensen, C. (2009, July). Iran: networked dissent. *Le Monde diplomatique*. Retrieved January 07, 2011, from http://mondediplo.com/blogs/iran-networked-dissent

Cleaver, H. (1998). The Zapatista effect: The internet an the rise of an alternative political fabric. *Journal of International Affairs*, *51*(2), 621–640.

Cottle, S. (2011). Media and the Arab uprisings of 2011: Research notes. *Journalism*, *12*(5), 647–659. doi:10.1177/1464884911410017

Couldry, N., & Curran, J. (Eds.). (2003). *Contesting media power: Alternative media in a networked world*. Lanham, MD: Rowman Littlefield Publishers.

della Porta, D. (2007). *The global justice movement. Cross national and transnational perspectives*. London: Paradigm Publisher.

della Porta, D. (2012). Mobilizing against the crisis, mobilizing for 'another democracy': comparing two global waves of protest. *Interface: A Journal for and about Social Movements, 4*(1), 274-277.

della Porta, D., & Diani, M. (2006). *Social movements: An introduction*. Malden, MA: Blackwell.

Dongwon, J. (2010). Real-time networked media activism in the 2008 Chotbul protest. *Interface: A Journal for and about Social Movements, 2*(2), 92-102.

Downing, J. (1984). *Radical media: The political experience of alternative communication*. Boston: South End Press.

Downing, J. (2001). *Radical media: Rebellious communication and social movements* (2nd ed.). Thousand Oaks, CA: SAGE.

Downing, J. (2003). The independent media center movement center and the anarchist socialist tradition. In N. Couldry & J. Curran (Eds.), Contesting media power: Alternative media in a connected world (pp. 243–258). Oxford, UK: Rowman & Littlefield Publishers.

Downing, J. (2008). Social movement theories and alternative media. *Communication, Culture & Critique*, *1*(1), 40–50. doi:10.1111/j.1753-9137.2007.00005.x

Downing, J. (2013, March). *Recent (2012) approaches to social movement media: A critique*. Paper presented at the conference Social Movements, Media, Networking and Politics, Izmir, Turkey.

Duncombe, S. (1997). *Notes from underground: Zines and the politics of alternative culture*. London: Verso.

Eagleton-Pierce, M. (2001). The internet and the Seattle WTO protests. *Peace Review*, *13*(3), 386–401. doi:10.1080/13668800120079027

El-Nawawy, M., & Khamis, S. (2012). Political Activism 2.0: Comparing the role of social media in Egypt's "Facebook revolution" and Iran's "Twitter uprising". *CyberOrient, 6*(1). Retrieved March 14, 2013, from http://www.cyberorient.net/article.do?articleId=7439

Fuchs, C. (2014). *Social media: A critical introduction*. London: Sage. doi:10.4135/9781446270066.n2

Gerbaudo, P. (2012). *Tweets and the streets: Social media and contemporary activism.* Retrieved from Amazon.com

Ghonim, W. (2012). *Revolution 2.0: The power of people is greater than the people in power: A memoir.* New York: Houghton Mifflin Harcourt.

Gitlin, T. (1980). *The whole world is watching: Mass media in the making and unmaking of the New Left.* Berkeley: University of California Press.

Gladwell, M. (2010, October). Small change Why the revolution will not be tweeted. *The New Yorker*, 42–49.

Goldstein, J. (2007). *The role of digital networked technologies in the Ukrainian orange revolution.* The Berkman Center for Internet & Society at Harvard University, Research Publication No. 2007-14. Retrieved January 11, 2011, from http://cyber.law.harvard.edu/sites/cyber.law.harvard.edu/files/Goldstein_Ukraine_2007.pdf

Graeber, D. (2013). *The democracy project: A history, a crisis, a movement.* London: Allen Lane.

Hardt, M., & Negri, A. (2000). *Empire.* Cambridge, MA: Harvard University Press.

Hardt, M., & Negri, A. (2005). *Multitude: War and democracy in the age of empire.* New York: Penguin Books.

Hardt, M. & Negri, A. (2012). *Declaration.* Retrieved from Amazon.com

Hollander, E., & Stappers, J. (1992). Community media and community communication. In J. Jankowski, O. Prehn, & J. Stappers (Eds.), *The People's Voice: Local Radio and Television in Europe* (pp. 17–27). London: John Libbey.

Huesca, R. (1995). A procedural view of participatory communication: Lessons from Bolivian tin miners' radio. *Media Culture & Society, 17*(1), 101–119. doi:10.1177/016344395017001007

Juris, J. S. (2005). The new digital media and activist networking within anti-corporate globalization movements. *The Annals of the American Academy of Political and Social Science, 597*(1), 189–208. doi:10.1177/0002716204270338

Kahn, R., & Kellner, D. (2004). New media and internet activism: From the 'Battle of Seattle' to blogging. *New Media & Society, 6*(1), 87–95. doi:10.1177/1461444804039908

Kavada, A. (2005). Exploring the role of the internet in the 'movement for alternative globalization': The case of the Paris 2003 European Social Forum. *Westminster Papers in Communication and Culture, 2*(1), 72–95.

Keane, J. (1998). *Civil society: Old images, new visions.* Stanford, CA: Stanford University Press.

Kidd, D. (2012, June). *#Occupy in the San Francisco bay.* Paper presented at Cities are Us Conference, Coimbra, Portugal.

Langman, L. (2013). Occupy: A new new social movement. *Current Sociology, 61*(4), 510–524. doi:10.1177/0011392113479749

Leitner, H., Sheppard, E., & Sziarto, K. (2008). The spatialities of contentious politics. *Transactions of the Institute of British Geographers*, *33*(2), 157–172. doi:10.1111/j.1475-5661.2008.00293.x

Leoontidou, L. (2010). Urban social movements in 'weak civil societies': The right to the city and cosmopolitan activism in southern Europe. *Urban Studies (Edinburgh, Scotland)*, *47*(6), 1179–1203. doi:10.1177/0042098009360239

Mattoni, A. (2013). Repertoires of communication in social movement processes. In B. Cammaerts, A. Mattoni, & P. McCurdy (Eds.), *Mediation and protest movements* (pp. 39–56). Bristol: Intellect.

Mattoni, A., & Trerè, E. (2014). Media practices, mediation processes, and mediatization in the study of social movements. *Communication Theory*, *24*(3), 252–271. doi:10.1111/comt.12038

McAdam, D., & Jr Sewell, W. H. (2001). It's about time: Temporality in the study of contentious politics. In R. Aminzade (Ed.), *Silence and voice in the study of contentious politics*. Cambridge, UK: Cambridge University Press. doi:10.1017/CBO9780511815331.005

Melucci, A. (1996). *Challenging codes: Collective action in the information age*. Cambridge, UK: Cambridge University Press. doi:10.1017/CBO9780511520891

Morozov, E. (2011). *The net delusion: The dark side of Internet freedom*. New York: PublicAffairs.

Olesen, T. (2004). The transnational Zapatista solidarity network: An infrastructure analysis. *Global Networks - A Journal of Transnational Affairs, 4*(1), 89-107.

Papacharissi, Z. (2010). *A private sphere: Democracy in a digital age*. Cambridge, MA: Polity.

Perugorría, I., & Tejerina, B. (2013). Politics of the encounter: Cognition, emotions, and networks in the Spanish 15M. *Current Sociology*, *61*(4), 424–442. doi:10.1177/0011392113479743

Postill, J. (2011). Democracy in the age of viral reality. *Media/Anthropology*. Retrieved 16 March, 2013 from http://johnpostill.com/2011/11/07/democracy-in-the-age-of-viral-reality-3/

Psimitis, M. (2011). The Protest cycle of spring 2010 in Greece. *Social Movement Studies*, *10*(2), 191–197. doi:10.1080/14742837.2011.562365

Rennie, E. (2006). *Community media: A global introduction*. Oxford, UK: Rowman & Littlefield Publishers.

Rheingold, H. (2002). *Smart mobs*. Cambridge, MA: Perseus Books.

Rodriguez, C. (2001). *Fissures in the mediascape: An international study of citizens' media.* Hampton Press.

Sabety, S. (2010). Graphic content: The semiotics of a YouTube uprising. In I. Y. Kamalipour (Ed.), *Media, power, and politics in the digital age: The 2009 presidential election uprising in Iran* (pp. 119–124). Roman & Littlefield Publishers.

Servaes, J. (1999). *Communication for development: One world, multiple cultures*. Cresskill, NJ: Hampton Press.

Shihadem M., Fominaya, C. & Cox, C. (2012). The season of revolution: the Arab spring and European mobilizations. *Interface: A Journal for and about Social Movements, 4*(1), 1-16.

Shirky, C. (2008). *Here comes everybody: How change happens when people come together*. London: Penguin.

Shirky, C. (2011). The political power of social media. *Foreign Affairs*, *90*(1), 28–41.

Simiti, M. (2014, February). Rage and protest: The case of the Greek indignant movement. *Hellenic Observatory Papers on Greece and Southeast Europe*. London School of Economics and Political Science (LSE). Retrieved September 22, 2014, from: http://www.lse.ac.uk/europeanInstitute/research/hellenicObservatory/CMS%20pdf/Publications/GreeSE/GreeSE-No82.pdf

Smith, J. (2001). Globalizing resistance: The of Seattle and the future of social movements. *Mobilization: An International Journal*, *6*(1), 1–19.

Stelter, B. (2011, December 1). Camps are cleared, but '99 percent' still occupies the lexicon. *The New York Times*, p. A1.

Tapscott, D. (2011, February 14). The debate on social media and revolutions. Reality steps in. *HuffPost*. Retrieved January 14, 2013, from http://www.huffingtonpost.com/don-tapscott/social-media-key-to-revol_b_823043.html

Tarrow, S. (1994). *Power in movement: Collective action, social movements and politics*. Cambridge, UK: Cambridge University Press.

Tejerina, B., Perugorría, I., Benski, T., & Langman, L. (2013). From indignation to occupation: A new wave of global mobilization. *Current Sociology*, *61*(4), 377–392. doi:10.1177/0011392113479738

Tilly, C. (1978). *From mobilization to revolution*. Reading, MA: Addison-Wesley.

Tsagarousianou, R. (1998). Electronic democracy and the upblic sphere: Opportunities and challenges. In R. Tsagarousianou, D. Tambini, & C. Bryan (Eds.), *Cyberdemocracy: Technology, Cities and Civic Networks* (pp. 167–178). London: Routledge. doi:10.4324/9780203448847

Vatikiotis, P. (2005). Communication theory and alternative media. *Westminster Papers in Communication and Culture*, *2*(1), 5–29.

Vatikiotis, P. (2011). Networking activism: Implications for Greece. *Estudos em Comunicação. Communication Studies*, *10*, 169–185.

Vatikiotis, P., & Yörük, Z. (2013, April). *Arab spring: A networked social imaginary?* Paper presented at New Media – New Politics: (post) Revolutions in Theory and Practice Conference, London, UK.

Walgrave, R., & van Aelst, P. (2004). New media, new movements? The role of the internet in shaping the anti-globalization movement. In W. van de Donk, L. D. Loader, P. G. Nixon, & D. Rucht (Eds.), *Cyberprotest. New media, citizens and social movements* (pp. 97–122). London: Routledge.

Wilson, C., & Dunn, A. (2011). Digital media in the Egyptian revolution: Descriptive analyses from the Tahrir data set. *International Journal of Communication*, *5*, 1248–1272.

Wolfsfeld, G., Segev, E., & Sheafer, T. (2013). Social media and the Arab Spring: Politics comes first. *The International Journal of Press/Politics*, *20*(10), 1–23.

Section 2

Grassroots Social Movements, Institutionalized Politics, and Mediatized Political Communication

Chapter 4
Radical Political Communication and Social Media:
The Case of the Mexican #YoSoy132

Lázaro M. Bacallao-Pino
National Autonomous University of Mexico, Mexico

ABSTRACT

This chapter aims to analyze the practices of radical political communication within the context of social mobilizations whose emergence and initial spreading are inherently associated to social media. On the basis of a case study -the #YoSoy132, a university student mobilization during the 2012 electoral campaign in Mexico- the text analyzes the main uses of social media as part of the mobilizations and the interrelationships between online (communication) and offline collective action. The author concludes that, despite the importance of social media and the collective actions based on their use, even the participants recognize the necessity of going beyond the online space. Although social media pluralize the actors of political communication and even force its traditional actors to participate in alternative communication spaces, collective communicative action cannot be confined to the digital space, but it must be understood within the processes of social mobilization, in all its articulations and mediations.

INTRODUCTION

The increasing role of the information and communication technologies (ICTs) in everyday practices of communication in general and, particularly, in political communication, has become a relevant topic of research in contemporary societies (Bentivegna, 2006). At the same time, social movements and mobilizations have also become a relevant issue for social theories and research. In the articulation of these two trends, the analyses on the ICTs have underlined, on the one hand, its contribution for enabling processes of participation and democratic dynamics and, on the other hand, have criticized certain tendencies to a technological determinism. Those debates have increased with the emergence of social media, associated to openness, freedom and horizontality and a richer user experience and an architecture of participation (Vickery & Wunsch-Vincent, 2007).

DOI: 10.4018/978-1-4666-9879-6.ch004

Social mobilizations put in practice a significant appropriation of ICTs as part of their collective action that has been associated to the emergence of new cyber-based repertoires of contention and the development of horizontal forms of organization by those collective actors. This tendency leads to the peculiarities of the political communication as part of this collective phenomena. In that regard, the chapter aims to critically analyze the appropriation of social media as resources for radical political communication within the context of social mobilizations by people who are not traditional political militants. Radical political communication refers to the specifically sociopolitical-oriented communicative practices by counterhegemonic groups, that aim at explicitly questioning and challenging the mainstream political communication — i.e., the political communication by institutional hegemonic groups, such as political parties.

If social movements are counter-institutions — this is, absolute negations of the institutions that try to configure another institutional regime, alternative to the modern one (Alonso, 1986) — that give a significant importance to the communicative dimension (Kavada, 2005), then these collective actors may be considered as particularly challenging agents against the practices of communication by institutional political groups. Social movements have traditionally associated with practices of alternative communication (Alfaro, 2000), a notion that has been widely discussed. From a complex perspective, alternative communication refers to a participatory communicational model and, consequently: 1) it cannot be understood in terms of a communicational or technical alternative, nor a simple alternative use of media; and 2) "true alternative political communication projects" must have "a globalizing presence at the macro-political level" (Capriles, 2006, p. 305).

In that regard, radical political communication: 1) implies a participatory model of alternative communication; 2) overcomes an understanding of the communicational practices of social mobilizations and movements that is limited to a "citizen" and "non political" nature, a tendency derived from certain simplistic conceptualizations of these collective agents that place them out from politics; 3) goes beyond traditional concepts of radical political communication that are based on a very simple communication model and accept the idea that "whomsoever possesses the senders can control the throughs of humans" (Autonome a.f.r.i.k.a gruppe, 2003, p. 87); and 4) implies also an alternative understanding of politics, not as the activity associated with the traditional political agents such as political parties, but as "a space of accumulation of social, cultural and directly political forces" (Sader, 2001).

From this perspective, the text examines the main tendencies and dimensions mediating the online practices of digital radical political communication, in particular the online/offline tension, through the study of a relevant case of use of social media in the context of an electoral campaign: the Mexican #Yosoy132 (English: #Iam132). This was a mobilization led by students from both private and public universities that took place against the then presidential candidate of the Partido Revolucionario Institucional (PRI, English: Institutional Revolutionary Party) and current Mexican President, Enrique Peña Nieto, during the 2012 electoral campaign. The analysis focuses on the period between 23 May and 1 July 2012, when the #YoSoy132 published its foundational statement and elections were held, respectively. During this period, mobilizations and the electoral campaign coincided in time.

THEORETICAL AND CONTEXTUAL BACKGROUND

Social movements and mobilizations put in practice, as part of their collective action, certain repertoires of contention (Tarrow, 1998; Tilly, 1995), a notion that firstly focused on "public display of disruptive action", while most recent works have moved towards "broader contentious performances, stressing the constant innovation in the various forms of contentious politics" (Della Porta, 2013). The uses of ICTs for collective action have lead to the configuration of an online repertoire of contention — including online sit-ins, signing online petitions, hacking, defacing web pages, email floods, etc.—, in what has been defined as cyber-activism (Van Laer & Van Aelst, 2009).

The new digital communicative scenario has fundamental effects on politics, in such a way that communication becomes the main space of politics (Castells, 2000). Discussions on the political impact of the ICTs have ranged from the analysis of the consequences of the Internet on traditional representative democracy (Davis et al., 2002), to the Internet's potential to revitalize the public sphere and produce a new regime of participatory democracy (Thornton, 2001) and a new scenario for democratic dynamics, the so-called cyberspace (Poster, 1997). As part of these debates, for instance, some approaches have discussed how the online practices contribute in advancing democratic dynamics beyond its conceptualizations within the liberal-capitalist political context (Dahlberg & Siapera, 2007), or the extension and pluralization of the public sphere as a result of cyberspace practices (Dahlgren, 2005). In a context characterized by diverse and even opposite perspectives (see Morozov, 2011; Dahlgren, 2005), these debates bring us to the impact of the ICTs —and, particularly, social media— in the current dynamics of political communication.

Social Media and Political Communication

Political communication is an extremely complex notion that refers to a vast field. In an overview of this concept and as part of an effort to operationalize it, Franklin (1995, p. 225) defines political communication as the study of "the interactions between media and political systems, locally, nationally, and internationally", arguing that it focuses on the analysis of the following dimensions: 1) the political context of the media; 2) the actors and agencies involved in the production of media content; 3) the impact of political media content on the audience and/or on policy development; 4) the impact of the political system on the media one; and 5) the impact of the media system on the political one. Norris (2004) also defines political communication as "an interactive process concerning the transmission of information among politicians, the news media and the public" that "operates down-wards from governing institutions towards citizens, horizontally in linkages among political actors and also upwards from public opinion towards authorities".

This interactive nature of political communication is relevant for the proposed analysis, since —as aforementioned— social media are associated with the increase of the enabling conditions for interactivity. At the same time, these Web 2.0 platforms emerge in a context that has been described in terms of "media malaise", a notion that refers to negative impact of the process of political communication has upon civic engagement, by considering that "common practices in political communications by the news media and by party campaigns hinder 'civic engagement', meaning citizens learning about public affairs, trust in government, and political activism" (Norris, 2000, p. 4).

Given this scenario — and in line with the shared interactive nature of social media and political communication — different authors have underlined that the emergence of the Web 2.0 — including communicational resources such as blogs, wikis and social networks — has produced relevant changes in political communication, its structures and dynamics (Feenstra & Casero-Ripollés, 2014), by providing to the citizens technological resources that enable them not only to consume but also to produce their own communicative products and spaces (Dylko & McCluskey, 2012). These technological resources empower people since they can find new spaces of autonomy on the Internet (Castells, 2009; Jenkins, 2006) and open the information environment to multiple groups that can create or incorporate new issues or topics into the public debate (Casero-Ripollés, 2010; Chadwick, 2011), fostering this way transparency as well as facilitating many-to-many communication processes and promoting citizen's interactivity (McNair, 2006).

However, there have been also some debates on the potential of social media as a source of change for political communication: while some authors consider that the role of social media in collective action generates "a new fetishism of technology", distracting people from the core contradictions of contemporary capitalism (Fuchs, 2012), others highlight that social media have generated new communicational practices, bringing new dynamism to public mobilization, fueling revolts and bringing about political transformation (Bardici, 2012).

On the one hand, previous analyses have discussed, for instance, the capacities of the Internet as community builder in a context of raising political disengagement and disenchantment (Davis et al., 2002). In this scenario, although the use of social networks — such as Twitter — for political communication has been considered as "another arena for already established societal actors", it has been noted that this use "also helps broadening the public debate, because chances for 'ordinary' citizens to get in touch and discuss with the establishment of political communication are much higher on Twitter than in traditional contexts of interaction" (Maireder et al., 2012, p. 160). But, at the same time, despite the general recognition of the increasingly important role played by social media in shaping political communication in contemporary societies (e.g., Aday et al., 2010; Tumasjan et al., 2011), other authors have noted that "until now the potentials of political discussions in social media involving political institutions could not be exploited sufficiently" (Stieglitz & Dang-Xuan, 2012). In the same line, Macnamara and Kenning (2011, p. 19) suggested that, although the raising level of use of social media and the volume of social media content used for political communication, "Web 2.0-enabled social media are being used primarily in election-related political communication for one-way transmission of messages, rather than engaging in listening, dialogue, consultation and collaboration", resembling mass media communication and the practices of journalism, advertising and public relations.

These debates add new polemic dimensions to previous debates on the communication of social movements, a dimension that, although recognized as a central one for these collective actors, has been been under-theorized and under-researched by the theories on collective action (Kavada, 2005). In that regard, the uses of social media by recent episodes of social mobilizations offer a complex view of the communicative dimension of collective action, overcoming these trends, and it also provides a relevant analytical scenario for the understanding of what can be considered as a social media-based radical political communication. While, as a result of its technological characteristics — user-generated content, architecture of participation, openness, freedom and horizontality —, there is a trend to underline the positive impact of social media in the communicational democratization, as we have seen before, a more complex perspective of it is needed.

A particularly relevant dimension of analysis is the online/offline tension within social media-based practices of radical political communication. Since these episodes of collective action are political performatives — in the sense of that "participants start to experience what they strive to become" (Arditi, 2012), in this case through the online communication — then online collective action becomes, at the same time, a space of radical political communication. In that regard, there are opposite positions regarding the interrelationships between the online and the offline dimensions of collective action. While some previous studies have shown cases in which social networks have been used to mobilize online movements that moved offline (Harlow, 2012), other researches suggested that "a significant increase in the use of the new media is much more likely to follow a significan amount of protest activity that to precede it" (Wolfsfeld, Segev, & Sheafer, 2013: 115).

From this perspective and taking into account these debates, we aim to analyze — through the case study of the #YoSoy132 — how the uses of social media mediate the configuration of collective action's practices of radical political communication. We will focus on the tension between online and offline communicative collective actions, proposing that it will mediate, in a central way, the enabling conditions for these social mobilizations to become sustained practices for citizen participation and, consequently, practices of radical political communication that challenge the mainstream one.

#YoSoy132 and the Mexican Political and Communicative Context

The emergence and initial spreading of the #YoSoy132 are inherently linked to social media. It emerged as a result of the popular support, via Twitter, to a university students' protest against the Mexican presidential candidate Enrique Peña Nieto, during the electoral campaign in 2012. A video of the protest — that took place on May 11, 2012, during his visit to the Ibero-American University, Mexico City — was uploaded onto social media, but mainstream Mexican television channels and newspapers reported that protesters were not students, in an effort to discredit the manifestation. Then, 131 students from the Ibero-American University published a video on YouTube identifying themselves by their university ID card and people showed their support to them by symbolically stating, mainly on Twitter, that they were the "132nd student," thus creating a hashtag #YoSoy132 giving birth and naming to the social mobilization.

The relevance of that mobilization for the analyses of the social media-based enabling conditions for the emergence of radical political communication is derived largely from the Mexican political system and media system context. The latter is characterized by a high level of concentration — the better example of this is Televisa, the largest Mexican multimedia mass media company and, after Organizações Globo (Brazil), the largest one in Latin America and the first of Spanish-speaking world — where social media offer new enabling possibilities for the development of autonomous dynamics of communication. Some studies have examined how the use and appropriation of ICTs — and, particularly, social networks sites — by the Mexican civil society can be considered as the basis for a process of democratization of mainstream media, fostering pluralism and triggering important processes related to political culture within the Mexican context (García & Treré, 2014).

There is a particular articulation between this media system concentration and the hegemonic Mexican politics. It has been dominated by the PRI for 71 years in the last century, being the party in power from 1929 to 2000. Due this, the PRI has been described by some scholars as a "state party" (MacLeod, 2005; Russell, 2009), a term that describes both the non-competitive history and character of the party itself, and the inextricable connection between the PRI and the Mexican nation-state for much of the 20th century. It configured an authoritarian system characterized by PRI's anti-democratic practices such as vote buying, electoral fraud and clientelism (Gómez Vilchis, 2013).

In the context where previous studies (LAPOP/Barómetro de las Américas 2010; Latinobarómetro, 2009) have noted that the Mexicans are profoundly disappointed of their democratic regime, different authors (Vázquez, 1997; Villamil, 2012) have analyzed the complicity among the media system — in particular the Televisa Group — and the PRI, describing it as "the perfect dictatorship", an institutional one where media groups defined themselves as "soldiers of the PRI" (Vargas Llosa, 1990). In this scenario, some authors have underlined the increasing importance of social media for political and social activism in Mexico, highlighting in particular the role of Twitter in influencing government decision-making and shaping the interrelationships between different socio-political actors, including governments, politicians, citizens and other stakeholders. In that regard, the #YoSoy132 has been considered a new influential actor within Mexican politics that have shown how, based on social media, political movements can emerge and evolve, by using those technological resources to communicate certain concerns and organize protests (Sandoval-Almazan & Gil-Garcia, 2013).

In that scenario, the #YoSoy132 becomes a relevant case for the analysis of the specificities of social media as sources for radical political communication both in content and form, since, on the one hand, it is a social media-based mobilization and, on the other hand, its primary and foundational claim was the democratization of communication and the freedom of expression. Besides this, it emerged in the context of an election campaign, that can be considered the most densely political communication scenario. Although some authors have proposed the notion of political marketing for the analysis of communicative processes "in the context of political communication in the immediate pre-election period" (Lock & Harris, 1996, p. 27), we prefer to notion of radical political communication since, although the #YoSoy132 was a social mobilization that emerged in the context of an election campaign and one of its goals was to avoid the election of the PRI's candidate, the objective of a democratization of communication points out to a social actor aiming for cultural change and a general process of transformation of the political communication.

In that regard, although the #YoSoy132 is understood here — following the Norris' (2000) typology — as a specific campaign organization in the context of the short-term period of election campaign, which is characterized by purposive political communication with the aim of struggle for power, its general goal of a political communication transformation becomes a relevant underlying mediation that must be taken into account from the analytical perspective of the social media-based radical political communication.

METHODS AND DATA

The case study research uses a qualitative methodological perspective, involving mainly the discourse analysis of texts linked to the #YoSoy132 (declarations, interviews, speeches and other texts). If, as Castells (2004) affirms, social movements are what they say they are, then discourse analysis is an appropriate method for examining the issue. Discourse analysis has become a significant method for understanding social movements (Taylor & Whittier, 2004), as part of an increasing concern about the processes of meaning construction, "aware of this complexity and try to creatively approach the multiplicity of levels implied in a collective discourse" (Melucci, 2004, p. 57), and tend to focus on movement-related texts in the effort to identify patterns, linkages and structures of ideas related to these collective agents (Jonhston, 2002).

From a complex perspective of discourse analysis that is adequate for the proposed research, Franzosi (1998, p. 527) suggested to focus on the narrative dimension of discourse since it provides a point of view centered on actors as well as on discourse structures. This perspective transcends the focus on the search for the meaningful and moves on to the meanings contained in the structure and the narrative sequences of texts, in a transition "from variables to actors, away from regression-based statistical models to networks, and away from a variable-based conception of casualty to narrative sequences".

In the discourse analysis we included three types of texts, all from secondary sources and from 23 May to 1 July 2012. These three types of discourse are: 1) interviews with participants in the movement, taken from both mainstream and online alternative media (a total of 5 interviews with participants of the movement, published by 7 different media, were included in the analysis); 2) texts that appeared on social network sites (Facebook) and microblogging sites (Twitter) associated with the #YoSoy132 (these texts include tweets, posts, videos, pictures, etc. published during the analyzed period); and 3) public declarations and other documents by the #YoSoy132 (it includes the First Declaration of the #YoSoy132, its public declaration about the occupation of Televisa and the Counter-report of September 1st, 2012). We focussed particularly on three dimensions of the discourse: 1) references to mainstream political communication and other social dimensions associated with it (democracy, citizen participation, etc.); 2) comments on social media and its role as part of the emergence of a radical political communication; and 3) reflections on the tensions between online and offline actions as part of collective action.

The following section discusses the main findings of the study, aiming at provide a thorough understanding of some of the main characteristics, challenges, tensions and complexities of the interrelationships between social media and the emergence of practices of radical political communication, taking into account some of the main aforementioned theoretical tensions, in particular the online/offline one. Although a case study does not allow to obtain statistically representative results that can be generalized, it provides a thorough analysis of the more relevant characteristics of social media-based radical political communication. Despite the pros and cons of the discursive analysis approach (Paltridge, 2012), the study is relevant given the analytical significance of the #YoSoy132, a social media-based mobilization that emerges in the context of an election campaign focuses on the democratization of communication, challenging the mainstream political communication.

POLITICAL COMMUNICATION AND SOCIAL MEDIA-BASED MOBILIZATION: #YoSoy132

Democracy and Participation: Criticism and Alternatives from the Perspective of the Social Mobilization

The #YoSoy132 is defined as "a nonpartisan movement, with no leaders or ringleaders, a horizontal one" (Teyve de Lara, participant in the #YoSoy132, in Moraga, 2012) and, as part of these characteristics, social media are regarded by the participants as an enabling condition that allows "that now we do not depend on nothing nor nobody for communicating between us, as citizens" (Comment, #YoSoy132's profile on Facebook, 3 June 2012). Consequently, participants put in practice singular repertoires of contention, both online and offline ones, that has a special communicational nature and symbolical dimension —such as protest, manifestations and occupations— making an important effort for putting in practice participatory and horizontal forms of organization and decision-making.

In line with this tendency, democracy and participation have been central notions on the discourses of the movement and its participants. From the first declaration, the #YoSoy132 claimed for "the empowerment of common citizens through information," since it was considered as a "necessary condition" that allows citizens to "demand and criticize —based on arguments— their government, political actors, entrepreneurs and society". The #YoSoy132 "makes the right of information and freedom of expression to be its main demands", by considering that social democratization and a conscious and participatory citizenship requires "the democratization of the mass media of communication" (#YoSoy132, 28 May 2012).

The Mexican democracy was qualified as a "farce", given the absolute divorce between politicians and citizens, questioning a political dynamic that is limited to "vote every six years, [and] although even that is not respected", according to (Attolini, 2012), another participant in the #YoSoy132. Participants in the protests explained the mobilization as a result of "being full of indignation" about what the presidential candidates' in particular the PRI's one, represent (Protester, in Attolini, 2012). In that regard, the mobilization sets a radical opposition between this questioned representative democracy and what is considered as a real democracy, but also between two different practices of political communication associated to each one of these typologies of democratic regimes. In that oppositeness, social media and mobilizations are considered as core and articulated dimensions, since protests — resulting from, and inherently linked to online collective action — are seen as "healthy expressions for any democracy" (Teyve de Lara, in Moraga, 2012).

Comments by the users in the social network sites underline, on the one hand, the immediate purpose of avoiding that "the television channels impose me a candidate" (Comment, #YoSoy132's profile on Facebook, 24 May 2012), given advices about the strategies for their communicative practices: "instead of shouting insults to the candidates (…), we should give real facts about their frauds" (Comment, #YoSoy132's profile on Facebook, 25 May 2012). But, on the other hand, users also highlight "the marvelous opportunity given by social networks and the Internet in general for the organization and diffusion of this authentic and important movement" (Comment, #YoSoy132's profile on Facebook, 20 May 2012). From a more long-term perspective, the goal of the radical political communication developed by the social media-based mobilization is "to reassess the symbolic dimension of politics" against a political communication that is based on "empty figures and oxidized speeches", as part of the process of building "an authentic democracy, just right know" (Attolini, 2012). In the new democratic order, and as part of renewed scenario of political communication, the main objetive of the #YoSoy132 is associated with a certain practice of radical political communication, as agents of permanent political questioning: to become "the shadow of those one who would be the decision-makers" (Alina Rosa Duarte, participant in the #YoSoy132, in Moraga, 2012).

The Tension among Online and Offline Collective Action

Offline collective action is seen as a space for this new democratic regime, thanks to the radical political communication that is made possible by the appropriation of social media. In that regard, social networks sites are considered as "a fabulous way for fostering social mobilizations" (Diego Dante, participant in the #YoSoy132, in Goche, 2012), but also a space for a different model of political communication, since in these Web 2.0 platforms "no one is more important than another; we are all 140 characters" (Rodrigo Serrano, participant in the #YoSoy132, in Goche, 2012). The interrelationship between online and offline collective action —given the appropriation of social media as resources for spreading the protests, as well as their association with a horizontal and netlike structure— is underlined in tweets and comments in Facebook: "IMPORTANT - Let's spread this WARNING! # YoSoy132 – RT!" (@ElPsicosofo); "A decentralized movement is impossible to be cancelled or infiltrated" (@anonopshispano); "we must communicated through social media or mobile phones, so one can inform all the other people if one sees something rare during the election" (Comment, #YoSoy132's profile on Facebook, 27 June 2012); "we are organizing us in such a way that we can have an online platform ready for all the areas of work, so we can join ourselves in groups throughout the whole country" (Post, #YoSoy132's profile on Facebook, 1 July 2012).

In line with the role of social media in the emergence of the #YoSoy132, the participants give a particular importance to the online collective action, to the extent that the participation of some individuals in the mobilizations "takes place completely in the social networks" (Tania, participant in the #YoSoy132, in De Mauleón, 2012). However, despite the importance of the online dimension of radical political communication, participants also underlined the necessity of taking the mobilization from social networks sites into the streets, by putting in practice offline practices of radical political communication. Although individuals identify a trend to the decrease of the number of people attending the offline meeting spaces once online activity diminishes, in what is considered a prove of the capacities of online social networks "as a tool for organization and diffusion" (Diego Dante, in Goche, 2012), at the same time they also recognize that there is the need of creating offline communicational spaces, considered as sources for reinforcing the organizational capabilities of the movement and its national spreading. In that regard, even the online spaces, the users highlight that "we have to go to the streets, squares, restaurants, and all available places, and hand out leaflets" (Comment, #YoSoy132's profile on Facebook, 27 May 2012).

There are callings to "create informative groups that bring all what we know and share here in social networks to those people that only see Televisa" (Comment, #YoSoy132's profile on Facebook, 19 May 2012), since "we must take into account that, unfortunately, few people have access to the Internet, so each one of us must replicate and spread all what we comment here among the people around oneself" (Comment, #YoSoy132's profile on Facebook, 10 June 2012). The digital divide is also included as a main topic in the public declarations of the movement. The #YoSoy123 demands that "the access to Internet has to become an effective constitutional right" (#YoSoy132, 28 May 2012), denouncing the failure of the commitments regarding the bridging of the digital divide, underlining the hight costs of the access, the lack of telecommunication infrastructure and the inefficient computer literacy (#YoSoy132, 1 September 2012).

The offline spaces of radical political communication are important, in the view of the participants, because "what we want is not only to complain about what is not currently happening, but also to begin to make proposals about what we want to happen" (José Miguel Barberena, participant in the #YoSoy132, in Notimex, 2013). Although the radical political communication associated to the online collective action through social media has certain organizational dimension, the individuals underline, above all, its importance as resource of visibility. The tension between online and offline collective action mediates, in a central way, the enabling conditions for the continuity of the collective action after the end of the cycle of protest (Tarrow, 1995).

In that regard, the offline political communicative actions are considered as a step that goes beyond the online ones, a guarantee for the configuration of permanent spaces of radical political communication and the inclusion of the transformation of the mainstream communicative system in the public agenda. Participants underline that the #YoSoy132 "has [also] a very specific agenda, for example with regard to media law" (Teyve de Lara, in Moraga, 2012). The long-term goal, after the end of the election campaign, is to organize and consolidate the movement, in order "to become something like a citizen oversight, very active politically speaking, to propose agendas on issues of reforms" (Alina Rosa Duarte, in Moraga, 2012), underlining this way the objective of becoming a permanent collective action focused on the development of a radical political communication.

Social Media and Mobilization: Towards a Radical Political Communication?

As above-mentioned, the #YoSoy132's main and foundational claim was the democratization of communication. Traditional political communication in Mexico was put into question from the very beginning of the mobilizations, particularly through their spaces in social media. Participants frequently claim a new political communication in their posts and comments in social media: "Those who are not prepared to listen, have the reward of not learn anything", "I want a free Mexico, where my voice is heard", "Why keep quiet if I was born screaming?" (Post, #YoSoy132's profile on Facebook, 16 May 2012). There is a narrative in social media that associates this new political communication with a change in democracy: "Fair media, free minds," "Truth will make us free" (Post, #YoSoy132's profile on Facebook, 27 May 2012).

As we have seen before, social media are considered main sources for sharing information in a participatory way. There is a permanent concern about "spreading and forwarding all this information to those who did not have access to it during these elections", a demand of accurate information and a request for media "to stop the manipulation and the imposition of a candidate" (Post, #YoSoy132's profile on Facebook, 23 May 2012) and an explicit purpose of developing communicative spaces by "us, the people from below, against those ones above" (@Soy132MX).

However, both the context of electoral campaign and the sense of radicalness centrally mediate the development of this communicational collective action through social media. On the one hand, participants underline their apolitical position, denying any commitment with Mexican political parties and describing the #YoSoy132 as a movement from below, "without any party, without [political] colors, without violence" (Post, #YoSoy132's profile on Facebook, 23 May 2012). But, on the other hand, the use of social media is not an apolitical one: for instance, there are many complaints about the efforts made by political parties for co-opting the mobilization for their own electoral advantage. In that regard, previous analyses have noted that what was new during the 2012 electoral campaign, was the creation of "digital armies, responsible for opening electoral fronts in the Internet" that included false profiles, paid twitterers or the use of bots for creating trending topics in Twitter or placing topics in the public agenda (De Mauleón, 2012).

During the analyzed period, participants continuously denounce those trends through social media, in what are considered as "attempts to hijack the movement and use it by political parties for their own political capital" (@Soy132MX). Social media are regarded as resources for opposing these tendencies, since these Web 2.0 platforms can be used to "share, communicate, inform, criticize, participate" (@Soy132MX). Consequently, social media are considered main resources for the "transformation of the Mexican society" towards "a real democracy" where "the conscious, informed, active and purposeful participation defines the political life of the country" (Comment, #YoSoy132's profile on Facebook, 15 June 2012).

Social media become a relevant resource for a new democratic scenario, given its contribution for the configuration of practices of radical political communication. During the analyzed period, there is an intense activity in the both the Facebook's profile and the Twitter's account of the #YoSoy132. Most of the posts in Facebook are marked as "Like", commented and shared hundreds and even thousands of times. The profile is used for six surveys and the creation and diffusion of events (manifestations, assemblies, occupations), or asking celebrities and leaders for supporting the mobilizations. There are tweets that underline the emotional dimension — "I have already joined the movement! What are you waiting for?", "Hey! Do you follow @Soy132MX? It is the account of all of us!" (@Soy132MX) — and the hashtag #YoSoy132 became a trending topic for six days, occupying the first place within global trends from May 17-19, 2012.

The participants in the mobilizations organized an alternative debate among the presidential candidates and, during the debate, the three main hashtags on Twitter were: #debate132 (10225 tweets and 8152 users), #YoSoy132 (7659 tweets and 6031 users) and #DebateYoSoy132 (4389 tweets and 3590 users). The last one remained as global trending topic for more than 14 hours after the end of the debate (Capital Social Investigaciones, 2012). Many tweets also underline the importance of social media as resources for processes of communication from below: "What we do know is that a tweet replicated by key people will reach virtual media and then the traditional media too, continuing from there to television and reaching the people without access to networks. The elections showed us this chain. How we can fill a square. How we can trust unknown people who, nevertheless, have our same interests. There is no censorship in the Internet; nothing can stop the spreading of messages" (@lvloon, in De Mauleón, 2012).

Previous studies on the #YoSoy132 (De Mauleón, 2012; Salgado Andrade, 2013) agree in considering that some of the trending topics determined the media agenda during the electoral campaign. These analyses have highlighted that mobilizations made the Twittersphere to become an electoral thermometer, arguing that, for instance, the online collective action forced the mainstream media —particularly the television stations — to include the protests in their agenda and also made three of the candidates —all of them but Enrique Peña Nieto, to participate in the citizen debate organized and moderated by university students. This shows that social media did not only pluralized the actors of the political communication by giving voice to the students, but also became platforms from where the traditional actors of the political communication, i.e. the presidential candidates, were compelled to participate in spaces of radical political communication, such as a citizen debate. At the same time, since the participants "don not accept the representation that the power tries to impose to us as reality" (Comment, #YoSoy132's profile on Facebook, 5 June 2012), the social media-based radical political communication also include the transmission of offline collective actions, such as occupations and debates, through the technological resources available (streaming or Youtube).

But the objetive of developing a radical political communication goes beyond the period of election campaign. In that regard, the #YoSoy132 denounce the criminalization of "the citizen efforts for the creation of their own media", spaces that are considered main resources for the democratization of communication and the emergence of a radical political communication since these communicative experiences "give voice to the less favored groups in the society, bringing them information in line with their needs", becoming "an excellent tool for the communities to exercise their right to the information and freedom of expression" (#YoSoy132, 1 September 2012). Even the #YoSoy132 has an expression of continuity in an alternative communicational space: Colectivo Másde131 (English: CollectiveMoreThan131; see it at http://www.colectivo131.com.mx/). Created on May, 2014, it is defined as a space of alternative communication working for "the empowerment of the voice —from citizen to citizen— through projects aiming to strengthen our social networks", with the objective of developing "complaints accompanied by conscious actions, through the participation of all the Mexicans" in order to achieve "well informed citizens" and "an authentic democracy" (Colectivo Másde131, 2014).

SOLUTIONS AND RECOMMENDATIONS

The analysis sets a number of issues with regard to the practices of radical political communication associated to social mobilizations that are particularly based on social media. In particular, the case provides some relevant perspectives in the context of the debates regarding the impact of the uses of the ICTs in political communication. The Internet has been considered as a source of destabilization of political communication systems from a positive perspective, associated with the dispersion of older patterns of political communication and the extension and pluralization of the public sphere (Dahlgren, 2005). The ICTs are regarded as the cause of a new age of political communication, characterized by the reshaping of it through five trends: the intensification of professionalizing imperatives, the increase of competitive pressures, the emergence of anti-elitist populism, a process of "centrifugal diversification", and significant changes in how people receive politics (Bloomer & Kavanagh, 1999).

The #YoSoy132 shows that the appropriation of social media as part of collective action may destabilize traditional political communication, particularly in the scenario of a highly concentrated media system that is inherently articulated with an institutional politics characterized by corruption, clientelism and the hegemony of only one political party. Social media provide the technological resources for, on the hand, generating spaces of radical political communication from below and, on the other hand, forcing the traditional political communicative practices to open its agenda, by including the collective action on it and even compel their actors (such as presidential candidates) to participate in spaces of radical political communication.

Previous studies on social media have analyzed the increasing use of these technological resources during political campaigns and its impact on contemporary political communication, as well as the use of social media by some specific social groups, specifically in relation to political self-efficacy and situational political involvement in certain particular scenarios, such as election campaigns (Kushin & Yamamoto, 2010). The analysis of the #YoSoy132 shows that, as part of this process, the online/offline tension should be considered a central mediation, at least in the case if social mobilizations that emerge from the cyberspace. On the hand, this tension mediates aspects underlined by previous studies, such as the need of moving beyond the informational functions of social media on contentious politics, towards their roles as organizing mechanisms for collective action (Segerberg & Bennett, 2011). On the other hand, it also mediates the development of the collective action itself, in particular the weight given to the creation of spaces of alternative communication that are sources of radical political communication.

While the analysis proves that we are far from the days when initial studies spoke in terms of a cyber-diffusion of contention and it is clear that the cyberspace has become an autonomous scenario for specific cyber-repertoires of action, the online/offline tension remains as a core aspect of the configuration of a radical political communication as part of online-based social mobilizations. This tension will mediate the development of the social mobilization and its communicative dimension. Since the online dimension is particularly important during the emergence and initial spreading of collective action, this will increase the importance of the radical political communication as a dimension in the long-term development of collective action and its continuity beyond the period of greater activity of protest.

But, at the same time, participants in social mobilizations also believe that communicative collective action through social media is not enough for guaranteeing the continuity of the mobilizations. The transition from social media into the streets is regarded as a necessity and this becomes an important challenge to be borne in mind for a complex analysis of the radical political communication associated with social media-based collective action. In particular, it must take into account that the radicalness of this political communication is associated with both its content, i.e. the criticisms towards mainstream political communication, and its form, i.e. horizontality and participatory dynamics enabled by the characteristics of social media, but also with its inherent and crucial interlinkage between radical political communication and collective action.

FUTURE RESEARCH DIRECTIONS

Radical political communication articulates multiple dimensions and tensions. In particular, the centrality of the online/offline tension and the way in which it is managed as part of the development of collective action, are core aspects for a complex understanding of the issue. The study of this tension and its mediation is a relevant topic of research for future analyses of the consequences of social media for political communication. Another significant dimension of analysis is the articulation of radical political communication within the general collective action, in order to examine how being part of these social media-based mobilizations mediate these communicative practices, in particular their radicalness. This analytical perspective would be relevant for overcoming technology-centered approach to the re-configuration of political communication as a consequence of the use of social media, by including the socio-political context of these uses and the general aims of the collective action within which this technological appropriation takes place.

CONCLUSION

Radical political communication is a significant and core dimension of social media-based collective action. For the participants, given their interactivity and participatory architecture, social media enable the pluralization of the political communicative actors, challenge the manipulation and concentration of media system and open the public sphere to people from below, a relevant trend particularly in scenarios characterized by high levels of media concentration and complicity among the hegemonic institutional politics and mainstream media, as well as in contexts of electoral campaigns.

However, the importance of the online dimension in the case of social media-based episodes of collective action, there is a remaining technological determinism finds it expression in the online/offline tension. Although social media are used for a wide number of purposes — emotional mobilization, diffusion of information, denouncement of manipulation by mainstream political communication, share of resources for collective action, or pushing traditional political actors for them to participate in alternative spaces of communication — there is certain trend to underline the use of these Web 2.0 platforms as resources of visibility. At the same time, despite the importance given by the participants to the articulation between online and offline action — an even the transition from the former to the latter — it is hard to achieve this articulation/transition.

Although there is an explicit recognition of the need of putting into practice offline spaces of radical political communication, the prevailing trend is towards online radical political communication through the use of social media. On the one hand, the necessity of this transition from social media into the streets shows the limits — at least in the imaginary of the individuals — of the use of these technological resources for the transformation of the general practices of political communication. On the other hand, this online/offline tension can be understood in the light of the processes of social change that collective action tries to develop and its context. In the case of the #YoSoy132, the long-term main goal is precisely the democratization of communication but the immediate objective is to avoid the election of the PRI's candidate.

Consequently, the radical political communication will be mediated, in the short-term period of the election campaign, by the necessity of achieving the greatest possible influence and, in a very concentrated mainstream media system, social media are the most important channel available for this. However, the digital divide that characterizes the Mexican context forces to take into account the people who does not have access to the Internet. From a long-term perspective, the goal of the democratization of communication will find expression in the relevance of the communicative dimension as part of the continuity of the collective action, in particular through the creation of spaces of alternative communication that can be considered as experiences of radical political communication. While the impact of the short-term and social media-based radical political communication seems to be limited in the case analyzed, given the victory of the PRI's candidate in the election, the long-term consequences of these spaces of alternative communication — as radical political communication — in the mainstream political communication will need further research.

REFERENCES

Aday, S., Farrel, H., Lynch, M., Sides, J., Kelly, J., & Zuckerman, E. (2010). *Blogs and bullets: New media in contentious politics. Technical report*. U.S. Institute of Peace.

Alfaro, R. M. (2000). Culturas populares y comunicación participativa. *Revista Caminos*, *20*, 13–20.

Alonso, L. E. (1986). La mediación institucional y sus límites en el capitalismo avanzado. *Revista Espanola de Investigaciones Sociologicas*, *35*(35), 63–79. doi:10.2307/40183154

Arditi, B. (2012). Insurgencies don't have a plan – they are the plan: Political performatives and vanishing mediators in 2011. *Journalism, Media and Cultural Studies, 1*, 1-16. Retrieved from http://www.cardiff.ac.uk/jomec/jomecjournal/1-june2012/arditi_insurgencies.pdf

Attolini, A. (2012, September 19). Por una democracia auténtica, #YoSoy132. *ADN Político*. Retrieved from http://www.adnpolitico.com/opinion/2012/09/19/antonio-attolini-por-una-democracia-autentica-yosoy132

Autonome k. a. gruppe. (2003). What is Communication Guerrilla. In J. Richardson (Ed.), Anarchitexts: Voices from global digital resistance (pp. 86-91). New York: Autonomedia.

Ayres, J. M. (1999). From the streets to the Internet: The cyber-diffusion of contention. *The Annals of the American Academy of Political and Social Science*, *566*(1), 132–143. doi:10.1177/000271629956600101l

Bardici, M. V. (2012). A Discourse Analysis of the Media Representation of Social Media for Social Change - The Case of Egyptian Revolution and Political Change. (Master dissertation). Malmö University. Retrieved from http://muep.mah.se/handle/2043/14121

Bentivegna, S. (2006). Rethinking politics in the world of ICTs. *European Journal of Communication*, *21*(3), 331–343. doi:10.1177/0267323106066638

Blumler, J. G., & Kavanagh, D. (1999). The third age of political communication: Influences and features. *Political Communication, 16*(3), 209–230. doi:10.1080/105846099198596

Capital Social Investigaciones. (2012, June 20). *Algunos datos sobre la actividad en Twitter del debate de YoSoy132*. Retrieved from http://capitalsocialmexico.com/2012/06/20/algunos-datos-sobre-la-actividad-en-twitter-del-debate-de-yosoy132/

Capriles, O. (2006). Alternative communication, horizontal communication, alternative use of media, participant communication: Which is the paradigm? In A. Gamucio-Dragon & T. Tufte (Eds.), *Communication for Social Change Anthology: Historical and Contemporary Readings* (pp. 302–305). Communication for Social Change Consortium.

Casero-Ripollés, A. (2010). El despertar del público?: Comunicación política, ciudadanía y web 2.0. In M. Martin Vicente & D. Rothberg (Eds.), *Meios de comunicaçao e cidadania* (pp. 107–122). São Paulo: Cultura Académica.

Castells, M. (2000). Materials for an exploratory theory of the network society. *The British Journal of Sociology, 51*(1), 5–24. doi:10.1080/000713100358408

Castells, M. (2004). *The network society: A cross-cultural perspective*. Northampton, MA: Edward Elgar Publishing. doi:10.4337/9781845421663

Castells, M. (2009). *Communication power*. Oxford, UK: Oxford University Press.

Chadwick, A. (2011). The political information cycle in a hybrid news system: The British prime minister and the "bullygate" affair. *The International Journal of Press/Politics, 16*(1), 3–29. doi:10.1177/1940161210384730

Colectivo Másde131. (2014). *Sobre nosotros* [About us]. Retrieved from http://www.colectivo131.com.mx/

Dahlberg, L., & Siapera, E. (Eds.). (2007). *Radical Democracy and the Internet: Interrogating Theory and Practice*. Basingstoke, UK: Palgrave Macmillan. doi:10.1057/9780230592469

Dahlgren, P. (2005). The Internet, public spheres, and political communication: Dispersion and deliberation. *Political Communication, 22*(2), 147–162. doi:10.1080/10584600590933160

Davis, S., Elin, L., & Reeher, G. (2002). *Click on Democracy: The Internet's Power to Change Political Apathy into Civic Action*. Boulder, CO: Westview Press.

De Mauleón, H. (2012, September 1). De la red a las calles. *Nexos*. Retrieved from http://elecciones2012mx.wordpress.com/2012/09/01/de-la-red-a-las-calles-hector-de-mauleon-blog-nexos-en-linea/

Della Porta, D. (2013). Repertoires of contention. In D. A. Snow, D. Della Porta, B. Klandermans, & D. McAdam (Eds.), *The Wiley-Blackwell Encyclopedia of Social and Political Movements*. Malden, MA: Blackwell; doi:10.1002/9780470674871.wbespm178

Della Porta, D., & Diani, M. (2006). *Social movements: An introduction*. Malden, MA: Blackwell Publishing.

Dylko, I., & McCluskey, M. (2012). Media effects in an era of rapid technological transformation: A case of user-generated content and political participation. *Communication Theory*, *22*(3), 250–278. doi:10.1111/j.1468-2885.2012.01409.x

Feenstra, R., & Casero-Ripollés, A. (2014). Democracy in the Digital Communication Environment: A Typology Proposal of Political Monitoring Processes. *International Journal of Communication*, *8*, 2448–2468. Retrieved from http://ijoc.org/index.php/ijoc/article/view/2815

Franklin, B. (1995). A bibliographical essay. *Political Communication*, *12*, 223–242. doi:10.1080/10584609.1995.9963067

Franzosi, R. (1998). Narrative analysis -Or why (and how) sociologists should be interested in narrative. *Annual Review of Sociology*, *24*(1), 517–554. doi:10.1146/annurev.soc.24.1.517

Fuchs, C. (2012). Social media, riots, and revolutions. *Capital and Class*, *36*(3), 383–391. doi:10.1177/0309816812453613

García, R. G., & Treré, E. (2014). The# YoSoy132 movement and the struggle for media democratization in Mexico. *Convergence (London)*, *1354856514541744*. doi:10.1177/1354856514541744

Goche, F. (2012, September 11). Yo soy 132, movimiento del siglo XXI. *Contralínea.* Retrieved from http://contralinea.info/archivo-revista/index.php/2012/09/11/yo-soy-132-movimiento-del-siglo-xxi/

Gómez Quintero, N. (2014, May 15). ¿Qué ocurrió con #YoSoy132? *El Universal.* Retrieved from http://www.eluniversal.com.mx/nacion-mexico/2014/historias-que-ocurrio-con-39yosoy132-39-1010493.html

Gómez Vilchis, R. R. (2013). El regreso del dinosaurio: Un debate sobre la reciente victoria del PRI en la elección presidencial de 2012. *Estudios Politicos*, *28*, 45–161. doi:10.1016/S0185-1616(13)71443-4

Harlow, S. (2012). Social media and social movements: Facebook and an online Guatemalan justice movement that moved offline. *New Media & Society*, *14*(2), 225–243. doi:10.1177/1461444811410408

Jenkins, H. (2006). *Convergence culture: Where old and new media collide*. New York, NY: NYU Press.

Jonhston, H. (2002). Verification and proof in frame and discourse analysis. In B. Klandermans & S. Staggenborg (Eds.), *Methods of social movement research* (pp. 61–91). Minneapolis, MN: University of Minnesota Press.

Kavada, A. (2005). Exploring the role of the internet in the 'movement for alternative globalization': The case of the Paris 2003 European Social Forum. *Westminster Papers in Communication and Culture, 2*(1), 72-95.

Kushin, M. J., & Yamamoto, M. (2010). Did social media really matter? College students' use of online media and political decision making in the 2008 election. *Mass Communication & Society*, *13*(5), 608–630. doi:10.1080/15205436.2010.516863

LAPOP/Barómetro de las Américas. (2010). *Consolidación democrática en las Américas en tiempos difíciles: Informe sobre las Américas*. Retrieved from http://lapop.ccp.ucr.ac.cr/pdf/ReportontheAmericasSpanish2.pdf

Latinobarómetro. (2009). *Encuesta Latinobarómetro 2009*. Retrieved from http://latino-barometro.org/latino/LATDatos.jsp

Lock, A., & Harris, P. (1996). Political marketing - vive la difference. *European Journal of Marketing*, *30*(10-11), 21–31.

MacLeod, D. (2005). *Downsizing the state: Privatization and the Limits of Neoliberal Reform in Mexico*. Pennsylvania, PA: Penn State Press.

Macnamara, J., & Kenning, G. (2011). E-electioneering 2010: Trends in social media use in Australian political communication. *Media International Australia*, *139*, 7–22.

Maireder, A., Ausserhofer, J., & Kittenberger, A. (2012). Mapping the Austrian Political Twittersphere. How politicians, journalists and political strategists (inter-)act on Twitter. In P. Parycek, N. Edelmann & M. Sachs (Eds.), *CeDEM12. Proceeding of the International Conference for E-Democracy and Open Government* (pp. 151-163). Krems: Edition Donau-Universität Krems.

Melucci, A. (2004). The process of collective identity. In H. Jonhston & B. Klandermans (Eds.), *Social movements and culture* (pp. 41–63). Minneapolis, MN: University of Minnesota Press.

Moraga, S. (2012, July 24). #YoSoy132 busca ser la sombra del poder en México. *ADN Político*. Retrieved from http://www.adnpolitico.com/2012/2012/07/21/el-yosoy132-busca-ser-la-sombra-del-poder-en-mexico

Morozov, E. (2011). *The Net Delusion: The Dark Side of Internet Freedom*. New York: PublicAffairs.

Norris, P. (2000). *A Virtuous Circle: Political Communication in Post-Industrial Democracies*. New York: Cambridge University Press. doi:10.1017/CBO9780511609343

Norris, P. (2004). Political Communications. In *Encyclopedia of the Social Sciences*. Retrieved from http://www.hks.harvard.edu/fs/pnorris/Acrobat/Political%20Communications%20encyclopedia2.pdf

Notimex (2013, February 11). Afirman que movimiento "Yo Soy 132" carece de fecha de caducidad. *Crónica*. Retrieved from http://www.cronica.com.mx/notas/2012/664356.html

Paltridge, B. (2012). *Discourse analysis: an introduction* (2nd ed.). London: Bloomsbury.

Pérez de Acha, G. (2012, September 19). La democracia de #YoSoy132. *Animal Político*. Retrieved from http://www.animalpolitico.com/blogueros-blog-invitado/2012/09/19/la-democracia-de-yosoy132/#ixzz33PD7zyBc

Poster, M. (1997). Cyberdemocracy: Internet and the public sphere. In D. Porter (Ed.), *Internet culture* (pp. 201–218). New York: Routledge.

Russell, J. W. (2009). *Class and Race Formation in North America*. Toronto: University of Toronto Press.

Sader, E. (2001). Hegemonía y contra-hegemonía para otro mundo posible. In J. Seoane & E. Taddei (Eds.), *Resistencias Mundiales* [De Seattle a Porto Alegre] (pp. 23–45). Buenos Aires: CLACSO.

Salgado Andrade, E. (2013). Twitter en la campaña electoral de 2012. *Desacatos*, *42*, 217–232.

Sandoval-Almazan, R., & Gil-Garcia, J. R. (2013, January). Cyberactivism through Social Media: Twitter, YouTube, and the Mexican Political Movement I'm Number 132. In *Proceedings of the 46th Hawaii International Conference on System Sciences (HICSS)* (pp. 1704-1713). Wailea, HI: IEEE. doi:10.1109/HICSS.2013.161

Segerberg, A., & Bennett, W. L. (2011). Social media and the organization of collective action: Using Twitter to explore the ecologies of two climate change protests. *Communication Review*, *14*(3), 197–215. doi:10.1080/10714421.2011.597250

Stieglitz, S. & Dang-Xuan, L. (2012). Social media and political communication: a social media analytics framework. *Soc. Netw. Anal. Min.*, published online 25 August 2012. doi: 10.1007/s13278-012-0079-3

Tarrow, S. (1995). Cycles of Collective Action: Between Moments of Madness and the Repertoire of Contention. In M. Traugott (Ed.), *Repertoires and Cycles of Collective Action* (pp. 89–116). Durham, NC: Duke University Press.

Tarrow, S. (1998). *Power in Movement: Social Movements and Contentious Politics*. Cambridge, UK: Cambridge University Press. doi:10.1017/CBO9780511813245

Taylor, V., & Whittier, N. (2004). Analytical approaches to social movements culture: The culture of the women's movement. In H. Jonhston & B. Klandermans (Eds.), *Social movements and culture* (pp. 163–187). Minneapolis, MN: University of Minnesota Press.

Thornton, A. L. (2001). Does the Internet create democracy? *Ecquid Novi: African Journalism Studies*, *22*(2), 126–147. doi:10.1080/02560054.2001.9665885

Tilly, Ch. (1995). *Popular Contention in Great Britain, 1758-1834*. Cambridge, MA: Harvard University Press.

Tumasjan, A., Sprenger, T., Sandner, P., & Welpe, L. (2011). Election forecasts with Twitter: How 140 characters reflect the political landscape. *Social Science Computer Review*, *29*(4), 402–418. doi:10.1177/0894439310386557

Van Laer, J., & Van Aelst, P. (2009). Cyber-protest and civil society: the Internet and action repertoires in social movements. In Y. Jewkes & M. Yar (Eds.), *Handbook on Internet Crime* (pp. 230–254). Portland, OR: Willan Publishing.

Vargas Llosa, M. (1990, September 1). México es la dictadura perfecta. *El País*. Retrieved from http://elpais.com/diario/1990/09/01/cultura/652140001_850215.html

Vázquez, J. J. M. (1997). *La televisión y el poder político en México*. Madrid: Diana.

Vickery, G., & Wunsch-Vincent, S. (2007). *Participative web and user-created content: Web 2.0 wikis and social networking*. OECD.

Villamil, J. (2012). *El sexenio de Televisa: conjuras del poder mediático*. México: Random House Mondadori.

Wolfsfeld, G., Segev, E., & Sheafer, T. (2013). Social Media and the Arab Spring. Politics Comes First. *The International Journal of Press/Politics*, *18*(2), 115–137. doi:10.1177/1940161212471716

#YoSoy132. (2012a, May 28). *Manifiesto del #YoSoy132*. Retrieved from https://www.youtube.com/watch?v=igxPudJF6nU

#YoSoy132. (2012b, September 1). *Contrainforme presidencial*. Retrieved from http://www.sinembargo.mx/01-09-2012/352855

KEY TERMS AND DEFINITIONS

Electoral Campaign: In representative democracies, refers to the period previous to election, wherein representatives are chosen or referendums are decided, characterized for an intense activity of political communication. In modern politics, the highest electoral campaigns are focused on candidates for head of state or government.

Mainstream Media System: The prevailing current media (or media groups) in a given country or region, often associated to the hegemonic economic and political groups.

Offline Collective Action: A notion that has been defined from many areas of the social sciences (psychology, sociology, anthropology, political science and economics), it refers, in a general sense, to any action taken together by a group of people, aiming at enhance their status and achieve some common objectives.

Online Collective Action: ICTs-based actions, which is commonly referred as cyberactivism, held by some collective or social group, as part of its strategies for demanding some kind of resources or changes.

Online Social Networks: Web-based platforms that allow individuals to create a public profile as well as a list of users with whom to share connections and interact through Internet-based resources such as email and instant messaging, viewing and crossing the connections within the online system. Online social networks connect people who share interests, activities, backgrounds or real-life connections, through different tools, including mobile connectivity, photo/video/sharing or blogging.

Radical Political Communication: Practices of communication generally developed by people out of traditional political structures, which have a political nature, opposing mainstream political communication, and propose radical changes in politics and society.

Social Mobilization: Also known as mass or popular mobilization, it refers to the mobilizations of civilian population, often used by social movements, as part of their strategies of contentious politics, usually by meetings, marches, protests and demonstrations.

Uses (of ICTs): It refers to the diverse kind of actions made by individuals or groups for some purpose, by employing the ICTs as technological resources associated to some function.

Chapter 5
Reformulating Government–Citizen Relations in a Digitally Connected World:
The Twitter Ban Phenomenon in Turkey

Helin Alagöz Gessler
The Business and Information Technology School Berlin, Germany

ABSTRACT

This chapter analyses the effects of social media on political communication and the role they play in government-citizen relations by focusing on the Twitter ban phenomenon in Turkey in March 2014. The chapter asks the reasons of government intervention in social media, particularly Twitter. It argues that Twitter makes, on the one hand, a significant contribution to the evolution of political participation as it diversifies the process and methods of political communication. On the other hand, it introduces a new type of security dilemma which encourages governments to consider taking measures against social media to protect their authority.

INTRODUCTION

The rapid rise of social media is one of the most prominent developments of the last two decades not only because it represents an advancement in communication technology but also because of how it impacts the way people interact with each other and with political actors and institutions (Gainous & Wagner, 2014, p. 4). In this regard, there is a close link between social media and political communication.

Graber (2005) defines political communication as "the construction, sending, receiving, and processing of messages that potentially have a significant direct or indirect impact on politics" (p. 479). The growth of social media provided a new environment for political communication in which such messages can be constructed, processed, sent, and received by anyone, including governments, politicians, interest groups, activists, journalists, and ordinary citizens.

DOI: 10.4018/978-1-4666-9879-6.ch005

By lowering the cost of information acquisition, social media made it easier for citizens to follow the news and to become immediately aware of national and international issues. Several case studies show that the more people use online social networks, the more political awareness increases (Kanagavel & Chandrasekaran, 2014, p. 78; Reuter & Szakonji, 2015, p. 48). For instance, the results of Parmelee and Bichard's (2012) US survey of 426 people over 18 who were following at least one political leader on Twitter indicates that 89.2% of respondents were researching on the information given in the tweet posted by their political leader on Twitter. Of these, 60.7% retweeted the information and 61% took action, such as contributing to a campaign or signing a petition (p. 105). This proves that social media not only informed those people about political issues but also stimulated their political engagement.

The interactivity provided by social media has increased the demand for more democratic and accountable governance as digitally interconnected citizens, who now have the ability to generate and spread information quickly and easily, started questioning political decisions in cyberspace. Ordinary citizens could freely voice their opinions about public issues by tweeting or posting messages on other social media platforms. They could communicate with others with similar or different opinions. Social media provided an alternative way of criticizing political decisions and decision makers other than waiting for the next election to show their dissatisfaction. Many recent global social movements, particularly those in developing democracies such as the Arab Spring countries, illustrate how social media can help civil society groups and activists report on human rights violations, campaign across borders, access global information, and gain support to strengthen their position (Jørgensen, 2013, p. 121).

Policymakers have also discovered the power of social media as a political communication tool. Many political parties and leaders, including US President Barack Obama (@BarackObama; https://www.facebook.com/barackobama), Indian Prime Minister Pranab Mukherjee (@RashtrapatiBhvn; https://www.facebook.com/presidentofindiarb), Mexican President Enrique Peña Nieto (@EPN; https://www.facebook.com/EnriquePN), and Rwandan President Paul Kagame (@PaulKagame; https://www.facebook.com/PresidentPaulKagame), have social media accounts to increase their support and popularity, share their political activities, run their campaigns, and communicate with the electorate. The concern about losing prestige and authority by drawing the reaction of mobilized masses through social media can also be considered a source of motivation for decision makers to be more accountable.

As elsewhere, the use of social media in Turkey is growing rapidly and is shaping political life (TurkStat, 2014; We are social, 2014). Since the establishment of the Republic, the elitist nature of Turkish political culture, which has given priority to citizens' responsibilities to the state rather than their rights and freedoms, has resulted in the passive political participation of citizens and a weak civil society. However, this has changed, mostly due to Turkey's candidacy for EU membership. As part of the harmonization process, the government launched several constitutional reform packages in the early 2000s because Turkey, as a candidate for EU membership, was obliged to adopt EU laws, known as the acquis communautaire. The reforms included lifting the state of emergency and the death penalty, broadening freedom of expression, and prioritizing supranational treaties over domestic law (Aydın-Düzgit & Keyman, 2012, p. 7). In this context, social media can contribute to the development of civil society and political participation in Turkey by improving the diffusion of information and mobilization.

Recent evidence of the increasing effect of social media on political participation was the use of Twitter to mobilize and organize demonstrators during the Gezi Park events in Istanbul in 2013, which started as an environmentalist protest against the removal of the park to build a shopping mall. This initial protest turned into a wave of nationwide anti-government demonstrations. During the events, for the first time in

Turkish politics, social media coverage overtook mainstream media coverage. Moreover, the mainstream media was often called "yandaş medya" ("slanted media") and was blamed for not being objective and for supporting the government (Medya faresi, 2013; We fight censorship, 2013; Uzun, 2013).

This chapter concentrates on the reformulation of government–citizen relations through social media, especially Twitter, by transforming the political culture and the methods of political communication. Twitter provided Turkish citizens a way of expressing their political views and dissatisfaction with policies and policymakers. In this sense, and although there is no proof that social networking sites can directly provoke policy changes, social media can tarnish a government's image by presenting a challenge against its authority. The perception of Twitter as a threat was made clear by the Twitter ban phenomenon that occurred between 20 March and 2 April, 2014 in Turkey. The ban was implemented shortly after claims about government corruption spread across social media in the run-up to local elections.

The chapter addresses the research question of why states intervene in social media by focusing on the Twitter ban phenomenon in Turkey. Here, it is shown that Twitter has, on the one hand, contributed incontrovertibly to advancing political participation by changing the political communication process. On the other hand, Twitter has created a security dilemma for developing democracies like Turkey that are conflicted in terms of achieving the goal of democratization while maintaining authority.

Although there has been significant media coverage about the temporary Twitter ban in Turkey, there is no academic work addressing the issue. Therefore, the objective of this chapter is to lay the groundwork for future academic studies with regard to social media and Internet freedom in Turkey.

Regarding methodology, an exploratory and descriptive research design is employed to answer the research question. The qualitative case study method is used for an in-depth study of the Twitter ban phenomenon in Turkey to understand the introduction of social media as a new way of political communication in citizen–government relations. While benefiting from an extensive literature review of scholarly work for the theoretical part of the chapter, due to the lack of academic sources about the Twitter ban, data are mostly derived from 2014 statistics concerning social media and Internet usage in Turkey, national and international media coverage, and current legislation.

The author first examines the emergence of social media as a new method of political communication. Second, the author reconsiders government–citizen relations vis-à-vis Twitter. The issue is examined both from the perspective of policy makers and of citizens. The author then explains how social media can cause conflict between government and citizens. Finally, the Twitter ban phenomenon in Turkey is explored by analyzing the impact of social media, specifically Twitter, on Turkish political culture.

WEB 2.0: A NEW WAY OF POLITICAL COMMUNICATION

The world of the Internet in the late 20th century has rapidly carried global human activity from physical space to virtual space. This development soon affected the political realm. The early stage of cyber politics was mainly based on hyperlinked websites characterized by static political content.

Banaji and Buckingham (2013) state that websites tend to reflect the overall political objectives of their producers, as well as their own intended functions (p. 129). In their analysis of seven different case studies about the websites of the youth wings of formal political parties, activist sites, and the sites that do not explicitly suggest a program referring to government and public policy, Banaji and Buckingham argue that despite being a powerful medium for politics, the Internet's power depends on its capacity for convincing users to engage in the offline world (2013, p. 130). Put another way, the Internet may function as a significant political tool only if it has the power to motivate people to participate in the actual political process. In this regard, the Web 2.0. presents many more opportunities for political engagement due to its interactive nature.

With the introduction of the Web 2.0, the Internet has acquired a new dimension by moving beyond static websites. Social media, which allow users to generate content in virtual communities and to share information through social networking sites or blogging, are a relatively recent phenomenon. More than a technological advance, social media "present an entirely new paradigm on how people engage with each other" and with political actors and institutions (Gainous & Wagner, 2014, p. 3). Therefore, the implications of social media for political participation have aroused considerable scholarly interest in the last several years. It is possible to find scholarly works that analyze the relationship between social media use and political participation. For instance, Gainous and Wagner's (2011) study deals with the impact of Facebook and Twitter on the US Congress, political parties, and the American public. The authors state that social media are neither "the panacea for democracy" nor "the mind-numbing wasteland or corporate supermarket that many have feared. Social media does bring a great opportunity for open interaction in our democracy and greater means and impetus to participate" (p. 159). In other research touching upon the issue of the digital divide, Gainous, Marlowe, and Wagner (2013) argue that although the "have-nots" are more engaged in online social networking, the "haves" in the US have a greater tendency to use social media for political participation. Zúñiga, Jung, and Valenzuela (2012) focus on the relationship between social media use for news and individuals' social capital, civic engagement, and political participation using original survey data collected in the US. They claim that social media "can foster norms of reciprocity and trust and, therefore, create opportunities for civic and political engagement" (p. 331).

In other words, by making users feel connected to a community and increasing their knowledge of other members, social networking servicescan foster norms of reciprocity and trust and therefore create opportunities for civic and political engagement. In principle, social media enable everyone to interact. They provide a new multidimensional domain in politics where the government and citizens communicate interactively. In other words, they remove the national and territorial borders of states, and that makes them one of the most effective communication tools to reach out to the public, promote ideas, and encourage discussion on an open platform. The process by which people locate, organize, and coordinate groups of individuals with common interests; the amount, nature, and flow of information; available sources of news; and the ability to share opinions about various topics have changed dramatically with the rise of social media (Agrawal, Budak, & Abbadi, 2011, para. 1). Information flows continually between individuals. Today, posting a message with a simple click can increase awareness of any issue within seconds.

However, we must not forget that social media only exist in the presence of Internet access and that access to information and communication technologies (ICTs) is not the same in every geographical region or for every group in society. That is, there is a "digital divide". The Organization for Economic Cooperation and Development refers to the digital divide as "the gap between individuals, households, businesses and geographic areas at different socioeconomic levels with regard both to their opportunities to access ICTs and to their use of the Internet for a wide variety of activities" (OECD, 2001). This digital divide plays a crucial role in the use of Twitter or any other social medium in the political process. Thus, the real impact of social media on political communication can only be understood by bridging the digital divide.

In the case of Turkey, the presence of a digital divide, which limits a complete assessment of the impact of social media, should be taken into consideration. The findings of a 2014 Turkish Statistical Institute survey demonstrate that Turkish citizens encounter several aspects of digital divide. One is the gender digital divide; that is, males use the Internet more than females. During the period of January to March 2014, 53.8% of the Turkish population used the Internet, 63.5% of which were male and 44.1% of which were female. The percentage of females who had never used the Internet was 55.9%, and the percentage of males who had never used the Internet was 36.5% (TurkStat, 2014). The survey results also reveal a significant gap between age groups in terms of computer and Internet usage. The average computer usage rate is 70.3% and the Internet usage rate is 73.0% for the 16–24 age group. The rate for both computer and Internet usage is just 5.0% for the 65–74 age group (TurkStat, 2014). Education level is a significant factor affecting Internet usage. The rate of Internet usage for people with higher education is 93.6% and is 22.4% for people with only primary education (TurkStat, 2014). There is also a considerable divide across the regions of Turkey. For example, 57.2% of people in East Marmara use computers and 58.3% use the Internet, whereas in Central East Anatolia, only 37.7% of the population use computers and 37.6% use the Internet. Compared to all other regions in Turkey, Istanbul has the highest percentage of computer users at 64.0% and Internet users at 64.4% (TurkStat, 2014). Thus, the digital divide in Turkey limits the scope of this study to people who have access to social media and the ability to use it.

Despite the digital divide, studying the implications of social media for political communication is still important in analyzing how the ICT changes affect government–citizen relations. Microblogging services and social network sites, particularly Twitter and Facebook, have created a new domain in politics where the government and citizens can communicate interactively. In the next section, Twitter is examined to understand the impact of social media on government–citizen relations.

TWITTER AND RECONSIDERING GOVERNMENT–CITIZEN RELATIONS

There is a growing body of research focusing on the role of Twitter in politics. This is because a country's Twitter analytics can help in understanding the structural character of its government–citizen relations and its democratic status (Parmalee & Bichard, 2012; Maireder & Ausserhofer, 2014; Larsson & Moe, 2014). In particular, the 2011 uprisings in North Africa and the Middle East raised the question of whether Twitter can provoke revolution. There is insufficient evidence to support this; however, social media can contribute to anti-regime mobilization in authoritarian states as increased awareness of government malfeasance turns more citizens against the regime (Reuter & Szakonji, 2015, p. 48). Based on reports by bloggers, activists, and others, social media did not cause the revolutions but provided an important platform for expressing views, sharing information, and mobilizing people (Jørgensen, 2013, p. 119).

In such a context, Twitter can facilitate democracy by serving as a mediator; that is, it can publicize both government policies and the policy demands of citizens. Recently, Twitter has helped establish a two-way communication channel between the government and citizens. Although dissemination of information in this way does not guarantee interactivity, it offers the potential for communication. Given that public opinion and citizens' behaviordepend on the information they receive, Twitter is a source of information about the government that can affect the attitudes of citizens towards government policies. Im et al. (2012 p. 741) point out that citizens' level of trust in government and their compliance decrease when they spend more time on the Internet. Most of the studies dealing with Twitter and politics look at the impact of Twitter use on political behavior either from the perspective of government or citizens. The following section contains a brief review of both perspectives.

Twitter Usage by Policymakers

During the last decade, social media has become part of election campaigns in many countries. Government use of social media, particularly Twitter, started with the US Congress and spread. Several studies analyzing the content of tweets from US Congress members note that US politicians consider Twitter a platform for self-promotion and use it primarily to share information (particularly links to news articles about themselves and to their blog posts), to report on their daily activities, and to run their campaign prior to elections (Stieglitz & Dang-Xuan, 2012).

There are many studies on the use of Twitter by political parties and politicians. Parties and candidates in the UK, the Netherlands, and France benefited by using Twitter in their general election campaigns in 2010 and 2012 (Graham, Jackson, & Broersma, 2014; Greffet, 2013, p. 73). A 2012 study of Labour Party lords in the UK shows that the peers enthusiastically adopted Twitter as a communication tool to promote party policy, although they tended to "work in small, clustered networks of self-interest as opposed to collectively" (Adi, Erickson, & Lilleker, 2014, pp. 22–24). In Romania, candidates' Twitter presence during and after the 2009 political campaign was significant; most Romanian candidates opened a Twitter account prior to the elections (Mocanu, Aldea, & Rawal, 2013, p. 109). Even in African countries suffering from poverty and where illiteracy is high and Internet access is low, it is still common to find mainstream media reporting the Twitter posts of political parties or politicians (Salgado, 2013, p. 124). The Sinn Fein party in Northern Ireland used Twitter effectively to engage more closely with voters, especially during recent elections (Reilly, 2013, p. 162). In Australia, politicians use Twitter for political engagement, and those who use it not only for broadcasting but also for conversing appear to gain more political benefit than others (Grant, Moon, & Grant, 2010). The number of case studies on Twitter use by political parties and governments will increase in the future as the effects of Twitter become more visible and the need for comparative studies increases.

Twitter Usage by Citizens in Political Contexts

Recent studies of digital politics concentrate on the role of social media in empowering citizens. The emergence of the "Fifth Estate", which could be defined as a new estate where individuals shape the modes of governance using online social networking, is a highly remarkable phenomenon. It is even observable in countries like China, where the state takes explicit measures to control press coverage and the Internet (Huan, Dutton, & Shen, 2013). In their study investigating how networked individuals could shape policy and practice, Huan, Dutton, and Shen (2013) examine three cases in China in which social media mobilized individuals when state media and news reporting failed to meet the expectations of the public (p. 43). Blocking the Xiamen PX project, challenging news coverage of the Nanjing gas explosion, and disclosures about a publicly funded visit abroad made it clear that the Fifth Estate in China can play a role in enhancing democratic accountability and in reframing issues and the scope of debate (Huan et al., 2013).

There are also various case studies in the literature that specifically look into the political use of Twitter from the perspective of citizens, particularly during elections or social movements. For instance, a study about the 2009 presidential election in Iran and its aftermath proves that Twitter was effectively used by Iranians to express their political opinions. It helped them keep in touch with the Iranian diaspora and the rest of the world, although the regime had prevented foreign journalists from covering the election. Twitter also supported Iranian users in this critical time by scheduling maintenance that would render the service unavailable (Elson, Yeung, Roshan, Bohandy, & Nader, 2012, p. 12). In his study about social media and blogging in Australian politics, Jericho (2012) states that the introduction of social media such as Twitter has resulted in broader and deeper coverage of politics in Australia (pp. 286–287).Departing from the premise that the goal of improving democracy can only be achieved by the participation of dissenting citizens, in principle, it is possible that political mobilization through social media can significantly facilitate democratization.

However, so far, there is little proof that social media has an impact on power relations between the elite and ordinary citizens. As Margolis and Moreno-Riano (2013) state, the new Internet technologies changed people's habits for gathering and communicating information. However, they had "relatively little impact upon the power and liberties exercised by established elites in Euro-American democracies compared to those of ordinary citizens and especially those of the poor" (pp. 39–40).

One cannot claim that individuals or groups acting in social media approach the power of state; however they can help change the scope and outcome of political conflicts. This is because they can undermine the ability of the authorities to define the conflicts and the scope of conflicts by generating their own content (Huan et al., 2013, p. 55).

Government–Citizen Clash in Cyberspace: Why Restrict Social Media?

The supply and demand patterns of digital political communication often diverge. To a large extent, this stems from the diverse interests and perceptions of the actors. Assuming that both the government and citizens are rational actors capable of a cost-benefit analysis, there might be clashes when one's cost would be the other's benefit. Put another way, the government would prefer to act accountably and fulfill the expectations of citizens for the patterns of political communication on social media platforms as long as they do not conflict with its interests. In this regard, one should ask the question whether we can expect that governments will engage with civic commons, which refer to an enduring structure in cyberspace that could realize more fully the democratic potential of the new interactive media, while developing policies and making decisions (Blumler & Coleman, 2001, p. 16; Coleman & Blumler, 2009, p. 184). The gap between the growing expectations of the citizens, especially in developing democracies, and the capability or willingness of the government to meet them can mobilize dissident citizens to use social media to protest against the government and demand more.

Citizen dissidence in cyberspace can threaten the government as it tarnishes the image and reputation of the government and of national and international decision makers. In this regard, unlike other methods of political participation, the global nature of social media empowers citizens against governments and enables them to play the legitimacy card to persuade governments to institute reforms.

Today, the capability of insurgent movements to unsettle the leadership in countries without liberal democratic regimes and a free press increases with the increase in emotive reactions stemming from the growing connectedness of populations via social media (Bolt, 2012, p. 223). This assumption was evidenced in recent anti-governmental protests in many parts of the world, such as in the Arab Spring countries and in Spain. Activists in those countries used social media as a tool to bypass the mainstream media and to make their voices heard directly (Flesher Fomiyana, 2014, p. 179).

To avoid the spread of anti-government sentiments in cyberspace, some autocratic states prefer to take pre-emptive measures against Internet use and online social networks, including Twitter. Twitter access is currently blocked in North Korea, China, and Iran (Freedom House, 2014; Wei, 2014; Shaheed, 2014). However, Internet users can still find ways to access Twitter. Many Chinese users circumvent the ban and continue tweeting at all costs, such as the Chinese woman who was sentenced to a year in labor camp due to a Twitter post (Shahid, 2010, para. 2).

Controlling social media is not peculiar to autocratic states. Developing democracies and advanced democratic states are also skeptical about the freedom provided by social media when sensitive political issues are at stake. For instance, Jørgensen (2013) points out that Denmark has blocked specific website content since 2005. However, there has been no political will to revise the practice or to provide judicial or other independent review of the blocked content (p. 123).

As Bolt (2012) puts it, the potential spread of "infectious ideas" through online global networks at an alarming speed is problematic for states with rigid administrative structures as they lack the ability to respond quickly to fast moving emotional and cognitive changes and subjects (pp. 196–197). Therefore, despite the differences in participation patterns and access across regions, "the possibilities of effective control over *who* transmits, *what* is transmitted, *when*, *how* and with *what effects*" (Choucri, 2012, p. 51) are at the center of states' concern about social media. The US, Russia, France, and many other developed countries have already demanded censorship from Twitter with regard to some content they claim is illegal (Twitter, n.d.). According to the Transparency Report published by Twitter, during the period January 1 to June 30, 2014, the company received 107 removal requests from France, 32 from Russia, 26 from the US, 14 from the UK, 6 from Japan, and 5 from India. Twitter reports that removal requests increased from 6 to 432 between 2012 and 2014 (Twitter, n.d.). In most cases, Twitter accepted the complaints about illegal tweets and blocked those accounts (Twitter, n.d.).

In short, the global, anonymous, fast, and user friendly nature of Twitter has resulted in a potentially powerful political tool in the hands of the public, whereas it represents a new security challenge for governments that is not easily addressed. Governments thus resorted to filtering, controlling, or blocking access as a defense mechanism.

THE TWITTER BAN PHENOMENON IN TURKEY

To analyze the temporary Twitter ban in Turkey, the structure of Turkish political culture must be examined in detail as the emergence of social media, in this case Twitter, has sparked the transformation of Turkish political communication. This section first briefly examines Turkish political culture and then examines Twitter use in Turkey and its impact on Turkish politics. It concentrates on the Twitter ban phenomenon and gives insight into the latest state of Internet freedom in Turkey.

Turkish Political Culture

Almond and Verba (1963) define political culture as "the pattern of individual attitudes and cognitive, affective and evaluative orientations toward politics among the members of a given political system" (p. 16). As in many countries, these orientations in Turkey are mostly shaped by the historical developments and socio-economic structure of the country. Given the fact that political culture is the key factor affecting political behavior, providing an overview of Turkish political culture is important in understanding the nature of political participation in Turkey.

The military played a crucial role in shaping political culture in Turkey until the 2000s. Frequent military interventions resulted in a slow-growing electoral democracy and fragile political parties that lack robust institutionalization. In particular, the 1980 coup restricted active political participation by prohibiting all political activities. Following the coup all political parties were shut down, the party leaders were imprisoned, and the constitution was abolished. In 1982, a new constitution increasing the authority of the state at the expense of the democratic rights and liberties of individuals was introduced under the military rule (Akça, 2013, pp. 185–187). Avoiding political activism, the 1982 Constitution "served to depoliticize the system" (Ince, 2012, p. 142). Because freedom of expression was restricted, there was no governmental accountability and military involvement in politics was not resisted. Furthermore, the military acted as the guardian of the Kemalist state and could interrupt civilian political authority for the sake of Kemalist principles, such as secularism. This reduced the public's trust in political parties. The political parties were perceived as fragile political actors unable to avoid anarchy and chaos in the face of ideological polarization rather than as actors representing the democratic will of people. This resulted in a statist political culture based on duties and responsibilities rather than on the rights of citizens (Turan, 1986, pp. 479–487).

The socio-cultural legacy of the Ottoman Empire along with a strong state culture, a geographical location between Asia and Europe, the past experiences of modernization and westernization, rural societal origins, a mixed ethnic and religious demographic structure, a medium education level, and a growing economy combined to form a sui generis political culture. The sensitive political issues in Turkish politics, such as the Kurdish question, secularism, and minority rights, are all related to this structural combination that results in certain types of political behavior.

Briefly, the mainstream Turkish political culture can be characterized by the prevalence of state interests over fundamental human rights, the model of passive, deferential citizen, the lack of tolerance for cultural, religious and ethnic diversity, the exalted role of the military and bureaucratic elite as guardian of the Western and secular character of the state and society (Grigoriadis, 2004, para. 6).

All these characteristics explain the insufficient political participation in Turkey. Ordinary Turkish citizens perceive politics as an elite business in which they should not be involved. Acknowledging the idea of a state's supremacy over its citizens and defining citizenship based on duties and obligations rather than on individual rights and freedoms undermines individuals' confidence in expressing their personal political opinions about government policies or issues on the political agenda. The fear of being punished if labeled as "anti-government" makes them act collectively, which eliminates diversity and lets groupthink dominate over individual ideas.

With the emergence of social media, the political activity of ordinary Turkish people is likely to increase. In this regard, the problematic structure of political communication between Turkish citizens is undergoing a transformation.

Twitter in Turkey

In parallel to the global trends, Internet and social media penetration is steadily increasing in Turkey. A survey by Global Digital Statistics (We are social, 2014) shows that in 2014 Internet penetration in the country was 43% (the global average was 41%). Social media penetration constitutes 47% of total Internet usage. The survey indicates that Turkish people use social media mostly for reading, spending an average of 2 hours and 37 minutes on social media every day (We are social, 2014). Being connected has accelerated the spread of information across Turkish society. Today, few would dispute the dramatic penetration of social media into daily life.

Twitter started operating in Turkish in April 2011. In three years' time it has become the second most used digital social networking site in Turkey after Facebook. As of the second quarter of 2014, 72% of Internet users in Turkey owned a Twitter account (94% for Facebook) (Statista, 2014). Of those Twitter users, 76% visit their account every day and 56% interact on Twitter a few times every day (Dijital Ajanslar, 2014).

Nielson and Genart's survey results provide a demographic profile of Twitter users in Turkey; 60% of the users are male and 50% are under 34 and hold a university degree (Dijital Ajanslar, 2014). This shows that there is a divide in terms of Twitter use in Turkey. It is mainly preferred by young, educated men.

The survey results also indicate that 41% of Twitter users tweet about politics (Dijital Ajanslar, 2014). Tweeting provides an alternative way of political communication by enabling the creation of powerful trends and mobilizing society. It stands out as a source of real-time information and a platform to discuss current issues in Turkish politics.

The anonymity factor was also important in Twitter gaining popularity. The fact that Twitter accepts all usernames and requires no personal data gave ordinary citizens the opportunity to voice their opinions about the political agenda of Turkey in 140 key strokes. In this context, users' ability to control the privacy of the data on their profiles facilitated political participation and activism via Twitter, which did not happen prior to the 2010.

The world recognized the significant role of Twitter in Turkish political communication for the first time during the Gezi Park incidents in Istanbul. This series of popular uprisings and mass demonstrations around the world was facilitated and organized via social media. In the summer of 2013, about 3.5 million people took to the streets in 79 out of 81 Turkish provinces (Rettman, 2014a, para. 6). The Gezi Park case exemplified the shift in the methods of political communication between people and their elected leaders and governments to a new, virtual dimension that is effective in promoting political change and socio-cultural globalization. The use of force by the police turned the peaceful demonstrations, the original aim of which was to stop the government from replacing the park with a shopping mall, into nationwide anti-government protests. Social media witnessed an even more intensive political activism than the actual place of the demonstration as it was supported globally. The violent clashes between the police and the protestors, which cost the lives of several people and resulted in serious injuries, increased the tension.

During the protests that lasted more than three months, the mainstream Turkish mass media (with the exception of a few small-scale media companies) were heavily criticized for aligning with the government and reporting very little about what was going on (Öktem, 2013). Convinced that they had no other source of information, most people turned to social media. Those who had resisted joining social network websites opened Twitter and Facebook accounts to follow the Gezi news. Hashtags such as #occupygezi, #direngeziparki, and #geziparki broadcasted continuously during the protests. During the events, the nature of the communication among the demonstrators in online networks was based on a division of labor between those generating content and those disseminating content (*SMaPP Data Report*, 2013, p. 5). The Gezi Park events showed the ability of Twitter in Turkey to mobilize young people and to increase political engagement.

Twitter Ban Phenomenon

In the aftermath of the Gezi Park protests, Twitter continued to be part of daily political communication in Turkey with roughly 12 million users (Yetkin, 2014, para. 1). This included the government institutions and politicians that had already been using Twitter before the protests to make policy statements. In the meantime, growing tension between the government and Twitter became more prominent as most of the dissidents continued expressing their anti-government opinions on Twitter. This prompted the government to perceive Twitter as a security threat challenging its authority and causing a rift between itself and Turkish citizens. As a result, the government put a defense mechanism in place to counter Twitter and to control the Internet and social media.

Background

In fact, the key figures of the Turkish government had joined Twitter well before the Gezi Park events. Both Abdullah Gül (president from 2007 to 2014) and Tayyip Erdoğan (prime minister from 2003 to 2014 and president since 28 August 2014) opened their personal Twitter accounts "@cbabdullahgu" and "@RT_Erdogan" in 2009 and still use them. Following them, Ahmet Davutoğlu (foreign minister from 2009 to 2014 and prime minister since 28 August 2014) joined Twitter in 2010 and is currently the owner of three Twitter accounts in Turkish, English, and Arabic. In addition to personal accounts, The Turkish Presidency and the Turkish Foreign Ministry opened institutional Twitter accounts in different languages (@tccankaya, @trpresidency, @TC_Disisleri, @MFATurkey, @MFATurkeyFrench, @MFATurkeyArabic).

Tayyip Erdoğan, being the first Turkish leader to join Twitter (23 August 2009) is among the top ten most followed world leaders on Twitter (Twiplomacy, 2014). He has used Twitter mainly to post tweets about his political activities. However, he seems to have a negative attitude towards Twitter since the Gezi Park protests. In his public statement about the events he criticized the widespread use of Twitter with the words: "There is now a menace which is called Twitter. The best examples of lies can be found there. To me, social media is the worst menace to society" (Letsch, 2013, para. 4). Actually, those words heralded the beginning of a duel between the government and Twitter that would occupy the agenda in the next months.

Compared to Erdoğan, Abdullah Gül has always had a moderate stance vis-à-vis social media and Twitter usage in Turkey. He has used his Twitter account mostly to inform people about his presidential activities and has not tweeted comments about daily news items except in the case of the Gezi Park protests when he tweeted links to relevant press releases on the website of the Turkish presidency, such as: "Gül calls for more maturity so that events in Taksim Square cool down" (Twiplomacy, 2014).

Introduction of the Ban

On 20 March 2014, Erdoğan gave a speech at a campaign rally in Bursa in which he stated that his government would eradicate Twitter regardless of what the international community said and that everyone would witness the power of the Turkish Republic (*Hürriyet*, 2014). His perception of a power struggle between the government and Twitter can be clearly seen in this speech. On the same day, shortly before midnight, Twitter was shut down by the Telecommunication Directorate (TIB), working under Turkey's Transport, Maritime, and Communication Ministry. The ban was based on three court rulings and one prosecutor decision, particularly the ruling of the Anatolia 5th Criminal Court of Peace. The court issued ruling number 2014/181 in response to a complaint by former Minister of Transport, Maritime, and Communication Binali Yıldırım and his son (*Hürriyet Daily News*, 2014). As the principle of separation of powers allows the courts in Turkey to operate independently and as the executive and legislative bodies are obliged to obey the court, the ban came into effect within hours, depending on the Internet service provider.

The Twitter ban has its roots in the aftermath of the Gezi Park protests, a chain of events that paved the way for the increased tension between the government and social media. The timing of the ban was remarkable as it was enforced less than two weeks before the March 30 local elections in Turkey.

A central issue that occupied the government following the Gezi protests was the activities of the Gülen movement led by the powerful Turkish cleric Fethullah Gülen. The clash between the government and the Gülen movement was revealed when the movement disagreed with Erdoğan's attitude towards anti-government protests during the Gezi events and turned against him. Erdoğan accused followers of the Gülen movement in the police and judiciary of staging a "judiciary coup" against his government and called the followers of the movement having senior bureaucratic and judicial positions as "parallel state" (Zalewski, 2014). The government's decision to close Gülenist schools in Turkey intensified the political power struggle.

When the sons of the interior minister, the economy minister and the environment minister as well as many businessmen were arrested by Turkish police on 17 December 2014 as part of an investigation into bribery relating to public tenders, many speculated this was a response by the Gülen movement to government plans to abolish their schools (Zalewski, 2014). After this incident, hundreds of law enforcement officers were transferred, judges and police officers investigating the case were dismissed, and a series of judicial changes were made. Nevertheless, virtual attacks against the government soon appeared on Twitter as it provided a safe haven for anti-government activities. As the government established political control over police and judicial appointments, attention was focused on Twitter. For instance, Mat (2014) claims that an Azerbaijani journalist from a newspaper known as the main press organ of the Gülen movement was extradited and that his re-entry into Turkey was forbidden because of his tweets criticizing the government (para. 12).

Another significant point is that the Twitter ban came after the Turkish Parliament passed a controversial law on 6 February 2014 that amended Law no. 5651 on the Fight against the Regulations Concerning the Publications Made on the Internet Environment and the Crimes Committed through These Publication, known as the Internet Act. The 2007 Internet Act, "initially designed to protect children from illegal and harmful content", had already been criticized for its "infamous blocking orders in regards to freedom of information, expression and thought" (Akdenizli, 2015, p. xvi). The 2014 amendment to the Internet Act created more concern about individual freedoms as it strictly limits Internet use in Turkey by enabling the authorities to block access to websites if there are complaints of privacy violation. This happened after a Twitter account called "Haramzadeler" (meaning "son of thieves") started publishing a series of leaked documents, including audio files on alleged corruption cases involving people in government circles.

The new Internet law made the TIB responsible for monitoring privacy violations on the Internet. Accordingly, the TIB can block URLs, including upon the request of individual citizens when it considers privacy is violated. Service providers must block specified URLs within four hours of notification. However, the TIB is required to submit its judgment to the court within 24 hours of a block, a change made by President Gül. Moreover, during the court's assessment within the following 48 hours, the website remains inaccessible (Mat, 2014, para. 4–5). Additionally, the law obliges providers to preserve the traffic data of users for one to two years and obliges companies to join a union of providers to avoid bypassing the blocking of banned sites and to remain at the disposal of the TIB for any information requests. Thus, the law forces providers to comply with TIB directives (Mat, 2014, para. 6–8).

One week after the Twitter ban and only days before the local elections, the TIB also blocked the video-sharing site YouTube for leaking a conversation between top government officials in which they discussed the possibility of going to war with Syria. This heated up existing debates on freedom of expression in Turkey.

Criticisms and Cancellation of the Ban

The Twitter ban prompted harsh criticism in Turkey and condemnation around the world. The EU Commissioner of Digital Affairs, Neelie Kroes, tweeted that the international community would see it as censorship (Rettman, 2014b, para. 1). EU Commissioner for Enlargement, Štefan Füle, stated his concerns and pointed out that freedom of communication is a "fundamental EU value" (Raymundo, 2014, para. 10). White House Press Secretary Jay Carney stated that the restriction undermined the ability of Turkish people to exercise freedom of expression and added that Obama administration officials urged the Turkish government to restore full access to Twitter (as cited in Gaudin, 2014, para. 3–4). Even President Gül got around the ban and expressed disapproval in his tweets (Jones, 2014).

The ban was not effective. As soon as access was blocked, people discovered ways to circumvent the ban. Using a virtual private network, operating on a non-public channel, using programs that hide location by rerouting traffic to servers around the world, and sending tweets from mobile phones were popular workarounds to access Twitter (Koh & Yadron, 2014). The latter was suggested by Twitter itself. The hashtag #TwitterisblockedinTurkey, which came from inside Turkey despite the ban, became the top trend of worldwide Twitter postings. The ban backfired as it encouraged people to tweet even more to mock the government's Twitter policy.

Eventually, Turkey's constitutional court issued a ruling on 2 April 2014 ordering the authorities to lift the ban because it breached freedom of expression (Yurdakul, 2014, para. 4). The YouTube ban was lifted a short time later on 9 April 2014 with the condition that 15 links be removed (Karapinar, 2014, para. 4). The court decisions were welcomed by millions of Twitter users and by Twitter authorities.

The Twitter ban phenomenon in Turkey shows that social media have become a legitimate method of political communication between citizens and government. Any restriction of these digital communication tools could cause citizens to perceive it as a restricting access to information, censorship, or an attack on freedom of expression. This, in turn, would decrease the level of trust in government and cause citizens to question the legitimacy of the government.

Ironically, as of June 2014, despite the Twitter ban phenomenon, Abdullah Gül and Tayyip Erdoğan were the sixth and seventh most followed world leaders on Twitter with more than four million followers (Twiplomacy, 2014). This proves that when government and politicians perceive social media as an opportunity rather than as a threat and utilize these services instead of restricting them, social media can help them improve their relationships with the electorate.

Nonetheless, Turkey ranks first among the countries that requested Twitter remove content during the period of January 1 to June 30, 2014. Twitter received 65 court orders and 121 government requests to remove content in Turkey "regarding violations of personal rights and defamation of both private citizens and government officials" (Twitter, n.d.) When the number of requests from Turkey to remove content for the first and the second halves of 2013 and the first half of 2014 are compared, a significant increase is observed for the first half of 2014. During the first half of 2013, there were 3 court orders, 4 government requests, and 30 specified accounts. During the second half of 2013, there were just 2 court orders and approximately 10 specified accounts (Twitter, n.d.) This shows that the number of content removal requests made by the judicial and political organs of the Turkish government increased in the immediate aftermath of the Gezi incidents.

CONCLUSION

Freedom of speech remains limited in developing democracies. As a result, communication between these state and their citizens can be problematic. In such countries, social media can be one of the most effective methods of political communication by increasing the degree of citizens' political awareness, courage, participation, and activism. This in turn results in social change and democratization. In this sense, the findings of this study might be applicable to other countries whose path to democracy was interrupted by military coups in their recent history. However, social media also presents a security dilemma for governments as it facilitates the spread of dissidence, which could create political instability by affecting the balance of power.

As social media penetration increases worldwide and social media platforms continue to help transform developing democracies into information societies, how governments will respond will be critical in determining what kind of social change will occur.

As rational actors, governments must decide between two types of behavior, both having costs and benefits. On the one hand, they may choose to implement stronger measures against social networking sites, such as Twitter, to secure their authority and avoid conspiracies. This was the case with Turkey's Twitter ban phenomenon. However, this action also suppresses dissident citizens who are essential components of a functioning democracy. Even if governments justify this action as a security measure to prevent the breach of its' citizens' personal rights through the opening of fake accounts or to protect the country from social unrest, many will consider this censorship. The result is societal discontent and distrust.

On the other hand, governments may let information flow freely via social media. Their authority can be challenged as they will no longer be able to control who says what, when they say it, or how they say it. When this approach is taken, democracy progresses, even if it might result in a new government, as dissent and demands for political accountability are vital aspects of political participation. They consolidate relations between government and citizens and function as the control mechanisms of good governance. Although free social media does not necessarily lead to perfect political communication in which citizens' policy change demands are always understood and accepted by governments, it has that potential.

REFERENCES

Adi, A., Erickson, K., & Lilleker, D. (2014). Elite tweets: Analyzing the Twitter communication patterns of Labour Party peers in the House of Lords. *Policy & Internet*, *6*(1), 1–27. doi:10.1002/1944-2866.POI350

Agrawal, D., Budak, C., & Abbadi, A. E. (2011). Information diffusion in social networks: Observing and influencing societal interests. In *Proceedings of the 37th International Conference on Very Large Data Bases*. Seattle, WA: VLDB. Retrieved September 10, 2014, from http://www.cs.ucsb.edu/~cbudak/social-tutorial.pdf

Ajanslar, D. (2014). *Türkiye Twitter kullanıcı istatistikleri-2014*. Retrieved January 15, 2015, from https://twitter.com/search?q=%23whousestwitter%20Turkey&src=typd

Akça, I. (2013). *Türk siyasal hayatı*. Eskişehir: Anadolu Üniversitesi.

Akdenizli, B. (2015). Introduction. In B. Akdenizli (Ed.), *Digital transformations in Turkey: Current perspectives in communication studies* (p. ix–3). Lanham, MD: Lexington Books.

Almond, G., & Verba, S. (1963). *Civic culture: Political attitudes and democracy in five nations*. Princeton: Princeton University Press.

Aydın-Düzgit, S., & Keyman, E. F. (2012). *EU-Turkey relations and the stagnation of Turkish democracy* (Working Paper No. 2). Rome: IAI. Retrieved May 10, 2015, from http://mercury.ethz.ch/serviceengine/Files/ISN/156275/ipublicationdocument_singledocument/ff7f8ab1-6376-4be1-817f-c1a2228fe918/en/GTE_WP_02.pdf

Banaji, S., & Buckingham, D. (2013). *The civic web. Young people, the Internet and civic participation*. Cambridge, MA: The MIT Press.

Blumler, J. G., & Coleman, S. (2001). *Realising democracy online: A civic commons in cyberspace*. London: IPPR. Retrieved May 12, 2015, from http://www.gov2u.org/publications/10_coleman-realising%20democracy.pdf

Bolt, N. (2012). *The violent image. Insurgent propaganda and the new revolutionaries*. London: Hurst and Company.

Choucri, N. (2012). *Cyberpolitics in international relations*. Cambridge, MA: The MIT Press.

Coleman, S., & Blumler, J. G. (2009). *The Internet and democratic citizenship: Theory, practice and policy*. Cambridge, UK: Cambridge University Press. doi:10.1017/CBO9780511818271

Elson, S. B., Yeung, D., Roshan, P., Bohandy, S. R., & Nader, A. (2012). *Using social media to gauge Iranian public opinion and mood after the 2009 election*. Santa Monica, CA: Rand Corporation.

Faresi, M. (2013). *Yandaş medyaya göre Taksim'de hiçbir şey olmamış!* Retrieved February 22, 2014, from http://www.medyafaresi.com/haber/Yandas-medyaya-gore-Taksimde-hicbir-sey-olmamis_109002.html

Flesher Fomiyana, C. (2014). *Social movements and globalization. How protests, occupations and uprisings are changing the world*. London: Palgrave Macmillan.

Gainous, J., Marlowe, A. D., & Wagner, K. M. (2013). Traditional cleavages or a new world: Does online social networking bridge the political participation divide? *International Journal of Politics Culture and Society*, *26*(2), 145–158. doi:10.1007/s10767-013-9130-2

Gainous, J., & Wagner, K. M. (2011). *Rebooting American politics: The Internet revolution*. Lanham, MD: Rowman and Littlefield.

Gainous, J., & Wagner, K. M. (2014). *Tweeting to power. The social media revolution in American politics*. New York: Oxford University Press.

Gaudin, S. (2014, March 24). White House urges end to Turkey's Twitter ban. *Computer World*. Retrieved August 8, 2014, from http://www.computerworld.com/article/2488934/social-media/white-house-urges-end-to-turkey-s-twitter-ban.html

Graber, D. A., & Smith, J. M. (2005). Political communication faces the 21st century. *Journal of Communication*, *55*(3), 479–507. doi:10.1111/j.1460-2466.2005.tb02682.x

Graham, T., Jackson, D., & Broersma, M. (2014). New platform, old habits? Candidates' use of Twitter during the 2010 British and Dutch general election campaigns. *New Media & Society*, 1–19. doi:10.1177/1461444814546728

Grant, W. J., Moon, B., & Grant, J. B. (2010). Digital dialogue? Australian politicians' use of the social network tool Twitter. *Australian Journal of Political Science*, *45*(4), 579–604. doi:10.1080/10361146.2010.517176

Greffet, F. (2013). New techniques, new mobilizations? French parties in the Web 2.0 era. In P. G. Nixon, R. Rawal, & D. Mercea (Eds.), *Politics and the Internet in comparative context. Views from the cloud* (pp. 59–75). London: Routledge Taylor and Francis Group.

Grigoriadis, I. N. (2004). *Turkish political culture and minorities*. Paper presented at Nationalism, Society and Culture in post-Ottoman South East Europe, Oxford, UK. Retrieved September 30, 2014, from http://www.sant.ox.ac.uk/esc/esc-lectures/Grigoriadis.pdf

Huan, S., Dutton, W. H., & Shen, W. (2013). The semi-sovereign netizen. The fifth estate in China. In P. G. Nixon, R. Rawal, & D. Mercea (Eds.), *Politics and the Internet in comparative context. Views from the cloud* (pp. 43–59). London: Routledge Taylor and Francis Group.

Hürriyet. (2014, March 21). *Erdoğan: Twitter, mwitter kökünü kazıyacağız*. Retrieved August 12, 2014, from http://www.hurriyet.com.tr/gundem/26050109.asp

Hürriyet Daily News. (2014, March 29). *Twitter wins key case against Turkish government*. Retrieved August 10, 2014, from http://www.hurriyetdailynews.com/twitter-wins-key-case-against-turkish-government.aspx?PageID=238&NID=64273&NewsCatID=339

Im, T., Wonhyuk, C., Porumbescu, G., & Park, J. (2012). Internet, trust in government, and citizen compliance. *Journal of Public Administration: Research and Theory*, *24*(3), 741–763. doi:10.1093/jopart/mus037

Ince, B. (2012). *Citizenship and identity in Turkey: From Atatürk's republic to the present day*. New York: I. B. Tauris.

Jericho, G. (2012). *The rise of the fifth estate. Social media and blogging in Australian politics*. Victoria: Griffin Press.

Jones, B. (2014, March 24). Turkey's Twitter ban condemned-even by nation's own president. *CNN*. Retrieved August 8, 2014, from http://edition.cnn.com/2014/03/21/world/europe/turkey-twitter-ban-condemned/

Jørgensen, R. F. (2013). Freedom of expression in the Internet era. In U. Carlson (Ed.), *Freedom of expression revisited. Citizenship and Journalism in the Digital Era* (pp. 119–131). Göteborg: Nordicom.

Kanagavel, R., & Chandrasekaran, V. (2014). Creating political awareness through social networking – An empirical study with special reference to Tamil Nadu elections, 2011. *Journal of Social Media Studies*, *1*(1), 71–81. doi:10.15340/214733661177

Karapınar, T. (2014, April 9). YouTube yasağı kalktı. *Milliyet*. Retrieved August 8, 2014, from http://www.milliyet.com.tr/Gundem/SonDakika.aspx?aType=SonDakika&ArticleID=1864631&Date=09.04.2014&Kategori=gundem&b=Youtube%20erisime%20acildi

Koh, Y., & Yadron, D. (2014, March 21). What Turkish users are doing to evade the Twitter ban. *Digits*. Retrieved August 12, 2014, from http://blogs.wsj.com/digits/2014/03/21/how-users-evade-turkeys-twitter-ban/

Larsson, A. O., & Moe, H. (2014). Twitter in politics and elections: Insights from Scandinavia. In K. Weller, A. Bruns, J. Burgess, M. Mahrt, & C. Puschmann (Eds.), *Twitter and society* (pp. 319–331). New York: Peter Lang.

Letsch, C. (2013, June 3). Social media and opposition to blame for protests, says Turkish PM. *The Guardian*. Retrieved September 3, 2013, from http://www.theguardian.com/world/2013/jun/02/turkish-protesters-control-istanbul-square

Maireder, A., & Ausserhofer, J. (2014). Political discourse on Twitter: Networking topics, objects, and people. In K. Weller, A. Bruns, J. Burgess, M. Mahrt, & C. Puschmann (Eds.), *Twitter and society* (pp. 305–319). New York: Peter Lang.

Margolis, M., & Moreno-Riano, G. (2013). The Internet and the decline of the Euro-American democracy. In P. G. Nixon, R. Rawal, & D. Mercea (Eds.), *Politics and the Internet in comparative context. Views from the cloud* (pp. 26–43). London: Routledge Taylor and Francis Group.

Mat, F. (2014, February 27). Turkey, the web divide. *Osservatorio balcani e caucaso*. Retrieved March 26, 2014, from http://www.balcanicaucaso.org/eng/Regions-and-countries/Turkey/Turkey-the-web-divide-148380

Mocanu, M., Aldea, A., & Rawal, R. (2013). Why fix it when it is not broken? Continuity and adaptation in Romanian presidential e-campaigning. In P. G. Nixon, R. Rawal, & D. Mercea (Eds.), *Politics and the Internet in comparative context. Views from the cloud* (pp. 75–95). London: Routledge Taylor and Francis Group.

OECD. (2001). *Understanding the digital divide*. Retrieved October 23, 2014, from http://www.oecd.org/internet/ieconomy/1888451.pdf

Öktem, K. (2013). Why Turkey's mainstream media chose to show penguins rather than protests. *The Guardian*. Retrieved July 18, 2014, from http://www.theguardian.com/commentisfree/2013/jun/09/turkey-mainstream-media-penguins-protests

Parmalee, J. H., & Bichard, S. L. (2012). *Politics and the Twitter revolution. How tweets influence the relationship between political leaders and the public*. Plymouth: Lexington Books.

Raymundo, S. (2014, March 21). Twitter users mock Turkish government over attempted social media ban. *Latin Post*. Retrieved August 8, 2014, from http://www.latinpost.com/articles/9285/20140321/twitter-users-mock-turkish-government-over-attempted-social-media-ban.htm

Reilly, P. (2013). Ourselves alone (but making connections): The social media strategies of Sinn Fein. In P. G. Nixon, R. Rawal, & D. Mercea (Eds.), *Politics and the Internet in comparative context. Views from the cloud* (pp. 154–169). London: Routledge Taylor and Francis Group.

Rettman, A. (2014a, June 11). Turkey at 'crossroads' to authoritarian rule, Amnesty says. *EU Observer*. Retrieved July 18, 2014, from http://euobserver.com/foreign/124551

Rettman, A. (2014b, March 21). Turkey's Twitter can prompt instant EU criticism. *EU Observer*. Retrieved August 8, 2014, from http://euobserver.com/foreign/123564

Reuter, O. J., & Szakonyi, D. (2015). Online social media and political awareness in authoritarian regimes. *British Journal of Political Science*, *45*(1), 29–51. doi:10.1017/S0007123413000203

Salgado, S. (2013). Online party politics: Studying the presence of some African political parties on the Internet. In P. G. Nixon, R. Rawal, & D. Mercea (Eds.), *Politics and the Internet in comparative context. Views from the cloud* (pp. 118–135). London: Routledge Taylor and Francis Group.

Shaheed, A. (2014). *Layers of Internet censorship in Iran*. Retrieved October 2, 2014, from http://shaheedoniran.org/english/blog/layers-of-internet-censorship-in-iran/

Shahid, A. (2010). Chinese woman, Cheng Jianping, sentenced to a year in labor camp over Twitter post. *NY Daily News*. Retrieved August 8, 2014, from http://www.nydailynews.com/news/world/chinese-woman-cheng-jianping-sentenced-year-labor-camp-twitter-post-article-1.454253

SMaPP Data Report. (2013). *A breakout role for Twitter? The role of social media in the Turkish protests*. Retrieved September 10, 2014 from http://smapp.nyu.edu/reports/turkey_data_report.pdf

Statista. (2014). *Penetration of selected social networks in Turkey as of 2nd quarter 2014*. Retrieved September 10, 2014, from http://www.statista.com/statistics/284503/turkey-social-network-penetration/

Stieglitz, S., & Dang-Xuan, L. (2012). Social media and political communication: A social media analytics framework. In *Social Network Analysis and Mining*. Springer-Verlag. Retrieved September 11, 2014, from www.researchgate.net/publication/235632721_Social_Media_and_Political_Communication_-_A_Social_Media_Analytics_Framework/links/09e41512111a26d3f3000000

Turan, I. (1986). Türkiye'de siyasal kültürün oluşumu. In E. Kalaycıoğlu & A. Y. Sarıbay (Eds.), *Türk siyasal hayatının gelişmesi* (pp. 461–487). Istanbul: Beta.

Turkey, T. (n.d.). *Website*. Retrieved October 11, 2014, from http://twiplomacy.com/info/europe/turkey/

TurkStat. (2014, August 22). *Hanehalkı bilişim teknolojileri kullanım araştırması*. Retrieved December 12, 2014, from http://www.tuik.gov.tr/PreHaberBultenleri.do?id=16198

Twitter. (n.d.). *Transparency report*. Retrieved December 23, 2014, from https://transparency.twitter.com/removal-requests/2014/jan-jun

Uzun, S. (2013, December 2). Gezi parkı iddianamesinde 'Erdoğan' sansürü. *Hürriyet*. Retrieved January 20, 2015, from http://www.hurriyet.com.tr/gundem/25259300.asp

We are Social. (2014, July 24). *Digital landscape: Middle East, North Africa and Turkey*. Retrieved September 10, 2014 from http://wearesocial.net/tag/social-media/

We Fight Censorship. (n.d.). *Wave of dismissals after Gezi Park protests*. Retrieved January 22, 2015, from http://wefightcensorship.org/censored/wave-dismissals-after-gezi-park-protestshtml.html#forbidden-content

Wei, S. (2014, December 17). Inside the firewall: Tracking the news that China blocks. *ProPublica*. Retrieved January 5, 2014, from https://projects.propublica.org/firewall/

Yetkin, M. (2014, March 21). Turkish Twitter users defy Erdogan's ban. *Hürriyet Daily News*. Retrieved March 28, 2014, from http://www.hurriyetdailynews.com/turkish-twitter-users-defy-erdogans-ban.aspx?pageID=238&nID=63899&NewsCatID=409

Yurdakul, M. (2014, April 3). Twitter yasağı kalktı. *Milliyet*. Retrieved August 8, 2014, from http://www.milliyet.com.tr/twitter-yasagi-kalkiyor-mu /gundem/detay/1861721/default.htm

Zalewski, P. (2014, May 6). Erdoğan turns on Gulenists' "parallel state" in battle for power. *Financial Times*. Retrieved August 8, 2014, from http://www.ft.com/cms/s/0/0e7a3854-cc98-11e3-ab9900144feabdc0.html#axzz3GOGlssxv

Zúñiga, H. G., Jung, N., & Valenzuela, S. (2012). Social media use for news and individuals' social capital, civic engagement and political participation. *Journal of Computer-Mediated Communication*, *17*(3), 319–336. doi:10.1111/j.1083-6101.2012.01574.x

Chapter 6
Imperfect Bipartisanship and Spanish Pluralism:
The Keys to Success of Podemos on Twitter

Marta Pérez Escolar
Catholic University of Murcia, Spain

ABSTRACT

The objective of this research is to find if the success of Podemos in the 2014 European Parliament Elections and its activity on Twitter agrees with the theoretical perspectives that Dahlgren (2011) and De Ugarte (2007) developed or if there is a new civic participation paradigm that determines the success of the current political communication strategies. In order to verify this proposal, this study not only has applied Dahlgren and De Ugarte's theories, but it has also developed a tweets sampling methodology that permits collection and analysis of information from Podemos' tweets from the 25th March 2014 to the 24th May 2014. The main conclusion of this research is that there is not a 'new civic participation model', but there are some emerging social and collective trends that De Ugarte and Dahlgren did not consider in their approaches, but that offer a context for the development of a new concept of "politics".

INTRODUCTION

Cultural convergence has changed the public landscape from a technological, economic, social and global perspective (Jenkins, 2006). Information and communications technology has emerged as a result of this cultural convergence and it has transformed the structure of social relationships and the political communication process. Lasswell's (1948) communication theory is obsolete within this postmodern society where emerging technologies have motivated the birth of a "participative communication" model (Servaes, 1996; Servaes & Malikhao, 2005).

Barack Obama's campaign in 2008 demonstrated the strength of social networks, like *Twitter* or *Facebook*, as powerful tools to create communities of volunteers who worked together toward a greater good. Voters felt part of the campaign; they could collaborate and participate in the political process as

DOI: 10.4018/978-1-4666-9879-6.ch006

never before. Obama knew how to take the sense of belonging to new and stronger levels; for that reason, Obama's campaign was a turning point that defined a new way to understand the relationship between politics and new technology, between representatives and citizens.

John Daniel, the vice-chancellor of the Open University (UK), said in a conference about the new information society: "Ladies and gentlemen, the new technologies are the answer. What was the question?" This is a good consideration about "the great expectations generated in many different areas of our lives by the prospect of the application of information and communication technology, but at the same time the prevailing disconcertion over their possible uses and impacts" (Subirats, 2002, p. 228). This expression is also an anecdote that reminds the story about Marconi, the father of the Wireless. He was working a long time on the telegraph connections and, one day, when one of his collaborators realized what they have just got, he said: "Marconi, we can talk to Florida!" Marconi turned to him and he responded: "But do we have anything to say to the people in Florida?"

In the same way, we are all hopeful and excited about how digital revolution could improve the democratic system, "but we should first think about the problems facing us today and in the potential and real uses of the information and communication technologies" (Subirats, 2002, p. 228).

The success of *Podemos* during the European Parliament Elections in 2014 is the result of a set of political and communication strategies. However, *Podemos* stood up because of the online communication methods used during the campaign. According to Howard's (2006) thesis, *Podemos* organized a "hypermedia campaign" where citizens kept the power. In this sense, the hypothesis of this chapter suggests understanding if the success of *Podemos* in the 2014 European Parliament Elections and its activity on Twitter are influenced by the hypothesis developed by Dahlgren (2013) and De Ugarte (2007) or if there is a new civic participation paradigm that determines the successful of the current political communication strategies. So, this research should be understood as a theoretical approach that aims to compare the activity of *Podemos* on Twitter with Dahlgren's (2013) and De Ugarte's (2007) paradigms about political participation and civic engagement. This framework is expected to be useful to give some final recommendations about the main ingredients an online campaign should have.

CONTEXTUAL BACKGROUND

May 15, 2011 was a coordinated day of protests in many Spanish cities. It was the day of the *#spanishrevolution* when citizens took to the street expressing their opposition to the political elite. It was a networked movement popularly known as the *15M*. The *15M movement* was born digital. The call to occupy the streets came from many bloggers and online activists that spread their outrage against the Spanish government and their controversial laws[1] on *Twitter*, *Facebook* and other online platforms. The movement was not a single entity, but a blend of different intentions. They were the *Spanish indignados*[2] and they stood in for a great part of society that was growing apart from political institutions (Walzer, 1984).

One of the most powerful and repetitive mottos of the *15M movement* held that Spanish politicians "do not represent us". This was not a populist movement that tried to destabilize the democracy system and to shake the foundation of the Welfare State, but a protest that was warning that our politicians were neither devoting time nor efforts to get what they pledged to citizens. Politicians who represent citizens are supposed to share our values, our needs and our interests (Subirats, 2012); "to represent" is "to be alike", so this means that our representatives should look like us, citizens, because it is the only way they can understand our problems, our worries and our lifestyle.

Then, the *15M movement* was just claiming a democratic renovation and a political change: politicians were more interested in how to get more power and how to get promoted inside the political institutions than in how to satisfy the requirements of citizens. For those reasons, the *15M movement* demanded more transparency, more direct civic participation and to drive out the mediation of lobbies and chambers. The future of democracy was at stake here. How to get this renovation in the Spanish democratic society? Do they, politicians, really represent us, citizens?

The model of welfare mix (Evers & Wintersberger, 1990) could be defined as an alternative path where the political clear-out could start from. In the Spanish case, citizens must understand first how their representatives have been elected and second, how they are exerting their authority and their influences (Presno Linera, 2012). On the one hand, the Spanish representation voting system is not a proportional method. The *D'Hondt law* discriminates under-represented political parties in favor of over-represented ones; this electoral method does not guarantee a real representative and proportional system[3]. That is why the current political sphere is not a pluralist arena, but a monochromatic stage. The political scene should be like a puzzle made by different pieces and where each piece represents different preferences and social opinions. Voting should be understood like the tool that makes proportional representation possible. In this regard, Hirschman (1991, p.169) claimed that "a democratic regime achieves legitimacy to the extent that is decisions result from full and open deliberation among its principal groups, bodies, and representatives". Following the same idea, Narud and Esaisson (2013) considered that:

Democracy works best if citizens are not only voters, but also act as quality-controllers between elections. [...] The better the communication between citizens and representatives, the better the quality of the representation will be. Negotiation and deliberation between elections can be considered as critical for good representation. Political participation serves as an important tool for citizen input in the democratic process and it enables citizens to pressure politicians to take this information into account when making political decisions. (Mansbridge, 2003)

Then, if the intention is to figure out the democratic crisis and to create a trustful relationship between society and government, why can citizens not set up a 'deselect system' that permits individuals oust an elected official before his official term has ended? (Subirats, 2012). Other countries like Canada, Switzerland or some places in United State have already celebrated *recall elections* or *recall referendums*. According to the *Oxford dictionary*, the *recall* is a method of election in which voters can use when they want to remove and replace an elected official before his official term has ended. This procedure begins when sufficient voters sign a petition and it means to change "ordinary people" (Hibbing & Theis Morse, 2002) into "monitorial citizen" (Schudson, 1998) to ensure politicians functions properly (Narud & Esaisson, 2013). It is a democratic duty of citizens. *Monitoring* means the demolition of the *panoptic model* developed by Bentham in 1791 and the end of the role of political actors as a big brother, regarding the novel *1984* by George Orwell. According to Feenstra and Casero-Ripollés (2014), "monitoring, defined as the exercise of public scrutiny toward power centers and relations, is considered a rising trend due to the potential enabled by the new digital communication structure" (p. 2450).

On the other hand, regarding representative's functions and responsibilities, it is important first to point out the role of the representatives as a vehicle for expressing the wishes and choices of citizens and for promoting the civic participation. Democracy should not be understood like a scenario occupied only by professional politicians, but like an *infocracy* (Zuurmond, 1998). The coming of *infocracy* will imply a less hierarchical, more flexible and opener democratic system. "In a more 'constructive' sense, *informatization* is associated with a resurgence and renewal of democracy. More specifically, *informatization* is expected to facilitate all kinds of (direct as well as participatory) digital democracy. [...] ICTs are, furthermore, said to contribute to the transparency of power, to favour interactive decision-making and the empowerment of citizens". (Van de Donk, 2000, p. 139)

Occidental societies are living so a digital revolution that is making up the current *Information age*. Castells (2004) named this model of social organization the *«network society»*, in which citizens live in a global, interconnected and informed community based on a free, open and liberalizing culture. The traditional hierarchical structure is obsolete nowadays and a new decentralised democratic model is emerging. The main characteristic of this new social organization system is to provide lateral and multidirectional communication flows. The *network society* is composed of proactive or *prosumers* (McLuhan & Barrington, 1972; Toffler, 1980) that want to participate in the public sphere creating their own content, sharing information and interacting with other users of the web 2.0.

In this volatile context, activists from the *15M movement* protested against those politicians that "do not represent us". Government responsibility in public welfare is a deeply rooted idea in Spain, but activists from the *15M movement* believed that the main tenets of the Spanish democracy were living a tricky period because of the lack of civic involvement. According to their manifesto, Spanish democracy needed to conform to the new rules of the *network society*. For those reasons, the *15M movement* understood that the opportunity to set up their own political party had already arrived. *Podemos* was born with the aim of monitoring dishonest politicians and giving more power to the people.

In conclusion, in the same way the presidential campaign of Barack Obama in 2008 shined for the use of the Internet and social networks, the phenomenon *Podemos* excelled as a different political party that knew how to defend their political strategies skillfully on social networks, especially on Twitter. In their public manifesto, they demanded a deep political renovation and more opportunities for civic participation. Twitter was a useful tool for giving and receiving feedback from voters and although other Spanish candidates like Jose Luis Rodrígez Zapatero (PSOE), Mariano Rajoy (PP), or Rosa Díez (UPyD) had previously used social networks as a means of political expression, the effects of these last ones were less popular. The main advantage of *Podemos* lies in the level of argumentation, the discursive strategies, the coherence and the empathy of their online messages. They were not just disseminating a political ideology among voters (self-promotion), but the idea that the civic empowerment was the main step for reaching social and democratic changes.

CONCEPTUAL BACKGROUND

Postmodern societies have developed a new collective identity influenced by the technological, economic, social and global convergence (Jenkins, 2006). *Network society* has changed the rules of the political and public debate. Candidates and political parties who aspire to take advantage of the strength of networks must be aware of the logic of the new democratic society. In this sense, De Ugarte (2007) has configured the 'empowering people model' as a political strategy that parties should include in their electoral campaigns in order to connect with the new electorate. According to De Ugarte (2007), the 'empowering people model' depends on the strength of the following factors: swarming, speeches, tools and visibility.

1. Swarming. Arquilla and Ronfeldt (2000, p. 5) argued that swarming "is already emerging as an appropriate doctrine for networked forces to wage information-age conflict". It could seem an

amorphous multitude, but it is a deliberately structured, coordinated, strategic way to strike from all directions (Arquilla & Ronfeldt, 2000). Swarming is so the new power structure of the network society. It is a concept that explains the new organizational system of democratic citizenships in which people transfer their values and culture from virtual environment to reality. Thus, swarming depends upon communication and information flows that shape the structure of the network society. However, there is a conflict within the network society; it is called the "social netwar" (Ronfeldt, Arquilla, Graham Fuller & Melissa Fuller, 1998) and it is led by small units or nodes that interact with each other to coordinate their actions and to ensure the effectiveness of the movement. Online communities and virtual conversations follow the logic of swarming, but it is difficult to start a movement on the Web and then to shift it into reality, like a protest or a demonstration that occupies the streets. For that reason, new political parties should know how to be part of the swarming and how to bring that voices round to their point of view.

2. Speeches. The new speeches on social networks must be focused on the empowering people strategy. Online speeches do not aim to set a strict hierarchy of values, a doctrine or a creed; but they suggest ranges or perspectives from which we can understand the social reality. Political speeches should narrate individual stories or relate stories about small group of people that change the public space using the ingenious and the imagination (political storytelling). These new speeches keep the main postmodern ingredients that ensures the success of the narrations on the web: a strong identity component, decentralized flows of communication (information is not mediated by any single agent) and the common idea that defines "activism" as a "social hacking" form.
3. Tools. The main idea is to provide useful tools for users in order to encourage them to participate in any kind of movement that parties or political actors could organize. In this context, it is important that new political parties show their attitude to reach consensus among the online community and their ability to divulgate and spread their ideas on the global net. It is a strategy that will help politicians to find virtual allies.
4. Visibility. It is the last step of the empowering people strategy. Citizens must gain visibility on virtual spaces and offline environments. Network visibility is the key to achieve the "tipping points" (Gladwell, 2006). Ideas, products, messages, trends and behaviors spread on the Internet like viruses do, but there is a moment when the epidemic reaches the top point, the moment when the popularity of that information reaches a climax. That is the *tipping point phenomenon* and political strategies should be focused on researching that point.

On the other hand, Dahlgren (2013) understands that "democracies today do not automatically guarantee extensive participation of citizens, either in electoral or extra-parliamentarian contexts. Democratic systems in fact offer varying patterns of what are called structures of opportunity for participation" (p.11); but participation also depends on the initiatives that citizens take by themselves. Then the concept of «participation» is defined as a social conduct inherent to democratic systems. Civic participation is one of the most representative behaviours attached to the tenets of citizenship and democracies (Dahlgren, 2013).

Online civic participation is nowadays one of the main values to understand the evolution of democracy and the development of political participation and civic engagement. In this context, Dahlgren (2013) has reflected on the key elements of the online participation and the importance of each parameter within the democratic ecosystem. These factors also determine the success of the empowering people model and the popularity of movements or political speeches on the Internet. According to Dahlgren (2013), these parameters that define the democracy and the online and offline civic participation are:

1. Terrains of engagement: the borderlands. Public sphere is a terrain that is limited by three borders basically: *consumption*, *popular culture* and *civil society*. The *consumption* is a vast term that is connected with the logic of markets. This concept means that we participate because we are trying to find satisfaction and pleasure. "Consumption is a powerful gravitational force, and it is not surprising that our identities as consumers are generally much more easily mobilized that of citizens" (Dahlgren, 2013, p. 38). *Popular culture* is often entangled with consumption since it is a massive and heterogeneous terrain that has a compelling allure, but it is also a borderland that invites participation: invites citizens to engage in many questions having to do with how we should live and what kind of society people want. Popular culture "allows us to process, to work through positions having to do with contested values, norms and identities in a turbulent late modern socio-cultural milieu" (Dahlgren, 2013, p. 33). The idea of *civil society* refers to "a terrain that in some or other involves free association for common purpose outside both the market and the private sphere of the home" (Dahlgren, 2013, p. 33). Democracies must guarantee that the people share their interest with friends, communities or social networks without any commercial or political purpose. "Democracy should be a celebration of an involved public" (Dalton, 2002, p. 32). The freedoms associated with civil society are absolutely essential for democratic public spheres. However, civil society is always a potentially vulnerable terrain and, in this context, political participation must be understood as a tool to defend civil society against antidemocratic trends. "We often equate political participation with the act of voting, but if you view politics from the citizen's perspective, participation is not limited to voting, nor is voting necessarily the most effective means of influencing the political process. Instead of waiting several years until the next election, you might try to contact political elites directly, or you might work with others who share your interests, or you might find other ways to advocate your cause" (Dalton, 2002, p. 33).
2. Visibility and Intervisibility. The notion of *visibility* is not simply a question of being visible or invisible. Visibility is an important aspect of participation. Brighenti (2010) developed two models that conceptualize this term within the public sphere. On the one hand, the first model refers to the public sphere as a mode of visibility where one can be in public, "that is where the 'synchronicity of attention' can be said to (in its better moments) five rise to a certain regime of democracy visibility" (Dahlgren, 2013, p. 40). On the other hand, the second model is "the public realm of social visibility, of interaction, where the gaze and recognition of general or significant others becomes central to the constitution of self, of identity" (ibid. p. 40). Dahlgren (2013) called this last kind of model "*intervisibility*" and it is related to the idea of "how our sense of self emerges through interaction or the 'presentation of self'" (ibid. p. 40). Then, from the perspective of democratic participation, public sphere *visibility* and social *intervisibility* remain both conditions for participation.
3. Voice. Couldry (2010) described the concept of *voice* as a process in which particular perspectives and opinions are acknowledged; but voice is also a value that favours forms of social organization in political contexts. Nevertheless, in this contemporary context, voice and other social values and visions "become marginalized by political design and economic rationality, voices becomes something to be protected, to be promoted, to give witness to the human reality behind" (Dahlgren, 2013, p. 39). From the perspective of democratic participation, public sphere visibility and social intervisibility remain both conditions of participation.
4. Sociality. Political participation is a social action based on human communication and contingent upon sociality. Doing politics in an effective way requires a degree of social skills and competences; it is common to undervalue the importance of the sociability but we should understand this

> concept as a tool to motivate political participation and to improve networked interaction. Social interaction is the first requirement for supporting participation. However, the dreadful use of the web is obviously not a form of democratic political participation; it yet victimizes many people on the web. "There are many unfortunate examples of how not just baleful individuals but even entire symbolic 'lynch mobs' can emerge in social media. [...] In any case, sociality cannot be legislated, but there remains the regulatory challenge of dealing with anonymous harassment that can stifle public discussion, but in a way that will still safeguard freedom of legitimate speech." (Dahlgren, 2013, p. 35).

Regarding this characteristics (Dahlgren, 2011; De Ugarte, 2007), we understand that political participation on the Web is a mechanism of knowledge sharing and mutual learning. Traditional and conservatives political principles are becoming obsolete and less effective. The potential of political micro-blogging should not be underestimated; in fact, Twitter and other micro-blogging platforms are considered extraordinary tools to connect voters with candidates, but not everybody is capable enough to develop a political micro-blogging strategy.

The majority of online actions by political actors are more likely to seem an "electronic brochure" (Jackson & Lilleker, 2009) than an attempt to connect with the interests and needs of citizens. Politicians tend to use blogs as "campaign gimmicks" (Lilleker & Malagón, 2010) or tweets as a "vehicles for self-promotion" (Goblbeck, Grimes & Rogers, 2010), "while micro-blogging in general has evolved towards becoming more conversational and collaborative" (Larsson & Moe, 2011).The model of political participation proposed by Dahlgren (2011) and De Ugarte (2007) suggests increasing the power of individual through political micro-blogging use and the empowering people phenomenon. It is an open paradigm that enhances civic ability to share information and knowledge with other online users via social media.

METHOD

Social media data is difficult to obtain. Nevertheless, this research has developed a tweets sampling methodology that permits collection and analysis of information from *Podemos*' tweets. This method will provide an overview of the political participation strategy of *Podemos*' on Twitter. In order to verify this proposal, we will not only expound the strategies we have identified, but also we are going to compare those characteristics with De Ugarte's and Dahlgren's theoretical hypothesis.

This analysis will track tweets sent from *@ahorapodemos* and *@pablo_iglesias_* Twitter accounts two months before the European Parliament Elections 2014. In order to carry out this tweets collection, this work is going to use *Topsy* application, since we believe it is a suitable online tool for obtaining tweets and information according to our specific needs. The tweet search range we have employed it starts the 25th March 2015 and ends the 24th May 2014, two months before the day of the European Parliament Elections. We also point out that we have needed to translate the tweets from Spanish to English in order to make the speech understandable.

But why Twitter? Twitter is a micro-blogging system that has become one of the most relevant communication platforms for the new politics. Originally, this service was created as a web page in which users exchange personal messages (Barberá & Rivero, 2012), but nowadays, Twitter has become a massive phenomenon with more than 271 million online users[4].Twitter is the social network that better foreshadow the interrelationships that are shared on the Internet between citizens, representatives and prominent opinion movers. Twitter´s potential relies on the fact that messages are spread in a quick and massive way, viral phenomenon or "massive phenomenon" (Barberá & Rivero, 2012), and thus, they can get to a bigger and varying amount of public than direct followers. It is a platform made up of a structure difficult to find in other social networks that are more connected and introspective.

Moreover, the open nature of conversations in Twitter leaves us the chance to study the politic strategy carried out in elections and other political campaigns. In short, "Twitter is a relevant source of political information; it has been a battlefield during electoral campaigns, a deliberation forum and a path of political expression" (Barberá & Rivero, 2012).

RESULTS

The elections to the European Parliament, which took place on 25th May 2014, were a remarkable occasion to know the Spanish people's opinion. For the first time in almost three years, political parties were subjected to elector´s evaluation. It happened within a context of economic crisis which would predictably lead to several consequences that would affect the currently ruling party (*PP party*) and the previous party on the Government (*PSOE party*).

The European Elections made up the perfect scenario to test whether the citizens were still faithful to the two biggest political parties in Spain (imperfect two-party system) even in critical situations. Although civic participation was low in these elections -according to the Spanish Home Office, the participation rate was 45, 86%-, the event became the perfect alibi to apply the *protest vote*. The supporting rate of the two biggest parties (*PP party* and *PSOE party*) decreased significantly in comparison to the previous electoral meetings reaching records never seen before in the European elections.

Figure 1 shows the evolution of two-party system in Spain. PP party and PSOE party rates across the European Parliament elections (1987 – 2014)

Figure 1. The evolution of two-party system in Spain. PP party and PSOE party rates across the European Parliament elections (1987 – 2014)
Source: Boix Palop and López García (2014)

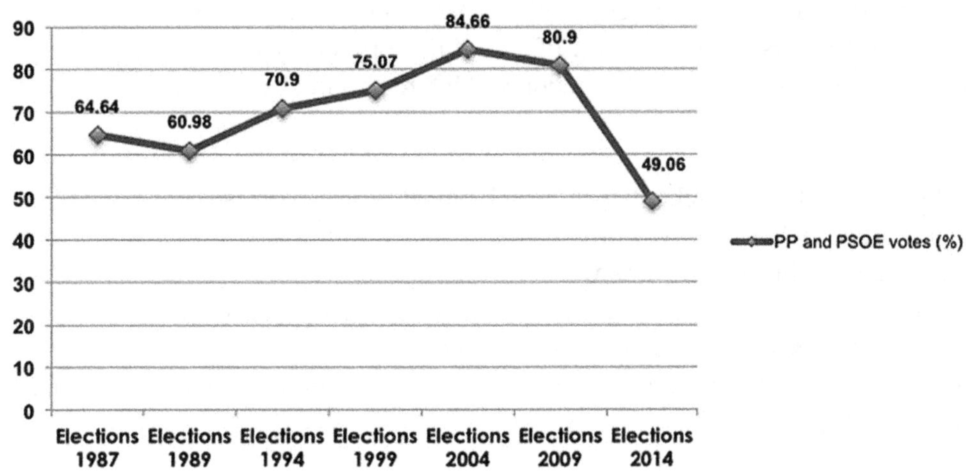

In this breeding ground, new parties emerged gaining importance in the politic scene, such as *Vox, Ciudadanos, Movimiento Red, Primavera europea, Partido X* or *Podemos*. One of the better rated parties was *Podemos.* They got almost the 8% of the votes. This electoral success made them one of the starring political groups in Spanish political outlook. These changes drove into deeper transformations as well, such as the resignation of the chief of staff from *PSOE*, Alfredo Pérez Rubalcaba. Following the tendencies the electorate showed in the European Elections, the *PSOE* agreed that the new presidency had to be replaced by someone young, who seemed to be worried about the real needs of the people and disappointed with the current political situation. This description matched with Pedro Sánchez, who started an overhauling process in the party, clearly aiming to recover citizen´s trust and improve the deteriorated reputation of socialist party.

Podemos could be also defined as a "hacktivist party" since we understand this political group was born from an activist movement (the *15M movement*), but they are not a protest demonstration anymore. They are a political party that is using the rules of cyber-activism and the hacker culture to create and set up another political participation model – more democratic, transparent and collaborative.

In this context, the concept of "hacker party" is connected with the idea of "hacktivism". The term *hacktivism* comes from the marriage of "hacking" and "activism": "*Hacktivism* is the emergence of popular political action, of the self-activity of group of people, in cyberspace. It is a combination of grassroots political protest with computer hacking. *Hacktivism* operate within the fabric of cyberspace, struggling over what is technologically possible in virtual lives, and reaches out of cyberspace utilizing virtual powers to mould offline life. Social movements and popular protest are integral parts of twenty-first-century societies. *Hacktivism* is activism gone electronic". (Jordan & Taylor, 2004, p. 1)

However, *hacktivism* does not mean any politic institution associated with cyberspace, "in which case all politics would be *hacktivist* [...]. *Hacktivism* is a specific social and cultural phenomenon, in which the popular politics of direct action has been translated into virtual realms" (Jordan & Taylor, 2004, p.1). The hacker culture is subject to seven values or characteristics that have a significant role in the formation of our new society and that represent the hacker ethics and the spirit of *informationalism* (Himanen, 2001). According to Himanen (2001), those seven values are:

1. Passions. Hackers enjoy what they do. They believe they are doing something interesting and there is not a higher stage of motivation than that belief.
2. Freedom. Hackers do not organize their lives in terms of a continuously optimized workday, but in terms of a dynamic flow between creative work and life's other passions.
3. Social worth. Hackers want to be part of an online community and to work together with other users in order to not only share information and interests, but also to create something valuable to society.
4. Openness.
5. The value of activity. The technological development of the Information Age provides open communication flows where freedom of expression does not find any limit, but where hackers must respect a code of ethical conduct as well.
6. Caring. The new challenge of hackers is to get that everybody participates in the network society and to make citizens feel responsible for the consequences and benefits of being part of the network society. Hackers who live according to the hacker ethic become a true hero and gain the community's highest respect.
7. Creativity.

On the other hand, following the conceptual approach that *Podemos* is a "*hacktivist* party", indeed we define them as a cyber-activist political party too. *Cyber-activism* is a new civic behavior model in which citizens develop a strong collective consciousness that encourage them to interact and discuss public affairs with other users on the Web. Cyber-activism is also considered the most evident manifestation of social movements; it is a phenomenon that requires political reforms in order to adapt the current democratic system to the new demands of the contemporary society. Tascón and Quintana (2012) described cyber-activism as a collective action made up by "individual activists who use online platforms and social networks to publish their protest, look for allies and face antagonists" (p. 9). Thus, a cyber-activist is "someone who uses the Internet and the blogosphere above all, to spread a speech and to make available to citizenship the tools that give the power and the visibility that is now monopolized by the institutions back to the people" (De Ugarte, 2007, p. 66).

Pablo Iglesias used Twitter frequently since he sang up on Twitter in November 2010. That was one of the main factors that helped him to gain more followers a year before the European Parliament Elections in 2014. Digital citizens understood that Pablo Iglesias did not create his Twitter account just for political goals, but maybe for activist purposes as well. However, one of his weaknesses was that he did not replay to his followers when they mentioned him for asking questions about his political proposals or about the manifesto of *Podemos*.

Pablo Iglesias was quite active on Twitter and he used this platform for making direct political communication flows, but also for promoting changes in the public sphere. However, it is suggested to improve the feedback since it is important citizens feels that representatives listen to their claims and petitions.

Then, in order to show some examples of the hacktivist behavior of *Podemos* and Pablo Iglesias (like transparency, protest actions, encouraging civic participation, informing against political corruption, etc.) we have collected some tweets we include below:

Figure 2 is an example of the hacker culture and the activist attitude of 'Podemos'

Figure 3 is an example of the hacker culture and the activist attitude of 'Podemos'

Podemos sought to get visibility and "intervisibility" (Dahlgren, 2013). Following the hypothesis of De Ugarte (2007), *Podemos* wrote their tweets and spread their ideas, behaviors or trends like viruses do. They tried to divulgate their messages like if they were an epidemic and infect citizens with their political ideas. Then, visibility helps to gain intervisibility, that is "how our sense of self emerges through interaction or the 'presentation of self'" (Dahlgren, 2013, p. 40).

Figure 2. Tweet published by @ahorapodemos the 27th March, 2014
Translation: "The problem is not the scoundrels, but the corruption as a form of government", Pablo Iglesias

Figure 3. Tweet published by @ahorapodemos the 5th May, 2014
Translation: "It is time to put civil laws before the interest of lobbies and privates campaigns", Pablo Iglesias

PODEMOS
@ahorapodemos

"Es hora de anteponer los derechos ciudadanos a los intereses de los lobbies y compañías privadas"
Pablo Iglesias

Responder Retwittear Favorito ••• Más

RETWEETS 27 FAVORITOS 20

2:58 - 5 de may. de 2014

Visibility could be significant improved using a suitable speech and voice. The following example may illustrate these ideas about how *Podemos* use Twitter to gain visibility and intervisibility among online users (they added the link to the TV program where Pablo Iglesias participated and they also included a headline that attracted attention) and offline citizens (he first participated on the TV program and then he used Twitter to publish and communicate his messages to whom did not watch the program; there is feedback relation between information broadcasted on TV and the one given on the Internet).

Figure 4 is an example of visibility and intervisibility on Twitter

Figure 4. Tweet published by @ahorapodemos the 6st May, 2014
Translation: "We cannot overcome this crisis impoverishing the population", intervention of Pablo Iglesias in Cuatro: bit.ly/1nhxSWK

PODEMOS
@ahorapodemos

"De la crisis no se sale empobreciendo más a la gente", intervención de Pablo Iglesias en Cuatro: bit.ly/1nhxSWK

Responder Retwittear Favorito ••• Más

Cuatro

Pablo Iglesias: "Aquí, parece que para que te vaya bien te tienes ...

Tras escuchar el testimonio de Miguel, un hombre en paro desde hace cinco años y tras la acusación de Compromís al PP asegurando que emplea en el Instituto Valenciano de la Juventud a miembros de...

Ver en la web

RETWEETS 60 FAVORITOS 30

13:08 - 6 de may. de 2014

Hence, Pablo Iglesias also used his own Twitter account as a way to improve the visibility and intervisibility of *Podemos*. Since this political party was born, they started strengthening the figure of Pablo Iglesias as a recognizable face on micro-blogging platforms and TV programs. His presence on Twitter has been active and constant; he showed to be a competent user and a skilled cyber-activist. Doubtlessly this fact helped *Podemos* to gain followers, visibility and intervisibility faster during the European Parliament campaign.

Figure 5 shows the development of Pablo Iglesias on Twitter

The speech of *Podemos* on Twitter was clearly focused on favoring the empowering people phenomenon. The speech of postmodern societies, as De Ugarte (2007) and Dahlgren (2013) explained

Figure 5. Figures about the development of Pablo Iglesias on Twitter
Source: Elaborated by the authors and based on López García (2014)

	Pablo Iglesias (@Pablo_Iglesias_)
First tweet date	11th November, 2010
Months on Twitter before the European Parliament campaign started	41.94
Published tweets until the 9th May, 2014	7,271
Tweets per day (before the European Parliament campaign started)	5.70
Published tweets until the 26th May, 2014	7,600
Published tweets during the campaign	329
Tweets per day during the campaign	18.28
Frequency variation (%)	220.51%
Retweets during the campaign	96
Retweets during the campaign (%)	29,18%
Replays during the campaign	4
Replays during the campaign (%)	1.22%
References to other users during the campaign	69
Hastags during the campaign	98
Retweeted times	73,225
Followers (until the 9th May, 2014)	149,147
Followers (until the 26th May, 2014)	264,892
Followers variation	115,745
Followers variation (%)	77,60%

should keep a strong identity component and contribute to create new forms of social organization in the political debate. The information given by *Podemos* was not mediated by any media; they provided decentralized flows of communication on Twitter and other micro-blogging platforms. The voice of *Podemos* acknowledged particular perspectives and opinions:

Figure 6 is an example of speech and voice on Twitter

Figure 7 is an example of speech and voice on Twitter

The speech of *Podemos* on Twitter was a political strategy that deals about the idea of vanquishing the bipartisanship and the political "caste"[5] that were damaging society. In this context, *Podemos* emerged to bring change and hope. Pablo Iglesias sent tweets to the leaders of the other political parties as well –like the PP party and the PSOE party- to remark the outrage of the Spanish citizens. *Podemos* believed that most of the people who used to vote to the *PP* or the *PSOE* were disenchant and they felt cheated by the "caste", so the Spanish society needed a deep political and social transformation: Spanish people were finding another kind of politicians who really "represent them" following the slogan of the *15M movement* (López García, 2014).

On the other hand, *Podemos* put different kinds of online tools on public scenario to encourage civic participation. Twitter was, in this sense, the most useful vehicle for communicating people how they could

Figure 6. Tweet published by @ahorapodemos the 3rd May, 2014
Translation: More than 300 circles created by honest and anonymous people that do politics daily. This is the right way: We can!

Figure 7. Tweet published by @ahorapodemos the 4th April, 2014
Translation: "What we are defending is the democracy system" Pablo Iglesias

participate in the public debate and which were the online tools that were available to them: links and *#hashtags* were used for redirecting users to other platforms or websites. These tools not only enhanced the empowering people phenomenon, but they were also a means for organizing social demonstrations, finding allies on the virtual arena and spreading ideas and knowledge. A successful message follows the logic of *transmediality*.

On the other hand, it is worth mentioning here that sociality (Dahlgren, 2013) has also shown to be an effective tool for *Podemos* strategy on Twitter. Sociality is a form of democratic political participation that motivates political participation and improves networked interaction.

Figure 8 is an example of online tools

Figure 9 is an example of online tools

On the official website of *Podemos*, activists could also find other online tools for participating and collaborating in political decisions, public debates, forums, etc. They opened a section called "Asamblea ciudadana" (*Citizens' Assembly*) where people could vote decisions and propose ideas; moreover, they have also deployed other cyber-activist tools and platforms like *Reddit, Loomio, Appgree, Agora voting*

Figure 8. Tweet published by @pablo_iglesias_ the 12th April, 2014
Translation: Today is an important day for @ahorapodemos. Join our meeting and participate.

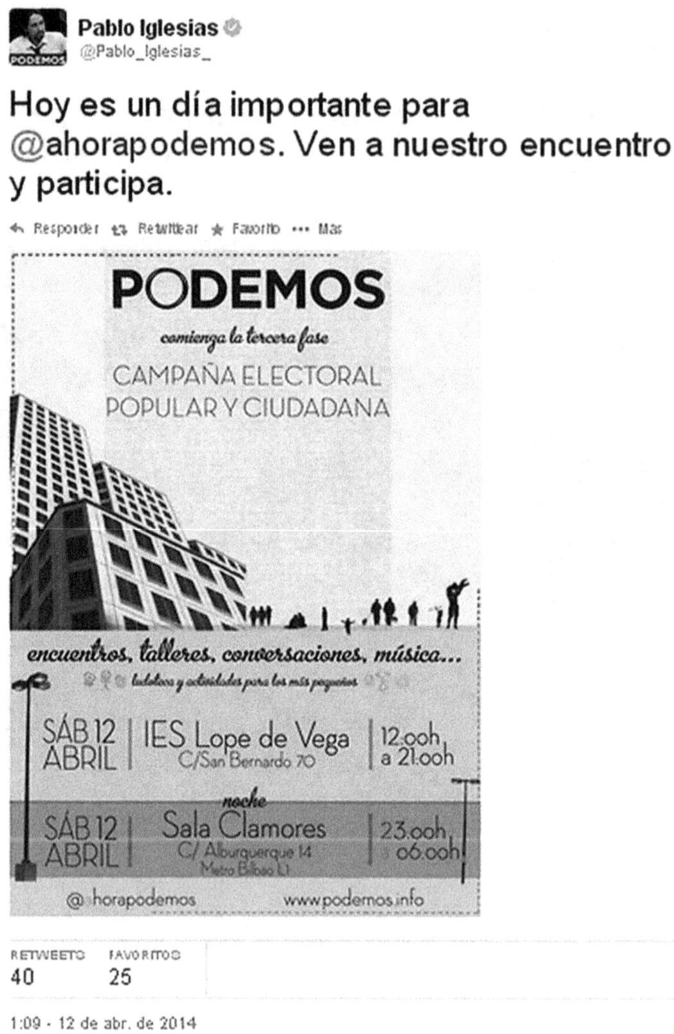

Figure 9. Tweet published by @pablo_iglesias_ the 11th April, 2014
Translation: Tomorrow there will be an awesome meeting of @ahorapodemos. I will give a Political Communication workshop (12:30 – assembly room) Join us! RT

system or *TitanPad*. Another significant space of civic participation was the "Banco de talentos" (Talent bank), where citizens explained their abilities and described how they thought they could collaborate in the organization and management of *Podemos*. In short, the official website of *Podemos* could be defined as a *crowdsourcing* and a *co-working* platform.

Eventually, we sum up that the presence of *Podemos* on Twitter has been notable during the two months before the European Parliament Elections in 2014. "Just 48 hours after they got five seats in the European Parliament, they became the Spanish political party with more followers on Twitter" (Gómez & Viejo, 2014). The Twitter account @ahorapodemos exceeded the followers of other political forcers like the *PP* party, *PSOE*, *UPyD* or *Izquierda Unida*.

Gustavo Entrala, brand strategist of 'Agencia 101' and creator of the Twitter account of the Pope (@ Pontifex) agreed that the successful of *Podemos* was an unexpected phenomenon in the communication field. Pablo Iglesias caused the same fascination than his party on the online scenario. One of the most remarkable characteristics is that they developed a strategy based on networks of interactionsto to encourage the dialogue with the citizens. As Rita Maestre argued: "The net must be an element of interaction. It is not just to launch a tweet", our representatives should understand the value to give feedback and replay to the users (Gómez & Viejo, 2014).

SOLUTIONS AND RECOMMENDATIONS

The popularity of *Podemos* was a sudden phenomenon. The party started being an unknown political group in the social sphere, but soon they realized their reputation was disseminating among citizens and they became the third most influential political force in Spain, that is behind *PP* party and *PSOE* party. *Podemos* is a "hacktivist party" which showed to have important advantages over traditional political parties; nevertheless, since they are an emerging political model, their civic participation strategy also presents some flaws that could harm their proposals and messages in the public online debate. For those reasons, this research aims to describe the most common defects of the political participation communication model of *Podemos* and suggests some solutions and recommendations that could relieve future negative effects:

Heterogeneity. The organizational model of *Podemos* is based on the heterogeneity. This means that there are different political opinions and a great number of ideological perspectives in the internal political debate – *Podemos* did not have political delegations; they were organized in local "circles" that followed a determinate ideology -. Pluralism is a good element in democratic societies since it is the key to understand and reconstruct liberal democratic politics. Groups are viewed as the means to acquiring political power and the role of those groups, communities and associations plays in self-development is central to political pluralism (Eisenberg, 1995).

Equally, there is a connection between this idea and the term developed by Francis Galton in 1906: "wisdom of crowds" or "crowdsourcing". Galton affirmed that decisions taken by groups or communities are often better than the information given by any single member of a group (Surowiecki, 2005). The *crowd* is intelligent because the decision making process is a collective action where bad decisions are rejected by the majority.

Nevertheless, - this opportunity is also a disadvantage, because not everybody is qualified to participate in the decision making process. Putnam (2001) argued that there are two characteristics that determine the motivation of citizens to participate in the political sphere: political knowledge and civic engagement. Citizens are not supposed to be political experts (Stoker, 2006), but they must show a basic political knowledge level that guarantee that their decisions are based on rational arguments. Civic engagement is important to motivate civic participation; citizens must be aware of the dreadful consequences of the electoral abstinence. Then, as Putnam (2001) claimed: "If you do not know the rules of the game and the players and do not care about outcome, you are unlikely to try playing yourself" (p. 35).

Therefore, it follows that heterogeneity is a positive value since we understand the multitude as a "wisdom crowd", but it might be also dangerous because not everybody is motivated to participate in the political affairs or they do not just know how to do it –lack of political knowledge-. So then, if we want to pursuit a real political pluralism, *Podemos* should start educating and training people before giving them political responsibilities that exceed their cognitive abilities.

The concept of democracy as an ambiguous term. Democracy is a polysemic concept. There is not a universal definition since we could establish standard tenets and characteristic of a perfect democratic system; each society demands different needs and so, each democracy should encompass different principles that satisfy those social petitions.

One of the most used proposals of *Podemos* which comes from the *15M movement* is to set up a "real democracy" in Spain. But, what do they understand when they say "real democracy"? They do not make the main tenets of a "real democracy" clear; there is not a common manifesto that includes a definition about how a democratic system, especially Spanish democracy, should be. *Podemos* uses this empty term without following any guideline or criterion and let people believe in the kind of democracy they would like to live in; but that is an individual perception that could not fit with the democratic ideals of other citizens. In fact, there are different local circles in *Podemos* that claim different models of democracy, for example, "Deepening democracy", "We could participate more", "Direct democracy" or "Anticapitalist Left". Some of those social circles tend to go towards radicalisms, although they do not divulgate radical or extreme ideas.

Yet, some of those movements also proclaim a direct democratic system when, indeed, direct democracy is a utopian model of social organization that was just feasible in the Ancient Greek civilization (Hamilton, Madison & Jay, 2012; Merino, 2001). Then, we suggest *Podemos* does encourage "direct participation", and not direct democracy, as a vehicle for giving power to citizens. Direct participation means that citizens turn into active actors that play an important role in the political process –it is a feasible model of popular sovereignty-. It is not just about voting during the elections; it is about collaborating in democratic decisions through social media, for example. Twitter provides interesting opportunities for online deliberation, as we have demonstrated; so as a "hacktivist party", *Podemos* should set up common values and definitions that users could share on the Internet, because the ideological chaos that is being generated by the different local circles makes people feel confused.

Superficial speech. The speech of *Podemos* on Twitter is sometimes offensive and radicalized. They use the term "caste" to label politicians who are not making politics. It is a pejorative concept that they use randomly when they want to discredit someone who are not using political power to help citizens. The concept of "caste" is a good resource to point out bad political praxis, without euphemisms. However, it would be better if *Podemos* also emphasis their political proposals instead of going on stressing the bad behavior of others political actors.

On the other hand, the speech of *Podemos* is like a plebiscite process and sometimes, their messages lack of preciseness and rigorous information. It seems their messages are written like tweets. For that reason, we suggest *Podemos* adjusting their speeches depending on the context and the target. Young people may appreciate tweets instead of rigorous speeches, but *Podemos* should not forget the importance of communicating quality messages and educating people in political issues.

From all this, it follows that even though *Podemos* has shown to innovate the traditional political participation model in Spain, there are still some behaviors we suggest they should improve, like the chaotic political pluralism, the lack of conciseness in their messages about democracy and civic participation, and the superficial speeches that look like tweets.

FUTURE RESEARCH DIRECTIONS

This research sets out to investigate the political participation model developed by Podemos during the European Parliament campaign 2014. However, we are aware that this study does not consider some others points from which we could also analyze this political strategy. Thus, we will discuss directions for future researches and emerging trends in this epigraph.

1. *An analysis of the narrative strategy from the perspective of storytelling.* The potential of stories demonstrates that the storytelling is one of the most powerful means of communication available in contemporary societies. "Stories are more efficient and effective vehicle for communicating factual, conceptual, emotional and tacit information" (Haven, 2007, p.122) than other political strategies. However, storytelling can be used to enlighten the reality or to conceal information. Salmon (2010) criticized that "in hypermedia society" the ability to build a political identity by telling stories, instead of using rational arguments, is the key to achieve power. Yet, storytelling is a management tool that is bewitching the human mind (Salmon, 2010). Politicians use a manipulative technique to influence opinion and behaviors. That is the power of stories. Stories have effects upon us. Instead of using stories to communicate, the political actors use a speech in which the force of language and the emotional plot seek to persuade citizens. "This is not written experience, and it is not experience based on rational thinking. Instead, storytelling is based on experience passed on from mouth to mouth" (Benjamin, 1999, p. 86).

However, this political narrative has not succeeded in Spain. During the presidential campaign in 2008, the electoral candidate Mariano Rajoy used this communicative strategy against Jose Luis Rodíguez Zapatero, who was the President of the government in that period, in a face to face TV Spanish program. Rajoy ended his speech telling a story about a girl who needed to grow up in a better society. That story reminded the 'Ashley's story' told by George Bush after the *11M* attack, but there was an important different: Rajoy was not able to transmit emotions, it seemed that he did not believe in the story he was telling. So, although it was a brave attempt to get something different, the strategy failed because Rajoy was not able to be a good storyteller.

In this regards, we consider that one important future research direction must investigate the storytelling strategy of *Podemos*. Pablo Iglesias, the leader of this political party, is a good speaker, but he has trouble building emotional connections with the audience. So then, it could be interesting to guess if the storytelling is an important point in his political strategy or if it is a strategy that could damage the image of the political party.

2. *Tracking the Spanish presidential campaign in 2015.* After the unexpected success of *Podemos* in the European Parliament elections in 2014, it is considered important to analyze the next political campaign in Spain. Twitter clearly constitutes a new arena for the public debate nowadays. Micro-blogging has shown to be an important tool for increasing political participation among previously unengaged citizens (Castells, 2007); however, it is still uncertain the next online communication strategy of *Podemos* for the presidential campaign in 2015.

CONCLUSION

The main conclusion of this research is that there is not a real 'new civic participation model' in the sense that the model is completely new, but there are emerging some social and collective trends that Dahlgren (2011) and De Ugarte (2007) did not consider in their approaches that means the reconsideration of some characteristics. Digital culture and new civic participation forms have led to several transformations in contemporary societies. Common knowledge and new collaboration forms offer a new context for the development of a new concept of "politics". In this participative ecosystem, Dahlgren (2013) and De Ugarte (2007) suggest that civic participation must be funded in the "empowering people" phenomenon and in understanding the democratic system like an opportunity for improving offline and online political participation. According to De Ugarte (2007), the 'empowering people model' depends on the strength of the following factors: swarming, speeches, tools and visibility. On the other hand, Dahlgren (2013) understands online civic participation is nowadays one of the main values to understand the evolution of democracy and the development of political participation and civic engagement. He also argues that the 'empowering people model' depends on the strength of some factors inherent to the democracy and the online and offline civic participation: consumption, popular culture, civil society, visibility, intervisibility, voice and sociality.

Nevertheless, Dahlgren (2013) and De Ugarte (2007) theoretical perspectives do not include some innovative and inherent to *network society* characteristics and inherent to *network society* (Castells, 2004). The electoral campaign in 2014 helped to change the traditional way of understanding and doing politics. The success of *Podemos* has made a turning point, its actual politic model and its campaign strategy has established a precedent for every new party that wants to make its own way through the actual politic scene.The analysis of the activity of *Podemos* on Twitter during the previous two months of the 2014 European Elections has shown that there are new trends that new politicians should also implement in their online strategies in order to improve their relation with voters and with the aim to connect with the real interest of the new electorate. These new elements could be summarized in the following proposal:

- Be a *hacktivist party*, not just a political party. Twitter is not only a tool for political purposes; it is also a vehicle for helping citizens. A *hacktivist* candidate should communicate with other users and provide feedback to their followers. The strength of any 'hackivist party' relies on their promise of setting up the empowering people model in the postmodern society.
- Spread your ideas, products, messages or behaviors on micro-blogging platforms like viruses do.
- Create your online self through the interaction with users and community on the Internet.
- Provide first hand information. It is important to not let media gives information before you do. Twitter and other online platforms are decentralized flows of communication that favour forms of social organization in political contexts and acknowledge a multitude of perspectives and opinions.

- Provide online tools for people who want to participate in the political debate. Twitter is a good vehicle for promoting these tools.
- Create democratic spaces for encouraging political participation and civic engagement. As a Twitter user, it is important to use sociality in the public and political debate.
- Set up a party that works like a net of interaction –where all the users and actors give feedback-, with a non-hierarchal structure.
- Be honest, transparent and open-minded. Be like ordinary people are, because it is the only way to know what are the real needs and interests of citizens.
- Motivate the sense of belonging. Create an affect effect, emotions in politics; but never forget the importance of being at the service of what citizens need.

REFERENCES

Arquilla, J., & Ronfeldt, D. (2000). *Swarming and the future of conflict.* Retrieved from: http://goo.gl/uAOxr0

Barberá, P., & Rivero, G. (July, 2012). *¿Un tweet, un voto? Desigualdad de la discusión política de Twitter.* Symposium presented by at I Congreso Internacional en Comunicación Política y Estrategias de Campaña, Madrid, Spain.

Benjamin, W. (1999). The Storyteller - Reflections on the work of Nikolai Leskov. In H. Arendt (Ed.), *Illuminations* (pp. 83–107). London: Pimlico.

Bentham, J. (2001). Farming defended. In M. Quinn (Ed.), *Writings on the Poor Laws* (Vol. 1, pp. 276–290). Oxford, UK: Oxford University Press.

Brighenti, A. M. (2010). *Visibility in social theory and social research.* London: Palgrave Macmillan. doi:10.1057/9780230282056

Castells, M. (2004). *The network society: A cross-cultural perspective.* Northampton: Edward Elgar Pub. doi:10.4337/9781845421663

Castells, M. (2007). Communication, power and counter-power in the network society. *International Journal of Communication, 1*(1), 238–266.

Couldry, N. (2010). *Why voice matters: Culture and Politics after Neoliberalism.* London: Sage.

Dahlgren, P. (2013). *The Political Web: Media, Participation and Alternative Democracy.* Hampshire: Macmillan Publisher. doi:10.1057/9781137326386

Dalton, R. J. (2002). *Citizen politics. Public opinion and political parties in advanced industrial democracies.* New York: Chatham House Publishers.

De Ugarte, D. (2007). *El poder de las redes. Manual ilustrado para personas, colectivos y empresas abocados al ciberactivismo.* Retrieved from: http://goo.gl/evRfYO

Eisenberg, A. I. (1995). *Reconstructing political pluralism.* Albany, NY: State University of New York Press.

Ever, A., & Wintersberger, H. (1990). *Shifts in the Welfare Mix. Their impact on work, social services and Welfare policies.* Westview Press.

Feenstra, R. A., & Casero-Ripollés, A. (2014). Democracy in the Digital Communication Environment: A Typology Proposal of Political Monitoring Processes. *International Journal of Communication*, (8): 2448–2468.

Gladwell, M. (2006). *The Tipping Point: How little things can make a big difference.* Boston: Little, Brown and Company.

Golbeck, J., Grimes, J. M., & Rogers, A. (2010). Twitter use by the US Congress. *Journal of the American Society for Information Science and Technology*, *61*(8), 1612–1621. doi:10.1002/asi.21344

Gómez, L., & Viejo, M. (2014, May 30). Las redes de arrastre de Podemos. *El País*. Retrieved from: http://goo.gl/KzF8fJ

Hamilton, A., Madison, J., & Jay, J. (2012). *El federalista*. México: Fondo de Cultura Económica.

Haven, K. (2007). *Story proof: The science behind the starling power of story.* Westport: Libraries Unlimited.

Hibbing, J. R., & Theiss-Morse, E. (2002). *Stealth democracy: Americans' beliefs about how government should work.* Cambridge, UK: Cambridge University Press. doi:10.1017/CBO9780511613722

Himanen, P. (2001). *The hacker ethic and the spirit of the Information Age*. New York: Random House.

Howard, P. N. (2006). *New media campaigns and the managed citizen.* Cambridge, UK: Cambridge University Press.

Jackson, N. A., & Lilleker, D. G. (2009). Building an architecture of participation? Political parties and Web 2.0 in Britain. *Journal of Information Technology & Politics*, *6*(3-4), 232–250. doi:10.1080/19331680903028438

Jenkins, H. (2006). Convergence Culture: Where Old and New Media Collide. New York University Press.

Jordan, T., & Taylor, P. A. (2004). *Hacktivism and Cyberwars: Rebel with a cause?* London: Routledge.

Larsson, A., & Moe, H. (2011). *Who tweets? Tracking microblogging use in the 2010 Swedish election campaign.* Paper presented at the 19th European Conference on Information Systems (ECIS 2011), Helsinki, Finland

Lasswell, H. D. (1948). The structure and function of communications in society. In L. Bryson (Ed.), The communication of ideas (pp.37-51). New York: Harper & Row.

Lilleker, D. G., & Malagón, C. (2010). Levels of Interactivity in the 2007 French Presidential Candidates' websites. *European Journal of Communication*, *25*(1), 25–42. doi:10.1177/0267323109354231

López García, G. (2014). *Estrategias de movilización política de los partidos para un público desmotivado: Internet y las Elecciones Europeas de 2014*. Paper presented at the III Congreso Internacional de Comunicación Política y Estrategias de Campaña 2014 de la Asociación Latinoamericana de Investigadores en Campañas Electorales (ALICE), Madrid, Spain.

McLuhan, M., & Barrington, N. (1972). *Take today. The executive as dropout*. New York: Harcourt Brace Jovanovich.

Merino, M. (2001). *La participación ciudadana en la democracia*. México: Instituto Federal Electoral.

Presno Linera, M. A. (2012). ¿Nos representan o no? *Anales de la Cátedra Francisco Suárez*, (46), 93-109.

Putnam, R. D. (2001). *Bowling alone*. Simon and Schuster.

Ronfeldt, D., Arquilla, J., Fuller, G., & Fuller, M. (1998). *The Zapatista 'Social Netwar' in Mexico*. Santa Monica: RAND.

Salmon, C. (2010). *Storytelling. Bewitching the modern mind*. London: Verso.

Schudson, M. (1998). *The Good Citizen: A History of American Public Life*. The Free Press.

Servaes, J. (1996). Participatory communication research with new social movements: A realistic utopia. In J. Servaes, T. L. Jacobson & S. A. White (Eds.), Participatory communication for social change (pp.82-108). New Delhi: Sage.

Servaes, J., & Malikhao, P. (2005). Participatory communication: The new paradigm? In O. Hemer & T. Tufte (Eds.), Media & Global change. Rethinking communication for development (pp. 91-103). Buenos Aires: Consejo Lationamericano de Ciencias Sociales.

Stoker, G. (2006). *Why politics matters: making democracy work*. Basingstoke, UK: Palgrave Macmillan.

Subirats, J. (2002). The dilemmas of an inevitable relationship: democratic innovation and the information and communication technology. In J. Jordana (Ed.), *Governing Telecommunications and the New Information Society in Europe* (pp. 228–250). Edward Elgar Publishing. doi:10.4337/9781781950463.00021

Subirats, J. (2012). ¿Qué democracia tenemos? ¿Qué democracia queremos? *Anales de la Cátedra Francisco Suárez*, (46), 155-180

Surowiecki, J. (2005). *The Wisdom of Crowds: Why the Many Are Smarter Than the Few and How Collective Wisdom Shapes Business, Economies, Societies and Nations*. Anchor Books.

Tascón, M. & Quintana, Y. (2012). *Ciberactivismo. Las nuevas revoluciones de las multitudes conectadas*. Madrid: Los libros de la Catarata.

Toffler, A. (1980). *La tercera ola*. Bogotá: Plaza & Janes.

Van de Donk, W. (2000). Infocracy or infopolis? In J. Hoff, I. Horrocks, & P. Tops (Eds.), *Democratic Governance and New Technology* (pp. 138–154). London: Routledge.

Walzer, M. (1984). Liberalism and the Art of separation. *Political Theory*, *12*(3), 315–330. doi:10.1177/0090591784012003001

KEY TERMS AND DEFINITIONS

Civic Engagement: The virtue of participating in social and political issues. It expresses the motivation and the aptitude of citizens to take part in the political decision making process in order to improve the tenets of society and the democratic community.

Cyber-Activism: Also known as «digital activism», is a form of activism in which activists use online platforms and social media for organizing protests and political mobilizations. Cyber-activists use online technologies to share messages and ideas and to reach common goals.

Cyber-Democracy: The virtual arena where online users can share their knowledge and their interests. This kind of democracy keeps a non-hierarchal structure and people could participate in any political proposal or social aims; there is not a central authority that controls the power; power is distributed equally among citizens on the Internet.

Empowerment: An action that gives power to the people. The ability of social communities or individuals to take decisions and to start those decisions up.

Micro-Blogging: An online platform that allows share brief information, images and video links quickly.

Political Campaign: A political strategy that seeks to influence on voting behavior. Candidates explain their political proposals and promises in order to win votes.

Political Participation: An activity leaded by citizens in which society shows interest in participating in the political sphere in order to get political purposes and change social conditions.

Social Movement: A collective behavior that supports a social goal. Every protester has an individual explanation for their actions, but they join the multitude because they all share the same feeling of outrage and frustration and they are searching for opportunities of change.

ENDNOTES

1 One of the most powerful movements was *#donotvotethem* (*#nolosvotes*) that encouraged people to protest against the *Sinde Law* or *Sustainable Economy Law*. According to this regulation, web contents and web sites must be limited in order to protect the intellectual propriety. However, as *Wikileaks* disclosed later, this law was a political strategy orchestrated by intellectual propriety lobbies, the music industry and the government of North America.

2 The tag *Spanish indignados* is a catch-all term, an ambiguous expression, because it does not defines the ideological identity of activists of the *15M demonstration*. The movement brought different kind of people together and the term *indignados* (indignant or anger) does not give us so much information about why they decided to join the protest, their opinions about the political and social situation. However, we must understand this catch-all term as an expression of outrage against the political system. The book of Stéphane Hessel, *Time for Outrage*! was the inspiration for the *Spanish Indignados* and other international movements like the American *Occupy Wall Street* protest.

3 The Council of Spanish State published an official report where they recognize that the Spanish representation voting system is not a proportional method and that the best solution is to encourage the civic participation in political affairs (Consejo de Estado, 2009).

4 Information updated in October 2014. This date is available on the Twitter official website: https://about.twitter.com/company

5 *Podemos* usually uses the term "casta" (an approximate translation could be caste or political class) to name politicians who are too much time in the power and forgot their responsibilities as political representatives. This term keeps negative connotations because it also refers to politicians who believe that they belong to such a select elite that they do not care to become into a corrupt person.

Section 3

Strategic Communication of Political Actors on Micro-Blogging Outlets and its Ability to Empower Democracy

Chapter 7
Political Communication and Twitter in Greece:
Jumps on the Bandwagon or an Enhancement of the Political Dialogue?

Stamatis Poulakidakos
University of Athens, Greece

Anastasia Veneti
Bournemouth University, UK

ABSTRACT

Social media already serve as a new place for the development of a "public sphere", hence the exchange of argumentation on issues of public interest. More specifically, Twitter has been rather frequently used by politicians and parties in their attempt to establish a new way of communicating with the electorate. Drawing on the concepts of public sphere and propaganda and by conducting content and thematic analysis on the tweets of the two biggest Greek political parties, New Democracy (ND) and the Coalition of the Radical Left (SYRIZA), this chapter examines Twitter as a platform of information dissemination and dialogue. The aspiration of this study is to contribute to a growing volume of research that seeks to examine the potential of microblogging to animate political communication and to increase political participation.

INTRODUCTION

Internet has transformed the way political communication has been conducted in most parts of the world. Information Communication Technologies (ICTs) have provided politicians with a wealth of opportunities to campaign and communicate with their electorate in novel and creative ways. The use of internet for political communication purposes has been studied by many scholars including Hill & Hughes, 1998; Jones, 1998; Blumler & Kavanagh, 1999; Livingstone, 1999; McChesney, 2000; Norris, 2001; Mcnamara, 2008; Vaccari, 2008; Schweitzer, 2008; Lev-On, 2011; Lilleker & Jackson 2010, 2011;

DOI: 10.4018/978-1-4666-9879-6.ch007

Towner & Dulio, 2012). As any new communication practice, the use of ICTs in political communication has both triggered hopes of its potential democratic impact, as well as raised concerns for impending adversities. In particular, the studies dated prior to 2004 have designated the risks of such a development, pointing out the threats in social consistency and the debate over the digital divide (Hoffman & Novak, 1998; Wellman, 2000). Nonetheless, many of these studies were prior to the communication applications offered by Web 2.0. The advent of social media such as YouTube, Facebook and Twitter led to a modernisation of political communication (Bimber & Davis, 2003; Carpenter, 2010). Politicians around the world have increasingly sought to capitalize on the new opportunities offered by the Web 2.0 applications and they embarked on new campaigning strategies, new modes of fundraising, mobilization and information gathering.

Studies that supervened the 2004 US presidential election (Macnamara, 2008; Smith & Rainie, 2008; Chen & Walsh, 2009; Dahlgren, 2009), which according to Xenos & Moy (2007, p. 704) was "a critical turning point" in the use of social media, have been more optimistic. The innovative and extensive use of social media such as Facebook, YouTube, Twitter and MySpace in the 2008 and 2012 U.S. presidential campaigns has been the watershed event for modern political communication. In the 2004 U.S. presidential campaigns, Vermont Governor Howard Dean successfully used the new applications for fundraising and mobilization (Trippi, 2004; Carpenter, 2010; Veneti, 2014). The Obama campaign in 2008 U.S. presidential elections created its own social networking site, My.BarackObama.com (MyBO) and the McCain campaign followed some time later with McCainSpace. Both MyBO and McCainSpace allowed individuals to create their own profiles, interact with others, donate funds, join groups and arrange events (Towner, 2012; Chadwick, 2008; Carpenter, 2010). Several studies on the use of social media in politics suggest that the new technologies provide a fertile new ground for new forms of public participation, political mobilization and information diffusion (Graham, Broersma & Hazelhoff, 2013; Smith, 2009; Lilleker & Jackson, 2010, 2011). Despite the flourishing use of ICTs in political campaigning, there are still questions over their substantial capabilities to empower democracy by fostering greater participation, encouraging political conversation and improving interactive information-sharing (Coleman, 2001; Jackson, 2007). As such, there is a pertinent need for more studies to examine if and how the new media have a democratic impact.

This chapter contributes to a growing volume of research that seeks to examine the potential of microblogging to animate political communication, increase political participation and provide a new repertoire of collective action (Castells, 2007, p. 255; Chadwick, 2008; Larsson & Moe, 2011; Jackson & Lilleker, 2011; Adi, Erickson & Lilleker, 2014). Twitter has been heralded as a new tool of online campaigning and electorate engagement. In Greece, during the last two years, Twitter has been rather frequently used by party members and press offices of the most significant political parties, in order to establish a new way of communicating with the electorate (Burgess & Bruns, 2012; Hutchins, 2011; Neuhaus & Webmoor, 2012; Ovadia, 2009, Heinrich, 2012; Hermida, Fletcher, Korell, & Logan, 2012; Small, 2011). In Greece, mainstream media are considered unreliable due to vested interests between the media moguls and politicians (Veneti & Karadimitriou, 2013), whilst at the same time there is a growing number of internet users which increases exponentially (OECD, 2015; "Greece", 2015). Throughout 2014, there were 418.700 active Twitter users in Greece – 257.700 more than 2012- with 6 tweets per second (Trending.gr, 2015). Moreover, similar statistics showed that Greek Twitter users' attention was primarily on socio-political issues such as #skouries, #occupyert, #ertopen, #killahp etc. Therefore, it seems reasonable to assume that Twitter provides Greek politicians with a novel digital tool that could go beyond traditional modes of communication and look more appealing to the electorate.

The Greek economic crisis, part of the on-going European debt crisis, has been amongst other things the result of a malfunctioning public sector, corruption, tax evasion and overly high structural deficits and debt-to-GDP levels on public accounts (Triandafyllidou, Gropas, & Kouki, 2013) for almost three decades. In May 2010, the Greek government signed the bailout treaty [Memorandum of Understanding (MoU)] with the "troika", i.e. the European Union, the International Monetary Fund and the European Central Bank (Poulakidakos, 2014; Varoufakis, 2014). In simple terms, this treaty offered guaranteed loans to Greece, but in return Greece should practice severe economic policies - among which austerity measures and deep structural reforms - so as to diminish the country's fiscal debt. As a result of the crisis and the ensuing economic policies, the political realm in Greece has undergone significant transformations (Triandafyllidou et al., 2013). The two big political parties (PASOK, social-democratic party, and New Democracy, conservative right wing party), which used to gain the elections for a period of more than 30 years (since 1974), have both suffered significant losses and new political parties have emerged. Within this political context, the radical left wing party (SYRIZA) has dramatically increased its political power, from 4.6% of the electoral body in the 2009 general elections, to almost 27% in 2012, when it became the major opposition party. In January 2015, SYRIZA was the winner of the general elections, becoming the first ever left- wing party to win general elections in Greece. From the former dominant political parties, only New Democracy managed to 'survive' politically, as PASOK barely entered the parliament. As a result of the political climate, there are two main elements that characterize contemporary Greek politics:

1. During the last four years, public discourse in Greece has focused on the economic crisis, its causes and the ways to confront it. Despite the intense interest of politicians, journalists and citizens, the quantitative generalization of public discussions has not contributed to a qualitative enhancement of public discourse on vital issues of public interest.
2. Another feature is the intensity of the political debate between the newly established left political power of SYRIZA and the traditional right-wing New Democracy. This intensity is being augmented both by the crisis context and the ideological distance of these parties (left vs. right).

These two characteristics along with the predominance of a sentimental approach in the political discourse (Poulakidakos, 2014; Poulakidakos & Veneti, forthcoming) have resulted in the creation of a state of tension and polarization in the Greek society or as Doxiadis (2013) puts it, they have created a polarized public sphere.

In this chapter, we examine Twitter as a platform of information dissemination and dialogue by conducting content and thematic analysis on the tweets of the two biggest Greek political parties, New Democracy (ND) and the Coalition of the Radical Left (SYRIZA) over a period of one month before the 2014 European elections. Elaborating on the concepts of public sphere and propaganda, we seek to examine whether the political messages 'broadcast' in Twitter contribute in a positive way to the public discussion on issues of public interest. We also examine whether these messages promote the exchange of rational argumentation instead of the sentimental approach on the crisis that conquers other- unilateral- media content; further to this, we discuss whether Twitter can be conceived as a new immaterial public space wherein prolific political discussions could possibly be generated.

TWITTER AND POLITICS

Confronted with declining citizen interest and participation along with a burgeoning distrust of politicians (Rosanvallon, 2008; Coleman & Blumler, 2009; Dahlgren, 2009), political parties in Western democracies have turned into the potentials of the new media in order to revive their relationship with the citizens. This relationship in free fall has also been affected by the citizen's scepticism towards the mainstream media (Ladd, 2012; Kamens, 2012). As both Habermas (2006, pp.421-2) and Dahlgren (2009) argued, the lack of opportunities for citizens' engagement in the political dialogue, the infotainment approach to political discussions and the exposure of the few selected media – favourite 'voices' contributed to the alienation of citizens from politics. Taking these into consideration, both citizens and politicians are increasingly bypassing the traditional modes of political communication and as Carpenter (2010, p. 221) elucidates, they "are utilizing the blogosphere as a way to participate and engage with others."

Social media like Facebook and Twitter increasingly form part of everyday communication, social coordination and news consumption for citizens worldwide (Burgess & Bruns, 2012, p.384). Facebook and Twitter enable users to hook up with others in virtually any connected spot on earth. Within the interactive spheres of such networks, links are shared, information distributed and news are commented on a scale not seen before (Heinrich, 2012, p. 2; Hermida et al. 2012, p. 2). Internet technologies, collectively described as Web 2.0, have facilitated the involvement of audiences in the observation, selection, filtering, distribution and interpretation of events (Hermida et al., 2012, p. 2). Participation in these environments is becoming increasingly important as a means of communicating directly to the public in a professional capacity, especially during times of heightened political activity like elections (Burgess & Bruns, 2012, p. 384).

Twitter is one of a range of new social media technologies that allow for the online and instant dissemination of short fragments of data from a variety of official and unofficial sources (Hermida, 2010, p.297). Established in 2006 (Neuhaus & Webmoor, 2012, p. 48), twitter is a microblogging site (Hutchins, 2011, p. 238), which allows its members to publish direct messages of up to 140 characters (Ovadia, 2009, p. 202). Interest in politicians' use of Twitter took off when Barack Obama and John Edwards used it to let their supporters know where they were and of upcoming events during the Democratic Party primaries in the United States (Jackson & Lilleker, 2011, p.88). Twitter-involvement of political parties, based on the number of tweets, shows that contemporary parties are more likely to use Twitter extensively (Verweij, 2012, p. 10), raising the question of whether politicians feel that Twitter is a bandwagon they need to jump on. Alternatively, they might view Twitter as a strategic communication channel, a way of reaching key audiences efficiently and effectively (Jackson & Lilleker, 2011, p.86).

In particular, twitter has become a digital space for the conduct of public discussions about issues of common interest (Juris, 2012). Twitter's role as a platform which supports the ad hoc formation of large online publics debating such topics is aided in part by its underlying structure: the #hashtag system, in particular, makes it possible for users to follow and contribute to such public debates easily even if they have no established connections with (or even knowledge of) other participating users (Ovadia, 2009). Additionally, participants are able to direct public messages in Twitter terms, an @reply*to any user whom they encounter during these debates, again without needing to formally "follow" or "friend" the recipient first. This positions Twitter as a site for the potentially rapid emergence of politically engaged publics that may include ordinary citizens, political actors and professional journalists (Burgess & Bruns, 2012, pp. 384-5; Grant et al., 2010, p. 580).

Several political and communication scholars have examined this new form of political communication (Lassen & Brown, 2011; Burgess & Bruns, 2012; Larsson & Moe, 2011; Small, 2011, Vergeer, Hermans & Sams, 2011; Graham, Jackson & Broersma, 2014; Adi, Erickson & Lilleker, 2014). What these studies denote is that there is not a unanimous way in which we can conceive the function and the effectiveness of twitter in the political field. The richness of the findings of these researches sheds light into the disparities that exists across countries with regard to the use of twitter by the politicians, the citizens' engagement in different socio-cultural contexts and the potential influence that the use of twitter may have in the electoral outcome.

TWITTER: AN IMMATERIAL PUBLIC SPACE FOR POLITICAL DIALOGUE

Since the mid-1990s, we identify growing discussions (Kahn & Kellner, 2005; Castells, 2009) on how the new media affect politics and the degree of the impact these might have on participatory democracy. For the scope of this study, we examine Twitter as a possible immaterial public space wherein fruitful political discussions could possibly be generated and citizens' engagement in political action may also be enhanced (Juris, 2012; Grant et al., 2010; Kirk & Schill, 2011). In order to contextualize our analysis of Twitter in political communication, we draw theoretically on the idea of public sphere. However, since the concept of public sphere is a very complex term which has been extensively used in various ways (Splichal, 2006; Marx Ferree et al., 2002), this research does not seek to offer an exhaustive review of this theoretical construct, but rather aims to focus on certain aspects of this theoretical framework, and its relevant debates, that best serve the purposes of this study.

Following Habermas' (1989) definition, in very generic terms, public sphere is a space where citizens come together and engage in a series of rational-critical debates. The 'bourgeois public sphere' (17th century onwards) refers to a kind of forum which is situated between the private sphere (economy and family) and the sphere of the public authorities (the state and the judiciary). Habermas' definition of the public sphere has undergone revisions and has been criticized on the ground that it represents a rather utopian and imaginative perception of the public dialogue procedure. Moreover, later studies (Murdock, 1992; Meyrowitz, 1985; Garnham, 2003) on the intersection between the public sphere and mass media highlighted the means and methods of manipulation of the public and its consequences. The emergence of the digital, interactive media and more specifically social media, like Twitter, introduced discussions regarding their ability to form a digital public sphere. Of course, most kinds of ICTs are influenced by economic interests and as Murdock (1993, p. 534) argues "They are, therefore, more usually viewed not as technologies of control or of freedom, but as the site of continual struggles over interpretation and use. At the heart of these struggles, lies the shifting boundary between the public and the private spheres. (...).". Nonetheless, the importance of Habermas's initial description of the public sphere lies in the definition of the ideal public sphere, which societies should approach, and not to his attempt of realistically describing an existing situation.

Based on the original concept of the public sphere (as introduced by Habermas), there are two elements which are important to our analysis of Twitter: firstly, (a) the public sphere entails a 'forum' which is accessible to as many people as possible (providing an opportunity for participatory communication), and secondly, (b) the debates taking place should be characterized by rational argumentation. The philosopher Immanuel Kant (1795/1983) also mentioned public sphere as the space for "public use of reason" (referring here to mutual respect among the interlocutors, ability to negotiate and other principles of reasonable and just public debate). Furthermore, drawing on the work of Kirk & Schill's (2011) about the new communication technologies as a digital agora, this study further argues that Twitter incorporates and synthesizes the essential elements which could possibly constitute this online application as a digital public sphere. Kirk & Schill (2011, p. 326) examine the digital agora created by citizen participation and in this sense "the agora resulted in a discursive space where citizens found voice, directly questioned candidates, and engaged each other in political discussions." Up to date, the interactive nature of Twitter has triggered intense debates about whether its employment enhances or not political dialogue and political participation. Nevertheless, one should also take into account the substantial differences between participation and interaction as the one does not necessarily guarantees the other (Carpentier, 2012).

Twitter's potential has been eulogized by many scholars. Kennedy (2008) argues Twitter has become a powerful tool for campaign reporting and mobilizing and Davis (2010) that it is a significant platform for the diffusion of news and information. Coleman and Blumler (2009, p. 80) argued that social media could offer a more intimate and conversational relationship between politicians and citizens, and Graham, Broersma and Hazelhoffas (2013) coined the term 'connected representation' explaining that Twitter make it possible for representation to be rooted in lasting connections between citizens and politicians and it also creates a sense of proximity, visibility and continuity. Praising the dynamic of Twitter, Carpenter (2010, p.222) claims that "Twitter has proven to be amazingly adept at two things: politically engaging the average citizen and empowering its users to participate as citizen journalists. [...]Twitter is a one-to-one and one-to many communications powerhouse available to anyone with a cell phone or computer. It is a link to real-time constituent consciousness, and it is marketed as a technology that directly taps into this collective consciousness." Twitter has the potential to contribute to political conversation. First, followers are able to respond to others. This process is known as @replies. Honeycutt & Herring (2009) found that around 30 per cent of tweets were @replies. Another aspect of Twitter that is considered interactive is retweeting. Retweets are the re-posting of the tweets of another sender, similar to e-mail forwarding, therefore a way of maximizing the reach of a certain message. In addition, a retweet is a type of conversation: While retweeting can simply be seen as the act of copying and rebroadcasting, the practice contributes to a conversational ecology in which conversations are composed of a public interplay of voices that give rise to an emotional sense of shared conversational context (Small, 2011, p. 878). Moreover, retweeting particular messages- such as party self – promotional tweets- could also be seen as a persuasion or propaganda activity employed in order to influence people in a unilateral way.

Nonetheless, extensive literature identifies that there is considerable hesitation with regard to the potential of Twitter to foster the political dialogue while several scholars are rather coy regarding the over appraisal surrounding Twitter as a new tool of political communication. Magolis & Resnick (2000), having examined the effects of the Internet on American politics, they argued that the American political system tends to normalize political activity, and thus we witness new media in which old patterns of political behavior and information flows are played out. To further illustrate this case, Larsson & Moe (2011) having examined Twitter users in the 2010 Swedish election campaign stated that " our findings indicate that Twitter falls somewhat short of the expectations held by those most optimistic on behalf of the democratic and disruptive potential of new web tools." (p. 742). In the same line, Golbeck, Grimes, and Rogers (2010, p. 1620) coined the term 'vehicles for self-promotion' to label the tweets they examined from Members of the US Congress. The term denotes a use of Twitter which resembles more a one-way, top-down communication rather than a citizen engaging function. Mcnamara & Kenning's (2011) analysis of Australian politicians' use of Twitter further supports Golbeck et al. (2010) findings. Mcnamara & Kenning (2011) found that, apart from a few exceptions, politicians used social media as a one-way transmission of political messages, rather than citizen engagement indicating that much of "the social media content was comprised of election slogans, attacking opponents, and political rhetoric – much of it of a banal nature" (p. 9). Moreover, another important observation of their research is the correlation between "followers" and "following" as an indicator of reciprocal interest and listening. Mcnamara & Kenning (2011, pp. 9-10) argue that there is a vast discrepancy between followers and following for most politicians on Twitter; giving the example of the Australian Opposition Leader Tony Abbott who had 19,083 followers in the week before the election, but was following just 20 other Twitter users. Tumasjan, Sprenger, Sandner, and Welpe. (2010, p. 4) who studied tweets related to the 2009 German federal election claimed that 'while Twitter is used as a forum for political deliberation, this forum is dominated by a small number of heavy users'.

INFORMATION, PROPAGANDA AND POLITICS

Political parties have found in the new media- Twitter among them- new ways of managing and disseminating political views and information. Information management constitutes a strategy followed by political mechanisms, in order to enhance and maintain their cohesion, as well as to reproduce their power structures. "The control of information constitutes an effort of utmost importance for political powers in order to manage public opinion and maintain public control" (Tumber, 1993). Nowadays, a major part of information is actually misinformation, due to various interests -especially political powers and financially strong factors- that have created and formed its presentation (Webster, 2006, p. 162). Certain communication systems[1] transmit carefully managed information in order to influence public opinion. Such actions, basically driven by the vested interests between mainstream media and politicians, may well lead to propaganda (Lippmann, 1927; Jackall, 1995; Edelstein, 1997; Webster, 2006, p.168).

Information revolution has led to a plethora of available information for citizens (Pratkanis & Aronson, 2001; Taylor, 2004). The persuasive power of the broadcasted information lies on: a. the sophistocated presentation of arguments (persuasion), and b. the use of symbols and techniques causing sentimental reactions (such as the one-sided presentation of evidence, the selective presentation of the aspects of a certain issue, even with lies, characteristics that lead to the domain of propaganda). In order to discriminate propaganda from persuasion, we need to study them as part of the systems (e.g. institutions, organizations, communication) to which they belong, rather than treat them as decontextualized phenomena (Marková, 2008, p. 49). For a most possible precise definition of propaganda, we locate it in the field of political discourse and political communication and distinct it from persuasion. Even though propaganda and persuasion may well co-exist (Marková, 2008), the latter is an effort of dissemination of views and opinions on behalf of the communicator, through interaction and satisfaction of the intentions of both the pursuer and the pursuee (Jowett & O'Donnell, 1995; Barker, 2002). On the contrary, propaganda makes (rather intense) use of the sentimental factor and seeks to persuade in order to serve the aims of the propagandist by disseminating a certain ideology or doctrine (Jowett & O'Donnell, 1995; Taylor, 2004, Poulakidakos & Armenakis, 2014; Marková, 2008).

Propaganda is being exercised in a more intense way during periods of crisis (Lehmann, 2003; Thussu & Freedman, 2003, p. 235). During such periods, a wide use of propaganda methods takes place (one-sided presentation of events, mainly sentimental argumentation, generalizations) so as to influence the audiences in favor of certain interests. Given the fact that political elites form the developments during crisis periods, they need propaganda more than any other occasion, as a means of legalizing their decisions and practices before citizens. Main target of the political elites and the mainstream Media is not to inform wide publics on facts, but to mobilize their audiences in order to support specific policies (Thussu & Freedman, 2003), trying to legalize those policies in the eyes of the citizens (Allan & Zelizer, 2004). In addition, propaganda is a phenomenon adaptive to different social contexts. Hence, it is adaptive to the media it utilizes, trying to take advantage of their structure and operational culture, so as to serve its purposes (Miotto, 1953; Ellul, 1973; Hiotis, 1986).

Propaganda is a part of contemporary reality. It constitutes a rational, mainly political, communication process, exercised through the dissemination of information via the Media (Poulakidakos 2014, Poulakidakos & Armenakis, 2014). It can actually be considered as a foundation element of the "construction" of social, political and financial "realities" and of the exercise of influence -in favor of the propagandist- in a unilateral way to the views, opinions and behaviors of the subjects that act within these realities (Doxiadis, 2013). Propagandistic methods which have been implemented throughout the centuries are characterized by a Manichean rationale for viewing the world. Thus propaganda divides the world in "good" and "bad" people, in "friends" and "enemies", in "us" and "them", in "solutions" and "dead ends", in "progress" and "regressiveness". In this sense, propaganda seeks to influence people in a unilateral way (Poulakidakos, 2014). The more public opinion constitutes a factor that influences politics, including the race of political parties to gain public acceptance and support, the more intense will be the need for persuasion of the civilians in terms of the acceptance of political decisions or even already implemented policies (Corner, 2007).

According to Snow (2002, p.40), basic propaganda characteristics are its "intentional communication practice, planned to influence the behavior of the target audience and the dissemination of unilateral information. Propaganda techniques include the selective publication of evidence or partly presented facts; they stress out threats or dangers; they "demonize" the enemy and interpret the facts in very specific ways; they take advantage of methods and arguments aiming at both the rationale and the sentiments of the receivers (Theodorakopoulos, 2006). Among the variety of propagandistic methods, we underline some basic characteristics (Corner, 2007, pp. 674-675):

1. Dissemination of specific- usually unilateral- information.
2. The use of exaggeration aiming at the distortion of either positive or negative (for the propagandist) information.
3. The direct or indirect evocation to fear, hope or desire (evocation to feelings).
4. The use of rhetoric frames so as to promote generic notions (e.g. trust, discreetness) and to organize the meaning and values in ways beyond rational argumentation

RESEARCH QUESTIONS

To understand how social media are being used in political communication in a contemporary context, two types of research questions were developed for this study, one relating to quantitative factors (how many), and one relating to qualitative factors (in what way). Based on the above mentioned theoretical framework our main research questions are:

RQ1: Do the tweets of New Democracy (conservative party) and SYRIZA (left wing party) promote the public dialogue within Twitter on issues of public interest?
RQ2: Do the tweets of the two Greek political parties, New Democracy and SYRIZA, contain propagandistic characteristics?

These two main research questions are further analyzed in several quantitative and qualitative additional research questions. The quantitative questions seek to examine how many retweets has a specific tweet and how many users have characterized it as a favorite. The qualitative research questions, deal with the existence of propagandistic elements in the tweets, such as the use of specific linguistic schemata (metaphors, transfers), the demonization of the political rival, the appeal to fear or to hope, the existence or not of logical argumentation and the different thematics that the tweets focus on.

METHODOLOGY

The current research is conducted through the combined use of quantitative content analysis and thematic analysis, since our analysis focuses on both quantitative and qualitative aspects of the political discourse within Twitter. Content analysis transforms content of quantitative and qualitative nature into a form of data with either qualitative or quantitative form. It can be briefly defined as the systematic, based on scientific criteria, quantitative or qualitative analysis of the characteristics of various messages (Berelson, 1952; Kiriazi, 2001; Neuendorf, 2002, p. 1). It constitutes a systematic, reproducible technique of transforming the words of a text[2] into fewer categories of meaning, based on specific codification rules (Stemler, 2001; Miller & Brewer, 2003), allowing the researchers to examine big amounts of data through a systematic methodology (Poulakidakos, 2014).

The primary target of content analysis is the systematic research of the content of the unit of analysis (text, image, news item, advertisement, web page etc.). Thus, the content is being examined in a holistic way and the categories used to encode the text are clearly defined, so as to enable the repetition and control of the whole procedure. Researches making use of content analysis focus on the main thematics of a text, their comparative meaning, the "space" and time dedicated to these thematics and other content characteristics that respond to the main research question and the research hypotheses (Berelson, 1971). Quantitative content analysis is conducted with the use of a coding protocol[3] and aims at the production of quantitative data out of a specific sample. The development of the coding frame was the result of a combined approach to developing an organizing system for the data.

Thematic analysis is a method for identifying, analyzing, and reporting patterns (themes) within data. It minimally organizes and describes a data set in detail (Aguinaldo, 2012; Ponnam & Dawra, 2013). However, it frequently goes further than this by interpreting various aspects of the research topic (Braun & Clarke, 2006). It can be used within different theoretical frameworks, and can be used to do different things within them. Thematic analysis can be an essentialist or realist method, which reports experiences, meanings and the reality of participants (Attard & Coulson, 2012, p. 501; Ponnam & Dawra, 2013, p. 30), or, it can be a constructionist method, which examines the ways in which events, realities, meanings, experiences and so on are the effects of a range of discourses operating within society (Braun & Clarke, 2006).

The most important element in the conduction of thematic analysis is the theme. A theme captures something important about the data in relation to the research question, and represents some level of patterned response or meaning within the data set (Braun & Clarke, 2006). The 'keyness' of a theme is not necessarily dependent on quantifiable measures, but rather on whether it captures something important in relation to the overall research question (Braun & Clarke, 2006, p. 82). The goal of thematic analysis is simply to paraphrase and summarize the dataset as a whole or in part in relation to particular research questions. Analysis typically involves steps that a) identify the content of the data, b) reduce redundancy, and c) group data into representative categories that articulate or describe a particular social phenomenon (Aguinaldo, 2012, p. 768; Sanderson, 2013, p. 494). The final themes for analysis emerge through a systematic process of studying, coding and analyzing the research data in accordance to the theoretical background supporting the research (Braun & Clarke, 2006; Aguinaldo, 2012, p. 768; Attard & Coulson, 2012; McParland & Whyte, 2008, p. 613). A thematic analysis approach can be extended at the latent level of a text going beyond the semantic content of the data, and starting to identifying or examining the underlying ideas, assumptions, conceptualizations and ideologies that are theorized as shaping or informing the semantic content of the data (Braun & Clarke, 2006, p. 84), Thus, for latent thematic analysis, the development of the themes themselves involves interpretative work, and the analysis that is produced is not just description, but is in- depth and already theorized (Braun & Clarke, 2006, p. 84).

The main research questions will be answered through the use of quantitative content analysis and qualitative thematic analysis on the tweets of specific twitter accounts administered by the parties of New Democracy (governing party at the time of the research, ND) and SYRIZA (Coalition of the Radical Left, major opposition party at the time of the research) for the pre-electoral period of the 2014 European and Municipal elections in Greece, namely from April 24th to May 24th 2014 (N= 437). With the complementary use of these two methods, we seek to quantify the characteristics of the examined tweets and embed them at the same time into the political context of the pre-electoral period. The accounts we examined are: @PrimeministerGR and @statheramprosta of ND, and @a.tsipras of SYRIZA. Our coding unit is the tweet (see Appendix 1). The elaboration of the quantitative results was conducted with the use of SPSS 22.0. The statistic tests used for testing the statistical significance of the results are chi-square and Fisher's exact tests (Gnardellis, 2003; Siomkos & Vasilakopoulou, 2005). The test used to measure the inter-coder reliability is the North, Holsti, Zaninovich and Zinnes test (North et al., 1963).[4]

FINDINGS AND DISCUSSION

In order to make clear how the different methodological approaches, employed here, have contributed to this scholarship, our findings are presented as follows: firstly, we present the quantitative data produced by the content analysis. In this section, findings mainly refer to the nature of the tweets, a numerical depiction of the activity in Twitter (tweets and retweets) as well as a presentation of the various propagandistic characteristics that were found in the political discourse that was developed in Twitter. Secondly, we present the data produced from the thematic analysis. In this section, the focus lies on the qualitative dimension of the political discourse.

Online Activity (Retweets and Favorites) and the Nature of Political Tweets

Starting with the quantitative research questions, our results demonstrated a rather limited dissemination of the political messages of the tweets of the two contemporary biggest parties (based on the electoral results of the national elections 2012 and 2015) in Greece. Given that the accounts of both parties have several thousands of followers (34.6k for @a.tsipras (the party leader of SYRIZA) and 81k for the two accounts administered to the political party of New Democracy, @PrimeministerGR and @statheramprosta) the retweets and favorites of the published tweets appear extremely low. Contrary to what Kirk and Schill (2011, p. 326) describe in their study of the 2008 US presidential elections, Twitter in Greece was not transformed into a participatory space. American citizens used the new communication technologies to receive messages and information and most importantly they were engaged both with the candidates and with each other in discussions about their nation's future (Kirk & Schill, 2011). The low retweet rate in the Greek case is an indication that an exploitation of the new platform for civic engagement and further dissemination of political messages by the citizens/followers was not so successful, especially compared to other occasions, such as the Greek indignants, where the retweeting rate appeared to be much higher (Theocharis, Lowe, van Deth, & Garcia-Albacete, 2015, p. 215). This implies that low retweeting is not necessarily connected to a generic "Greek culture" of Twitter use, but rather connected to the reasons and the aim of the use.

According to Figure 1, the average number of retweets for New Democracy is 1,76 per tweet and for SYRIZA 10,06. The same very low numbers, compared to the total number of followers of these accounts, appear in the favorites category too, i.e. the cases in which a follower marks a specific tweet as favorite. The average favorite bookmarks per tweet is 2,76 for the two New Democracy accounts and 8,84 for the account of SYRIZA's leader Alexis Tsipras. These numbers demonstrate a lack of 'secondary', user generated, dissemination- conducted by the followers- of the political messages of the two parties.

A first parameter to be examined is to whom each tweet refers. As shown in Figure 2, New Democracy's tweets focus exclusively on its own actions or political views, while SYRIZA's tweets refer primarily to its own actions and political views (48,9%), secondarily to opposing parties (31,7%) and thirdly to the people- voters (15,6%). These findings can partly be explained by the fact that ND –at that time, the governmental party- was primarily interested in highlighting the governmental achievements, whilst SYRIZA, being the opposition party, wished firstly, to persuade the electorate of its own political views and secondly, to underline the inability of the government.

Figure 1. Re-tweets and favorites average per tweet, per party (t-test p. value= .000)

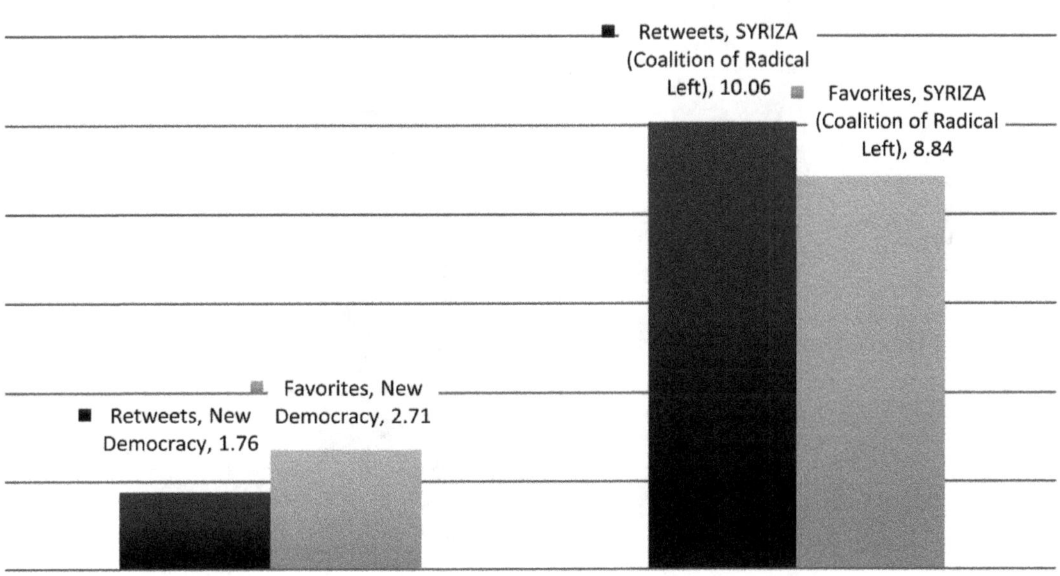

In addition, the tweets of the two parties seem to differ significantly in terms of their either positive or negative character. According to Figure 3, New Democracy tweets mostly in a positive way (73,8%), since it presents its own views, whereas SYRIZA tweets in all different ways in almost balanced percentages (positive, negative and neutral), since a significant part of its communication strategy in Twitter seems to be the negative reference to its political rivals.

The difference of the Twitter political discourse between New Democracy and SYRIZA is visible in the case of the debating/downgrading of political rivals as well. According to Figure 4, only SYRIZA appears to adopt a negative rhetoric towards its political rivals in about one third of its tweets.

Figures 2, 3 and 4 depict quite clearly the diachronically established difference in the political discourse between governing parties and opposing parties. Governing parties seek primarily to promote their own achievements, using a mostly "positive" rhetoric focused on their own political views and practices, while their opponents' rhetoric seeks to undermine the governing incumbents, since the institutional roles of political parties define the formation of their political discourse as well (Van Dijk, 2001).

Propagandistic Characteristics of Tweets

Another characteristic of propaganda in discourse is the use of linguistic schemas, such as transfers and metaphors,[5] which are used to promote generic notions (e.g. trust, mistrust, discreetness) and to organize the meaning and values in ways beyond rational argumentation (Theodorakopoulos, 2006; Corner, 2007). According to Figure 5, SYRIZA appears to use such linguistic methods in the majority of its tweets (51,1%), whereas New Democracy relies on such linguistic schemas in the 36,1% of its tweets.

Figure 2. Whom do the tweets refer to? (per party) (chi square p. value= .000)

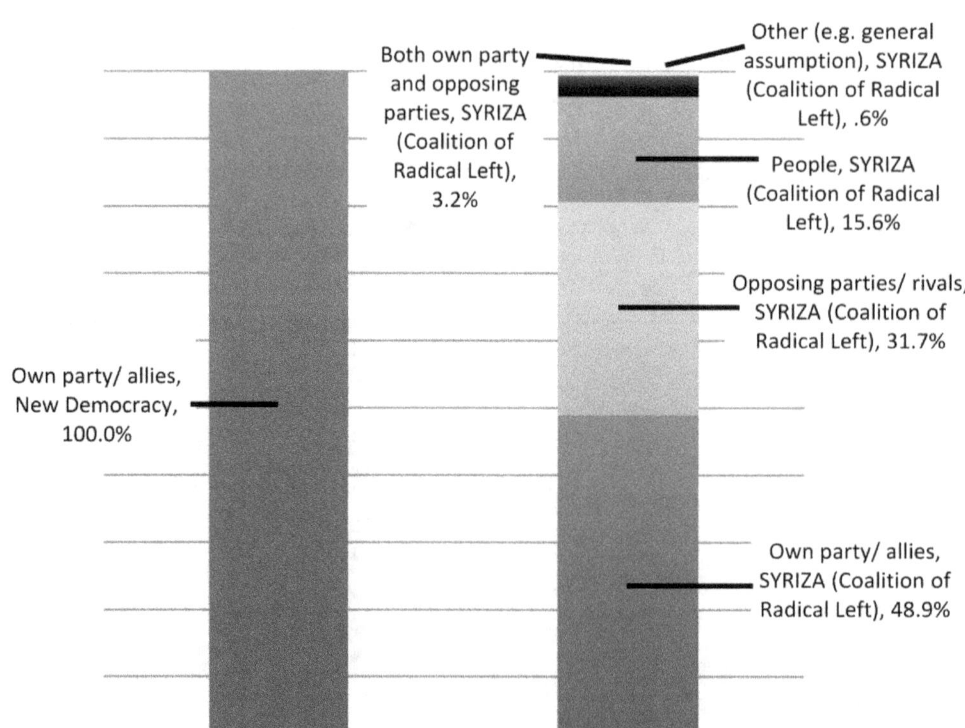

Figure 3. Positive or negative character of the tweet per party (chi- square p. value= .000)

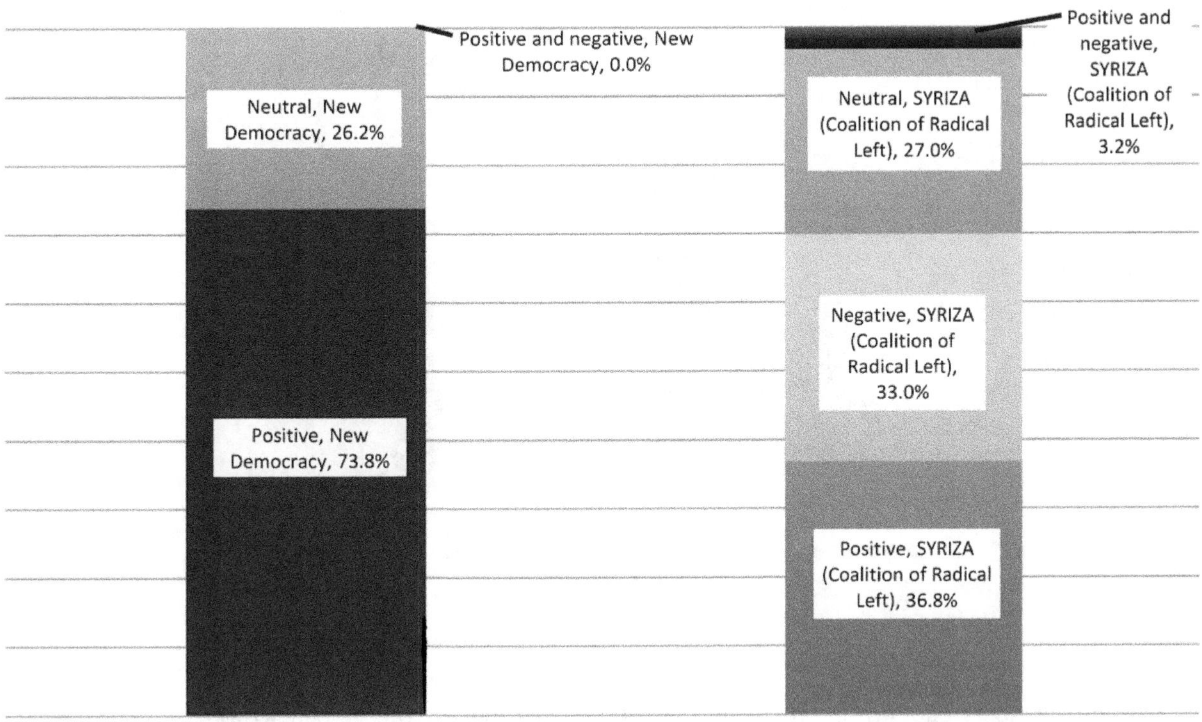

Figure 4. Does the tweet try to debate/"downgrade" political rivals? (per party) (Fischer's exact test p. value= .000)

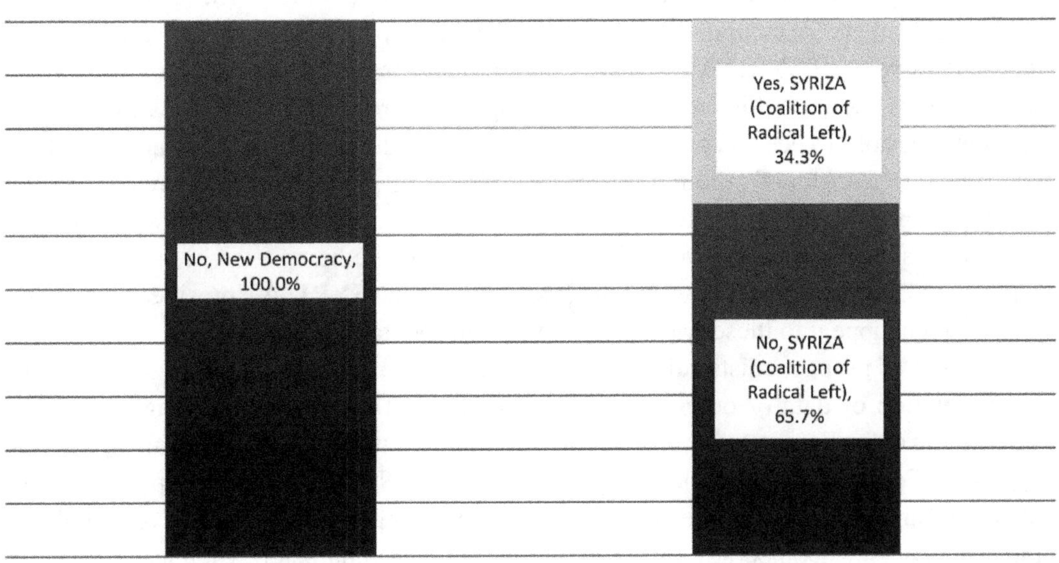

Figure 5. Use of transfers and metaphors per party (chi- square p. value= .005)

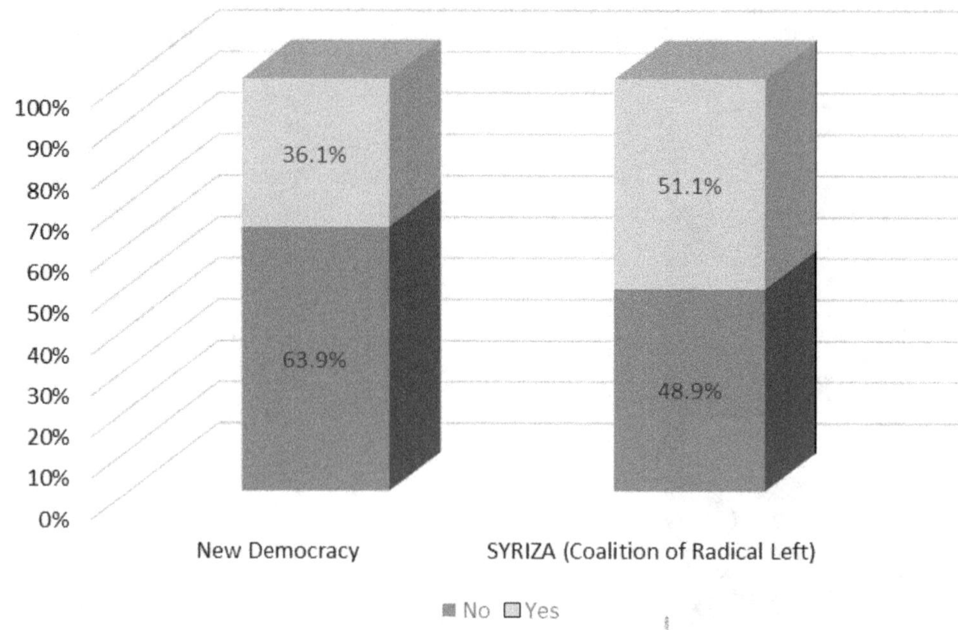

Among the most frequently deployed propagandistic methods are the "appeal to hope" and the "appeal to fear/threat",[6] aiming at the evocation to the feelings of the voters (Snow 2002, Corner, 2007), usually in terms of a better or worse/dystopic future. On one hand, both parties seem to make use of "hope" in quite similar percentages (ND 30,3%, SYRIZA 26%) (see Figure 6). Though these percentages do not appear to be very high, the "appeal to hope" can still be traced in a rather significant percentage of the total amount of the tweets we examined. On the other hand, "appeal to fear/threat" can be traced almost exclusively in the tweets of SYRIZA (12,1%). This fact reflects the positive rhetoric followed by New Democracy, since as shown in Figure 3, the governing party prefers to promote its own work and the positive perspectives of Greece, according to its own argumentation. On the contrary, SYRIZA makes use of the "appeal to fear/threat", though in significantly lower percentage compared to the "appeal to hope", since among its aims was the downgrading of the government. An overview of the total use of "hope" and "fear" shows that these two basic sentiments alone are being used in more than 30% of the tweets of the New Democracy accounts and in almost 40% of the SYRIZA's presidential tweets, implying a rather frequent appeal to these two fundamental sentimental states.

Another aspect of propagandistic discourse is the use of unilateral rational argumentation, by the selective presentation of data or other rational arguments on behalf of the propagandist.[7] Similar to previous research findings concerning the use of "rational" argumentation on behalf of governing and opposing parties (Poulakidakos, 2014), the governing party of New Democracy appears to make use of unilateral rational arguments in a far greater percentage than their political opponents of SYRIZA. Almost 30% of the tweets of New Democracy appear to have a "rational" character, whereas a mere 2,5% of the tweets of SYRIZA can be characterized as rational. In that way the major opposition party appears to rely heavily on the sentimental discourse, a result that coincides with previous empirical findings on the

Figure 6. "Appeal to hope" and "appeal to fear/threats" per party [Fischer's exact test p. values= .402 (hope) & .000 (fear/threats)]

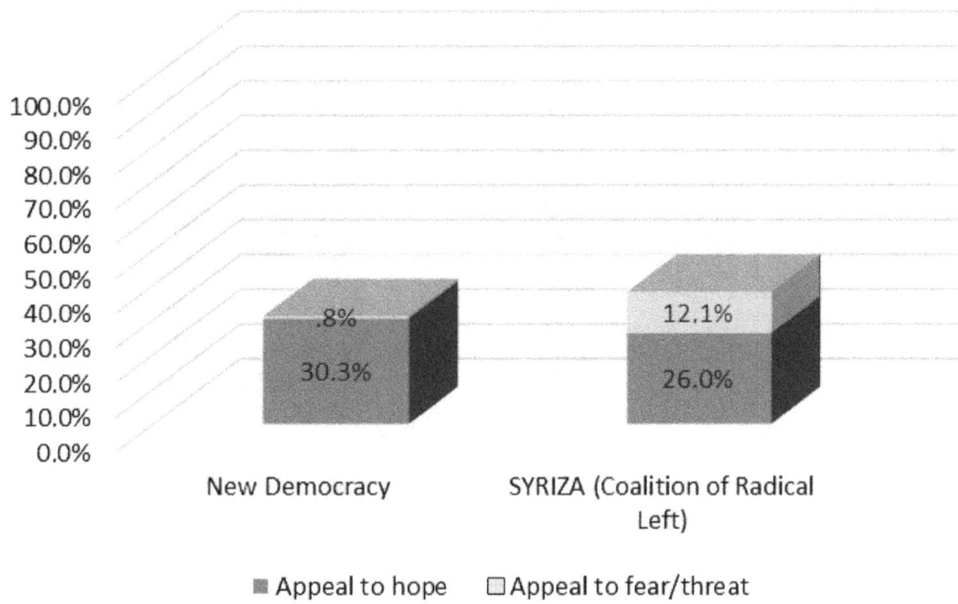

political discourse of the leftist parties in Greece (Poulakidakos, 2014) (see Figure 7). It is important to note that the total amount of tweets of both parties are characterized by a unilateral rationale, since both rivals try to either promote their own party's "advantages", or criticize the opponents' disadvantages.

Thematic Analysis: Public Dialogue and the Main Themes Emerging from the Tweets

The thematic analysis we deployed for the analysis of the main themes, (Aguinaldo, 2012; Ponnam & Dawra, 2013) emerging from the tweets of the two parties, provided us with some significant results related to the communicational strategy of the two parties within Twitter, and our main research question on the existence or not of propagandistic elements in the political discourse of the two parties expressed through their tweets. Once again, we have to note, that the unilateral, hence propagandistic character of the tweets is more than evident in the examined tweets. In Table 1, we can see the main thematics that emerged from the examined tweets. These thematics are analysed in relation to the parties' communication strategies in this section.

Table 1. Thematics emerging by the examined tweets

	Presenting their Own Achievements/Proposals	Presenting their Own Pre-Electoral Activity	Appealing to the People	Downgrading/Accusing Political Rivals
New Democracy	√	√	X	X
SYRIZA	√	√	√	√

Figure 7. Use of unilateral rational argumentation per party (Fischer's exact test p. value= .000)

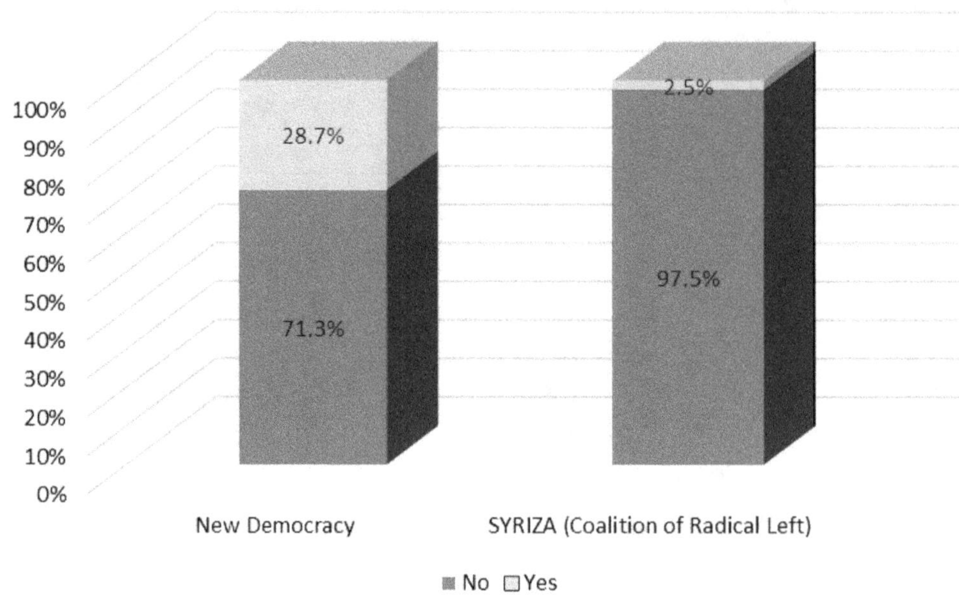

The governing party of New Democracy appears to focus on two basic themes: First the positive perspectives of the Greek economy (as result of the government's policies), through the account @ statheramprosta (steadily ahead) - the central catchphrase of New Democracy's pre-electoral campaign. In a way, these tweets could have also served as an attempt by the government both to reverse the negative public image and to set the stage of the electoral campaign. Second, the pre-electoral activity of the Prime Minister Antonis Samaras through his personal twitter account @PrimeministerGR, since almost the sum of the twitted messages refered to the places and the events that the PM visited and gave speeches as part of his pre-electoral program. Research in Germany has indicated that Twitter was used as a tool by members of the Reichstag for informing both the electorate and the media, delivering particular messages and setting the agenda of a campaign (Jungherr, 2009).

These tweets focus on presenting the prime minister having meetings with key different financial, political and social actors, as well as with citizens' organizations. Among others the prime minister - according to the tweets of his official account - took part in a conference organized by the Greek Organization of Tourist Enterprises; had a discussion with several women from the city of Lamia; attended several national highway construction sites, which were presented as closely connected to the development of the Greek economy; visited an echelon of Frontex based on the island of Lesvos; attended several political events of his own party in order to express his support for his party's candidates and inspected the central police administration of Epirus. These tweets, announcements contained audiovisual material from all the prime minister's pre-electoral public appearances, seeking to promote the basic axes of the party's political views, expressed mainly by the PM himself.

The other official account set up by New Democracy @statheramprosta focused mainly on the achievements of the current government and the already tangible results of the policies implemented during the last two years of the New Democracy administration. In order to appear even more convincing the tweets re-produced comments on Greece and the Greek economy made by mostly foreign actors praising the positive perspectives of Greece, which is in the neat of overcoming the financial crisis. Such tweets are: "The European Commission foresees development and lower unemployment", "there is an increased interest for investments in Greece", "positive reference to the Greek economy by Wall Street Journal", "14,8 bn. Euros invested in Greece by foreign funds", "prediction of 40 million tourists to visit Greece during 2025!", "2014 will be the year that Greece will escape the crisis". These stand as the most characteristic tweets of a handful of similar messages focusing first and foremost on the financial sector, since the public discourse has been conquered by the discussion concerning the overcoming of the financial crisis. Should we want to further elaborate on the different thematics of the positive financial perspectives, we could argue that these belong to three different categories: the tweets having to do with the tourist development of Greece, the positive comments on behalf of key political, financial and journalistic actors both from Greece and abroad and the politics, which will be followed so as to diminish the austerity measures.

SYRIZA's tweets appear to have a rather multidimensional focus: Firstly, they try to promote the pre-electoral activity of the party leader, who at the same time was a candidate for the European Commission presidency. Secondly, they promote several basic policies that the party will seek to implement, if SYRIZA take the cabinet. Thirdly, SYRIZA seeks to attack both the governmental policies and the prime minister himself as well as the foreign political actors that supported the austerity policies. Finally, the party seeks to address the voters, especially the young ones, in order to support SYRIZA through their votes with the aim to cease the implementation of austerity policies. It is important to note that the majority of the tweets are quotes taken from A. Tsipras's speeches during his pre-electoral campaign.

The first dimension, being a common one with the tweets of New Democracy, refers to the tweets that "follow" Alexis Tsipras during his tour around Greece and Europe, since he was a candidate for the Presidency of the European Commission as well. Graham et al., (2013) in their analysis of political tweets during the 2010 U.K. General Election have argued that Twitter is frequently used as a promotion tool for the politician, the party and/or its performance. Hence there are tweets presenting the different stops of the tour, still in quite a few cases promoting the leftist ideological identity of the party. Instead of saying "today we are in Portugal", the relevant tweet says that "today in Portugal at 21.30 we celebrate the 40-year anniversary of the Carnation Revolution", or "speech at Charles University. We discuss with the youth about the Europe of austerity and the response of the new generation", and "In Brussels for the 99% of Europeans, we understand their concerns and we'll bring them to the @EVNDebate tonight".

The second aim of SYRIZA's tweets is to present the most important policies that the party supports that should be implemented so as to improve the financial situation of those in need because of the crisis. Such tweets are: "We put an end to uncertainty and insecurity. We restore the lowest salary at 751 euros for everyone", "we put an end to austerity in order to re-gain democracy. To build our own Europe", "we will restore pensions, starting from the lowest ones. Free public education and health system", "A public social insurance system", "tax reduction of small and middle incomes", "financial support programmes for the farmers", "favorable settlements for the debts to the banks and the public sector". These tweets on the implementation of specific policies in support of the lower incomes are escorted by a series of tweets promising the guarantee of the public character of several public assets, such as water, electricity and public access to the beachside. These last policies aim at the same time at downgrading the privatization program of public resources boosted by the government of New Democracy.

As we saw in our quantitative results, one of the most important points of SYRIZA's tweets is the downgrading of its political rivals, allegedly the governing party of New Democracy, the Greek Prime Minister Antonis Samaras, as well as their political and financial allies, such as Angela Merkel and Wolfgang Schauble. What is noteworthy is the fact that due to Twitter's nature (limitations of 140 characters), we witness mostly superficial attacks as opposed to substantial critical arguments on issues (Graham et al., 2013). There are indeed many tweets attacking all those political rivals either in person or through the implemented austerity policies. Such tweets are: "The new memorandum is Samaras' secret program", "in the aftermath of Thatcher, Merkel and her allies say there is no alternative to austerity. They will be refuted in these elections", "they threaten Greek people with harsh punishments in case they don't support Mr. Samaras and the far-right group of his colleagues", "turn off the TV sets. Through their propagandistic news bulletins they try to rescue the political and financial system of corruption", "Go back, Mrs Merkel, Mr. Schauble, ladies and gentlemen of the conservative nomenclature of Europe. Greece is not a guinea pig", "Mr. Samaras is afraid to confront the problems he created", "they take us back to the Miserables of Victor Hugo and Jean Ajean, being proud at the same time. They call it reformation and progress", "does Mr. Samaras agree that people's needs and the resolution of the humanitarian crisis come in the first place and the loaners follow?". These stand among the most characteristic tweets attacking the political rivals of SYRIZA, the conservative political and financial status quo in Greece and Europe.

The fourth important thematic of SYRIZA tweets is the address to the voters and especially young people of Greece and Europe so as to overthrow, with their votes, the conservative governments and the austerity policies throughout Europe. Such tweets include: "On May 25th we vote for @EsquerdaNet @ syriza_gr and @europeanleft to re-gain our lives", "the vote of the young people is very important in these elections. They vote for their future against the policy, which dramatically raised unemployment", "the young people must take the situation in their hands and defy the policies that attacked democracy and created unemployment", "give one and only order to the government of vassalage: GO AWAY! One and only order to the neo-liberal powers throughout Europe. GO AWAY", "we want you on our side. On the streets. At the three ballot boxes. For the great overthrow. Victories everywhere", "we do not forget and we should not forget: The people is powerful when they are united and decided", "the Greek people aims, through their vote, to overthrow the ones that during the last 4 years deceive and humiliate them", "you scare them, we @syriza_gr, scare them. You and us together, people and @syriza_gr together, we terrify them". These tweets stand as some of the most characteristic ones in terms of addressing the voters to join SYRIZA in its attempt to overthrow the austerity policies and the corrupt elites of the past. Table one attempts a categorization of the main themes emerging from the tweets of both parties we examined.

CONCLUSION

Though it would have been naïve to consider that a sporadic or fragmented engagement in a political discussion on Twitter equates the nascence of a grounded civic participation, it is indeed important to accept that such discussions can enhance participation. However, it is equally significant to consider the quality of this participation in terms of the kind of interaction between citizens and politicians as well as the type of discourse that is being developed in Twitter.

Based on the data of the research that was conducted, despite the fact that Greek politicians use Twitter extensively, it seems that this has not changed much of the old trends of communicating politics. In the same line with other studies such as that of Margolis & Resnick (2000), McNamara & Kenning(2011), Larsson & Moe (2011), neither the examined Greek politicians and parties nor their constituents exploit the new platform in order to immerse themselves in an interlocutory environment. Rather, what is apparent from the thematic analysis of the data is the unfolding of perpetual parallel monologues. In terms of responses and conversations, most of the politicians on Twitter used their tweets in order to broadcast their messages rather than respond or engage in conversation. The great bulk of tweets focused on: attacking the opponent, promoting the party, the politician or particular policies, setting the agenda for the electoral campaign, fostering campaign slogans or election promises. What is noteworthy is that –in the examined sample of tweets- there were no personalised responses.

In addition, New Democracy's and SYRIZA's communication through Twitter includes propagandistic characteristics, since the parties did not avoid the promotion of unilateral views, mainly of sentimental and of logical rationale, so as to promote their political views. Well established and diachronic propagandistic methods – such as the dissemination of unilateral information, the use of rhetoric schemas, so as to either promote own party's views, or downgrade the political opponents, the effort to appeal in either positive (e.g. hope) or negative (e.g. fear/dead-end) sentiments- appeared quite frequently in the tweets of the abovementioned political parties in Greece. Moreover, the conduction of parallel monologues and the extreme unilaterality rate of the expressed views on behalf of both parties prove that the abilities of the medium are not the sole factor needed to improve the quality of political public discourse. The most decisive factor is the way users take advantage of each new technological potential. In our case, Greek political parties seem to fail – at least up to now – to understand the interactive character of the new medium, since they engage in a dissemination of political information under the rationale of the traditional one-way political rhetoric. The modernization of political discourse and the promotion of political – civic dialogue in the digital public space require a fundamental change in the approach of the political discourse itself by its main carriers, the political parties.

In spite of the possibilities offered by the interactive nature of Twitter, Greek political parties appear to be short of ideas so as to take advantage of this emerging potentiality and boost political dialogue and citizen participation, through the exchange of logical and substantial argumentation with the citizens. In a broader context, we could argue that the politicians' failure to profit from the capabilities of Twitter is also linked to the wider political circumstances. On the one hand, New Democracy (governing party at the time of this research) was anxious to maintain its political and electoral power (taking into consideration its low popularity status due to the imposition of austerity measures). On the other hand, SYRIZA emphasized the weaknesses and incapability of the government and was struggling to create and highlight a leadership profile along with the introduction of alternative methods of governance that would bring an end to austerity and economic asphyxia. Following the pre-electoral period, a spirit and climate of hostility dominated Twitter to the extent that both parties were so much absorbed by their need to promote themselves and eventually neglected the necessity of igniting fruitful political discussion and the engagement with the public.

Based on a combination of research methods (quantitative content analysis and qualitative thematic analysis), we managed to address the research objective of this study, that is to assess the use of Twitter by Greek political parties. We tried to highlight how Greek politicians used Twitter as a one-way diffusion of messages. They failed to exploit it as a forum of participatory communication where they could have the chance to engage in a (possibly) prolific dialogue with the citizens. Currently, the employment of Twitter by the Greek politicians is more a jump on the bandwagon rather than a digital public space where political dialogue can be enhanced. Nevertheless, the fact that our examination took place during a very polarized pre-electoral period strengthens our belief that further research that would include a longer period would greatly contribute to a better understanding of the use of Twitter by Greek political parties. The use of Twitter in political communication remains a very important field for future examination. Taking into account the new practices and structures that have been developed with the advent of the new media, further and comparative research amongst different contexts and countries could contribute with interesting insights regarding the employment of Twitter in political communication.

REFERENCES

Adi, A., Erickson, K., & Lilleker, D. (2014). Elite Tweets: Analyzing the Twitter Communication Patterns of Labour Party Peers in the House of Lord. *Policy & Internet*, *6*(1), 1–27. doi:10.1002/1944-2866.POI350

Aguinaldo, P. J. (2012). Qualitative analysis in Gay Men's Health Research: Comparing Thematic, Critical Discourse, and Conversation Analysis. *Journal of Homosexuality*, *59*(6), 765–787. doi:10.1080/00918369.2012.694753 PMID:22853179

Allan, S., & Zelizer, B. (Eds.). (2004). *Reporting War: Journalism in Wartime*. London: Taylor & Francis.

Attard, A., & Coulson, S. N. (2012). A thematic analysis of patient communication in Parkinson's disease online support group discussion forums. *Computers in Human Behavior*, *28*(2), 500–506. doi:10.1016/j.chb.2011.10.022

Barker, D. C. (2002). *Rushed to Judgment. Talk Radio, Persuasion and American Political Behavior*. New York: Columbia University Press.

Berelson, B. (1952). *Content Analysis in Communication Research*. New York: Free Press.

Berelson, B. (1971). *Content Analysis in Communication Research*. New York: Hafner Publishing Company.

Bimber, B., & Davis, R. (2003). *Campaigning online: The Internet in U.S. elections*. New York, NY: Oxford University Press.

Blumler, J. G., & Kavanagh, D. (1999). The Third Age of Political Communication: Influences and Features. *Political Communication*, *16*(3), 209–230. doi:10.1080/105846099198596

Braun, V., & Clarke, V. (2006). Using thematic analysis in psychology. *Qualitative Research in Psychology*, *3*(2), 77–101. doi:10.1191/1478088706qp063oa

Burgess, J., & Bruns, A. (2012). '(Not) The Twitter election: The dynamics of the #ausvotes conversation in relation to the Australian media ecology'. *Journalism Studies*, *6*, 384–402.

Carpenter, A. C. (2010). The Obamachine: Technopolitics 2.0. *Journal of Information Technology & Politics*, *7*(2-3), 216–225. doi:10.1080/19331681003765887

Carpentier, N. (2012). The concept of participation. If they have access and interact, do they really participate. *Revista Fronteiras – Estudos Midiáticos, 14*(2), 164-177.

Castells, M. (2007). Communication, power and counter-power in the network society. *International Journal of Communication, 1*(1), 238–266.

Castells, M. (2009). *Communication Power*. Oxford, UK: Oxford University Press.

Chadwick, A. (2008). Web 2.0: New challenges for the study of e-democracy in an era of informational exuberance. *I/S: A Journal of Law and Policy for the Information Society, 5*(1), 9–41.

Chen, P., & Walsh, L. (2009). E-election 2007: Political competition online. *Australian Cultural History*, *28*(1), 47–54.

Coleman, S. (2001). Online campaigning. In P. Norris (Ed.), *Britain Votes 2001*. Oxford, UK: Oxford University Press. doi:10.1093/parlij/54.4.679

Coleman, S., & Blumler, J. G. (2009). *The Internet and Democratic Citizenship: Theory,Practice and Policy*. Cambridge, UK: Cambridge University Press. doi:10.1017/CBO9780511818271

Corner, J. (2007). Mediated politics, promotional culture and the idea of "propaganda". *Media Culture & Society*, *29*(4), 669–677. doi:10.1177/0163443707078428

Dahlgren, P. (2009). *Media and Political Engagement: Citizens, Communication and Democracy*. New York: Cambridge University Press.

Davis, A. (2010). *Political Communication and Social Theory*. London, UK: Taylor & Francis.

Doxiadis, K. (2013). Political Discourse in Contemporary Greece. Network for Political Discourse Analysis: Working Texts, 1, 1-22.

Edelstein, A. (1997). *Total Propaganda: From Mass Culture to Popular Culture*. London: Lawrence Erlbaum Associates Publishers.

Ellul, J. (1973). *Propaganda, the Formation of Men's Attitudes*. New York: Vintage Books.

Garnham, N. (2003). *Emancipation and Modernity*. Athens: Kastaniotis.

Gnardellis, Ch. (2003). *Applied Statistics*. Athens: Papazisis.

Golbeck, J., Grimes, J. M., & Rogers, A. (2010). Twitter use by the US Congress. *Journal of the American Society for Information Science and Technology*, *61*(8), 1612–1621.

Graham, T., Broersma, M., & Hazelhoff, K. (2013). CLOSING THE GAP? Twitter as an instrument for connected representation. In R. Scullion, R. Gerodimos, D. Jackson, & D. Lilleker (Eds.), *The Media, Political Participation and Empowerment*. London: Routledge.

Graham, T., Jackson, D., & Broersma, M. (2014). New platform, old habits? Candidates' use of Twitter during the 2010 British and Dutch general election campaigns. *New Media & Society*, 1–19. doi:10.1177/1461444814546728

Grant, J., Moon, B., & Busby Grant, J. (2010). Digital Dialogue? Australian Politicians' use of the Social Network Tool Twitter. *Australian Journal of Political Science*, *45*(4), 579–604. doi:10.1080/10361146.2010.517176

Greece: Internet Usage and Marketing Report. (n.d.). Retrieved January 27, 2015, from Internet World Stats website, http://www.internetworldstats.com/eu/gr.htm

Habermas, J. (1962/1989). *The Structural Transformation of the Public Sphere*. Cambridge, UK: Polity.

Habermas, J. (2006). Political communication in media society: Does democracy still enjoy an epistemic dimension? The impact of normative theory on empirical research. *Communication Theory*, *16*(4), 411–426. doi:10.1111/j.1468-2885.2006.00280.x

Heinrich, A. (2012). Foreign reporting in the sphere of network journalism. *Journalism Practice*, 1-10.

Hermida, A. (2010). Twittering the news: The emergence of ambient journalism. *Journalism Practice*, *4*(3), 297–308. doi:10.1080/17512781003640703

Hermida, A., Fletcher, F., Korell, D., & Logan, D. (2012). Share, Like, Recommend: Decoding the social media news consumer. *Journalism Studies*, 1–10.

Hill, K., & Hughes, J. (1998). *Cyperpolitics: Citizen Activism in the Age of the Internet*. New York: Rowman & Littlefield.

Hiotis, A. (1986). *Propaganda: Methods and Technique*. Self Published.

Hoffman, D., & Novak, T. (1998). Information access: Bridging the racial divide on the internet. *Science*, *280*(5362), 390–391. doi:10.1126/science.280.5362.390

Honeycutt, C., & Herring, S. C. (2009). Beyond Microblogging: Conversation and Collaboration via Twitter. In *Proc. HICSS 42*. IEEE Press.

Hutchins, B. (2011). The acceleration of media sports culture: Twitter, telepresence and online messaging. *Information Communication and Society*, *14*(2), 237–257. doi:10.1080/1369118X.2010.508534

Jackall, R. (1995). *Propaganda*. London: Palgrave. doi:10.1007/978-1-349-23769-2

Jackson, N. (2007). Political parties, the Internet and the 2005 General Election: Third time Lucky? *Internet Research*, *17*(3), 249–271. doi:10.1108/10662240710758911

Jackson, N., & Lilleker, D. (2011). Microblogging, constituency service and impression management: UK MPs and the use of Twitter. *Journal of Legislative Studies*, *17*(1), 86–105. doi:10.1080/13572334.2011.545181

Jones, S. (Ed.). (1998). *Cybersociety 2.0: Revisiting Computer-mediated communication and Community*. Thousand Oaks, CA: Sage.

Jowett, G. S., & O' Donnell, V. (1995). *Propaganda and Persuasion*. London: Sage.

Jungherr, A. (2009). Twitternde Politiker: Zwischen buntem Rauschen und Bu¨ rgerna¨he 2.0. In C. Bieber, M. Eifert, T. Groß, & J. Lamla (Eds.), *Soziale Netze in der Digitalen Welt: Das Internet zwischen Egalitaerer Beteiligung und Oekonomischer Macht* (pp. 99–127). Frankfurt am Main: Campus Verlag.

Juris, S. J. (2012). Reflections on #Occupy Everywhere: Social media, public space, and emerging logics of aggregation. *American Ethnologist*, *39*(2), 259–279. doi:10.1111/j.1548-1425.2012.01362.x

Kahn, R., & Kellner, D. (2005). Oppositional politics and the Internet: A critical reconstructive approach. *Cultural Politics*, *1*(1), 75–100. doi:10.2752/174321905778054926

Kamens, H. D. (2012). *Beyond the Nation-State: The Reconstruction of Nationhood and Citizenship*. London, UK: Emerald Group. doi:10.1108/S1479-3539(2012)18

Kant, I. (1983). To perpetual peace. In I. Kant (Ed.), *Perpetual peace and other essays on politics, history, and morals* (pp. 107–144). Indianapolis, IN: Hackett. (Original work published 1795)

Kennedy, J. (2008). Twitter and Digg to introduce social media to U.S. election coverage. *Silicon Republic*. Retrieved September 11, 2014, from http://www.siliconrepublic.com/news/article/11712/new-media/twitter-and-digg-to-introduce-social-media-to-uselection-coverage

Kirk, R., & Schill, D. (2011). A Digital Agora: Citizen Participation in the 2008 Presidential Debates. *The American Behavioral Scientist*, *55*(3), 325–347. doi:10.1177/0002764210392167

Kyriazi, N. (2001). *Sociological Research: Critical Evaluation of Methods and Techniques*. Athens: Greek Letters.

Ladd, M. J. (2012). *Why Americans Hate the Media and How It Matters*. Princeton University Press.

Larsson, O. A., & Moe, H. (2011). Studying political microblogging: Twitter users in the 2010 Swedish election campaign. *New Media & Society*, *14*(5), 729–747. doi:10.1177/1461444811422894

Lassen, D., & Brown, A. (2011). Twitter: The electoral connection? *Social Science Computer Review*, *29*(4), 419–436. doi:10.1177/0894439310382749

Lehmann, I. A. (2003). Exploring the Transatlantic Media Divide over Iraq: How and Why U.S. and German Media Differed in Reporting on UN Weapons Inspections in Iraq, 2002-2003. *Press/Politics* *10*(1), 63-89.

Lev-On, A. (2011). Campaigning online: Use of the Internet by parties, candidates and voters in national and local election campaigns in Israel. *Policy & Internet*, *3*(1), 1–28. doi:10.2202/1944-2866.1045

Lilleker, D. G., & Jackson, N. A. (2010). Toward a more participatory style of election campaigning: The impact of Web 2.0 on the U.K. 2010 general election. *Policy & Internet*, *2*(3), 69–98. doi:10.2202/1944-2866.1064

Lilleker, D. G., & Jackson, N. A. (2011). *Political campaigning, elections and the Internet: Comparing the U.S., U.K., France and Germany*. New York: Routledge.

Lippmann, W. (1927). *The Phantom Public*. New York: MacMillan.

Livingstone, S. (1999). New media, new audiences. *New Media & Society*, *1*(1), 59–66. doi:10.1177/1461444899001001010

Macnamara, J. (2008). The internet and the public sphere: The 2007 Australian e-electioneering experience. *Media International Australia*, *129*, 7–19.

Margolis, M., & Resnick, D. (2000). *Politics as Usual: The Cyberspace Revolution*. London: Sage.

Marková, I. (2008). Persuasion and Propaganda. One or two processes? Persuasion, propaganda and rhetoric. *Diogenes*, *217*(1), 37–51. doi:10.1177/0392192107087916

Marx Ferree, M., Gamson, W. A., Gerhards, J., & Rucht, D. (2002). Four models of the public sphere in modern democracies. *Theory and Society*, *31*(3), 289–324. doi:10.1023/A:1016284431021

McChesney, R. (2000). *Rich Media, Poor Democracy: Communication Politics in Dubious Times*. New York: New Press.

Mcnamara, J., & Kenning, G. (2011). E-electioneering 2010: Trends in social media use in Australian political communication. *Media International Australia*, *139*, 7–22.

McParland, L. J., & Whyte, A. (2008). A thematic analysis of attributions to others for the origins and ongoing nature of pain in community pain sufferers. *Psychology Health and Medicine*, *13*(5), 610–620. doi:10.1080/13548500701842966 PMID:18942015

Meyrowitz, J. (1985). *No Sense of Place. The Impact of Electronic Media on Social Behavior*. New York, Oxford: Oxford University Press.

Miller, L. R., & Brewer, J. D. (Eds.). (2003). *The A-Z of Social Research*. London: Sage.

Miotto, A. (1953). *Psicologia della Propaganda*. Florence: Editrice Universitaria.

Murdock, G. (1992). Citizens, consumers and public culture. In M. Skovmand & J. C. Schroder (Eds.), *Media Cultures. Reappraising Transnational Media* (pp. 17–41). London, New York: Routledge.

Murdock, G. (1993). Communications and the constitution of modernity. *Media Culture & Society*, *15*(4), 521–539. doi:10.1177/016344393015004002

Neuendorf, K. A. (2002). *The Content Analysis Guidebook*. London: Sage.

Neuhaus, F., & Webmoor, T. (2012). Agile ethics for massified research and visualization. *Information Communication and Society*, *15*(1), 43–65. doi:10.1080/1369118X.2011.616519

Norris, P. N. (2001). *Digital Divide, Civic Engagement, Information Poverty and the Internet Worldwide*. Cambridge, UK: Cambridge University Press. doi:10.1017/CBO9781139164887

North, R., Holsti, O. R., Zanninovich, M. G., & Zinnes, D. A. (1963). *Content analysis*. Northwestern University Press.

OECD: Selected Indicators for Greece. (n.d.). Retrieved January 27, 2015, from OECD website, http://data.oecd.org/greece.htm#profile-innovationandtechnology

Ovadia, S. (2009). Exploring the potential of Twitter as a research tool. *Behavioral & Social Sciences Librarian*, *28*(4), 202–205. doi:10.1080/01639260903280888

Ponnam, A., & Dawra, J. (2013). Discerning product benefits through visual thematic analysis. *Journal of Product and Brand Management*, *22*(1), 30–39. doi:10.1108/10610421311298669

Poulakidakos, S. (2014). *Propaganda and Public Discourse. The presentation of the MoU by the Greek Media.* Athens: DaVinci Books.

Poulakidakos, S., & Armenakis, A. (2014). Propaganda in Greek Public Discourse. Propaganda Scales in the presentation of the Greek MoU-bailout agreement of 2010. *Revue des Sciences Politiques*, *41*, 126–140.

Poulakidakos, S., & Veneti, A. (forthcoming). The sentimental element in public discourse as a factor of formation of polarization in Greece. In F. Morandau & D. Stefenel (Eds.), Understanding local and global trans-formations across cultures. Research and practice in social and human sciences. Academic Press.

Pratkanis, A., & Aronson, E. (2001). *Age of Propaganda: The Everyday Use and Abuse of Persuasion.* New York: Owl Books.

Rosanvallon, P. (2008). *Counter-Democracy. Politics in an Age of Distrust.* Cambridge University Press. doi:10.1017/CBO9780511755835

Sanderson, J. (2013). From Loving the Hero to Despising the Villain: Sports fans, Facebook and Social Identity Treats. *Mass Communication & Society*, *16*(4), 487–509. doi:10.1080/15205436.2012.730650

Scbweitzer, E. J. (2008). Innovation or normalization in e-campaigning? Structural analysis of German party Websites in the 2002 and 2005 national elections. *European Journal of Communication*, *23*(4), 449–470. doi:10.1177/0267323108096994

Siomkos, G. I., & Vasilakopoulou, A. (2005). *Implementation of Analysis Methods in Market Research.* Athens: Ath. Stamoulis.

Small, T. (2011). What the hashtag? A content analysis of Canadian politics of Twitter. *Information Communication and Society*, *14*(6), 872–895. doi:10.1080/1369118X.2011.554572

Smith, A. (2009). *The Internet's Role in Campaign 2008, Pew Internet & American Life Project.* Retrieved September 11, 2013, from http://pewinternet.org/Reports/2009/6--The-Internets-Role-in-Campaign-2008.aspx

Smith, A., & Rainie, L. (2008). *The internet and the 2008 election', Pew Internet & American Life Project.* Retrieved September 11, 2013, from http://www.pewinternet.org/PPF/r/252/report_display.asp

Snow, N. (2002). *Propaganda Inc.: Selling America's culture to the world.* New York: Seven Stories Press.

Splichal, S. (2006). In search of a strong European public sphere: Some critical observations on conceptualizations of publicness and the (European) public sphere. *Media Culture & Society*, *28*(5), 695–7147. doi:10.1177/0163443706067022

Splichal, S. (2011). *Transnationalization of the Public Sphere and the Fate of the Public (Euricom Monographs).* Hampton Press.

Stemler, S. (2001). *An Introduction to Content Analysis.* ERIC Digest. ERIC Clearinghouse on Assessment and Evaluation College Park MD. Retrieved December 6, 2011, from http://www.ericdigests.org/2002-2/content.htm

Taylor, P. (2004). *War and International Relations in the Information Age*. Athens: Papazisis.

Theocharis, Y., Lowe, W., van Deth, J. W., & Garcia-Albacete, G. (2015). Using Twitter to mobilize protest action: Online mobilization patterns and action repertoires in the Occupy Wall Street, Indignados, and Aganaktismenoi movements. *Information Communication and Society*, *18*(2), 202–220. doi:10.1080/1369118X.2014.948035

Theodorakopoulos, Ch. (2006). *Propaganda the Glorious*. Athens: Sideris.

Thussu, D. K., & Freedman, D. (2003). *War and the Media: Reporting Conflict 24/7*. London: Sage.

Towner, L. T., & Dulio, A. D. (2012). New Media and Political Marketing in the United States: 2012 and Beyond. *Journal of Political Marketing*, *11*(1-2), 95–119. doi:10.1080/15377857.2012.642748

Trending.gr. (n.d.). *Power by Monitor*. Retrieved April 18, 2015, from http://trending.gr/

Triandafyllidou, A., Gropas, R., & Kouki, H. (Eds.). (2013). *The Greek Crisis and European Modernity*. Palgrave Macmillan. doi:10.1057/9781137276254

Trippi, J. (2004). *The revolution will not be televised: Democracy, the Internet and the overthrow of everything*. New York, NY: Harper Collins.

Tumasjan, A., Sprenger, T. O., Sandner, P. G., & Welpe, I. M. (2010.) *Predicting elections with Twitter: What 140 characters reveal about political sentiment*. Paper presented at the Fourth International AAAI Conference on Weblogs and Social Media, Washington, DC.

Tumber, H. (1993). Taming the Truth. *British Journalism Review*, *4*(1), 37–41.

Vaccari, C. (2008). Surfing to the Elysee: The Internet in the 2007 French Elections. *French Politics*, *6*(1), 1–22. doi:10.1057/palgrave.fp.8200139

Van Dijk, T. A. (2001). *Political discourse and ideology*. Paper presented at Jornadas del Discurso Politico, Barcelona, Spain.

Varoufakis, Y. (2014). *The Birth of Memorandum Greece: A chronicle of the crisis*. Athens: Gutenberg.

Veneti, A. (2014). Campaigns, Virtual. In H. Kerric & G. J. Geoffrey (Eds.), *Encyclopedia of Social Media and Politics* (pp. 214–218). London, UK: Sage.

Veneti, A., & Karadimitriou, A. (2013). Policy and Regulation in the Media Landscape: The Greek Paradigm Concentration of Media Ownership versus the Right to Information. *Management Dynamics in the Knowledge Economy*, *1*(3), 439–457.

Vergeer, M., Hermans, L., & Sams, S. (2011). Online social networks and micro-blogging in political campaigning: The exploration of a new campaign tool and a new campaignstyle. *Party Politics*, 477–501.

Verweij, P. (2012). Twitter links between Politicians and Journalists. *Journalism Practice*, 1-12.

Webster, F. (2006). *Theories of the Information Society* (3rd ed.). London: Routledge.

Wellman, B. (2000). Physical place and cyberspace: The rise of networked individualism. *International Journal of Urban and Regional Research, 25*(2), 227–252. doi:10.1111/1468-2427.00309

Xenos, M., & Moy, P. (2007). Direct and differential effects of the internet on political and civic engagement. *Journal of Communication, 57*(4), 704–718. doi:10.1111/j.1460-2466.2007.00364.x

ENDNOTES

1 As communication systems we consider Mass Communication Media, such as Press, Radio, Television, Cinema, and all applications allowing mass or private communication within the internet environment (news sites, various content sites, social media, applications such as e-mails and chat applications). Our focus is mainly in communication systems based on commercial rationale which end up offering infotainment through the dissemination of information that serves specific interests of sponsors, advertisers, public relations and the intense information management by political actors, corporations and other factors.

2 The term "text" is not being used here with the specific essence of written discourse, but includes many different forms of communication, which might be meaningful such as interviews, letters, diaries, fiction stories, proceedings, audiovisual content etc.

3 The full coding frame used for the current research can be found in the appendix. In the results we present the main findings of our research, focusing on the variables of the coding frame that appeared to be of greater importance for the presentation of the pre-electoral use of twitter. Hence, several variables, e.g. the week of the tweet, have been omitted in the presentation of the results, due to their lack of importance regarding the presentation of the pre-electoral twitter ecology.

4 R= 2(C1,C2)/C1+C2, with 70% as the lowest level of credibility. The conduction of the test on both coders provided us with an average of 80% inter-coder reliability.

5 Metaphor examples: "the new austerity measures will be a pogrom against the greek society" (@a.tsipras). "(Mr. Samaras) amputates democracy…" (@a.tsipras). "Landing of millions of British tourists this year in Greece" (@statheramprosta). Transfer examples: "They take us back to the Miserables of Hugo and Jean Ajean" (@a.tsipras). "Greece walks the road of Chile and Pinochet" (@a.tsipras).

6 Appeal to fear example: "You have agreed for lay-offs in the public sector, reduction of pensions, privatization of everything" (@a.tsipras). Appeal to hope examples: "2014 will be a year that Greece and Europe will exit the crisis" (@statheramprosta). "A ray of hope for Greece, according to German economist" (@statheramprosta).

7 Selective rational argumentation examples" "Focus mag.: EIB supports small businesses in Greece with 50 million euros" (@statheramprosta). "10,3 bn. Euros surplus in the 2013 travel balance" (@statheramprosta). "30000 new jobs in the next two years" (@statheramprosta).

APPENDIX

Variables of the coding frame

1. Name of the account
2. Party-owner of the account
3. Week of tweet
4. Is it an original tweet or is it a retweet?
5. If a retweet, is it retweeted from another party related account or from an account not belonging to the party?
6. How many times is the tweet re-tweeted?
7. How many times is it marked as "favorite"?
8. Whom does the tweet refer to? (own party/ party allies, political rivals, people)
9. Is the tweet positive or negative?
10. Does it try to debate-"demonize" the political rivals?
11. Does it use transfers, metaphors and other linguistic schemas?
12. Does it include appeal to hope (e.g. bright future)?
13. Does it include appeal to fear/threats (e.g. dark future)?
14. Does it include rational argumentation with the use of data?

Chapter 8
The Performative Role of Hashtags in the Politicization of Europe:
Twitter and European Elections in 2014

Maria Francesca Murru
Università Cattolica del Sacro Cuore di Milano, Italy

ABSTRACT

The chapter analyses Twitter as one of the several fora where the general public sphere manifests itself. The Twitter debate generated in Italy during the campaign for EP2014 is used as a prism for looking in depth into the mutual shaping between the specific grammar of the micro-blogging platform and the ongoing politicization of the EU within and across national politics. The contribution looks at the ways in which specific socio-communicative features of Twitter have became deeply interlaced with the emergence of Europe-related structure of meanings. Special attention is paid to the performative role of hashtags in summoning publics and in triggering a peculiar kind of ambient affiliation that is more than mere connectivity and rather involves the opening of a discursive space where negotiation of meanings becomes possible.

INTRODUCTION

The chapter analyses Twitter as one of the several fora where the general public sphere manifests itself. The Twitter debate, which was generated in Italy during the campaign for European Parliament elections in 2014 (EP2014), is used as a prism to look into the mutual shaping between the specific grammar of the micro-blogging platform and the ongoing politicization of the EU within and across national politics (Statham & Trenz, 2012). The starting assumption is that the dominant features of political life on Twitter can be efficaciously grasped turning the analytical perspective towards moments of remarkable political unrest. EP2014 represent an exemplary case in point because they were characterized by the exceptional combination of unprecedented dynamics, both on the communicative and the political side.

DOI: 10.4018/978-1-4666-9879-6.ch008

Twitter as a communicative phenomenon, which is expected to radically shape rules and stakes of political life, is at the core of an expanding strand of literature on media and communication (for an extensive and interdisciplinary overview, see Jungherr 2014). The scientific interest is paralleled by a growing attention on the part of institutions which ever more consider the popular micro-blogging platform as a unique opportunity to actively involve citizens in the practices and the rituals of democracy. During EP2014, many European institutions arranged ad hoc communication strategies on the popular micro-blogging platforms. The European Parliament launched a special *elections night website* which promised to release «fact, polls, quotes, trivia, social media buzz, pictures, videos from all 28 members states and the European Parliament»[1] during the four elections days. The special attention that EP paid to social media during the elections is further confirmed by a special twitter tool - the Twitter dashboard[2] - which collected all the tweets with the official European election hashtag #EP2014 and similar national hashtags. It showed mentions and accounts of the candidates for the Commission Presidency, registering the number of election-related tweets per minute and hour and the most mentioned topics on Twitter. Rather than being just one among other communication tools, Twitter became a communicative event in itself worth being represented through a new form of storytelling made of infographics, visual resources and metrics describing candidates' popularity and users' participation rates. Many other European institutions, such as the European Broadcasting Union, the Commission and all the European parties, took part in the Twitter debate, using official hashtags, promoting Twitter accounts and making use of specialized companies that provide analytics of Twitter.

However, all these remarkable investments from both the scientific and institutional side run the risk of appearing paradoxical if we take into account the niche diffusion that this social medium has across the wider population. While social media continue to grow rapidly around the world, with active users accounts that are almost equating 29% of the world's population (We are social, 2015), Twitter is still behind the top ranking with 284 million of monthly active users against the 1.4 billion of Facebook users and 300 million of Instagram users (Cosenza, 2015). To quote just some data, consider that in 2014 the percentage of Twitter users of the entire population in Italy, Germany and France did not overcome 10%, while a higher diffusion amounting to 19% was registered in the UK (We are social, 2015).

The objective of the chapter is to build a theoretical and empirical route towards the understanding of the social and political value attached to Twitter. Having acknowledged that this value clearly does not coincide with its capillary diffusion, it will be argued that it can be grasped if assessed in the light of the complex processes that sustain the wider public sphere. Consequently, the primary issue to be dealt with is whether Twitter conversations that unfolded during EP2014 hosted processes that can be ascribed to the wider public sphere. If so, it becomes relevant to explore and explain the relationship that connects Twitter to the wide-ranging discursive practices through which topics of common interests are framed and made visible. An issue like this one can be legitimately raised only within a cultural paradigm of the public sphere that considers it in its plural declination, as a multiplicity of public spheres, associations and communities nested within one another and also within a putative larger national sphere (Alexander & Jacobs, 1998). Besides acknowledging both the indisputable empirical existence and the ethical need of a multiplicity of public spheres (Fraser, 1992), this paradigm turns away from the exclusive understanding of public sphere as a place for rational processes of reaching consensus. Rather, it conceives it as «a cultural space in which different individuals and groups jockey to "narrate the social" and where citizens actively construct their own understandings of real and ideal civil society by filtering overarching discourse and narratives through multiple public spheres and communities» (Alexander & Jacobs, 1998, p. 29). Analyzing how the social is narrated through a stream of Twitter conversations means taking into account not only the patterns of meaning but also the way in which the discursive articulation is affected by the architectural affordances of a connective space that is network-shaped and performance-oriented (Van Dijck, 2013). To look for the main features of Twitter as a public sphere implies examining those communicative processes through which specific narrations have acquired a collective echo and a special symbolic force. The focus will thus be on the emergence of Twitter publics intended as «social production of shared attention» (Dayan, 2005, p. 44) that enhance these same narrations and give them the symbolic strength of being worth following and sharing. While taking into account the recent literature that has pointed out the networked nature of these peculiar publics (boyd, 2011), their being awareness systems that can be conducive to communities of knowledge (Hermida, 2010) and to issue networks (Marres, 2007), the present contribution addresses the peculiar "ambient affiliation" (Zappavigna, 2014) that arises from the performative function exerted by hashtags. As linguistic markers that summon publics and trace their thematic route, hashtags are supposed to trigger the emergence of publics by providing them with an affiliative and value-laden space of discourse whereby meanings and stances can be negotiated.

After an extensive theoretical discussion of the performative function exerted by hashtags, the chapter will further develop the argument while exploring the kind of relationship that connects the negotiation of meaning taking place within Twitter publics to the wider European public sphere. In the long debate about the need and the concrete existence of European Public Sphere (Bärenreuter et al. 2009), the concept of "Europeanization" has been used to examine how much the European democratic deficit is gradually bridged by an increasing presence of Europe in collective identities, public debates and citizens' participation to the policy process. While several categories have been produced to distinguish between horizontal and vertical processes of Europeanization, what is more pertinent here is the «Europeanization of meaning structures» (Trenz, 2008, p. 6) within which the public sphere is seen as an arena where discourses and interpretations are framed, identities and relations are generated and shaped. From this point of view, what is relevant is the degree to which «issues are discussed under a common frame of interpretation, which includes the identification of problems of shared relevance (...). Europe is thus conceived as an interpretative space in which meaning structures converge, common standpoints are crystallised and a collective self develops». Abandoning the principle of convergence, which seems to still be linked to an ideal of public sphere uniquely devoted to consensus and community integration (Trenz, 2012), the notion of Europeanization of meaning structures orient attention to the ways in which discourses spread on Twitter during 2014 electoral campaign have contributed to incorporate Europe in a structure of meanings that comprises both values and themes.

All these issues will be then empirically problematized through the discussion of the ethnographic study of the hashtags and related stream of contents that were published in the Italian Twitter-sphere during and around EP2014. The discussion of the empirical case study will disentangle the methodological challenges that should be faced when looking for ambient affiliation within a discursive material that is fragmented and uneven by its nature. It will be argued that ethnography of communication represents a valuable methodological approach to study a dynamic of affiliation which resides in the mutual implication of content and context that characterizes communicative events happening in Twitter. Finally, the interpretative reading of the findings will offer an answer to the issues raised at the beginning of the chapter. The analysis of tweets will demonstrate that Twitter acted as a public sphericule (Gitlin, 1988) which gave stage to the increasing politicization of the European Union. However, when focusing on its connection to the wider public sphere, Twitter emerged as a complementary rather than autonomous interactional arena, whose main value resided in funneling and channeling attention towards what was happening outside and beyond itself.

NETWORKED PUBLICS IN TWITTER: AMBIENT AFFILIATION AND DISCURSIVE NEGOTIATIONS

In order to understand in which terms Twitter conversations can become a component of the general public sphere, it should be considered how publics emerge within social networking sites and how their founding dynamics of aggregation and thickening of attention are affected by the technological affordances of the platforms hosting them. A very common issue in recent literature on networked publics is the thematic focus which is supposed to act as one of the main drivers of social gathering within this multi-channel environment (Maireder and Schloegl, 2014). Just as relevant appears to be the possibility of a "peripheral awareness and ambient community" (Erikson, 2010, p. 1194) that, without necessarily requiring direct participation, is sustained by differentiated practices of background, reciprocal and delegated listening (Crawford, 2009). Similarly, Hermida (2010) describes Twitter as a an awareness system, a peculiar medium of co-presence that allows users to receive news information in the periphery of their awareness and to activate full attention just when they feel the need to communicate.

This background awareness opens the way for the emergence of issue publics: social groups who share attention towards the same issue and that are able to exploit connective potentialities of social media in order to develop communication exchanges around shared topics or interests. Marres and Rogers (2005) have argued for the need to renew conceptualization of issue publics through the notion of *issue networks*, in order to take into account the double articulation of code (platform, software, networks, informational dynamics) and politics (political discourses, political cultures, citizens ...) (Langlois et al. 2009). Drawing upon Dewey and Lippman as well as ANT (Latour & Weibel, 2005), Marres (2007) inquires *issues networks* as heterogeneous assemblages that include human and not-human actors and that come into being through marking the scope of a problem of common interest. Thanks to their affordances that allow for hyperlinking and traceability of communication practices, networking media are meant to act as an integral part of those specific conjunctural dynamics that bring issue-publics into being. While algorithms, software and protocols that manage attentive structure (Mejias, 2008; Hogan, 2013) can be rightfully considered as decisive actors in the constitution of issues networks within the technocultural spaces of social networking sites, this chapter chooses to focus attention on hashtags, as linguistic markers that exert a performative function in summoning publics and tracing their thematic boundaries.

In their basic function, hashtags are keywords included in the tweets' text in order to mark them as relevant to specific known themes and topics. They embody the communicative intent of addressing an imagined community of users who is following and willing to discuss a specific topic. Insofar as hashtags allow us to extend the reach of a tweet beyond the established follower/following network of a user, they incorporate the potentiality of communication in broadcasting mode into Twitter. Therefore, they are essential tools in those mechanisms of "social production of shared attention" (Dayan, 2005, p. 44) we are looking for and decisive philters in selecting, among the myriads of discursive frames circulating in Twitter, those that can acquire the symbolic force of being *worth sharing, worth following*.

Hashtags and their Performative Function

In 2007 when Chris Messina originally proposed a system of channel tags using the symbol of pound or hash (Messina, 2007), he aimed at introducing a kind of content filtering that would have allowed people to orient selective attention towards their topics of interest. Therefore, hashtags were originally conceived as a system of channels in which to organize and disseminate the stream of contents on the basis of thematic coherence rather than on membership to networks of social relations. If it is true that this primary orientation to content still represents the main feature of Twitter, for instance, if compared to Facebook, the popular use of the hashtags that takes hold in the following years has largely exceeded the original idea of Messina. Hashtags can emerge spontaneously from within the Twitter community, or they can be pre-planned by media, political, public relations intermediaries as part of their strategies to manage the thematic frame of the topic that is going to be commented (as during electoral campaigns or within second-screen television). They can offer coordination and rapid insight during natural disasters and emergency management (Flew et al. 2013) or they can become the object of carnivalesque subversion and playful jokes as in "meme" circulation (Huang et al. 2010). In either case, they easily become a thematic umbrella that offers the possibility of visibility, recognition and mutual awareness to discursive communities. Their function of isolating and signifying topics can determine the life-time of ad hoc publics - short-lived communicative gatherings that gain their momentum exactly thanks to the adoption of a popular hahstag (Bruns and Burgess, 2011) - or can give a new communicative substance to broad and enduring issue publics that may exist at the same time in other public spheres such as politics, political culture, or mainstream media (Maireder and Schlögl, 2014).

Beyond the deep layer of differentiated communicative and social habits of the Twitter user community, several taxonomies of Twitter hashtags have been identified and classified. Bruns and Stieglitz (2011) distinguish between *ad hoc* ones - hashtags that emerge in response to breaking news or other unforeseen events - *recurring* ones - hashtags employed by users in order to contribute to a long-lasting topic that attract continuous attention - and *praeter hoc* ones - launched and promoted by relevant organisations in order to channel and aggregate all the comments produced about a particular event, for example, conferences or TV shows.

All the three types of hashtag identified by Bruns and Stieglitz can be considered "topical" hashtags, differentiated by the reason that bring them into Twitter stream but equated by the common focus on a circumscribed thematic area. However, it would be reductive to consider hashtags as merely headlines suggesting which thematic category the tweet should be referred to. It is increasingly common to see non-topical use of hashtags, such as #facepalm or #fail, where the hash symbol is used as a linguistic marker both to give special emphasis to a specific content of the message and to express emotional involvement (Bruns and Moe, 2013). This is a clear example of linguistic generativity within which the original significance of hashtags is subverted and metaphorically readapted in order to symbolize the "loudness" of discourse. They continue to be markers of collective resonance but, rather than addressing a wider community, they are used to emphasize a message that is made so strong as to be metaphorically heard beyond the established network of senders and receivers. Therefore, if the function carried out by hashtags is that of marking contextual embedding of a tweet, this contextualization is referred not only to the specific thematic domain it deals with, but also to the relational context it wants to address. It starts to be plausible to conceive hashtags in their performative role, as linguistic markers that can contain, in specific circumstances, information dealing with the relational configuration within which the tweet is or wants to be entailed.

In their analysis of the conversations' stream gathered around the hashtag #hagchatoz, a farmer advocacy Twitter community based in Australia, Burgess and Sauter (2014) contend that there is still room to consider the performative role of the hashtag in materially shaping and coordinating public communication on specific issues, within and across social media platforms. According to their findings, the *praeter hoc* hashtags of #hagchatoz has organized a peculiar structure of discussion that is akin to those "hybrid fora" where, according to the description by Michel Callon, heterogeneous groups of experts, politicians, laypersons, come together to discuss different options in technological development.

The performative function of hashtags is not so far from the attitudes, the qualities and cultural predisposition usually associated to the so-called networked publics. In Ito (2008), participants to networked publics are thought to be dynamic players who act as (re)actors, (re)makers and (re)distributors of content within complex communication networks. According to boyd (2011), users imagine their receivers less as a target audience and more as collectives with whom to engage for civic and cultural purposes. From a more critical perspective, Page (2012) acknowledges the conversational nature of hashtags (Huang et al. 2010) but specifies that it has to do less with face-to-face dialogue and more with the para-social simulations of conversationality found in broadcast talk. She shows as, in the micro-celebrity field, *conversationality* has become a commodity in the linguistic marketplace of Twitter, used to build social and economic capital of those already in a powerful position.

Being primarily interested in how linguistic practices create social bonds, Zappavigna (2001) coined the concept of "ambient affiliation" in order to give an account of the role played by hashtags in calling for potential discourse communities. If a tweet constitutes an instance of language use, a tag is language about language "enacting the following social relation: search for me and affiliate with my value!" (p. 789). The affiliative function performed by hashtags is the result of a cultural shift from searching purely the content to searching what other people are saying online and forming communities of shared value. This shift towards a stronger interpersonal meaning in searching activities has resulted in the emergence of *searchable talk*, that is, online discourse where the primary function appears to be affiliation via 'findability'. Increasing the likelihood that the tweet will be found, hashtags seem to enhance the "loudness" of the content giving an additional semiotic pull that makes it hyper-charged. From this point of view, more than thematic areas, hashtags mark the call for affiliation implied by the tweet, the invitation to consider, recognize and share the values it contains. The community building function performed by hashtags is characterized by peculiar features. It is "ambient" in the sense that users do not have to interact directly, they don't know each other and they might not start to interact after the bound and determined encounter that has been possible under the same hashtag. However, the absence of direct interaction does not undermine the communitarian value built in a hashtag. Quite the opposite, Zappavigna argues that affiliation is something more than mere connection: "it is about negotiating meaning within genres of language use" (p. 804).

Following this line of reasoning, hashtags can thus be examined as a mechanism of social production of shared attention (Dayan, 2005) that enhances specific narrations and gives them the symbolic strength of being worth following and sharing. Drawing upon the linguistic analysis of Zappavigna, shared attention that is conducive to publics is expected to be produced though the call for affiliation to a shared discursive space where negotiation of meanings can occur.

TWITTER FRAMING EUROPE: THE EMERGENT PUBLIC SPHERE AND THE EUROPEANIZATION OF MEANINGS

These processes of affiliation and summoning that organize and sustain networked publics, are expected to become even more visible and observable during electoral periods. As liminal stages that challenge agendas and political understandings that are usually taken for granted (Herzog, 1987), electoral campaigns are designed to set up an active arena where political cognition, social meanings and symbolic representations of the political world are presented, moulded and negotiated. This is particularly true for the European elections in 2014 which were characterized by unprecedented innovation both on the political and the communicative side.

Besides being marked by relevant changes in institutional and contextual conditions, as the fielding of candidates for Commission President or the exacerbation of the financial crisis, EP2014 took place in the middle of an increasing and irreversible politicization of the European Union (de Wilde and Zürne, 2011). In general terms, politicization indicates the act of transporting an issue from the realm of necessity or the private sphere to the public sphere: it is "the process by means of which decision-making powers and the associated authoritative interpretations of facts and circumstances are brought into the political sphere" (de Wilde and Zürne, 2011, p. 142). Politicization of EU is a general but uneven trend that took off in the late 1980s as a function of the expanded authority that was bestowed upon European institutions. De Wilde and Zürne (2011) notice that more recently politicization of EU has acquired a stronger discursive dimension consisting of an increasing controversy of issues and narratives together with the widening of the audiences interested and actively engaged in EU affairs. De Wilde (2011) underlines that the crystallization of conflicts within politicization is the result of a general practice of competitive representatives claims-making within which actors present themselves as representatives publicly and thereby contest other representatives. As a result, the discursive dimension of politicization emerges as an agonistic and value-laden field where political actors make their claims about EU and compete to affirm their representativeness. While a thorough assessment of politicization as it has evolved during EP2014 is far beyond the scope of this contribution, rather what matters here is to explore whether and eventually how Twitter has become a relevant stage for the politicization of institutions and issues of EU.

With regards to the communicative innovation, several analyses that have been produced during all the electoral campaign converge in registering the high intensity of the Twitter debate. According to Topsy.com[3], during the month of May the hashtag #EP2014 gathered over a million tweets, which is half of those of the Eurovision song contest (#eurovision) but ten times those sent during the television debate between the four candidates held on May 15 (#telleurope)[4].

Starting two months prior to the election, the think-thank created by the University of Vienna together with GfK, has identified 1,346,647 tweets that contained the words "European election" and "European Parliament" in all official EU languages or used similar hashtags (Maireder, Schlögl, et al. 2014). The mapping of the followers networks – which emerges from the aggregation of individual choices on whom to follow – has pointed out the presence of a central trans-European sphere which acted as a bridge between the several nation-based clusters and was responsible for most of the European-wide information diffusion. This central sphere consisted mainly of accounts directly related to the European Union, such as the official account of the Commission, several accounts of commissioners as well as several European Parliament members and candidates. However, if the structure was predisposed to give higher centrality to accounts that have strong institutional connections to the European Union (institutional bodies, representatives or candidates), national parties, and especially those that were critical of the common currency or had a distinctly anti-EU orientation, attracted the greatest part of social conversations (Pew Research Center, 2014). Examining the sentiment and the most discussed topics surrounding the EP2014 on a sample of more than 1.2 million tweets in English, French and German, the research by the Pew Center shows that national parties, and especially those with an explicitly anti EU platform, draw more attention than individual candidates.

So far, the available data show highly intense social conversations which, on the one hand, have been strategically encouraged by institutions and, on the other hand, have been mostly catalyzed by centres of gravity that are national and opinion-oriented. It is commonly acknowledged that Twitter communication cannot be considered as a representative sample of the general public. Those using social networking sites to express their opinion comprise a small slice of the entire public and Twitter seems to have hosted more discontent against EU than what was recently registered by Pew research on a sample that was representative of seven EU nations (Pew Research Center, 2013; 2014). And yet, despite its lack of representativeness, these first studies that have just been briefly outlined show that the peculiar segment of political discussion that took shape in Twitter during EP2014 had been entangled in larger discursive phenomena that involved both institutionalized communication harbored by the EU and opinion-oriented publics gathered around radical disagreement against those same institutions. This peculiar position points out that the symbolic value that is stratifying in this micro-blogging platform goes beyond the mere social representativeness of opinions that are expressed. The aim of the following paragraph is to give a contribution to the understanding of this symbolic value, through the analysis of the mutual shaping between the specific grammar of the micro-blogging platform and the ongoing politicization of the EU as it has taken shape within the fluxes of Twitter conversations generated in Italy during the campaign for EP2014.

FRAMING THROUGH AFFILIATION: THE ITALIAN TWITTER-SPHERE AROUND EP2014

The empirical study here presented has explored the flux of conversations that took place in the Italian Twitter-sphere during the European elections campaign. Although relatively lower than 2009, the Italian turnout reached 58% which is still higher than the EU average (42.54%)[5]. The considerable political significance these elections acquired, faithfully mirrored the turbulent political situation that was being experienced in the national context. Since the beginning, the European elections were framed as a two-horse race between the newborn Government of Matteo Renzi (Democratic Party), in office since February 2014, and the anti-establishment and populist 5 Star Movement, led by the former comedian Beppe Grillo and hugely strengthened by the spectacular success obtained in 2013's general election. In front of the strong pro-European stance taken by Matteo Renzi and his party, an heterogeneous coalition of no-euro opinion-leaders gradually emerged in a grey-zone, allegedly independent but variously contiguous to right-wing parties as Brothers of Italy – National Alliance (Fratelli D'Italia – Alleanza Nazionale) and Northern League. This no-euro coalition was composed of academics, bankers and bureaucrats who were previously unknown to the public but whom, during the election campaign, started to become more and more popular thanks to sophisticated media synergies between their personal blogs, their social media profiles and a regular presence in television talk-shows. The election returns registered a resounding victory of the Prime Minister, whose centre-left Democratic Party won more than 40% of the vote, and a disappointing performance of 5 Star Movement which didn't overcome 22% of the vote. Not successful but still noteworthy were the returns of the no-euro parties, with 6% obtained by the Northern League and 3% obtained by Brothers of Italy-National Alliance.

The theoretical premises that have been illustrated in the preceding paragraphs, have conceptually supported the peculiar approach to empirical inquiry that is going to be addressed now. The discursive dimension of EU politicization has been described as a competitive and potentially conflicting claim-making process characterized by an increasing polarization of opinions, interests and values. When deployed in Twitter, this process of claim-making has to rely on the specific socio-technical features of the platform which entail the performative function of hashtags and the peculiar call for affiliation they allow. The claim-making becomes thus possible within a network of publics that have been convened and invited to participate in an affiliative and value-laden space of discourse whereby meanings, identities and issues of Europe can be negotiated. The empirical inquiry has started with the collection of all the hashtags related to EP2014 that were used in the Italian Twitter-sphere during the period April 25th and May 25th. The collection followed a snowball technique. Daily monitoring of the Twitter profiles of all the Italian candidates, hashtags used by them were primarily identified; then, a second set of hashtags was identified following the stream of tweets gathered around primary hashtags; at the same time, the main general hashtags used in Italy -#elezionieuropee, #euro2014, #EP2014, #Europee - were constantly monitored looking for other hashtags that would have not been otherwise caught. On the whole, a sample of 189 hashtags were collected (selected as pertinent to EP2014 among the 221 originally collected). The first analytical step consisted of a classification of all the hashtags in four main categories, inductively elaborated on the basis of their topical domain: *evenemential, thematic, satiric, catchphrase*. The "evenemential" were those hashtags that expressed the main frame of the event, such as -#elezionieuropee, #euro2014, #EP2014, #Europee. They were used as large containers of all the tweets related to the political event, without any specific value or political identity connotation. "Thematic" hashtags were those which collected tweets about specific topics connected to EP2014. It is already a relevant finding to realize that they were mainly linked to the debate about Euro currency and that they articulated the opposition between those defending it and those fiercely opposing it[6]. Few exceptions were registered, as #stopvivisection, or #riparteilfuturo, the latter being a hashtag launched by Libera, a NGO fighting against *mafia* that, during EP2014, promoted a petition through change.org and a campaign against political corruption. "Satiric" hashtags were used mainly in the dispute between Democratic Party and 5 Star Movement[7]. Although massively sustained by both constituencies, satiric hashtags were initially launched by the parties' official accounts or by accounts of parties' communication managers. They used the strategy of subversion and détournement on the adversary's slogan in order to ridicule and delegitimize it. Finally, the hashtags "catchphrase" were used by each political fraction to spread the slogans of their electoral campaign[8]. The empirical research that was conducted consisted of an ethnographic observation of the stream of tweets gathered around thematic, satiric and catchphrase hashtags. While collecting hashtags and inductively identifying the typologies to classify them, the researcher accessed to Twitter through her personal account and daily followed and read all the tweets and related hyperlinks. At the end of the month, the sequences of visualized tweets were saved and accessed for a further analysis which was supported by all the ethnographic notes taken during daily observation.

This kind of observation has structural limitations insofar as the number of tweets effectively produced often exceed those that are visible and accessible by a single Twitter account. These relevant structural limits that are linked to technical mediation of observant's position, precluded the development of an exhaustive and comprehensive examination of what happened in the Italian Twitter-sphere during EP2014. However, the purpose was to develop an in-depth, contextual and contingent understanding that can be complementary to web content analysis of large data sets or social network analysis that are more commonly applied to the study of communicative process unfolding in social media. The ethnographic observation has thus been conceived as a theoretically-informed exploration into an empirical area that hasn't yet been deeply examined. As Zappavigna (2011) highlights, while studies of online discourse are relatively established, the processes though which linguistic patterns in social media contribute to "build affiliation and communitarian bonds is still an emergent area of inquiry" (p. 789). According to Herring (2013), large-scale automated analysis can and should coexist with ethnographic case studies, at least until online environments are not understood well enough to distill parameters that can be subjected to systematic and quantitative analysis. The ethnographic exploration here discussed has been informed by the aim of identifying the kind of affiliation that is created by the sequence of tweets containing the same hashtag. If, following Zappavigna, the hashtag can be considered as a meta-text that entails the summons of a potential discursive community, then what is the kind of affiliation concretely established by hashtags used during EP2014? Moreover, we know that this affiliation is something different than connection or direct interaction between people and rather coincides with the establishing of a common discursive space where negotiation of meaning is possible. Is it therefore plausible to expect that, within this affiliation framework, structure of meanings concerning Europe have been shaped and negotiated?

METHODOLOGY

The first issue to be dealt with is how to find dynamics of affiliation, cohesion and unity in a discursive material that is extremely fragmented, discontinuous and disjointed. The text that should be explored is not a dialogue, neither a narration; it is rather a mosaic assembled through the hyper-textuality of bricolage, an endless process of textual manipulation consisting of "personalized, continuous and more or less autonomous assembly, disassembly and reassembly of mediated reality" (Deuze, 2006, p. 66). As Chouliaraki (2010) argues, "a key characteristic of technologisation of textualities of mediation is its mutation into discourse without narrative, without a cohesive structures of story-telling so essential to traditional forms of public communication" (p. 230). Therefore, if the aim is to look for that affiliation which allows structures of meanings to be shaped and negotiated, it is not analytically plausible to find it in a cohesive narrative structure that tidily lays out issues, identities and values, neither in the logical accumulation of arguments that is typical of deliberative conversations. Consequently, the assumption that has guided the ethnographic exploration discussed here presumes that affiliation resides not in context, nor in content, rather it should be searched for in the mutual implication between content and context. Beyond the circumscribed content of the single tweet, the meanings of communication are embodied in the entire stream of tweets within which a single message is incorporated.

This is the reason why the approach of ethnography of communication has appeared to be the best equipped methodology to explore how the affiliation instantiated by hashtags is concretely translated into negotiation of meanings. Adoption of ethnographic methodology to online spaces and practices is not new and a growing body of literature (Hine, 2000, 2008; Juris, 2012; Marwick and Boyd, 2011) has been dealing with the challenge of "adapting" methods (Hine, 2000) to the new routes to knowledge that are introduced by online/offline engagements. In order to adapt it to the peculiar communicative context of Twitter, it has been useful to go back to the essential grounds of ethnography of communication, as an approach, a perspective and a method that studies «culturally distinctive means and meanings of communication» (Carbaugh, 2007, p. 1). In orienting attention towards the socially situated uses and meanings of words, their relations and sequential forms of expression, ethnography of communication offers procedures for analyzing communication practices as formative of social life. Several concepts, like communication event, communication act, communication situation and speech community, have been introduced to analyse communication in context (Hymes, 1972). In this context, what appears more relevant for the exploration of affiliation within hashtags, is the combination between the *communicative act*, defined as a single interactional function, such as a referential statement, a request, or a command, and the *communicative event*, considered as a sequential structuring of acts involving culturally bounded aspects of social life. This combination can be grasped through one of the components towards which ethnography of communication usually pays attention; the component is the *act sequence* that is involved in and for the communicative practice: "The practice is part of social interaction. When does it arise and as part of what sequence? And further, what are the content of the practice and its form? This component invites a careful look at the sequential organization of the practice, its message content, and form" (Carbaugh, 2007, p. 4).

While a tweet can be indisputably thought of as a communicative act, the adaptation of the notion of communicative event to Twitter is not as uncontroversial. In the original formulation, a communicative event is "defined by a unified set of components, beginning with the same general purpose of communication, the same general topic, and involving the same participants, generally using the same language variety, maintaining the same tone or key and the same rules for interaction, in the same setting" (Saville-Troike, 2003; p. 23). However, the definition seems to be too much rigid to be applied to the open, fragmented, patchy and hyper-textual communicative environment of Twitter and other social media: participants can constantly evolve, increasing or decreasing their number according to contingent conditions, involving or excluding specific social identities; expressivity entails a wide range of linguistic styles and rules for interaction are constantly, and sometimes hardly, negotiated between participants. What can be still found in Twitter is the sharing of the same general topic and this is exactly the clue that perhaps can legitimize to consider the entire stream of tweets grouped by the same hashtag as a communicative event in itself. If the affiliation cannot be found in the narrative cohesion neither in the dialectic dialogue, then it can be searched for in the *act sequence*, in how form and content of the message are included in a sequential organization of acts. Rather than considering the single tweet as unit of analysis, the ethnographic observation has thus paid attention to the sequential articulation of tweets within the same hashtags. Following the rule of studying communication in context, the purpose was to look if and how the sequence contained redundancies, repetitions, coherence, referred to content, to form or to both of them. The theoretical premise of ambient affiliation brought the analysis to identify any component that was unitarily shared by a great majority of tweets, independently from the direct interactions concretely occurring between different participants. The analytic aim was to check if a kind of cohesion could be detected and whether this same cohesion worked as a possible entry point towards a shared discursive space where the negotiation of meanings was possible. The identification of coherences within the same sequence made use of a generic text analysis focused on three main aspects: the occurrence of discernible patterns in texts' thematic structure, the presence of appeals to partisan or shared values, the establishment of credibility and trust in relation to the structuring of knowledge[9].

RITUALIZATION AND RATIONALIZATION

In both the conversations gathered around the ironic and catchphrase hashtags, a principle of coherence was detected in the sequential repetition of a similar linguistic structure, within which a limited margin of creative personalization was allowed. In the tweets containing those hashtags related to the slogans of the electoral campaigns, the sequence of tweets appeared to act as a sounding board for the main values heralded by parties' leaders.

Common to the different political factions was the repeated affirmation of the campaign's slogan together with a rich variety of pictures showing the several electoral events taking place in physical spaces, the smiling faces of people involved or other panoramic pictures metaphorically alluding to the wholeness of the general will, that soon would have materialized in votes (see Figure 1). The visual richness of the messages, with the assertiveness in personally reaffirming the values of the slogans, were the main components of a cohesive sequence of self-disclosure's practices. These practices added to the ideal principles of the leader's electoral discourses the concreteness of a smiling face or a crowded room, ideally offering a perceptible embodiment of the main narration displayed by the political campaign. These sequences thus revealed multiple internal coherences in all the three aspects that were explored: in the text's thematic structure, which dealt with the facts and the events of the election campaign, in the appealing to partisan values, and in the establishment of trust and credibility that strongly relied on providing documentary evidence of the narrated facts.

Figure 1. Three examples of tweets containing catchphrase hashtags and referred respectively (from the left) to the Democratic Party, Brothers of Italy- National Alliance, The Other Europe with Tsipras.

The discursive phenomena that took place under the ironic hashtag developed a linguistic mechanism that was similar to *meme* (Shifman, 2012). Movimento 5 Stelle kicked off the sarcastic dispute, subverting the main Democratic Party's slogan. The PD's slogan said #celochieditu ("this is what you are asking of us") and circulated in the form of a poster where it was associated to images of ordinary people and to the several topics of the electoral program. Since the ideation, this slogan was conceived purposefully as a participatory motto through which citizens were invited to complete the sentence expressing their specific instances[10]. Therefore, #celochieditu sounded as if the party's candidates were racing to give voice to citizens. Few days after the launch of the slogan, Movimento 5 Stelle, through the official account of the leader Beppe Grillo, launched a parody of it where the voices and instances by citizens were replaced by the private interests of corrupt businessman and politicians. An example of this was #celochiedeSilvio ["This is what Silvio (Berlusconi) is asking of us] but the variations on theme were several and involved all the main targets of Beppe Grillo's complaints against political and financial corruption. Then, the Democratic Party replied with a counter-hashtag #celochiedebeppe ("this is what Beppe Grillo is asking of us") sarcastically alluding to the non-democratic leadership of Beppe Grillo; even in this case, a long wave of tweets followed, remembering all the circumstances in which Beppe Grillo took controversial political stances without consulting Movimento 5 Stelle's constituency. This mocking dispute allowed both political factions to incisively display all the main contrastive arguments that each of them was sustaining in order to delegitimize the adversary. Ultimately, it served to cement an already established opposition *us* vs *them*.

In both ironic and catchphrase streams, cohesion clearly emerged through the repetition of the same discursive articulation – the sarcastic parody of adversary's discourse, in the first case, and a personal endorsement of the slogan through claims and faces in the second case – which was in turn accompanied by personalized variations on theme. It seems that affiliation was therefore achieved through a peculiar form of ritualized communication consisting of an endless reiteration of the same script. The reiteration progressively involved an increasing number of people and the script was double articulated into a standardized component and a variable one, the latter being imperatively delegated to the personalization and creative appropriation by participants. It seems that a kind of normative dimension was at stake in ensuring the internal coherence within the sequence of tweets: the inclusion of those specific hashtags within the tweet was meaningful only if accompanied by the reproposition of the same discursive structure that was prevailing in the rest of the sequence. This is something very similar to the social processes that underpin the participation to rituals.

While the notion of rituals remains a controversial sociological category, the definition proposed by Rothenbuhler (1998) can offer some coordinates for applying it to the realm of social media. Drawing upon a large review of literature, Rothenbuhler explains rituals as intentional performances which show a patterned behavior and participate to the serious life (Durkheim, 1912) of society. Three elements in this definition are worth focusing on here.

The first one regards the relevance of behavioral script. The ritual performance should be carried out following a script that is stereotyped and pre-codified and cannot be originally reinvented during each execution. The original model that inspires it, is also a criterion for assessing adequacy of the performance. What happened within the two monitored hashtags, can therefore be understood as a process by which political parties and parties' activists have incorporated in their communication strategies the vernacular model of "mimicking culture" (Shifman, 2011).

While the concept of *meme* was used long before the digital era (Hull, 1982) to define units of culture that spread from person to person by means of copying or imitation, "mimicking culture" points out the widespread phenomenon of popular clips that generate extensive user engagement by way of creative derivatives. Its working mechanism materializes the participatory logic of convergence culture (Jenkins et al. 2007) within which, the content is endlessly reconfigured and publicly displayed in parodies, mashups, remixes and other derivative formats. Unlike viral content that spread to the masses via digital word-of-mouth without significant changes, "memetic videos" attract «participation through mimesis» (Shifman, 2011, p. 190) whereby users are engaged in both imitation (parroting elements from a video) and re-mix (technologically-afforded re-editing of the video) of the original content.

Inviting users to embody values of the electoral campaign or to creatively subvert the original slogans, both the catchphrase and ironic hashtags involved people in a ritualized communication whose original model belongs to the vernacular culture of the web.

The second element taken from Rothenbuhler's definition of rituals specifies that rituals are personal fulfillments which need personal will and awareness in order to be accomplished. Each participant has the possibility of personally calibrating the orthodoxy of performance, of slightly varying the style and the enthusiasm of the script's enactment. While the model of inspiration cannot be contingently decided by the participant, the enactment of the ritual basically depends on the will of participants and on their attitude to recognize themselves in the symbolic world evoked by the ritual. In a very similar way, each tweet that was referred to the ironic and catchphrase hashtags, showed the relevance of the original contribution that each participant gave to the choral representation of both the adversary and his/her own faction. Each of them emphasized a different aspect of the main political narrations that were simultaneously circulating in the wider and multi-media communicative event of European electoral campaigns. In this way, the single communicative act that was involved in the communicative sequence of each hashtag, also entailed a set of practices of self-disclosure and personal expression. From this point of view, the participation to this kind of ritualized communication can be understood as an organizational mechanism through which individual contributions are made to flow into a collective discursive endeavor.

Finally, the third point from Rothenbuhler is that rituals take part in the serious life (Durkheim, 1912) of society. What distinguishes the ritual from the ordinary behavior is the patterned and codified form it should enact in order to become meaningful. The script performed by the ritual does not have an intrinsic meaning, it is rather a sign of something else that exists beyond the *hic et nunc* of the performance. The rituals participate in the serious life of society because the distilled evidence of its cultural forms symbolizes and materializes specific values.

Values were explicitly stated in catchphrase hashtags but they were also indirectly implied in the ironic ones and in their specific way of addressing criticisms to the adversary. Their symbolic strength was enhanced by the ritualized communication based both on reiterated scripts and creative derivatives. This is possibly the clue that allows us to go back to the notion of ambient affiliation as a form of cohesion that has to do less with interactional connection and more with creating discursive space where meaning is negotiated. The final hypothesis that has emerged from the ethnographic exploration is that the kind of ambient affiliation created by catchphrase and ironic hashtags consisted in a peculiar form of communicative ritualization. These communicative rituals drew upon a set of practices commonly diffused in the vernacular culture of the web and allowed the opening of a symbolic space where Europe-related meaning have been negotiated. Ultimately, Europe and EP2014 have been framed into a structure of values that found its roots in the national politics and its antagonisms.

Something different happened within thematic hashtags, which were focused on approvals/refusals of the Euro currency and gathered heterogeneous groups of participants who only partially overlapped constituencies of established parties. A decisive role in the shaping of this strand of conversation was played by the No-Euro coalition, and mostly by its peculiar types of opinion-leaders which, as previously stated, were external to politics and with a professional background in academia and/or in finance. Flaunting their expert knowledge and simultaneously assuming an educational attitude, these opinion-leaders were the main sources of discursive fragments that repeatedly circulated in the sequences of tweets and that framed Yes/No Euro debate in technical and (apparently) politically neutral terms. Besides a portion of assertive claims, the great majority of tweet founds its internal cohesion in a discursive structure that was argumentative and informational. Links to news media, to explanatory articles or diagrams were frequently used to argue for the necessity to stay in or exit from the Euro area. Rather than reaffirming and symbolically strengthening values, as was the case in ironic and catchphrase hashtags, the sequence of tweets generated within the thematic hashtags contributed to the cooperative building of a system of knowledge where subjectivities and logics of action related to financial and economic domains were ordered within an intelligible representation. In Yes/No Euro quarrel, the structure of meanings that framed Europe was not made of values, rather by a sequence of circumscribed issues and of explanations claiming for cognitive legitimization. A certain idea of Europe was thus legitimized through rationalization (Van Leeuwen, 2007), by reference to the social knowledge that endows institutionalized social actions with cognitive validity.

The ethnography of sequences of tweets gathered under the same hashtag, has thus shown the emergence of two different kinds of affiliation: one is based on the ritualistic reinforcement of values that guide and differentiate political discourses, while the other one revolves around accumulation of practical argumentations and technical knowledge apparently impermeable to political values. This difference has been in turn conducive of two different processes of politicization of European issues. Where ritualistic affiliation prevails, EU politicization occurs through a nationally filtered language of claims that resonate with national political context. The salience of EU-related issues is completely dependent from those political narratives that are functional to the fierce competition between national parties. According to both Democratic Party and 5 Star Movement, Europe is not an issue *per se* but appears to be one of the several agonistic fields where they have to translate their representativeness and to fight for hegemony. On the contrary, it is within the more divisive quarrel between Yes/No Euro factions, that politicization of EU arises with greater salience and fierce polarization. The debate around the currency developed through practical argumentations and expert knowledge; relying mainly on technical information apparently devoid of values, it tried to gain credibility through its claimed indifference towards national political controversies. As a relevant but not unique stage of the EU-politicization, the Italian Twittersphere during EP2014 has shown that the «Europeanization of meaning structure» (Trenz, 2008, p. 6) becomes strongest when mediated by highly contentious issues that, rather than consolidating a shared framework, push for the breakdown of general political order.

TWITTER AS A SOUNDING BOARD

The chapter has examined Twitter as a public sphere where citizens narrate the social and actively construct their own understandings of the reality that surround them. It has developed a theoretical and empirical approach that aims at taking into account both the patterns of meanings that attract shared attention on the platform and the socio-technical affordances that constitute their conditions of possibility. Among the several elements that shape the techno-cultural spaces of Twitter, the contribution has focused attention on the hashtags and on the performative function they exert in summoning publics and tracing their

Figure 2. Three examples of tweets containing thematic hashtags and arguing pro and against Euro

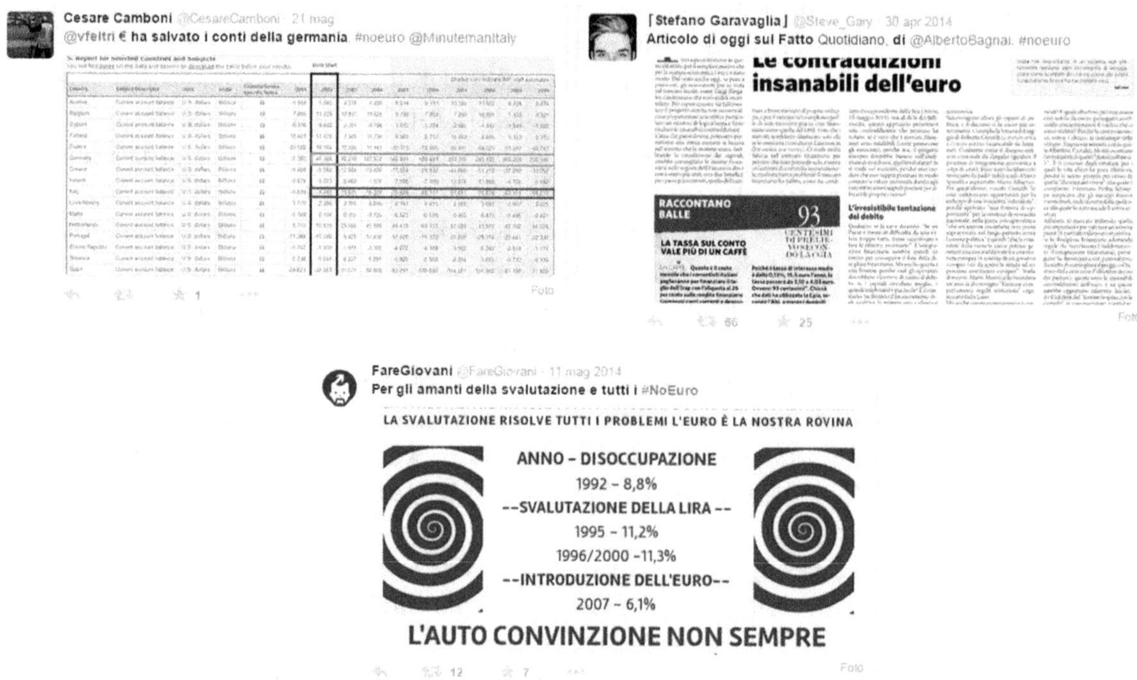

thematic route. Hashtags as linguistic markers that entail a call for affiliation, are supposed to open a space of shared attention where meaning can be negotiated and claims can be antagonistically confronted. Twitter conversations generated in Italy during the EP2014 have been used as a privileged viewpoint for the analysis of the relationship between the discursive processes taking place in Twitter and the wider European public sphere, currently invested by an uneven yet irreversible politicization of stances and identities. The empirical research has confronted with the methodological challenge of looking for that collective dimension of the discourse wherein affiliation is established through discursive commonality rather than through direct interaction. While in current literature on Twitter the relational dimension generated within social media is mainly studied through social network analysis pointing both at the network of followers and the network interactively generated by mentions and/or re-tweets, the research here discussed has privileged the less haunted path of ethnography. Ethnography of communication, with its focus on communication in context, has revealed itself to be the most suited methodology to study affiliation as a special kind of social relation that resides in the mutual implication between the content of the single tweet and the contextual stream where it is incorporated. While the empirical findings of the research cannot be generalized, neither can they be considered as an exhaustive examination of all that happened in the Italian Twitter-sphere during EP2014, the study has been conceived as a propaedeutic step towards more systematic analyses of the performative function of hashtags.

Analysing in depth a limited set of hashtags and the related sequences of tweets produced in the month prior to the elections, the research has identified two main patterns of affiliation - ritualization and rationalization - and explained how they are conducive to different paths to politicization of European issues. Findings have shown that Twitter effectively acted as a forum of the wider public sphere insofar as it offered a polyphonic stage for the competitive claims-making process that brings Europe in the conflicting arena of public debate. However, the specific way in which this happened has illuminated the kind of connections that link Twitter to the other several fora of the public sphere. The thematic analysis has indeed revealed that Twitter did not convey facts, information and knowledge that wouldn't have been otherwise publicly available on other online platforms or even in physical spaces. On the contrary, it incorporated already existing content, symbols and facts in its streams of affiliation, enhancing their symbolic value both through the collective rituals of memes and through the pressing accumulation of practical argumentations pro and against the Euro. It has thus been possible to grasp one of the several aspects that are likely to underline that indefinite symbolic value of Twitter which is confirmed by the considerable strategic and institutional investment it receives but simultaneously denied by its objective lack of capillary diffusion and social representativeness. Rather than as an autonomous sphericule (Gitlin, 1998), Twitter has therefore emerged as a sounding board for the wider public sphere, as a complementary interactional arena where publics are summoned and the symbolic capital of shared attention is produced, exchanged and claimed.

REFERENCES

Alexander, J. C., & Jacobs, R. N. (1998). Mass Communication, Ritual and Civil Society. In T. Liebes & J. Curran (Eds.), *Media, ritual, and identity* (pp. 23–41). London: Routledge.

Bärenreuter, C., Brüll, C., Mokre, M., & Wahl-Jorgensen, K. (2009). *An Overview of Research on the European Public Sphere*. Online Working Paper No. 03.

Benkler, Y. (2006). *The Wealth of Networks: How Social Production Transforms Markets and Freedom*. New Haven, CT: Yale University Press.

Boyd, D. (2011). Social network sites as networked publics. In Z. Papacharissi (Ed.), *Networked Self: Identity, Community, and Culture on Social Network Sites* (pp. 39–58). New York: Routledge.

Bruns, A., & Burgess, J. E. (2011). The use of Twitter hashtags in the formation of ad hoc publics. In *6th European Consortium for Political Research General Conference*. University of Iceland.

Bruns, A., & Moe, H. (2013). Structural Layers of Communication on Twitter. In K. Weller, A. Bruns, J. Burgess, M. Mahrt, & C. Puschmann (Eds.), *Twitter and Society* (pp. 15–28). New York, NY: Peter Lang.

Bruns, A., & Stieglitz, S. (2012). Quantitative approaches to comparing communication patterns on Twitter. *Journal of Technology in Human Services*, *30*(3-4), 160–185. doi:10.1080/15228835.2012.744249

Burgess, J., & Sauter, L. (2014). *Hashtag as hybrid forum: the case of #agchatoz*. Paper presented at the Conference "Social Media and the Transformation of Public Space", Amsterdam.

Callon, M., Lascoumes, P., & Barth, Y. (2001). *Acting in an Uncertain World. An Essay on Technical Democracy*. Cambridge, MA: MIT Press.

Carbaugh, D. (2007). Ethnography of Communication. In W. Donsbach (Ed.), *International Encyclopedia of Communication*. Hoboken, NJ: Wiley Blackwell. Retrieved October, 15, from http://works.bepress.com/donal_carbaugh/12

Chouliaraki, L. (2010). Self-mediation: New media and citizenship. *Critical Discourse Studies*, *7*(4), 227–232. doi:10.1080/17405904.2010.511824

Couldry, N. (2012). *Media, Society, World*. Cambridge, MA: Polity Press.

Crawford, K. (2009). Following you: Disciplines of listening in social media. *Continuum (Perth)*, *23*(4), 525–535. doi:10.1080/10304310903003270

Dayan, D. (2005). Mothers, Midwives and Abortionists. Genealogy and obstetrics of Audiences and Publics. In S. Livingstone (Ed.), *Audiences and Publics. When Cultural Engagement matters for the Public Sphere* (pp. 43–76). Bristol, CT: Intellect Press.

De Wilde, P. (2011). No Polity for Old Politics? A Framework for Analyzing the Politicization of European Integration. *Journal of European Integration*, *33*(5), 559–575. doi:10.1080/07036337.2010.546849

De Wilde, P., & Zürn, M. (2012). Can the Politicization of European Integration Be Reversed? *Journal of Common Market Studies*, *50*(1), 137–153. doi:10.1111/j.1468-5965.2011.02232.x

Deuze, M. (2006). Participation, remediation, bricolage: Considering principal components of a digital culture. *The Information Society*, *22*(2), 63–75. doi:10.1080/01972240600567170

Erickson, I. (2010). Geography and community: New forms of interaction among people and places. *The American Behavioral Scientist*, *53*(8), 1194–1207. doi:10.1177/0002764209356250

Fairclough, I., & Fairclough, N. (2012). *Political Discourse Analysis: A Method for Advanced Students*. London: Routledge.

Fairclough, N. (1995). *Critical Discourse Analysis*. London: Longman.

Flew, T., Bruns, A., Burgess, J. E., Crawford, K., & Shaw, F. (2013). *Social media and its impact on crisis communication: Case studies of Twitter use in emergency management in Australia and New Zealand*. In ICA Regional Conference "Communication and Social Transformation", Shanghai, China.

Fraser, N. (1992). Rethinking the Public Sphere: a Contribution to the Critique of Actually Existing Democracy. In C. Calhoun (Ed.), *Habermas and The Public Sphere* (pp. 109–142). Cambridge, MA: The MIT Press.

Gerhards, J., & Schäfer, M. (2010). Is the Internet a better public sphere? Comparing old and new media in the USA and Germany. *New Media & Society*, *12*(1), 143–160. doi:10.1177/1461444809341444

Gitlin, T. (1998). Public Sphere or Public Sphericules? In T. Liebes & J. Curran (Eds.), *Media, Ritual, and Identity* (pp. 168–174). London: Routledge.

Hermida, A. (2010). From TV to Twitter: How ambient news became ambient journalism. *M/C Journal*, *13*(2). Retrieved from: http://journal.media-culture.org.au/index.php/mcjournal/article/viewArticle/220

Herring, S. (2013). Discourse in Web 2.0: Familiar, reconfigured, and emergent. In D. Tannen & A. M. Tester (Eds.), *Discourse 2.0: Language and new media* (pp. 1–26). Washington, DC: Georgetown University Press.

Hine, C. (2000). *Virtual Ethnography*. London: Sage.

Hine, C. (2008). Overview: Virtual ethnography: modes, varieties, affordances. In N. G. Fielding, R. M. Lee, & G. Blank (Eds.), *Handbook of Online Research Methods* (pp. 257–270). London: Sage. doi:10.4135/9780857020055.n14

Hogan, B. (2013). Comment on Elena Pavan/1: Considering Platforms as Actors. *Sociologica, 3*. doi:10.2383/75767

Huang, J., Thornton, C., & Efthimiadis, E. N. (2010). Conversational Tagging in Twitter. In *Proceedings of the 21st ACM Conference on Hypertext and Hypermedia*. Toronto, Canada. doi:10.1145/1810617.1810647

Hull, D. L. (1982). The naked meme. In Learning, Development and Culture: Essays in Evolutionary Epistemology (pp. 273–327). New York: John Wiley and Sons.

Hutter, S., & Grande, E. (2014). Politicizing Europe in the National Electoral Arena: A Comparative Analysis of Five West European Countries, 1970–2010. *JCMS: Journal of Common Market Studies, 52*(5), 1002–1018.

Hymes, D. (1972). Models of the interaction of language and social life. In J. Gumperz & D. Hymes (Eds.), *Directions in sociolinguistics: The ethnography of communication* (pp. 35–71). New York: Holt, Rinehart and Winston.

Ito, M. (2008). Introduction. In K. Varnelis (Ed.), *Networked Publics* (pp. 1–14). Cambridge, MA: MIT Press. doi:10.7551/mitpress/9780262220859.003.0001

Jenkins, H., Clinton, K., Purushotma, R., Robinson, A. J., & Weigel, M. (2007). *Confronting the Challenges of Participatory Culture: Media Education for the 21st Century*. Chicago, IL: The MacArthur Foundation.

Jungherr, A. (2014). *Twitter in politics: a comprehensive literature review*. Available at: http://papers.ssrn.com/sol3/papers.cfm?abstract_id=2402443

Juris, J. (2012). Reflections on #Occupy Everywhere: Social Media, Public Space, and Emerging Logics of Aggregation. *American Ethnologist, 39*(2), 259–279. doi:10.1111/j.1548-1425.2012.01362.x

Koopmans, R., & Erbe, J. (2004). Towards a European public sphere? *Innovation (Abingdon), 17*(2), 97–118. doi:10.1080/1351161042000238643

Krosnick, J. A. (1990). Government policy and citizen passion: A study of issue publics in contemporary America. *Political Behavior, 12*(1), 59–92. doi:10.1007/BF00992332

Langlois, G., Elmer, G., McKelvey, F., & Devereaux, Z. (2009). Networked Publics: The Double Articulation of Code and Politics on Facebook. *Canadian Journal of Communication, 34*(3), 415–434.

Latour, B., & Weibel, P. (2005). *Making things public: Atmospheres of democracy*. Cambridge, MA: The MIT Press.

Maggini, N. (2014). A turnout like in 2009 but with many "Europes" within the EU. In L. De Sio, V. Emanuele, & N. Maggini (Eds.), *The European Parliament Elections of 2014* (pp. 31–36). Rome: CISE.

Maireder, A., & Schlögl, S. (2014). 24 hours of an #outcry: The networked publics of a socio-political debate. *European Journal of Communication*, *29*(6), 687–702. first published online onSeptember22014. doi:10.1177/0267323114545710

Maireder, A., Schlögl, S., Schütz, F., Karwautz, M., & Waldheim, C. (2014). *The European Political Twittersphere*. Retrieved October, 15, 2014, from www.gfk.com/twitter

Marres, N. (2007). The issues deserve more credit: Pragmatist contributions to the study of public involvement in controversy. *Social Studies of Science*, *37*(5), 759–780. doi:10.1177/0306312706077367

Marwick, A., & Boyd, D. (2011). To See and Be Seen: Celebrity Practice on Twitter. *Convergence*, *17*(2), 139–158.

Mejias, U. (2008). *Networks and the politics of the para-nodal*. Paper presented at Politics: Web 2.0: An International Conference, Royal Holloway, Egham, UK.

Messina, C. (2007a). Groups for Twitter; or A Proposal for Twitter Tag Channels. *FactoryCity*. Retrieved October, 15, 2014, from http://factoryjoe.com/blog/2007/08/25/groups-for-twitter-or-a-proposal-for-twitter-tag-channels/

Page, R. (2012). The Linguistics of Self Branding and Micro-celebrity in Twitter: The Role of Hashtags. *Discourse and Communication*, *6*(2), 181–201. doi:10.1177/1750481312437441

Pew Research Centre. (2014). *The EU Elections on Twitter: Mixed Views about the EU and Little Passion for the Candidates*. Retrieved October 15, 2014, from http://www.journalism.org/files/2014/05/2014-05-22_The-EU-Elections-on-Twitter.pdf

Reif, K., & Schmitt, H. (1980). Nine Second-Order National Elections. A Conceptual Framework for the Analysis of European Election Results. *European Journal of Political Research*, *8*(1), 3–44. doi:10.1111/j.1475-6765.1980.tb00737.x

Rothenbuhler, E. W. (1998). *Ritual Communication. From Everyday Conversation to Mediated Ceremony*. Sage.

Saville-Troike, M. (2003). *The Ethnography of Communication*. Malden, MA: Blackwell Publishing. doi:10.1002/9780470758373

Shifman, L. (2012). An anatomy of a YouTube meme. *New Media & Society*, *14*(2), 187–203. doi:10.1177/1461444811412160

Statham, P., & Trenz, H.-J. (2012). *The Politicization of the European Union: Media Discourse, Political Contestation and the Public Sphere*. London: Routledge.

Trenz, H.-J. (2008). Measuring the Europeanisation of Public Communication. *European Political Science*, *7*(3), 273–284. doi:10.1057/eps.2008.19

van Dijck, J. (2013). *The Culture of Connectivity. A Critical History of Social Media*. Oxford, UK: Oxford University Press. doi:10.1093/acprof:oso/9780199970773.001.0001

Van Leeuwen, T. (2007). Legitimation in discourse and communication. *Discourse & Communication*, *1*(1), 91–112. doi:10.1177/1750481307071986

We are Social. (2014). *European Digital Landscape in 2014.* Available at: http://wearesocial.net/blog/2014/02/social-digital-mobile-europe-2014/

We are Social. (2015). *Digital, Social and Mobile in 2015.* Available at: http://wearesocial.net/blog/2015/01/digital-social-mobile-worldwide-2015/

Zappavigna, M. (2014). Enacting identity in microblogging through ambient affiliation. *Discourse and Communication*, *8*(2), 209–228. doi:10.1177/1750481313510816

ENDNOTES

1 http://www.europarl.europa.eu/news/en/news-room/content/20140525STO48301/html/The-European-elections-live-on-our-special-site

2 http://electionsnight2014.eu/twitterdashboard

3 Topsy.com is a real-time search engine which provides access to metrics for any term mentioned on Twitter via its free analytics service at analytics.topsy.com, where users can compare up to three terms for content in the past hour, day, week or month.

4 The comparison between the three hashtags has been created by Nikos Smyrnaios, University of Toulouse, and published in his personal blog: http://ephemeron.eu/wpcontent/uploads/2014/05/Topsy_eurovision_EP2014_telleurope.png

5 http://www.europarl.europa.eu/elections2014-results/en/election-results-2014.html

6 #euroexit; #noeuro; #noUE; #noeurostorm; #noUEtweetstorm; #sieuro; #proeuro#eurosi; #euroNO.

7 Some examples: #celochiedesilvio, #celochiedebeppe, #sevincegrillo.

8 Some examples: #altraeuropa; #alzalatesta; #bastaeuro; #celochieditu; #europacambiaverso; #ineuropaprimalitalia; #IoCambio; #IostoconlaMeloni ; #LaltraEuropa; #oltrelobiettivo; #Osiamo; #popolosovrano; #primagliitaliani; #SceglilEuropa; #SceltaEU; #sovrana; #vinciamonoi; #senza-paura; #sipuofare; #pugnisultavolo

9 Without strictly following any specific methodology of text analysis, this ethnography is properly inspired by two of the several analytical coordinates that have been elaborated by critical discourse analysis approach (Fairclough, 1995): the attention to the ways in which discourses build systems of knowledge and meanings, relying on values or practical argumentations (Fairclough and Fair-clough, 2012), and the contextualization of the text in the discourses and genres that are articulated in its production. The decision of using these well-established conceptual tools as loose sensitizing concepts, finds its reason in the peculiar design of the research, which has to be intended as an exploratory ethnography that is propaedeutic to more standardized analyses.

10 There has been also a website allowing citizens to personalize the posters with their faces and their political requests. It is still accessible at the following link: http://www.celochieditu.eu/#

Chapter 9

Post as Much and as Diversely as Possible: Intensity and Innovation in the Application of Twitter by Political Parties during the 2014 Slovenian National Election Campaign

Alem Maksuti
University of Ljubljana, Slovenia

Tomaž Deželan
University of Ljubljana, Slovenia

ABSTRACT

The daily interaction between political parties and voters is a driving force in election campaigns and can influence their outcomes. The theory of campaign intensity holds that the timing of message delivery in an election campaign is a key component of the strategies used by political actors. However, this theory also warns political actors to be cautious about the timing of different types of messages sent during the election campaign. Our objective is to examine the intensity and types of messages Slovenian political actors communicated through Twitter during different stages in the 2014 national election campaign. Our study conducts a content analysis of 7,113 tweets posted during the last four weeks of the official election campaign. It includes 17 official accounts of Slovenian parties, party leaders, and influential party twitterians. The results indicated that the stage of the campaign and the differences between established and fringe political parties significantly influenced the intensity of Twitter communications during the study period. The results also revealed that the political actors tweeted different types of political messages (e.g., to inform and to persuade voters) during different stages of the campaign.

DOI: 10.4018/978-1-4666-9879-6.ch009

INTRODUCTION

After failing to introduce important tax reforms and resolve leadership issues in the main governmental party in 2014, the left-wing government of Prime Minister Alenka Bratušek caused a second consecutive pre-term national election. Increased dissatisfaction with politics in general and the immense distrust of the party elites resulted in the emergence of new political parties that put forward seemingly different agendas based on higher moral grounds. The reduced campaign budgets of the established political parties showed scars of the continuing financial crisis, economic contraction, and recurring pre-term elections, thus playing into the hands of the new parties. Hence, the entire political establishment was forced to use free online self-promotional communication tools, such as websites and social networks (Oblak Črnič & Amon-Prodnik, 2014). One of the latter, Twitter was a widely utilized and influential communication tool in the Slovenian election campaign (see Deželan et al., 2014).

Twitter is popular among politicians, journalists, and opinion makers. As in the election campaign held two and a half years earlier, all political parties made extensive use of Twitter during the 2014 election campaign. All Slovenian parliamentary parties actively used Twitter on a more or less continuous basis, and key party leaders and visible party members chirpily joined the flock of tweeps and twitterians.[1] Traditional[2] and labor-intensive election campaign tools had been used in Slovenian election campaigns since the introduction of political pluralism in the late 1980s. However, the parties began to resort to post-modern tools of political campaigning because they are less capital-intensive than the costly advertising in the mass media, particularly television (see Deželan et al., 2010). Even though there still is the prevailing belief that nothing can replace television, this currently "immoral"[3] option has forced the parties to draft strategies combining the tools available with social media outlets and traditional canvassing with the free-of-charge air time guaranteed by the election campaign legislation. Consequently, election campaigns have become shorter, and they have focused on an officially defined 30-day campaign period, which has frequently been shorter (see CoARS, 2015).

Previous studies have shown that Twitter has been accepted as an integrative element of Slovenian party campaign strategies, which are focused on political interactions with voters and journalists and opinion makers in particular (e.g. Deželan et al., 2014). Informing voters about the party's position on particular issues emerged as the dominant mode of campaigning in the national election in 2011, which indicates that they still had not completely mastered the tool (ibid., p. 152). This also was indicated by their propensity to "visualize" this micro-blogging tool by appending photographic material to update voters on the campaign's progress and the activities that were performed offline (Tomanić-Trivundža, 2014). Additionally, the use of Twitter began to define the negotiation process in politico-journalistic relations (Vobič et al., 2014) and frequently revealed instances of journalists becoming an extended arm of the parties' propaganda machines (i.e., exaggerated re-tweeting of tweets posted by a particular party or by its highest echelons) (Mance, 2014). Predictably, studies also have revealed that parties have restrained from hiring professionals to run their Twitter accounts, even during the most intensive stages of campaigning. However, it is particularly surprising that they engage in their Twitter adventures without using serious strategies (Deželan et al., 2014). This has resulted in a haphazard political battlefield that is probably best understood by the actual audience—engaged network citizens (see Xenos et al., 2014).

Deželan, Vobič, and Maksuti (2014, p. 157) revealed that during election campaigns, the direct communication by politicians with voters, journalists, and opinion makers, which comprised approximately one third of their entire Twitter communication, ranged between expressions of affection and conflict. This finding supports the argument that the utilization of Twitter, particularly to convey emotions, contributes to increasing the campaign dynamics (Carsey, 2001), which is often the rule in "hard-fought" election races during the last days of election campaigns (Kahn & Kenney, 1997). Even though substantial and coherent Twitter campaign strategies have been virtually absent from the Slovenian political realm, the use of interviews in 2011 indicated that the parties intuitively tried to integrate Twitter into their overall campaign strategies.

By examining the intensity of the use of Twitter by political parties and their key representatives, this study aims to investigate the centrality of Twitter in contemporary election campaigning in Slovenia. The study will also review some key theories of campaign intensity. It is therefore necessary to re-examine the hypothesis of campaign intensity (see Kahn & Kenney, 1997, 1999; Sulkin, 2001), which posits that "intense electoral races are characterized by high candidate visibility, a real competition for votes, and a large, and balanced information flow" (Sulkin 2001, p. 609). Grounded in the theory of political psychology, the intensity hypothesis supports the assumption that the timing of message delivery in an election campaign is a key component of the strategy used by political actors. Messages that are received the closest to Election Day are expected to have a greater effect on the behavior of voters than messages received earlier in the campaign (Panagopoulos, 2011, p. 82).

In the case of Twitter, intensity refers to the increased flow of information (Sulkin, 2001, p. 609; Aragón et al., 2013, p. 189; Kruikemeier, 2014, p. 135). It is therefore reasonable to expect that political campaigners will increase the frequency of communicated messages as the election day approaches. Furthermore, message timing and tactics (i.e., the mode of mediation) are also important in understanding the kinds of messages political actors send to voters. In the context of the rational (strategic) behavior of parties during an election campaign, message timing and tactics present several dilemmas: when to send (tweet) information about their campaign activities and urge voters to the pools (Panagopoulos, 2011); when to take a stance on "valence" issues (Stokes, 1992); when to increase the salience of issues in which particular parties have a relative advantage (Carsey, 2001; Carsey et al., 2011; Sides, 2006); when to attack their political counterparts; and which voter contact tactics to employ, directly or indirectly (Shea, 1996, p. 170).

Finally, it seems reasonable to determine whether there were differences in Twitter usage among the parties and whether it would be possible to talk about common features of Twitter usage in election campaigns. This study assumes that political parties aim to be, and to appear to be, modern and up-to-date. They emulate each other and follow the leading actors, which could be explained by the copycat theory of party web campaigning (Gibson et al., 2003).

This chapter is divided into three parts. The first part explores the theoretical premises of election campaign intensity and online party politicking during election campaigns. The second part elaborates the methods applied in the study, such as the sampling procedure and the computer-assisted data gathering process. The third part presents the results. It is divided into three sections: (a) the intensity of Twitter usage in the election campaign and in different campaign stages, (b) the character of Twitter communication in the election campaign, and (c) differences between major and fringe political parties in online campaign intensity and communication type. The study concludes with a discussion of the effects of party campaigning on Twitter in the context of the selected relevant theories of online political communication.

THEORETICAL BACKGROUND

Stages in Voters' Perceptions of Campaigners

Election campaigns are complex processes of purposive political communication that originates in political actors and is disseminated to the entire electorate or to targeted segments of it (Schmitt-Beck & Farrell, 2002, p. 5). Regardless of the effects of election campaigns on the political preferences of voters (see e.g. Holbrook, 1996), the strategy of communicating with voters directly towards the end of election campaigns is the most commonly applied communication strategy (Panagopoulos, 2011, p. 80).

Intensity and message timing are important elements of every campaign. During any election, voters' attitudes go through three distinct phases: cognition, affect, and evaluation (Salmore & Salmore, 1989; Parker, 1981; Shea, 1996; Lau & Relawsk, 2006). First, cognition refers to the level at which voters become aware that the candidate is running, that is, "a simple name identification or raw recognition" (Shea, 1996, p. 168). Campaign appearance, speeches, and political ads are designed to promote candidate visibility and to enhance the constituent's contact with the candidate. This contact provides numerous channels for voters to gain and form impressions of the candidate (Parker 1981, p. 219). The second phase occurs when voters form opinions about the competing candidates, which are often affected by on a "host of rational or foolish cues" (see Lau and Redlawsk, 2006). These opinions are often based on party affiliation, social-demographics, issues, candidate's image, and so forth (Lewis-Beck et al., 2011, pp. 22-24). For some voters, the formation of opinions is a complex process that requires examination, such as identifying alternatives, searching for information about them, and identifying a method for making a choice (Lau & Redlawsk, 2006, p. 30). Third, the evaluation phase occurs when voters make their final decision. When voters evaluate candidates, they are interested not only in how each candidate meets their personal preferences but also in how each candidate performs in comparison with the other candidates (Lau & Redlawsk, 2006, p. 182). Indeed, comparison is an explicit part of the activation of cues. For example, the minority status of one candidate compared to others—whether ideological, partisan, ethnical, or sexual—may encourage voters to apply the cues associated with the minority group to the individual. For example, the "conservative label" would be a more salient cue in a field of candidates where one was a conservative and the rest were moderates and liberals (Conover, 1981, p. 433). One feature of the theoretical model presented in this study is its linear conception. The sequence of phases is clearly ordered and cannot be skipped or reordered.

Hence, political actors should be aware of the process of the formation of voters' attitudes. For example, candidates cannot base their campaigns on arguments of why he or she is better than their political counterparts are or engage in bi-directional communication with the electorate before the voters actually know that the candidates are running for office. Campaign themes, appeals, and issues only have a limited electoral impact until the voters gain a minimal awareness of the candidate (Parker 1981, p. 219). Hence, name recognition must precede thematic and issue messages regardless of the type of communication tool utilized (Shea, 1996, p. 168).

The effects of message timing on voters' behavior can be inferred from the theory of cognitive psychology. According to this theory, messages encountered the earliest have a memory advantage because they compete against fewer messages for the limited memory capacity of the individual. This means that the messages encountered the latest have the advantage because they are more readily available in short-term memory, which results in recent effects (Panagopoulos, 2011, p. 80). Political psychologists have used the same theoretical framework to develop parallel arguments about how the exposure to political messages influences voters' behavior (see Zaller, 1992; Mitchell, 2012; Wessels et al., 2014). Messages encountered closest to Election Day are expected to affect voters' behavior more than earlier messages do. Hence, political actors increase the frequency and repeat their mobilizing messages and political ads close to the day of election (Dale & Strauss, 2009; Holman & McLoughlin, 2001).[4]

In addition, research has shown that parties try to increase the amount of information about salient issues in which the political actors have a relative advantage (Carsey, 2001; Carsey et al., 2011; Sides, 2006). They also try to increase the amount of information about valence issues during the last period of the election campaign in order to be separate from their political opponents (Green, 2007). Hence, candidates devote the most attention to the valence issues that offer them a relative advantage on the Election Day. In doing so, candidates attempt to create what Riker (1990) called a "heresthetic change" in the issue-space of the election. This alters the nature of the issue space for voters so that they are encouraged to shift their support from one candidate to another (Carsey, 2001, p. 15). However, unlike the traditional spatial model of party competition, such changes do not imply that candidates should change their stance on a particular issue (Downs, 1957; Stokes, 1963). This strategy merely leads each candidate to find a dimension that, if made sufficiently salient relative to other dimensions, improves that candidate's chance of winning. Candidates disseminate information in order to create this shift. Thus, the election campaign becomes a race among candidates to provide information to voters as they try to define the most important issues.

Because the election campaign takes place immediately before voters deliver a true political decision—based on different cues (see Lewis-Beck et al., 2011; Lau & Redlawsk, 2006)—this common knowledge typically heightens voters' attention to politics in direct relation to the proximity of the event. Thus, issue saliency is more likely to register in voters' minds as Election Day approaches (Brady et al., 2006, p. 2).

Salient issues tend to exclude all voters on the "other side" of the issue, whereas valence issues tend to be inclusive. Obviously, campaign themes, whenever possible, should be centered on valence issues (Shea, 1996, p. 151) because everyone agrees to these issues in contrast to positional issues about which voters and political actors are split. Stokes (1963, 1992) claimed that valence issues are highly important to party competition and political choice because consensus on these issues shifts attention to the ability to deliver (Green 2007, p. 629). The valence model stresses that political actors have strategic initiatives to position themselves differently, depending on their valence advantages *vis-à-vis* their electoral counterparts (Groseclose, 2001). Following this logic, the first hypothesis is posited:

H1: *The first two weeks of the election campaign are marked by the predominance of informative campaign messages,*[5] *whereas the last two weeks are characterized by personal messages related to politics,*[6] *direct communication with voters, and advocacy information about (salience and valence) policy issues.*

Another important assumption concerns the "recency hypothesis" (Panagopoulos, 2011), which posits that the impact of persuasive messages dissipates over time. Hence, in election campaigns, persuasive messages should be sent temporally close to the point of decision or action (ibid., p. 81), that is, just before the evaluation phase in the process of formulating voters' attitudes (Shea, 1996). Accordingly, in election campaigns, parties should *ceteris paribus* send more advertising messages just before Election Day (Panagopoulos, 2011, p. 81, see also O'Keefe, 2015; Benoit & Benoit, 2008).[7] Based on the importance of timing in communicating campaign messages, the second hypothesis is posited:

H2: *Slovenian political parties continuously increase the number of posted tweets as the Election Day approaches.*

Online Party Politicking: Equalization and Normalization Perspectives

In the age of "mediatized politics" (see Esser & Strömbäck, 2014), it is reasonable to expect that political actors at the beginning of their campaigns, especially if they are less known (e.g. political newcomers), use all available political communication tools in order to send identification messages and increase their visibility among the electorate. In this case, Twitter could prove very useful because the actors might invest more effort in using this tool than the already established parties would. In addition to the limited exposure in traditional media outlets,[8] the entry costs are negligible to non-existent, and the traditional media recognize the daily reports on political actors' actions and whereabouts (e.g., launch of the list of candidates, rallies, conventions and other offline campaign activities). Hence, the range of influence is not limited to the undersized Slovenian Twittersphere but reaches even voters who have never heard of this tool.

The increased intensity of Twitter utilization by challengers, in our case fringe parties and political newcomers, may be elucidated in the work of "equalization" theorists, who anticipated that the Internet would facilitate a participatory style of politics, which would draw a greater number of people and underrepresented groups, such as youth, into the democratic process, and bring politicians and the electorate closer together (Baxter & Marcella, 2013, p. 191). This revolutionary or cyber-optimistic (Wright, 2012, p. 245) wave symbolizes initial utopian deliberations on the effects of the Internet on politics. In addition to empowered participatory politics (Hosch-Dayican et al., 2014), equalization theory predicts that the Internet and social networks are equalizing communication platforms for political competition among parties. In this theory, the move online challenges existing political bonds and introduces different types of political engagement, which differs from traditional off-line activities (Norris, 2003, p. 22–23).[9] Hence, the third hypothesis is posited:

H3: *New and fringe political parties communicate a greater number of messages through Twitter than established political parties do, which is especially evident in the first half of the official election campaign.*

The second wave of skeptical "normalization" theorists, which closely followed the utopian wave, argued that the Internet simply reflects and reinforces existing patterns of offline political behavior (Baxter & Marcella, 2013, p. 191). Accordingly, in their seminal book titled *Politics as Usual,* Margolis and Resnick (2000) argued that the revolutionary potential of politics would be normalized by the socio-political reality. Their "normalization hypothesis" rejects revolution in the conduct of politics and emphasizes the simple transfer of the offline features of politics to the Internet. Their main complaint about the utopian idea of cyber-optimists is related to their hope that new politics would spill out of the computer and revitalize the initial idea of citizenship and democracy. This view has been shattered by ordinary politics and commercial activity, which have been invaded and captured by cyberspace (ibid., p. 2). They argued that there was a brief revolutionary "golden age" based on altruism rather than money with equal personal positions, internally regulated behavior, and without government interference. However, this golden age quickly faded and fell under the influence of the state, market regulation, and political forces that wished to tame it (see Wright, 2012, p. 247).[10] Accordingly, normalization theorists believe that political actors in favorable positions in the offline world will also enjoy similar status and attention online (Larsson & Moe, 2014, p. 2). This "rich-get-richer" logic therefore stresses that major political actors also will dominate the numerous platforms on the Internet because cyberspace does not exist in a vacuum. To test these convictions, the fourth hypothesis is posited:

H4: *Major parties with sizeable parliamentary contingents and larger campaign budgets have utilized Twitter more intensively and exploited a greater set of features than fringe parties with smaller campaign budgets have.*

METHODOLOGY

In order to analyze the use of Twitter by Slovenian political parties during the 2014 campaign for the national election, we employ the framework of Golbeck et al. (2010) to examine the content of microblogs in the political realm. An extremely important method for research in political communication (Benoit, 2011), content analysis has been used to describe the content of political communication messages. In addition to investigate televised political advertising (e.g. Kaid & Johnston, 2001) news coverage (e.g. De Vreese et al., 2006), and online media releases (e.g. Norris, 2003; Gibson & Ward, 2000), content analysis is commonly used to examine Twitter microblogs, which are used extensively by politicians during election campaigns (Kruikemeier, 2014; Graham et al., 2013, 2014; Adams & McCorkindale, 2013; Medina & Muños, 2014). With the objective of detecting latent campaign communication strategies in Slovenia, we prepared a codebook that identified different features of collected tweets as analyzed units. By taking into consideration the essentials of campaign communication strategies (O'Keefe & Atwood, 1981; Meadow, 1980), the codebook was prepared based on the coding scheme of Golbeck et al. (2010) to provide the internal content of analyzed tweets. The codebook was based on the additional elaboration of some classified categories in order to distinguish how parties communicated, (spontaneously, with @, mention [.@] or by a RT [retweet]) and/or what they talked about ("folksonomically" categorized content [#]). In this regard, the codebook integrates the indicators of both election campaign communication and Twitter communication:

- DAT (Date and Time): Date and time when tweets were posted on the timeline of official political actors' Twitter accounts.
- DC (Direct Communication): A message directed at a specific person or institution identified with the @username convention. DC was divided into five subclasses: DC1, internal communication with members of the party; DC2, external communication with media (DC2a) or journalists (DC2b); DC3, external communication with citizens (DC3a) or opinion makers (DC3b); DC4 internal communication within the institution (ministry); and DC5, communication with oppositional politicians from other parties.
- PM (Personal Message): A message or note with personal expressions. PM was divided into two subclasses: PMI, personal messages with a non-political character; and PMP, messages with a political campaign character.
- CAMPACT (Campaign Activities): A message reporting on a person's or institution's 'offline' campaign activities. This was divided into two subclasses: OB, official and predictable campaign activities; and LA, non-official or unpredicted activities.

- INF (Information): A message providing a fact, opinion, or attitude expressed on Twitter.
- RA (Requesting Action): A message providing a request to take action, such as voting on elections, signing a petition, and attending rallies.
- FU (Fundraising): A message asking for donations and contributions.
- OTHER (Unknown): A message that cannot be classified, such as a single-character post.
- LINK: A message that provides a link to other websites that have been also coded, such as a link to a personal blog, personal/party Facebook account, political party website, state, or European institution website, news website, YouTube, Instagram, or another social network.
- RT (Retweet): A message that provides a repost of tweets posted by others, usually accompanied by the abbreviation 'RT'.
- HT (Hashtag): A message containing a word or a phrase prefixed with the symbol #, which is a form of metadata tag for grouping similar messages.
- MENTION: A message that includes the mention of oppositional politicians and/or other actors (.@username).

The codebook was finalized after meetings of the study's co-authors in the Faculty of Social Sciences at the University of Ljubljana. Two independent coders conducted the coding of the captured tweets in October and November 2014. The intercoder reliability calculations were conducted on a sample of 100 tweets. They calculated using intra- and inter-coder reliability indexes (Krippendorf, 2003; Benoit, 2011).[11] Using this apparatus (the first version was previously verified in Deželan et al. 2014), we analyzed tweets from the official accounts of all political parties using Twitter, party leaders involved in social media communication, or prolific party twitterians[12] during the official election campaign. All tweets posted during this period were included in the analysis. For the computer-assisted data collection, the web browser extension NCapture in the QDA software NVivo was used to export the captured tweets to a data source. The data collection resulted in 7,113 tweets, which were analyzed to measure the usage intensity of the Twitter social media outlet. Seventeen accounts were searched:

- Eleven political party accounts (@ZaveznistvoAB—577 tweets; @strankaSD—703; @StrankaSLS—823; @strankaSDS—1531; @NovaSlovenija—481; @strankaDeSUS—47; @zdruzenalevica—762; @strankaTRS—50; @PozitivnaSlo—234; @strankaDL—323; @piratskastranka—190);
- Seven party leaders' accounts (@ABratusek—301 tweets; @MiroCerar—241; @JJansaSDS—579; @gregor_virant—54); and
- Two prolific party twitterians (@UrosJausevec—191; @JernejVrtovec—26).

POLITICAL COMMUNICATION ON TWITTER DURING THE 2014 NATIONAL ELECTION CAMPAIGN IN SLOVENIA

Brief Contextualization of the 2014 Pre-Term Election

The second consecutive pre-term national election in Slovenia was conducted in a specific political environment. It included the entry of several influential newcomers to the political scene. Several long-term implications may arise from the election results. The party-affiliated proportion of the electorate has shrunk, which indicates the weakening of old party loyalties. The balance of powers, particularly on the left, has been completely reorganized for the second time in the last three years. Because of an internal split, the former dominant party, Positive Slovenia (PS), failed to pass the parliamentary threshold. A splinter group of deputies lead by former Prime Minister Alenka Bratušek formed its own party, The Alliance of Alenka Bratušek (ZAAB), and managed to enter the chamber in the 2014 national election. The erosion of support to the PS has given way to Miro Cerar and his party (SMC) to dominate the political landscape. At the same time, the weakened position of Social Democrats (SD), formerly a key player in the left of the political spectrum, allowed the entry of another political newcomer in the parliament—the United Left (ZL).[13]

In the center to the center-right of the ideological spectrum, the classical liberal Civic List (DL) failed to pass the parliamentary threshold after only three years in parliament. Similarly, the right wing Christian democratic Slovenian People's Party (SLS) dropped out of parliament for the first time since the introduction of political pluralism in 1989. The Christian democratic New Slovenia (NSI) and the conservative Slovenian Democratic Party (SDS) were more or less in the same position prior to election campaign. The central point of the campaign was the imprisonment of the former Prime Minister (PM) and leader of the opposition SDS party, Janez Janša. He was sentenced to two years in prison for his involvement in a corruption scandal related to bribery in a Patria weapons deal only a month before Election Day. Hence, this issue was issue central in the campaign agenda.

Intensity of Twitter Usage: Evolution of the Number of Tweets and Communication Types

To verify the first two hypotheses, we analyzed the number of tweets posted per week to identify the variations in the intensity of usage as well as the specific Twitter usage by political parties during the election campaign. Based on the analysis of 7,113 tweets, the coded messages were divided into six different categories: direct communication, personal message, campaign activity, information, requesting action, fundraising, and "other." The examination of the four-week election campaign week by week revealed substantial differences in intensity as well as in types of posted campaign messages. Figure 1 indicates the intensity of tweets by week and the types of posted tweets.

Figure 1 demonstrates the continuous increase in the number of posted tweets as Election Day approached. In the first two weeks of the official campaign, the intensity of the posted tweets remained more or less the same. During the second week, only 57 tweets more than during the first week were posted. However, the last two weeks of the election campaign proved to be a period of immense party activity on Twitter. As Figure 1 indicates, the number of postings increased from the second to the third week of the campaign by 54.8% (876 tweets). A similar increase in intensity was recorded for the fourth week of the campaign, which showed an additional increase of 39% in the number of posted tweets compared to the previous week (third week). Therefore, the second hypothesis is supported.

The increased frequency of tweets requesting action during the last week of the campaign also demonstrates the mobilization efforts made by the parties (e.g., calls on the early voting). Although their frequency was moderate compared to other categories (only 217 in four weeks), the number of tweets of this type in the last days of the election campaign supports the recency hypothesis, which is also supported by the evidence of partisan mobilization. As predicted by the recency assumption, the results showed that the political parties increased the intensity of Twitter campaigning as Election Day approached during the 2014 pre-term election campaign.

Figure 1. Number of tweets and categories of political actors' tweets per week

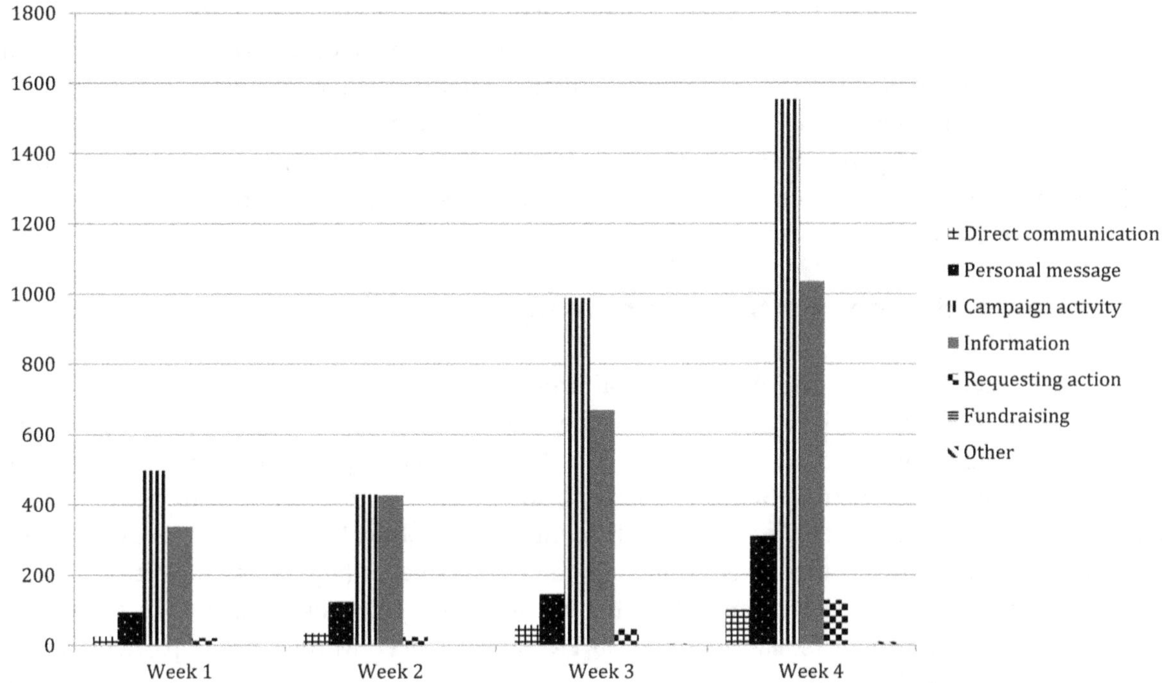

Furthermore, the types of tweets posted by the political actors were predominantly related to campaign activity, with the exception of the second week of the observed election campaign when the tweets providing a fact, opinion, or attitude expressed on Twitter were the most numerous (see Figure 1). Tweets indicating campaign activities or information about facts, opinions, or attitudes about the political parties and their key representatives dominated the entire campaign. Tweets about campaign activity comprised almost half (49.1%) and informative tweets comprised more than a third (35%) of all posted tweets in the dataset. Other categories of tweets, such as personal messages, direct communication, and requests for action, were posted in considerably smaller numbers, and fundraising activities using Twitter were almost non-existent. Contrary to our first hypothesis, which stipulated a change in the predominant type of tweets as the campaign progressed, the results showed that all four weeks of the election campaign were marked by tweets covering the campaign activities of political actors, promoting lists of candidates, promoting individual candidates, repeating party slogans, and so forth. As Election Day approached, the number of this type of tweets increased, which culminated in the fourth week (see Figure 1).

It is therefore impossible to assert that the last two weeks of the election campaign were characterized by personal messages related to politics, direct communication with voters, and advocacy information about policy issues. We should not ignore, however, that the number of tweets in the three categories continued to increase as the campaign was finishing. This finding indicates that the political parties were aware of the importance of the last days of the election campaign, but they did not devise campaign strategies that would prioritize types of messages according to the campaign period. Even though the increase in the number of personal messages related to politics does revealed that they wanted to dominate the political debate and have deeper (direct) connections with voters, the focus on messages about campaign activities indicates that the strategic capacity of parties on Twitter was insufficient.

Nevertheless, it must be acknowledged that the results revealed evidence of the rising occurrence of informing practices about a fact, opinion, or attitude of the parties and candidates regarding certain policy issues. The parties attempted to posts more tweets about issues in order to be separate from other competitors and to devote attention to topics that offered them a relative advantage on Election Day because of increased salience of those issues. Although the first hypothesis is not supported, the results provide evidence that the parties tried to pay increased attention to personal messages related to politics and direct communication with voters. Moreover, they advocated key policy issues in the last two weeks of the election campaign.

Did the New and Fringe Parties do Anything Different?

As previously mentioned, the Slovenian political scene was caught "off guard" during the election campaign because of the scandal related to the weapons deal with a Finnish army vehicle manufacturer and the imprisonment of the former PM Janez Janša. This event also opened the way for the increased personalization of political parties. Some well-known individuals, albeit without any true organizational support, decided to enter the electoral race by forming a new political party, which is evident in the names of several new parties that opted to include the leader's name (e.g., Party of Miro Cerar, now Party of the Modern Centre [SMC] and The Alliance of Alenka Bratušek [ZAAB]). In addition, the winning SMC party chose to personalize its official Twitter account (@MiroCerar). In particular, during the election campaign, SMC did not have an official party Twitter account, but it posted tweets through the account of its leader. In addition, the majority of candidates on the SMC list of candidates either did not have a Twitter account or did not use Twitter during the election campaign. Some SMC candidates were elected in the most competitive electoral district without posting a single tweet, hanging a single poster, making a single TV appearance, or buying a single ad. This phenomenon accentuates the fact that the examined campaign was highly personalized, and it confirms the validity of the "personalization hypotheses," which emphasized the role of personality politics in democratic elections (see Costa Lobo & Crutice, 2015). It also raises questions about the actual impact of social networks on political communication, particularly during election campaigns when the amount of political information floods political communities.

In this changed political atmosphere, established parties with impressive organizational capacity and resources (e.g., SD and SDS) competed against paper tigers (e.g., PS and DL) with a numerous contingent of deputies in the national parliament, but decreasing electoral support. Fringe parties competed for minor slices of the electoral pie (e.g., SLS, NSI, DESUS, and PIR), and new parties emerged from this politically unpredictable situation (SMC, ZAAB and ZL).

Contrary to our third hypothesis (i.e., that new and fringe parties communicate more frequently through Twitter than established ones do), the results shown in Figure 2 demonstrated that during all four weeks of the election campaign, the established parties were more active on Twitter than the fringe and new parties were. Of all political parties, SDS used this social media outlet the most extensively. For example, in the last week of the election campaign, SDS posted more tweets than all the other parties posted during the entire four weeks of the campaign. On average, the established parties posted more tweets than the fringe and new parties did. Combined, SDS and SD posted exactly 50% of all tweets during the first and the second weeks of the campaign. This finding suggests that in general the new and fringe Slovenian parties did not recognize Twitter as a new communication platform for political competition, that is, a tool for promoting equalization as some had predicted. It needs to be said, however,

Figure 2. Absolute number of tweets posted by parties during the last four weeks of the 2014 election campaign

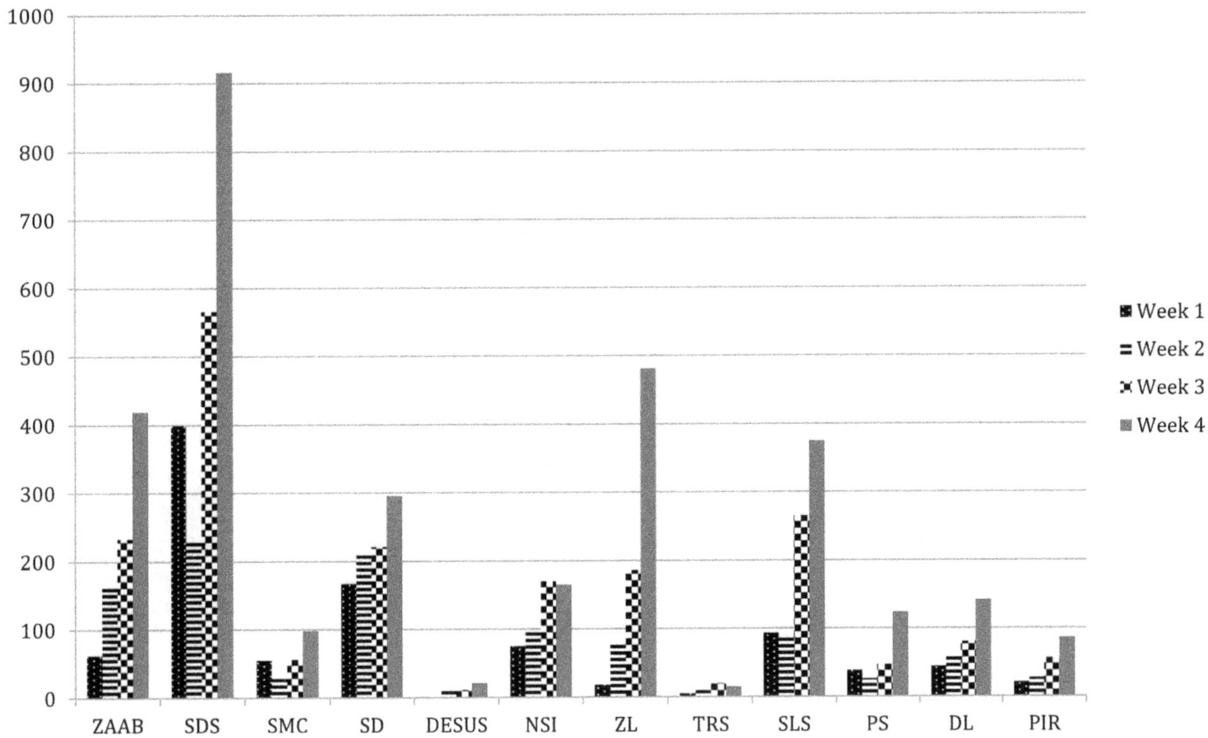

that two new parties, ZAAB and ZL—the former with a US-proven campaign strategist and the latter with a large assemblage of tech-savvy supporters and activists—utilized Twitter almost as intensively as the established parties did. They managed to equalize their structural deficiencies by either adapting campaign strategies or utilizing specific attributes of the party's nucleus of activists. Regardless, they clearly were aware of Twitter's potential influence on the election campaign and the eventual results of the election.

Another important element of using Twitter in elections campaigns is that the parties communicated messages to voters and other relevant actors. They communicated through different types of tweets, which also revealed much about their communication strategy. Figure 3 clearly shows the types of tweets that political parties preferred on a weekly basis as the campaign progressed. During the first week of the campaign, the majority of parties tweeted about campaign activities and promoted candidates and candidate lists. The exception was ZAAB, which focused on the advocacy of selected policy issues that were relevant to the party. ZAAB retained this strategy throughout all four weeks of the election campaign. The reasons for this strategy were that ZAAB was headed by Alenka Bratušek, the PM at the time, and the list did not need extensive information about the candidates and their platforms. In addition, ZAAB chose a somewhat negative campaign strategy by trying to make corruption a salient campaign issue because some of the main political contenders faced corruption charges or allegations. ZAAB posted the highest number of tweets regarding excessive pressure on the Supreme Court caused by Janez Janša and his supporters. The following is an example:

Figure 3. Number of tweets posted by parties and the type of communication per week

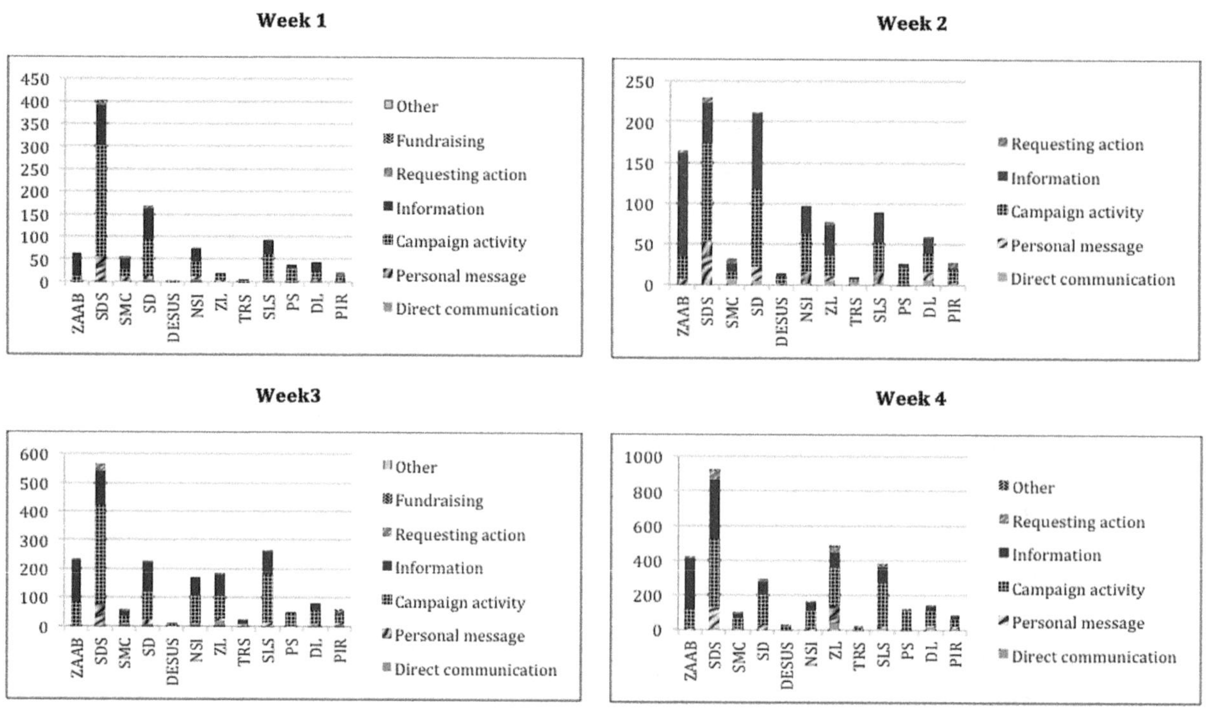

@ABratusek: If you are convicted longer than six months you cannot be even a civil servant, let alone to lead the country. #soočenje

With the exception of tweets about campaign activities and promoting candidates and candidate lists, the parties therefore rarely used other types of tweets during the first week of the campaign. "Fundraising," "requesting message" and "direct communication" were not features of Twitter communication, and only SDS posted some truly personal messages related to politics, which consisted of mostly negative, emotional, and sarcastic remarks targeted at political opponents and the political system in general. Negative elements dominated the SDS election campaign regardless of the communication tool (posters, TV debates, party website, or candidate blogs) Twitter was no exception. An example is the following tweet posted by SDS:

@strankaSDS: Aggressors exempt, defenders in jail. Who does not understand where we are? http://t.co/TvpyD5nByT

During the second week of the campaign, the parties rarely changed the way they utilized Twitter. The only noticeable difference is the proportion of messages promoting candidate lists with names, photos, and messages about parties' preferences regarding policy issues. Compared to the first week, the difference between these two categories was reduced because the parties posted an increasing number of tweets about their policy positions. In the transition to the second half of the campaign, the parties were urged to post more self-promoting messages on Twitter. The "campaign activity" tweets flooded the

Twittersphere because most political parties relentlessly posted this type of content. With the exception of ZAAB and DL, which chose to post policy-oriented tweets, only SDS posted personal messages related to politics, more than half of which were negative (63 of 121) and targeted journalists. The following is an example of a tweet that targeted a highly esteemed political anchor on public television:

@JJansaSDS: This is a statement of PR worker from the domestic agency of SD party, characterized as an expert by public television (@RTV_Slovenija). A shame, @SBobovnik http://t.co/Am3Vkx2RAp

In the final leg of the electoral race on Twitter during the fourth week of the campaign, the same pattern was revealed. The promotion of party lists and candidates was predominant. Nevertheless, there was also increased attention to policy positions (category "information"), and there were more attempts to mobilize voters (see Figure 3). Personal messages related to politics were used as emotionally charged cues by which the parties tried for the last time to persuade voters. In addition to the established parties SDS and SD, the new ZL used this type of communication. The same party also dominated the field in terms of direct communication with voters. During the fourth week, 43% of all tweets posted by ZL were direct communications with voters or other actors in the Twittersphere.

As reported in previous studies on campaign intensity (e.g., Sulkin, 2001; Kahn & Kenney, 1999) and the intensity of Twitter usage in election campaigns (Aragón et al., 2013; Kruikemeier, 2014), the proximity of Election Day influences the intensity of party activity on Twitter. In the Slovenian case, the established parties communicated more messages through Twitter than the new or fringe parties did. This also was the case during the first two weeks of the official campaign, which contradicts the third hypothesis. With few exceptions, the parties tweeted mainly about their candidates and candidate lists. To a slightly lesser extent, they tried to present their positions on the policy issues that were vital to them. The findings showed that the Slovenian political parties did not find any revolutionary potential in Twitter campaigning (see Margolis & Resnick, 2000). Indeed, the new and fringe parties used Twitter less intensively than the established parties did but in almost the same way. The two examples that deviated from this pattern were ZAAB, with its aggressive, negative strategy focusing on corruption as a salient policy issue, and ZL, with its strategy of direct communication during the last week of the election campaign.

"posteno#" and the Capacity to use Twitter as a Political Communication Tool

The general perception is that extensive campaign spending is inappropriate during economic hardship, the political parties in Slovenia constantly stressed they opted for a less capital-intensive campaign in 2014. Previously conducted research on Twitter campaigning in Slovenia indicates that the political parties indicated the desire to use Twitter extensively and with a large set of features, but they did not have the capacity to do so (Deželan et al., 2014). This was particularly the case with political newcomers, who lack not only money but also skilled personnel. The findings showed that this shortcoming resulted in less professional communication and the less diverse use of the features of Twitter by the new and fringe parties with smaller campaign budgets.

Figure 4 shows that there were some differences in the micro-blogging activities of the Slovenian political parties. The established SD and SDS, fringe SLS and NSI, new parties ZAAB and ZL, and DL and PIR utilized more or less all the features of Twitter communication to a high degree (mention (@

Figure 4. Features used in party communications on Twitter

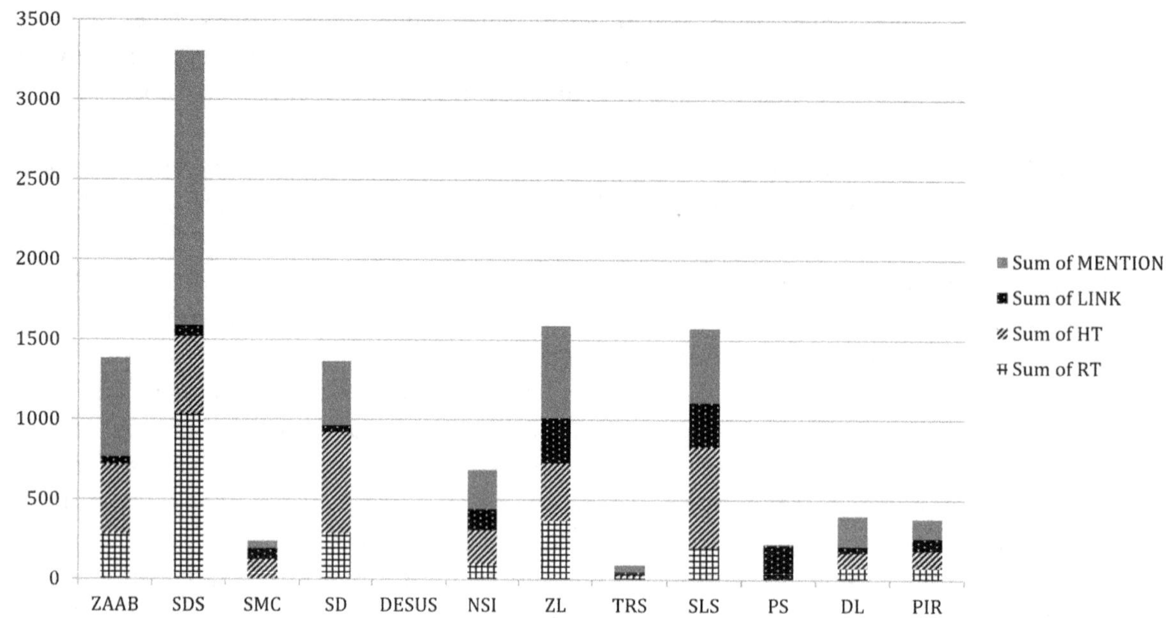

username) as an integral part of their tweets, hashtags (#), and function retweets (RT)). However, some fringe and new parties failed to utilize certain Twitter conventions. DESUS (party of the pensioners) is a particularly interesting example. This party posted only "simple" messages such as the following:

@strankaDeSUS: Everybody from Žalec for Karel Erjavec.

This party was entirely distanced from promoting interaction and social conversation on Twitter (see Medina & Muñoz, 2014). It did not use retweets to share information with others by spreading it beyond its original audience. It did not mention function as a mechanism of two-way communication, and it did not use extra linked information as a resource to add content value. However, the same could be said for some other parties (e.g., TRS). A similar example of unusual campaigning was PS. Throughout the entire campaign, this party did not use the retweet function or hashtags. Although they tried once, the sign '#' was put in the wrong place. An example of the lack of capacity to exploit Twitter as a political communication tool is demonstrated by the following inappropriate use of the hashtag convention:

@PozitivnaSlo: Supporters of PS in Slovenj Gradec. posteno#

Based on the data about PS's campaign budget, it would difficult to argue that this paper tiger did not have enough money to hire a professional administrator to manage the party's official Twitter account. The unprofessional and *ad hoc* nature of Twitter usage, which was already a feature of the 2011 national election (Deželan et al., 2014), indicates the parties' reluctance to take campaigning online seriously.

A somewhat different rationale was identified in the case of the most influential newcomer and the eventual winner, the SMC. This party used Twitter extremely cautiously. Because it wanted to retain control over the communication process, it avoided using Twitter. Although the party was new, and voters were not familiar with its candidates and ideological preferences, SMC opted not to risk direct communications to explain its electoral manifesto. Nevertheless, the SMC enjoyed immense public support when its president Miro Cerar announced that he would run for parliament. From the perspective of an effective political strategy, this kind of behavior is rational because parties that enjoy substantial leads in the polls are not expected to confront their opponents directly (see Shea, 1996; Kahn & Kenney, 1999).

In contrast to the new and fringe parties, the established SDS used Twitter the most, taking advantage of all the features offered by this social media outlet. Figure 4 indicates SDS's extensive use of the "mention" feature, which promoted interactions and social conversations during the campaign. Among the many possible explanations is that as a challenger running in a close contest, SDS used Twitter to target its opponents and involve the public in newly initiated discussion. The findings showed that 81.4% of SDS tweets contained at least one mention (.@username). SDS also tried to control the campaign agenda by promoting Twitter hashtags (e.g. #freeJJ, #freeSLO) across different campaign tools, which enabled them to have a visible influence on the formation of the agenda.

The results supported some theoretical premises of the fourth hypothesis but contradicted others. Some established parties with a sizeable parliamentary contingent and large campaign budgets (e.g., SDS) utilized Twitter more extensively and exploited a greater set of features than the fringe and new parties with smaller campaign budgets. However, the results showed similarities in the context of micro-blogging activities between the established and the new and fringe parties (e.g., SD and ZAAB). This finding appears to contradict the fourth hypothesis. However, although newly established, ZAAB devoted an extensive budget to its campaign to re-elect the PM. Consequently, it utilized more professional expertise than any other established party. In contrast, ZL was based on a core of tech-savvy young activists who were digital natives. Therefore, compared to the established parties, the human resource capacity of ZL compensated for its structural deficiencies.

CONCLUSION

The findings of the study showed that Slovenian political parties have not entirely accepted the full potential of Twitter as an online political communication tool. However, the results indicate that Twitter will remain an integral part of the campaign strategies of all Slovenian political parties in the near future.

This study also offers new evidence to support the idea that increased intensity and message timing are important elements of election campaigns because they influence election race dynamics, voting behavior, and consequently the results of the election. Most notably, this study demonstrated that the use of Twitter by all political parties during the campaign for the Slovenian national election in 2014 significantly increased as Election Day approached. This finding confirms the campaign intensity hypothesis and the recency hypothesis based on the assumption that the timing of message delivery in election campaign is a key component of the strategy of political actors (Panagopoulos, 2011). Therefore, the most important findings of our study has significance for theories of effective campaign strategies and fundamental theories of political psychology and voting behavior.

With regard to the equalization vs. normalization debate, the findings did not yield the expected answers. Although the online political communication patterns of the new and fringe parties were equal to the political communication patterns of the established parties, no dominance was identified in the volume and use of Twitter-specific features in the clusters of new and fringe parties. On the contrary, the established parties dominated the field (particularly SDS), thus supporting the relevance of the normalization hypothesis. The findings of the content analysis of the Twitter communications showed that the established parties had the advantage, particularly in terms of using the range of features in Twitter. In fact, there were signs of the relevance of both hypotheses. Larsson and Moe's (2014) "middle road" between the two extremes of revolution and normalization seems to be the most acceptable solution to this dilemma. Although the new and fringe parties intended to make themselves heard in the Twittersphere, their voices were largely overshadowed by the established competitors, which had larger campaign budgets and greater overall capacities.

Although there was evidence of the overall pattern of the increased campaign intensity of political communications on Twitter, further work is needed to obtain a precise estimate of causality. This study is only one in a series of case studies focused on the application of Twitter during election campaigns; nevertheless, it has provided an empirical demonstration of the impact of the utilization of Twitter on campaign intensity, and it has discussed Twitter's implications for campaign equality and uniformity. Although it would be feasible to continue to use the current approach, future research might find it equally useful to take into account the content of tweets (e.g., hashtags as dynamic entities suitable for her esthetic change in campaign agenda).

REFERENCES

Adams, A., & McCorkindale, T. (2013). Dialogue and transparency: A content analysis of how the 2012 presidential candidates used twitter. *Public Relations Review*, *39*(4), 357–359. doi:10.1016/j.pubrev.2013.07.016

Aragón, P., Kappler, K. E., Kaltenbrunner, A., Laniado, D., & Volkovich, Y. (2013). Communication Dynamics in Twitter during Political Campaigns: The Case of the 2011 Spanish National Election. *Policy & Internet*, *5*(2), 183–206. doi:10.1002/1944-2866.POI327

Baxter, G., & Marcella, R. (2013). Do Online Election Campaign Sway the Vote? A Study of the 2011 Scottish Parliamentary Elections. *Libri*, *63*(3), 190–205. doi:10.1515/libri-2013-0015

Benoit, W. L. (2011). Content Analysis in Political Communication. In E. P. Bucy & R. L. Holbert (Eds.), *The Sourcebook for Political Communication Research: Methods, Measures, and Analytical Techniques* (pp. 268–279). New York: Routledge.

Benoit, W. L., & Benoit, P. J. (2008). *Persuasive Messages: The Process of Influence*. Malden, MA: Blackwell Publishing.

Berleson, B., Lazarsfeld, P. F., & McPhee, W. N. (1954). *Voting: Study of Opinion Formation in a Presidential Campaign*. Chicago: University of Chicago Press.

Brady, H. E., Johnston, R., & Sides, J. (2006). The Study of Political Campaigns. In H. E. Brady & R. Johnston (Eds.), *Capturing Campaign Effects* (pp. 1–26). Ann Arbor, MI: The University of Michigan Press.

Carsey, T. M. (2001). *Campaign Dynamics: The Race for Governor.* The University of Michigan Press.

Carsey, T. M., Jackson, R. A., Stewart, M., & Nelson, J. P. (2011). Strategic Candidates, Campaign Dynamics, and Campaign Advertising in Grubernatorial Races. *State Politics & Policy Quarterly*, *11*(3), 269–298. doi:10.1177/1532440011413085

CoARS. (2015). *Archive of Court of Audit of the Republic of Slovenia audit reports*. Retrieved February 1, 2015, from http://www.rs-rs.si/rsrs/rsrseng.nsf/RevizijeArhiv?OpenForm&appSource=AA288C363EA722B2C125715C001B5795

Conover, P. J. (1981). Political Cues and the Perception of Candidates. *American Politics Quarterly*, *9*(4), 427–445. doi:10.1177/1532673X8100900403

Costa Lobo, M., & Curtice, J. (Eds.). (2015). *Personality Politics? The Role of Leader Evaluations in Democratic Elections*. Oxford, UK: Oxford University Press.

Dale, A., & Strauss, A. (2009). Don't Forget to Vote: Text Message Reminders as a Mobilization Tool. *American Journal of Political Science*, *53*(4), 787–804. doi:10.1111/j.1540-5907.2009.00401.x

De Vreese, C. H., Banducci, S. A., Semetko, H. A., & Boomgaarden, H. G. (2006). The News Coverage of the 2004 European Parliamentary Election Campaign in 25 Countries. *European Union Politics*, *7*(4), 477–504. doi:10.1177/1465116506069440

Deželan, T., Krašovec, A., & Kovačič, M. (2010). Volilna kampanja po slovensko. In S. Kustec Lipicer (Ed.), *Politične vsebine in volilna kampanja: slovenska izkušnja z volitev v Evropski parlament 2009* (pp. 53–70). Ljubljana: FDV.

Deželan, T., Vobič, I., & Maksuti, A. (2014). Twitter Campaigning in the 2011 National Election in Slovenia: Strategy and Application of the Twitter Social Media Outlet in Party Election Campaigns. In B. Patrut & M. Patrut (Eds.), *Social Media in Politics: Case Studies on the Political Power of Social Media* (pp. 141–163). Cham: Springer. doi:10.1007/978-3-319-04666-2_9

Downs, A. (1957). *An economic theory of democracy*. New York: Harper Collins.

Esser, F., & Strömbäck, J. (Eds.). (2014). *Mediatization of Politics: Understanding the Transformation of Western Democracies*. London: Palgrave Macmillan. doi:10.1057/9781137275844

Gibson, R., & McAllister, I. (2014). Normalising or Equalising Party Competition? Assessing the Impact of the Web on Election Campaigning. *Political Studies*, *2014*, 1–19.

Gibson, R., Nixon, P., & Ward, S. (Eds.). (2003). *Political parties and the Internet net gain?* London, New York: Routledge.

Gibson, R., & Ward, S. (2000). A proposed methodology for studying the function and effectiveness of party and candidate Web sites. *Social Science Computer Review*, *18*(3), 301–319. doi:10.1177/089443930001800306

Goldbeck, J., Grimes, J. M., & Rogers, A. (2010). Twitter use by the U.S. Congress. *Journal of the American Society for Information Science and Technology*, *61*(8), 1612–1621.

Graham, T., Broersma, M., Hazelhoff, K., & van 't Haar, G. (2013). Between Broadcasting Political Messages and Interacting with Voters: The use of Twitter during the 2010 UK general election campaign. *Information Communication and Society, 16*(5), 692–716. doi:10.1080/1369118X.2013.785581

Graham, T., Jackson, D., & Broersma, M. (2014). New Platform, old habits? Candidates' use of Twitter during the 2010 British and Dutch general election campaigns. *New Media & Society, 0*(0), 1–19.

Green, J. (2007). When Voters and Parties Agree: Valence Issues and Party Competition. *Political Studies, 55*(3), 629–655. doi:10.1111/j.1467-9248.2007.00671.x

Groseclose, T. (2001). A Model of Candidate Location When One Candidate Has a Valence Advantage. *American Journal of Political Science, 45*(4), 862–886. doi:10.2307/2669329

Holbrook, T. M. (1996). *Do Campaigns Matter?* Thousand Oaks, CA: Sage.

Holman, C. B., & McLoughlin, L. P. (2001). *Buying Time 2000: Television Advertising in the 2000 Federal Elections*. New York: Brennan Center for Justice at New York School of Law.

Hosch-Dayican, B., Amrit, C., & Aarts, K. (2014). How Do Online Citizens Persuade Fellow Voters? Using Twitter During the 2013 Dutch Parliamentary Election Campaign. *Social Science Computer Review, 0*(0), 1–18.

Kahn, K. F., & Kenney, P. J. (1997). A Model of Candidate Evaluations in Senate Elections: The Impact of Campaign Intensity. *The Journal of Politics, 59*(4), 1173–1205. doi:10.2307/2998597

Kahn, K. F., & Kenney, P. J. (1999). *The Spectacle of U.S. Senate Campaigns*. Princeton, NJ: Princeton University Press.

Kaid, L. L., & Johnston, A. (2001). *Videostyle in Presidential Campaigns: Style and Content of Televised Political Advertising*. Westport, CT: Praeger.

Krippendorff, K. (2003). *Content analysis: an introduction to its methodology. Thousand Oaks etc.* Sage Publications.

Kruikemeier, S. (2014). How political candidates use Twitter and the impact of votes. *Computers in Human Behavior, 34*, 131–139. doi:10.1016/j.chb.2014.01.025

Lau, R. R., & Redlawsk, D. P. (2006). *How Voters Decide: Information Processing in Election Campaigns*. Cambridge, UK: Cambridge University Press. doi:10.1017/CBO9780511791048

Larsson, O. A., & Moe, H. (2014). Triumph of the Underdogs? Comparing Twitter Use by Political Actors During Two Norwegian Election Campaigns. *Sage Open, 4*(4), 2158–2440. doi:10.1177/2158244014559015

Lazarsfled, P. F., Berelson, B., & Gaudet, H. (1944). *The People's Choice: How the Voter Makes Up His Mind in a Presidential Campaign*. New York: Duell, Sloan and Pierce.

Lewis-Beck, M. S., Jacoby, W. G., Norpoth, H., & Weisberg, H. F. (2011). *The American Voter Revisited*. Ann Arbor, MI: The University of Michigan Press.

Mance, B. (2014). Odnosi med novinarji in politiki na twitterju: od profesionalizma do »odmevne komore«. *Javnost - The Public, 21*(Supplement), 23–40.

Margolis, M., & Resnick, D. (2000). *Politics as usual: the cyberspace 'revolution*. Thousand Oaks, CA: Sage Publications.

Meadow, R. G. (1980). *Politics as communication*. Norwood, NJ: Abalex Publishing Corporation.

Medina, R. Z., & Muñoz, C. Z. (2014). Campaigning on Twitter: Towards the "Personal Style" Campaign to Activate the Political Engagement During the 2011 Spanish General Elections. *Communicatio Socialis*, *27*(1), 83–106.

Mitchell, D.-G. (2012). It's About Time: The Lifespan of Information Effects in a Multiweek Campaign. *American Journal of Political Science*, *56*(2), 298–311. doi:10.1111/j.1540-5907.2011.00549.x

Norris, P. (2000). *A virtuous circle: political communication in postindustrial societies*. Cambridge, UK: Cambridge University Press. doi:10.1017/CBO9780511609343

Norris, P. (2002). Campaign communications. In L. LeDuc, R. G. Niemi, & P. Norris (Eds.), *Comparing democracies 2: new challenges in the study of elections and voting* (pp. 127–147). London: SAGE.

Norris, P. (2003). Preaching to the converted? Pluralism, participation and party websites. *Party Politics*, *9*(1), 21–45. doi:10.1177/135406880391003

O'Keefe, G. J. (2015). Persuasion: Theory and Research (3rd ed.). Los Angeles, CA: Sage.

O'Keefe, G. J., & Atwood, L. E. (1981). Communication and Election Campaigns. In D. D. Nimmo & K. R. Sanders (Eds.), *Handbook of Political Communication* (pp. 329–357). Beverly Hills, CA: Sage Publications.

Oblak Črnič, T., & Amon-Prodnik, J. (2014). Samopromocijski novičarski mediji? Analiza spletnih mest slovenskih političnih akterjev. *Teorija in Praksa*, *51*(6), 1321–1343.

Panagopoulos, C. (2011). Timing is Everything? Primacy and Recency Effects in Voter Mobilization Campaigns. *Political Behavior*, *33*(1), 79–93. doi:10.1007/s11109-010-9125-x

Parker, G. R. (1981). Interpreting Candidate Awareness in U. S. Congressional Elections. *Legislative Studies Quarterly*, *6*(2), 219–233. doi:10.2307/439646

Radio-Television of Slovenia. (2014). *Roles of Slovenian public broadcasting services for the use of airtime for the presentation of candidate lists or candidates for MP's election in National Assembly in 13th July 2014* [in Slovenian]. Retrieved January 1, 2015, from https://www.rtvslo.si/files/novice_zavoda/pravila_-_drzavni_zbor-2014.pdf

Riker, W. H. (1990). Heresthetic and Rhetoric in the Spatial Model. In J. M. Elenow & M. J. Hinich (Eds.), *Advances in the Spatial Theory of Voting* (pp. 46–65). Cambridge, UK: Cambridge University Press. doi:10.1017/CBO9780511896606.005

Salmore, B. G., & Salmore, S. A. (1989). *Candidates, Parties, and Campaigns*. Washington, DC: Congressional Quarterly Press.

Schmitt-Beck, R., & Farrell, D. M. (2002). Studying political campaigns and their effects. In D. M. Farrell & R. Schmitt-Beck (Eds.), *Do Political Campaigns Matter? Campaign Effects in Elections and Referendums* (pp. 1–21). London: Routledge. doi:10.4324/9780203166956_chapter_1

Shea, D. M. (1996). *Campaign Craft: The Strategies, Tactics, And Art of Political Campaign Management*. Westport, CT: Praeger.

Sides, J. (2006). The Origins of Campaign Agendas. *British Journal of Political Science, 36*(3), 407–436. doi:10.1017/S0007123406000226

Stokes, D. E. (1963). Spatial Models of Party Competition. *The American Political Science Review, 57*(2), 368–377. doi:10.2307/1952828

Stokes, D. E. (1992). Valence Politics. In D. Kavanaugh (Ed.), *Electoral Politics* (pp. 141–164). New York: Oxford University Press.

Sulkin, T. (2001). Explaining Campaign Intensity. *American Politics Research, 29*(6), 608–624. doi:10.1177/1532673X01029006004

Tomanić Trivundža. I. (2014). Vernakularna vizualna politična kultura: vizualni tviti v predvolilni kampanji za EP 2014. *Javnost - The Public, 21*(Supplement), 41–58.

Vobič, I., Maksuti, A., & Deželan, T. (2014). *Social negotiation of roles on Twitter : analysing journalists-politicians conversations before national elections.* Paper presented at Open Conference of the COST Action IS0906 "Transforming audiences, transforming societies: the future of audience research: agenda, theory and societal significance", University of Ljubljana, Slovenia, February 5-7, 2014.

Wessels, B. (2014). Voters' Motivations: How and Why Short-Term Factors Grow in Importance. In B. Wessels, H. Rattinger, S. Rossteutscher, & R. Schmitt-Beck (Eds.), *Voters on the Move or the Run* (pp. 238–262). Oxford, UK: Oxford University Press. doi:10.1093/acprof:oso/9780199662630.001.0001

Wright, S. (2012). Politics as usual? Revolution, normalization and a new agenda for online deliberation. *New Media & Society, 14*(2), 244–261. doi:10.1177/1461444811410679

Xenos, M., Vromen, A., & Loader, B. (2014). The great equalizer? Patterns of social media use and youth political engagement in three advanced democracies. *Information Communication and Society, 17*(2), 151–167. doi:10.1080/1369118X.2013.871318

Zaller, J. R. (1992). *The nature and origins of mass opinion.* New York: Cambridge University Press. doi:10.1017/CBO9780511818691

ENDNOTES

1 All parliamentary parties in Slovenia communicate through official Twitter accounts, which are maintained by the parties' public relations officers. Similarly, all party presidents except Karel Erjavec, the leader of the Democratic Party of Pensioners of Slovenia (DESUS), have a functioning account directly operated either by themselves or their personal assistants. In addition, 47 out of 90 current members of parliament (2014–) actively use their personal Twitter accounts.

2 For an extensive elaboration of different campaign tools in accordance with the modernization of political communication, see Norris (2000, 2002).

3 Political parties do not want to appear as big spenders in the eyes of voters during an economic downturn.

4 Following this logic, approximately 60% of all US federal election TV ads are broadcasted in the six weeks prior to the election (Holman & McLoughlin, 2001, p. 53).

5 E.g., promoting a candidate list with names and photos, fundraising online, repeating party slogans, and using hashtags

6 E.g., emotions, reactions, remarks, and sarcasm

7 Classical theory about the minimal campaign effects (Lazarsfled et al., 1944; Berelson et al., 1954) and theories of individual decision making (Lau & Relawsk, 2006) emphasize that increased campaign intensity is relevant only for certain types of voters that make "fast and frugal" or "intuitive" decisions inside the frame of bounded rationality (Lau & Relawsk, 2006, p. 8).

8 In line with the legislation, during election campaigns, Slovenia's public broadcasting service (Radio-Television of Slovenia) provides free-of-charge slots for the presentation of lists of candidates and political parties. The rules set by Radio-Television of Slovenia for the 2014 election to the National Assembly of the Republic of Slovenia favored political parties having members in the national or the European parliament. To be precise, non-parliamentary parties were entitled to just one third of the amount of time reserved for the election race (Radio-Television of Slovenia, 2014, p. 1).

9 A good example are Green parties, which have been found to offer websites that often surpass those of rival major parties in terms of content richness and levels of interactivity (Gibson & McAllister, 2014, p. 3).

10 It is necessary to point out that Margolis and Resnick (2000) did not argue that normalization of the Internet would have no impact on the political process.

11 A sample of 100 randomly selected tweets was coded by two independent coders both before the coding process (inter-coder reliability) and after the coding process (intra-coder reliability). The inter-coder reliability analysis was performed using Krippendorf's Alpha to determine the consistency among and within coders. The inter-coder reliability for two coders for all utilized variables was found to be at least Krippendorf's alpha (nominal) = 0.83, while the intra-coder reliability for all utilized variables did not drop below Krippendorf's alpha (nominal) = 0.93.

12 If the president of political party did not hold or actively use its Twitter account, we selected the party functionaries—most frequently party press officers—with the largest number of Twitter followers.

13 The United Left is a left wing electoral alliance between the Democratic Labor Party (DSD), the Party for Sustainable Development of Slovenia (TRS), and the Initiative for Democratic Socialism (IDS). It was formed to contest 2014 European Parliament election held in May 2014 as a socialist and Eurosceptic list. The alliance also took part in the Slovenian national elections held in July 2014. The Twitter accounts of the ZL (@zdruzenalevica) and TRS party (@strankaTRS) were included in our analysis because both accounts had more than 1,000 followers, and both were actively used during the election campaign.

Section 4

Utilization of Facebook as a Strategic Election Campaign Tool

Chapter 10
European Elections and Facebook:
Political Advertising and Deliberation?

Lucia Vesnic-Alujevic
Independent Researcher, Italy

ABSTRACT

This chapter deals with the political advertising strategies used on Facebook during the elections campaigns for the European Parliament in 2009 and 2014. It explores and examines the posts of 11 political parties and comments they received during the last two weeks before the elections. The focus of the chapter is on possible interactions among citizens and politicians or citizens themselves that would support the idea that online deliberation could function as an improvement over other types of campaigning dialogues and the ways in which individuals used Facebook. The chapter explores possible similarities and differences in campaigning of political parties with the same national and ideological background, if any. It also makes a comparison between the campaigns in 2009 and 2014.

INTRODUCTION[1]

Over the last decade and since the appearance of social media, research in political communication has been examining how campaigns are carried out in new media. Also, if they create new possibilities for overcoming the democratic deficit by including citizens in decision-making processes. Political advertising on Facebook started to be systematically introduced during the electoral campaign for the 2008 US elections. Although it is difficult to estimate the achievements of an online campaign, social media were rapidly included in the European context as well. However the use of political advertising on social media for the European Parliament elections has not been widely studied.

In parallel to the growing presence of European political parties on Facebook, in 2009 slightly over 60 million (33%) of Facebook users were from the European Union, which meant that one in eight Europeans used Facebook (Lorica, 2009). Five years later, (Internet World Stats, 2014), the number tripled. There were 194.3 million Facebook users in Europe, meaning that one in two-three Europeans

DOI: 10.4018/978-1-4666-9879-6.ch010

now use Facebook. Based on the use of Facebook by political parties and the number of Facebook users in Europe, we were interested in discovering how Facebook was used in political advertising during the 2009 and 2014 campaigns for the European Parliament elections.

This chapter also draws on the concept of deliberative democracy, because it is considered relevant for studying political communication in the web 2.0 environment. The interactive features of social media are a fertile ground for dialogue and the application of some of the ideals of deliberative democracy and can be seen as a new public sphere where citizens gather to discuss issues that matter to them. Therefore we were eager to discover if there was any interaction between citizens and politicians and citizens themselves that would support the idea of online deliberation that could prove to be an improvement over other types of dialogues among politicians and citizens; and the ways in which individuals who participate in these pages used Facebook. We also looked for differences related to ideology or home country with regard to party strategies on Facebook.

The original contribution of this paper is seen in its efforts to reveal the campaign strategy for the European Parliament elections on Facebook and compare two consecutive electoral campaigns, which were previously not studied and based on that, to conclude if Facebook could be useful in campaigning for the European Parliament.

SOCIAL MEDIA, POLITICAL ADVERTISING AND ONLINE DELIBERATION

Political advertising is a major tool for political actors to communicate with citizens in order to influence their voting decisions (Kaid, 1999). According to Kaid (1999), it takes place through the channels of mass communication, in any written/audio/visual format, either as paid or unpaid advertising and it is completely controlled by the message producer (Kaid, 1999). Media management of electoral campaigns is used in order for political messages to be transmitted to the audience (Lilleker, 2006). Accordingly, media agenda is attempted to be controlled by the campaign manager (Lilleker, 2006). However, we are not interested in indirect campaigning through traditional mass media that can control the content of information. Instead, we focus on direct ways of advertising through online communicative channels.

Social media are not classic media but the so-called *read-write web* or *user-generated content*, in which the audiences are not just passive viewers of the content but become participants that contribute to the creation of content. Many citizens nowadays are more interested in the less formal, conversational campaign that is facilitated by means of the Internet (Scoble & Israel, 2006). Cardenal (2013) suggests that, since the beginning of 2000, political parties have perceived online tools as useful for political mobilization, but the exact benefits of online advertising remain mostly uncertain. Similarly, Williams and Gulati (2012) argue that voters can effectively be mobilized through social media and mentions their significant role in the US 2008 congressional elections.

The use of the Internet in electoral campaigns has developed over time. An important factor of the convenience of online tools in a campaign is the interaction with the electoral environment (electoral norms and rules) and party organizations (Anstead & Chadwick, 2009). From a political actors' point of view in an electoral process, a positive aspect of the Internet is certainly the possibility of avoiding restrictions and regulations adhered to in traditional media, especially television (Anstead & Chadwick, 2009). We consider political advertising over the Internet to be a sort of bridge between paid and free of charge advertising. Although the use of social media is free of charge, it is more similar to traditional paid advertising whereby a candidate or a party can determine the content and the style of messages placed online which have the possibility of affecting the outcome and influence the messages (Kaid & Holtz-Bacha, 1995). Chadwick (2006) argues that the candidate can tailor their program better, according to voters' needs. He has also noticed that the distinction between an "online" and "offline" citizen is diminishing and considers online interaction "in many ways more real and rewarding than the average campaign rally" (Chadwick, 2006, p. 172). We can assume the scale that political actors on the EU level started to use it massively was in 2009, based on its role in electoral campaign for the 2008 US elections.

Scholarships on online political communication are divided about the role of Internet. For instance, Larsson (2014) argues that the low cost of Internet usage can be seen as suitable for fringe parties that would be able to participate more. On the contrary, Hindman (2009) argues inequalities in gaining access to an audience are replicated online. His data shows that poorly resourced organizations, or organizations not given priority within the mainstream media such as EU institutions, fail to redress these imbalances online. In a study of political parties' websites in several countries, Sudulich (2013) argues that bigger parties provide more informative and interactive content for users which speaks in favour of the normalization hypothesis as well as that left-wing parties provide more interaction between the party and the electorate.

The potentials of online political advertising can be further evaluated through four different communicative features, a concept developed by Foot et al. (2009). The *informing* feature informs the audiences or communicates a specific message. This is the most basic feature. The *interacting* feature implies two-way communication, both among politicians and citizens and among citizens themselves. The *engaging* feature suggests the active participation of visitors in an online platform, based on interactive games, sharing etc. The *mobilizing* has the goal of mobilizing visitors of a website or social media profile in this case. Although all four features are present in online political advertising, mobilizing as many webpage visitors as possible should be the ultimate goal of every political party, especially during the electoral campaign. For the purpose of this paper we will now continue discussing the interactive feature more in depth, which connects well to the ideal of deliberative democracy, through equal participation in collective reasoning and equal distribution of power in collective decision making. Many studies hypothesize that participating in politics, taking participation as any behaviour that can be defined as active as opposed to passive, leads to further participation as well as feelings of empowerment. Engaging in discussions provokes greater self confidence in talking about politics online and offline and can act as a springboard to greater involvement in some form of political activity. Likewise, Gastil (2000) argues that the, deliberation on political issues can increase political efficacy among its participants and stimulate political engagement. Lately the focus has switched to the potential of social media in sustaining this kind of open communication, interaction and deliberation (Graham, forthcoming).

One of the advantages of the online environment is the heterogeneous character of an online debate, where individuals have access to many different views and opinions (besides the similar ones) (Jansens & Kees, 2005). Political discussion is equally important for offering exposure to multiple viewpoints (Mutz & Martin, 2001), and can lead to further discussion and dialogue. Also, social media reinforce the potential for political parties to include citizens interested in the discussion on various issues and their views on certain topics, providing them with mobilizing, interactive and engagement tools. As Lilleker and Koc Mihalska (2014) argue: "Social media appear to provide a gateway into some forms of political participation, some of which are simplistic, but that may actually have impact upon the participant, who might like a picture or statement from a candidate, and their online contacts who view the item that has been liked." (p. 298). In this sense, social media could be seen as a new place for deliberation and interaction among citizens and politicians and consequently lead to the increase of political participation in the offline world as well. Furthermore Cammaerts (2007) suggests that new technologies are diversifying citizens' media practices and activities in the public sphere and consequently they could be seen as "key for participation in a public discourse".

In this chapter, we focus on Facebook, as a specific social media site. A Facebook profile page is considered "a dialogic feature with great potential" (Sweetser & Weaver Lariscy, 2008, p. 182). Lilleker & Koc Mihalska (2014) argue that the more posts a party puts on their profile page, the more audience, their attention and participation they will have. Similarly, Williams and Gulati (2012) suggest that Facebook goes beyond informing the electorate on how to participate in the campaign and elections and encourages discussion.

CAMPAIGNING FOR EUROPEAN PARLIAMENT

The use of Facebook and other social media in political communications on the EU level has not been researched extensively. At the same time, research on transnational elections in Europe is largely lacking (Strömbäck, Maier & Kaid, 2011). Although national elections are often believed to be more important for politicians, and even though the level of personalization is low (voting for a party and not a person), the European Parliament elections provide a good opportunity for comparative research because they are held at the same time across 28 European countries. They are also interesting because of their "hybrid" character: because of the actors and themes, they are at the same time both European and national (Strömbäck, Maier & Kaid, 2011).

One of the first comparative studies on the European Parliament elections was performed by Blumler in 1979 (Blumler, 1983). Those elections were the first ever elections for the European Parliament, and the study questioned the role of television in the electoral campaign. Overall, the differences in political systems in various European countries and other factors have forestalled comparative research of the European Parliament electoral campaigns and elections (Holtz-Bacha, 2004).

The European Parliament elections are considered to be elections of a "second" order in comparison to the national elections; this means that the electorate is not as engaged as it is during national elections, and political parties do not invest much money in supranational elections. As a result, campaigns are badly organized, and turnout and media coverage are low (Holtz-Bacha, 2004). Based on several studies, Banducci (2005) believes that visibility in mass media can increase voter's engagement and participation, thereby increasing turnout. Consequently we think that, although usually excluded from "traditional" media, the appearance of European politicians on new media, could increase their visibility and along with it bring more political engagement among EU citizens.

According to Davidson-Schmich and Davidson-Schmich (2005), the campaigns for the European Parliament elections do not discuss EU issues, but national ones, and "serve as referenda on current national governments" (p. 2). National issues are at the forefront because many parties start a larger overall campaign with the EU elections and then continue the themes from the campaign during the national election's campaign. This is especially true in the case of opposition parties, who obtain an extra opportunity to criticize the government (Davidson-Schmich & Davidson-Schmich, 2005).

Social media were first used in EP electoral campaigns before the 2009 EP elections. At that time, some parliamentarians and their political consultants began to exploit the advantages and strengths that social media may have over traditional media in the realm of political communication. The following elections were held in 2014.

Therefore, the main research question in this chapter is connected to the comparison of Facebook pages of political parties: we wanted to discover similarities and differences between these two campaigns, as well as connections (if any) between different strategies based on ideology or nationality.

RQ1: *What are the differences between the use of social media in electoral campaigning for the EP elections in 2009 and 2014?*

Based on Foot et al. (2009) and Jackson et al. (2010) concept of four communicative features, we were interested to see which feature was dominant. Also if there can be any connection with national and/or ideological background. Therefore the second research question was:

RQ2: *Which party used Facebook the most for political advertising and what feature was dominant?*

We were also interested in discovering to what extent deliberative and interactive potentials were being used on the Facebook pages. This was explored by analyzing comments and interaction between various participants in the conversation. Therefore, the third research question was:

RQ3: *To what extend did the interaction between the page owner/moderator and page fans or between fans themselves exist and what kind of content was posted?*

DATA COLLECTION

The research focused on the comparison of the two-week period that preceded the elections in 2009 (20/5/2009-3(6)/6/2009) and in 2014 (9/5/2014-23/5/2014), which should represent the peak of the electoral campaign. It embraced eleven different political parties from four EU countries and three different political groups in the European Parliament placed differently in the political spectrum (Table 1). The data was gathered by copy-pasting all the relevant material into a word document before the analysis began.

As the project was restricted in time and resources, a small number of countries were selected in order to represent different types of political advertising, electoral systems etc. in the best possible way, allowing for the identification of the impact of specific political, social and cultural contexts in Europe.

Table 1. List of analysed political parties' profiles, grouped according to political group in the EP and to country

	European People's Party (EPP)	Alliance of Socialists and Democrats in the EP (S&D)	Alliance of Liberals and Democrats for Europe (ALDE)
France	Union pour un mouvement populaire (UMP)	Parti socialiste (PS)	Mouvement Democrate (MD)
Ireland	Fine Gael (FG)		Fianna Fail (FF)
Italy	Popolo della liberta- Forza Italia[2] (PdL-FI)	Partito democratico (PD)	Italia dei valori (IdV)
Slovenia	Slovenska demokratska stranka (SDS)	Socialni demokrati (SD)	Liberalna demokracija Slovenije (LDS)

Various political systems, national cultures, and degrees of modernization are considered to be factors that influence campaign techniques (Baines 1999; Plasser et al. 1999). Out of these four countries, two are the founding members of the European community (France and Italy), Ireland joined in 1973 and Slovenia joined the EU in 2007. Two are Western European countries, one is Southern and one is Central European. Gibson and Römmele (2007) suggest that different national political systems could produce varying patterns of online behavior. Out of the chosen states, Ireland, Italy and Slovenia are parliamentary republics and France is a semi-presidential republic. With regards to the electoral system, one has a closed list, two semi-open with preferential vote and one open. There is also a difference in political advertising. France was among the first countries in Europe that started with a modern approach to campaigning in 1965, by developing the so-called French "school" of political advertising, a model of advertising different to the US one (Vesnic-Alujevic, 2011), Italy and Ireland adopted the US model and Slovenia started using it only after gaining the independence in 1991. The level of trust in the European Parliament in all four countries is the same as the level of distrust, between 40 and 50%, which is also the EU average (Eurobarometer, 2012).

These 4 countries in total have a population of 130.7 million citizens (France 64.3, Italy 60, Ireland 4.4, and Slovenia 2), this figure represents roughly 25% of the EU citizens (500 million). Between 2004 and 2009, the turnout dropped in degree for the four countries studied, ranging from a 0.3% decline (Slovenia) to an 8.05% decline (Italy). Between 2009 and 2014, the turnout increased only in France, while in other countries it dropped between 7.83% (Italy) and 3.78% (Slovenia). The digital divide in the four countries is mostly above the EU average (60.7%, according to Internet world stats (2009) and 68.6% according to the Internet World Stats (2014)). Also in Table 2 we can see which party was in power in their respective country before the electoral turn in 2009 and in 2014, which provide us with an indication of the political climate at the given moment.

Table 2. Turnout (2004, 2009), electoral system, digital divide, and number of allocated seats (2004, 2009) in the analyzed countries

Country	Date of accession	Turnout (2009)	Turnout (2014)	Electoral system	Digital divide	Number of seats (2009)	Number of seats (2014)	In power on national level (2009)	In power on national level (2014)
France (UMP, PS, MD)	1957	40.5%	42.4%	List-PR system, closed list	69.3%	49/72	40/74	UMP	PS
Italy (PdL-FI, PD, IdV)	1957	65.0%	57.2%	List PR-system, semi-open list (preferential vote)	51.7%	57/72	44/73	PdL-FI	PD
Ireland (FG, FF)	1973	57.6%	52.4%	STV, Open list	67.3%	7/12	5/11	FF	FG
Slovenia (SDS, SD, LDS)	2004	28.3%	24.5%	List-PR system, Semi-open (preferential vote)	64.8%	5/7	4/8	SDS	SD (in coalition)

We have chosen three political groups which were the biggest political groups at the European Parliament before the 2009 elections. Roughly speaking, the European People's Party (EPP) is a centre-right party group, the Progressive Alliance of Socialists and Democrats (S&D) is a left and centre-left (social-democrats) party group and Alliance of Liberals and Democrats for Europe (ALDE) is a centre party group. The relevance of the selected parties is determined by the number of seats they won in the EP elections in 2004 and 2009. In 2004, the selected parties won 65.7% of all seats in those 4 countries; in 2009, this same set of parties won 72.4% of the seats. However, this percentage lowered in 2014 to 57% and Slovenian LDS became a fringe party.

Comparison of the electoral strategies and campaigns of the 11 political parties chosen for our analysis must account for all the potential differences that can exist in parties and in electoral systems. All of these differences have an impact on the creation and formation of electoral campaigns.

METHODS

Similarly to other social media, analysing Facebook content is not an easy task. The methods, such as content analysis, discourse analysis and similar, need to be rethought and adjusted to online settings and features offered by the medium. Besides the content posted by the page owner that consists of textual, visual and audio-visual material, likes, shares, comments and replies posted by participants are equally important and thus need to be taken into consideration. This is why our analysis is based on computer-mediated discourse analysis (CMDA), which is a type of content analysis adjusted to online environment (Herring, 2009). Herring (2009) argues that CMDA can be applied to four levels of language: structure, meaning, interaction, social behaviour, to which she adds a fifth domain as participation patterns. By this she understands the frequency and length of posted messages and responses received in threads (Herring, 2009). Based on this, we can conclude that CMDA is used for studying the online behaviour of participants in their discussions, interactions, in-group language, speech acts. Thus, its focus is on the language and its use, with special focus on participation in online communication (Herring, 2009).

By means of quantitative exploration followed by qualitative analysis, we have analysed Facebook profiles of 11 political parties in France, Italy, Ireland, and Slovenia. The qualitative analysis of political parties' posts included the four communicative features developed by Foot et al. (2010) in the coding scheme.

As there are often several profile pages for one party on Facebook (created either by political party, supporters, or adversaries), we took pages with some indication that they were official profile pages for the political parties in question into account. If this could not be explicitly determined, research was performed using the page with the greatest number of fans.

The unit of analysis was one post.

We analysed two weeks before the elections, as the last couple of weeks usually represent the peak of an electoral campaign. The qualitative analysis allowed us to take a better look at the deliberative potential of these pages.

RESULTS

Number of Facebook Fans/Friends for Each Political Party

In 2009, most pages had between 1000 and 5000 fans/friends (6) (e.g. Italian PdL), while there were some with less than 500 (4) (e.g., Irish Fianna Fáil). Only one page had more than 5000 fans (French UMP with 5374 fans). In 2014, the number of fans grew dramatically (as well as the number of Facebook users on a global scale), and the most profiles had over 50.000 fans, although there were still two parties with less than 5.000 (both Slovenian parties, SD and LDS). If we compare these data with the population of a respective country as well as the number of Facebook users in the same country as is shown in Table 3, we can see that the biggest percentage of both citizens and Facebook users is linked to Slovenian political parties (in 2009 1.03% and in 2014 2.12% of Slovenian Facebook users are members of these three groups), while in other countries the percentage is considerably lower and quite similar (between 0.075% of Italian Facebook users and 0.13% of French Facebook users in 2009 and between 0.75% of Irish Facebook users and 1.07% of Italian Facebook users) and this is neither related to the ideological background. However the number increased 10 times in these five years. The fact that the numbers constantly change should be taken into account. Another important fact is that 2009 was marked as the beginning of the use of Facebook by political actors in Europe for the European Parliament elections' campaign (Vesnic-Alujevic, 2011). Nevertheless, we can see that the figures are generally small in terms of the number of participants in the general population and within the reach of political advertising through this channel of communication.

Table 3. Number of fans of analyzed parties in relation to the number of citizens and Facebook fans in every country in %

Country	Political party	Nr. of fans		% of fans in population of a country		%fans in total number Facebook users in a country	
		2009	2014	2009	2014	2009	2014
France	UMP	5,374	92,060	0.008%	0. 14%	0.056%	0.37%
	PS	4,742	90,482	0.007%	0.14%	0.049%	0.36%
	MD	2,367	6,672	0.004%	0.01%	0.025%	0.03%
Italy	PdL-FI	1,820	93,258	0.003%	0.16%	0.020%	0.40%
	PD	1,279	143,596	0.002%	0.24%	0.014%	0.62%
	IdV	1,301	12,243	0.002%	0.02%	0.015%	0.05%
Ireland	FG	368	8,565	0.008%	0.19%	0.057%	0.43%
	FF	349	6,461	0.008%	0.15%	0.054%	0.32%
Slovenia	SDS	2,024	10,270	0.10%	0.51%	0.69%	1.41%
	SD	649	4,484	0.03%	0.22%	0.22%	0.61%
	LDS	347	730	0.02%	0.04%	0.12%	0.10%

Structure of a Political Party's Profile Page

We also looked at the structure of a political party's page. In 2009, some of these pages were constructed as "groups", whilst others as "pages", but in 2014 they all had a unified profile page (due to Facebook design changes that abolished groups as such).

If they were constructed as "pages", one could have become a "fan" of a certain "page", with the possibility of reading posts of the owner/moderator of a "page", writing their own comments, "liking" posts of others, etc. The following profiles were constructed as "pages": French UMP and MD, Italian PD and PdL-FI, Slovenian SDS and LDS.

On the other hand, profiles constructed as "groups" had a slightly different page design and features. A group usually contained only posts by members of the group; there was no interaction in the sense that someone else could comment on a post, or "like" the page; rather, individuals had to write a new post to respond to a previous post. Out of the analysed profiles, the following five were constructed as groups: Slovenian SD, French PS, Irish FG, Irish FF, and Italian IdV. In this case, understanding a political party's strategy was not possible from the "wall" section; rather, the thoughts of other participants (i.e. fans), and what they wanted to share, was the main information that we were able to work from.

The choice of creating a profile page as either "page" or "group" could have been a result of party strategy, lack of skills, knowledge or understanding social media or have been a random factor. However groups did not have either classical advertising by posting their own material or providing a possibility for interaction which is a considerable distinction from the pages.

In 2014, they were all designed as pages, which allowed for the same greater amount of interaction and the inclusion of citizens in designing the content of the pages (commenting, interacting and posting their own content).

Political Parties' Posts on Facebook

While focusing on the topic and number of posts, as well as on comments they received, it is important first to note: 1. which profile pages had no posts, 2. which pages blocked the possibility of writing comments and 3. which were actively posting various textual, visual or audio-visual material.

In 2009, pages constructed as groups (Slovenian SD, French PS, Irish FG and FF and Italian IdV) had only a "recent news" section with hyperlinks to news published on the website that dealt with the elections or provided an explanation of a particular party's attitudes regarding various issues. Only one of them (PS) also had: 1. a "photos" section; this section displayed photos from the campaign, such as candidates' ones; 2. a links' section to press releases; 3. an events' section in which electoral events were announced, and 4. a videos' section where videos that deal with party leaders and policies were posted.

On the contrary in 2014, during the observed period, the PS had 23 posts, so it was among the parties that posted the most. The content consisted of YouTube links, posters and mostly pictures from public gatherings followed by a link to the official website where an article on that topic could have been found. The topics were current issues in French politics and campaigning. One of the rare posts that could be considered as interactive was posted on the page of PS, as an invitation to citizens to chat with a candidate for Commission president on Twitter and the other to meet a candidate for the elections in person.

Vous souhaitez poser une question à Martin Schulz? Sur Twitter, utilisez le hashtag #askmartin. Il vous répond à 12h30, aujourd'hui, sur le site du SPD. [Do you have a question for Martin Schulz? Use the hashtag [hashtag] on Twitter, he will reply today at 12.30 on the website of SPD] (Parti Socialiste, 19 May 2014)

For the same period in 2014, Italian IdV, Slovenian SD and Irish FF were moderately active. They had between 8 and 14 posts. For instance, SD only posted their pictures from public gatherings and different activities they were involved in, followed by a couple of lines of text explaining the event on the pictures.

Although in 2009 they did not post anything, in 2014 FG was one of the most active analysed parties. It had 29 posts that consisted of (informal) photos of candidates, official campaign posters, YouTube material, links to the official webpage with a longer article and so on. Nevertheless it should be noted that local elections were taking place on the same day, which probably influenced the campaign. But, the topics were still mainly national ones and the main slogan "Fine Gael for Jobs, Stability and Growth" was not connected to the European Parliament any elections. A very small amount of posts were dedicated to mobilization. They mainly contained direct invitations to vote for them at the European elections, e.g.:

Hang Out Your Brightest Colours! Today, vote Fine Gael (Fine Gael, 23 May 2014)

Despite having the possibility of posting content on their profile page in 2009, the UMP page had neither posts nor comments on its profile page, although the number of fans was quite high in comparison to others (more than 5000), which speaks in favour of their popularity. This could be considered a missed opportunity. We should also bear in mind that the UMP was a party in power in France in that period, but it is also a centre-right party, member of the EPP group; in general, centre-right parties tend to use social media less than others do in the political spectrum (Sudulich, 2013). Another explanation for this may be that the account had recently been added to Facebook shortly before the monitored period. In 2014, on the contrary, the UMP was an opposition party in France. During the two observed weeks, it had 13 posts (almost one per day). The party posted mainly videos that can be found on YouTube as well: their official video for the 2014EP campaign, a video against the current French president as a sort of negative campaign, a video from the campaign, from party's youth etc. Besides, it announced TV appearances of candidates, public gatherings, pictures and links to the articles published on their website, e.g.

Jean-François Copé sera l'invité de "des Paroles et des Actes », spéciale Européennes, ce soir sur France 2 à 20h40 [Jean-François Copé will be guest of 'About words and acts', special edition on European elections, tonight on France 2 at 20h40]. (UMP, 22 May 2014)

These posts were informative but many of them were also engaging and mobilizing. Therefore we can say that the situation changed considerably. The content was mainly national issues and campaign reports.

The Italian party PdL-FI, another EPP centre-right party that was in power in 2009, had only one post during the observed period, possibly for the same reasons. Its only post was: "europee 2009 [European 2009]" which could be interpreted as a reminder or an invitation for their fans to vote. In that sense we could say that it held a slightly mobilizing message. However in 2014, the political situation for this party significantly changed. Similarly to UMP, it became the opposition party on a national level. During the two weeks monitored, it had 11 posts. They were mostly links to articles posted on the party's official website, where different candidates expressed their opinion on various mainly national issues. The party also used negative campaign strategy, against their opponents on a national level. Therefore the posts were engaging for the most part as well as informing.

Another Italian party, this time from S&D group, the PD had only one post in 2009, in which they announced the preparation for the elections and wrote nothing more, which can be seen as purely informing. This changed considerably in 2014 with 28 posts, on average 2 per day. It provided hyperlinks to web streamings of public gathering, to some YouTube audio-visual campaign material, pictures from public gatherings, and links to the articles on the official website. Almost every post contained the word "Europe" but also "Italy", which means that topics represented a blend of national issues but always remained in connection on a European level. They were informative and engaging.

In 2009, the two ALDE parties, Slovenian LDS and French MD (except for 3 posts) posted only titles and the first couple of lines with hyperlinks leading to their respective official websites, where the entire articles that were uploaded by the political party could be found. For example, LDS's posts invited citizens to vote while providing information about political campaigns by their leaders and on various awards their leaders had won. MD provided announcements about the public appearance of its leaders, in first place, its president François Bayrou, and reviews of public meetings already held along with an invitation to vote. In 2014, LDS did not post anything during the monitored period and MD had 8 posts. Between 2009 and 2014 LDS became a fringe party and despite the possibilities of developing a strong advertising campaign on Facebook, as an unofficial channel, they did not do anything. This speaks in favour of the normalization thesis (Sudulich, 2013). MD posted links to the articles either on their own website or via online newspapers (euronews.com, lemonde.fr). As opposed to the majority of other parties, the topics were mostly European (place of France in Europe, European project, importance of European elections, European foreign policy and so on). These posts were engaging for the most part.

The engaging posts were nothing more than informative posts about their stand regarding various issues and visits but contained a hyperlink to the party website or YouTube, where it was possible to read the entire article, e.g.

MARIELLE DE SARNEZ était l'invitée du 13h de LCP. Elle est revenue sur l'importance des élections du 25 mai ainsi que sur la crise ukrainienne. Retrouvez l'intégralité de l'interview sur notre site. [hashtag] [hyperlink] [Marielle De Sarnez was LCP invitee at 13h. She talked about the importance of the elections in 25 May but also about the Ukraine crisis. Find the whole interview on our website [hashtag] [hyperlink] (Mo Dem, 12 May 2014)

However going to another webpage (the official website or YouTube) had the potential of attracting other content to visitors as well.

The most active profile page in 2009 was a page from SDS with 26 posts. This party used several different advertising formats: posters, text, photos, and audio-visual material. This was the only party (among the ones analysed) with a clear Facebook strategy, and the intention to use it in order to attract participants to the issues they considered important. SDS used Facebook mostly as a complementary channel (besides the invitations to vote, nothing new was posted on Facebook, but only copied from either the official website or other "traditional" media such as campaign video ads and posters). The content was informative. In 2014, SDS had 21 posts, less than in 2009 but again a noteworthy number.

Overall, during the period analysed in 2009, seven profiles did not have any post, one had only one, two between five and 10 posts; and one more than 20. In 2014, four had less than 10, three between 10 and 20 and four between 20 and 30. In the majority of cases (especially in 2009), this should be considered as an inadequate use of Facebook for any political party regardless of its country or ideological background, especially when compared to the usual rhythm of postings on Facebook, and the fact that this type of political advertising is free of charge and could have been exploited better. However there was a huge advance in the campaigning methods between 2009 and 2014. Table 4 gives an overview of all posts grouped according to the type of post (informing, mobilizing, engaging, interacting). From Table 4, we see that the majority of posts were either informative or engaging and to some extent mobilizing.

Comments

When it comes to comments, as presented in Table 5, in 2009 the UMP and PD profile pages had no posts, hence no comments or "likes"; the LDS profile page turned off the option of leaving comments, which left only the possibility of sharing the content with other Facebook "friends". MD had a similar tactic, opening the profile page for comments only on May 31 and on June 5-6. An interesting fact is that both LDS and MD are political parties from ALDE group; as liberal parties espousing ideologies at the centre of the political spectrum, they would generally be expected to use more web 2.0 features than right-wing parties in determining their online presence (Vesnic-Alujevic and Van Bauwel, 2014). However, comparing these parties, we argue that there is no difference in either the country they come from or at an ideological level.

In Table 5, we see that the percentage of active group members grew considerably. For instance, Italian PD or Irish FG had 40% of active group members. However there were some group members still inactive for the most part (such as IdV, PS or MD group members).

We wanted to test the profiles with respect to the distinction between partial and full interaction, whereby partial interaction would mean only putting "likes" under a post (and, in more general terms, becoming a fan of a certain profile page) or "sharing" the post on their own wall (this button did not

Table 4. Analysed political parties and type of posts they shared on Facebook during the weeks analysed

Party/Type of Posts	Informing		Engaging		Mobilizing		Interacting	
	2009	2014	2009	2014	2009	2014	2009	2014
UMP	/	3	/	4	/	/	/	/
PS	/	/	/	22	/	/	/	1
MD	1	/	7	8	/	/	/	/
PdL-FI	/	3	/	6	1	/	/	/
PD	/	9	/	19	/	/	/	/
IdV	/	2	/	4	/	2	/	/
FG	/	2	/	16	/	11	/	/
FF	/	3	/	4	/	1	/	/
SDS	6	16	17	3	3	3	/	1
SD	/	12	/	1	/	1	/	/
LDS	2	/	5	/	/	/	/	/

Table 5. Number of comments, likes and shares[3] according to political party

Political party	Participation in General		Comments		Likes		Shares
	2009	2014	2009	2014	2009	2014	2014
PdL-FI	0.5%	11.3%	3	871	5	7,458	2,189
PD	0	39.4%	0	10,080	0	36,204	10,304
UMP	0	7.0%	0	474	0	4,550	1,105
MD	3%	6.0%	19	12	49	309	80
LDS	0	0	0	0	0	0	0
SDS	5%	17.4%	25	105	87	1,617	63
SD	0.6%	20.3%	4	60	/	804	48
PS	0.2%	3.7%	9	345	/	2,622	391
FG	0.5%	40.1%	2	1,134	/	2,052	252
FF	1.1%	13.7%	4	152	/	560	176
IdV	1.5%	1.2%	20	20	/	132	1

exist in 2009), and full interaction would mean writing comments under posts (Vesnic-Alujevic, 2012). In 2009, on four profile pages, both partial and full interaction were observed; one had only partial, and three (as we already mentioned) no interaction at all. There were, roughly, 2–3 times more likes than comments. In 2014, all but one had both partial and full participation. As Table 5 shows, the number of "likes" occurred several times (sometimes even more than 10 times) more than the number of comments. This finding speaks in favour of the thesis that citizens who participate on these pages are not interested in interacting, explaining their arguments and opinions and thus participating on a more in depth level; or if they are, they prefer to limit their engagement to putting "likes" or alternatively "share" parties' material. This measures a party's visibility dramatically as all "friends" of the person who shares party's content will see it, because it appears in their news feeds.

The aforementioned proportions of "likes" and comments again show that several profile pages differ from others through their activity (both by the profile page manager, and by participants). The parties that stand out again are Slovenian SDS in 2009, an EPP group party, and Italian PD in 2014, an S&D group party. They also had the largest percentage of fans, compared to the total number of Facebook users in their respective countries. SDS was part of the opposition party blocs in its home country in 2009. However, PD was the party in power in its home country in 2014. To provide a possible explanation for this, it may be considered that Italy is an "old" democracy, with developed political marketing strategies, so it is not surprising that they have introduced new online campaigning strategies as well. However, maybe more significant and interesting is that a "new" democracy such as Slovenia already in 2009 had parties that used new web 2.0 applications as a part of their campaigns and on a higher level than French, Italian or Irish ones.

In 2009, most comments were supportive of the political party's page they were on, while one sixth of comments consisted of negative statements about other politicians and political parties. For instance, this is a comment that was posted on the MD French liberal political party, in line with their policies:

Oui à une Europe allant vers une veritable cohesion! [Yes to a Europe that will reach a true cohesion] (SJ, 31 May 2009 on MoDem page)

A similar comment could have been found on other pages as well:

Samo pogumno naprej....MI smo z vami. [Just bravely forward... We are with you] (IL, 5 June 2009 on SDS page)

In 2014, there were also supportive comments, such as:

Emozioni grandissime, fatti concreti e parole semplici: Matteo è senz'altro il mio Presidente del consiglio! Orgogliosa di votare PD! [Huge emotions, concrete facts and simple words: Matteo is certainly my president of the government! Proud to vote PD] (GA, 22 May 2014 on PD)

as well as many short comments, such as: "continue like this", "Non ti fermare" [don't stop], "grande [great]", "go ahead", "SDS rules", etc.

This speaks in favour of the fact that people join groups they support, and that there is no discussion among people who hold different opinions. This is in accordance with the concept of "collective action" (Marwell & Oliver, 1993). Also, previous studies have shown that comments written on a candidate's wall are usually rare, superficial, supportive, and have a positive tone (Sweetser & Weaver Lariscy, 2008). An interesting observation from 2009 was that on the most active pages, citizens discussed issues that go beyond mere support for their political party during the elections. For instance, comments posted on the PS group dealt with the elections, but were also expressions of opposition to the government; The IdV group, most of the comments were also anti-government (as IdV was an opposition party), even though they also provided support to the IdV and invited other members of the group to vote.

Five years later, in 2014, it is significant to note that, besides supportive comments, there were many heterogeneous opinions. Although the supporters of political parties are still clearly in a majority, there were also opponents registered on a party's profile page as fans, who were very active in posting comments opposing the respective party. For instance:

Do ye really think people are going fall twice for your propaganda? Just give us a general election and let us show you how we feel about you (TR, 10 October 2014, on Fine Gael profile page)

In 2014, we had, for the first time, interaction between the participants. For instance, while answering to one Partito Democratico post, one user wrote:

È LA PRIMA VOLTA CHE CHE UN POLITICO ADDIRITURA UN PREMIER ESPRIME AD ALTA VOCE TUTTI I MIEI PENSIERI MATTEO INSISTI TANTE RESISTENZE MI FANNO PENSARE CHE SEI SULLA STRADA GIUSTA [It is the first time that a politician, even prime minister, expresses all my thoughts aloud. Matteo insists! Many resistances make me think you are on the right track- emphasis by the author] (RP, 22 May 2014 on PD)

And then he received a reply from another user:

il problema è che restano solo pensieri.. [the problem is that they remain only as thoughts] (answer to the first one, NR, 22 May 2014)

This comment is just an illustration of the new and interesting phenomenon of opposing comments that were present on all analysed pages. Some of them were explicitly based on disappointment about how some issues were dealt with by a party, especially when that party was in power in the relevant country.

Another novelty is the interaction among participants. Here is an example. The original post was a picture of a candidate with the message "Vote Fine Gael in Ireland South on 23rd May". Among many comments we chose one as an illustration, as well as 3 replies that the comment got. The comment was:

Job bridge and internships aren't jobs they are a way of fudging the numbers on the live register, ye think we're all that stupid to not realise what ye are doing when telling us there's so so many off the register each quarter (AF, 19 May 2014 on Fine Gael page)

This comment got 8 likes and 2 replies. The first reply was:

77.000 new jobs in the last 2 years. Do you think the CSO are lying and making up the figures? (BW, 19 May 2014)

This reply got one like. Then a third person replied to the previous one:

Get real Barry, most politicans do not realise how stretched people are, unemployment at its lowest in 5 years!!!,no mention of the thosands of people who have emigrated, back to work schemes, gone back to collage, social universal charges to go up for people on average income but the super rich get a cut, hospitals understaffed and closing, people with severe disabilities having medical cards taken off them, do you agree with these stats???? (DO 19 May 2014)

This last reply got 10 likes.

Therefore, we can say that there is an interaction, both via replies and likes, among participants on a page, and what is even more important, among those who do not share the same opinion. In fact, we have seen many comments that are opposed to the opinions of the party which created the page. Unfortunately, the conversations were often neither constructive nor founded on a solid basis but mostly superficial, showing either the support to a party or the opposition, often expressed through personal insults ("you idiot!", "you don't know anything", "yes, vote for a lout and convict") or swear words.

CONCLUSION

Although political parties' profiles on Facebook are constantly changing and although campaigning on Facebook becomes more and more organized and 'professional', we wanted to explore the possibility of political advertising on Facebook during the electoral campaign for the 2009 EP elections, at the beginning of its use for such purposes. The studied period was of particular interest because almost all candidates in the election created their Facebook profile just a couple of months before the beginning of the campaign. Therefore, for most parties, this was the first web 2.0 campaign. Then we compared it with the 2014 campaign, which was the following electoral turn, held 5 years later, to see what had changed in the parties' social media strategies. It was certainly important to explore and examine the changes that this 5-year period brought in the usage of social media both by political parties and citizens.

In 2009, in most cases, research showed that the Facebook campaign was not well developed, and there was no clear strategy for approaching the target group (in this case, Facebook members). Topics of the posts mainly provided information about the elections. Some of them provided more engaging material with mobilizing potential. Therefore, the essence of these posts was mainly informative. In 2014, Facebook became a sort of mainstream campaigning medium that political parties started to use in a more systematic way and the content proved to be much richer. They all had audio-visual material (mostly campaign advertising videos posted on YouTube), many visuals, hyperlinks to lengthier published articles and other material on their own website, hyperlinks to newspapers' articles, invitations to public gatherings, voting and to some extent invitations to interact with politicians. The informative posts contained mainly information from the campaign with many pictures, their take on some issues or information of when and where a candidate would present his program or appear on a television program. Engaging posts were very similar to the informative ones but contained links to other websites where more information could be found. Posts with mobilizing content were less present and interactive ones almost non-existent. Therefore, based on the type of posts used, we can conclude that, both in 2009 and 2014 Facebook was used more as a means of informing the public rather than persuading the participants on their pages. This could be explained by the fact that political parties assumed that fans of their pages are mainly their supporters. Based on this, supporters needed to be informed about the campaign events more than invited to vote and be mobilized in the campaign.

Parties that used Facebook the most were SDS in 2009 and PD in 2014. In 2009 SDS had 26 posts and in 2014 PD had 28. Both parties have various advertising formats and posts, which were mainly informative and engaging with links leading to their official websites and YouTube videos. At the rhythm of two or more posts per day and given the diversity of material, we can say that Facebook was used well, as a complementary channel. As these two parties come from different countries and belong to different political groups, it would be wrong to conclude that the ideological or national background played a role in this behaviour.

It is often assumed that social media should support dialogical communication which can be used during electoral campaigns and online deliberation (Sweetser & Weaver Lariscy, 2008). Even though possibilities for deliberation and interaction through Facebook are numerous, they were not adequately exploited by the political parties. In 2009, comments were rare and not expanded on, even though they were generally supportive and positive. There was also no reciprocal communication between page members, a fact already observed in a previous study on Facebook (Sweetser & Weaver Lariscy, 2008). As we have seen, only 1% to 7% of group members were active, while others were merely spectators. This changed in 2014. As the number of fans rose considerably, the number of their comments increased too. Comments were longer and more clearly expounded when compared to 2009. Also a greater number of fans actually participated in the discussions. The discussions were often tense and people exchanged their opinions more widely. This leads us to the conclusion that Facebook can be seen as a good place for encouraging deliberation among citizens on political issues. However, the discussion was often superficial and not a "rational-critical" debate that could lead to solving problems, which is an ideal of deliberative democracy (Habermas, 1996).

At the same time, it is important to stress that there was no interaction at all between political parties and their fans either in 2009 or in 2014. This is in accordance with the view of Lilleker and Koc Mihalska (2014) who argue that parties do not see added value in communicating with their fans and avoid interpersonal contact on social media which is uncensored. .

The greatest number of involved persons and comments was on the pages of SDS in 2009 and PD in 2014. These were also the parties that posted the most. Therefore we can agree that more active pages attract more attention and participation of citizens (Williams & Gulati, 2012; Lilleker & Koc Mihalska, 2014).

While there is a certain level of difference in the use of Facebook between different political parties, this study did not conclusively establish any relationship between strategies of parties from the same country, or from the same ideological background. These findings were in spite of the fact that research has suggested that parties on the center-right area of the political spectrum tend to make less use of web 2.0 interactive technologies in the political arena (Sudulich, 2013).

The difference in the use of Facebook in 2009 and 2014 is seen mainly in the type of material that was posted. The 2014 campaign was richer with visual and audio-visual material and links to other websites. The major difference was the number and the content of comments, i.e. the greater engagement of citizens.

Nevertheless, if the aim of this type of campaign is to attract more voters, campaigning on Facebook should become more professional and make use of its possibility to communicate directly with the electorate. The interactive component of this type of campaigning could lead more to deliberative democracy goals and greater engagement of citizens in political processes. The advantage of free advertising should also be put to stronger use.

REFERENCES

Anstead, N., & Chadwick, A. (2009). Parties, Election Campaigning and the Internet: Toward A Comparative Institutional Approach. In A. Chadwick & P. N. Howard (Eds.), *The Handbook of Internet Politics* (pp. 56–71). London: Routledge.

Banducci, S. (2005). *Media Exposure, Media Content and Voter Mobilization: Implications for the Lijphart Thesis*. Annual Meeting of the American Political Science Association, Washington, DC.

Blumler, J. (1983). *Communicating to Voters: Television in the First European Parliament Elections*. London: Sage.

Cammaerts, B. (2007). Citizenship, the Public Sphere and Media. In Reclaming the Media: Communication Rights and Democratic Media roles (pp. 1-8). Bristol: Intellect Books.

Cardenal, A. (2013). Why mobilize support online? The paradox of party behavior online. *Party Politics*, *19*(1), 83–103. doi:10.1177/1354068810395059

Chadwick, A. (2006). *Internet Politics: States, Citizens, and New Communication Technologies*. Oxford, UK: Oxford University Press.

Davidson-Schmich, L., & Davidson-Schmich, M. (2005). *The Content of European Parliament Election Campaigns: A Framework for Analysis and Evidence from Germany in 2004*. University of Miami, EU Center Working Paper.

Flew, T., & Young, G. (2005). *From E-Government to Online Deliberative Democracy*. Presented on the International Conference on Engaging Communities, Brisbane, Australia.

Foot, K., Xenos, M., Schneider, S., Kluver, R., & Jankowski, N. (2009). Electoral web production practices in cross-national perspective: The relative influence of national development, political culture, and web genre 2008. In A. Chadwick & P. Howard (Eds.), *Handbook of Internet politics* (pp. 40–55). London, UK: Routledge.

Gastil, J. (2000). Is Face-to-Face Citizen Deliberation a Luxury or a Necessity? *Political Communication, 17*(4), 357–361. doi:10.1080/10584600050178960

Graham, T. (forthcoming). Everyday Political Talk in the Internet-Based Public Sphere. In S. Coleman & D. Freelon (Eds.), *Handbook of Digital Politics*. Cheltenham, UK: Edward Elgar.

Habermas, J. (1996). *Between Facts and Norms: Contributions to a discourse theory of law and democracy*. Cambridge, MA: Polity Press.

Herring, S. (2009). Web content analysis: Expanding the paradigm. In J. Hunsinger, M. Allen, & L. Klastrup (Eds.), *The International Handbook of Internet Research*. Springer Verlag. doi:10.1007/978-1-4020-9789-8_14

Hindman, M. (2009). *The myth of digital democracy*. Princeton, NJ: Princeton University Press.

Holtz-Bacha, C. (2004). Political campaign communication. In Comparing Political Communication: Theories, Cases, Challenges (pp. 213-230). Cambridge, UK: Cambridge University Press.

Internet World Stats. (2014). *Internet Users in the European Union in December 31, 2013*. Retrieved from http://www.internetworldstats.com/stats9.htm

Janssens, D., & Kies, R. (2005). Online Forums and Deliberative Democracy. *Acta Politica, 40*(3), 317–335. doi:10.1057/palgrave.ap.5500115

Kaid, L. L. (1999). Political Advertising: A Summary of Research Findings. In B. Newman (Ed.), *The Handbook of Political Marketing* (pp. 423–438). Thousand Oaks, CA: Sage Publications.

Kaid, L. L., & Holtz-Bacha, C. (1995). Political Advertising Across Cultures: Comparing Content, Styles, and Effects. In L. L. Kaid & C. Holtz-Bacha (Eds.), *Political Advertising in Western Democracies: Candidates and Parties on Television* (pp. 206–227). Thousand Oaks, CA: Sage Publications.

Larsson, A. (2014). Online, all the time? A quantitative assessment of the permanent campaign on Facebook. *New Media & Society*. doi:10.1177/1461444814538798

Lilleker, D. (2006). *Key Concepts in Political Communication*. London: Sage.

Lilleker, D., & Koc-Michalska, K. (2014). Online Election Campaigning: Exploring Supply and Demand During the France 2012 Presidential Election. In A.Solo (Ed.), Political Campaigning in the Information Age (pp. 287-304). Hershey, PA: IGI Global.

Lorica, B. (2009). *Facebook is growing fast in Asia, Europe and the Middle East*. Retrieved May 13, 2010 from http://radar.oreilly.com/2009/03/facebook-is-growing-fast-in-asia-europe-middleeast.html

Mutz, D., & Martin, P. (2001). Facilitating Communication Across Lines of Political Difference: The Role of Mass Media. *The American Political Science Review, 95*(1), 97–114.

Scoble, R., & Israel, S. (2006). *Naked Conversations: how blogs are changing the way businesses talk to customers*. Hoboken, NJ: John Wiley and Sons.

Strömbäck, J., Maier, M., & Kaid, L. L. (2011). Political communication and election campaigns for the European Parliament. In M. Maier, J. Strömbäck, & L. L. Kaid (Eds.), *Political Communication in European Parliamentary Elections* (pp. 3–16). Aldershot, UK: Ashgate.

Sudulich, M. (2013). Do ethos, ideology, country and electoral strength make a diffence in cyberspace? In P. Nixon, R. Rawal & D. Tercea (Eds.), Politics and the Internet in Comparative Context: Views from the Cloud (pp. 75-94). Routledge.

Sweetser, K., & Weaver Lariscy, R. (2008). Candidates make good friends: An analysis of candidates' uses of Facebook. *International Journal of Strategic Communication*, *2*(3), 175–198. doi:10.1080/15531180802178687

Vesnic-Alujevic, L. (2011). *The Role of Internet in Political Communication: A Case Study of the 2009 European Parliament Elections*. Gent: University Press (doctoral dissertation).

Williams, C., & Gulati, G. (2013). Social networks in political campaigns: Facebook and the congressional elections of 2006 and 2008. *New Media & Society*, *15*(1), 52–71. doi:10.1177/1461444812457332

ENDNOTES

1 A part of this research was conducted at Ghent University during the author's PhD studies.

2 The party changed the name from Partito della Liberta' to Forza Italia

3 "Shares" option did not exist in 2009

Chapter 11
One of Many Tools to Win the Election:
A Study of Facebook Posts by Presidential Candidates in the 2012 Election

Ashik Shafi
Wayne State University, USA

Fred Vultee
Wayne State University, USA

ABSTRACT

Presidential campaigns today are increasingly integrating social media such as Facebook as an efficient tool to communicate with the public and organize their supporters. In a bid to explore how the Facebook is used by the politicians during election campaigns, this chapter explored official Facebook posts by two presidential candidates ahead of the 2012 US presidential election. The findings suggest Facebook was used in the campaign as a platform to organize like-minded voters, and reporting a virtual presence to the voters. Facebook was used strategically to resonate with the real-life campaign, and disseminate instant messages, rather than engaging in discussion with the public. The two candidates had only minor difference in the characteristics of their Facebook contents. The implication of the research for the online political agenda-building tactics is discussed.

INTRODUCTION

New media have profoundly changed the nature of political communication. Online and wireless communication has allowed an abundance of virtual political activities with high interactivity and instantaneity, which has altered the way politicians used to plan and build their campaigns. Scholars have studied the impact of new media in political campaigns and looked at the use of social media by politicians and the public (Vitak et al., 2011; Quintelier & Theocharis, 2013; Heaney, Newman & Sylvester, 2011). Politicians were quick to adapt to the environment of new media communication in the early 2000s, as

DOI: 10.4018/978-1-4666-9879-6.ch011

the Internet spread as a major form of mass and interpersonal communication. Politicians have been found using various types of social media as a part of their election campaigns (Heaney, Newman & Sylvester, 2011). As scholars have investigated the content and rhetoric of social media messages by politicians (Parmelee, 2014; Vital et al., 2011; Campbell & Jamieson, 2008), the strategic use of social media during elections deserves further attention. This study explores Facebook posts by Mitt Romney and Barack Obama during the 2012 election campaign and relates the findings to agenda-setting theory and the concept of agenda-building. The findings underscore the importance of looking at the role of social media as a part of larger political campaigns. This chapter emphasizes that the Internet can be used by politicians and elites as a top-down, center-to-peripheral channel of mass communication, besides its use by the audience as a mass user-based network.

EMERGENCE OF ONLINE POLITICAL CAMPAIGNS

Since the advent of television, political campaigns in the US have relied on two major components as ways of avoiding what 2008 vice presidential candidate Sarah Palin derided as "media filters": advertisements and televised debates (Craig & Hill, 2010). The massive expansion of the Internet in recent times has added online outlets as a third arena in which campaigns can spread their messages without their being reshaped by journalists. Online political activities include information consumption and sharing on social networks, website publishing, online advertisements, email marketing and online fundraising. Online political activities came to public attention for the first time in the 1996 presidential election, when political parties opened their official websites and quickly rose to popularity (Heaney, Newman & Sylvester, 2011).

The Pew Center for Internet Research found that 4% of the public visited online sources for political information in 1995, but that number reached 18% in 2000, 37% in 2004 and 46% in 2008 (Raine, Horrigan & Cornfield, 2005; Raine & Smith, 2008; Kohut & Raine, 2000). Voters used the Internet to seek information online, donate electronically, share political thoughts among their virtual networks, campaign in social and user-generated media, and discuss politics on online forums. During the 2012 US presidential election, around 22% of registered voters let others know how they voted on a social networking site, 30% were encouraged to vote by their friends or families, and 20% encouraged others to vote by posting on social networking sites (Raine, 2012). Scholars have concluded that politicians in the US since the 1990s have been using the Internet as a vital tool to disseminate their messages, contact the voters and the campaign team, influence mass media and mass-interpersonal media, collect funds and organize supporters (Heaney, Newman & Sylvester, 2011).

Among different Internet platforms, social networking sites (SNS) have become notable due to their features of interactivity, immediacy, convergence across various platforms and ability to host large number of users. Facebook has become the most popular social networking site for political campaign because of its immense number of users. As of March, 2013, 1.11 billion people reportedly used it every month, 665 million people logged in every day, and 751 million people accessed it via mobile devices (Facebook, 2013). Its size, spread and ease of access have attracted scholars to explore Facebook as an arena of political communication.

A number of studies have explored political use of social media. Most have explored the content of social media messages (Vergeer, 2013; Heaney, Newman & Sylvester, 2011), the rhetoric in the communication (Gurevitch, Coleman & Blumler, 2009; Williams & Gulati, 2013) or social network activities by authoritarian regimes (Youmans & Yorks, 2012; Wolfsfeld, Segev & Sheafer, 2013). Scholars have also investigated how users themselves use social media, including their consumption and sharing of political information and their online political discussion (Binder, Howes & Smart, 2012; Vitak & Ellison, 2013; Han, 2008; Freelon, 2010).

USING SOCIAL MEDIA AS A CAMPAIGN TOOL

Social networking sites (SNS) are now immensely popular, and thus an attractive choice for politicians who want to reach a large number of voters instantly. Many of the social network pages published by politicians have more subscribers than a medium-sized newspaper. As of October 11, 2013, around 36 million people had liked the Facebook pages of Obama and 11 million liked Romney's. (https://www.facebook.com/barackobama and https://www.facebook.com/mittromney). As SNSs complement, and in some cases supplant, traditional media in the political communication process, an analysis of the rhetoric, features and content on the two candidates' Facebook pages can help reveal how politicians use Facebook as a communication medium and offer insights on the use of SNS as a political mass communication medium.

AGENDA-BUILDING BY POLITICIANS THROUGH SOCIAL MEDIA

The agenda-building concept states that journalists' stories and public opinion can be shaped by outside forces (Parmelee, 2014), often by politicians who are concerned about their coverage in the media. The concept is related to the agenda-setting theory of mass communication, which contends that the media agenda influences the public agenda by transferring salience of issues into the public mind (McCombs & Shaw, 1972; Wanta & Hu, 1994; Wu & Coleman, 2009). In practical terms, the agenda-building process is understood as politicians' effort to control and shape the media agenda, which in turn, is supposed to shape the public agenda.

The work of agenda-building usually consists of information subsidies provided by the politicians or their campaign teams to journalists. The subsidies may be given directly through press releases or recordings, or indirectly through informal interviews, personal communications or framing of events (Lancendorfer & Lee, 2010). A large number of studies have documented politicians' agenda-building efforts, such as the top issues in 2008 election (Kim, Xiang & Kiousis, 2011), during the 2006 gubernatorial election (Kiousis, Kim, McDevitt & Ostrowski, 2009), during the policy process on health-care reform in 2009 (Kiousis, Park, Kim & Go, 2013) and in international affairs (Kiousis & Wu, 2008).

Previous literature on political agenda-setting research has outlined a complex relationship among the audience, mass media, public relations organizations and the news environment (Rogers & Dearing, 1988, Atwater, Fico & Pizante, 1987). Several researchers from the early 2000s reported that politicians influence the media agenda through public relations and the media work to influence the public agenda (Lanosga, 2008; Sweetser, Golan & Wanta, 2008). Through the process of inter-media agenda-setting, newspapers can set the agenda of other types of media, such as cable television and wire services (Golan, 2006). Recent studies have found that the agenda-setting process works by the mass media influencing the agenda of smaller communication networks around the citizens, such as social, user-generated and interpersonal communication media (Lei, Hong & McCombs, 2012).

The unique technical capacities of new media allow politicians to reach both the media and the public instantly and make it an effective tool in agenda-building. In traditional forms of political communication, such as face-to-face speeches, politicians depended on the mass media for their messages to reach a national audience. With online media, politicians can directly reach national and global audiences and bypass the gatekeeping of mass media. This capacity allows politicians to strategically use social media in election campaigns and to influence the public and media agendas in a scale greater than before. Looking at the process of social media use by the politicians during elections can offer valuable insights into their strategies and agenda-building efforts in political campaign strategies.

Politicians have been found to use social media as agenda-building tool by disseminating information subsidy through different SNS that helps to influence the media agenda. Politicians frequently post Tweets, Facebook status or YouTube videos which are used by the journalist as a source of news, and are included in the afterward news story. Exploring the agenda-building function of political tweets, Parmelee (2014) interviewed 11 journalists from US national newspapers and found they frequently use political tweets in preparing for their stories as the tweets offer the politicians' unique views of a particular event, provide authentic quotes, reveal possible story errors and provide better understanding of political events. The journalists reported following the tweets of political bloggers, think tanks and interest groups (ibid, 2014). In another study, some 18% business journalists reported that they utilize the social media when writing a story, while 4% reporting that blogs and Tweeter are their most important news source (Lariscy et al., 2009). The findings show that social media is deemed as an important and authentic source in news gathering, suggesting an agenda-building purpose by the politicians. However, additional studies are needed with controlling media and the public agenda to determine the influence of the social media on the news media.

RHETORICAL CONTENTS OF DEMOCRATS AND REPUBLICAN CAMPAIGN MESSAGES

Studies have looked at the rhetorical performance of presidents on occasions such as presidential nomination acceptance addresses (Ritter, 1980), inaugural speeches, farewell addresses, war, denial of charges and impeachment trials (Campbell & Jamieson, 2008) and at classical democracy in ancient Greece (Yunis, 1996). The politicians have been found strategically choosing different rhetorical messages during contesting as incumbent and challengers (Lowry & Naser, 2010); as winner and loser candidates (Stein & Church, 2007) and running as Democrats and Republicans (Benoit, 2004).

Democrats and Republicans have been found to differ in the references made in their campaign messages, as well as the rhetorical language. Several of the studies have found that Democrats more refer to policy, both their own and their opponents, compared to Republicans, who focus more on their suggested superior character and the tainted morality of their opponents (Benoit, 2004; Benoit et al., 2013; Lowry & Naser, 2010). A content analysis of primary and general presidential debates, television spots and acceptance speeches from 1948 to 2000 revealed that Democrats discussed policy more and character less than Republicans in all kinds of texts combined, including general debates, TV spots and primary debates (Benoit, 2004). Both Democrats and Republicans discussed the issues "owned" by their respective parties more than other issues. In regard to character utterances Democrats were found using more sincerity and morality and less empathy and drive than Republicans. Democratic candidates have been found to refer to policy more often (86% vs. 72%) than their Republican counterparts, who referred more to character (28% vs. 13%) during the 2008 election (Benoit et al., 2013). The study also found that the Democrats focused on general goals (44%), past deeds (24%) and future plans (20%), whereas the Republicans focused nearly equally on past deeds and general goals (Benoit et al., 2013). Democrats have also been found to refer to more to rhetorical verbose of numerical terms, contemporary concerns and diversity more than the Republicans, who cited more inspiration and complexity (Lowry & Naser, 2010).

Quantitative analysis of rhetorical content has revealed that Democrats have used more "collective focus" and "similarity to followers" in their campaigns in terms of conveying a charismatic image of their candidates in the 2008 election (Schroedel et al., 2013). In terms of employing charismatic language in campaign messages, the Democrats have been found to refer the present situation as a continuation of the past more and invoke value and moral justification less than the Republicans (Schroedel et al., 2013). Both of the candidates have been found to frequently refer to intangible future goals. The winning candidates used more "direct entitlement" strategies --, stating self-responsibility for achievements -- and less "enhancement." which is stating the achievement greater in significance than the losers (Lowry & Naser, 2010; Stein & Church, 2007).

The difference in the content of the campaign messages of the two parties are originated in their disparate political ideologies, distinct intended audiences and particular motivation of their voters. The Democrats emphasize the diversity in American society, take stands for immigration, minority and civil rights, which are percolated in their mentions of collectivism, rapport and commonality. On the other hand, the Republicans assert American exceptionalism, takes a conservative stance on issues involving minorities and welfare, and underline the influence of religion on public life, which are manifested in their weight on personality appeals, self-reference and present concern. These explorations suggest the importance of looking more closely into political campaigns in online environments to understand campaign strategies as well as the changing nature of politicians' interaction with the audience.

HYPOTHESIS AND RESEARCH QUESTIONS

This chapter explores use of social media in political campaigns by analyzing official Facebook posts by the Democratic and Republican candidates during the US presidential election campaign in 2012. Agenda-building studies have found evidence that the politicians are able to influence the media agenda by communicating and campaigning about political issues (Sheafer & Weimann, 2005). As studies have found that the mass media agenda exerts significant influence over that of the blogs and social networks (Meraz, 2011), it is worth investigating how politicians' messages on Facebook, as an example of social media, resemble patterns found in the mass media. A strong correlation between the presidential candidates' Facebook messages and the media agenda will suggest a social media agenda-building activity. Investigating the two candidates Facebook posts in the 2012 election, this study asks the following question:

RQ1: *How do the presidential candidates' agendas on Facebook resemble the mass media agenda?*

Previous literature suggests that the Republic and Democratic candidates talk about fairly similar issues during election campaigns, and do not strongly differ in terms of their frequency of discussions (Petrocik, Benoit & Hansen, 2003). The two parties are found to refer to issues such as defense policies, taxing, crime and social welfare issues during their acceptance speeches from 1952 to 2000. Literature on political issue formation and issue dynamics of the two parties found the two parties have been debating mostly on the same list of the issues in last 30 years although the party position on the issues have changed considerably (Stimson, 2004). Based on the literature, it can be inferred that the two candidates will be similar in their reference of issues in the Facebook posts. Thereby, this study hypothesizes the following:

H1: *Obama and Romney will be similar in the issue agendas presented in their Facebook posts ahead of the 2012 elections.*

Literature suggests that elements in presidential rhetoric include references to policy, achievements, personal characteristics, and values, along with affirming patriotic statements, stating commitments and using metaphors (Campbell & Jamieson, 2008). In their examination of presidential speeches in recent decades, Campbell and Jamieson (2008) found that presidents use emotion and patriotic appeals to influence public opinion and cite facts and statistics to construct arguments in support of their own position. Previous literature suggests that winning and the losing candidates differ in the rhetoric of their campaign speeches (Lowry & Naser, 2010; Benoit, 2004). Thereby, as an exploratory study into political posts on Facebook, this study asks the following research question:

RQ2: *What were the major rhetorical references in the Facebook posts of Obama and Romney ahead of the 2012 election?*

Studies have concluded that although Democratic and Republican candidates debate about similar issues, the rhetorical references in the speeches and their framing of the issues have strong differences (Petrocik, Benoit & Hansen, 2003). The winning and losing candidates have been found differ in their campaign messages (Lowry & Naser, 2010). This study hypothesizes that Obama and Romney will differ in the rhetorical elements in their Facebook posts, and tests the following statement:

H2: *Obama and Romney will significantly differ in the major rhetorical references in their Facebook posts.*

Social media are increasingly used as a mass-interpersonal medium, where prominent personalities, organizations or institutions connect with large number of people instantly and interactively (Vitak & Ellison, 2013). Studies found when people post on Twitter, they imagine about different groups of people among their network of audience, and attempt to strategically use Twitter posts to communicate with the different groups (Marwick & Boyd, 2011). The users have been found to navigate between different imagined groups of people, such as friends, co-workers, family and acquaintances, and compose their tweets targeting the different types audiences. Drawing from this concept of imagined mode of address to the audience, As the two to communicate with the voters, it can be inferred that the presidential candidates in 2012 in their Facebook posts approached the audience in three ways: 1) As an individual partner in interpersonal communication, 2) as a part of a geographic or demographic group, or 3) as a part of the mass public that constitute American voters. The three approaches to the audience can be counted as individual, local and national, depending on how they were addressed by the politicians.

Thereby, it can be suggested that a politician addressing the audience using second-person personal pronouns, such as *you*, would indicate that they are addressing the audience from individual level. Addressing the audience naming a particular geographic location, such as "Join us tomorrow at Denver", may be counted as a local mode of address. Finally, addressing the audience using collective terms such as *Americans* and *the nation* would indicate a national mode of address, and suggest the politician is using Facebook as a mass medium, aiming to reach a large audience regardless of distance or demographic differences. Tracking how the politicians changed their mode of address to the audience throughout the election time are likely to reveal valuable information about the chronological development of the online public relation campaign.

Scholars have discussed a timing effect in election campaign that states the messages encountered closer to the voting day have stronger effect on the voters than earlier ones (Panagopoulos, 2011). Broadly, public opinion has been found to be strongly based on accessibility of the information received, as noted by Zaller (1992). As on an online environment the accessibility of information may in fact increase due to the citizen's constant connection with news information thanks to 24/7 social and electronic media. As studies have found that around 8% of voters in the 2012 national election were found to decide their vote within three weeks prior to the election (Hickey, 2012), changes in the content or target of SNS appeals could shed light on how candidates are positioning themselves for "undecided" voters. Previous literature suggests that presidential candidates change the characteristics of their message during the course of the campaign. In the beginning stage, the candidates concentrate on policy debates, but in the finishing stage they focus more in contacting the voters and urging them to vote (Sides, Shaw, Grossmann, & Lipsitz, 2013). The mass-interpersonal use of social media and the changing pattern of campaign during the time of the election lead this chapter to ask the following research question:

RQ3: *How did the approach to the audience in Obama and Romney's Facebook posts change over time during the election campaign?*

As the two candidates will want to expend most of their influence as Election Day appears, it can be assumed that they will address the audience more by individual level address, such as second-person pronouns, than by other terms. Thus, the following statement is hypothesized:

H3: *The two candidates used national or local approach of address for the audience closer to the election day than earlier, when they used individual approach.*

METHODS

All official Facebook posts from Barack Obama and Mitt Romney were retrieved from the addresses http://www.facebook.com/barackobama and http://www.facebook.com/mittromney for content analysis. Shared posts and comments were not analyzed since they are not considered the original work of the candidates. Considering that the presidential campaigns reaches a peak in October, this chapter selected Facebook posts from October 1 to Election Day, November 6, for coding. One author of this paper acted as the main coder. In total 233 posts, 154 from Romney and 79 from Obama, were analyzed.

An undergraduate student acted as the main coder for this study and was personally trained on the materials by the first author. The coding task was done using personal computers. Intercoder reliability was determined with the help of two other graduate students. Agreement using Scott's pi, which accounts for agreement by chance, ranged from .71 to .84. All the Facebook messages were available during coding. Users' comments on the posts were not coded.

Variables

Common media agenda: As a benchmark for a commonly known agenda in the mass media during the presidential election, this study used a list of major issues in the 2012 election prepared by CNN. The list had the following 12 issues according to importance: economy, healthcare, immigration, foreign policy, education, abortion, same-sex marriage, social security, gun control, environment, terrorism, role of government. (CNN Politics, 2012). This study did not gather original data on the agenda of the mass media.

Agenda in Facebook posts: The main topic or subject on the post was coded. The list of 12 issues prepared to explore the media agenda was used as a basis. The Facebook posts were checked for whether they have any of the twelve issues. Scott's pi for this variable was .77.

References in Facebook posts: The personality versus politics dichotomy is a well studied debate in political science (Brunk & Fishkin, 1982; Latimer, 1984). There has been debate about whether the mass media focus on the candidate's personal characteristics more than policies, whether the candidates' messages are factual and whether patriotism is overly used in political campaigns used appeal in political advertising. Latimer (1984) found that the politicians have been found to use more personality appeals than policy messages during election advertising in general. The winners who were incumbents are found to use more personality appeals, whereas the winners who were challengers use more policy messages. To look into the characteristics of the campaign messages on SNSs, this study measured the different types of references made in the Facebook posts by Romney and Obama. References to policy or achievement was operationalized as mentioning any kind of specific policy related past achievement or future plan. References to facts/statistics was measured by citing one or more factual or statistical information. In case of a presence of both fact and policy, the post was categorized as the latter, because examine the presence of factual information in the campaign messages is a priority in this study. References to personal characteristics was operationalized by mentioning personal character, trait or appearance, reference to values by mention of value, morality, social norm, and reference to American glory by mentioning American achievement, national glory and matter of pride. Scott's Pi for these five variables was .78, .81, .75, .71 and .84 respectively.

Approach to the audience in Facebook posts: The approach of a Facebook post the audience tells us about each poster's intended relationship with the audience and the perception of the messages by the audience. Thus, this study measured the nature of the appeal to the audience in Facebook posts with the following options: 1) Individual, when the post appeals to the audience as individuals, such as, asking the audience to be personally active or to help the candidate; 2) Local, if the post appeals to the audience from a particular region, such as addressing all Texans or all residents from Denver; 3) National, if the post appeals to a national audience. Scott's Pi for this variable was .78.

FINDINGS

Romney posted almost twice as often as Obama (154 vs. 79) on Facebook. Romney's Facebook page did not yield any data from October 1 to October 10, but the challenger was more prolific in posting on Facebook as a whole than Obama.

RQ1 asked how the candidates' agendas on Facebook resemble the common media agenda. Candidates' references to different agenda items were ranked by frequency. The majority of the posts—44%

for Obama and 65% for Romney—did not talk about any of the major agenda topics on the media agenda (see Table 1) and were listed as "no specific issue". Most of these messages were mere campaign messages those urged the audience to vote for them, shared information about voting or asked the audience to take part in their campaign. Facebook pages mentioned the economy the second most, with 25% for Obama and 22% for Romney. The other issues in the media, such as health care, foreign policy, the role of government, social security and the status of women, were mentioned only a few times and accounted for less than 5 percent of the total. The economy was the only issue that had the similar top priority by both the candidates and the media (CNN in this study). Thus, the priorities of the candidates for the eight issues explored in this study did not resemble that in the mass media, showing the candidate's agenda not reflective of the media agenda, and not supporting the assumption of agenda-building. Testing H1, the Spearman Rho correlation coefficient between the candidates' ranking of media agendas was not found significant (Rho = .46, $p > .24$), suggesting only an inconsistent association in the salience of items the two discussed. Moreover, a chi-square test between the percentages of frequency of posts was statistically significant, χ^2 (7, N = 100) = 37.4, p < .001, suggesting there is statistically significant difference between the two candidates regarding their number of Facebook posts on the issues. Thus, H1 was not supported by the findings.

RQ2 inquired about the frequencies of the candidates' references to various rhetorical appeals, such as policies, values/emotion, patriotism, facts/statistics and asking for donations, votes or participation. This study counted the number of references to each of those categories and compared the two candidates (see Figure 1). Obama referred most often to policy/achievements, followed by facts/statistics and asking for donations; Romney most often asked for donations, votes or participation, followed by references to policy/achievements and facts/statistics. It should be noted that because Romney posted almost twice as often as Obama, he had more posts than Obama in all categories. Figure 1 shows the distribution of references for the two candidates. Obama proportionately referred more to policy/achievements and facts/statistics than Romney, who proportionately referred more to values/emotion and patriotism.

*Table 1. Ranking of major issues mentioned in the Facebook posts of the Obama and Romney campaigns**

Issues	Obama (Percentages in Parenthesis)	Rank	Romney (Percentages in Parenthesis)	Rank
No specific issue	41 (46.1)	1	101 (65.2)	1
Economy	23 (25.8)	2	35 (22.6)	2
Education	5 (5.6)	3	2 (1.3)	6
Health	5 (5.6)	3	3 (1.9)	5
Women	5 (5.6)	3	3 (1.9)	5
Government	3 (3.4)	4	5 (3.2)	3
Foreign policy	3 (3.4)	4	4 (2.6)	4
Energy	3 (3.4)	4	2 (1.3)	6
Social security	1 (1.1)	5	-	
Total	89		155	

**Note:* Spearman rho = .46, $p > .24$; χ^2 (7, N = 100) = 37.4, p < .001. The numbers may add up differently than the total number of posts because some posts had more than one topic.

Figure 1. Comparison of frequency of different categories of references in the Facebook posts by Obama and Romney

Note: Values in the Y axis are percentages of frequencies. Chi-square statistics between Obama and Romney = 7.1, df = 5, p = .20.

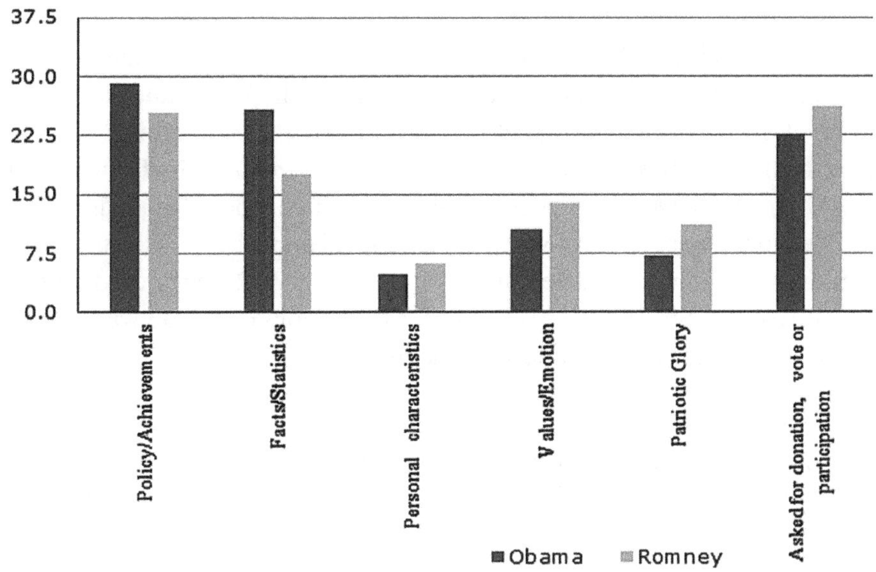

H2 predicted that the two candidates would differ in the characteristics of their Facebook posts mentioned above. This hypothesis was tested with chi-square for the frequencies of the six categories of references from the two candidates. The results found no significant different among the candidates in their frequencies of references to the rhetorical categories of policies, values/emotion, patriotism, facts/statistics and asking for donations, votes or participation (χ^2 = 7.1, df = 5, p = .20). H2 was not supported; the two candidates were similar in the characteristics of their Facebook posts.

RQ3 asked how the content of the candidates' Facebook posts changed over time as Election Day approached. To answer that question, the frequencies of appeals to the audience from individual, local and national perspectives were calculated, and presented in the Table 2. The results show that both of the candidates appealed to the audience from a national perspective (49% for Obama and 46% for Romney) most often, followed by individual and local perspectives. Differences in the proportion of appeals were not statistically significant (χ^2 = .65, p = .72), indicating the two candidates used a similar approach to the audience.

Table 2. Comparison of Obama and Romney on different levels of appeals to the audience in Facebook posts

	Obama (Percentages in Parenthesis)	Romney (Percentages in Parenthesis)
Individual	28 (35.4)	54 (35.1)
Local	12 (15.2)	28 (18.2)
National	39 (49.4)	72 (46.7)

Note: (χ^2 = .65 df = 2, p > .72). The frequencies may not add up to the total number of posts because remaining posts were coded as having none of these three appeals and were left out.

H3 predicted that the candidates will use the individual appeal to the audience in the latter stages of the campaign and collective appeal in the beginning stage. To compare the usage of different levels of appeal along with time, a time series plot was prepared using date as the independent variable and approach to the audience as the dependent variable. The approach to the audience was considered an ordinal level variable, with the breadth of the candidates' approach to the audience measured from individual level (narrowest) to local (medium) and national (broadest). Both Obama and Romney used *individual appeal* around 35% of the time. Obama appealed to the audience *locally* around 15.2% of the time and Romney 18.2% of the time. Both Obama and Romney used *national appeals* the most often, 49% and 46% respectively. Although the two candidates used all of the three types of appeals during the five weeks period before the election, Obama almost stopped using local appeals in the last week of the campaign and used individual appeals more at the beginning than at the end. Romney used all three types evenly throughout the period (see Figure 2a and 2b). Thereby, assumptions of the H3 was supported for Obama, but not for Romney, indicating partial support for the hypothesis.

Figure 2a. Time series of nature of appeal in Obama Facebook posts
Note: The values on the Y axis indicate approach to the audience, with 1, 2, and 3 indicating local, group and national level respectively. The X axis indicates weekly time up to 6th November.

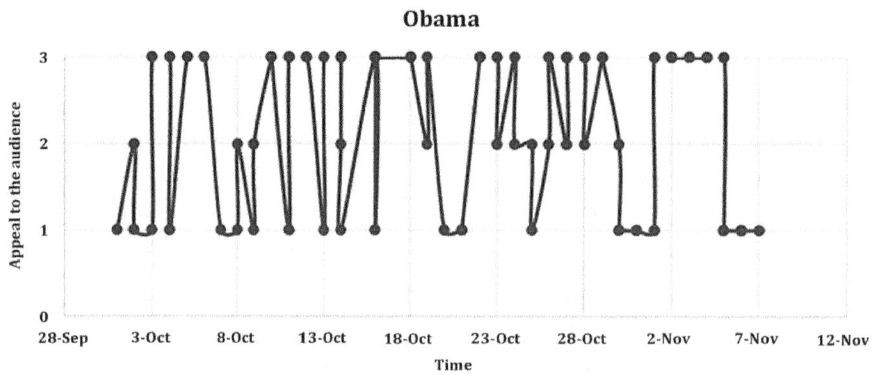

Figure 2b. Time series of nature of appeal in Romney Facebook posts
Note: The values on the Y axis indicate approach to the audience, with 1, 2, and 3 indicating local, group and national level respectively. The X axis indicates weekly time up to 6th November.

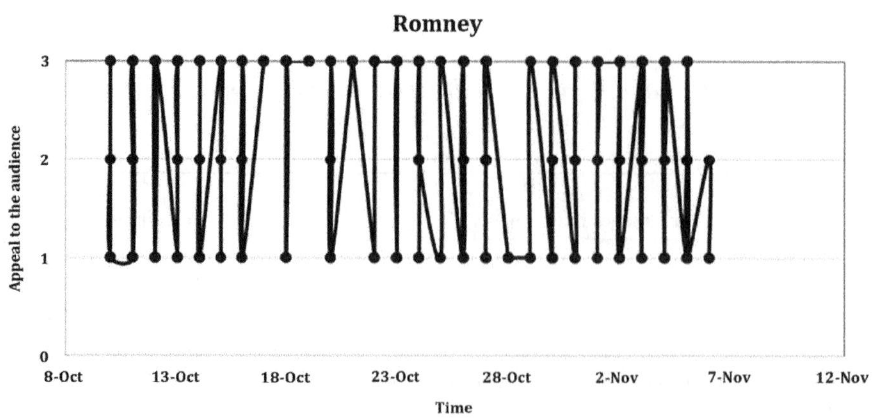

To search for possible correlations among different kinds of categories, correlation matrixes for the variables of appeal to the audiences, references to policies/achievements, facts/statistics, personal characteristics/values/emotion, patriotic appeals and asking the audience to vote, for donation or participation were prepared (Tables 3 and 4). For both Obama and Romney, appeal to the audience was positively correlated with reference to policy/achievements and mentioning of facts/statistics ($r = .474, p < .01$; $r = .284, p < .05$ for Obama and $r = .66, p < .01$; $r = .59, p < .01$ for Romney), but was negatively correlated with asking for donations, votes or participation ($r = -.6, p < .01$ for Obama and $r = -.34, p < .01$ for Romney). For both of the candidates, reference to policy/achievement was significantly correlated with mentioning facts/statistics (Obama: $r = .56, p < .01$; Romney: $r = .75, p < .01$). For Obama, neither references to policy/achievement nor mentioning facts/statistics was statistically correlated with using values/emotion and patriotic glories, meaning his posts mentioning policies did not use value appeal or patriotic glory. Romney, on the other hand, used values/emotions when discussing policy/achievements; his references to policy/achievement are statistically correlated with appeal to values/emotion and usage of patriotic glories ($r = .23, p < .01$; $r = .17, p < .05$).

For both Obama and Romney, the use of values/emotion was correlated with patriotic glories ($r = .27, p < .05$ and $r = .41, p < .01$ respectively): both used emotion and patriotism in appeals. Also, for both candidates, asking for donations, votes or participation was negatively correlated with all other characteristics, meaning those types of posts did not have any other types of characteristics, and therefore, were distinctive in nature.

Table 3. Zero order bivariate correlation between different characteristics of Facebook posts by Obama

Appeal to audience	1						
Policy/ Achievement	.474**	1					
Facts/ Stats	.284*	.562**	1				
Personal characteristics	.219	-.166	-.225*	1			
Values or Emotion	.270*	.005	-.150	.259*	1		
Patriotic glories	-.011	-.088	-.204	.048	.271*	1	
Asked to donate, vote or participate	-.608**	-.572**	-.376**	-.113	-.115	.067	1

Table 4. Zero order bivariate correlation between different characteristics of Facebook posts by Romney

Appeal to audience	1						
Policy/ Achievement	.661**	1					
Facts/ Stats	.597**	.758**	1				
Personal characteristics	.055	-.091	-.107	1			
Values or Emotion	.347**	.231**	.120	.267**	1		
Patriotic glories	.223**	.177*	.092	.031	.412**	1	
Asked to donate, vote or participate	-.345**	-.397**	-.378**	-.055	-.262**	-.149	1

DISCUSSION

"If you log in with Facebook, now the campaign has connected you with all your relationships" (Pilkington & Michel, 2012). This was a comment from one of the top strategists of the Obama campaign team published on The Guardian ahead of the November election. The 2012 election has been described as the data election, where contesting parties used Facebook and computer databases as the backbone to reach voters. The campaign teams raced to contact voters individually instead of treating them as blocks of people (Pilkington & Michel, 2012). The emphasis on social media is evident from comment of another Obama strategist: "Facebook is ubiquitous. Whichever candidate uses Facebook the most effectively could win the war" (2012). The findings in this chapter support the idea that political campaign teams now use social media as a campaign tool to disseminate mainly personality and character appeals and organize supporters.

Three key characteristics of online political communication are evident from this study. First, the candidates in their Facebook posts seemed to be barely reflecting the mainstream media agenda. The issues they prioritized on the Facebook posts do not seem to be resembling with the major media agenda such as the CNN's. Most of the time, the candidates did not talk about any news issue, but rather referred to their personal characteristics, cited American exceptionalism or asked for votes or support. (See Figure 1.) The nature of the Facebook posts suggest that the candidates use Facebook as a strategic public relations tool, rather than as a source of information. The candidates mostly attempted to show their presence, uphold their personality, appeal to the audience or engage in cyber-rallying, rather than debating and discussing about their issue policies.

Although previous research on agenda-building has found that politicians considerably influence the media agenda (Weaver & Elliot, 1985) and are able to set the agenda in the new media to a certain extent (Hong & Nadler, 2012; Meraz, 2011), this study did not find any noticeable efforts by Obama and Romney to use SNSs to prioritize issues for the mass media. The candidates talked only a quarter of the time to talk about the top media issue, economy, whereas the other major news issues such as defense or immigration are scantly mentioned. Novel issues – ones that candidates might want to get past the often-discussed "filters" of the 2008 campaign – were not part of the picture. Rather, mobilization seems to be primary objective in the Facebook campaigns, as both of the candidates posted around 25% of the posts asking for joining a program, buying campaign merchandises or straightly, donation.

Second, Obama and Romney slightly differed in the issue agenda on their Facebook posts. Both of them emphasized the economy, but Obama focused on the education and health issues to emphasize his success records, while Romney referred to the role of the government and foreign policy issues to underscore the perceived weakness of his opponents. The difference, as seen in Table 1, is not very wide. Rather, the candidates seem to strongly differ in the rhetoric of their Facebook posts. Obama used more appeals based on facts/statistics than his counterpart, who used more that drew on on emotional and value attributes (see Figure 1), which supports previous findings about rhetoric of past Democratic and Republican presidential candidates (Benoit et al., 2013; Lowry & Naser, 2010). Obama seemed to use numerical information and to mention specific policies undertaken by his administration that benefited Americans in his posts. Romney on the other hand, focused more on using value-ridden appeals, using patriotic and nationalistic remarks and mentioning personality characteristics to persuade the voters. Supporting previous findings that the Internet is increasingly used as a mobilizing tool, both candidates used around a quarter of their Facebook posts to ask for donations or participation. Overall, the findings show that the rhetoric in the new media platforms closely follows that in the face-to-face and other mediated forms.

Third, this study found that like real-life campaigns, online campaigns also change their focus and forms of address to the audience as Election Day approaches. Obama shifted his appeal to the audience from local to national in the final week of the campaign; Romney maintained local and individual appeal. Previous literature on presidential campaigns show that the candidates do more negative attacks and focus on personality characteristics as Election Day gets closer (West, 2013). These findings suggest a pattern: During the last weeks, the candidates focused on mobilizing the audience to come out and vote and hence, used individual appeals. During the early days of the campaigns, candidates use more national appeals to explain policy issues.

The candidates' Facebook messages do seem to follow certain characteristics. Obama and Romney used three common types of Facebook posts: 1) posts urging donations or votes, addressing the audience individually; 2) posts talking about policies, using facts or statistics and addressing a national audience; and 3) posts pointing to the candidates' personal and physical characteristics and appealing to the audience nationally. Although both candidates almost equally submitted the first type of post, Obama posted more in the second category and Romney more in the third category. Campaign messages on SNSs thus appear less diverse than those in the mass media, as the candidates limit their SNS communication to maintaining an apparent contact with the audience and assembling supporters virtually, compared to communication in face-to-face and traditional media, where they engage in debating issues and influencing the mass media agenda.

In this sense, the interplay of candidate, media, and audience issue agendas probably resembles past campaigns more than it differs. Further, campaigns are primarily run by campaign professionals whose influence on the character and nature of new media communication will probably produce similar results, regardless of a difference in candidate ideologies. Those factors await further exploration in future studies.

This study states that social media messages by the politicians are part of the information subsidy provided by the politicians. Although in the case of information subsidies, the politicians have to depend on the journalists for their description of the political messages, the politicians can directly reach the public, through social media. However, the politicians can only gather a limited feedback from the public through social media due to its chaotic nature and its huge number of users. Compared to social media, the campaign teams can have more detailed feedback from mass media by studying their portrayal in the media. In political campaigns, social media messages are "thrown in" to accentuate to actual information subsidies provided to journalists (press releases or in-depth interviews) or direct communication with the public (public rallies). However, the public social media messages are not likely to have any serious messages other than accentuating the already provided messages in the information subsidies. Thereby, this study suggests an intermediary role of social media, which is more a follower of traditional media relations tactics rather than a leader in the election campaigns.

LIMITATIONS AND SUGGESTIONS FOR FUTURE RESEARCH

This study used a single report from CNN to represent a perceived major agenda in mass media. A content analysis of major content would provide a more valid and reliable index of the media agenda. Also, this study explored only Facebook as a type of social media. Those findings are unlikely to represent the full range of social media – either other popular sites, like Instagram, Twitter and YouTube, or yet-unconceived sites that will draw their own millions of users during the campaigns of 2016 and 2020.

Future studies should also explore the relationship among social network agendas of the presidential candidates, the media agenda and the public agenda in greater detail by exploring the direction and casual influence of the agenda from one medium to other. Also, the time gap between publishing of stories on mass media and the candidates' social network could tell about the candidates' strategy in agenda-building with new media along with time. For rhetorical study, content and references in the candidates' posts in social network and other platforms can be compared. For understanding the interaction among the users and the politicians, user comments on Facebook posts or other interactive outlets can be analyzed.

REFERENCES

Atwater, T., Fico, F., & Pizante, G. (1987). Reporting on the state legislature: A case study of inter-media agenda-setting. *Newspaper Research Journal*, *8*(2), 53–61.

Benoit, W. L. (2004). Political Party Affiliation and Presidential Campaign Discourse. *Communication Quarterly*, *52*(2), 81–97. doi:10.1080/01463370409370183

Benoit, W. L., Henson, J., Davis, C., Glantz, M., Phillips, A., & Rill, L. (2013). Stumping on the Internet 2008 Presidential primary candidate campaign webpages. *Human Communication*, *16*(1), 1–12.

Binder, J. F., Howes, A., & Smart, D. (2012). Harmony and tension on social network sites. *Information Communication and Society*, *15*(9), 1279–1297. doi:10.1080/1369118X.2011.648949

Brunk, G. G., & Fishkin, J. A. (1982). Media coverage of presidential candidates: A study of popularity prior to the 1976 national nominating conventions. *Communication Research*, *9*(4), 525–538. doi:10.1177/009365082009004002

Campbell, K. K., & Jamieson, K. H. (2008). *Presidents creating the presidency: Deeds done in words*. Chicago, IL: University of Chicago Press.

Craig, S. C., & Hill, D. B. (Eds.). (2010). *The Electoral Challenge: Theory Meets Practice*. Sage Publications.

Erikson, R. S., & Wlezien, C. (1999). Presidential polls as a time series: The case of 1996. *Public Opinion Quarterly*, *63*(2), 163–177. doi:10.1086/297709

Facebook. (2013). *Investor relations: Facebook reports first quarter 2013 results*. Retrieved from http://investor.fb.com/releasedetail.cfm?ReleaseID=761090

Fisher, E. (2010). *Media and new capitalism in the digital age: The spirit of networks*. Basingstoke, UK: Palgrave Macmillan. doi:10.1057/9780230106062

Freelon, D. G. (2010). Analyzing online political discussion using three models of democratic communication. *New Media & Society*, *12*(7), 1172–1190. doi:10.1177/1461444809357927

Golan, G. (2006). Inter-media agenda setting and global news coverage. *Journalism Studies*, *7*(2), 323–333. doi:10.1080/14616700500533643

Gurevitch, M., Coleman, S., & Blumler, J. G. (2009). Political communication—Old and new media relationships. *The Annals of the American Academy of Political and Social Science*, *625*(1), 164–181. doi:10.1177/0002716209339345

Han, G. (2008). New media use, sociodemographics, and voter turnout in the 2000 presidential election. *Mass Communication & Society*, *11*(1), 62–81. doi:10.1080/15205430701587644

Heaney, M. T., Newman, M. E., & Sylvester, D. E. (2011). Campaigning in the internet age. In S. C. Craig & D. B. Hill (Eds.), *The electoral challenge: Theory meets practice*. Washington, DC: CQ Press.

Hong, S., & Nadler, D. (2012). Which candidates do the public discuss online in an election campaign?: The use of social media by 2012 presidential candidates and its impact on candidate salience. *Government Information Quarterly*, *29*(4), 455–461. doi:10.1016/j.giq.2012.06.004

Kim, J. Y., Xiang, Z., & Kiousis, S. (2011). Agenda building effects by 2008 presidential candidates on global media coverage and public opinion. *Public Relations Review*, *37*(1), 109–111. doi:10.1016/j.pubrev.2010.09.009

Kiousis, S., Kim, S.-Y., McDevitt, M., & Ostrowski, A. (2009). Competing for attention: Information subsidy influence in agenda building during election campaigns. *Journalism & Mass Communication Quarterly*, *86*(3), 545–562. doi:10.1177/107769900908600306

Kiousis, S., & Wu, X. (2008). International agenda-building and agenda-setting. *The International Communication Gazette*, *70*(1), 58–75. doi:10.1177/1748048507084578

Kohut, A., & Rainie, L. (2000, December 3). *Internet election news audience seeks convenience, familiar names*. Retrieved from http://www.pewinternet.org/Reports/2000/Internet-Election-News-Audience-Seeks-Convenience-Familiar-Names/Report.aspx

Lancendorfer, K. M., & Lee, B. (2010). Who influences whom? The agenda-building relationship between political candidates and the media in the 2002 Michigan governor's race. *Journal of Political Marketing*, *9*(3), 186–206. doi:10.1080/15377857.2010.497737

Lanosga, G. (2008). *Blogs and big media: A comparative study of agendas*. Paper presented at the annual conference of International Communication Association, Montreal, Canada.

Lariscy, R. W., Avery, E. J., Sweetser, K. D., & Howes, P. (2009). An examination of the role of online social media in journalists' source mix. *Public Relations Review*, *35*(3), 314–316. doi:10.1016/j.pubrev.2009.05.008

Latimer, M. K. (1984). Policy Issues and Personal Images in Political Advertising in a State Election. *The Journalism Quarterly*, *61*(4), 776–784. doi:10.1177/107769908406100405

Lei, G., Hong Tien, V., & McCombs, M. (2012). An expanded perspective on agenda-setting effects. Exploring the third level of agenda setting. *Revista De Comunicación*, *11*, 51–68.

Lowry, D. T., & Naser, M. A. (2010). From Eisenhower to Obama: Lexical characteristics of winning versus losing presidential campaign commercials. *Journalism & Mass Communication Quarterly*, *87*(3-4), 530–547. doi:10.1177/107769901008700306

Marwick, A. E., & boyd, . (2011). I tweet honestly, I tweet passionately: Twitter users, context collapse, and the imagined audience. *New Media & Society*, *13*(1), 114–133. doi:10.1177/1461444810365313

McCombs, M. E., & Shaw, D. L. (1972). The agenda-setting function of mass media. *Public Opinion Quarterly*, *36*(2), 176–187. doi:10.1086/267990

Meraz, S. (2011). Using time series analysis to measure intermedia agenda-setting influence in traditional media and political blog networks. *Journalism & Mass Communication Quarterly*, *88*(1), 176–194.

Panagopoulos, C. (2011). Timing is everything? primacy and recency effects in voter mobilization campaigns. *Political Behavior*, *33*(1), 79–93. doi:10.1007/s11109-010-9125-x

Parmelee, J. H. (2014). The agenda-building function of political tweets. *New Media & Society*, *16*(3), 434–450. doi:10.1177/1461444813487955

Payne, J., Golden, J. L., Marlier, J., & Ratzan, S. C. (1989). Perceptions of the 1988 Presidential and Vice-Presidential Debates. *The American Behavioral Scientist*, *32*(4), 425–435. doi:10.1177/0002764289032004008

Petrocik, J. R., Benoit, W. L., & Hansen, G. J. (2003). Issue Ownership and Presidential Campaigning, 1952-2000. *Political Science Quarterly*, *118*(4), 599–626. doi:10.1002/j.1538-165X.2003.tb00407.x

Pilkington, E., & Michel, A. (2012). Obama, Facebook and the power of friendship?: The 2012 data election. *The Guardian*. Retrieved from http://www.theguardian.com/world/2012/feb/17/obama-digital-data-machine-facebook-election

Politics, C. N. N. (2012). *America's choice: Issues*. Retrieved from http://www.cnn.com/election/2012/campaign-issues.html

Quintelier, E., & Theocharis, Y. (2012). Online political engagement, Facebook, and personality traits. *Social Science Computer Review*, 0894439312462802.

Raine, L., Horrigan, J., & Cornfield, M. (2005, March 6). *The Internet and campaign, 2004*. Retrieved from http://www.pewinternet.org/Reports/2005/The-Internet-and-Campaign-2004/1-Summary-of-Findings.aspx

Rainie, L. (2012, November 6). *Social media and young*. Retrieved from http://www.pewinternet.org/Reports/2012/Social-Vote-2012.aspx

Reilly, I. (2011). "Amusing Ourselves to Death?" Social Media, Political Satire, and the 2011 Election. *Canadian Journal of Communication*, *36*(3), 503–511.

Ritter, K. W. (1980). American political rhetoric and the jeremiad tradition: Presidential nomination acceptance addresses, 1960–1976. *Communication Studies*, *31*(3), 153–171.

Rogers, E. M., & Dearing, J. W. (1988). Agenda-setting research: Where has it been, where it is going. *Communication Yearbook*, *11*, 555–594.

Schroedel, J., Bligh, M., Merolla, J., & Gonzalez, R. (2013). Charismatic rhetoric in the 2008 presidential campaign: Commonalities and differences. *Presidential Studies Quarterly*, *43*(1), 101–128. doi:10.1111/psq.12005

Sheafer, T., & Weimann, G. (2005). Agenda building, agenda setting, priming, individual voting intentions, and the aggregate results: An analysis of four Israeli elections. *Journal of Communication*, *55*(2), 347–365. doi:10.1111/j.1460-2466.2005.tb02676.x

Sides, J., Shaw, D., Grossmann, M., & Lipsitz, K. (2013). *Campaigns & elections: Rules, reality, strategy, choice*. New York City: W. W. Norton & Company.

Smith, A., & Rainie, L. (2008, June 15). *The Internet and the 2008 election*. Retrieved from http://www.pewinternet.org/~/media/Files/Reports/2008/PIP_2008_election.pdf

Stein, K., & Church, S. (2007). *Success Strategies by Candidates in Presidential Debates, 1960-2004*. Paper presented in the annual convention of National Communication Association, Chicago, IL.

Stimson, J. A. (2004). *Tides of consent: How public opinion shapes American politics*. Cambridge, UK: Cambridge University Press. doi:10.1017/CBO9780511791024

Sweetser, K. D., Golan, G. J., & Wanta, W. (2008). Intermedia agenda setting in television, advertising, and blogs during the 2004 election. *Mass Communication & Society*, *11*(2), 197–216. doi:10.1080/15205430701590267

Vergeer, M. (2013). Politics, elections and online campaigning: Past, present . . . and a peek into the future. *New Media & Society*, *15*(1), 9–17. doi:10.1177/1461444812457327

Vitak, J. (2012). The impact of context collapse and privacy on social network site disclosures. *Journal of Broadcasting & Electronic Media*, *56*(4), 451–470. doi:10.1080/08838151.2012.732140

Vitak, J., & Ellison, N. B. (2013). 'There's a network out there you might as well tap': Exploring the benefits of and barriers to exchanging informational and support based resources on Facebook. *New Media & Society*, *15*(2), 243–259. doi:10.1177/1461444812451566

Vitak, J., Zube, P., Smock, A., Carr, C. T., Ellison, N., & Lampe, C. (2011). It's complicated: Facebook users' political participation in the 2008 election. *Cyberpsychology, Behavior & Social Networking*, *14*(3), 107-114. doi:10.1089/cyber.2009.0226

Wanta, W., & Hu, Y.-W. (1994). Time-lag differences in the agenda-setting process: An examination of five news media. *International Journal of Public Opinion Research*, *6*(3), 225–240. doi:10.1093/ijpor/6.3.225

Weaver, D., & Elliott, S. N. (1985). Who sets the agenda for the media? A study of local agenda-building. *The Journalism Quarterly*, *62*(1), 87–94. doi:10.1177/107769908506200113

West, D. M. (2013). *Air wars: Television advertising and social media in election campaigns, 1952-2012*. Washington, DC: CQ Press.

Williams, C. B., & Gulati, G. (2013). Social networks in political campaigns: Facebook and the congressional elections of 2006 and 2008. *New Media & Society*, *15*(1), 52–71. doi:10.1177/1461444812457332

Wlezien, C., & Erikson, R. S. (2002). The timeline of presidential election campaigns. *The Journal of Politics*, *64*(04), 969–993. doi:10.1111/1468-2508.00159

Wolfsfeld, G., Segev, E., & Sheafer, T. (2013). Social Media and the Arab Spring: Politics Comes First. *The International Journal of Press/Politics*, *18*(2), 115–137. doi:10.1177/1940161212471716

Wu, H. D., & Coleman, R. (2009). Advancing agenda-setting theory: The comparative strength and new contingent conditions of the two levels of agenda-setting effects. *Journalism & Mass Communication Quarterly*, *86*(4), 775–789. doi:10.1177/107769900908600404

Youmans, W., & York, J. (2012). Social media and the activist toolkit: User agreements, corporate interests, and the information infrastructure of modern social movements. *Journal of Communication*, *62*(2), 315–329. doi:10.1111/j.1460-2466.2012.01636.x

Yunis, H. (1996). *Taming democracy: Models of political rhetoric in classical Athens*. Cornell University Press.

Chapter 12
Facebook Photographic Images:
Political Tools of Self-Presentation during the 2014 European Parliament Elections in Romania

Camelia Cmeciu
University of Bucharest, Romania

ABSTRACT

"Act, react, impact" was the slogan of the 2014 European Parliament elections. A social media campaign focused on a solid informing practice may constitute the first step in attaining European citizens' actions and reactions. This chapter explores the visual Facebook presence of winning and losing Romanian candidates who stood for the 2014 EP elections. The visual framing analysis shows that the Romanian winning politicians preferred to visually promote themselves as statesmanlike candidates being surrounded by national influentials or by campaign entourage whereas the losing candidate framed themselves either as populist campaigners in the middle of larger audiences or as compassionate candidates interacting with individuals. The analysis of the visual categories highlights that both winning and losing EP candidates in Romania used a hybrid message. Despite the attempt to provide a visual presentation of European campaign paraphernalia, national identity features rendered through religious symbols and traditional elements prevailed.

INTRODUCTION

Although the main purpose of online campaigns is to involve, connect and mobilize citizens, the online engagement desired to be translated into an offline engagement is highly dependent on the informing practice. Besides the social media verbal content as a site of election campaign information, campaign photographs are also a means of citizens' engagement (Lilleker et al., 2011, p. 209). Facebook photographic images are important during election campaigns for three main reasons: first, contemporary elections are based on a visual foundation (Grabe & Bucy, 2009, p. 85); second, photographic images have the meaning potential of authenticity, integration, evidence (Bourdieu, 1990, p. 19), by framing

DOI: 10.4018/978-1-4666-9879-6.ch012

politicians as social actors performing certain actions; third, Facebook's Timeline provides a visibility of the strategic visual planning of the campaign by allowing citizens "to see what images were posted in what order during a specific period of time" (Goodnow, 2013, p. 1586).

Suzanne Schols[1] considers that a visual online European Parliament election campaign could potentially bring the EU closer to its citizens because candidates are given a face and complex policy issues are made easier to be grasped through infographics. Although photographs uploaded by politicians during EP election campaigns may trigger more likes, shares and comments than verbal posts, it is risky to state that an increasingly visual election campaign may help create a more positive, or at least a less negative image of the European Union. What Facebook photographic images may reveal is "the hybrid character of elections to the European Parliament" (Strömbäck, Maier, & Kaid, 2011, p. 5). The 2014 European Parliament elections took place in the context of a high skepticism regarding the European identity. The results of the Eurobarometer 77 (2012) showed that 49% of Europeans opted for an identity where their nationality comes before being European, 39% identified themselves with only their nationality, and 3% described themselves as European only. The candidates' visual choice may emphasize the extent to which national and/or European issues are visually framed and it may show what visual categories a candidate uses in his/her self-presentation to promote a national and/or European identity.

This chapter has a threefold objective: (a) to investigate the strategic visual planning of the EP candidates in Romania; (b) to provide a comparative analysis of the master frames and themes used by the Romanian candidates in their visual self-presentation; (c) to determine the visual categories used by the Romanian candidates for the most dominant frames and themes.

BACKGROUND

Used as a means of expression and communication, visual images are "as power-laden as words are" (Jewitt, 2008, p. 252) and "the pictorial representation of reality is as subjective as verbal statements are" (Messaris, 2012, p. 102). According to Kathleen German (2010), the pictorial turn has a new dimension with the new media. The online self-presentations have exploded with the increasing use of new and social media and the new visual technologies have gradually been used in "constituting us, our interaction, our identities and our relationships" (Graham et al., 2011, p. 90). Facebook, "the platform to see and to be seen" (Caers et al., 2013, p. 984) has significantly contributed to "the increased publicness of personal images" (Van House, 2011, p. 128).

Throughout the years, political candidates have become aware of the significant role that visuals, especially photographic images, play in election campaigns. Conveying attributes associated with realism, credibility, believability, and truthfulness (Moriarty & Popovich, 1991), candidate images may mediate voter thoughts about political messages since "voters respond more to their perceptions than to objective realities about candidates" (Hacker, 1995, p.xi). "The photo opportunity" (Barnhurst & Quinn, 2012) has become an important election tool since citizens are likely to view rather than listen to candidates (Miller, 2013; Verser & Wicks, 2006). The publicly open "glasshouse" structure of Facebook (Papacharissi, 2002, p. 215) has allowed candidates to stage various photo opportunities which frame them as more prominent than their opponents.

Contextual Background

After the fall of communism in 1989, Romania has become a semi-presidential representative democratic republic. Romania joined the EU in 2007 and the first European Parliament elections took place in 2009. In 2014, 15 Romanian political parties and 8 independent candidates took part in the EP elections and the results showed that there were only six winners and they occupied 32 seats in the European Parliament (see Table 1). The surprise of these EP elections in Romania was the victory of an independent candidate (4th position) who outscored well-known Romanian politicians. In my analysis of the visual self-presentation of Romanian candidates to the EP elections, I will focus both on the six winners and on the following six candidates who lost the elections (see Table 1). I will select the leaders of the lists of candidates from the national parties which ran for the EP elections.

Literature Review on Political Candidates' Visual Self-Presentation

In the *Review of Visual Communication in the Field of Political Communication,* Dan Schill (2012) mentions that the visual aspects of political communication remain one of the least studied. Authors (Schill, 2012; Barnhurst & Quinn, 2012) make a plea for a blending of critical-cultural, semiotic, rhetorical, media and behavioral approaches, which may provide challenging insights both at the level of visual content and at the level of emotional appeal. Since photographic images "enable voters to form impressions, opinions, and beliefs about political candidates" (Verser & Wicks, 2006, p. 179), research on political visual communication (Banwart, 2002; Bystrom & Kaid, 2002; Foot & Schneider, 2006; Verser & Wicks, 2006; Goodnow, 2013; Miller, 2013; Stromer-Galley, 2014) focused on the content of self-presentation photographs used by candidates during election campaigns in advertisements, TV spots, Web 1.0 and Web 2.0.

The study of gender-based stereotypes in female and male candidates' websites was one strand of research. Female candidates for the US Congress in the 2000 and 2002 elections seem to have shifted (Dolan, 2005) their issue priorities from a set of gender-stereotypical issues (education, health care, social security/medicare, environment, family issues, women's issues, abortion, and ethics/government reform), which reflect compassion traits, to a set of topics similar to those of their male counterparts, which reflect competence (business, economy, foreign affairs, defense/military issues, agriculture). Research on campaign websites (Dolan, 2005) highlights that the dominance of certain issues in the self-presentation of female candidates should be mainly associated with party-based stereotypes rather than with gender-based stereotypes.

Another strand of research focused on the types of attributes that may be (de)coded in an image. Starting from Moriarty and Popovich's attributes (1991) used in the analysis of candidates' images, Rebecca Verser & Robert H. Wicks (2006) extended the number of attributes and grouped them in three clusters of variables: *visual imagery related to human interaction, visual imagery relating to photographic setting and appearance* and *visual imagery relating to photographic production values.* The findings of their analysis of the web photographs of Al Gore and George W. Bush during the 2000 elections showed that Gore presented himself as a candidate conveying a sense of activity, interacting with others, the photographs focusing more frequently on his years in public years whereas Bush was presented as less active and alone in photographs but trying to provide a visual insight into his personal and professional development through a montage from boyhood through college leading to leadership roles in business and as the Governor of Texas. Trischa Goodnow (2013) considers that neither Grabe and Bucy's study

Table 1. Romanian candidates - 2014 European Parliament Elections

	EP candidates	Party affiliation	Position in the party	Incumbent position	Results by national party[4]	No of Facebook photographic images
2014 EP winning candidates in Romania	Corina Crețu	PSD + PC + UNPR - Coalition Social Democratic Party (PSD), Conservative Party (PC), National Union for the Progress of Romania (UNPR)	Vice-President	EMP (2007-present)	37.60%	485
	Norica Nicolai	PNL - National Liberal Party	Member	EMP (2009-present)	15%	384
	Theodor Stolojan	PDL - Democratic Liberal Party	Member; former Prime Minister (1991-1992)	EMP (2007-present)	12.23%	800
	Mircea Diaconu	Independent	Former member of PNL	-	6.81%	321
	Iuliu Winkler	UDMR - Democratic Union of Hungarians in Romania	Member	EMP (2007-present)	6.30%	No Facebook account
	Cristian Preda	PMP - People's Movement Party	Member	EMP (2009-present)	6.21%	55
2014 EP losing candidates in Romania	Dan-Cristian Diaconescu	PPDD - People's Party – Dan Diaconescu	Leader	-	3.67%	136
	Corneliu Vadim Tudor	PRM - Greater Romania Party	Leader	EMP (2009-2014)	2.70%	3
	Mihai-Răzvan Ungureanu	FC - Civic Force	President; Former Prime Minister (2012)	-	2.60%	375
	Radu Moraru	PER - Romanian Ecologist Party	Member	-	1.18%	No Facebook account
	Florin Simion	ANA - National Farmers Alliance	Member	-	0.95%	No posts on Facebook accounts
	Aurelian Pavelescu	PNTCD - Christian Democratic National Peasants' Party	Leader	-	0.91%	47
					TOTAL	2606

of ideal, populist and sure loser frames nor Verser and Wicks's approach on visual imagery through human interaction, setting and production values offer sufficient explanation to the reasons for which the content of the images may produce meanings for the audience. Goodnow considers that the ideational, interpersonal and textual metafunctions of the social semiotic perspective may be applied to Grabe and Bucy's schema work in order to understand how the meaning potentials of a candidate's Facebook photos may be conveyed to voters. Her micro-analysis of Obama's and Romney's photos on their Facebook Timelines during the 2012 presidential elections showed that although both candidates used the ideal candidate frame, their visual credibility was differently presented from a social semiotic perspective. A semiotic analysis may provide a better understanding into how a frame is visually constructed. From a voter perspective, possessing (representation of participants on the left side of an image) is stronger than borrowing (representation of participants on the right side of an image) and thus an analysis on the image composition may reveal how a stronger identification with a candidate is produced within a certain frame (Goodnow, 2013). Whereas Romney borrowed credibility by associating himself with patriotic images or revered veterans, Obama visually shaped his credibility through symbols that were given by election, for example the Oval Office.

Studies on Romanian Political Candidates' Visual Self-Presentation

The fall of communism in 1989 in Romania brought a new perspective on election campaigns. Since 1990 Romanian citizens have been the spectators of challenging confrontations between candidates and with the increase of internet use, they have become generators of content for or against a candidate. The visual self-presentations of the first four general elections candidates were dominated by posters and advertisements and the visual studies focused on a marketing perspective or on rhetoric and structural semiotic approaches (Ghilezean, 2000; Stoiciu, 2000; Cmeciu, 2005). The analysis of the content and composition of political advertisements during the 2000 elections showed that the Romanian politicians used three types of visual representations (Cmeciu, 2005): 'the parent', 'the redeemer' or 'the youth'. Since 2004, the year when internet has been first used during election campaigns in Romania, Romanian politicians have become more aware of the advantages of the online self-presentation and of downplaying their opponents' attributes. Traian Băsescu, the incumbent president in 2014, has been the first Romanian candidate to exploit the internet as a political communication tool during the 2004 presidential elections (Guțu, 2007, p. 167). His website had a twofold means: to represent himself as the ideal candidate and to engage Romanian citizens in generating visual content as a form of digital guerrilla against his opponents. The 2008, 2009 and 2012 (presidential or parliamentary) election campaigns focused on extensive online campaigns and the candidates have gradually become aware that a visual communication has a double function: on the one hand, to reveal a strategic planning of their campaign with photos depicting their rallies throughout the country, and on the other hand, to evaluate the citizens' engagement through the number of likes and comments that photos may get. Nicoleta Ionescu's comparative study (2013) on the relation between Facebook image upload and the citizen's engagement factor showed that the Romanian politicians' Facebook pages using more images have a higher response rate from the public. Analyzing the types of images posted by Romanian politicians, the findings showed that Romanian politicians prefer to promote their political activity rather than to be associated with family members and that images of religious and patriotic symbols are frequently used by Romanian politicians. Camelia Cmeciu and Monica Pătruț's study (2014) of the visual framing of Romanian women politicians in personal campaign blogs during the 2012 Romanian parliamentary elections focused on a social semiotic approach to the function of blog photography. The analysis of the represented participants, types of shots and camera angles highlighted two aspects: (a) the party-stereotyped issues, the candidate and the context may determine the dominance of certain female and male traits (compassion trait - Social Democratic Party and Democratic Liberal Party candidates versus competence trait - National Liberal Party candidate), and (b) the prevalence of a certain socio-demographic category (members of the clergy, elderly persons) should be related to the Romanian social and political context.

Studies on European Parliament Elections

Within the context of a democratic and symbolic deficit associated with the European Union, the majority of studies focused on how national media covered the EP elections or other European events. In their review of the 1979, 1999 and 2004 EP elections, Claes H. de Vrees and Hajo G. Boomgaarden (2012, p. 331) consider that the national news coverage of European affairs provides significant cross-national and outlet-specific variations. The studies on the news coverage of the 2004 EP elections in the 25 EU countries (de Vrees et al., 2006; de Vrees & Boomgaarden, 2012) showed four important aspects: (a) elections were more visible in the 10 new member states than in the old EU member states; (b) the news stories focused more on national political actors and not on EU actors; (c) a negative attitude on EU prevailed in the old EU-15 whereas a mixed pattern was found in the new EU countries; (d) news about the EP elections are more visible on TV newscasts (public broadcasting and commercial television) than on quality and tabloid press front pages. The scarce visibility of EU actors in news coverage highlight the domestic orientation of these elections (de Vrees et al., 2006) and their hybrid nature (Strömbäck, Maier, & Kaid, 2011): beyond the same rules applied across countries, the EP elections tend to be treated as second-order national elections.

Another strand of research focuses on the content analysis of the websites of parties and/or EP candidates (Lilleker et al., 2011; Vergeer et al., 2012). The cross-national examination of the main functions of the campaign websites during the 2009 EP elections in four EU member states (Lilleker et al., 2011) suggested that (a) although Web 1.0 predominated, Web 2.0 features would clearly become important elements within the design of political websites; (b) besides the information function which was well served by all campaign sites, the engagement function increased its delivery modes; (c) right-wing parties offer the greatest number of opportunities for interaction and not libertarian parties as expected; (d) nations with longer traditions of democratic engagement in elections demonstrated more innovative online strategies; (e) parties providing the most innovative websites had the greatest resources at their disposal. Vergeer et al.'s study is in line with the previous research on how technology was used to inform, to involve and to mobilize the EU citizens. The comparative website-feature analysis of the 2009 EP candidates and party websites from 17 EU member states (Vergeer et al., 2012) showed that the 'informing' and 'personal reputation' dimensions of the web features were more dominant than social networking (connecting and sharing) and audio-visualization supply dimensions.

Insights into Studies of European Parliament Elections in Romania

In the study on the website-feature analysis of the 2009 EP candidates and parties (Vergeer et al., 2012), Romania occupied the sixth position (out of 17) in the salient utilization of the four dimensions of website features and the mostly used dimensions by Romanian candidates and parties were the personal reputation, informing and audio-visualization supplies, the social networking being the less used dimension.

Within the same strands of research (news coverage and candidates' online communication), studies have been made at a Romanian micro-level as well. Viorela Dan and Aurora Iorgoveanu's study (2013) on the media representation of the four most prominent male and female Romanian candidates for the 2009 European Elections showed that trivialization and issue were the main frames associated with female candidates whereas the horse race frame was used both for depicting male and female candidates. Romanian candidates' online communication in the 2014 EP elections has been also studied (Buturoiu, 2014; Cmeciu, 2014). Unlike in the 2009 EP elections when the social networking dimension through sharing and connecting was scarcely used by Romanian candidates, the 2014 EP elections brought more disclosure of candidates and more engagement with Romanian citizens. Raluca Buturoiu's analysis of the Facebook pages of the four political parties which won the highest number of seats in the 2014 EP elections showed that Romanian parties' social media sites have not shaped a proper European public sphere yet and that communication on social media, as a means of attracting possible voters, is preferred by the newly founded parties/coalition. Although Facebook was not used as a space of debating with Romanian citizens during the 2014 EP elections, it was extensively used as an online environment where they may promote their Facebook identity in pictures. The visual framing analysis of the photos uploaded by three EP candidates from three main Romanian parties (Cmeciu, 2014) showed that Romanian candidates preferred to visually present themselves more as ideal statesmen and then as compassionate persons, they used national political actors and celebrities more than EU actors, and religious symbols seemed to have been extensively used in their FB photographic images. These findings are consistent with de Vrees et al.'s study (2006) which highlighted a domestic orientation of the EP elections.

FACEBOOK IDENTITY PERFORMANCE IN PHOTOGRAPHIC IMAGES

Since 2004 each political campaign in the US has continued "the history-making trend by deeply entrenching social media as an essential outlet in the campaign process" (Goodnow, 2013, p. 1584). As Trischa Goodnow mentions, the 2008 and 2012 elections proved that candidates' Facebook pages have turned into a public place where users discuss politics, endorse politicians and where they may learn about the candidates' positions and/or about the chronological development of their campaign.

Romanian political candidates have gradually become aware of the visibility benefits that social media campaigns may bring to their self-presentation. The endeavor of Romanian political actors to become up-to-date with the online political communication may have three explanations: (1) Romanians' rapid internet usage[2]: from 35.5% in 2010 to 49.8% in 2013 and half of the internet users (10,812,784) have Facebook accounts; (2) a higher visibility of offline features of politics; (3) the tendency to follow the leading actors' online strategy. Whereas the first explanation lies in the social change that internet has brought in each country, the second and third explanations reside in Margolis and Resnick's normalization hypothesis of cyberspace (2000). The two authors consider that the spread of the Web will reinforce rather than reinvent traditional offline patterns of political life and that the Internet would not contribute to the mobilization of new voters. This increase of internet usage did not lead to Romanians' offline participation to the vote (Momoc, 2014) but it provided politicians with a new environment of unfolding themselves. As M. Margolis and D. Resnick (2000) highlighted, major party Web sites are increasingly more dominant on the internet relative to minor party Web sites and the minor party politicians tend to apply a 'copycat' strategy by following the leading actors' online strategy.

Although involving, mobilizing and connecting (Foot & Schneider, 2006) are the great advantages of social networking sites, these three functions involve a ladder of engagement. Adam Conner[3], manager for Public Policy in Facebook's DC Office and US Elections Social Media Strategist, considers that for some citizens, this ladder of engagement may turn into an offline engagement if and only if the practice of informing is sufficiently convincing. Thus besides the advantages of a coproduction of content and an interaction between politicians and citizens, the online practice of informing still remains "foundational to and part of all other Web practices" (Foot & Schneider, 2006, p. 47). The emphasis on a high degree of self-presentation associated with Facebook (Kaplan & Haenlein, 2010) coincides with the metaphorical representation of Facebook as a 'glasshouse' (Papacharissi, 2002, p. 215). The Facebook publicly open structure, used especially during election campaigns, allows users either 'to peep' into the candidate's 'political house' or to interact with other users and get involved in the ongoing debates during the election campaigns. A constant flow of well-documented information about politicians during election campaigns may determine citizens to participate online and eventually offline. Besides biography, issue positions, campaign news, speech texts, or campaign ads, photographic images play a significant role for the shaping of a politician's image during campaigns since voters respond more to their perceptions of visual images than to objective realities (Hacker, 1995, p. xii) related to the candidate.

SCOPE AND METHODOLOGY

This chapter seeks to reveal the online visual frames used by Romanian candidates during the 2014 EP elections. I intend to provide a comparative visual analysis of the Facebook photographic images of the six winning and six losing EP candidates in Romania, posted during the four weeks (April, 25 - May 24, 2014) leading up to European Parliament Election Day (May 25, 2014). The analysis focused on the leaders of the lists of candidates from political parties or on the independent candidates. As observed in Table 1, out of the twelve candidates selected, only nine candidates had a Facebook account or posted on their Facebook accounts during the EP elections and six of the twelve candidates were members of the European Parliament (EMP).

As Table 1 shows, not all winning candidates had a Facebook account and two of the losing candidates posted more photos than some of the winning candidates. This illustrates Margolis and Resnick's (2000) normalization hypothesis, namely that the online communication would not contribute to a higher voters' offline participation and thus the Romanian politicians' victory to European Parliament did not depend on the online campaign, but to some contextual factors which might have contributed to the image projected upon the candidate. Two cases may be mentioned:

(a) M.R. Ungureanu (FC) had an intensive visual online election campaign with daily visual and verbal updates, but this did not trigger the winning of a seat in the European Parliament. Part of Ungureanu's failure may be linked to the representation with which media associated him. As a former Prime Minister of Romania, M.R. Ungureanu was accused by media (Antena 3 TV station) of having lavishly spent on protocol during his 78 days in the government office.

(b) The victory of I. Winkler (UDMR) should not be explained in terms of the presence or absence of a Facebook election campaign, but on his political affiliation. Belonging to the Democratic Union of Hungarians in Romania, I. Winkler or any candidate of UDMR will know the percentage he/she would get due to the fact that the party mainly relies of the ethnic community of Hungarians.

Analytical Framework: Visual Framing Theory

Considered "schemata of interpretation" (Goffman, 1974, p. 21), frames are used to make sense of information or an occurrence, providing "principles for the organization of social reality" (Hertog & McLeod, 2001, p. 140). During election campaigns, candidates and the campaign staff select those aspects of a perceived reality and make them more salient in a Facebook post. Thus political Facebook accounts convey the candidates' opinions on various issues, but at the same time they provide the candidates' visual portrayals whose meaning potential is to craft "enduring images that affect electoral support" (Grabe & Bucy, 2009, p. 85).

Starting from the (political) visual framing (Messaris & Abraham, 2001; Grabe & Bucy, 2009; Verschueren, 2012; Goodnow, 2013; Cmeciu & Pătruţ, 2014; Cmeciu, 2014), I use a multilevel frame analysis of the Facebook photographic images posted by nine Romanian candidates to the 2014 EP elections. The multilevel frame analysis belongs to Paul Verschueren (2012), but in my analysis, I will associate each of the three levels with other theories on visual framing (Jewitt & Oyama, 2001 - the analysis of the represented participants; Grabe & Bucy, 2009 and Goodnow, 2013 - the analysis of themes and frames) and I will show that the categories of each visual frame should be culture specific.

The first level implies an observation of the *scene* which consists of a process (action, event, state of being), some participants and a circumstance (setting, means, accompaniments). The analysis focuses on the representational meaning potential. The participants belonging to different socio-demographic categories may be depicted within certain narrative structures (for example, a politician helping a citizen to plant a tree or shaking hands with voters). The presence or absence of a socio-demographic category is relative to the social, economic and cultural context of the country the candidate represents. For example, Grabe and Bucy (2009) did not include the category 'elderly people' in their coding instrument, but this category has been used by Romanian politicians during previous election campaigns (Cmeciu & Pătruţ, 2014).

The second level implies a generalization of the scene into a *theme*. A politician helping or caressing a child may be associated with the compassion theme. The last level focuses on a generalization of a theme into a *master frame* or *ideological orientation* with which the represented participants are to be associated. In my analysis, I use Grabe and Bucy's three master frames (the ideal candidate, the populist candidate, the sure loser). Since the analysis does not focus on politicians' visual news coverage, but on politicians' self-appraising presentation through Facebook photographic images, I consider that Grabe and Bucy's sure loser frame should refer to the photographic images highlighting the opponent's weak points.

Method

The comparative visual framing analysis of the Facebook photos focused on all the photos posted and shared on the Timeline of the Romanian EP candidates with a Facebook account (see Table 1), during the four weeks (April, 25 - May 24, 2014) leading up to European Parliament Election Day (May 25, 2014). I collected all the photographs posted and shared by the candidate and the campaign staff and on all the photographic images posted by some other persons on the candidates' Timeline. The final sample included 2606 photographic images. Table 1 shows the distribution of the FB photos for all the nine Romanian candidates who had a FB account during the 2014 EP elections.

The study employs both a deductive and an inductive method. The inductive method was used for an in-depth analysis of the photographs in order to find the types of represented participants, the dressing code, and the gestures that may render Grabe and Bucy's themes and frames. As mentioned above, this first level of analysis is specific to a particular social, economic, and cultural context. For example, in the coding scheme, I inserted members of the clergy and churches because Romanians continue to trust the Church (over 65%) more than politicians, according to an INSCOP survey[5]. I coded participants in four categories and they included either the people, places, concrete or abstract things:

1. Political party staff (candidate, party members, party high officials, political opponents, indexical objects depicting a candidate's profession);
2. Local authorities (town/city officials);
3. Socio-demographic categories (elderly citizens, middle-aged persons, families, children, students, members of the clergy, doctors, disabled people, factory workers, ethnic groups, young bloggers, crowds);
4. Buildings (historical buildings, churches, European buildings);
5. Dressing code (suit & tie, shirt, blue-jeans & T-shirt, Romanian folk costume).

I used a deductive method by seeking to find how these five categories and Grabe & Bucy's categories visualize the three master frames (ideal candidate, populist candidate and sure loser) and the four associated themes (statesmanship, compassion, mass appeal, ordinariness) within the nine Romanian candidates' self-presentation for the 2014 European Parliament Elections. In the coding scheme, I adapted Grabe and Bucy's coding instrument to the context of Romania and the final coding scheme included 26 categories. For example, I included the social category of elderly persons in the compassion theme because the low pensions is a sensitive issue in Romania. As mentioned above, the sure loser frame was associated with opponents visually depicted as losers.

The first master frame, the ideal candidate, includes two themes: statesmanship and compassion. For the statesmanship theme, I coded the following variables: *elected officials and other influentials* (European, national and local high-ranking members); *patriotic symbols* (monuments, memorials, flags, statues); *symbols of progress* (images of economic and technological progress: manufacturing plants, buildings); *identifiable entourage* (political aides, volunteers, campaign caravan, reporters); *campaign paraphernalia* (posters, banners, party clothing and campaign transportation) and *formal attire* (suits). For the compassion theme, I coded the following variables: social categories (*children, family members, admiring women, elderly persons*); *ethnic communities* (gypsies); *religious symbols* (members of the clergy, crosses, candles, churches, monasteries); behavioral gestures (*interaction with voters* - engaging with supporters without physical contact, *physical embraces* - hugging, shaking hands, embracing).

The second frame, the populist candidate, includes two theme: the mass appeal and ordinariness. For the mass appeal theme, I coded the following variables: *celebrities* (movie stars, TV personalities, musicians, well-known athletes), *large audiences* (a mass of supporters, who are not party members, attending a candidate's meeting with citizens), *approving audiences* and *interaction with crowds* (shots of the candidate giving rapid, anonymous handshakes, grips, or touches to groups of supporters without individualized or fixed engagement with anyone in particular). For the ordinariness theme, I coded the following variables: *informal attire* (the candidate wearing a tie without a jacket), *casual dress* (the candidate wearing jeans, T-shirts or other casual garment), *traditional folk clothing* (the candidate or people wearing folk costumes), *ordinary people* (common folk, visits to disadvantaged communities, or to manufacturing plants), and *traditional dishes* (the candidate eating traditional food). In the ordinary people category I included all the photographs depicting the candidates visiting the work places of ordinary people (manufacturing plants, factories, vegetable markets, schools, universities etc.). When coding the photographs with ordinary persons, I made a distinction between interaction with individuals and physical embraces (the 'compassion' theme), on the one hand, and ordinary people (the ordinariness theme), on the other hand. In the first category, I included those photographs depicting citizens in the streets, for example, and in the latter category, I included those photographs depicting citizens at their work place.

The third frame, the sure loser candidate, focuses on the opponents and the two variables coded are: *opponent - a weak candidate* (a visual display of weakness through a caricature or through a photo having a negative connotation) and *defiant gestures* (opponent's campaign staff performing some inappropriate gestures - to remove other candidates' glued posters etc.).

Cohen's *kappa* was employed to check reliability of the data. About 10% of the Facebook photos was used to calculate inter-coder reliability. Two expert coders were used to code the Facebook images according to the 26 visual variables. The coders were trained in applying the defined criteria for each variable by orienting them to the codebook and discussing examples of each code. *Kappa* was computed to .94 for statesmanship, .85 for compassion, .89 for mass appeal, .86 for mass appeal and .88 for sure loser.

The present study addresses the following research questions:

RQ1: What master frames were present in the photographic images on the Romanian candidates' Facebook Timeline?

RQ2: What types of themes prevail in their online photographic images?

FINDINGS: VISUAL FRAMING OF ROMANIAN CANDIDATES TO 2014 EUROPEAN ELECTIONS

To better understand the visual categories, themes and frames, mean values were calculated to determine how often they were used by the nine Romanian candidates. As indicated in Table 2, all nine candidates portrayed themselves as ideal candidates. The self-presentation as ideal candidates was significantly more salient than the self-presentation as populist candidates, the only exception being Dan Diaconescu (PPDD) who tried to provide a visual balance between the two visual frames (RQ2).

Table 2 and Figure 1 show that the differences appear within the framing of the four themes belonging to the two master frames (RQ3). Unlike his eight opponents who presented themselves more as statesmanlike, M.R. Ungureanu (FC) chose to portray himself more as a compassionate candidate ($m = 6.80$). Within the populist candidate frame, all nine candidates preferred the ordinariness theme and Theodor Stolojan (PDL) was shown with the highest level of ordinariness ($m = 6.07$). The sure loser frame was not frequently used by the nine candidates, only two candidates attempted to visually attack their opponents, the verbal attacks being more salient than the visual ones. Mircea Diaconu (Indep.) and M.R. Ungureanu (FC) uploaded photos depicting their opponents' supporters while ungluing Diaconu's and Ungureanu's posters.

The Ideal Candidate Master Frame: The Statesmanship Theme

Three main dimensions were used in the framing of the statesmanship theme (Figure 2): elected officials and other influentials, identifiable entourage, and campaign paraphernalia. Corina Crețu, Norica Nicolai, and Theodor Stolojan used visual associations with elected officials and other influentials, with

Table 2. Mean values for categories, themes and frames by 2014 EP candidates in Romania

Frames/ Themes/ Categories	Romanian candidates to 2014 European Parliament Elections								
	Winning candidates					Losing candidates			
	Corina Crețu PSD+ PC+ UNPR	**Norica Nicolai PNL**	**Theodor Stolojan PDL**	**Mircea Diaconu INDEP.**	**Cristian Preda PMP**	**Dan Diaconescu PPDD**	**Corneliu V. Tudor PRM**	**Mihai R. Ungureanu FC**	**Aurelian Pavelescu PNTCD**
Ideal Candidate	14.22	11.37	21.83	8.61	1.18	2.80	.11	10.03	1.26
Statesmanship	8.19	7.11	13.64	6.80	.65	1.92	.11	3.23	1.14
Elected officials & other influentials	4.47	4.57	5.61	.00	.30	.34	.00	.73	.43
Patriotic symbols	.42	.15	.03	1.19	.00	.23	.00	1.03	.00
Symbols of progress	.03	.34	.03	.11	.00	.00	.00	.00	.03
Identifiable entourage	1.03	1.23	5.07	.57	.15	.53	.07	.76	.19
Campaign paraphernalia	.49	.42	1.15	4.92	.15	.73	.00	.53	.45
Formal attire	1.74	.38	1.73	.00	.03	.07	.03	.15	.03
Compassion	6.03	4.26	8.18	1.80	.53	.88	.00	6.80	.11
Children	.65	.26	.00	.19	.00	.00	.00	1.19	.03
Family associations	.42	.00	.00	.00	.00	.00	.00	.00	.00
Admiring women	.46	.46	.00	.30	.00	.15	.00	.11	.00
Elderly people	.42	.53	2.11	.07	.00	.00	.00	.30	.00
Ethnic communities	.00	.00	.11	.00	.00	.00	.00	.00	.00
Religious symbols	.61	.26	.19	.30	.00	.07	.00	.19	.00
Interaction with individuals	1.23	1.23	4.19	.53	.53	.57	.00	2.99	.03
Physical embraces	2.24	1.49	1.57	.38	.00	.07	.00	1.99	.03
Populist Candidate	4.42	3.38	8.92	3.49	.92	2.42	.00	4.11	.53
Mass Appeal	2.03	1.38	2.84	2.69	.76	2.03	.00	.99	.00
Celebrities	.15	.42	.15	.73	.00	0.11	.00	.15	.49
Large audiences	.96	.57	2.65	.00	.53	1.23	.00	.84	.00
Approving audiences	.03	.00	.00	.19	.00	.00	.00	.00	.00
Interaction with crowds	.88	.38	.03	1.76	.15	.69	.00	.00	.00
Ordinariness	2.38	1.99	6.07	.80	.15	.38	.00	3.11	.03
Informal attire	.07	.07	.30	.11	.07	.00	.00	.34	.00
Casual dress	.00	.00	.00	.15	.03	.00	.00	.15	.00
Folk costume	.19	.00	.00	.11	.00	.38	.00	.42	.00
Manufacturing costume	.00	.00	.07	.00	.00	.00	.00	.00	.00
Ordinary people	2.11	1.92	5.69	.19	.03	.00	.00	1.53	.03
Traditional dishes	.00	.00	.00	.23	.00	.00	.00	.65	.00
Sure Loser	.00	.00	.00	.23	.00	.00	.00	.26	.00
Opponent - weak candidate	.00	.00	.00	.00	.00	.00	.00	.03	.00
Defiant gestures	.00	.00	.00	.23	.00	.00	.00	.23	.00

Figure 1. Visual framing of themes - Romanian candidates to 2014 EP elections

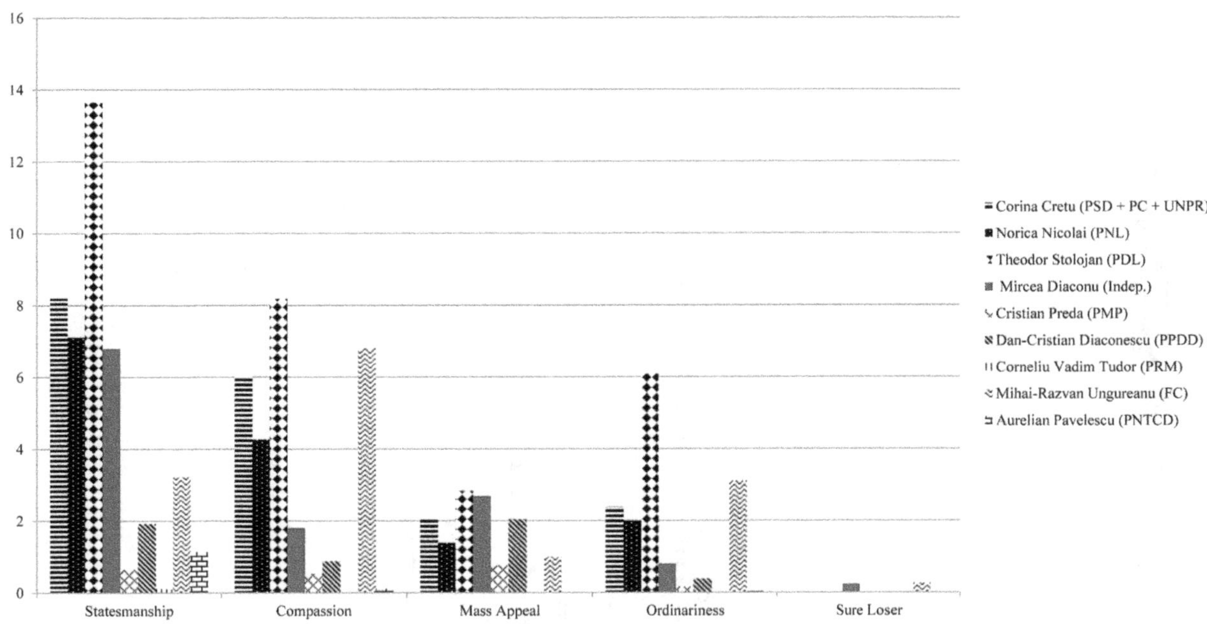

Stolojan at a higher level ($m = 5.61$). Within this social category, Grabe and Bucy (2009, pp. 289–290) include “people with power, status, and money, whether on the national or local level.” Each of the three Romanian candidates used photographic images with national and local high-ranking members of their party: Corina Crețu accompanied by Victor Ponta, the Romanian Prime Minister and the PSD president; Norica Nicolai accompanied by Crin Antonescu, the PNL president; or Theodor Stolojan accompanied by Vasile Blaga, the PDL president. Unlike the other two candidates, Corina Crețu (PSD) posted photos with Martin Schultz (Leader of the Progressive Alliance of Socialists and Democrats and the incumbent President of the European Parliament). The use of the European, national and local high-ranking members implies a transfer of credibility through status upon the candidate. The endorsement function associated with these elected officials and influentials relies on what Ronald Smith (2002) identifies as “the audience’s deference to the social position or prestige of a message source” (p. 119). It was interesting to observe that none of the Romanian candidates included in their photos the social category of people with money, because this type of influentials may trigger the negative meaning potential of corruption upon the respective candidate, corruption being a sensitive social issue in the Romanian context.

The identifiable entourage and the campaign paraphernalia dimensions showed two discrepancies among the nine candidates. Theodor Stolojan’s Facebook page contained the highest level of photos linked to entourage ($m = 5.07$). Stolojan used photographs depicting him accompanied by political aides and volunteers throughout his rallies in Romanian cities and towns and he even adapted to the social online media trend of selfies. The strategy of a political selfie was also used by two other candidates (Norica Nicolai - PNL and M.R. Ungureanu - FC). Photos linked to campaign paraphernalia were dominant on Mircea Diaconu’s Facebook page ($m = 4.92$). Besides posters informing citizens when and where the independent candidate would be present in Romanian cities and towns, M. Diaconu was the only candidate who highly provided visual associations with the campaign transportation. The slogan of his campaign (“Mircea Diaconu face ocolul României în 22 de zile”/”Mircea Diaconu - Around Romania

Figure 2. Visual categories of the statesmanship theme

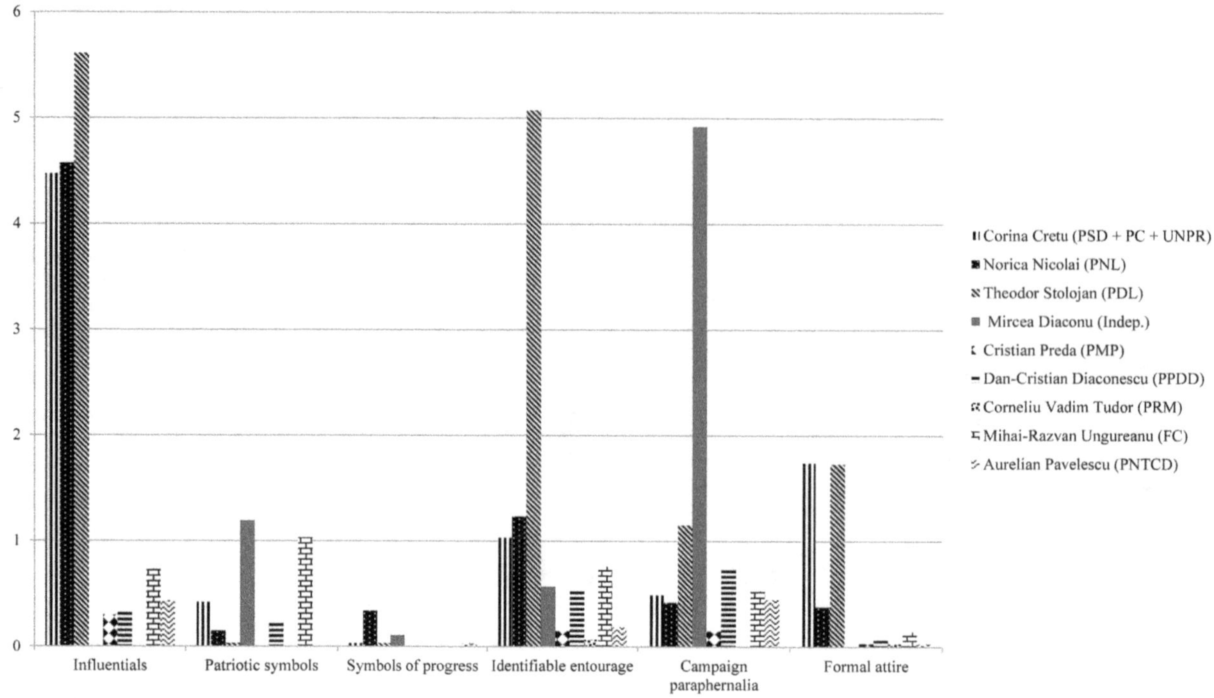

in 22 days") was the intertextual interpretation of Jules Verne's classic adventure novel *Around the World in Eighty Days*. The verbal message was visually accompanied by the image of his personal car (a yellow Romanian off-road vehicle). The independent candidate used his yellow car as his means of transport during the rallies in Romania and throughout the whole campaign he provided a metaphorical representation of his yellow car as his campaign companion.

The candidates did not fully exploit the meaning potential of patriotic symbols and symbols of progress especially on May 9, when Europe Day and Romania's State Independence Day are celebrated. Two candidates (Mircea Diaconu and M.R. Ungureanu) outscored the other seven candidates on the dimension of patriotic symbols. Ungureanu greatly used photos of traditional Romanian sites (The Peasant Museum or The Museum of Dacian and Roman Civilization in Deva). Photos linked to progress were not fully exploited. The photographic images depicting Norica Nicolai accompanied by aircrafts and pilots who took part in military missions may be associated with the meaning potential of progress and, at the same time, are consistent with her EP position as the vice-chair of the Subcommittee on Security and Defense.

The Ideal Candidate Master Frame: The Compassion Theme

Using the compassion theme, candidates represent themselves as "warm and benevolent personalities who should be loved and adored by voters" (Grabe & Bucy, 2009, p. 104). There are three main categories which may guarantee the framing of benevolence: (1) the visual association of candidates with social categories that trigger the meaning potential of benevolence (children, family, admiring women, elderly people, ethnic communities); (2) nonverbal gestures (interaction with individuals and physical embraces); (3) visual association with religious symbols (members of the clergy, crosses, candles, churches, monasteries).

The primary visual category used by all candidates focused on a behavioral display of interaction and physical embraces with voters (Figure 3). The difference in the use of these nonverbal gestures lay in the degree of physical contact. The presence or absence of physical contact may be explained in terms of gender stereotypes. Women are more likely to be perceived as compassionate, and they seem to be associated with compassion traits (education, health care, social security/medicare, environment, family issues, women's issues, abortion; Dolan, 2005). Unlike their male opponents who uploaded photos containing interaction with individuals, both women candidates (Corina Crețu and Norica Nicolai) had a high level of the physical contact dimension, displaying a variety of physical embraces from shaking hands to hugging and even kissing supporters.

The most visible social category in all photographs posted by three of the winning candidates was elderly persons. Many of the photos depicted them while talking with elderly people either from the countryside or in the markets. The salience of this socio-demographic category showed their compassion and portrayed the candidates as protective children. Theodor Stolojan outscored all his opponents in the usage of elderly people ($m = 2.11$)

A significant discrepancy may be noticed in the usage of the category of children. As Grabe and Bucy (2009, p. 104) highlight, the link to children "supports the mythology of family" and this value is dominant not only in American culture, but in Romanian culture as well. Only four Romanian candidates used the category of children to frame themselves as compassionate. M.R. Ungureanu, a male candidate, outscored his two female candidates and he was the only male candidate who self-presented as a protective father.

Figure 3. Visual categories of compassion theme

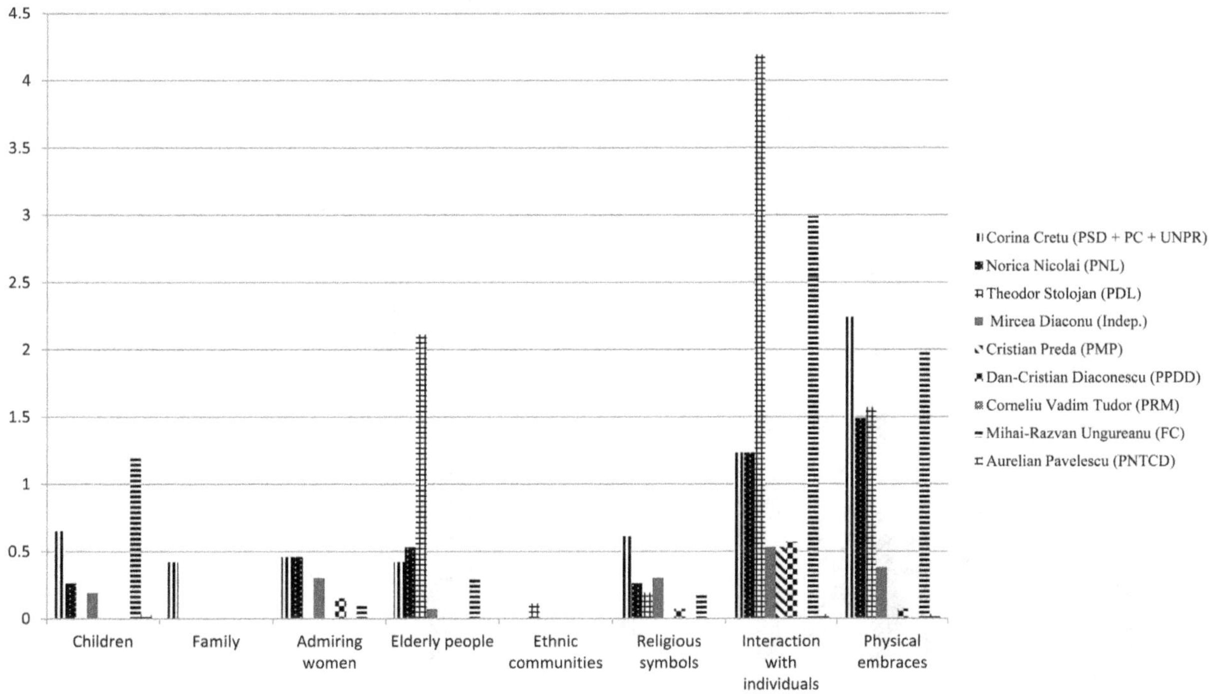

Religious symbols were pervasive in the photos of seven Romanian candidates. The visual choice of clergy, churches, and monasteries may be explained in terms of the collectivist society that prevails in Romania. Since Romanians trust the Church more that politicians,[6] the EP candidates used "members of the clergy as participants in their photos in order to highlight their closeness to traditional values in the Romanian society and to attract the elderly religious voters" (Cmeciu, Pătruţ, 2014).

Unlike Western and American candidates who are portrayed with their family members in order to "evoke the frame of the ideal surrogate father of the nation" (Grabe & Bucy, 2009, p. 104), Romanian candidates prefer not to expose their families to possible media scrutiny. Corina Creţu was the only candidate who used visual associations to family members and historical family ties: photographs of Corina Creţu and her husband baptizing a child and photographs depicting her at her father's grave while paying homage to his memory.

The Populist Candidate Master Frame: The Mass Appeal Theme

As Grabe and Bucy (2009, p. 105) mention, "the populist narratives are built on the idea that ordinary people [...] stand in opposition to an aristocratic and self-serving elite." The mass appeal was the least used theme in the self-appraising presentation of the Romanian candidates to the 2014 EP elections. Three main variables were used: large audiences, interaction with crowds, and celebrities (Figure 4).

The first two visual categories were visually obtained in the same way for all six candidates who used them. The category of large audiences was visually obtained through shots of supporters tightly packed into a space, especially in the street or in a building (a school or a village cultural centre). Theodor

Figure 4. Visual categories of the mass appeal theme

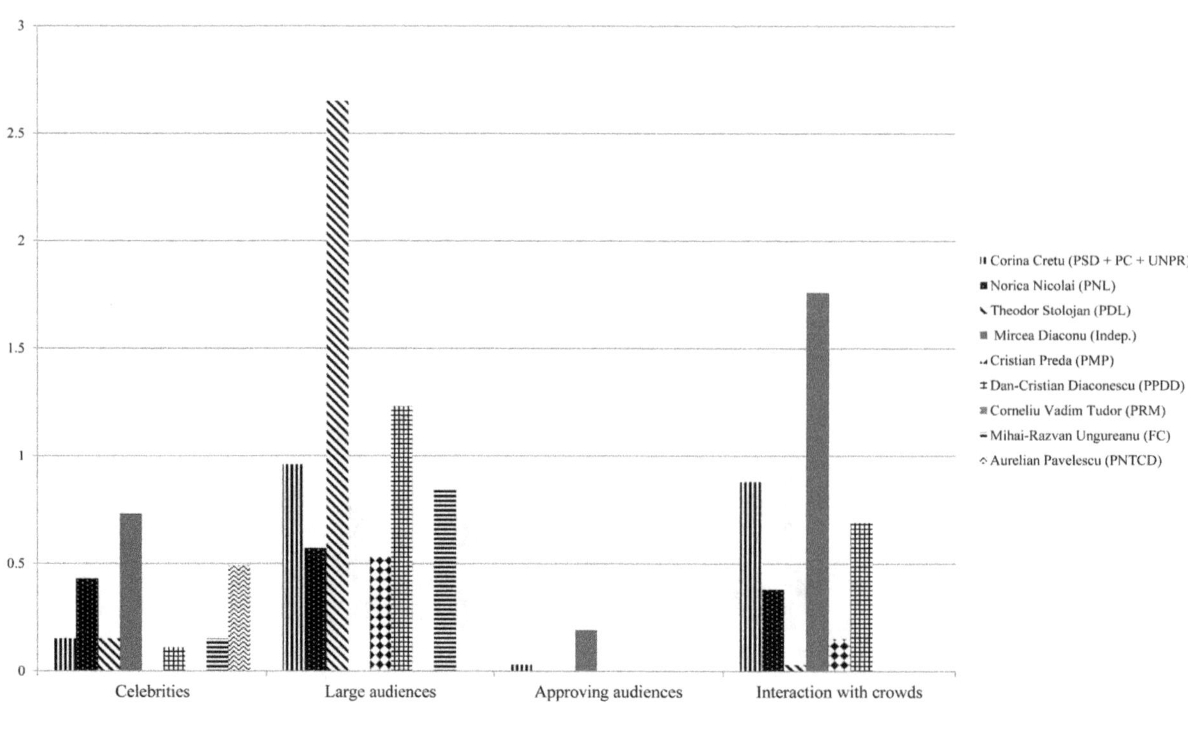

Stolojan outscored (*m* =2.65) all the other candidates in the visual usage of large audiences. The supporters were not PDL members, but anonymous citizens attending the political rallies of the candidate who was neither the centre of the frame, nor the main focus.

Seven candidates used celebrities as a mass appeal attribute. Grabe and Bucy (2009, p. 107) consider that celebrities are "symbols of populist devotion" and they "transfer their cultural appeal to political candidates [...]." Mircea Diaconu (Indep.), Aurelian Pavelescu (PNTCD) and Norica Nicolai (PNL) had the highest levels with this visual category. Two types of celebrities were visible during the EP elections in Romania: members of the Romanian Royal Family and famous actors. The visual associations with celebrities depicted, on the one hand, Mircea Diaconu, an actor, reminding the movies of other famous Romanian actors, and on the other hand, Norica Nicolai and Aurelian Pavelescu, as representatives of historical parties, with members of the Romanian Royal Family who took part at the Centenary of Corneliu Coposu (a conservative Romanian politician who was the victim of the communist regime).

The Populist Candidate Master Frame: The Ordinariness Theme

For the Romanian candidates, the primary common dimensions of the ordinariness theme (Figure 5) were the visual appearances with regular folks at their work places and traditional items (folk costume or traditional dishes).

The ordinary people category was visually obtained through photographs depicting the six candidates visiting various work places of Romanian citizens. Theodor Stolojan was the only candidate who mostly exploited this frame (*m* = 5.69). He visited more than ten work places, from vegetable, flower, or diary

Figure 5. Visual categories of the ordinariness theme

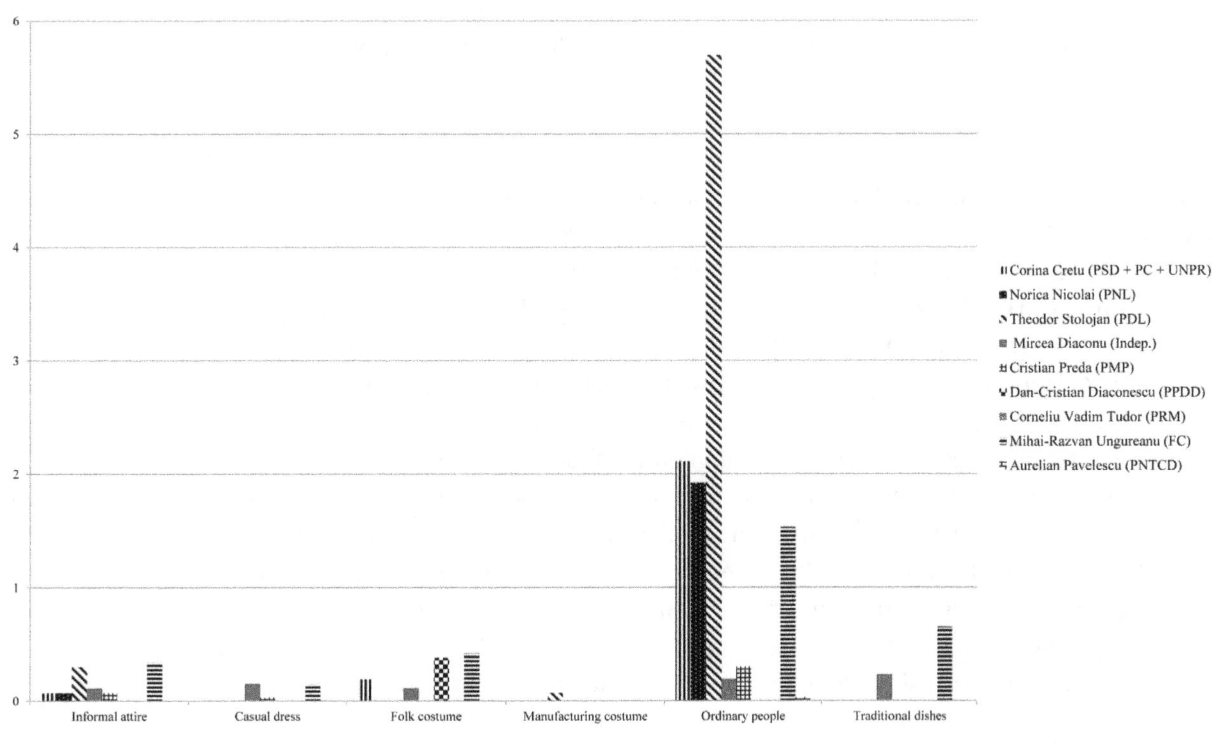

markets to ready-made garments factories, metallurgy manufacturing plants, or universities. These visits seemed consistent with the PDL slogan (*Europa în fiecare casă/Europe in every house*) and with his EP position as the Vice-Chair of the Committee on Economic and Monetary Affairs, since the meaning potential of these interactions with different working class representatives was to frame the PDL candidate as a supporter of the economic development of the respective plants, factories, or academic institutions. Although the photo albums of Corina Crețu and Norica Nicolai did not focus so much on visits to Romanian citizens' work places, the photographs posted were accompanied by verbal messages which mentioned either that the factory was raised through European funds (Norica Nicolai visiting the water pumping station at Repedea, Maramures), or that the candidate would become a promoter of the Romanian brand (Corina Crețu visiting the Jolidon factory in Cluj-Napoca).

Four candidates used visual associations with tradition (folk costumes and traditional dishes), but Corina Crețu was the only candidate who developed a style of dress specific to Romania and which was actually in line with the party slogan (*Mândri că suntem români/Proud to be Romanians*). Throughout several rallies in the country, Corina Crețu was wearing a traditional Romanian folk blouse ("ie"), thus establishing empathy with common folk, and representing herself as a preserver of Romanian traditions. This traditional folk style of dress was consistent with the traditional Romanian embroidery pattern to be found on the PSD election poster for the 2014 European Parliament elections.

CONCLUSION AND DISCUSSION

One of the purposes of this chapter was to study the way in which Romanian winning and losing candidates used Facebook photographic images during the 2014 European Parliament Elections. The analysis showed that only six out of twelve candidates tried to provide a visual insight into their online campaign and that a social network communication campaign does not imply winning the EP elections. This clearly reflects what Margolis and Resnick (2000) have highlighted in their study: the online visibility does not trigger an offline mobilization of voters.

Aware of the public exposure on Facebook and of their target-public (Romanian citizens), the EP candidates in Romania focused their content visibility on a hybrid message where the national identity features prevailed. This finding may be associated with the studies on the news coverage of the EP elections (de Vrees et al., 2006; de Vrees & Boomgaarden, 2012) which revealed that the news stories focused more on national political actors and not on EU actors.

Starting from Grabe and Bucy's visual framing theory, I have adapted the ideal and populist candidate frames and the four visual themes (statesmanship, compassion, mass appeal, ordinariness) to the Romanian EP elections context. In terms of research methodology, the refinement of the visual categories used for the political frames and themes seems important since the analysis will reveal some categories that are contextual specific. In the Romanian political context of the 2014 EP elections, the category of 'people with money' belonging to the statesmanship theme was excluded because it has the meaning potential of corruption, a social issue with which Romanian candidates do not want to be linked. 'Elderly people' was a social category highlighting the compassion theme within the Romanian context, five winning candidates using this social category in their visual presentation. Five winning candidates and two losing candidates exploited the category of religious symbols (compassion theme) being aware of the trust that Romanians show towards church than towards politicians.

The comparative analysis of the use of frames and themes by Romanian candidates during the 2014 EP elections showed a salience of the ideal candidate frame both for the winning and losing candidates. Within the ideal candidate frame, the statesmanship theme was more visible than the compassion theme. No significant difference was noticed between the winning and losing candidates in the usage of the frames and themes, the variation mainly lay in the dominance of visual categories associated with these themes and frames. The losing candidates mostly used the category of interaction with individuals, thus portraying themselves as compassionate campaigners. The winning candidates preferred the visual category of elected officials and other influentials (the winning national party candidates), and of campaign paraphernalia (the winning independent candidate). Unfortunately, the majority of the elected officials' visual appearances did not include European leaders or other important persons at a European level. The endorsement was mainly made at a national and local level, highlighting the domestic orientation of the EP elections in Romania. The visual category of physical embraces within the compassion theme revealed a prevalence of physical contact with citizens (hugging or kissing) in the self-presentations of women candidates. We may imply that the physical embraces of Romanian EP candidates may be explained in terms of gender stereotypes, thus highlighting that women politicians portray themselves as more compassionate than their male opponents.

In the EP elections in Romania, the populist candidate frame was activated through the visual categories of large audiences, interaction with crowds and celebrities for the mass appeal theme and the regular folks and traditional items for the ordinariness theme. The prevalence of crowds is consistent with the contextual setting of a campaign (visits to Romanian cities and towns), whereas celebrities highlight a degree of nationality by laying an emphasis on context-specific visual categories (the use of members of the Romanian Royal Family in candidate's photos). Traditional folk costume within the ordinariness theme may be associated with a high degree of nationality. Although the visual appearance of the PSD+PC+UNPR candidate wearing a traditional Romanian folk blouse may have been consistent with a representation of patriotism, it did not seem appropriate within the context of an increasing phenomenon of Euroskepticism. The analysis showed an implicit tackling of European issues in the ordinariness theme. The category of ordinary people revealed that the Romanian candidates chose to post photographs of their visits to Romanian citizens' work places. This seems to be an appropriate visual strategy as long as it is connected to a verbal message which may suggest the connection between the respective organization and some European issues. One important remark should be made regarding the way in which the Romanian EP candidates visually exploited their positions as former members of the European Parliament (EMP). Although six out of the twelve candidates were former EMP, only three candidates (Corina Crețu, Norica Nicolai and Theodor Stolojan) framed their visual messages depicting themselves as competent European Parliament members.

Hybridity was the main feature which characterized the 2014 EP candidates' self-presentations in Romania. The visual hybrid message promoted by the Romanian candidates is consistent with the hybrid character of elections to the European Parliament, found in Strömbäck, Maier, & Kaid's study of EP elections in other European countries. By blending visual categories belonging to Europe (EU officials) with national identity features (religious symbols or traditional elements), Romanian politicians tried to reduce citizens' high skepticism regarding the European identity but at the same time to promote a pre-election presidential campaign which took place in Romania in November, 2014.

FUTURE RESEARCH DIRECTIONS

Although this study was limited to the visual framing analysis of political candidates' Facebook photographic images during the 2014 EP elections in Romania, further research may be carried out: a comparative analysis of the visual images posted by EP candidates from other East-European countries, the visual media coverage of the Romanian candidates to the EP elections, or the Romanians' online engagement towards the candidates' visual self-representation through an analysis of their comments on the photos uploaded. This last aspect should be related to a combination between a quantitative and a qualitative analysis of the political candidates' Facebook photographs. Despite the advantage of a quantitative analysis of the visual frames and themes which showed a certain pattern of the visual strategic planning for each Romanian candidate, a qualitative analysis of Facebook photographs is also valuable. Although certain photos may not be salient within a frame and theme, they have a meaning potential which may have a greater impact for voters (for example, Stolojan's photo with a Rroma woman triggered a higher degree of engagement through likes and shares).

REFERENCES

Banwart, M. C. (2002). *Videostyle and webstyle in 2000: Comparing the gender differences of candidate presentations in political advertising and on the internet.* (Unpublished PhD Dissertation). University of Oklahoma, Oklahoma.

Barnhurst, K. G., & Quinn, K. (2012). Political visions: Visual studies in political communication. In H. A. Semetko & M. Scammell (Eds.), *The SAGE handbook of political communication* (pp. 276–291). Thousand Oaks, CA: Sage. doi:10.4135/9781446201015.n23

Bourdieu, P. (1990). *Photography. A middle-brow art* (S. Whiteside, Trans.). Cambridge, MA: Polity Press.

Buturoiu, R. (2014). Every comments counts. The 2014 EP elections in Romania on Facebook. *Sfera Politicii/The Sphere of Politics, 179*(3), 46-55.

Bystrom, D., & Kaid, L. L. (2002). Are women candidates transforming campaign communication? A comparison of advertising videostyles in the 1990s. In C. S. Rosenthal(Ed.), *Women Transforming Congress* (pp. 146–169). Norman, OK: University of Oklahoma Press.

Caers, R., De Feyter, T., De Couck, M., Stough, T., Vigna, C., & Du Bois, C. (2013). Facebook: A literature review. *New Media & Society, 15*(6), 982–1002. doi:10.1177/1461444813488061

Cmeciu, C. (2005). *Strategii persuasive în discursul politic/Persuasive strategies in political discourse.* Iaşi. *Universitas*, XXI.

Cmeciu, C., & Pătruţ, M. (2014). The visual framing of Romanian women politicians in personal campaign blogs during the 2012 Romanian parliamentary elections. In M. Raicheva-Stover & E. Ibroscheva (Eds.), *Women in politics and the media: Perspectives from nations in transition* (pp. 181-198). London: Bloomsbury.

Cmeciu, C. (2014). Beyond the online faces of Romanian candidates for the 2014 European Parliament Elections - A visual framing analysis of Facebook photographic Images. In G. Horvath, R. K. Bako, & E. Biro-Kaszas (Eds.), *Ten years of Facebook* (pp. 405–434). Debrecen: Debrecen University Press.

Dan, V., & Iorgoveanu, A. (2013). Still on the beaten path: How gender impacted the coverage of male and female Romanian candidates for European Office. *The International Journal of Press/Politics*, *18*(2), 208–233. doi:10.1177/1940161212473508

de Vrees, C. H., Banducci, S. A., Semetko, H. A., & Boomgaarden, H. G. (2006). The news coverage of the 2004 European parliamentary election campaign in 25 countries. *European Union Politics*, *7*(4), 477–504. doi:10.1177/1465116506069440

de Vrees, C. H., & Boomgaarden, H. G. (2012). Comparing news on Europe: Elections and beyond. In F. Esser & Th. Hanitzsch (Eds.), *Handbook of Comparative Communication Research* (pp. 327–340). New York: Routledge.

Dolan, K. (2005). Do women candidates play to gender stereotypes? Do men candidates play to women? candidate sex and issues priorities on campaign websites. *Political Research Quarterly*, *58*(1), 31–44. doi:10.1177/106591290505800103

Foot, K. A., & Schneider, S. M. (2006). *Web campaigning*. Cambridge, MA: MIT Press.

German, K. (2010). Bush/Gore photos reveal differing styles, strategies. *Newspaper Research Journal*, *31*(4), 48–61.

Ghilizean, M. (2000). *Cum să reuşeşti în viaţa politică – manual de campanie electorală./How to succeed in political life - A guide to election campaign*. Bucureşti: Active Vision.

Goffman, E. (1974). *Frame analysis: An essay on the organization of experience*. Cambridge, MA: Harvard University Press.

Goodnow, T. (2013). Facing off: A comparative analysis of Obama and Romney Facebook timeline photographs. *The American Behavioral Scientist*, *57*(11), 1584–1595. doi:10.1177/0002764213489013

Grabe, M. E., & Bucy, E. P. (2009). *Image bite politics: News and the visual framing of elections*. Oxford: Oxford University Press. doi:10.1093/acprof:oso/9780195372076.001.0001

Graham, C., Laurier, E., O'Brien, V., & Rouncefield, M. (2011). Guest editors' introduction. New visual technologies: Shifting boundaries, shared moments. *Visual Studies*, *26*(2), 87–91. doi:10.1080/1472586X.2011.571883

Guţu, D. (2007). New Media. Bucureşti: Comunicare.ro.

Hacker, K. L. (1995). *Candidate images in presidential elections*. Westport, CT: Praeger.

Hertog, J. K., & McLeod, D. M. (2001). A multiperspectival approach to framing analysis: A field guide. In S. D. Reese, O. H. Gandy, & A. E. Grant (Eds.), *Framing public life: Perspective on media and our understanding of the social world* (pp. 139–162). Mahwah, NJ: Lawrence Erlbaum Associates.

INSCOP Survey. (2013). *The Barometer of Public Opinion – the Truth about Romania*. Retrieved from http://www.inscop.ro/septembrie-2013-increderea-in-institutii/

Ionescu, N. (2013).Online political communication: The role of image upload on Facebook. *Revista română de jurnalism şi comunicare/Romanian Review of Journalism and Communication, 8*(1), 53-58.

Jewitt, C. (2008). Multimodality and literacy in school classrooms. *Review of Research in Education, 32*(1), 241–267. doi:10.3102/0091732X07310586

Jewitt, C., & Oyama, R. (2001). Visual meaning: A social semiotic approach. In T. van Leeuwen & C. Jewitt (Eds.), *Handbook of visual analysis* (pp. 134–156). Los Angeles, CA: Sage.

Kaplan, A. M., & Haenlein, M. (2010). Users of the world, unite! The challenge and opportunities of social media. *Business Horizons, 53*(1), 59–68. doi:10.1016/j.bushor.2009.09.003

Lazarsfeld, P. P., Berelson, B., & Gaudet, H. (2004). *Mecanismul votului. Cum se decid alegătorii într-o campanie electorală/The people's choice: How the voter makes up his mind in a presidential campaign.* Bucureşti: comunicare.ro.

Margolis, M., & Resnick, D. (2000). *Politics as usual: The "Cyberspace Revolution"*. Thousand Oaks, CA: Sage.

Messaris, P. (2012). Visual "literacy" in the digital age. *The Review of Communication, 12*(2), 101–117. doi:10.1080/15358593.2011.653508

Messaris, P., & Abraham, L. (2001). The role of images in framing news stories. In S. D. Reese, O. H. Gandy, & A. E. Grant (Eds.), *Framing public life: Perspective on media and our understanding of the social world* (pp. 215–226). Mahwah, NJ: Lawrence Erlbaum Associates.

Miller, J. (2013). *Visual framing and social networking: A content analysis of the 2012 Barack Obama and Mitt Romney Facebook pages.* (Unpublished MA Thesis). The University of Alabama.

Momoc, A. (2014). Social networks - Public space or political tool? Voters and candidates on Facebook during the elections for the European Parliament. In G. Horvath, R. K. Bako, & E. Biro-Kaszas (Eds.), *Ten years of Facebook* (pp. 435–456). Debrecen: Debrecen University Press.

Moriarty, S. E., & Popovich, M. N. (1991). Newsmagazine visuals and the 1988 presidential election. *The Journalism Quarterly, 68*(3), 371–380. doi:10.1177/107769909106800307

Pabst, S. (2014, May 15). *Europoliticians take on social media.* Retrieved from http://www.dw.de/euro-politicians-take-on-social-media/a-17627641

Papacharissi, Z. (2002). The virtual sphere. The internet as public sphere. *New Media & Society, 4*(1), 9–27. doi:10.1177/14614440222226244

Schill, D. (2012). The Visual image and the political image: A review of visual communication research in the field of political communication. *The Review of Communication, 12*(2), 118–142. doi:10.1080/15358593.2011.653504

Schols, S. (2014, April 10). *A more visual EU elections?* Retrieved from http://europedecides.eu/2014/04/a-more-visual-eu-election/

Smith, R. D. (2002). *Strategic Planning for Public Relations.* Mahwah, NJ: Lawrence Erlbaum Associates.

Stoiciu, A. (2000). *Comunicarea politică – cum se vând idei şi oameni./Political communication - How to sell ideas and people*. Bucureşti: Humanitas-Libra.

Strömbäck, J., Maier, M., & Kaid, L. L. (2011). Political communication and election campaigns for the European Parliament. In M. Maier, J. Strömbäck, & L. L. Kaid (Eds.), *Political communication in European Parliamentary elections* (pp. 3–16). Farnham, MD: Ashgate.

Stromer-Galley, J. (2014). *Presidential campaigning in the internet age*. Oxford, UK: Oxford University Press. doi:10.1093/acprof:oso/9780199731930.001.0001

Van House, N. A. (2011). Personal photography, digital technologies and the uses of the visual. *Visual Studies*, *26*(2), 125–134. doi:10.1080/1472586X.2011.571888

Vergeer, M., Hermans, L., & Cunha, C. (2012). Web campaigning in the 2009 European Parliament elections: A cross-national comparative analysis. *New Media & Society*, *15*(1), 128–148. doi:10.1177/1461444812457337

Verschueren, P. (2012). *Picturing Afghanistan: The photography of foreign conflict*. New York: Hampton Press.

Verser, R., & Wicks, R. H. (2006). Managing voter impressions: The use of images on presidential candidate web sites during the 2000 campaign. *Journal of Communication*, *56*(1), 178–197. doi:10.1111/j.1460-2466.2006.00009.x

KEY TERMS AND DEFINITIONS

Hybridity: The intermingling of several items belonging to different domains, sites, cultures etc.

Ideal Candidate Frame: A pattern presenting the candidate as a statesman and as a compassionate person.

Populist Candidate Frame: A pattern presenting the candidate as an ordinary man in opposition to an aristocratic and self-serving elite.

Romania: Country in Eastern Europe, member of the European Union since 2007.

Sure Loser Candidate Frame: A pattern presenting the opponent as a weak candidate.

Visual Framing: The process of making salient some aspects of reality by using images.

Visual Categories: Elements of visual nature which may be used in the framing of an issue.

ENDNOTES

1 As communication systems we consider Mass Communication Media, such as Press, Radio, Television, Cinema, and all applications allowing mass or private communication within the internet environment (news sites, various content sites, social media, applications such as e-mails and chat applications). Our focus is mainly in communication systems based on commercial rationale which end up offering infotainment through the dissemination of information that serves specific interests

of sponsors, advertisers, public relations and the intense information management by political actors, corporations and other factors.

2 The term "text" is not being used here with the specific essence of written discourse, but includes many different forms of communication, which might be meaningful such as interviews, letters, diaries, fiction stories, proceedings, audiovisual content etc.

3 The full coding frame used for the current research can be found in the appendix. In the results we present the main findings of our research, focusing on the variables of the coding frame that appeared to be of greater importance for the presentation of the pre-electoral use of twitter. Hence, several variables, e.g. the week of the tweet, have been omitted in the presentation of the results, due to their lack of importance regarding the presentation of the pre-electoral twitter ecology.

4 R= 2(C1,C2)/C1+C2, with 70% as the lowest level of credibility. The conduction of the test on both coders provided us with an average of 80% inter-coder reliability.

5 Metaphor examples: "the new austerity measures will be a pogrom against the greek society" (@ a.tsipras). "(Mr. Samaras) amputates democracy…" (@ a.tsipras). "Landing of millions of British tourists this year in Greece" (@statheramprosta). Transfer examples: "They take us back to the Miserables of Hugo and Jean Ajean" (@ a.tsipras). "Greece walks the road of Chile and Pinochet" (@ a.tsipras).

6 Appeal to fear example: "You have agreed for lay-offs in the public sector, reduction of pensions, privatization of everything" (@ a.tsipras). Appeal to hope examples: "2014 will be a year that Greece and Europe will exit the crisis" (@statheramprosta). "A ray of hope for Greece, according to German economist" (@statheramprosta).

7 Selective rational argumentation examples" "Focus mag.: EIB supports small businesses in Greece with 50 million euros" (@statheramprosta). "10,3 bn. Euros surplus in the 2013 travel balance" (@statheramprosta). "30000 new jobs in the next two years" (@statheramprosta).

8 Schols, S. (2014, April 10). A more visual EU elections? Retrieved from http://europedecides.eu/2014/04/a-more-visual-eu-election/

9 Internet World States. Retrieved from http://www.internetworldstats.com/stats4.htm

10 Debating Europe - How is social media changing politics? Retrieved from http://www.debatingeurope.eu/2013/01/22/how-is-social-media-changing-politics/#.U3b9BPmSyfg.

11 European Parliament/Results of the 2014 European elections. Retrieved from http://www.results-elections2014.eu/en/country-results-ro-2014.html.

12 INSCOP survey "The Barometer of Public Opinion – the Truth about Romania." (2013) Retrieved from http://www.inscop.ro/septembrie-2013-increderea-in-institutii/

13 The findings of an INSCOP (Institutul National de Sondare a Cetăţenilor şi a Opiniei Publice/The National Institute of Citizens and Public Opinion Survey) survey show that Romanians continue to trust the Church (over 65 per cent) more than politicians (retrieved from http://www.inscop.ro/septembrie-2013-increderea-in-institutii/).

Related References

Aas, B. G. (2012). What's real? Presence, personality and identity in the real and online virtual world. In N. Zagalo, L. Morgado, & A. Boa-Ventura (Eds.), *Virtual worlds and metaverse platforms: New communication and identity paradigms* (pp. 88–99). Hershey, PA: Information Science Reference; doi:10.4018/978-1-60960-854-5.ch006

Aceti, V., & Luppicini, R. (2013). Exploring the effect of mhealth technologies on communication and information sharing in a pediatric critical care unit: A case study. In J. Tan (Ed.), *Healthcare information technology innovation and sustainability: Frontiers and adoption* (pp. 88–108). Hershey, PA: Medical Information Science Reference; doi:10.4018/978-1-4666-2797-0.ch006

Acilar, A. (2013). Factors affecting mobile phone use among undergraduate students in Turkey: An exploratory analysis. In I. Lee (Ed.), *Strategy, adoption, and competitive advantage of mobile services in the global economy* (pp. 234–246). Hershey, PA: Information Science Reference; doi:10.4018/978-1-4666-1939-5.ch013

Adams, A. (2013). Situated e-learning: Empowerment and barriers to identity changes. In S. Warburton & S. Hatzipanagos (Eds.), *Digital identity and social media* (pp. 159–175). Hershey, PA: Information Science Reference; doi:10.4018/978-1-4666-1915-9.ch012

Adeoye, B. F. (2013). Culturally different learning styles in online learning environments: A case of Nigerian university students. In L. Tomei (Ed.), *Learning tools and teaching approaches through ICT advancements* (pp. 228–240). Hershey, PA: Information Science Reference; doi:10.4018/978-1-4666-2017-9.ch020

Agarwal, N., & Mahata, D. (2013). Grouping the similar among the disconnected bloggers. In G. Xu & L. Li (Eds.), *Social media mining and social network analysis: Emerging research* (pp. 54–71). Hershey, PA: Information Science Reference; doi:10.4018/978-1-4666-2806-9.ch004

Aiken, M., Wang, J., Gu, L., & Paolillo, J. (2013). An exploratory study of how technology supports communication in multilingual groups. In N. Kock (Ed.), *Interdisciplinary applications of electronic collaboration approaches and technologies* (pp. 17–29). Hershey, PA: Information Science Reference; doi:10.4018/978-1-4666-2020-9.ch002

Aikins, S. K., & Chary, M. (2013). Online participation and digital divide: An empirical evaluation of U.S. midwestern municipalities. In *Digital literacy: Concepts, methodologies, tools, and applications* (pp. 63–85). Hershey, PA: Information Science Reference; doi:10.4018/978-1-4666-1852-7.ch004

Al Disi, Z. A., & Albadri, F. (2013). Arab youth and the internet: Educational perspective. In F. Albadri (Ed.), *Information systems applications in the Arab education sector* (pp. 163–178). Hershey, PA: Information Science Reference; doi:10.4018/978-1-4666-1984-5.ch012

Al-Dossary, S., Al-Dulaijan, N., Al-Mansour, S., Al-Zahrani, S., Al-Fridan, M., & Househ, M. (2013). Organ donation and transplantation: Processes, registries, consent, and restrictions in Saudi Arabia. In M. Cruz-Cunha, I. Miranda, & P. Gonçalves (Eds.), *Handbook of research on ICTs for human-centered healthcare and social care services* (pp. 511–528). Hershey, PA: Medical Information Science Reference; doi:10.4018/978-1-4666-3986-7.ch027

Al-Khaffaf, M. M., & Abdellatif, H. J. (2013). The effect of information and communication technology on customer relationship management: Jordan public shareholding companies. In R. Eid (Ed.), *Managing customer trust, satisfaction, and loyalty through information communication technologies* (pp. 342–350). Hershey, PA: Business Science Reference; doi:10.4018/978-1-4666-3631-6.ch020

Al-Nuaim, H. A. (2012). Evaluation of Arab municipal websites. In *Wireless technologies: Concepts, methodologies, tools and applications* (pp. 1170–1185). Hershey, PA: Information Science Reference; doi:10.4018/978-1-61350-101-6.ch505

Al-Nuaim, H. A. (2013). Developing user profiles for interactive online products in practice. In M. Garcia-Ruiz (Ed.), *Cases on usability engineering: Design and development of digital products* (pp. 57–79). Hershey, PA: Information Science Reference; doi:10.4018/978-1-4666-4046-7.ch003

Al Omoush, K. S., Alqirem, R. M., & Shaqrah, A. A. (2013). The driving internal beliefs of household internet adoption among Jordanians and the role of cultural values. In A. Zolait (Ed.), *Technology diffusion and adoption: global complexity, global innovation* (pp. 130–151). Hershey, PA: Information Science Reference; doi:10.4018/978-1-4666-2791-8.ch009

Al-Shqairat, Z. I., & Altarawneh, I. I. (2013). The role of partnership in e-government readiness: The knowledge stations (KSs) initiative in Jordan. In A. Mesquita (Ed.), *User perception and influencing factors of technology in everyday life* (pp. 192–210). Hershey, PA: Information Science Reference; doi:10.4018/978-1-4666-1954-8.ch014

AlBalawi, M. S. (2013). Web-based instructions: An assessment of preparedness of conventional universities in Saudi Arabia. In M. Khosrow-Pour (Ed.), *Cases on assessment and evaluation in education* (pp. 417–451). Hershey, PA: Information Science Reference; doi:10.4018/978-1-4666-2621-8.ch018

Alejos, A. V., Cuiñas, I., Expósito, I., & Sánchez, M. G. (2013). From the farm to fork: Information security accomplishment in a RFID based tracking chain for food sector. In P. Lopez, J. Hernandez-Castro, & T. Li (Eds.), *Security and trends in wireless identification and sensing platform tags: Advancements in RFID* (pp. 237–270). Hershey, PA: Information Science Reference; doi:10.4018/978-1-4666-1990-6.ch010

Alkazemi, M. F., Bowe, B. J., & Blom, R. (2013). Facilitating the Egyptian uprising: A case study of Facebook and Egypt's April 6th youth movement. In N. Azab (Ed.), *Cases on web 2.0 in developing countries: Studies on implementation, application, and use* (pp. 256–282). Hershey, PA: Information Science Reference; doi:10.4018/978-1-4666-2515-0.ch010

Almutairi, M. S. (2012). M-government: Challenges and key success factors – Saudi Arabia case study. In Wireless technologies: Concepts, methodologies, tools and applications (pp. 1698-1717). Hershey, PA: Information Science Reference. doi:10.4018/978-1-61350-101-6.ch611

Alyagout, F., & Siti-Nabiha, A. K. (2013). Public sector transformation: Privatization in Saudi Arabia. In N. Pomazalová (Ed.), *Public sector transformation processes and internet public procurement: Decision support systems* (pp. 17–31). Hershey, PA: Engineering Science Reference; doi:10.4018/978-1-4666-2665-2.ch002

Amirante, A., Castaldi, T., Miniero, L., & Romano, S. P. (2013). Protocol interactions among user agents, application servers, and media servers: Standardization efforts and open issues. In D. Kanellopoulos (Ed.), *Intelligent multimedia technologies for networking applications: Techniques and tools* (pp. 48–63). Hershey, PA: Information Science Reference; doi:10.4018/978-1-4666-2833-5.ch003

Andres, H. P. (2013). Shared mental model development during technology-mediated collaboration. In N. Kock (Ed.), *Interdisciplinary applications of electronic collaboration approaches and technologies* (pp. 125–142). Hershey, PA: Information Science Reference; doi:10.4018/978-1-4666-2020-9.ch009

Andrus, C. H., & Gaynor, M. (2013). Good IT requires good communication. In S. Sarnikar, D. Bennett, & M. Gaynor (Eds.), *Cases on healthcare information technology for patient care management* (pp. 122–125). Hershey, PA: Medical Information Science Reference; doi:10.4018/978-1-4666-2671-3.ch007

Annafari, M. T., & Bohlin, E. (2013). Why is the diffusion of mobile service not an evolutionary process? In I. Lee (Ed.), *Mobile services industries, technologies, and applications in the global economy* (pp. 25–38). Hershey, PA: Information Science Reference; doi:10.4018/978-1-4666-1981-4.ch002

Anupama, S. (2013). Gender evaluation of rural e-governance in India: A case study of E-Gram Suraj (e-rural good governance) scheme1. In *Digital literacy: Concepts, methodologies, tools, and applications* (pp. 1059–1074). Hershey, PA: Information Science Reference; doi:10.4018/978-1-4666-1852-7.ch055

Ariely, G. (2013). Boundaries of socio-technical systems and IT for knowledge development in military environments. In J. Abdelnour-Nocera (Ed.), *Knowledge and technological development effects on organizational and social structures* (pp. 224–238). Hershey, PA: Information Science Reference; doi:10.4018/978-1-4666-2151-0.ch014

Arsenio, A. M. (2013). Intelligent approaches for adaptation and distribution of personalized multimedia content. In D. Kanellopoulos (Ed.), *Intelligent multimedia technologies for networking applications: Techniques and tools* (pp. 197–224). Hershey, PA: Information Science Reference; doi:10.4018/978-1-4666-2833-5.ch008

Artail, H., & Tarhini, T. (2013). Runtime discovery and access of web services in mobile environments. In I. Lee (Ed.), *Mobile services industries, technologies, and applications in the global economy* (pp. 193–213). Hershey, PA: Information Science Reference; doi:10.4018/978-1-4666-1981-4.ch012

Asino, T. I., Wilder, H., & Ferris, S. P. (2013). Innovative use of ICT in Namibia for nationhood: Special emphasis on the Namibian newspaper. In H. Rahman (Ed.), *Cases on progressions and challenges in ICT utilization for citizen-centric governance* (pp. 205–216). Hershey, PA: Information Science Reference; doi:10.4018/978-1-4666-2071-1.ch009

Atici, B., & Bati, U. (2013). Identity of virtual supporters: Constructing identity of Turkish football fans on digital media. In S. Warburton & S. Hatzipanagos (Eds.), *Digital identity and social media* (pp. 256–274). Hershey, PA: Information Science Reference; doi:10.4018/978-1-4666-1915-9.ch018

Azab, N., & Khalifa, N. (2013). Web 2.0 and opportunities for entrepreneurs: How Egyptian entrepreneurs perceive and exploit web 2.0 technologies. In N. Azab (Ed.), *Cases on web 2.0 in developing countries: Studies on implementation, application, and use* (pp. 1–32). Hershey, PA: Information Science Reference; doi:10.4018/978-1-4666-2515-0.ch001

Bainbridge, W. S. (2013). Ancestor veneration avatars. In R. Luppicini (Ed.), *Handbook of research on technoself: Identity in a technological society* (pp. 308–321). Hershey, PA: Information Science Reference; doi:10.4018/978-1-4666-2211-1.ch017

Baporikar, N. (2013). Critical review of academic entrepreneurship in India. In A. Szopa, W. Karwowski, & P. Ordóñez de Pablos (Eds.), *Academic entrepreneurship and technological innovation: A business management perspective* (pp. 29–52). Hershey, PA: Information Science Reference; doi:10.4018/978-1-4666-2116-9.ch002

Barroca, L., & Gimenes, I. M. (2013). Computing postgraduate programmes in the UK and Brazil: Learning from experience in distance education with web 2.0 support. In N. Azab (Ed.), *Cases on web 2.0 in developing countries: Studies on implementation, application, and use* (pp. 147–171). Hershey, PA: Information Science Reference; doi:10.4018/978-1-4666-2515-0.ch006

Barton, S. M. (2013). Facilitating learning by going online: Modernising Islamic teaching and learning in Indonesia. In E. McKay (Ed.), *ePedagogy in online learning: New developments in web mediated human computer interaction* (pp. 74–92). Hershey, PA: Information Science Reference; doi:10.4018/978-1-4666-3649-1.ch005

Barzilai-Nahon, K., Gomez, R., & Ambikar, R. (2013). Conceptualizing a contextual measurement for digital divide/s: Using an integrated narrative. In *Digital literacy: Concepts, methodologies, tools, and applications* (pp. 279–293). Hershey, PA: Information Science Reference; doi:10.4018/978-1-4666-1852-7.ch015

Bénel, A., & Lacour, P. (2012). Towards a participative platform for cultural texts translators. In C. El Morr & P. Maret (Eds.), *Virtual community building and the information society: Current and future directions* (pp. 153–162). Hershey, PA: Information Science Reference; doi:10.4018/978-1-60960-869-9.ch008

Bentley, C. M. (2013). Designing and implementing online collaboration tools in West Africa. In N. Azab (Ed.), *Cases on web 2.0 in developing countries: Studies on implementation, application, and use* (pp. 33–60). Hershey, PA: Information Science Reference; doi:10.4018/978-1-4666-2515-0.ch002

Berg, M. (2012). Checking in at the urban playground: Digital geographies and electronic flâneurs. In F. Comunello (Ed.), *Networked sociability and individualism: Technology for personal and professional relationships* (pp. 169–194). Hershey, PA: Information Science Reference; doi:10.4018/978-1-61350-338-6.ch009

Bers, M. U., & Ettinger, A. B. (2013). Programming robots in kindergarten to express identity: An ethnographic analysis. In *Industrial engineering: Concepts, methodologies, tools, and applications* (pp. 1952–1968). Hershey, PA: Engineering Science Reference; doi:10.4018/978-1-4666-1945-6.ch105

Binsaleh, M., & Hassan, S. (2013). Systems development methodology for mobile commerce applications. In I. Khalil & E. Weippl (Eds.), *Contemporary challenges and solutions for mobile and multimedia technologies* (pp. 146–162). Hershey, PA: Information Science Reference; doi:10.4018/978-1-4666-2163-3.ch009

Bishop, J. (2013). Cooperative e-learning in the multilingual and multicultural school: The role of "classroom 2.0" for increasing participation in education. In P. Pumilia-Gnarini, E. Favaron, E. Pacetti, J. Bishop, & L. Guerra (Eds.), *Handbook of research on didactic strategies and technologies for education: Incorporating advancements* (pp. 137–150). Hershey, PA: Information Science Reference; doi:10.4018/978-1-4666-2122-0.ch013

Bishop, J. (2013). Increasing capital revenue in social networking communities: Building social and economic relationships through avatars and characters. In J. Bishop (Ed.), *Examining the concepts, issues, and implications of internet trolling* (pp. 44–61). Hershey, PA: Information Science Reference; doi:10.4018/978-1-4666-2803-8.ch005

Bishop, J. (2013). Lessons from the emotivate project for increasing take-up of big society and responsible capitalism initiatives. In P. Pumilia-Gnarini, E. Favaron, E. Pacetti, J. Bishop, & L. Guerra (Eds.), *Handbook of research on didactic strategies and technologies for education: Incorporating advancements* (pp. 208–217). Hershey, PA: Information Science Reference; doi:10.4018/978-1-4666-2122-0.ch019

Blau, I. (2013). E-collaboration within, between, and without institutions: Towards better functioning of online groups through networks. In N. Kock (Ed.), *Interdisciplinary applications of electronic collaboration approaches and technologies* (pp. 188–203). Hershey, PA: Information Science Reference; doi:10.4018/978-1-4666-2020-9.ch013

Boskic, N., & Hu, S. (2013). Blended learning: The road to inclusive and global education. In E. Jean Francois (Ed.), *Transcultural blended learning and teaching in postsecondary education* (pp. 283–301). Hershey, PA: Information Science Reference; doi:10.4018/978-1-4666-2014-8.ch015

Botero, A., Karhu, K., & Vihavainen, S. (2012). Exploring the ecosystems and principles of community innovation. In A. Lugmayr, H. Franssila, P. Näränen, O. Sotamaa, J. Vanhala, & Z. Yu (Eds.), *Media in the ubiquitous era: Ambient, social and gaming media* (pp. 216–234). Hershey, PA: Information Science Reference; doi:10.4018/978-1-60960-774-6.ch012

Bowe, B. J., Blom, R., & Freedman, E. (2013). Negotiating boundaries between control and dissent: Free speech, business, and repressitarian governments. In J. Lannon & E. Halpin (Eds.), *Human rights and information communication technologies: Trends and consequences of use* (pp. 36–55). Hershey, PA: Information Science Reference; doi:10.4018/978-1-4666-1918-0.ch003

Brandão, J., Ferreira, T., & Carvalho, V. (2012). An overview on the use of serious games in the military industry and health. In M. Cruz-Cunha (Ed.), *Handbook of research on serious games as educational, business and research tools* (pp. 182–201). Hershey, PA: Information Science Reference; doi:10.4018/978-1-4666-0149-9.ch009

Brost, L. F., & McGinnis, C. (2012). The status of blogging in the republic of Ireland: A case study. In T. Dumova & R. Fiordo (Eds.), *Blogging in the global society: Cultural, political and geographical aspects* (pp. 128–147). Hershey, PA: Information Science Reference; doi:10.4018/978-1-60960-744-9.ch008

Burns, J., Blanchard, M., & Metcalf, A. (2013). Bridging the digital divide in Australia: The potential implications for the mental health of young people experiencing marginalisation. In *Digital literacy: Concepts, methodologies, tools, and applications* (pp. 772–793). Hershey, PA: Information Science Reference; doi:10.4018/978-1-4666-1852-7.ch040

Cagliero, L., & Fiori, A. (2013). News document summarization driven by user-generated content. In G. Xu & L. Li (Eds.), *Social media mining and social network analysis: Emerging research* (pp. 105–126). Hershey, PA: Information Science Reference; doi:10.4018/978-1-4666-2806-9.ch007

Camillo, A., & Di Pietro, L. (2013). Managerial communication in the global cross-cultural context. In B. Christiansen, E. Turkina, & N. Williams (Eds.), *Cultural and technological influences on global business* (pp. 397–419). Hershey, PA: Business Science Reference; doi:10.4018/978-1-4666-3966-9.ch021

Canazza, S., De Poli, G., Rodà, A., & Vidolin, A. (2013). Expressiveness in music performance: Analysis, models, mapping, encoding. In J. Steyn (Ed.), *Structuring music through markup language: Designs and architectures* (pp. 156–186). Hershey, PA: Information Science Reference; doi:10.4018/978-1-4666-2497-9.ch008

Carrasco, J. G., Ovide, E., & Puyal, M. B. (2013). Closing and opening of cultures. In F. García-Peñalvo (Ed.), *Multiculturalism in technology-based education: Case studies on ICT-supported approaches* (pp. 125–142). Hershey, PA: Information Science Reference; doi:10.4018/978-1-4666-2101-5.ch008

Carreras, I., Zanardi, A., Salvadori, E., & Miorandi, D. (2013). A distributed monitoring framework for opportunistic communication systems: An experimental approach. In V. De Florio (Ed.), *Innovations and approaches for resilient and adaptive systems* (pp. 220–236). Hershey, PA: Information Science Reference; doi:10.4018/978-1-4666-2056-8.ch013

Carter, M., Grover, V., & Thatcher, J. B. (2013). Mobile devices and the self: developing the concept of mobile phone identity. In I. Lee (Ed.), *Strategy, adoption, and competitive advantage of mobile services in the global economy* (pp. 150–164). Hershey, PA: Information Science Reference; doi:10.4018/978-1-4666-1939-5.ch008

Caruso, F., Giuffrida, G., Reforgiato, D., & Zarba, C. (2013). Recommendation systems for mobile devices. In I. Lee (Ed.), *Mobile services industries, technologies, and applications in the global economy* (pp. 221–242). Hershey, PA: Information Science Reference; doi:10.4018/978-1-4666-1981-4.ch014

Casamassima, L. (2013). eTwinning project: A virtual orchestra. In P. Pumilia-Gnarini, E. Favaron, E. Pacetti, J. Bishop, & L. Guerra (Eds.) Handbook of research on didactic strategies and technologies for education: Incorporating advancements (pp. 703-709). Hershey, PA: Information Science Reference. doi:10.4018/978-1-4666-2122-0.ch061

Caschera, M. C., D'Ulizia, A., Ferri, F., & Grifoni, P. (2012). Multiculturality and multimodal languages. In G. Ghinea, F. Andres, & S. Gulliver (Eds.), *Multiple sensorial media advances and applications: New developments in MulSeMedia* (pp. 99–114). Hershey, PA: Information Science Reference; doi:10.4018/978-1-60960-821-7.ch005

Catagnus, R. M., & Hantula, D. A. (2013). The virtual individual education plan (IEP) team: Using online collaboration to develop a behavior intervention plan. In N. Kock (Ed.), *Interdisciplinary applications of electronic collaboration approaches and technologies* (pp. 30–45). Hershey, PA: Information Science Reference; doi:10.4018/978-1-4666-2020-9.ch003

Ch'ng, E. (2013). The mirror between two worlds: 3D surface computing for objects and environments. In D. Harrison (Ed.), *Digital media and technologies for virtual artistic spaces* (pp. 166–185). Hershey, PA: Information Science Reference; doi:10.4018/978-1-4666-2961-5.ch013

Chand, A. (2013). Reducing digital divide: The case of the 'people first network' (PFNet) in the Solomon Islands. In *Digital literacy: Concepts, methodologies, tools, and applications* (pp. 1571–1605). Hershey, PA: Information Science Reference; doi:10.4018/978-1-4666-1852-7.ch083

Chatterjee, S. (2013). Ethical behaviour in technology-mediated communication. In J. Bishop (Ed.), *Examining the concepts, issues, and implications of internet trolling* (pp. 1–9). Hershey, PA: Information Science Reference; doi:10.4018/978-1-4666-2803-8.ch001

Chen, C., Chao, H., Wu, T., Fan, C., Chen, J., Chen, Y., & Hsu, J. (2013). IoT-IMS communication platform for future internet. In V. De Florio (Ed.), *Innovations and approaches for resilient and adaptive systems* (pp. 68–86). Hershey, PA: Information Science Reference; doi:10.4018/978-1-4666-2056-8.ch004

Chen, J., & Hu, X. (2013). Smartphone market in China: Challenges, opportunities, and promises. In I. Lee (Ed.), *Mobile services industries, technologies, and applications in the global economy* (pp. 120–132). Hershey, PA: Information Science Reference; doi:10.4018/978-1-4666-1981-4.ch008

Chen, Y., Lee, B., & Kirk, R. M. (2013). Internet use among older adults: Constraints and opportunities. In R. Zheng, R. Hill, & M. Gardner (Eds.), *Engaging older adults with modern technology: Internet use and information access needs* (pp. 124–141). Hershey, PA: Information Science Reference; doi:10.4018/978-1-4666-1966-1.ch007

Cheong, P. H., & Martin, J. N. (2013). Cultural implications of e-learning access (and divides): Teaching an intercultural communication course online. In A. Edmundson (Ed.), *Cases on cultural implications and considerations in online learning* (pp. 82–100). Hershey, PA: Information Science Reference; doi:10.4018/978-1-4666-1885-5.ch005

Chhanabhai, P., & Holt, A. (2013). The changing world of ICT and health: Crossing the digital divide. In *Digital literacy: Concepts, methodologies, tools, and applications* (pp. 794–811). Hershey, PA: Information Science Reference; doi:10.4018/978-1-4666-1852-7.ch041

Chuling, W., Hua, C. M., & Chee, C. J. (2012). Investigating the demise of radio and television broadcasting. In R. Sharma, M. Tan, & F. Pereira (Eds.), *Understanding the interactive digital media marketplace: Frameworks, platforms, communities and issues* (pp. 392–405). Hershey, PA: Information Science Reference; doi:10.4018/978-1-61350-147-4.ch031

Ciaramitaro, B. L. (2012). Introduction to mobile technologies. In B. Ciaramitaro (Ed.), *Mobile technology consumption: Opportunities and challenges* (pp. 1–15). Hershey, PA: Information Science Reference; doi:10.4018/978-1-61350-150-4.ch001

Cicconetti, C., Mambrini, R., & Rossi, A. (2013). A survey of wireless backhauling solutions for ITS. In R. Daher & A. Vinel (Eds.), *Roadside networks for vehicular communications: Architectures, applications, and test fields* (pp. 57–70). Hershey, PA: Information Science Reference; doi:10.4018/978-1-4666-2223-4.ch003

Ciptasari, R. W., & Sakurai, K. (2013). Multimedia copyright protection scheme based on the direct feature-based method. In K. Kondo (Ed.), *Multimedia information hiding technologies and methodologies for controlling data* (pp. 412–439). Hershey, PA: Information Science Reference; doi:10.4018/978-1-4666-2217-3.ch019

Code, J. (2013). Agency and identity in social media. In S. Warburton & S. Hatzipanagos (Eds.), *Digital identity and social media* (pp. 37–57). Hershey, PA: Information Science Reference; doi:10.4018/978-1-4666-1915-9.ch004

Comunello, F. (2013). From the digital divide to multiple divides: Technology, society, and new media skills. In *Digital literacy: Concepts, methodologies, tools, and applications* (pp. 1622–1639). Hershey, PA: Information Science Reference; doi:10.4018/978-1-4666-1852-7.ch085

Consonni, A. (2013). About the use of the DMs in CLIL classes. In F. García-Peñalvo (Ed.), *Multiculturalism in technology-based education: Case studies on ICT-supported approaches* (pp. 9–27). Hershey, PA: Information Science Reference; doi:10.4018/978-1-4666-2101-5.ch002

Constant, J. (2012). Digital approaches to visualization of geometric problems in wooden sangaku tablets. In A. Ursyn (Ed.), *Biologically-inspired computing for the arts: Scientific data through graphics* (pp. 240–253). Hershey, PA: Information Science Reference; doi:10.4018/978-1-4666-0942-6.ch013

Cossiavelou, V., Bantimaroudis, P., Kavakli, E., & Illia, L. (2013). The media gatekeeping model updated by R and I in ICTs: The case of wireless communications in media coverage of the olympic games. In M. Bartolacci & S. Powell (Eds.), *Advancements and innovations in wireless communications and network technologies* (pp. 262–288). Hershey, PA: Information Science Reference; doi:10.4018/978-1-4666-2154-1.ch019

Cropf, R. A., Benmamoun, M., & Kalliny, M. (2013). The role of web 2.0 in the Arab Spring. In N. Azab (Ed.), *Cases on web 2.0 in developing countries: Studies on implementation, application, and use* (pp. 76–108). Hershey, PA: Information Science Reference; doi:10.4018/978-1-4666-2515-0.ch004

Cucinotta, A., Minnolo, A. L., & Puliafito, A. (2013). Design and implementation of an event-based RFID middleware. In N. Karmakar (Ed.), *Advanced RFID systems, security, and applications* (pp. 110–131). Hershey, PA: Information Science Reference; doi:10.4018/978-1-4666-2080-3.ch006

D'Andrea, A., Ferri, F., & Grifoni, P. (2013). Assessing e-health in Africa: Web 2.0 applications. In N. Azab (Ed.), *Cases on web 2.0 in developing countries: Studies on implementation, application, and use* (pp. 442–467). Hershey, PA: Information Science Reference; doi:10.4018/978-1-4666-2515-0.ch016

de Guinea, A. O. (2013). The level paradox of e-collaboration: Dangers and solutions. In N. Kock (Ed.), *Interdisciplinary applications of electronic collaboration approaches and technologies* (pp. 166–187). Hershey, PA: Information Science Reference; doi:10.4018/978-1-4666-2020-9.ch012

Dhar-Bhattacharjee, S., & Takruri-Rizk, H. (2012). An Indo-British comparison. In C. Romm Livermore (Ed.), *Gender and social computing: Interactions, differences and relationships* (pp. 50–71). Hershey, PA: Information Science Publishing; doi:10.4018/978-1-60960-759-3.ch004

Díaz-Foncea, M., & Marcuello, C. (2013). ANOBIUM, SL: The use of the ICT as niche of employment and as tool for developing the social market. In T. Torres-Coronas & M. Vidal-Blasco (Eds.), *Social e-enterprise: Value creation through ICT* (pp. 221–242). Hershey, PA: Information Science Reference; doi:10.4018/978-1-4666-2667-6.ch013

Díaz-González, M., Froufe, N. Q., Brena, A. G., & Pumarola, F. (2013). Uses and implementation of social media at university: The case of schools of communication in Spain. In B. Pătruţ, M. Pătruţ, & C. Cmeciu (Eds.), *Social media and the new academic environment: Pedagogical challenges* (pp. 204–222). Hershey, PA: Information Science Reference; doi:10.4018/978-1-4666-2851-9.ch010

Ditsa, G., Alwahaishi, S., Al-Kobaisi, S., & Snášel, V. (2013). A comparative study of the effects of culture on the deployment of information technology. In A. Zolait (Ed.), *Technology diffusion and adoption: Global complexity, global innovation* (pp. 77–90). Hershey, PA: Information Science Reference; doi:10.4018/978-1-4666-2791-8.ch006

Donaldson, O., & Duggan, E. W. (2013). Assessing mobile value-added preference structures: The case of a developing country. In I. Lee (Ed.), *Strategy, adoption, and competitive advantage of mobile services in the global economy* (pp. 349–370). Hershey, PA: Information Science Reference; doi:10.4018/978-1-4666-1939-5.ch019

Douai, A. (2013). "In YouTube we trust": Video exchange and Arab human rights. In J. Lannon & E. Halpin (Eds.), *Human rights and information communication technologies: Trends and consequences of use* (pp. 57–71). Hershey, PA: Information Science Reference; doi:10.4018/978-1-4666-1918-0.ch004

Dromzée, C., Laborie, S., & Roose, P. (2013). A semantic generic profile for multimedia document adaptation. In D. Kanellopoulos (Ed.), *Intelligent multimedia technologies for networking applications: Techniques and tools* (pp. 225–246). Hershey, PA: Information Science Reference; doi:10.4018/978-1-4666-2833-5.ch009

Drucker, S., & Gumpert, G. (2012). The urban communication infrastructure: Global connection and local detachment. In *Wireless technologies: Concepts, methodologies, tools and applications* (pp. 1150–1169). Hershey, PA: Information Science Reference; doi:10.4018/978-1-61350-101-6.ch504

Drula, G. (2013). Media and communication research facing social media. In M. Pătruţ & B. Pătruţ (Eds.), *Social media in higher education: Teaching in web 2.0* (pp. 371–392). Hershey, PA: Information Science Reference; doi:10.4018/978-1-4666-2970-7.ch019

Dueck, J., & Rempel, M. (2013). Human rights and technology: Lessons from Alice in Wonderland. In J. Lannon & E. Halpin (Eds.), *Human rights and information communication technologies: Trends and consequences of use* (pp. 1–20). Hershey, PA: Information Science Reference; doi:10.4018/978-1-4666-1918-0.ch001

Dumova, T. (2012). Social interaction technologies and the future of blogging. In T. Dumova & R. Fiordo (Eds.), *Blogging in the global society: Cultural, political and geographical aspects* (pp. 249–274). Hershey, PA: Information Science Reference; doi:10.4018/978-1-60960-744-9.ch015

Dunn, H. S. (2013). Information literacy and the digital divide: Challenging e-exclusion in the global south. In *Digital literacy: Concepts, methodologies, tools, and applications* (pp. 20–38). Hershey, PA: Information Science Reference; doi:10.4018/978-1-4666-1852-7.ch002

Elias, N. (2013). Immigrants' internet use and identity from an intergenerational perspective: Immigrant senior citizens and youngsters from the former Soviet Union in Israel. In R. Luppicini (Ed.), *Handbook of research on technoself: Identity in a technological society* (pp. 293–307). Hershey, PA: Information Science Reference; doi:10.4018/978-1-4666-2211-1.ch016

Elizabeth, L. S., Ismail, N., & Tun, M. S. (2012). The future of the printed book. In R. Sharma, M. Tan, & F. Pereira (Eds.), *Understanding the interactive digital media marketplace: Frameworks, platforms, communities and issues* (pp. 416–429). Hershey, PA: Information Science Reference; doi:10.4018/978-1-61350-147-4.ch033

Erne, R. (2012). Knowledge worker performance in a cross-industrial perspective. In S. Brüggemann & C. d'Amato (Eds.), *Collaboration and the semantic web: Social networks, knowledge networks, and knowledge resources* (pp. 297–321). Hershey, PA: Information Science Reference; doi:10.4018/978-1-4666-0894-8.ch015

Ertl, B., Helling, K., & Kikis-Papadakis, K. (2012). The impact of gender in ICT usage, education and career: Comparisons between Greece and Germany. In C. Romm Livermore (Ed.), *Gender and social computing: Interactions, differences and relationships* (pp. 98–119). Hershey, PA: Information Science Publishing; doi:10.4018/978-1-60960-759-3.ch007

Estapé-Dubreuil, G., & Torreguitart-Mirada, C. (2013). ICT adoption in the small and medium-size social enterprises in Spain: Opportunity or priority? In T. Torres-Coronas & M. Vidal-Blasco (Eds.), *Social e-enterprise: Value creation through ICT* (pp. 200–220). Hershey, PA: Information Science Reference; doi:10.4018/978-1-4666-2667-6.ch012

Eze, U. C., & Poong, Y. S. (2013). Consumers' intention to use mobile commerce and the moderating roles of gender and income. In I. Lee (Ed.), *Strategy, adoption, and competitive advantage of mobile services in the global economy* (pp. 127–148). Hershey, PA: Information Science Reference; doi:10.4018/978-1-4666-1939-5.ch007

Farrell, R., Danis, C., Erickson, T., Ellis, J., Christensen, J., Bailey, M., & Kellogg, W. A. (2012). A picture and a thousand words: Visual scaffolding for mobile communication in developing regions. In W. Hu (Ed.), *Emergent trends in personal, mobile, and handheld computing technologies* (pp. 341–354). Hershey, PA: Information Science Reference; doi:10.4018/978-1-4666-0921-1.ch020

Fidler, C. S., Kanaan, R. K., & Rogerson, S. (2013). Barriers to e-government implementation in Jordan: The role of wasta. In A. Mesquita (Ed.), *User perception and influencing factors of technology in everyday life* (pp. 179–191). Hershey, PA: Information Science Reference; doi:10.4018/978-1-4666-1954-8.ch013

Filho, J. R. (2013). ICT and human rights in Brazil: From military to digital dictatorship. In J. Lannon & E. Halpin (Eds.), *Human rights and information communication technologies: Trends and consequences of use* (pp. 86–99). Hershey, PA: Information Science Reference; doi:10.4018/978-1-4666-1918-0.ch006

Fiordo, R. (2012). Analyzing blogs: A hermeneutic perspective. In T. Dumova & R. Fiordo (Eds.), *Blogging in the global society: Cultural, political and geographical aspects* (pp. 231–248). Hershey, PA: Information Science Reference; doi:10.4018/978-1-60960-744-9.ch014

Fischer, G., & Herrmann, T. (2013). Socio-technical systems: A meta-design perspective. In J. Abdelnour-Nocera (Ed.), *Knowledge and technological development effects on organizational and social structures* (pp. 1–36). Hershey, PA: Information Science Reference; doi:10.4018/978-1-4666-2151-0.ch001

Fleury, M., & Al-Jobouri, L. (2013). Techniques and tools for adaptive video streaming. In D. Kanellopoulos (Ed.), *Intelligent multimedia technologies for networking applications: Techniques and tools* (pp. 65–101). Hershey, PA: Information Science Reference; doi:10.4018/978-1-4666-2833-5.ch004

Freeman, I., & Freeman, A. (2013). Capacity building for different abilities using ICT. In T. Torres-Coronas & M. Vidal-Blasco (Eds.), *Social e-enterprise: Value creation through ICT* (pp. 67–82). Hershey, PA: Information Science Reference; doi:10.4018/978-1-4666-2667-6.ch004

Gallon, R. (2013). Communication, culture, and technology: Learning strategies for the unteachable. In R. Lansiquot (Ed.), *Cases on interdisciplinary research trends in science, technology, engineering, and mathematics: Studies on urban classrooms* (pp. 91–106). Hershey, PA: Information Science Reference; doi:10.4018/978-1-4666-2214-2.ch005

García, M., Lloret, J., Bellver, I., & Tomás, J. (2013). Intelligent IPTV distribution for smart phones. In D. Kanellopoulos (Ed.), *Intelligent multimedia technologies for networking applications: Techniques and tools* (pp. 318–347). Hershey, PA: Information Science Reference; doi:10.4018/978-1-4666-2833-5.ch013

García-Plaza, A. P., Zubiaga, A., Fresno, V., & Martínez, R. (2013). Tag cloud reorganization: Finding groups of related tags on delicious. In G. Xu & L. Li (Eds.), *Social media mining and social network analysis: Emerging research* (pp. 140–155). Hershey, PA: Information Science Reference; doi:10.4018/978-1-4666-2806-9.ch009

Gerpott, T. J. (2013). Attribute perceptions as factors explaining mobile internet acceptance of cellular customers in Germany: An empirical study comparing actual and potential adopters with distinct categories of access appliances. In I. Lee (Ed.), *Strategy, adoption, and competitive advantage of mobile services in the global economy* (pp. 19–48). Hershey, PA: Information Science Reference; doi:10.4018/978-1-4666-1939-5.ch002

Giambona, G. J., & Birchall, D. W. (2012). Collaborative e-learning and ICT tools to develop SME managers: An Italian case. In *Wireless technologies: Concepts, methodologies, tools and applications* (pp. 1606–1617). Hershey, PA: Information Science Reference; doi:10.4018/978-1-61350-101-6.ch605

Giannakos, M. N., Pateli, A. G., & Pappas, I. O. (2013). Identifying the direct effect of experience and the moderating effect of satisfaction in the Greek online market. In A. Scupola (Ed.), *Mobile opportunities and applications for e-service innovations* (pp. 77–97). Hershey, PA: Information Science Reference; doi:10.4018/978-1-4666-2654-6.ch005

Giorda, M., & Guerrisi, M. (2013). Educating to democracy and social participation through a "history of religion" course. In P. Pumilia-Gnarini, E. Favaron, E. Pacetti, J. Bishop, & L. Guerra (Eds.), *Handbook of research on didactic strategies and technologies for education: Incorporating advancements* (pp. 152–161). Hershey, PA: Information Science Reference; doi:10.4018/978-1-4666-2122-0.ch014

Goggins, S., Schmidt, M., Guajardo, J., & Moore, J. L. (2013). 3D virtual worlds: Assessing the experience and informing design. In B. Medlin (Ed.), *Integrations of technology utilization and social dynamics in organizations* (pp. 194–213). Hershey, PA: Information Science Reference; doi:10.4018/978-1-4666-1948-7.ch012

Gold, N. (2012). Rebels, heretics, and exiles: Blogging among estranged and questioning American Hasidim. In T. Dumova & R. Fiordo (Eds.), *Blogging in the global society: Cultural, political and geographical aspects* (pp. 108–127). Hershey, PA: Information Science Reference; doi:10.4018/978-1-60960-744-9.ch007

Görgü, L., Wan, J., O'Hare, G. M., & O'Grady, M. J. (2013). Enabling mobile service provision with sensor networks. In I. Lee (Ed.), *Mobile services industries, technologies, and applications in the global economy* (pp. 175–192). Hershey, PA: Information Science Reference; doi:10.4018/978-1-4666-1981-4.ch011

Gregory, S. J. (2013). Evolution of mobile services: An analysis. In I. Lee (Ed.), *Mobile services industries, technologies, and applications in the global economy* (pp. 104–119). Hershey, PA: Information Science Reference; doi:10.4018/978-1-4666-1981-4.ch007

Grieve, G. P., & Heston, K. (2012). Finding liquid salvation: Using the Cardean ethnographic method to document second life residents and religious cloud communities. In N. Zagalo, L. Morgado, & A. Boa-Ventura (Eds.), *Virtual worlds and metaverse platforms: New communication and identity paradigms* (pp. 288–305). Hershey, PA: Information Science Reference; doi:10.4018/978-1-60960-854-5.ch019

Guha, S., Thakur, B., Konar, T. S., & Chakrabarty, S. (2013). Web enabled design collaboration in India. In N. Kock (Ed.), *Interdisciplinary applications of electronic collaboration approaches and technologies* (pp. 96–111). Hershey, PA: Information Science Reference; doi:10.4018/978-1-4666-2020-9.ch007

Gulati, G. J., Yates, D. J., & Tawileh, A. (2013). Explaining the global digital divide: The impact of public policy initiatives on e-government capacity and reach worldwide. In *Digital literacy: Concepts, methodologies, tools, and applications* (pp. 39–62). Hershey, PA: Information Science Reference; doi:10.4018/978-1-4666-1852-7.ch003

Gupta, J. (2013). Digital library initiatives in India. In T. Ashraf & P. Gulati (Eds.), *Design, development, and management of resources for digital library services* (pp. 80–93). Hershey, PA: Information Science Reference; doi:10.4018/978-1-4666-2500-6.ch008

Gururajan, R., Hafeez-Baig, A., Danaher, P. A., & De George-Walker, L. (2012). Student perceptions and uses of wireless handheld devices: Implications for implementing blended and mobile learning in an Australian university. In *Wireless technologies: Concepts, methodologies, tools and applications* (pp. 1323–1338). Hershey, PA: Information Science Reference; doi:10.4018/978-1-61350-101-6.ch512

Gwilt, I. (2013). Data-objects: Sharing the attributes and properties of digital and material culture to creatively interpret complex information. In D. Harrison (Ed.), *Digital media and technologies for virtual artistic spaces* (pp. 14–26). Hershey, PA: Information Science Reference; doi:10.4018/978-1-4666-2961-5.ch002

Hackley, D. C., & Leidman, M. B. (2013). Integrating learning management systems in K-12 supplemental religious education. In A. Ritzhaupt & S. Kumar (Eds.), *Cases on educational technology implementation for facilitating learning* (pp. 1–22). Hershey, PA: Information Science Reference; doi:10.4018/978-1-4666-3676-7.ch001

Hale, J. R., & Fields, D. (2013). A cross-cultural measure of servant leadership behaviors. In M. Bocarnea, R. Reynolds, & J. Baker (Eds.), *Online instruments, data collection, and electronic measurements: Organizational advancements* (pp. 152–163). Hershey, PA: Information Science Reference; doi:10.4018/978-1-4666-2172-5.ch009

Hanewald, R. (2012). Using mobile technologies as research tools: Pragmatics, possibilities and problems. In *Wireless technologies: Concepts, methodologies, tools and applications* (pp. 130–150). Hershey, PA: Information Science Reference; doi:10.4018/978-1-61350-101-6.ch108

Hanewald, R. (2013). Professional development with and for emerging technologies: A case study with Asian languages and cultural studies teachers in Australia. In J. Keengwe (Ed.), *Pedagogical applications and social effects of mobile technology integration* (pp. 175–192). Hershey, PA: Information Science Reference; doi:10.4018/978-1-4666-2985-1.ch010

Hayhoe, S. (2012). Non-visual programming, perceptual culture and mulsemedia: Case studies of five blind computer programmers. In G. Ghinea, F. Andres, & S. Gulliver (Eds.), *Multiple sensorial media advances and applications: New developments in MulSeMedia* (pp. 80–98). Hershey, PA: Information Science Reference; doi:10.4018/978-1-60960-821-7.ch004

Henschke, J. A. (2013). Nation building through andragogy and lifelong learning: On the cutting edge educationally, economically, and governmentally. In V. Wang (Ed.), *Handbook of research on technologies for improving the 21st century workforce: Tools for lifelong learning* (pp. 480–506). Hershey, PA: Information Science Publishing; doi:10.4018/978-1-4666-2181-7.ch030

Hermida, J. M., Meliá, S., Montoyo, A., & Gómez, J. (2013). Developing rich internet applications as social sites on the semantic web: A model-driven approach. In D. Chiu (Ed.), *Mobile and web innovations in systems and service-oriented engineering* (pp. 134–155). Hershey, PA: Information Science Reference; doi:10.4018/978-1-4666-2470-2.ch008

Hernández-García, Á., Agudo-Peregrina, Á. F., & Iglesias-Pradas, S. (2013). Adoption of mobile video-call service: An exploratory study. In I. Lee (Ed.), *Strategy, adoption, and competitive advantage of mobile services in the global economy* (pp. 49–72). Hershey, PA: Information Science Reference; doi:10.4018/978-1-4666-1939-5.ch003

Hesapci-Sanaktekin, O., & Somer, I. (2013). Mobile communication: A study on smart phone and mobile application use. In I. Lee (Ed.), *Strategy, adoption, and competitive advantage of mobile services in the global economy* (pp. 217–233). Hershey, PA: Information Science Reference; doi:10.4018/978-1-4666-1939-5.ch012

Hill, S. R., Troshani, I., & Freeman, S. (2013). An eclectic perspective on the internationalization of Australian mobile services SMEs. In I. Lee (Ed.), *Mobile services industries, technologies, and applications in the global economy* (pp. 55–73). Hershey, PA: Information Science Reference; doi:10.4018/978-1-4666-1981-4.ch004

Ho, V. (2013). The need for identity construction in computer-mediated professional communication: A Community of practice perspective. In R. Luppicini (Ed.), *Handbook of research on technoself: Identity in a technological society* (pp. 502–530). Hershey, PA: Information Science Reference; doi:10.4018/978-1-4666-2211-1.ch027

Hudson, H. E. (2013). Challenges facing municipal wireless: Case studies from San Francisco and Silicon Valley. In A. Abdelaal (Ed.), *Social and economic effects of community wireless networks and infrastructures* (pp. 12–26). Hershey, PA: Information Science Reference; doi:10.4018/978-1-4666-2997-4.ch002

Humphreys, S. (2012). Unravelling intellectual property in a specialist social networking site. In A. Lugmayr, H. Franssila, P. Näränen, O. Sotamaa, J. Vanhala, & Z. Yu (Eds.), *Media in the ubiquitous era: Ambient, social and gaming media* (pp. 248–266). Hershey, PA: Information Science Reference; doi:10.4018/978-1-60960-774-6.ch015

Iglesias, A., Ruiz-Mezcua, B., López, J. F., & Figueroa, D. C. (2013). New communication technologies for inclusive education in and outside the classroom. In D. Griol Barres, Z. Callejas Carrión, & R. Delgado (Eds.), *Technologies for inclusive education: Beyond traditional integration approaches* (pp. 271–284). Hershey, PA: Information Science Reference; doi:10.4018/978-1-4666-2530-3.ch013

Igun, S. E. (2013). Gender and national information and communication technology (ICT) policies in Africa. In B. Maumbe & J. Okello (Eds.), *Technology, sustainability, and rural development in Africa* (pp. 284–297). Hershey, PA: Information Science Reference; doi:10.4018/978-1-4666-3607-1.ch018

Ikolo, V. E. (2013). Gender digital divide and national ICT policies in Africa. In *Digital literacy: Concepts, methodologies, tools, and applications* (pp. 812–832). Hershey, PA: Information Science Reference; doi:10.4018/978-1-4666-1852-7.ch042

Imran, A., & Gregor, S. (2013). A process model for successful e-government adoption in the least developed countries: A case of Bangladesh. In *Digital literacy: Concepts, methodologies, tools, and applications* (pp. 213–241). Hershey, PA: Information Science Reference; doi:10.4018/978-1-4666-1852-7.ch012

Ionescu, A. (2013). ICTs and gender-based rights. In J. Lannon & E. Halpin (Eds.), *Human rights and information communication technologies: Trends and consequences of use* (pp. 214–234). Hershey, PA: Information Science Reference; doi:10.4018/978-1-4666-1918-0.ch013

Iyamu, T. (2013). The impact of organisational politics on the implementation of IT strategy: South African case in context. In J. Abdelnour-Nocera (Ed.), *Knowledge and technological development effects on organizational and social structures* (pp. 167–193). Hershey, PA: Information Science Reference; doi:10.4018/978-1-4666-2151-0.ch011

Jadhav, V. G. (2013). Integration of digital reference service for scholarly communication in digital libraries. In T. Ashraf & P. Gulati (Eds.), *Design, development, and management of resources for digital library services* (pp. 13–20). Hershey, PA: Information Science Reference; doi:10.4018/978-1-4666-2500-6.ch002

Jäkälä, M., & Berki, E. (2013). Communities, communication, and online identities. In S. Warburton & S. Hatzipanagos (Eds.), *Digital identity and social media* (pp. 1–13). Hershey, PA: Information Science Reference; doi:10.4018/978-1-4666-1915-9.ch001

Janneck, M., & Staar, H. (2013). Playing virtual power games: Micro-political processes in inter-organizational networks. In B. Medlin (Ed.), *Integrations of technology utilization and social dynamics in organizations* (pp. 171–192). Hershey, PA: Information Science Reference; doi:10.4018/978-1-4666-1948-7.ch011

Januska, I. M. (2013). Communication as a key factor in cooperation success and virtual enterprise paradigm support. In P. Renna (Ed.), *Production and manufacturing system management: Coordination approaches and multi-site planning* (pp. 145–161). Hershey, PA: Engineering Science Reference; doi:10.4018/978-1-4666-2098-8.ch008

Jayasingh, S., & Eze, U. C. (2013). Consumers' adoption of mobile coupons in Malaysia. In I. Lee (Ed.), *Strategy, adoption, and competitive advantage of mobile services in the global economy* (pp. 90–111). Hershey, PA: Information Science Reference; doi:10.4018/978-1-4666-1939-5.ch005

Jean Francois, E. (2013). Transculturality. In E. Jean Francois (Ed.), *Transcultural blended learning and teaching in postsecondary education* (pp. 1–14). Hershey, PA: Information Science Reference; doi:10.4018/978-1-4666-2014-8.ch001

Jensen, S. S. (2012). User-driven content creation in second life a source of innovation? Three case studies of business and public service. In N. Zagalo, L. Morgado, & A. Boa-Ventura (Eds.), *Virtual worlds and metaverse platforms: New communication and identity paradigms* (pp. 1–15). Hershey, PA: Information Science Reference; doi:10.4018/978-1-60960-854-5.ch001

Johnston, W. J., Komulainen, H., Ristola, A., & Ulkuniemi, P. (2013). Mobile advertising in small retailer firms: How to make the most of it. In I. Lee (Ed.), *Strategy, adoption, and competitive advantage of mobile services in the global economy* (pp. 283–298). Hershey, PA: Information Science Reference; doi:10.4018/978-1-4666-1939-5.ch016

Kadas, G., & Chatzimisios, P. (2013). The role of roadside assistance in vehicular communication networks: Security, quality of service, and routing issues. In R. Daher & A. Vinel (Eds.), *Roadside networks for vehicular communications: Architectures, applications, and test fields* (pp. 1–37). Hershey, PA: Information Science Reference; doi:10.4018/978-1-4666-2223-4.ch001

Kale, S. H., & Spence, M. T. (2012). A trination analysis of social exchange relationships in e-dating. In C. Romm Livermore (Ed.), *Gender and social computing: Interactions, differences and relationships* (pp. 257–271). Hershey, PA: Information Science Publishing; doi:10.4018/978-1-60960-759-3.ch015

Kamoun, F. (2013). Mobile NFC services: Adoption factors and a typology of business models. In I. Lee (Ed.), *Mobile services industries, technologies, and applications in the global economy* (pp. 254–272). Hershey, PA: Information Science Reference; doi:10.4018/978-1-4666-1981-4.ch016

Kaneda, K., & Iwamura, K. (2013). New proposals for data hiding in paper media. In K. Kondo (Ed.), *Multimedia information hiding technologies and methodologies for controlling data* (pp. 258–285). Hershey, PA: Information Science Reference; doi:10.4018/978-1-4666-2217-3.ch012

Kastell, K. (2013). Seamless communication to mobile devices in vehicular wireless networks. In O. Strobel (Ed.), *Communication in transportation systems* (pp. 324–342). Hershey, PA: Information Science Reference; doi:10.4018/978-1-4666-2976-9.ch012

Kaye, B. K., & Johnson, T. J. (2012). Net gain? Selective exposure and selective avoidance of social network sites. In F. Comunello (Ed.), *Networked sociability and individualism: Technology for personal and professional relationships* (pp. 218–237). Hershey, PA: Information Science Reference; doi:10.4018/978-1-61350-338-6.ch011

Kaye, B. K., Johnson, T. J., & Muhlberger, P. (2012). Blogs as a source of democratic deliberation. In T. Dumova & R. Fiordo (Eds.), *Blogging in the global society: Cultural, political and geographical aspects* (pp. 1–18). Hershey, PA: Information Science Reference; doi:10.4018/978-1-60960-744-9.ch001

Kefi, H., Mlaiki, A., & Peterson, R. L. (2013). IT offshoring: Trust views from client and vendor perspectives. In J. Wang (Ed.), *Perspectives and techniques for improving information technology project management* (pp. 113–130). Hershey, PA: Information Science Reference; doi:10.4018/978-1-4666-2800-7.ch009

Khan, N. A., & Batoo, M. F. (2013). Stone inscriptions of Srinagar: A digital panorama. In T. Ashraf & P. Gulati (Eds.), *Design, development, and management of resources for digital library services* (pp. 58–79). Hershey, PA: Information Science Reference; doi:10.4018/978-1-4666-2500-6.ch007

Kim, P. (2012). "Stay out of the way! My kid is video blogging through a phone!": A lesson learned from math tutoring social media for children in underserved communities. In *Wireless technologies: Concepts, methodologies, tools and applications* (pp. 1415–1428). Hershey, PA: Information Science Reference; doi:10.4018/978-1-61350-101-6.ch517

Kisubi, A. T. (2013). A critical perspective on the challenges for blended learning and teaching in Africa's higher education. In E. Jean Francois (Ed.), *Transcultural blended learning and teaching in postsecondary education* (pp. 145–168). Hershey, PA: Information Science Reference; doi:10.4018/978-1-4666-2014-8.ch009

Koole, M., & Parchoma, G. (2013). The web of identity: A model of digital identity formation in networked learning environments. In S. Warburton & S. Hatzipanagos (Eds.), *Digital identity and social media* (pp. 14–28). Hershey, PA: Information Science Reference; doi:10.4018/978-1-4666-1915-9.ch002

Kordaki, M., Gorghiu, G., Bîzoi, M., & Glava, A. (2012). Collaboration within multinational learning communities: The case of the virtual community collaborative space for sciences education European project. In A. Juan, T. Daradoumis, M. Roca, S. Grasman, & J. Faulin (Eds.), *Collaborative and distributed e-research: Innovations in technologies, strategies and applications* (pp. 206–226). Hershey, PA: Information Science Reference; doi:10.4018/978-1-4666-0125-3.ch010

Kovács, J., Bokor, L., Kanizsai, Z., & Imre, S. (2013). Review of advanced mobility solutions for multimedia networking in IPv6. In D. Kanellopoulos (Ed.), *Intelligent multimedia technologies for networking applications: Techniques and tools* (pp. 25–47). Hershey, PA: Information Science Reference; doi:10.4018/978-1-4666-2833-5.ch002

Kreps, D. (2013). Performing the discourse of sexuality online. In S. Warburton & S. Hatzipanagos (Eds.), *Digital identity and social media* (pp. 118–132). Hershey, PA: Information Science Reference; doi:10.4018/978-1-4666-1915-9.ch009

Ktoridou, D., Kaufmann, H., & Liassides, C. (2012). Factors affecting WiFi use intention: The context of Cyprus. In *Wireless technologies: Concepts, methodologies, tools and applications* (pp. 1760–1781). Hershey, PA: Information Science Reference; doi:10.4018/978-1-61350-101-6.ch703

Kumar, N., Nero Alves, L., & Aguiar, R. L. (2013). Employing traffic lights as road side units for road safety information broadcast. In R. Daher & A. Vinel (Eds.), *Roadside networks for vehicular communications: Architectures, applications, and test fields* (pp. 118–135). Hershey, PA: Information Science Reference; doi:10.4018/978-1-4666-2223-4.ch006

Kvasny, L., & Hales, K. D. (2013). The evolving discourse of the digital divide: The internet, black identity, and the evolving discourse of the digital divide. In *Digital literacy: Concepts, methodologies, tools, and applications* (pp. 1350–1366). Hershey, PA: Information Science Reference; doi:10.4018/978-1-4666-1852-7.ch071

L'Abate, L. (2013). Of paradigms, theories, and models: A conceptual hierarchical structure for communication science and technoself. In R. Luppicini (Ed.), *Handbook of research on technoself: Identity in a technological society* (pp. 84–104). Hershey, PA: Information Science Reference; doi:10.4018/978-1-4666-2211-1.ch005

Laghos, A. (2013). Multimedia social networks and e-learning. In D. Kanellopoulos (Ed.), *Intelligent multimedia technologies for networking applications: Techniques and tools* (pp. 365–379). Hershey, PA: Information Science Reference; doi:10.4018/978-1-4666-2833-5.ch015

Lappas, G. (2012). Social multimedia mining: Trends and opportunities in areas of social and communication studies. In I. Ting, T. Hong, & L. Wang (Eds.), *Social network mining, analysis, and research trends: Techniques and applications* (pp. 1–16). Hershey, PA: Information Science Reference; doi:10.4018/978-1-61350-513-7.ch001

Lawrence, J. E. (2013). Barriers hindering ecommerce adoption: A case study of Kurdistan region of Iraq. In A. Zolait (Ed.), *Technology diffusion and adoption: Global complexity, global innovation* (pp. 152–165). Hershey, PA: Information Science Reference; doi:10.4018/978-1-4666-2791-8.ch010

Lawrence, K. F. (2013). Identity and the online media fan community. In S. Warburton & S. Hatzipanagos (Eds.), *Digital identity and social media* (pp. 233–255). Hershey, PA: Information Science Reference; doi:10.4018/978-1-4666-1915-9.ch017

Lee, M. J., Dalgarno, B., Gregory, S., Carlson, L., & Tynan, B. (2013). How are Australian and New Zealand higher educators using 3D immersive virtual worlds in their teaching? In B. Tynan, J. Willems, & R. James (Eds.), *Outlooks and opportunities in blended and distance learning* (pp. 169–188). Hershey, PA: Information Science Reference; doi:10.4018/978-1-4666-4205-8.ch013

Lee, S., Alfano, C., & Carpenter, R. G. (2013). Invention in two parts: Multimodal communication and space design in the writing center. In R. Carpenter (Ed.), *Cases on higher education spaces: Innovation, collaboration, and technology* (pp. 41–63). Hershey, PA: Information Science Reference; doi:10.4018/978-1-4666-2673-7.ch003

Leichsenring, C., Tünnermann, R., & Hermann, T. (2013). Feelabuzz: Direct tactile communication with mobile phones. In J. Lumsden (Ed.), *Developments in technologies for human-centric mobile computing and applications* (pp. 145–154). Hershey, PA: Information Science Reference; doi:10.4018/978-1-4666-2068-1.ch009

Lemos, A., & Marques, F. P. (2013). A critical analysis of the limitations and effects of the Brazilian national broadband plan. In A. Abdelaal (Ed.), *Social and economic effects of community wireless networks and infrastructures* (pp. 255–274). Hershey, PA: Information Science Reference; doi:10.4018/978-1-4666-2997-4.ch014

Leung, C. K., Medina, I. J., & Tanbeer, S. K. (2013). Analyzing social networks to mine important friends. In G. Xu & L. Li (Eds.), *Social media mining and social network analysis: Emerging research* (pp. 90–104). Hershey, PA: Information Science Reference; doi:10.4018/978-1-4666-2806-9.ch006

Li, B. (2012). Toward an infrastructural approach to understanding participation in virtual communities. In H. Li (Ed.), *Virtual community participation and motivation: Cross-disciplinary theories* (pp. 103–123). Hershey, PA: Information Science Reference; doi:10.4018/978-1-4666-0312-7.ch007

Li, L., Xiao, H., & Xu, G. (2013). Recommending related microblogs. In G. Xu & L. Li (Eds.), *Social media mining and social network analysis: Emerging research* (pp. 202–210). Hershey, PA: Information Science Reference; doi:10.4018/978-1-4666-2806-9.ch013

Liddell, T. (2013). Historical evolution of adult education in America: The impact of institutions, change, and acculturation. In V. Wang (Ed.), *Handbook of research on technologies for improving the 21st century workforce: Tools for lifelong learning* (pp. 257–271). Hershey, PA: Information Science Publishing; doi:10.4018/978-1-4666-2181-7.ch017

Liljander, V., Gummerus, J., Pihlström, M., & Kiehelä, H. (2013). Mobile services as resources for consumer integration of value in a multi-channel environment. In I. Lee (Ed.), *Strategy, adoption, and competitive advantage of mobile services in the global economy* (pp. 259–282). Hershey, PA: Information Science Reference; doi:10.4018/978-1-4666-1939-5.ch015

Litaay, T., Prananingrum, D. H., & Krisanto, Y. A. (2013). Indonesian legal perspectives on biotechnology and intellectual property rights. In *Digital rights management: Concepts, methodologies, tools, and applications* (pp. 834–845). Hershey, PA: Information Science Reference; doi:10.4018/978-1-4666-2136-7.ch039

Little, G. (2013). Collection development for theological education. In S. Holder (Ed.), *Library collection development for professional programs: Trends and best practices* (pp. 112–127). Hershey, PA: Information Science Reference; doi:10.4018/978-1-4666-1897-8.ch007

Losh, S. C. (2013). American digital divides: Generation, education, gender, and ethnicity in American digital divides. In *Digital literacy: Concepts, methodologies, tools, and applications* (pp. 932–958). Hershey, PA: Information Science Reference; doi:10.4018/978-1-4666-1852-7.ch048

Lovari, A., & Parisi, L. (2012). Public administrations and citizens 2.0: Exploring digital public communication strategies and civic interaction within Italian municipality pages on Facebook. In F. Comunello (Ed.), *Networked sociability and individualism: Technology for personal and professional relationships* (pp. 238–263). Hershey, PA: Information Science Reference; doi:10.4018/978-1-61350-338-6.ch012

Maamar, Z., Faci, N., Mostéfaoui, S. K., & Akhter, F. (2013). Towards a framework for weaving social networks into mobile commerce. In D. Chiu (Ed.), *Mobile and web innovations in systems and service-oriented engineering* (pp. 333–347). Hershey, PA: Information Science Reference; doi:10.4018/978-1-4666-2470-2.ch018

Maia, I. F., & Valente, J. A. (2013). Digital identity built on a cooperative relationship. In S. Warburton & S. Hatzipanagos (Eds.), *Digital identity and social media* (pp. 58–73). Hershey, PA: Information Science Reference; doi:10.4018/978-1-4666-1915-9.ch005

Maity, M. (2013). Consumer information search and decision-making on m-commerce: The role of product type. In I. Lee (Ed.), *Strategy, adoption, and competitive advantage of mobile services in the global economy* (pp. 73–89). Hershey, PA: Information Science Reference; doi:10.4018/978-1-4666-1939-5.ch004

Malinen, S., Virjo, T., & Kujala, S. (2012). Supporting local connections with online communities. In A. Lugmayr, H. Franssila, P. Näränen, O. Sotamaa, J. Vanhala, & Z. Yu (Eds.), *Media in the ubiquitous era: Ambient, social and gaming media* (pp. 235–250). Hershey, PA: Information Science Reference; doi:10.4018/978-1-60960-774-6.ch013

Mantoro, T., Milišic, A., & Ayu, M. (2013). Online authentication using smart card technology in mobile phone infrastructure. In I. Khalil & E. Weippl (Eds.), *Contemporary challenges and solutions for mobile and multimedia technologies* (pp. 127–144). Hershey, PA: Information Science Reference; doi:10.4018/978-1-4666-2163-3.ch008

Marcato, E., & Scala, E. (2013). Moodle: A platform for a school. In P. Pumilia-Gnarini, E. Favaron, E. Pacetti, J. Bishop, & L. Guerra (Eds.), *Handbook of research on didactic strategies and technologies for education: Incorporating advancements* (pp. 107–116). Hershey, PA: Information Science Reference; doi:10.4018/978-1-4666-2122-0.ch010

Markaki, O. I., Charalabidis, Y., & Askounis, D. (2013). Measuring interoperability readiness in south eastern Europe and the Mediterranean: The interoperability observatory. In A. Scupola (Ed.), *Mobile opportunities and applications for e-service innovations* (pp. 210–230). Hershey, PA: Information Science Reference; doi:10.4018/978-1-4666-2654-6.ch012

Martin, J. D., & El-Toukhy, S. (2012). Blogging for sovereignty: An analysis of Palestinian blogs. In T. Dumova & R. Fiordo (Eds.), *Blogging in the global society: Cultural, political and geographical aspects* (pp. 148–160). Hershey, PA: Information Science Reference; doi:10.4018/978-1-60960-744-9.ch009

Matei, S. A., & Bruno, R. J. (2012). Individualist motivators and community functional constraints in social media: The case of Wikis and Wikipedia. In F. Comunello (Ed.), *Networked sociability and individualism: Technology for personal and professional relationships* (pp. 1–23). Hershey, PA: Information Science Reference; doi:10.4018/978-1-61350-338-6.ch001

Matsuoka, H. (2013). Acoustic OFDM technology and system. In K. Kondo (Ed.), *Multimedia information hiding technologies and methodologies for controlling data* (pp. 90–103). Hershey, PA: Information Science Reference; doi:10.4018/978-1-4666-2217-3.ch005

McCarthy, J. (2013). Online networking: Integrating international students into first year university through the strategic use of participatory media. In F. García-Peñalvo (Ed.), *Multiculturalism in technology-based education: Case studies on ICT-supported approaches* (pp. 189–210). Hershey, PA: Information Science Reference; doi:10.4018/978-1-4666-2101-5.ch012

McDonald, A., & Helmer, S. (2013). A comparative case study of Indonesian and UK organisational culture differences in IS project management. In A. Mesquita (Ed.), *User perception and influencing factors of technology in everyday life* (pp. 46–55). Hershey, PA: Information Science Reference; doi:10.4018/978-1-4666-1954-8.ch005

McDonough, C. (2013). Mobile broadband: Substituting for fixed broadband or providing value-added. In I. Lee (Ed.), *Mobile services industries, technologies, and applications in the global economy* (pp. 74–86). Hershey, PA: Information Science Reference; doi:10.4018/978-1-4666-1981-4.ch005

McKeown, A. (2013). Virtual communitas, “digital place-making,” and the process of “becoming”. In D. Harrison (Ed.), *Digital media and technologies for virtual artistic spaces* (pp. 218–236). Hershey, PA: Information Science Reference; doi:10.4018/978-1-4666-2961-5.ch016

Medeni, T. D., Medeni, I. T., & Balci, A. (2013). Proposing a knowledge amphora model for transition towards mobile government. In A. Scupola (Ed.), *Mobile opportunities and applications for e-service innovations* (pp. 170–192). Hershey, PA: Information Science Reference; doi:10.4018/978-1-4666-2654-6.ch010

Melo, A., Bezerra, P., Abelém, A. J., Neto, A., & Cerqueira, E. (2013). PriorityQoE: A tool for improving the QoE in video streaming. In D. Kanellopoulos (Ed.), *Intelligent multimedia technologies for networking applications: Techniques and tools* (pp. 270–290). Hershey, PA: Information Science Reference; doi:10.4018/978-1-4666-2833-5.ch011

Mendoza-González, R., Rodríguez, F. Á., & Arteaga, J. M. (2013). A usability study of mobile text based social applications: Towards a reliable strategy for design evaluation. In M. Garcia-Ruiz (Ed.), *Cases on usability engineering: Design and development of digital products* (pp. 195–219). Hershey, PA: Information Science Reference; doi:10.4018/978-1-4666-4046-7.ch009

Metzger, M. J., Wilson, C., Pure, R. A., & Zhao, B. Y. (2012). Invisible interactions: What latent social interaction can tell us about social relationships in social network sites. In F. Comunello (Ed.), *Networked sociability and individualism: Technology for personal and professional relationships* (pp. 79–102). Hershey, PA: Information Science Reference; doi:10.4018/978-1-61350-338-6.ch005

Millo, G., & Carmeci, G. (2013). Insurance in Italy: A spatial perspective. In G. Borruso, S. Bertazzon, A. Favretto, B. Murgante, & C. Torre (Eds.), *Geographic information analysis for sustainable development and economic planning: New technologies* (pp. 158–178). Hershey, PA: Information Science Reference; doi:10.4018/978-1-4666-1924-1.ch011

Mingqing, X., Wenjing, X., & Junming, Z. (2012). The future of television. In R. Sharma, M. Tan, & F. Pereira (Eds.), *Understanding the interactive digital media marketplace: Frameworks, platforms, communities and issues* (pp. 406–415). Hershey, PA: Information Science Reference; doi:10.4018/978-1-61350-147-4.ch032

Miscione, G. (2013). Telemedicine and development: Situating information technologies in the Amazon. In J. Abdelnour-Nocera (Ed.), *Knowledge and technological development effects on organizational and social structures* (pp. 132–145). Hershey, PA: Information Science Reference; doi:10.4018/978-1-4666-2151-0.ch009

Modegi, T. (2013). Spatial and temporal position information delivery to mobile terminals using audio watermarking techniques. In K. Kondo (Ed.), *Multimedia information hiding technologies and methodologies for controlling data* (pp. 182–207). Hershey, PA: Information Science Reference; doi:10.4018/978-1-4666-2217-3.ch009

Montes, J. A., Gutiérrez, A. C., Fernández, E. M., & Romeo, A. (2012). Reality mining, location based services and e-business opportunities: The case of city analytics. In *Wireless technologies: Concepts, methodologies, tools and applications* (pp. 1520–1532). Hershey, PA: Information Science Reference; doi:10.4018/978-1-61350-101-6.ch601

Moreno, A. (2012). The social construction of new cultural models through information and communication technologies. In M. Safar & K. Mahdi (Eds.), *Social networking and community behavior modeling: Qualitative and quantitative measures* (pp. 68–84). Hershey, PA: Information Science Reference; doi:10.4018/978-1-61350-444-4.ch004

Morris, J. Z., & Thomas, K. D. (2013). Implementing BioSand filters in rural Honduras: A case study of his hands mission international in Copán, Honduras. In H. Muga & K. Thomas (Eds.), *Cases on the diffusion and adoption of sustainable development practices* (pp. 468–496). Hershey, PA: Information Science Reference; doi:10.4018/978-1-4666-2842-7.ch017

Mura, G. (2012). The MultiPlasticity of new media. In G. Ghinea, F. Andres, & S. Gulliver (Eds.), *Multiple sensorial media advances and applications: New developments in MulSeMedia* (pp. 258–271). Hershey, PA: Information Science Reference; doi:10.4018/978-1-60960-821-7.ch013

Murray, C. (2012). Imagine mobile learning in your pocket. In *Wireless technologies: Concepts, methodologies, tools and applications* (pp. 2060–2088). Hershey, PA: Information Science Reference; doi:10.4018/978-1-61350-101-6.ch807

Mutohar, A., & Hughes, J. E. (2013). Toward web 2.0 integration in Indonesian education: Challenges and planning strategies. In N. Azab (Ed.), *Cases on web 2.0 in developing countries: Studies on implementation, application, and use* (pp. 198–221). Hershey, PA: Information Science Reference; doi:10.4018/978-1-4666-2515-0.ch008

Nandi, B., & Subramaniam, G. (2012). Evolution in broadband technology and future of wireless broadband. In *Wireless technologies: Concepts, methodologies, tools and applications* (pp. 1928–1957). Hershey, PA: Information Science Reference; doi:10.4018/978-1-61350-101-6.ch801

Naser, A., Jaber, I., Jaber, R., & Saeed, K. (2013). Information systems in UAE education sector: Security, cultural, and ethical issues. In F. Albadri (Ed.), *Information systems applications in the Arab education sector* (pp. 148–162). Hershey, PA: Information Science Reference; doi:10.4018/978-1-4666-1984-5.ch011

Nemoianu, I., & Pesquet-Popescu, B. (2013). Network coding for multimedia communications. In D. Kanellopoulos (Ed.), *Intelligent multimedia technologies for networking applications: Techniques and tools* (pp. 1–24). Hershey, PA: Information Science Reference; doi:10.4018/978-1-4666-2833-5.ch001

Nezlek, G., & DeHondt, G. (2013). Gender wage differentials in information systems: 1991 – 2008 a quantitative analysis. In B. Medlin (Ed.), *Integrations of technology utilization and social dynamics in organizations* (pp. 31–47). Hershey, PA: Information Science Reference; doi:10.4018/978-1-4666-1948-7.ch003

Nishimura, A., & Kondo, K. (2013). Information hiding for audio signals. In K. Kondo (Ed.), *Multimedia information hiding technologies and methodologies for controlling data* (pp. 1–18). Hershey, PA: Information Science Reference; doi:10.4018/978-1-4666-2217-3.ch001

Norder, J. W., & Carroll, J. W. (2013). Applied geospatial perspectives on the rock art of the lake of the woods region of Ontario, Canada. In D. Albert & G. Dobbs (Eds.), *Emerging methods and multidisciplinary applications in geospatial research* (pp. 77–93). Hershey, PA: Information Science Reference; doi:10.4018/978-1-4666-1951-7.ch005

O'Brien, M. A., & Rogers, W. A. (2013). Design for aging: Enhancing everyday technology use. In R. Zheng, R. Hill, & M. Gardner (Eds.), *Engaging older adults with modern technology: Internet use and information access needs* (pp. 105–123). Hershey, PA: Information Science Reference; doi:10.4018/978-1-4666-1966-1.ch006

O'Hanlon, S. (2013). Health information technology and human rights. In J. Lannon & E. Halpin (Eds.), *Human rights and information communication technologies: Trends and consequences of use* (pp. 235–246). Hershey, PA: Information Science Reference; doi:10.4018/978-1-4666-1918-0.ch014

Odella, F. (2012). Social networks and communities: From traditional society to the virtual sphere. In M. Safar & K. Mahdi (Eds.), *Social networking and community behavior modeling: Qualitative and quantitative measures* (pp. 1–25). Hershey, PA: Information Science Reference; doi:10.4018/978-1-61350-444-4.ch001

Okazaki, S., Romero, J., & Campo, S. (2012). Capturing market mavens among advergamers: A case of mobile-based social networking site in Japan. In I. Ting, T. Hong, & L. Wang (Eds.), *Social network mining, analysis, and research trends: Techniques and applications* (pp. 291–305). Hershey, PA: Information Science Reference; doi:10.4018/978-1-61350-513-7.ch017

Omojola, O. (2012). Exploring the impact of Google Igbo in South East Nigeria. In R. Lekoko & L. Semali (Eds.), *Cases on developing countries and ICT integration: Rural community development* (pp. 62–73). Hershey, PA: Information Science Reference; doi:10.4018/978-1-60960-117-1.ch007

Ovide, E. (2013). Intercultural education with indigenous peoples and the potential of digital technologies to make it happen. In F. García-Peñalvo (Ed.), *Multiculturalism in technology-based education: Case studies on ICT-supported approaches* (pp. 59–78). Hershey, PA: Information Science Reference; doi:10.4018/978-1-4666-2101-5.ch005

Owusu-Ansah, A. (2013). Exploring Hofstede's cultural dimension using Hollins' structured dialogue to attain a conduit for effective intercultural experiences. In E. Jean Francois (Ed.), *Transcultural blended learning and teaching in postsecondary education* (pp. 52–74). Hershey, PA: Information Science Reference; doi:10.4018/978-1-4666-2014-8.ch004

Özdemir, E. (2012). Gender and e-marketing: The role of gender differences in online purchasing behaviors. In C. Romm Livermore (Ed.), *Gender and social computing: Interactions, differences and relationships* (pp. 72–86). Hershey, PA: Information Science Publishing; doi:10.4018/978-1-60960-759-3.ch005

Palmer, M. H., & Hanney, J. (2012). Geographic information networks in American Indian governments and communities. In S. Dasgupta (Ed.), *Technical, social, and legal issues in virtual communities: Emerging environments: Emerging environments* (pp. 52–62). Hershey, PA: Information Science Reference; doi:10.4018/978-1-4666-1553-3.ch004

Pande, R. (2013). Gender gaps and information and communication technology: A case study of India. In *Digital literacy: Concepts, methodologies, tools, and applications* (pp. 1425–1439). Hershey, PA: Information Science Reference; doi:10.4018/978-1-4666-1852-7.ch075

Park, J., Chung, T., & Hur, W. (2013). The role of consumer innovativeness and trust for adopting internet phone services. In A. Scupola (Ed.), *Mobile opportunities and applications for e-service innovations* (pp. 22–36). Hershey, PA: Information Science Reference; doi:10.4018/978-1-4666-2654-6.ch002

Parke, A., & Griffiths, M. (2013). Poker gambling virtual communities: The use of computer-mediated communication to develop cognitive poker gambling skills. In R. Zheng (Ed.), *Evolving psychological and educational perspectives on cyber behavior* (pp. 190–204). Hershey, PA: Information Science Reference; doi:10.4018/978-1-4666-1858-9.ch012

Paschou, M., Sakkopoulos, E., Tsakalidis, A., Tzimas, G., & Viennas, E. (2013). An XML-based customizable model for multimedia applications for museums and exhibitions. In D. Kanellopoulos (Ed.), *Intelligent multimedia technologies for networking applications: Techniques and tools* (pp. 348–363). Hershey, PA: Information Science Reference; doi:10.4018/978-1-4666-2833-5.ch014

Pauwels, L. (2013). Images, self-images, and idealized identities in the digital networked world: Reconfigurations of family photography in a web-based mode. In S. Warburton & S. Hatzipanagos (Eds.), *Digital identity and social media* (pp. 133–147). Hershey, PA: Information Science Reference; doi:10.4018/978-1-4666-1915-9.ch010

Peachey, A., & Withnail, G. (2013). A sociocultural perspective on negotiating digital identities in a community of learners. In S. Warburton & S. Hatzipanagos (Eds.), *Digital identity and social media* (pp. 210–224). Hershey, PA: Information Science Reference; doi:10.4018/978-1-4666-1915-9.ch015

Peixoto, E., Martins, E., Anjo, A. B., & Silva, A. (2012). Geo@NET in the context of the platform of assisted learning from Aveiro University, Portugal. In M. Cruz-Cunha (Ed.), *Handbook of research on serious games as educational, business and research tools* (pp. 648–667). Hershey, PA: Information Science Reference; doi:10.4018/978-1-4666-0149-9.ch033

Pillay, N. (2013). The use of web 2.0 technologies by students from developed and developing countries: A New Zealand case study. In N. Azab (Ed.), *Cases on web 2.0 in developing countries: Studies on implementation, application, and use* (pp. 411–441). Hershey, PA: Information Science Reference; doi:10.4018/978-1-4666-2515-0.ch015

Pimenta, M. S., Miletto, E. M., Keller, D., Flores, L. V., & Testa, G. G. (2013). Technological support for online communities focusing on music creation: Adopting collaboration, flexibility, and multiculturality from Brazilian creativity styles. In N. Azab (Ed.), *Cases on web 2.0 in developing countries: Studies on implementation, application, and use* (pp. 283–312). Hershey, PA: Information Science Reference; doi:10.4018/978-1-4666-2515-0.ch011

Pina, P. (2013). Between scylla and charybdis: The balance between copyright, digital rights management and freedom of expression. In *Digital rights management: Concepts, methodologies, tools, and applications* (pp. 1355–1367). Hershey, PA: Information Science Reference; doi:10.4018/978-1-4666-2136-7.ch067

Pitsillides, S., Waller, M., & Fairfax, D. (2013). Digital death: What role does digital information play in the way we are (re)membered? In S. Warburton & S. Hatzipanagos (Eds.), *Digital identity and social media* (pp. 75–90). Hershey, PA: Information Science Reference; doi:10.4018/978-1-4666-1915-9.ch006

Polacek, P., & Huang, C. (2013). QoS scheduling with opportunistic spectrum access for multimedia. In M. Ku & J. Lin (Eds.), *Cognitive radio and interference management: Technology and strategy* (pp. 162–178). Hershey, PA: Information Science Reference; doi:10.4018/978-1-4666-2005-6.ch009

Potts, L. (2013). Balancing McLuhan with Williams: A sociotechnical view of technological determinism. In J. Abdelnour-Nocera (Ed.), *Knowledge and technological development effects on organizational and social structures* (pp. 109–114). Hershey, PA: Information Science Reference; doi:10.4018/978-1-4666-2151-0.ch007

Prescott, J., & Bogg, J. (2013). Stereotype, attitudes, and identity: Gendered expectations and behaviors. In *Gendered occupational differences in science, engineering, and technology careers* (pp. 112–135). Hershey, PA: Information Science Reference; doi:10.4018/978-1-4666-2107-7.ch005

Preussler, A., & Kerres, M. (2013). Managing social reputation in Twitter. In S. Warburton & S. Hatzipanagos (Eds.), *Digital identity and social media* (pp. 91–103). Hershey, PA: Information Science Reference; doi:10.4018/978-1-4666-1915-9.ch007

Prieger, J. E., & Church, T. V. (2013). Deployment of mobile broadband service in the United States. In I. Lee (Ed.), *Mobile services industries, technologies, and applications in the global economy* (pp. 1–24). Hershey, PA: Information Science Reference; doi:10.4018/978-1-4666-1981-4.ch001

Puumalainen, K., Frank, L., Sundqvist, S., & Tuppura, A. (2012). The critical mass of wireless communications: Differences between developing and developed economies. In *Wireless technologies: Concepts, methodologies, tools and applications* (pp. 1719–1736). Hershey, PA: Information Science Reference; doi:10.4018/978-1-61350-101-6.ch701

Rabino, S., Rafiee, D., Onufrey, S., & Moskowitz, H. (2013). Retention and customer share building: Formulating a communication strategy for a sports club. In H. Kaufmann & M. Panni (Eds.), *Customer-centric marketing strategies: Tools for building organizational performance* (pp. 511–529). Hershey, PA: Business Science Reference; doi:10.4018/978-1-4666-2524-2.ch025

Rahman, H., & Kumar, S. (2012). Mobile computing: An emerging issue in the digitized world. In A. Kumar & H. Rahman (Eds.), *Mobile computing techniques in emerging markets: Systems, applications and services* (pp. 1–22). Hershey, PA: Information Science Reference; doi:10.4018/978-1-4666-0080-5.ch001

Ratten, V. (2013). Adoption of mobile reading devices in the book industry. In I. Lee (Ed.), *Strategy, adoption, and competitive advantage of mobile services in the global economy* (pp. 203–216). Hershey, PA: Information Science Reference; doi:10.4018/978-1-4666-1939-5.ch011

Ratten, V. (2013). Mobile banking in the youth market: Implications from an entrepreneurial and learning perspective. In I. Lee (Ed.), *Strategy, adoption, and competitive advantage of mobile services in the global economy* (pp. 112–126). Hershey, PA: Information Science Reference; doi:10.4018/978-1-4666-1939-5.ch006

Ratten, V. (2013). Social e-enterprise through technological innovations and mobile social networks. In T. Torres-Coronas & M. Vidal-Blasco (Eds.), *Social e-enterprise: Value creation through ICT* (pp. 96–109). Hershey, PA: Information Science Reference; doi:10.4018/978-1-4666-2667-6.ch006

Rego, P. A., Moreira, P. M., & Reis, L. P. (2012). New forms of interaction in serious games for rehabilitation. In M. Cruz-Cunha (Ed.), *Handbook of research on serious games as educational, business and research tools* (pp. 1188–1211). Hershey, PA: Information Science Reference; doi:10.4018/978-1-4666-0149-9.ch062

Reinhard, C. D. (2012). Virtual worlds and reception studies: Comparing engagings. In N. Zagalo, L. Morgado, & A. Boa-Ventura (Eds.), *Virtual worlds and metaverse platforms: New communication and identity paradigms* (pp. 117–136). Hershey, PA: Information Science Reference; doi:10.4018/978-1-60960-854-5.ch008

Rieser, M. (2013). Mobility, liminality, and digital materiality. In D. Harrison (Ed.), *Digital media and technologies for virtual artistic spaces* (pp. 27–45). Hershey, PA: Information Science Reference; doi:10.4018/978-1-4666-2961-5.ch003

Rodrigues, R. G., Pinheiro, P. G., & Barbosa, J. (2012). Online playability: The social dimension to the virtual world. In M. Cruz-Cunha (Ed.), *Handbook of research on serious games as educational, business and research tools* (pp. 391–421). Hershey, PA: Information Science Reference; doi:10.4018/978-1-4666-0149-9.ch021

Romm-Livermore, C., Somers, T. M., Setzekorn, K., & King, A. L. (2012). How e-daters behave online: Theory and empirical observations. In C. Romm Livermore (Ed.), *Gender and social computing: Interactions, differences and relationships* (pp. 236–256). Hershey, PA: Information Science Publishing; doi:10.4018/978-1-60960-759-3.ch014

Rosaci, D., & Sarnè, G. M. (2012). An agent-based approach to adapt multimedia web content in ubiquitous environment. In S. Bagchi (Ed.), *Ubiquitous multimedia and mobile agents: Models and implementations* (pp. 60–84). Hershey, PA: Information Science Reference; doi:10.4018/978-1-61350-107-8.ch003

Rosas, O. V., & Dhen, G. (2012). One self to rule them all: A critical discourse analysis of French-speaking players' identity construction in World of Warcraft. In N. Zagalo, L. Morgado, & A. Boa-Ventura (Eds.), *Virtual worlds and metaverse platforms: New communication and identity paradigms* (pp. 337–366). Hershey, PA: Information Science Reference; doi:10.4018/978-1-60960-854-5.ch022

Rouibah, K., & Abbas, H. A. (2012). Effect of personal innovativeness, attachment motivation and social norms on the acceptance of camera mobile phones: An empirical study in an Arab country. In W. Hu (Ed.), *Emergent trends in personal, mobile, and handheld computing technologies* (pp. 302–323). Hershey, PA: Information Science Reference; doi:10.4018/978-1-4666-0921-1.ch018

Ruiz-Mafé, C., Sanz-Blas, S., & Martí-Parreño, J. (2013). Web 2.0 goes mobile: Motivations and barriers of mobile social networks use in Spain. In N. Azab (Ed.), *Cases on web 2.0 in developing countries: Studies on implementation, application, and use* (pp. 109–146). Hershey, PA: Information Science Reference; doi:10.4018/978-1-4666-2515-0.ch005

Rybas, S. (2012). Community embodied: Validating the subjective performance of an online class. In H. Li (Ed.), *Virtual community participation and motivation: Cross-disciplinary theories* (pp. 124–141). Hershey, PA: Information Science Reference; doi:10.4018/978-1-4666-0312-7.ch008

Sabelkin, M., & Gagnon, F. (2013). Data transmission oriented on the object, communication media, application, and state of communication systems. In M. Bartolacci & S. Powell (Eds.), *Advancements and innovations in wireless communications and network technologies* (pp. 117–132). Hershey, PA: Information Science Reference; doi:10.4018/978-1-4666-2154-1.ch009

Sajeva, S. (2013). Towards a conceptual knowledge management system based on systems thinking and sociotechnical thinking. In J. Abdelnour-Nocera (Ed.), *Knowledge and technological development effects on organizational and social structures* (pp. 115–130). Hershey, PA: Information Science Reference; doi:10.4018/978-1-4666-2151-0.ch008

Salo, M., Olsson, T., Makkonen, M., & Frank, L. (2013). User perspective on the adoption of mobile augmented reality based applications. In I. Lee (Ed.), *Strategy, adoption, and competitive advantage of mobile services in the global economy* (pp. 165–188). Hershey, PA: Information Science Reference; doi:10.4018/978-1-4666-1939-5.ch009

Samanta, S. K., Woods, J., & Ghanbari, M. (2013). Automatic language translation: An enhancement to the mobile messaging services. In A. Mesquita (Ed.), *User perception and influencing factors of technology in everyday life* (pp. 57–75). Hershey, PA: Information Science Reference; doi:10.4018/978-1-4666-1954-8.ch006

Santo, A. E., Rijo, R., Monteiro, J., Henriques, I., Matos, A., Rito, C., & Marcelino, L. et al. (2012). Games improving disorders of attention deficit and hyperactivity. In M. Cruz-Cunha (Ed.), *Handbook of research on serious games as educational, business and research tools* (pp. 1160–1174). Hershey, PA: Information Science Reference; doi:10.4018/978-1-4666-0149-9.ch060

Sarker, S., Campbell, D. E., Ondrus, J., & Valacich, J. S. (2012). Mapping the need for mobile collaboration technologies: A fit perspective. In N. Kock (Ed.), *Advancing collaborative knowledge environments: New trends in e-collaboration* (pp. 211–233). Hershey, PA: Information Science Reference; doi:10.4018/978-1-61350-459-8.ch013

Sasajima, M., Kitamura, Y., & Mizoguchi, R. (2013). Method for modeling user semantics and its application to service navigation on the web. In G. Xu & L. Li (Eds.), *Social media mining and social network analysis: Emerging research* (pp. 127–139). Hershey, PA: Information Science Reference; doi:10.4018/978-1-4666-2806-9.ch008

Scheel, C., & Pineda, L. (2013). Building industrial clusters in Latin America: Paddling upstream. In J. Abdelnour-Nocera (Ed.), *Knowledge and technological development effects on organizational and social structures* (pp. 146–166). Hershey, PA: Information Science Reference; doi:10.4018/978-1-4666-2151-0.ch010

Sell, A., Walden, P., & Carlsson, C. (2013). Segmentation matters: An exploratory study of mobile service users. In D. Chiu (Ed.), *Mobile and web innovations in systems and service-oriented engineering* (pp. 301–317). Hershey, PA: Information Science Reference; doi:10.4018/978-1-4666-2470-2.ch016

Sermon, P., & Gould, C. (2013). Site-specific performance, narrative, and social presence in multi-user virtual environments and the urban landscape. In D. Harrison (Ed.), *Digital media and technologies for virtual artistic spaces* (pp. 46–58). Hershey, PA: Information Science Reference; doi:10.4018/978-1-4666-2961-5.ch004

Servaes, J. (2012). The role of information communication technologies within the field of communication for social change. In *Wireless technologies: Concepts, methodologies, tools and applications* (pp. 1117–1135). Hershey, PA: Information Science Reference; doi:10.4018/978-1-61350-101-6.ch502

Seth, N., & Patnayakuni, R. (2012). Online matrimonial sites and the transformation of arranged marriage in India. In C. Romm Livermore (Ed.), *Gender and social computing: Interactions, differences and relationships* (pp. 272–295). Hershey, PA: Information Science Publishing; doi:10.4018/978-1-60960-759-3.ch016

Shaffer, G. (2013). Lessons learned from grassroots wireless networks in Europe. In A. Abdelaal (Ed.), *Social and economic effects of community wireless networks and infrastructures* (pp. 236–254). Hershey, PA: Information Science Reference; doi:10.4018/978-1-4666-2997-4.ch013

Shen, J., & Eder, L. B. (2013). An examination of factors associated with user acceptance of social shopping websites. In A. Mesquita (Ed.), *User perception and influencing factors of technology in everyday life* (pp. 28–45). Hershey, PA: Information Science Reference; doi:10.4018/978-1-4666-1954-8.ch004

Shen, K. N. (2012). Identification vs. self-verification in virtual communities (VC): Theoretical gaps and design implications. In C. El Morr & P. Maret (Eds.), *Virtual community building and the information society: Current and future directions* (pp. 208–236). Hershey, PA: Information Science Reference; doi:10.4018/978-1-60960-869-9.ch011

Shi, Y., & Liu, Z. (2013). Cultural models and variations. In *Industrial engineering: Concepts, methodologies, tools, and applications* (pp. 1560–1573). Hershey, PA: Engineering Science Reference; doi:10.4018/978-1-4666-1945-6.ch083

Shiferaw, A., Sehai, E., Hoekstra, D., & Getachew, A. (2013). Enhanced knowledge management: Knowledge centers for extension communication and agriculture development in Ethiopia. In B. Maumbe & C. Patrikakis (Eds.), *E-agriculture and rural development: Global innovations and future prospects* (pp. 103–116). Hershey, PA: Information Science Reference; doi:10.4018/978-1-4666-2655-3.ch010

Simão de Vasconcellos, M., & Soares de Araújo, I. (2013). Massively multiplayer online role playing games for health communication in Brazil. In K. Bredl & W. Bösche (Eds.), *Serious games and virtual worlds in education, professional development, and healthcare* (pp. 294–312). Hershey, PA: Information Science Reference; doi:10.4018/978-1-4666-3673-6.ch018

Simour, L. (2012). Networking identities: Geographies of interaction and computer mediated communication1. In S. Dasgupta (Ed.), *Technical, social, and legal issues in virtual communities: Emerging environments: Emerging environments* (pp. 235–246). Hershey, PA: Information Science Reference; doi:10.4018/978-1-4666-1553-3.ch016

Singh, G. R. (2013). Cyborg in the village: Culturally embedded resistances to blended teaching and learning. In E. Jean Francois (Ed.), *Transcultural blended learning and teaching in postsecondary education* (pp. 75–90). Hershey, PA: Information Science Reference; doi:10.4018/978-1-4666-2014-8.ch005

Singh, M., & Iding, M. K. (2013). Does credibility count?: Singaporean students' evaluation of social studies web sites. In R. Zheng (Ed.), *Evolving psychological and educational perspectives on cyber behavior* (pp. 230–245). Hershey, PA: Information Science Reference; doi:10.4018/978-1-4666-1858-9.ch014

Singh, S. (2013). Information and communication technology and its potential to transform Indian agriculture. In B. Maumbe & C. Patrikakis (Eds.), *E-agriculture and rural development: Global innovations and future prospects* (pp. 140–168). Hershey, PA: Information Science Reference; doi:10.4018/978-1-4666-2655-3.ch012

Siqueira, S. R., Rocha, E. C., & Nery, M. S. (2012). Brazilian occupational therapy perspective about digital games as an inclusive resource to disabled people in schools. In M. Cruz-Cunha (Ed.), *Handbook of research on serious games as educational, business and research tools* (pp. 730–749). Hershey, PA: Information Science Reference; doi:10.4018/978-1-4666-0149-9.ch037

Siti-Nabiha, A., & Salleh, D. (2013). Public sector transformation in Malaysia: Improving local governance and accountability. In N. Pomazalová (Ed.), *Public sector transformation processes and internet public procurement: Decision support systems* (pp. 276–290). Hershey, PA: Engineering Science Reference; doi:10.4018/978-1-4666-2665-2.ch013

Siwar, C., & Abdulai, A. (2013). Sustainable development and the digital divide among OIC countries: Towards a collaborative digital approach. In *Digital literacy: Concepts, methodologies, tools, and applications* (pp. 242–261). Hershey, PA: Information Science Reference; doi:10.4018/978-1-4666-1852-7.ch013

Smith, P. A. (2013). Strengthening and enriching audit practice: The socio-technical relevance of "decision leaders". In J. Abdelnour-Nocera (Ed.), *Knowledge and technological development effects on organizational and social structures* (pp. 97–108). Hershey, PA: Information Science Reference; doi:10.4018/978-1-4666-2151-0.ch006

Smith, P. A., & Cockburn, T. (2013). Generational demographics. In *Dynamic leadership models for global business: Enhancing digitally connected environments* (pp. 230–256). Hershey, PA: Business Science Reference; doi:10.4018/978-1-4666-2836-6.ch009

Smith, P. A., & Cockburn, T. (2013). Leadership, global business, and digitally connected environments. In *Dynamic leadership models for global business: Enhancing digitally connected environments* (pp. 257–296). Hershey, PA: Business Science Reference; doi:10.4018/978-1-4666-2836-6.ch010

Sohrabi, B., Gholipour, A., & Amiri, B. (2013). The influence of information technology on organizational behavior: Study of identity challenges in virtual teams. In N. Kock (Ed.), *Interdisciplinary applications of electronic collaboration approaches and technologies* (pp. 79–95). Hershey, PA: Information Science Reference; doi:10.4018/978-1-4666-2020-9.ch006

Soitu, L., & Paulet-Crainiceanu, L. (2013). Student-faculty communication on Facebook: Prospective learning enhancement and boundaries. In B. Pătruţ, M. Pătruţ, & C. Cmeciu (Eds.), *Social media and the new academic environment: Pedagogical challenges* (pp. 40–67). Hershey, PA: Information Science Reference; doi:10.4018/978-1-4666-2851-9.ch003

Solvoll, T. (2013). Mobile communication in hospitals: What is the problem? In C. Rückemann (Ed.), *Integrated information and computing systems for natural, spatial, and social sciences* (pp. 287–301). Hershey, PA: Information Science Reference; doi:10.4018/978-1-4666-2190-9.ch014

Somboonviwat, K. (2013). Topic modeling for web community discovery. In G. Xu & L. Li (Eds.), *Social media mining and social network analysis: Emerging research* (pp. 72–89). Hershey, PA: Information Science Reference; doi:10.4018/978-1-4666-2806-9.ch005

Speaker, R. B., Levitt, G., & Grubaugh, S. (2013). Professional development in a virtual world. In J. Keengwe & L. Kyei-Blankson (Eds.), *Virtual mentoring for teachers: Online professional development practices* (pp. 122–148). Hershey, PA: Information Science Reference; doi:10.4018/978-1-4666-1963-0.ch007

Stevenson, G., & Van Belle, J. (2013). Using social media technology to improve collaboration: A case study of micro-blogging adoption in a South African financial services company. In N. Azab (Ed.), *Cases on web 2.0 in developing countries: Studies on implementation, application, and use* (pp. 313–341). Hershey, PA: Information Science Reference; doi:10.4018/978-1-4666-2515-0.ch012

Strang, K. D. (2013). Balanced assessment of flexible e-learning vs. face-to-face campus delivery courses at an Australian university. In M. Khosrow-Pour (Ed.), *Cases on assessment and evaluation in education* (pp. 304–339). Hershey, PA: Information Science Reference; doi:10.4018/978-1-4666-2621-8.ch013

Strömberg-Jakka, M. (2013). Social assistance via the internet: The case of Finland in the European context. In J. Lannon & E. Halpin (Eds.), *Human rights and information communication technologies: Trends and consequences of use* (pp. 177–195). Hershey, PA: Information Science Reference; doi:10.4018/978-1-4666-1918-0.ch011

Sultanow, E., Weber, E., & Cox, S. (2013). A semantic e-collaboration approach to enable awareness in globally distributed organizations. In N. Kock (Ed.), *Interdisciplinary applications of electronic collaboration approaches and technologies* (pp. 1–16). Hershey, PA: Information Science Reference; doi:10.4018/978-1-4666-2020-9.ch001

Sun, H., Gui, N., & Blondia, C. (2013). A generic adaptation framework for mobile communication. In V. De Florio (Ed.), *Innovations and approaches for resilient and adaptive systems* (pp. 196–207). Hershey, PA: Information Science Reference; doi:10.4018/978-1-4666-2056-8.ch011

Surgevil, O., & Özbilgin, M. F. (2012). Women in information communication technologies. In C. Romm Livermore (Ed.), *Gender and social computing: Interactions, differences and relationships* (pp. 87–97). Hershey, PA: Information Science Publishing; doi:10.4018/978-1-60960-759-3.ch006

Sylaiou, S., White, M., & Liarokapis, F. (2013). Digital heritage systems: The ARCO evaluation. In M. Garcia-Ruiz (Ed.), *Cases on usability engineering: Design and development of digital products* (pp. 321–354). Hershey, PA: Information Science Reference; doi:10.4018/978-1-4666-4046-7.ch014

Sylvester, O. A. (2013). Impact of information and communication technology on livestock production: The experience of rural farmers in Nigeria. In B. Maumbe & C. Patrikakis (Eds.), *E-agriculture and rural development: Global innovations and future prospects* (pp. 68–75). Hershey, PA: Information Science Reference; doi:10.4018/978-1-4666-2655-3.ch007

Taha, K., & Elmasri, R. (2012). Social search and personalization through demographic filtering. In I. Ting, T. Hong, & L. Wang (Eds.), *Social network mining, analysis, and research trends: Techniques and applications* (pp. 183–203). Hershey, PA: Information Science Reference; doi:10.4018/978-1-61350-513-7.ch012

Tai, Z. (2012). Fame, fantasy, fanfare and fun: The blossoming of the Chinese culture of blogmongering. In T. Dumova & R. Fiordo (Eds.), *Blogging in the global society: Cultural, political and geographical aspects* (pp. 37–54). Hershey, PA: Information Science Reference; doi:10.4018/978-1-60960-744-9.ch003

Taifi, N., & Gharbi, K. (2013). Technology integration in strategic management: The case of a micro-financing institutions network. In T. Torres-Coronas & M. Vidal-Blasco (Eds.), *Social e-enterprise: Value creation through ICT* (pp. 263–279). Hershey, PA: Information Science Reference; doi:10.4018/978-1-4666-2667-6.ch015

Talib, S., Clarke, N. L., & Furnell, S. M. (2013). Establishing a personalized information security culture. In I. Khalil & E. Weippl (Eds.), *Contemporary challenges and solutions for mobile and multimedia technologies* (pp. 53–69). Hershey, PA: Information Science Reference; doi:10.4018/978-1-4666-2163-3.ch004

Tamura, H., Sugasaka, T., & Ueda, K. (2012). Lovely place to buy!: Enhancing grocery shopping experiences with a human-centric approach. In A. Lugmayr, H. Franssila, P. Näränen, O. Sotamaa, J. Vanhala, & Z. Yu (Eds.), *Media in the ubiquitous era: Ambient, social and gaming media* (pp. 53–65). Hershey, PA: Information Science Reference; doi:10.4018/978-1-60960-774-6.ch003

Tawileh, W., Bukvova, H., & Schoop, E. (2013). Virtual collaborative learning: Opportunities and challenges of web 2.0-based e-learning arrangements for developing countries. In N. Azab (Ed.), *Cases on web 2.0 in developing countries: Studies on implementation, application, and use* (pp. 380–410). Hershey, PA: Information Science Reference; doi:10.4018/978-1-4666-2515-0.ch014

Teixeira, P. M., Félix, M. J., & Tavares, P. (2012). Playing with design: The universality of design in game development. In M. Cruz-Cunha (Ed.), *Handbook of research on serious games as educational, business and research tools* (pp. 217–231). Hershey, PA: Information Science Reference; doi:10.4018/978-1-4666-0149-9.ch011

Teusner, P. E. (2012). Networked individualism, constructions of community and religious identity: The case of emerging church bloggers in Australia. In F. Comunello (Ed.), *Networked sociability and individualism: Technology for personal and professional relationships* (pp. 264–288). Hershey, PA: Information Science Reference; doi:10.4018/978-1-61350-338-6.ch013

Tezcan, M. (2013). Social e-entrepreneurship, employment, and e-learning. In T. Torres-Coronas & M. Vidal-Blasco (Eds.), *Social e-enterprise: Value creation through ICT* (pp. 133–147). Hershey, PA: Information Science Reference; doi:10.4018/978-1-4666-2667-6.ch008

Thatcher, B. (2012). Approaching intercultural rhetoric and professional communication. In *Intercultural rhetoric and professional communication: Technological advances and organizational behavior* (pp. 1–38). Hershey, PA: Information Science Reference; doi:10.4018/978-1-61350-450-5.ch001

Thatcher, B. (2012). Borders and etics as units of analysis for intercultural rhetoric and professional communication. In *Intercultural rhetoric and professional communication: Technological advances and organizational behavior* (pp. 39–74). Hershey, PA: Information Science Reference; doi:10.4018/978-1-61350-450-5.ch002

Thatcher, B. (2012). Core competencies in intercultural teaching and research. In *Intercultural rhetoric and professional communication: Technological advances and organizational behavior* (pp. 318–342). Hershey, PA: Information Science Reference; doi:10.4018/978-1-61350-450-5.ch011

Thatcher, B. (2012). Distance education and e-learning across cultures. In *Intercultural rhetoric and professional communication: Technological advances and organizational behavior* (pp. 186–215). Hershey, PA: Information Science Reference; doi:10.4018/978-1-61350-450-5.ch007

Thatcher, B. (2012). Information and communication technologies and intercultural professional communication. In *Intercultural rhetoric and professional communication: Technological advances and organizational behavior* (pp. 97–123). Hershey, PA: Information Science Reference; doi:10.4018/978-1-61350-450-5.ch004

Thatcher, B. (2012). Intercultural rhetorical dimensions of health literacy and medicine. In *Intercultural rhetoric and professional communication: Technological advances and organizational behavior* (pp. 247–282). Hershey, PA: Information Science Reference; doi:10.4018/978-1-61350-450-5.ch009

Thatcher, B. (2012). Legal traditions, the universal declaration of human rights, and intercultural professional communication. In *Intercultural rhetoric and professional communication: Technological advances and organizational behavior* (pp. 216–246). Hershey, PA: Information Science Reference; doi:10.4018/978-1-61350-450-5.ch008

Thatcher, B. (2012). Organizational theory and communication across cultures. In *Intercultural rhetoric and professional communication: Technological advances and organizational behavior* (pp. 159–185). Hershey, PA: Information Science Reference; doi:10.4018/978-1-61350-450-5.ch006

Thatcher, B. (2012). Teaching intercultural rhetoric and professional communication. In *Intercultural rhetoric and professional communication: Technological advances and organizational behavior* (pp. 343–378). Hershey, PA: Information Science Reference; doi:10.4018/978-1-61350-450-5.ch012

Thatcher, B. (2012). Website designs as an indicator of globalization. In *Intercultural rhetoric and professional communication: Technological advances and organizational behavior* (pp. 124–158). Hershey, PA: Information Science Reference; doi:10.4018/978-1-61350-450-5.ch005

Thatcher, B. (2012). Writing instructions and how-to-do manuals across cultures. In *Intercultural rhetoric and professional communication: Technological advances and organizational behavior* (pp. 283–317). Hershey, PA: Information Science Reference; doi:10.4018/978-1-61350-450-5.ch010

Thirumal, P., & Tartakov, G. M. (2013). India's Dalits search for a democratic opening in the digital divide. In *Digital literacy: Concepts, methodologies, tools, and applications* (pp. 852–871). Hershey, PA: Information Science Reference; doi:10.4018/978-1-4666-1852-7.ch044

Thomas, G. E. (2013). Facilitating learning with adult students in the transcultural classroom. In E. Jean Francois (Ed.), *Transcultural blended learning and teaching in postsecondary education* (pp. 193–215). Hershey, PA: Information Science Reference; doi:10.4018/978-1-4666-2014-8.ch011

Tripathi, S. N., & Siddiqui, M. H. (2013). Designing effective mobile advertising with specific reference to developing markets. In I. Lee (Ed.), *Strategy, adoption, and competitive advantage of mobile services in the global economy* (pp. 299–324). Hershey, PA: Information Science Reference; doi:10.4018/978-1-4666-1939-5.ch017

Truong, Y. (2013). Antecedents of consumer acceptance of mobile television advertising. In A. Mesquita (Ed.), *User perception and influencing factors of technology in everyday life* (pp. 128–141). Hershey, PA: Information Science Reference; doi:10.4018/978-1-4666-1954-8.ch010

Tsuneizumi, I., Aikebaier, A., Ikeda, M., Enokido, T., & Takizawa, M. (2013). Design and implementation of hybrid time (HT) group communication protocol for homogeneous broadcast groups. In N. Bessis (Ed.), *Development of distributed systems from design to application and maintenance* (pp. 282–293). Hershey, PA: Information Science Reference; doi:10.4018/978-1-4666-2647-8.ch017

Tzoulia, E. (2013). Legal issues to be considered before setting in force consumer-centric marketing strategies within the European Union. In H. Kaufmann & M. Panni (Eds.), *Customer-centric marketing strategies: Tools for building organizational performance* (pp. 36–56). Hershey, PA: Business Science Reference; doi:10.4018/978-1-4666-2524-2.ch003

Underwood, J., & Okubayashi, T. (2013). Comparing the characteristics of text-speak used by English and Japanese students. In R. Zheng (Ed.), *Evolving psychological and educational perspectives on cyber behavior* (pp. 258–271). Hershey, PA: Information Science Reference; doi:10.4018/978-1-4666-1858-9.ch016

Unoki, M., & Miyauchi, R. (2013). Method of digital-audio watermarking based on cochlear delay characteristics. In K. Kondo (Ed.), *Multimedia information hiding technologies and methodologies for controlling data* (pp. 42–70). Hershey, PA: Information Science Reference; doi:10.4018/978-1-4666-2217-3.ch003

Usman, L. M. (2013). Adult education and sustainable learning outcome of rural widows of central northern Nigeria. In V. Wang (Ed.), *Technological applications in adult and vocational education advancement* (pp. 215–231). Hershey, PA: Information Science Reference; doi:10.4018/978-1-4666-2062-9.ch017

Usoro, A., & Khan, I. U. (2013). Trust as an aspect of organisational culture: Its effects on knowledge sharing in virtual communities. In R. Colomo-Palacios (Ed.), *Enhancing the modern organization through information technology professionals: Research, studies, and techniques* (pp. 182–199). Hershey, PA: Business Science Reference; doi:10.4018/978-1-4666-2648-5.ch013

Utz, S. (2012). Social network site use among Dutch students: Effects of time and platform. In F. Comunello (Ed.), *Networked sociability and individualism: Technology for personal and professional relationships* (pp. 103–125). Hershey, PA: Information Science Reference; doi:10.4018/978-1-61350-338-6.ch006

Vasilescu, R., Epure, M., & Florea, N. (2013). Digital literacy for effective communication in the new academic environment: The educational blogs. In B. Pătruţ, M. Pătruţ, & C. Cmeciu (Eds.), *Social media and the new academic environment: Pedagogical challenges* (pp. 368–390). Hershey, PA: Information Science Reference; doi:10.4018/978-1-4666-2851-9.ch018

Vladimirschi, V. (2013). An exploratory study of cross-cultural engagement in the community of inquiry: Instructor perspectives and challenges. In Z. Akyol & D. Garrison (Eds.), *Educational communities of inquiry: Theoretical framework, research and practice* (pp. 466–489). Hershey, PA: Information Science Reference; doi:10.4018/978-1-4666-2110-7.ch023

Vuokko, R. (2012). A practice perspective on transforming mobile work. In *Wireless technologies: Concepts, methodologies, tools and applications* (pp. 1104–1116). Hershey, PA: Information Science Reference; doi:10.4018/978-1-61350-101-6.ch501

Wall, M., & Kirdnark, T. (2012). The blogosphere in the "land of smiles": Citizen media and political conflict in Thailand. In T. Dumova & R. Fiordo (Eds.), *Blogging in the global society: Cultural, political and geographical aspects* (pp. 19–36). Hershey, PA: Information Science Reference; doi:10.4018/978-1-60960-744-9.ch002

Warburton, S. (2013). Space for lurking: A pattern for designing online social spaces. In S. Warburton & S. Hatzipanagos (Eds.), *Digital identity and social media* (pp. 149–158). Hershey, PA: Information Science Reference; doi:10.4018/978-1-4666-1915-9.ch011

Warren, S. J., & Lin, L. (2012). Ethical considerations for learning game, simulation, and virtual world design and development. In H. Yang & S. Yuen (Eds.), *Handbook of research on practices and outcomes in virtual worlds and environments* (pp. 1–18). Hershey, PA: Information Science Publishing; doi:10.4018/978-1-60960-762-3.ch001

Wasihun, T. A., & Maumbe, B. (2013). Information and communication technology uses in agriculture: Agribusiness industry opportunities and future challenges. In B. Maumbe & C. Patrikakis (Eds.), *E-agriculture and rural development: Global innovations and future prospects* (pp. 235–251). Hershey, PA: Information Science Reference; doi:10.4018/978-1-4666-2655-3.ch017

Webb, L. M., Fields, T. E., Boupha, S., & Stell, M. N. (2012). U.S. political blogs: What aspects of blog design correlate with popularity? In T. Dumova & R. Fiordo (Eds.), *Blogging in the global society: Cultural, political and geographical aspects* (pp. 179–199). Hershey, PA: Information Science Reference; doi:10.4018/978-1-60960-744-9.ch011

Weeks, M. R. (2012). Toward an understanding of online community participation through narrative network analysis. In H. Li (Ed.), *Virtual community participation and motivation: Cross-disciplinary theories* (pp. 90–102). Hershey, PA: Information Science Reference; doi:10.4018/978-1-4666-0312-7.ch006

White, J. R. (2013). Language economy in computer-mediated communication: Learner autonomy in a community of practice. In B. Zou, M. Xing, Y. Wang, M. Sun, & C. Xiang (Eds.), *Computer-assisted foreign language teaching and learning: Technological advances* (pp. 75–90). Hershey, PA: Information Science Reference; doi:10.4018/978-1-4666-2821-2.ch005

Whitworth, B., & Liu, T. (2013). Politeness as a social computing requirement. In J. Bishop (Ed.), *Examining the concepts, issues, and implications of internet trolling* (pp. 88–104). Hershey, PA: Information Science Reference; doi:10.4018/978-1-4666-2803-8.ch008

Wichowski, D. E., & Kohl, L. E. (2013). Establishing credibility in the information jungle: Blogs, microblogs, and the CRAAP test. In M. Folk & S. Apostel (Eds.), *Online credibility and digital ethos: Evaluating computer-mediated communication* (pp. 229–251). Hershey, PA: Information Science Reference; doi:10.4018/978-1-4666-2663-8.ch013

Williams, J. (2013). Social cohesion and free home internet in New Zealand. In A. Abdelaal (Ed.), *Social and economic effects of community wireless networks and infrastructures* (pp. 135–159). Hershey, PA: Information Science Reference; doi:10.4018/978-1-4666-2997-4.ch008

Williams, S., Fleming, S., Lundqvist, K., & Parslow, P. (2013). This is me: Digital identity and reputation on the internet. In S. Warburton & S. Hatzipanagos (Eds.), *Digital identity and social media* (pp. 104–117). Hershey, PA: Information Science Reference; doi:10.4018/978-1-4666-1915-9.ch008

Winning, R. (2013). Behind the sonic veil: Considering sound as the mediator of illusory life in variable and screen-based media. In D. Harrison (Ed.), Digital media and technologies for virtual artistic spaces (pp. 117-134). Hershey, PA: Information science reference. doi:10.4018/978-1-4666-2961-5.ch009

Wolfe, A. (2012). Network perspective on structures related to communities. In M. Safar & K. Mahdi (Eds.), *Social networking and community behavior modeling: Qualitative and quantitative measures* (pp. 26–50). Hershey, PA: Information Science Reference; doi:10.4018/978-1-61350-444-4.ch002

Worden, S. (2013). The earth sciences and creative practice: Exploring boundaries between digital and material culture. In D. Harrison (Ed.), *Digital media and technologies for virtual artistic spaces* (pp. 186–204). Hershey, PA: Information Science Reference; doi:10.4018/978-1-4666-2961-5.ch014

Xing, M., Zou, B., & Wang, D. (2013). A wiki platform for language and intercultural communication. In B. Zou, M. Xing, Y. Wang, M. Sun, & C. Xiang (Eds.), *Computer-assisted foreign language teaching and learning: Technological advances* (pp. 1–15). Hershey, PA: Information Science Reference; doi:10.4018/978-1-4666-2821-2.ch001

Xu, G., Gu, Y., & Yi, X. (2013). On group extraction and fusion for tag-based social recommendation. In G. Xu & L. Li (Eds.), *Social media mining and social network analysis: Emerging research* (pp. 211–223). Hershey, PA: Information Science Reference; doi:10.4018/978-1-4666-2806-9.ch014

Yakura, E. K., Soe, L., & Guthrie, R. (2012). Women in IT careers: Investigating support for women in the information technology workforce. In C. Romm Livermore (Ed.), *Gender and social computing: Interactions, differences and relationships* (pp. 35–49). Hershey, PA: Information Science Publishing; doi:10.4018/978-1-60960-759-3.ch003

Yang, Y., Rahim, A., & Karmakar, N. C. (2013). 5.8 GHz portable wireless monitoring system for sleep apnea diagnosis in wireless body sensor network (WBSN) using active RFID and MIMO technology. In N. Karmakar (Ed.), *Advanced RFID systems, security, and applications* (pp. 264–303). Hershey, PA: Information Science Reference; doi:10.4018/978-1-4666-2080-3.ch012

Yu, Z., Liang, Y., Yang, Y., & Guo, B. (2013). Supporting social interaction in campus-scale environments by embracing mobile social networking. In G. Xu & L. Li (Eds.), *Social media mining and social network analysis: Emerging research* (pp. 182–201). Hershey, PA: Information Science Reference; doi:10.4018/978-1-4666-2806-9.ch012

Zaman, M., Simmers, C. A., & Anandarajan, M. (2013). Using an ethical framework to examine linkages between "going green" in research practices and information and communication technologies. In B. Medlin (Ed.), *Integrations of technology utilization and social dynamics in organizations* (pp. 243–262). Hershey, PA: Information Science Reference; doi:10.4018/978-1-4666-1948-7.ch015

Zarmpou, T., Saprikis, V., & Vlachopoulou, M. (2013). Examining behavioral intention toward mobile services: An empirical investigation in Greece. In A. Scupola (Ed.), *Mobile opportunities and applications for e-service innovations* (pp. 37–56). Hershey, PA: Information Science Reference; doi:10.4018/978-1-4666-2654-6.ch003

Zavala Pérez, J. M. (2012). Registry culture and networked sociability: Building individual identity through information records. In F. Comunello (Ed.), *Networked sociability and individualism: Technology for personal and professional relationships* (pp. 41–62). Hershey, PA: Information Science Reference; doi:10.4018/978-1-61350-338-6.ch003

Zemliansky, P., & Goroshko, O. (2013). Social media and other web 2.0 technologies as communication channels in a cross-cultural, web-based professional communication project. In B. Pătruţ, M. Pătruţ, & C. Cmeciu (Eds.), *Social media and the new academic environment: Pedagogical challenges* (pp. 256–272). Hershey, PA: Information Science Reference; doi:10.4018/978-1-4666-2851-9.ch013

Zervas, P., & Alexandraki, C. (2013). The realisation of online music services through intelligent computing. In D. Kanellopoulos (Ed.), *Intelligent multimedia technologies for networking applications: Techniques and tools* (pp. 291–317). Hershey, PA: Information Science Reference; doi:10.4018/978-1-4666-2833-5.ch012

Zhang, J., & Mao, E. (2013). The effects of consumption values on the use of location-based services on smartphones. In I. Lee (Ed.), *Strategy, adoption, and competitive advantage of mobile services in the global economy* (pp. 1–18). Hershey, PA: Information Science Reference; doi:10.4018/978-1-4666-1939-5.ch001

Zhang, S., Köbler, F., Tremaine, M., & Milewski, A. (2012). Instant messaging in global software teams. In N. Kock (Ed.), *Advancing collaborative knowledge environments: New trends in e-collaboration* (pp. 158–179). Hershey, PA: Information Science Reference; doi:10.4018/978-1-61350-459-8.ch010

Zhang, T., Wang, C., Luo, Z., Han, S., & Dong, M. (2013). RFID enabled vehicular network for ubiquitous travel query. In D. Chiu (Ed.), *Mobile and web innovations in systems and service-oriented engineering* (pp. 348–363). Hershey, PA: Information Science Reference; doi:10.4018/978-1-4666-2470-2.ch019

Zhang, W. (2012). Virtual communities as subaltern public spheres: A theoretical development and an application to the Chinese internet. In H. Li (Ed.), *Virtual community participation and motivation: Cross-disciplinary theories* (pp. 143–159). Hershey, PA: Information Science Reference; doi:10.4018/978-1-4666-0312-7.ch009

Zhang, X., Wang, L., Li, Y., & Liang, W. (2013). Global community extraction in social network analysis. In G. Xu & L. Li (Eds.), *Social media mining and social network analysis: Emerging research* (pp. 156–171). Hershey, PA: Information Science Reference; doi:10.4018/978-1-4666-2806-9.ch010

Zhang, X., Wang, L., Li, Y., & Liang, W. (2013). Local community extraction in social network analysis. In G. Xu & L. Li (Eds.), *Social media mining and social network analysis: Emerging research* (pp. 172–181). Hershey, PA: Information Science Reference; doi:10.4018/978-1-4666-2806-9.ch011

Zulu, S. F. (2013). Emerging information and communication technology policy framework for Africa. In B. Maumbe & J. Okello (Eds.), *Technology, sustainability, and rural development in Africa* (pp. 236–256). Hershey, PA: Information Science Reference; doi:10.4018/978-1-4666-3607-1.ch016

Compilation of References

#YoSoy132. (2012a, May 28). *Manifiesto del #YoSoy132*. Retrieved from https://www.youtube.com/watch?v=igxPudJF6nU

#YoSoy132. (2012b, September 1). *Contrainforme presidencial*. Retrieved from http://www.sinembargo.mx/01-09-2012/352855

Abramowitz, A. (2010). *The disappearing center: Engaged citizens, polarization, and American democracy*. New Haven, CT: Yale University Press.

Abramowitz, A., & Saunders, K. (2008). Is polarization a myth? *The Journal of Politics*, *70*(2), 542–555. doi:10.1017/S0022381608080493

Adams, A., & McCorkindale, T. (2013). Dialogue and transparency: A content analysis of how the 2012 presidential candidates used twitter. *Public Relations Review*, *39*(4), 357–359. doi:10.1016/j.pubrev.2013.07.016

Aday, S., Farrel, H., Lynch, M., Sides, J., Kelly, J., & Zuckerman, E. (2010). *Blogs and bullets: New media in contentious politics. Technical report*. U.S. Institute of Peace.

Adi, A., Erickson, K., & Lilleker, D. (2014). Elite tweets: Analyzing the Twitter communication patterns of Labour Party peers in the House of Lords. *Policy & Internet*, *6*(1), 1–27. doi:10.1002/1944-2866.POI350

Agrawal, D., Budak, C., & Abbadi, A. E. (2011). Information diffusion in social networks: Observing and influencing societal interests. In *Proceedings of the 37th International Conference on Very Large Data Bases*. Seattle, WA: VLDB. Retrieved September 10, 2014, from http://www.cs.ucsb.edu/~cbudak/social-tutorial.pdf

Aguinaldo, P. J. (2012). Qualitative analysis in Gay Men's Health Research: Comparing Thematic, Critical Discourse, and Conversation Analysis. *Journal of Homosexuality*, *59*(6), 765–787. doi:10.1080/00918369.2012.694753 PMID:22853179

Ajanslar, D. (2014). *Türkiye Twitter kullanıcı istatistikleri-2014*. Retrieved January 15, 2015, from https://twitter.com/search?q=%23whousestwitter%20Turkey&src=typd

Akça, I. (2013). *Türk siyasal hayatı*. Eskişehir: Anadolu Üniversitesi.

Akdenizli, B. (2015). Introduction. In B. Akdenizli (Ed.), *Digital transformations in Turkey: Current perspectives in communication studies* (p. ix–3). Lanham, MD: Lexington Books.

Alexander, J. C., & Jacobs, R. N. (1998). Mass Communication, Ritual and Civil Society. In T. Liebes & J. Curran (Eds.), *Media, ritual, and identity* (pp. 23–41). London: Routledge.

Alfaro, R. M. (2000). Culturas populares y comunicación participativa. *Revista Caminos*, *20*, 13–20.

Allan, S., & Zelizer, B. (Eds.). (2004). *Reporting War: Journalism in Wartime*. London: Taylor & Francis.

Almond, G., & Verba, S. (1963). *Civic culture: Political attitudes and democracy in five nations*. Princeton: Princeton University Press.

Alonso, L. E. (1986). La mediación institucional y sus límites en el capitalismo avanzado. *Revista Espanola de Investigaciones Sociologicas*, *35*(35), 63–79. doi:10.2307/40183154

American National Election Studies. (2014). User's guide and codebook for the ANES 2012 time series study. Ann Arbor, MI: The University of Michigan and Stanford University

Anstead, N., & Chadwick, A. (2009). Parties, Election Campaigning and the Internet: Toward A Comparative Institutional Approach. In A. Chadwick & P. N. Howard (Eds.), *The Handbook of Internet Politics* (pp. 56–71). London: Routledge.

Aragón, P., Kappler, K. E., Kaltenbrunner, A., Laniado, D., & Volkovich, Y. (2013). Communication Dynamics in Twitter during Political Campaigns: The Case of the 2011 Spanish National Election. *Policy & Internet*, *5*(2), 183–206. doi:10.1002/1944-2866.POI327

Arceneaux, K., & Johnson, M. (2013). *Changing minds or changing channels: Partisan news in an age of choice*. Chicago: University of Chicago Press. doi:10.7208/chicago/9780226047447.001.0001

Arditi, B. (2012). Insurgencies don't have a plan – they are the plan: Political performatives and vanishing mediators in 2011. *Journalism, Media and Cultural Studies, 1*, 1-16. Retrieved from http://www.cardiff.ac.uk/jomec/jomecjournal/1-june2012/arditi_insurgencies.pdf

Arquilla, J., & Ronfeldt, D. (2000). *Swarming and the future of conflict*. Retrieved from: http://goo.gl/uAOxr0

Attard, A., & Coulson, S. N. (2012). A thematic analysis of patient communication in Parkinson's disease online support group discussion forums. *Computers in Human Behavior*, *28*(2), 500–506. doi:10.1016/j.chb.2011.10.022

Attolini, A. (2012, September 19). Por una democracia auténtica, #YoSoy132. *ADN Político*. Retrieved from http://www.adnpolitico.com/opinion/2012/09/19/antonio-attolini-por-una-democracia-autentica-yosoy132

Atton, A. (2002). *Alternative media*. London: Sage.

Atwater, T., Fico, F., & Pizante, G. (1987). Reporting on the state legislature: A case study of inter-media agenda-setting. *Newspaper Research Journal*, *8*(2), 53–61.

Autonome k. a. gruppe. (2003). What is Communication Guerrilla. In J. Richardson (Ed.), Anarchitexts: Voices from global digital resistance (pp. 86-91). New York: Autonomedia.

Aydın-Düzgit, S., & Keyman, E. F. (2012). *EU-Turkey relations and the stagnation of Turkish democracy* (Working Paper No. 2). Rome: IAI. Retrieved May 10, 2015, from http://mercury.ethz.ch/serviceengine/Files/ISN/156275/ipublicationdocument_singledocument/ff7f8ab1-6376-4be1-817f-c1a2228fe918/en/GTE_WP_02.pdf

Ayres, J. M. (1999). From the streets to the Internet: The cyber-diffusion of contention. *The Annals of the American Academy of Political and Social Science*, *566*(1), 132–143. doi:10.1177/0002716299566001011

Bamman, D., O'Connor, B., & Smith, N. (2012). Censorship and deletion practices in Chinese social media. *First Monday*, *17*(3). doi:10.5210/fm.v17i3.3943

Banaji, S., & Buckingham, D. (2013). *The civic web. Young people, the Internet and civic participation*. Cambridge, MA: The MIT Press.

Banducci, S. (2005). *Media Exposure, Media Content and Voter Mobilization: Implications for the Lijphart Thesis*. Annual Meeting of the American Political Science Association, Washington, DC.

Banwart, M. C. (2002). *Videostyle and webstyle in 2000: Comparing the gender differences of candidate presentations in political advertising and on the internet.* (Unpublished PhD Dissertation). University of Oklahoma, Oklahoma.

Barberá, P., & Rivero, G. (July, 2012). *¿Un tweet, un voto? Desigualdad de la discusión política de Twitter.* Symposium presented by at I Congreso Internacional en Comunicación Política y Estrategias de Campaña, Madrid, Spain.

Bardici, M. V. (2012). A Discourse Analysis of the Media Representation of Social Media for Social Change - The Case of Egyptian Revolution and Political Change. (Master dissertation). Malmö University. Retrieved from http://muep.mah.se/handle/2043/14121

Bärenreuter, C., Brüll, C., Mokre, M., & Wahl-Jorgensen, K. (2009). *An Overview of Research on the European Public Sphere.* Online Working Paper No. 03.

Barker, D. C. (2002). *Rushed to Judgment. Talk Radio, Persuasion and American Political Behavior.* New York: Columbia University Press.

Barnhurst, K. G., & Quinn, K. (2012). Political visions: Visual studies in political communication. In H. A. Semetko & M. Scammell (Eds.), *The SAGE handbook of political communication* (pp. 276–291). Thousand Oaks, CA: Sage. doi:10.4135/9781446201015.n23

Barry, E. (2009, April 8). Protests in Moldova explode, with help of twitter. *The New York Times*, p. A1.

Bauman, Z. (2000). *Liquid modernity.* Cambridge, MA: Polity Press.

Baumgarten, B. (2013). Geração à Rasca and beyond: Mobilizations in Portugal after 12 March 201. *Current Sociology, 61*(4), 457–473. doi:10.1177/0011392113479745

Baum, M. A., & Kernell, S. (1999). Has cable ended the golden age of presidential television? *The American Political Science Review, 93*(1), 99–114. doi:10.2307/2585763

Baxter, G., & Marcella, R. (2013). Do Online Election Campaign Sway the Vote? A Study of the 2011 Scottish Parliamentary Elections. *Libri, 63*(3), 190–205. doi:10.1515/libri-2013-0015

Benjamin, W. (1999). The Storyteller - Reflections on the work of Nikolai Leskov. In H. Arendt (Ed.), *Illuminations* (pp. 83–107). London: Pimlico.

Benkler, Y. (2006). *The Wealth of Networks: How Social Production Transforms Markets and Freedom.* New Haven, CT: Yale University Press.

Benkler, Y. (2006). *The wealth of networks: How social production transforms markets and freedom.* Yale University Press.

Bennett, W. L. (2003). Communicating global activism: Strengths and vulnerabilities of networked politics. *Information Communication and Society, 6*(2), 143–168. doi:10.1080/1369118032000093860a

Bennett, W. L., & Segerberg, A. (2012). The logic of connective action. *Information Communication and Society, 15*(5), 739–768. doi:10.1080/1369118X.2012.670661

Benoit, W. L. (2004). Political Party Affiliation and Presidential Campaign Discourse. *Communication Quarterly, 52*(2), 81–97. doi:10.1080/01463370409370183

Benoit, W. L. (2011). Content Analysis in Political Communication. In E. P. Bucy & R. L. Holbert (Eds.), *The Sourcebook for Political Communication Research: Methods, Measures, and Analytical Techniques* (pp. 268–279). New York: Routledge.

Benoit, W. L., & Benoit, P. J. (2008). *Persuasive Messages: The Process of Influence.* Malden, MA: Blackwell Publishing.

Benoit, W. L., Henson, J., Davis, C., Glantz, M., Phillips, A., & Rill, L. (2013). Stumping on the Internet 2008 Presidential primary candidate campaign webpages. *Human Communication, 16*(1), 1–12.

Bentham, J. (2001). Farming defended. In M. Quinn (Ed.), *Writings on the Poor Laws* (Vol. 1, pp. 276–290). Oxford, UK: Oxford University Press.

Bentivegna, S. (2006). Rethinking politics in the world of ICTs. *European Journal of Communication, 21*(3), 331–343. doi:10.1177/0267323106066638

Berelson, B. (1952). *Content Analysis in Communication Research*. New York: Free Press.

Berleson, B., Lazarsfeld, P. F., & McPhee, W. N. (1954). *Voting: Study of Opinion Formation in a Presidential Campaign*. Chicago: University of Chicago Press.

Best, S. J., & Krueger, B. S. (2005). Analyzing the representativeness of Internet political participation. *Political Behavior, 27*(2), 183–216. doi:10.1007/s11109-005-3242-y

Bimber, B., & Davis, R. (2003). *Campaigning online: The Internet in U.S. elections*. New York, NY: Oxford University Press.

Binder, J. F., Howes, A., & Smart, D. (2012). Harmony and tension on social network sites. *Information Communication and Society, 15*(9), 1279–1297. doi:10.1080/1369118X.2011.648949

Bishop, B. (2008). *The big sort*. Boston: Houghton Mifflin.

Blumler, J. G., & Coleman, S. (2001). *Realising democracy online: A civic commons in cyberspace*. London: IPPR. Retrieved May 12, 2015, from http://www.gov2u.org/publications/10_coleman-realising%20democracy.pdf

Blumler, J. (1983). *Communicating to Voters: Television in the First European Parliament Elections*. London: Sage.

Blumler, J. G., & Kavanagh, D. (1999). The third age of political communication: Influences and features. *Political Communication, 16*(3), 209–230. doi:10.1080/105846099198596

Bolt, N. (2012). *The violent image. Insurgent propaganda and the new revolutionaries*. London: Hurst and Company.

Bourdieu, P. (1990). *Photography. A middle-brow art* (S. Whiteside, Trans.). Cambridge, MA: Polity Press.

Boyd, D. (2011). Social network sites as networked publics. In Z. Papacharissi (Ed.), *Networked Self: Identity, Community, and Culture on Social Network Sites* (pp. 39–58). New York: Routledge.

Brady, H. E., Johnston, R., & Sides, J. (2006). The Study of Political Campaigns. In H. E. Brady & R. Johnston (Eds.), *Capturing Campaign Effects* (pp. 1–26). Ann Arbor, MI: The University of Michigan Press.

Braun, V., & Clarke, V. (2006). Using thematic analysis in psychology. *Qualitative Research in Psychology, 3*(2), 77–101. doi:10.1191/1478088706qp063oa

Brighenti, A. M. (2010). *Visibility in social theory and social research*. London: Palgrave Macmillan. doi:10.1057/9780230282056

Brunk, G. G., & Fishkin, J. A. (1982). Media coverage of presidential candidates: A study of popularity prior to the 1976 national nominating conventions. *Communication Research, 9*(4), 525–538. doi:10.1177/009365082009004002

Bruns, A., & Burgess, J. E. (2011). The use of Twitter hashtags in the formation of ad hoc publics. In *6th European Consortium for Political Research General Conference*. University of Iceland.

Bruns, A., & Moe, H. (2013). Structural Layers of Communication on Twitter. In K. Weller, A. Bruns, J. Burgess, M. Mahrt, & C. Puschmann (Eds.), *Twitter and Society* (pp. 15–28). New York, NY: Peter Lang.

Bruns, A., & Stieglitz, S. (2012). Quantitative approaches to comparing communication patterns on Twitter. *Journal of Technology in Human Services*, *30*(3-4), 160–185. doi:10.1080/15228835.2012.744249

Burgess, J., & Sauter, L. (2014). *Hashtag as hybrid forum: the case of #agchatoz*. Paper presented at the Conference "Social Media and the Transformation of Public Space", Amsterdam.

Burgess, J., & Bruns, A. (2012). '(Not) The Twitter election: The dynamics of the #ausvotes conversation in relation to the Australian media ecology'. *Journalism Studies*, *6*, 384–402.

Buturoiu, R. (2014). Every comments counts. The 2014 EP elections in Romania on Facebook. *Sfera Politicii/The Sphere of Politics, 179*(3), 46-55.

Bystrom, D., & Kaid, L. L. (2002). Are women candidates transforming campaign communication? A comparison of advertising videostyles in the 1990s. In C. S. Rosenthal(Ed.), *Women Transforming Congress* (pp. 146–169). Norman, OK: University of Oklahoma Press.

Caers, R., De Feyter, T., De Couck, M., Stough, T., Vigna, C., & Du Bois, C. (2013). Facebook: A literature review. *New Media & Society*, *15*(6), 982–1002. doi:10.1177/1461444813488061

Calhoun, C. (1993). Civil society and the public sphere. *Public Culture*, *5*(2), 267–267. doi:10.1215/08992363-5-2-267

Callon, M., Lascoumes, P., & Barth, Y. (2001). *Acting in an Uncertain World. An Essay on Technical Democracy*. Cambridge, MA: MIT Press.

Cammaerts, B. (2007). Citizenship, the Public Sphere and Media. In Reclaming the Media: Communication Rights and Democratic Media roles (pp. 1-8). Bristol: Intellect Books.

Campante, F., & Hojman, J. (2013). Media polarization: Evidence from the introduction of broadcast TV in the United States. *Journal of Public Economics*, *100*, 79–92. doi:10.1016/j.jpubeco.2013.02.006

Campbell, K. K., & Jamieson, K. H. (2008). *Presidents creating the presidency: Deeds done in words*. Chicago, IL: University of Chicago Press.

Capital Social Investigaciones. (2012, June 20). *Algunos datos sobre la actividad en Twitter del debate de YoSoy132*. Retrieved from http://capitalsocialmexico.com/2012/06/20/algunos-datos-sobre-la-actividad-en-twitter-del-debate-de-yosoy132/

Capriles, O. (2006). Alternative communication, horizontal communication, alternative use of media, participant communication: Which is the paradigm? In A. Gamucio-Dragon & T. Tufte (Eds.), *Communication for Social Change Anthology: Historical and Contemporary Readings* (pp. 302–305). Communication for Social Change Consortium.

Carbaugh, D. (2007). Ethnography of Communication. In W. Donsbach (Ed.), *International Encyclopedia of Communication*. Hoboken, NJ: Wiley Blackwell. Retrieved October, 15, from http://works.bepress.com/donal_carbaugh/12

Cardenal, A. (2013). Why mobilize support online? The paradox of party behavior online. *Party Politics*, *19*(1), 83–103. doi:10.1177/1354068810395059

Carpenter, A. C. (2010). The Obamachine: Technopolitics 2.0. *Journal of Information Technology & Politics*, *7*(2-3), 216–225. doi:10.1080/19331681003765887

Carpentier, N. (2012). The concept of participation. If they have access and interact, do they really participate. *Revista Fronteiras – Estudos Midiáticos, 14*(2), 164-177.

Carsey, T. M. (2001). *Campaign Dynamics: The Race for Governor.* The University of Michigan Press.

Carsey, T. M., Jackson, R. A., Stewart, M., & Nelson, J. P. (2011). Strategic Candidates, Campaign Dynamics, and Campaign Advertising in Grubernatorial Races. *State Politics & Policy Quarterly, 11*(3), 269–298. doi:10.1177/1532440011413085

Casero-Ripollés, A. (2010). El despertar del público?: Comunicación política, ciudadanía y web 2.0. In M. Martin Vicente & D. Rothberg (Eds.), *Meios de comunicaçao e cidadania* (pp. 107–122). São Paulo: Cultura Académica.

Castells, M. (2000). Materials for an exploratory theory of the network society. *The British Journal of Sociology, 51*(1), 5–24. doi:10.1080/000713100358408

Castells, M. (2004). *The network society: A cross-cultural perspective.* Northampton, MA: Edward Elgar Publishing. doi:10.4337/9781845421663

Castells, M. (2007). Communication, power and counter-power in the network society. *International Journal of Communication, 1*(1), 238–266.

Castells, M. (2009). *Communication power.* Oxford, UK: Oxford University Press.

Castells, M. (2009). *Communication Power.* Oxford, UK: Oxford University Press.

Castells, M. (2012). *Networks of outrage and hope: Social movements in the internet age.* Cambridge: Polity.

Castletrione, I. (2014). Facebook and political Information in Italy and the UK: An antidote against political fragmentation and polarization. *Online Journal of Communication and Media Technologies, 4*(1), 27–49.

Chadwick, A. (2008). Web 2.0: New challenges for the study of e-democracy in an era of informational exuberance. *I/S: A Journal of Law and Policy for the Information Society, 5*(1), 9–41.

Chadwick, A. (2006). *Internet Politics: States, Citizens, and New Communication Technologies.* Oxford, UK: Oxford University Press.

Chadwick, A. (2011). The political information cycle in a hybrid news system: The British prime minister and the "bullygate" affair. *The International Journal of Press/Politics, 16*(1), 3–29. doi:10.1177/1940161210384730

Chan, M., Wu, X., Hao, Y., Xi, R., & Jin, T. (2012). Microblogging, online expression, and political efficacy among young Chinese citizens: The moderating role of information and entertainment needs in the use of Weibo. *Cyberpsychology, Behavior, and Social Networking, 15*(7), 345–349. doi:10.1089/cyber.2012.0109 PMID:22780993

Chen, P., & Walsh, L. (2009). E-election 2007: Political competition online. *Australian Cultural History, 28*(1), 47–54.

Chomsky, N. (2012). *Occupy.* Retrieved from Amazon.com

Choucri, N. (2012). *Cyberpolitics in international relations.* Cambridge, MA: The MIT Press.

Chouliaraki, L. (2010). Self-mediation: New media and citizenship. *Critical Discourse Studies, 7*(4), 227–232. doi:10.1080/17405904.2010.511824

Christensen, C. (2009, July). Iran: networked dissent. *Le Monde diplomatique.* Retrieved January 07, 2011, from http://mondediplo.com/blogs/iran-networked-dissent

Claassen, B., & Highton, B. (2009). Policy polarization among party elites and the significance of political awareness in the mass public. *Political Research Quarterly, 62*(3), 538–551. doi:10.1177/1065912908322415

Cleaver, H. (1998). The Zapatista effect: The internet an the rise of an alternative political fabric. *Journal of International Affairs, 51*(2), 621–640.

Cmeciu, C., & Pătruţ, M. (2014). The visual framing of Romanian women politicians in personal campaign blogs during the 2012 Romanian parliamentary elections. In M. Raicheva-Stover & E. Ibroscheva (Eds.), *Women in politics and the media: Perspectives from nations in transition* (pp. 181-198). London: Bloomsbury.

Cmeciu, C. (2005). *Strategii persuasive în discursul politic/Persuasive strategies in political discourse*. Iaşi. *Universitas*, XXI.

Cmeciu, C. (2014). Beyond the online faces of Romanian candidates for the 2014 European Parliament Elections - A visual framing analysis of Facebook photographic Images. In G. Horvath, R. K. Bako, & E. Biro-Kaszas (Eds.), *Ten years of Facebook* (pp. 405–434). Debrecen: Debrecen University Press.

CoARS. (2015). *Archive of Court of Audit of the Republic of Slovenia audit reports*. Retrieved February 1, 2015, from http://www.rs-rs.si/rsrs/rsrseng.nsf/RevizijeArhiv?OpenForm&appSource=AA288C363EA722B2C125715C001B5795

Colectivo Másde131. (2014). *Sobre nosotros* [About us]. Retrieved from http://www.colectivo131.com.mx/

Coleman, S. (2001). Online campaigning. In P. Norris (Ed.), *Britain Votes 2001*. Oxford, UK: Oxford University Press. doi:10.1093/parlij/54.4.679

Coleman, S., & Blumler, J. G. (2009). *The Internet and democratic citizenship: Theory, practice and policy*. Cambridge, UK: Cambridge University Press. doi:10.1017/CBO9780511818271

Conover, P. J. (1981). Political Cues and the Perception of Candidates. *American Politics Quarterly*, *9*(4), 427–445. doi:10.1177/1532673X8100900403

Corner, J. (2007). Mediated politics, promotional culture and the idea of "propaganda". *Media Culture & Society*, *29*(4), 669–677. doi:10.1177/0163443707078428

Costa Lobo, M., & Curtice, J. (Eds.). (2015). *Personality Politics? The Role of Leader Evaluations in Democratic Elections*. Oxford, UK: Oxford University Press.

Cottle, S. (2011). Media and the Arab uprisings of 2011: Research notes. *Journalism*, *12*(5), 647–659. doi:10.1177/1464884911410017

Cotton, J. (1985). Cognitive dissonance in selective exposure. In D. Zillman & J. Bryant (Eds.), *Selective Exposure to Communication* (pp. 11–34). Hillsdale, NJ: Lawrence Erlbaum Associates.

Couldry, N. (2010). *Why voice matters: Culture and Politics after Neoliberalism*. London: Sage.

Couldry, N. (2012). *Media, Society, World*. Cambridge, MA: Polity Press.

Couldry, N., & Curran, J. (Eds.). (2003). *Contesting media power: Alternative media in a networked world*. Lanham, MD: Rowman Littlefield Publishers.

Craig, S. C., & Hill, D. B. (Eds.). (2010). *The Electoral Challenge: Theory Meets Practice*. Sage Publications.

Crawford, K. (2009). Following you: Disciplines of listening in social media. *Continuum (Perth)*, *23*(4), 525–535. doi:10.1080/10304310903003270

Dahlberg, L., & Siapera, E. (Eds.). (2007). *Radical Democracy and the Internet: Interrogating Theory and Practice*. Basingstoke, UK: Palgrave Macmillan. doi:10.1057/9780230592469

Dahlgren, P. (2005). The Internet, public spheres, and political communication: Dispersion and deliberation. *Political Communication*, *22*(2), 147–162. doi:10.1080/10584600590933160

Dahlgren, P. (2009). *Media and Political Engagement: Citizens, Communication and Democracy*. New York: Cambridge University Press.

Dahlgren, P. (2013). *The Political Web: Media, Participation and Alternative Democracy*. Hampshire: Macmillan Publisher. doi:10.1057/9781137326386

Dale, A., & Strauss, A. (2009). Don't Forget to Vote: Text Message Reminders as a Mobilization Tool. *American Journal of Political Science*, *53*(4), 787–804. doi:10.1111/j.1540-5907.2009.00401.x

Dalton, R. J. (2002). *Citizen politics. Public opinion and political parties in advanced industrial democracies*. New York: Chatham House Publishers.

Dan, V., & Iorgoveanu, A. (2013). Still on the beaten path: How gender impacted the coverage of male and female Romanian candidates for European Office. *The International Journal of Press/Politics*, *18*(2), 208–233. doi:10.1177/1940161212473508

Davidson-Schmich, L., & Davidson-Schmich, M. (2005). *The Content of European Parliament Election Campaigns: A Framework for Analysis and Evidence from Germany in 2004*. University of Miami, EU Center Working Paper.

Davis, A. (2010). *Political Communication and Social Theory*. London, UK: Taylor & Francis.

Davis, S., Elin, L., & Reeher, G. (2002). *Click on Democracy: The Internet's Power to Change Political Apathy into Civic Action*. Boulder, CO: Westview Press.

Dayan, D. (2005). Mothers, Midwives and Abortionists. Genealogy and obstetrics of Audiences and Publics. In S. Livingstone (Ed.), *Audiences and Publics. When Cultural Engagement matters for the Public Sphere* (pp. 43–76). Bristol, CT: Intellect Press.

De Mauleón, H. (2012, September 1). De la red a las calles. *Nexos*. Retrieved from http://elecciones2012mx.wordpress.com/2012/09/01/de-la-red-a-las-calles-hector-de-mauleon-blog-nexos-en-linea/

De Ugarte, D. (2007). *El poder de las redes. Manual ilustrado para personas, colectivos y empresas abocados al ciberactivismo*. Retrieved from: http://goo.gl/evRfYO

de Vrees, C. H., & Boomgaarden, H. G. (2012). Comparing news on Europe: Elections and beyond. In F. Esser & Th. Hanitzsch (Eds.), *Handbook of Comparative Communication Research* (pp. 327–340). New York: Routledge.

De Vreese, C. H., Banducci, S. A., Semetko, H. A., & Boomgaarden, H. G. (2006). The News Coverage of the 2004 European Parliamentary Election Campaign in 25 Countries. *European Union Politics*, *7*(4), 477–504. doi:10.1177/1465116506069440

De Wilde, P. (2011). No Polity for Old Politics? A Framework for Analyzing the Politicization of European Integration. *Journal of European Integration*, *33*(5), 559–575. doi:10.1080/07036337.2010.546849

De Wilde, P., & Zürn, M. (2012). Can the Politicization of European Integration Be Reversed? *Journal of Common Market Studies*, *50*(1), 137–153. doi:10.1111/j.1468-5965.2011.02232.x

Dean, J. (2003). Why the net is not a public sphere. *Constellations (Oxford, England)*, *10*(1), 95–112. doi:10.1111/1467-8675.00315

della Porta, D. (2012). Mobilizing against the crisis, mobilizing for 'another democracy': comparing two global waves of protest. *Interface: A Journal for and about Social Movements, 4*(1), 274-277.

della Porta, D. (2007). *The global justice movement. Cross national and transnational perspectives*. London: Paradigm Publisher.

Della Porta, D. (2013). Repertoires of contention. In D. A. Snow, D. Della Porta, B. Klandermans, & D. McAdam (Eds.), *The Wiley-Blackwell Encyclopedia of Social and Political Movements*. Malden, MA: Blackwell; doi:10.1002/9780470674871.wbespm178

della Porta, D., & Diani, M. (2006). *Social movements: An introduction*. Malden, MA: Blackwell.

Deuze, M. (2006). Participation, remediation, bricolage: Considering principal components of a digital culture. *The Information Society*, *22*(2), 63–75. doi:10.1080/01972240600567170

Dewey, J. (1927). *The Public and its problems*. New York: Holt.

Deželan, T., Krašovec, A., & Kovačič, M. (2010). Volilna kampanja po slovensko. In S. Kustec Lipicer (Ed.), *Politične vsebine in volilna kampanja: slovenska izkušnja z volitev v Evropski parlament 2009* (pp. 53–70). Ljubljana: FDV.

Deželan, T., Vobič, I., & Maksuti, A. (2014). Twitter Campaigning in the 2011 National Election in Slovenia: Strategy and Application of the Twitter Social Media Outlet in Party Election Campaigns. In B. Patrut & M. Patrut (Eds.), *Social Media in Politics: Case Studies on the Political Power of Social Media* (pp. 141–163). Cham: Springer. doi:10.1007/978-3-319-04666-2_9

Di Gennaro, C., & Dutton, W. (2006). The Internet and the public: Online and offline political participation in the United Kingdom. *Parliamentary Affairs*, *59*(2), 299–313. doi:10.1093/pa/gsl004

Dimaggio, P., Evans, J., & Bryson, B. (1996). Have Americans' social attitudes become more polarized? *American Journal of Sociology*, *102*(3), 690–755. doi:10.1086/230995

Dimmock, M., Kiley, J., Keeter, S., & Doherty, C. (2014). *Political polarization in the American public*. Retrieved July 27, 2014 from http://www.people-press.org/files/2014/06/6-12-2014-Political-Polarization-Release.pdf

Dolan, K. (2005). Do women candidates play to gender stereotypes? Do men candidates play to women? candidate sex and issues priorities on campaign websites. *Political Research Quarterly*, *58*(1), 31–44. doi:10.1177/106591290505800103

Dongwon, J. (2010). Real-time networked media activism in the 2008 Chotbul protest. *Interface: A Journal for and about Social Movements, 2*(2), 92-102.

Downey, J., & Fenton, N. (2003). New media, counter publicity and the public sphere. *New Media & Society*, *5*(2), 185–202. doi:10.1177/1461444803005002003

Downing, J. (2003). The independent media center movement center and the anarchist socialist tradition. In N. Couldry & J. Curran (Eds.), Contesting media power: Alternative media in a connected world (pp. 243–258). Oxford, UK: Rowman & Littlefield Publishers.

Downing, J. (2013, March). *Recent (2012) approaches to social movement media: A critique*. Paper presented at the conference Social Movements, Media, Networking and Politics, Izmir, Turkey.

Downing, J. (1984). *Radical media: The political experience of alternative communication*. Boston: South End Press.

Downing, J. (2001). *Radical media: Rebellious communication and social movements* (2nd ed.). Thousand Oaks, CA: SAGE.

Downing, J. (2008). Social movement theories and alternative media. *Communication, Culture & Critique*, *1*(1), 40–50. doi:10.1111/j.1753-9137.2007.00005.x

Downs, A. (1957). *An economic theory of democracy*. New York: Harper Collins.

Doxiadis, K. (2013). Political Discourse in Contemporary Greece. Network for Political Discourse Analysis: Working Texts, 1, 1-22.

Duncombe, S. (1997). *Notes from underground: Zines and the politics of alternative culture*. London: Verso.

Dylko, I., & McCluskey, M. (2012). Media effects in an era of rapid technological transformation: A case of user-generated content and political participation. *Communication Theory*, *22*(3), 250–278. doi:10.1111/j.1468-2885.2012.01409.x

Eagleton-Pierce, M. (2001). The internet and the Seattle WTO protests. *Peace Review*, *13*(3), 386–401. doi:10.1080/13668800120079027

Edelstein, A. (1997). *Total Propaganda: From Mass Culture to Popular Culture*. London: Lawrence Erlbaum Associates Publishers.

Eisenberg, A. I. (1995). *Reconstructing political pluralism*. Albany, NY: State University of New York Press.

Ellul, J. (1973). *Propaganda, the Formation of Men's Attitudes*. New York: Vintage Books.

El-Nawawy, M., & Khamis, S. (2012). Political Activism 2.0: Comparing the role of social media in Egypt's "Facebook revolution" and Iran's "Twitter uprising". *CyberOrient*, *6*(1). Retrieved March 14, 2013, from http://www.cyberorient.net/article.do?articleId=7439

Elson, S. B., Yeung, D., Roshan, P., Bohandy, S. R., & Nader, A. (2012). *Using social media to gauge Iranian public opinion and mood after the 2009 election*. Santa Monica, CA: Rand Corporation.

Erickson, I. (2010). Geography and community: New forms of interaction among people and places. *The American Behavioral Scientist*, *53*(8), 1194–1207. doi:10.1177/0002764209356250

Erikson, R. S., & Wlezien, C. (1999). Presidential polls as a time series: The case of 1996. *Public Opinion Quarterly*, *63*(2), 163–177. doi:10.1086/297709

Esser, F., & Strömbäck, J. (Eds.). (2014). *Mediatization of Politics: Understanding the Transformation of Western Democracies*. London: Palgrave Macmillan. doi:10.1057/9781137275844

Ever, A., & Wintersberger, H. (1990). *Shifts in the Welfare Mix. Their impact on work, social services and Welfare policies*. Westview Press.

Facebook. (2013). *Investor relations: Facebook reports first quarter 2013 results*. Retrieved from http://investor.fb.com/releasedetail.cfm?ReleaseID=761090

Facebook. (2014). *How news feed works*. Retrieved October 4, 2014 from https://www.facebook.com/help/327131014036297/

Fairclough, I., & Fairclough, N. (2012). *Political Discourse Analysis: A Method for Advanced Students*. London: Routledge.

Fairclough, N. (1995). *Critical Discourse Analysis*. London: Longman.

Faresi, M. (2013). *Yandaş medyaya göre Taksim'de hiçbir şey olmamış!* Retrieved February 22, 2014, from http://www.medyafaresi.com/haber/Yandas-medyaya-gore-Taksimde-hicbir-sey-olmamis_109002.html

Feenstra, R., & Casero-Ripollés, A. (2014). Democracy in the Digital Communication Environment: A Typology Proposal of Political Monitoring Processes. *International Journal of Communication*, *8*, 2448–2468. Retrieved from http://ijoc.org/index.php/ijoc/article/view/2815

Fiorina, M., Abrams, S., & Pope, J. (2010). *Culture war?: The myth of a polarized America* (3rd ed.). New York: Longman.

Fisher, E. (2010). *Media and new capitalism in the digital age: The spirit of networks.* Basingstoke, UK: Palgrave Macmillan. doi:10.1057/9780230106062

Flesher Fomiyana, C. (2014). *Social movements and globalization. How protests, occupations and uprisings are changing the world.* London: Palgrave Macmillan.

Flew, T., & Young, G. (2005). *From E-Government to Online Deliberative Democracy.* Presented on the International Conference on Engaging Communities, Brisbane, Australia.

Flew, T., Bruns, A., Burgess, J. E., Crawford, K., & Shaw, F. (2013). *Social media and its impact on crisis communication: Case studies of Twitter use in emergency management in Australia and New Zealand.* In ICA Regional Conference "Communication and Social Transformation", Shanghai, China.

Foot, K. A., & Schneider, S. M. (2006). *Web campaigning.* Cambridge, MA: MIT Press.

Foot, K., Xenos, M., Schneider, S., Kluver, R., & Jankowski, N. (2009). Electoral web production practices in cross-national perspective: The relative influence of national development, political culture, and web genre 2008. In A. Chadwick & P. Howard (Eds.), *Handbook of Internet politics* (pp. 40–55). London, UK: Routledge.

Franklin, B. (1995). A bibliographical essay. *Political Communication, 12*, 223–242. doi:10.1080/10584609.1995.9963067

Franzosi, R. (1998). Narrative analysis -Or why (and how) sociologists should be interested in narrative. *Annual Review of Sociology, 24*(1), 517–554. doi:10.1146/annurev.soc.24.1.517

Fraser, N. (1990). Rethinking the public sphere: A contribution to the critique of actually existing democracy. *Social Text*, (25/26): 56–80. doi:10.2307/466240

Fraser, N. (1992). Rethinking the Public Sphere: a Contribution to the Critique of Actually Existing Democracy. In C. Calhoun (Ed.), *Habermas and The Public Sphere* (pp. 109–142). Cambridge, MA: The MIT Press.

Freelon, D. G. (2010). Analyzing online political discussion using three models of democratic communication. *New Media & Society, 12*(7), 1172–1190. doi:10.1177/1461444809357927

Fuchs, C. (2012). Social media, riots, and revolutions. *Capital and Class, 36*(3), 383–391. doi:10.1177/0309816812453613

Fuchs, C. (2014). *Social media: A critical introduction.* London: Sage. doi:10.4135/9781446270066.n2

Gainous, J., Marlowe, A. D., & Wagner, K. M. (2013). Traditional cleavages or a new world: Does online social networking bridge the political participation divide? *International Journal of Politics Culture and Society, 26*(2), 145–158. doi:10.1007/s10767-013-9130-2

Gainous, J., & Wagner, K. M. (2011). *Rebooting American politics: The Internet revolution.* Lanham, MD: Rowman and Littlefield.

Gainous, J., & Wagner, K. M. (2014). *Tweeting to power. The social media revolution in American politics.* New York: Oxford University Press.

Gans, H. J. (2011). Multiperspectival news revisited: Journalism and representative democracy. *Journalism, 12*(1), 3–13. doi:10.1177/1464884910385289

García, R. G., & Treré, E. (2014). The# YoSoy132 movement and the struggle for media democratization in Mexico. *Convergence (London), 1354856514541744.* doi:10.1177/1354856514541744

Garnham, N. (2003). *Emancipation and Modernity.* Athens: Kastaniotis.

Garrett, R. (2009). Echo chambers online?: Politically motivated selective exposure among Internet users. *Journal of Computer-Mediated Communication*, *14*(2), 265–285. doi:10.1111/j.1083-6101.2009.01440.x

Gastil, J. (2000). Is Face-to-Face Citizen Deliberation a Luxury or a Necessity? *Political Communication*, *17*(4), 357–361. doi:10.1080/10584600050178960

Gaudin, S. (2014, March 24). White House urges end to Turkey's Twitter ban. *Computer World*. Retrieved August 8, 2014, from http://www.computerworld.com/article/2488934/social-media/white-house-urges-end-to-turkey-s-twitter-ban.html

Geoff, D. (2013). *US attacks China as Snowden stays free*. Retrieved from http://www.ft.com/cms/s/0/3861666e-dcbc-11e2-b52b-00144feab7de.html#axzz3PcyOgTbN

Gerbaudo, P. (2012). *Tweets and the streets: Social media and contemporary activism*. Retrieved from Amazon.com

Gerhards, J., & Schäfer, M. (2010). Is the Internet a better public sphere? Comparing old and new media in the USA and Germany. *New Media & Society*, *12*(1), 143–160. doi:10.1177/1461444809341444

German, K. (2010). Bush/Gore photos reveal differing styles, strategies. *Newspaper Research Journal*, *31*(4), 48–61.

Ghilizean, M. (2000). *Cum să reuşeşti în viaţa politică – manual de campanie electorală./How to succeed in political life - A guide to election campaign*. Bucureşti: Active Vision.

Ghonim, W. (2012). *Revolution 2.0: The power of people is greater than the people in power: A memoir*. New York: Houghton Mifflin Harcourt.

Gibbs, G. R. (2008). Analysing qualitative data. *Sage (Atlanta, Ga.)*.

Gibson, R., & McAllister, I. (2014). Normalising or Equalising Party Competition? Assessing the Impact of the Web on Election Campaigning. *Political Studies*, *2014*, 1–19.

Gibson, R., Nixon, P., & Ward, S. (Eds.). (2003). *Political parties and the Internet net gain?* London, New York: Routledge.

Gibson, R., & Ward, S. (2000). A proposed methodology for studying the function and effectiveness of party and candidate Web sites. *Social Science Computer Review*, *18*(3), 301–319. doi:10.1177/089443930001800306

Gitlin, T. (1980). *The whole world is watching: Mass media in the making and unmaking of the New Left*. Berkeley: University of California Press.

Gitlin, T. (1998). Public Sphere or Public Sphericules? In T. Liebes & J. Curran (Eds.), *Media, Ritual, and Identity* (pp. 168–174). London: Routledge.

Gladwell, M. (2010, October). Small change Why the revolution will not be tweeted. *The New Yorker*, 42–49.

Gladwell, M. (2006). *The Tipping Point: How little things can make a big difference*. Boston: Little, Brown and Company.

Gnardellis, Ch. (2003). *Applied Statistics*. Athens: Papazisis.

Goche, F. (2012, September 11). Yo soy 132, movimiento del siglo XXI. *Contralínea*. Retrieved from http://contralinea.info/archivo-revista/index.php/2012/09/11/yo-soy-132-movimiento-del-siglo-xxi/

Goffman, E. (1974). *Frame analysis: An essay on the organization of experience*. Cambridge, MA: Harvard University Press.

Golan, G. (2006). Inter-media agenda setting and global news coverage. *Journalism Studies*, *7*(2), 323–333. doi:10.1080/14616700500533643

Golbeck, J., Grimes, J. M., & Rogers, A. (2010). Twitter use by the US Congress. *Journal of the American Society for Information Science and Technology*, *61*(8), 1612–1621. doi:10.1002/asi.21344

Goldbeck, J., Grimes, J. M., & Rogers, A. (2010). Twitter use by the U.S. Congress. *Journal of the American Society for Information Science and Technology*, *61*(8), 1612–1621.

Goldstein, J. (2007). *The role of digital networked technologies in the Ukrainian orange revolution*. The Berkman Center for Internet & Society at Harvard University, Research Publication No. 2007-14. Retrieved January 11, 2011, from http://cyber.law.harvard.edu/sites/cyber.law.harvard.edu/files/Goldstein_Ukraine_2007.pdf

Gómez Quintero, N. (2014, May 15). ¿Qué ocurrió con #YoSoy132? *El Universal*. Retrieved from http://www.eluniversal.com.mx/nacion-mexico/2014/historias-que-ocurrio-con-39yosoy132-39-1010493.html

Gómez Vilchis, R. R. (2013). El regreso del dinosaurio: Un debate sobre la reciente victoria del PRI en la elección presidencial de 2012. *Estudios Politicos*, *28*, 45–161. doi:10.1016/S0185-1616(13)71443-4

Gómez, L., & Viejo, M. (2014, May 30). Las redes de arrastre de Podemos. *El País*. Retrieved from: http://goo.gl/KzF8fJ

Goodnow, T. (2013). Facing off: A comparative analysis of Obama and Romney Facebook timeline photographs. *The American Behavioral Scientist*, *57*(11), 1584–1595. doi:10.1177/0002764213489013

Grabe, M. E., & Bucy, E. P. (2009). *Image bite politics: News and the visual framing of elections*. Oxford: Oxford University Press. doi:10.1093/acprof:oso/9780195372076.001.0001

Graber, D. A., & Smith, J. M. (2005). Political communication faces the 21st century. *Journal of Communication*, *55*(3), 479–507. doi:10.1111/j.1460-2466.2005.tb02682.x

Graeber, D. (2013). *The democracy project: A history, a crisis, a movement*. London: Allen Lane.

Graham, C., Laurier, E., O'Brien, V., & Rouncefield, M. (2011). Guest editors' introduction. New visual technologies: Shifting boundaries, shared moments. *Visual Studies*, *26*(2), 87–91. doi:10.1080/1472586X.2011.571883

Graham, T. (forthcoming). Everyday Political Talk in the Internet-Based Public Sphere. In S. Coleman & D. Freelon (Eds.), *Handbook of Digital Politics*. Cheltenham, UK: Edward Elgar.

Graham, T., Broersma, M., & Hazelhoff, K. (2013). CLOSING THE GAP? Twitter as an instrument for connected representation. In R. Scullion, R. Gerodimos, D. Jackson, & D. Lilleker (Eds.), *The Media, Political Participation and Empowerment*. London: Routledge.

Graham, T., Broersma, M., Hazelhoff, K., & van 't Haar, G. (2013). Between Broadcasting Political Messages and Interacting with Voters: The use of Twitter during the 2010 UK general election campaign. *Information Communication and Society*, *16*(5), 692–716. doi:10.1080/1369118X.2013.785581

Graham, T., Jackson, D., & Broersma, M. (2014). New Platform, old habits? Candidates' use of Twitter during the 2010 British and Dutch general election campaigns. *New Media & Society*, *0*(0), 1–19.

Graham, T., Jackson, D., & Broersma, M. (2014). New platform, old habits? Candidates' use of Twitter during the 2010 British and Dutch general election campaigns. *New Media & Society*, 1–19. doi:10.1177/1461444814546728

Grant, W. J., Moon, B., & Grant, J. B. (2010). Digital dialogue? Australian politicians' use of the social network tool Twitter. *Australian Journal of Political Science*, *45*(4), 579–604. doi:10.1080/10361146.2010.517176

Greece: Internet Usage and Marketing Report. (n.d.). Retrieved January 27, 2015, from Internet World Stats website, http://www.internetworldstats.com/eu/gr.htm

Green, J. (2007). When Voters and Parties Agree: Valence Issues and Party Competition. *Political Studies*, *55*(3), 629–655. doi:10.1111/j.1467-9248.2007.00671.x

Greffet, F. (2013). New techniques, new mobilizations? French parties in the Web 2.0 era. In P. G. Nixon, R. Rawal, & D. Mercea (Eds.), *Politics and the Internet in comparative context. Views from the cloud* (pp. 59–75). London: Routledge Taylor and Francis Group.

Grigoriadis, I. N. (2004). *Turkish political culture and minorities*. Paper presented at Nationalism, Society and Culture in post-Ottoman South East Europe, Oxford, UK. Retrieved September 30, 2014, from http://www.sant.ox.ac.uk/esc/esc-lectures/Grigoriadis.pdf

Groseclose, T. (2001). A Model of Candidate Location When One Candidate Has a Valence Advantage. *American Journal of Political Science*, *45*(4), 862–886. doi:10.2307/2669329

Gurevitch, M., Coleman, S., & Blumler, J. G. (2009). Political communication—Old and new media relationships. *The Annals of the American Academy of Political and Social Science*, *625*(1), 164–181. doi:10.1177/0002716209339345

Guţu, D. (2007). New Media. Bucureşti: Comunicare.ro.

Habermas, J. (1992). Further reflections on the public sphere. *Habermas and the Public Sphere, 422.*

Habermas, J. (1962/1989). *The Structural Transformation of the Public Sphere*. Cambridge, UK: Polity.

Habermas, J. (1991). *The structural transformation of the public sphere: An inquiry into a category of bourgeois society*. MIT press.

Habermas, J. (1996). *Between Facts and Norms: Contributions to a discourse theory of law and democracy*. Cambridge, MA: Polity Press.

Habermas, J. (2006). Political communication in media society: Does democracy still enjoy an epistemic dimension? the impact of normative theory on empirical research. *Communication Theory*, *16*(4), 411–426. doi:10.1111/j.1468-2885.2006.00280.x

Hacker, K. L. (1995). *Candidate images in presidential elections*. Westport, CT: Praeger.

Hamilton, A., Madison, J., & Jay, J. (2012). *El federalista*. México: Fondo de Cultura Económica.

Han, G. (2008). New media use, sociodemographics, and voter turnout in the 2000 presidential election. *Mass Communication & Society*, *11*(1), 62–81. doi:10.1080/15205430701587644

Hardt, M. & Negri, A. (2012). *Declaration*. Retrieved from Amazon.com

Hardt, M., & Negri, A. (2000). *Empire*. Cambridge, MA: Harvard University Press.

Hardt, M., & Negri, A. (2005). *Multitude: War and democracy in the age of empire*. New York: Penguin Books.

Harlow, S. (2012). Social media and social movements: Facebook and an online Guatemalan justice movement that moved offline. *New Media & Society*, *14*(2), 225–243. doi:10.1177/1461444811410408

Haven, K. (2007). *Story proof: The science behind the starling power of story*. Westport: Libraries Unlimited.

Heaney, M. T., Newman, M. E., & Sylvester, D. E. (2011). Campaigning in the internet age. In S. C. Craig & D. B. Hill (Eds.), *The electoral challenge: Theory meets practice*. Washington, DC: CQ Press.

Heinrich, A. (2012). Foreign reporting in the sphere of network journalism. *Journalism Practice*, 1-10.

Hermida, A. (2010). From TV to Twitter: How ambient news became ambient journalism. *M/C Journal*, *13*(2). Retrieved from: http://journal.media-culture.org.au/index.php/mcjournal/article/viewArticle/220

Hermida, A. (2010). Twittering the news: The emergence of ambient journalism. *Journalism Practice*, *4*(3), 297–308. doi:10.1080/17512781003640703

Hermida, A., Fletcher, F., Korell, D., & Logan, D. (2012). Share, Like, Recommend: Decoding the social media news consumer. *Journalism Studies*, 1–10.

Herring, S. (2009). Web content analysis: Expanding the paradigm. In J. Hunsinger, M. Allen, & L. Klastrup (Eds.), *The International Handbook of Internet Research*. Springer Verlag. doi:10.1007/978-1-4020-9789-8_14

Herring, S. (2013). Discourse in Web 2.0: Familiar, reconfigured, and emergent. In D. Tannen & A. M. Tester (Eds.), *Discourse 2.0: Language and new media* (pp. 1–26). Washington, DC: Georgetown University Press.

Hertog, J. K., & McLeod, D. M. (2001). A multiperspectival approach to framing analysis: A field guide. In S. D. Reese, O. H. Gandy, & A. E. Grant (Eds.), *Framing public life: Perspective on media and our understanding of the social world* (pp. 139–162). Mahwah, NJ: Lawrence Erlbaum Associates.

Hetherington, M. (2007). Turned off or turned on? How polarization affects political engagement. In Red and Blue Nation? Consequences and Correction of America's Polarized Politics (vol. 2, pp. 1-53). Washington, DC: Brookings Institution Press.

Hetherington, M. (2001). Resurgent mass partisanship: The role of elite mass polarization. *The American Political Science Review*, *95*(3), 619–631. doi:10.1017/S0003055401003045

Hetherington, M., & Weiler, J. (2009). *Authoritarianism and polarization in American politics*. New York: Cambridge University Press. doi:10.1017/CBO9780511802331

Hibbing, J. R., & Theiss-Morse, E. (2002). *Stealth democracy: Americans' beliefs about how government should work*. Cambridge, UK: Cambridge University Press. doi:10.1017/CBO9780511613722

Hill, K., & Hughes, J. (1998). *Cyperpolitics: Citizen Activism in the Age of the Internet*. New York: Rowman & Littlefield.

Himanen, P. (2001). *The hacker ethic and the spirit of the Information Age*. New York: Random House.

Hindman, M. (2009). *The myth of digital democracy*. Princeton, NJ: Princeton University Press.

Hine, C. (2000). *Virtual Ethnography*. London: Sage.

Hine, C. (2008). Overview: Virtual ethnography: modes, varieties, affordances. In N. G. Fielding, R. M. Lee, & G. Blank (Eds.), *Handbook of Online Research Methods* (pp. 257–270). London: Sage. doi:10.4135/9780857020055.n14

Hiotis, A. (1986). *Propaganda: Methods and Technique*. Self Published.

Hoffman, D., & Novak, T. (1998). Information access: Bridging the racial divide on the internet. *Science*, *280*(5362), 390–391. doi:10.1126/science.280.5362.390

Hogan, B. (2013). Comment on Elena Pavan/1: Considering Platforms as Actors. *Sociologica*, *3*. doi:10.2383/75767

Holbrook, T. M. (1996). *Do Campaigns Matter?* Thousand Oaks, CA: Sage.

Hollander, E., & Stappers, J. (1992). Community media and community communication. In J. Jankowski, O. Prehn, & J. Stappers (Eds.), *The People's Voice: Local Radio and Television in Europe* (pp. 17–27). London: John Libbey.

Holman, C. B., & McLoughlin, L. P. (2001). *Buying Time 2000: Television Advertising in the 2000 Federal Elections*. New York: Brennan Center for Justice at New York School of Law.

Holmes, J. (2009). *21st century media effects: Choice, predispositions, and their impact on agenda setting and priming*. (Doctoral Dissertation). University of Minnesota. Retrieved from http://purl.umn.edu/58353

Holtz-Bacha, C. (2004). Political campaign communication. In Comparing Political Communication: Theories, Cases, Challenges (pp. 213-230). Cambridge, UK: Cambridge University Press.

Honeycutt, C., & Herring, S. C. (2009). Beyond Microblogging: Conversation and Collaboration via Twitter. In *Proc. HICSS 42*. IEEE Press.

Hong, S., & Nadler, D. (2012). Which candidates do the public discuss online in an election campaign?: The use of social media by 2012 presidential candidates and its impact on candidate salience. *Government Information Quarterly*, *29*(4), 455–461. doi:10.1016/j.giq.2012.06.004

Hosch-Dayican, B., Amrit, C., & Aarts, K. (2014). How Do Online Citizens Persuade Fellow Voters? Using Twitter During the 2013 Dutch Parliamentary Election Campaign. *Social Science Computer Review*, *0*(0), 1–18.

Howard, P. N. (2006). *New media campaigns and the managed citizen*. Cambridge, UK: Cambridge University Press.

Huang, J., Thornton, C., & Efthimiadis, E. N. (2010). Conversational Tagging in Twitter. In *Proceedings of the 21st ACM Conference on Hypertext and Hypermedia*. Toronto, Canada. doi:10.1145/1810617.1810647

Huan, S., Dutton, W. H., & Shen, W. (2013). The semi-sovereign netizen. The fifth estate in China. In P. G. Nixon, R. Rawal, & D. Mercea (Eds.), *Politics and the Internet in comparative context. Views from the cloud* (pp. 43–59). London: Routledge Taylor and Francis Group.

Huesca, R. (1995). A procedural view of participatory communication: Lessons from Bolivian tin miners' radio. *Media Culture & Society*, *17*(1), 101–119. doi:10.1177/016344395017001007

Hull, D. L. (1982). The naked meme. In Learning, Development and Culture: Essays in Evolutionary Epistemology (pp. 273–327). New York: John Wiley and Sons.

Hürriyet Daily News. (2014, March 29). *Twitter wins key case against Turkish government*. Retrieved August 10, 2014, from http://www.hurriyetdailynews.com/twitter-wins-key-case-against-turkish-government.aspx?PageID=238&NID=64273&NewsCatID=339

Hürriyet. (2014, March 21). *Erdoğan: Twitter, mwitter kökünü kazıyacağız*. Retrieved August 12, 2014, from http://www.hurriyet.com.tr/gundem/26050109.asp

Hutchins, B. (2011). The acceleration of media sports culture: Twitter, telepresence and online messaging. *Information Communication and Society*, *14*(2), 237–257. doi:10.1080/1369118X.2010.508534

Hutter, S., & Grande, E. (2014). Politicizing Europe in the National Electoral Arena: A Comparative Analysis of Five West European Countries, 1970–2010. *JCMS: Journal of Common Market Studies*, *52*(5), 1002–1018.

Hymes, D. (1972). Models of the interaction of language and social life. In J. Gumperz & D. Hymes (Eds.), *Directions in sociolinguistics: The ethnography of communication* (pp. 35–71). New York: Holt, Rinehart and Winston.

Im, T., Wonhyuk, C., Porumbescu, G., & Park, J. (2012). Internet, trust in government, and citizen compliance. *Journal of Public Administration: Research and Theory*, *24*(3), 741–763. doi:10.1093/jopart/mus037

Ince, B. (2012). *Citizenship and identity in Turkey: From Atatürk's republic to the present day*. New York: I. B. Tauris.

INSCOP Survey. (2013). *The Barometer of Public Opinion – the Truth about Romania*. Retrieved from http://www.inscop.ro/septembrie-2013-increderea-in-institutii/

Internet World Stats. (2014). *Internet Users in the European Union in December 31, 2013*. Retrieved from http://www.internetworldstats.com/stats9.htm

Ionescu, N. (2013).Online political communication: The role of image upload on Facebook. *Revista română de jurnalism şi comunicare/Romanian Review of Journalism and Communication, 8*(1), 53-58.

Isenberg, D. (1986). Group polarization: A critical review and meta-analysis. *Journal of Personality and Social Psychology*, *50*(6), 1141–1151. doi:10.1037/0022-3514.50.6.1141

Ito, M. (2008). Introduction. In K. Varnelis (Ed.), *Networked Publics* (pp. 1–14). Cambridge, MA: MIT Press. doi:10.7551/mitpress/9780262220859.003.0001

Iyengar, S., & Hahn, K. (2009). Red media, blue media: Evidence of ideological selectivity in media use. *Journal of Communication*, *59*(1), 19–39. doi:10.1111/j.1460-2466.2008.01402.x

Iyengar, S., Sood, G., & Lelkes, Y. (2012). Affect not ideology: A social identity perspective on polarization. *Public Opinion Quarterly*, *76*(3), 411–435. doi:10.1093/poq/nfs038

Iyengar, S., & Westwood, S. (2014). Fear and loathing across party lines: New evidence on group polarization. *American Journal of Political Science*. doi:10.1111/ajps.12152

Jackall, R. (1995). *Propaganda*. London: Palgrave. doi:10.1007/978-1-349-23769-2

Jackson, N. (2007). Political parties, the Internet and the 2005 General Election: Third time Lucky? *Internet Research*, *17*(3), 249–271. doi:10.1108/10662240710758911

Jackson, N. A., & Lilleker, D. G. (2009). Building an architecture of participation? Political parties and Web 2.0 in Britain. *Journal of Information Technology & Politics*, *6*(3-4), 232–250. doi:10.1080/19331680903028438

Jackson, N., & Lilleker, D. (2011). Microblogging, constituency service and impression management: UK MPs and the use of Twitter. *Journal of Legislative Studies*, *17*(1), 86–105. doi:10.1080/13572334.2011.545181

Janssens, D., & Kies, R. (2005). Online Forums and Deliberative Democracy. *Acta Politica*, *40*(3), 317–335. doi:10.1057/palgrave.ap.5500115

Jenkins, H. (2006). Convergence Culture: Where Old and New Media Collide. New York University Press.

Jenkins, H. (2006). *Convergence culture: Where old and new media collide*. New York, NY: NYU Press.

Jenkins, H., Clinton, K., Purushotma, R., Robinson, A. J., & Weigel, M. (2007). *Confronting the Challenges of Participatory Culture: Media Education for the 21st Century*. Chicago, IL: The MacArthur Foundation.

Jericho, G. (2012). *The rise of the fifth estate. Social media and blogging in Australian politics*. Victoria: Griffin Press.

Jewitt, C. (2008). Multimodality and literacy in school classrooms. *Review of Research in Education*, *32*(1), 241–267. doi:10.3102/0091732X07310586

Jewitt, C., & Oyama, R. (2001). Visual meaning: A social semiotic approach. In T. van Leeuwen & C. Jewitt (Eds.), *Handbook of visual analysis* (pp. 134–156). Los Angeles, CA: Sage.

Jia, L., & Fanxu, Z. (2014). Microblogging and Grassroots Surveillance in China. *China. International Journal (Toronto, Ont.)*, *12*(3), 55–71.

Jiang, M. (2010). Spaces of authoritarian deliberation: Online public deliberation in China. In The Search for Deliberative Democracy in China, (pp. 261-287). Academic Press.

Jones, B. (2014, March 24). Turkey's Twitter ban condemned-even by nation's own president. *CNN*. Retrieved August 8, 2014, from http://edition.cnn.com/2014/03/21/world/europe/turkey-twitter-ban-condemned/

Jones, J. (2014). *Obama's fifth year job approval ratings among most polarized*. Retrieved September 27, 2014 from http://www.gallup.com/poll/167006/obama-fifth-year-job-approval-ratings-among-polarized.aspx

Jones, S. G. (1997). The Internet and its social landscape. *Virtual Culture: Identity and Communication in Cybersociety*, 7-35.

Jones, S. (Ed.). (1998). *Cybersociety 2.0: Revisiting Computer-mediated communication and Community*. Thousand Oaks, CA: Sage.

Jonhston, H. (2002). Verification and proof in frame and discourse analysis. In B. Klandermans & S. Staggenborg (Eds.), *Methods of social movement research* (pp. 61–91). Minneapolis, MN: University of Minnesota Press.

Jordan, T., & Taylor, P. A. (2004). *Hacktivism and Cyberwars: Rebel with a cause?* London: Routledge.

Jørgensen, R. F. (2013). Freedom of expression in the Internet era. In U. Carlson (Ed.), *Freedom of expression revisited. Citizenship and Journalism in the Digital Era* (pp. 119–131). Göteborg: Nordicom.

Jowett, G. S., & O' Donnell, V. (1995). *Propaganda and Persuasion*. London: Sage.

Jungherr, A. (2014). *Twitter in politics: a comprehensive literature review*. Available at: http://papers.ssrn.com/sol3/papers.cfm?abstract_id=2402443

Jungherr, A. (2009). Twitternde Politiker: Zwischen buntem Rauschen und Bu¨ rgerna¨he 2.0. In C. Bieber, M. Eifert, T. Groß, & J. Lamla (Eds.), *Soziale Netze in der Digitalen Welt: Das Internet zwischen Egalitaerer Beteiligung und Oekonomischer Macht* (pp. 99–127). Frankfurt am Main: Campus Verlag.

Juris, J. S. (2005). The new digital media and activist networking within anti-corporate globalization movements. *The Annals of the American Academy of Political and Social Science*, *597*(1), 189–208. doi:10.1177/0002716204270338

Juris, S. J. (2012). Reflections on #Occupy Everywhere: Social media, public space, and emerging logics of aggregation. *American Ethnologist*, *39*(2), 259–279. doi:10.1111/j.1548-1425.2012.01362.x

Kahn, K. F., & Kenney, P. J. (1997). A Model of Candidate Evaluations in Senate Elections: The Impact of Campaign Intensity. *The Journal of Politics*, *59*(4), 1173–1205. doi:10.2307/2998597

Kahn, K. F., & Kenney, P. J. (1999). *The Spectacle of U.S. Senate Campaigns*. Princeton, NJ: Princeton University Press.

Kahn, R., & Kellner, D. (2004). New media and internet activism: From the 'Battle of Seattle' to blogging. *New Media & Society*, *6*(1), 87–95. doi:10.1177/1461444804039908

Kahn, R., & Kellner, D. (2005). Oppositional politics and the Internet: A critical reconstructive approach. *Cultural Politics*, *1*(1), 75–100. doi:10.2752/174321905778054926

Kaid, L. L. (1999). Political Advertising: A Summary of Research Findings. In B. Newman (Ed.), *The Handbook of Political Marketing* (pp. 423–438). Thousand Oaks, CA: Sage Publications.

Kaid, L. L., & Holtz-Bacha, C. (1995). Political Advertising Across Cultures: Comparing Content, Styles, and Effects. In L. L. Kaid & C. Holtz-Bacha (Eds.), *Political Advertising in Western Democracies: Candidates and Parties on Television* (pp. 206–227). Thousand Oaks, CA: Sage Publications.

Kaid, L. L., & Johnston, A. (2001). *Videostyle in Presidential Campaigns: Style and Content of Televised Political Advertising*. Westport, CT: Praeger.

Kamens, H. D. (2012). *Beyond the Nation-State: The Reconstruction of Nationhood and Citizenship*. London, UK: Emerald Group. doi:10.1108/S1479-3539(2012)18

Kanagavel, R., & Chandrasekaran, V. (2014). Creating political awareness through social networking – An empirical study with special reference to Tamil Nadu elections, 2011. *Journal of Social Media Studies*, *1*(1), 71–81. doi:10.15340/214733661177

Kant, I. (1983). To perpetual peace. In I. Kant (Ed.), *Perpetual peace and other essays on politics, history, and morals* (pp. 107–144). Indianapolis, IN: Hackett. (Original work published 1795)

Kaplan, A. M., & Haenlein, M. (2010). Users of the world, unite! The challenge and opportunities of social media. *Business Horizons*, *53*(1), 59–68. doi:10.1016/j.bushor.2009.09.003

Karapınar, T. (2014, April 9). YouTube yasağı kalktı. *Milliyet*. Retrieved August 8, 2014, from http://www.milliyet.com.tr/Gundem/SonDakika.aspx?aType=SonDakika&ArticleID=1864631&Date=09.04.2014&Kategori=gundem&b=Youtube%20erisime%20acildi

Kaufman, K., & Petrocik, J. (1999). The changing politics of American men: Understanding the sources of the gender gap. *American Journal of Political Science*, *43*(3), 864–887. doi:10.2307/2991838

Kavada, A. (2005). Exploring the role of the internet in the 'movement for alternative globalization': The case of the Paris 2003 European Social Forum. *Westminster Papers in Communication and Culture, 2*(1), 72-95.

Kavada, A. (2005). Exploring the role of the internet in the 'movement for alternative globalization': The case of the Paris 2003 European Social Forum. *Westminster Papers in Communication and Culture, 2*(1), 72–95.

Keane, J. (1995). Structural transformations of the public sphere. *Communication Review*, *1*(1), 1–22. doi:10.1080/10714429509388247

Keane, J. (1998). *Civil society: Old images, new visions*. Stanford, CA: Stanford University Press.

Kennedy, J. (2008). Twitter and Digg to introduce social media to U.S. election coverage. *Silicon Republic*. Retrieved September 11, 2014, from http://www.siliconrepublic.com/news/article/11712/new-media/twitter-and-digg-to-introduce-social-media-to-uselection-coverage

Kidd, D. (2012, June). *#Occupy in the San Francisco bay*. Paper presented at Cities are Us Conference, Coimbra, Portugal.

Kim, J. Y., Xiang, Z., & Kiousis, S. (2011). Agenda building effects by 2008 presidential candidates on global media coverage and public opinion. *Public Relations Review*, *37*(1), 109–111. doi:10.1016/j.pubrev.2010.09.009

Kim, Y. (2011). The contribution of social network sites to exposure to political difference: The relationships among SNSs, online political messaging, and exposure to cross-cutting perspectives. *Computers in Human Behavior*, *27*(2), 971–977. doi:10.1016/j.chb.2010.12.001

Kiousis, S., Kim, S.-Y., McDevitt, M., & Ostrowski, A. (2009). Competing for attention: Information subsidy influence in agenda building during election campaigns. *Journalism & Mass Communication Quarterly*, *86*(3), 545–562. doi:10.1177/107769900908600306

Kiousis, S., & Wu, X. (2008). International agenda-building and agenda-setting. *The International Communication Gazette*, *70*(1), 58–75. doi:10.1177/1748048507084578

Kirk, R., & Schill, D. (2011). A Digital Agora: Citizen Participation in the 2008 Presidential Debates. *The American Behavioral Scientist*, *55*(3), 325–347. doi:10.1177/0002764210392167

Knoblach-Westerwick, S. (2012). Selective exposure and reinforcement of attitudes and partisanship before a presidential election. *Journal of Communication*, *62*(4), 628–642. doi:10.1111/j.1460-2466.2012.01651.x

Koh, Y., & Yadron, D. (2014, March 21). What Turkish users are doing to evade the Twitter ban. *Digits*. Retrieved August 12, 2014, from http://blogs.wsj.com/digits/2014/03/21/how-users-evade-turkeys-twitter-ban/

Kohut, A., & Rainie, L. (2000, December 3). *Internet election news audience seeks convenience, familiar names*. Retrieved from http://www.pewinternet.org/Reports/2000/Internet-Election-News-Audience-Seeks-Convenience-Familiar-Names/Report.aspx

Koopmans, R., & Erbe, J. (2004). Towards a European public sphere? *Innovation (Abingdon)*, *17*(2), 97–118. doi:10.1080/1351161042000238643

Krippendorff, K. (2003). *Content analysis: an introduction to its methodology. Thousand Oaks etc.* Sage Publications.

Krosnick, J. A. (1990). Government policy and citizen passion: A study of issue publics in contemporary America. *Political Behavior*, *12*(1), 59–92. doi:10.1007/BF00992332

Kruikemeier, S. (2014). How political candidates use Twitter and the impact of votes. *Computers in Human Behavior*, *34*, 131–139. doi:10.1016/j.chb.2014.01.025

Kushin, M. J., & Yamamoto, M. (2010). Did social media really matter? College students' use of online media and political decision making in the 2008 election. *Mass Communication & Society*, *13*(5), 608–630. doi:10.1080/15205436.2010.516863

Kyriazi, N. (2001). *Sociological Research: Critical Evaluation of Methods and Techniques*. Athens: Greek Letters.

Ladd, M. J. (2012). *Why Americans Hate the Media and How It Matters*. Princeton University Press.

Lancendorfer, K. M., & Lee, B. (2010). Who influences whom? The agenda-building relationship between political candidates and the media in the 2002 Michigan governor's race. *Journal of Political Marketing*, *9*(3), 186–206. doi:10.1080/15377857.2010.497737

Langlois, G., Elmer, G., McKelvey, F., & Devereaux, Z. (2009). Networked Publics: The Double Articulation of Code and Politics on Facebook. *Canadian Journal of Communication*, *34*(3), 415–434.

Langman, L. (2013). Occupy: A new new social movement. *Current Sociology*, *61*(4), 510–524. doi:10.1177/0011392113479749

Lanosga, G. (2008). *Blogs and big media: A comparative study of agendas*. Paper presented at the annual conference of International Communication Association, Montreal, Canada.

LAPOP/Barómetro de las Américas. (2010). *Consolidación democrática en las Américas en tiempos difíciles: Informe sobre las Américas*. Retrieved from http://lapop.ccp.ucr.ac.cr/pdf/ReportontheAmericasSpanish2.pdf

Lariscy, R. W., Avery, E. J., Sweetser, K. D., & Howes, P. (2009). An examination of the role of online social media in journalists' source mix. *Public Relations Review*, *35*(3), 314–316. doi:10.1016/j.pubrev.2009.05.008

Larsson, A., & Moe, H. (2011). *Who tweets?Tracking microblogging use in the 2010 Swedish election campaign*. Paper presented at the 19th European Conference on Information Systems (ECIS 2011), Helsinki, Finland

Larsson, A. (2014). Online, all the time? A quantitative assessment of the permanent campaign on Facebook. *New Media & Society*. doi:10.1177/1461444814538798

Larsson, A. O., & Moe, H. (2014). Twitter in politics and elections: Insights from Scandinavia. In K. Weller, A. Bruns, J. Burgess, M. Mahrt, & C. Puschmann (Eds.), *Twitter and society* (pp. 319–331). New York: Peter Lang.

Larsson, O. A., & Moe, H. (2011). Studying political microblogging: Twitter users in the 2010 Swedish election campaign. *New Media & Society, 14*(5), 729–747. doi:10.1177/1461444811422894

Larsson, O. A., & Moe, H. (2014). Triumph of the Underdogs? Comparing Twitter Use by Political Actors During Two Norwegian Election Campaigns. *Sage Open, 4*(4), 2158–2440. doi:10.1177/2158244014559015

Lassen, D., & Brown, A. (2011). Twitter: The electoral connection? *Social Science Computer Review, 29*(4), 419–436. doi:10.1177/0894439310382749

Lasswell, H. D. (1948). The structure and function of communications in society. In L. Bryson (Ed.), The communication of ideas (pp.37-51). New York: Harper & Row.

Latimer, M. K. (1984). Policy Issues and Personal Images in Political Advertising in a State Election. *The Journalism Quarterly, 61*(4), 776–784. doi:10.1177/107769908406100405

Latinobarómetro. (2009). *Encuesta Latinobarómetro 2009*. Retrieved from http://latino-barometro.org/latino/LATDatos.jsp

Latour, B., & Weibel, P. (2005). *Making things public: Atmospheres of democracy*. Cambridge, MA: The MIT Press.

Lau, R. R., & Redlawsk, D. P. (2006). *How Voters Decide: Information Processing in Election Campaigns*. Cambridge, UK: Cambridge University Press. doi:10.1017/CBO9780511791048

Layman, G., Carsey, T., & Horowitz, J. (2006). Party polarization in American politics: Characteristics, causes, and consequences. *Annual Review of Political Science, 9*(1), 83–110. doi:10.1146/annurev.polisci.9.070204.105138

Lazarsfeld, P. P., Berelson, B., & Gaudet, H. (2004). *Mecanismul votului. Cum se decid alegătorii într-o campanie electorală/The people's choice: How the voter makes up his mind in a presidential campaign*. Bucureşti: comunicare.ro.

Lazarsfled, P. F., Berelson, B., & Gaudet, H. (1944). *The People's Choice: How the Voter Makes Up His Mind in a Presidential Campaign*. New York: Duell, Sloan and Pierce.

Lee, J., Choi, J., Kim, C., & Kim, Y. (2014). Social media, network heterogeneity, and opinion polarization. *Journal of Communication, 64*(4), 702–722. doi:10.1111/jcom.12077

Lehmann, I. A. (2003). Exploring the Transatlantic Media Divide over Iraq: How and Why U.S. and German Media Differed in Reporting on UN Weapons Inspections in Iraq, 2002-2003. *Press/Politics 10*(1), 63-89.

Lei, G., Hong Tien, V., & McCombs, M. (2012). An expanded perspective on agenda-setting effects. Exploring the third level of agenda setting. *Revista De Comunicación, 11*, 51–68.

Leighley, J., & Nagler, J. (1992). Socioeconomic class bias in turn out, 1964-1988: The voters remain the same. *The American Political Science Review, 86*(3), 725–736. doi:10.2307/1964134

Leitner, H., Sheppard, E., & Sziarto, K. (2008). The spatialities of contentious politics. *Transactions of the Institute of British Geographers, 33*(2), 157–172. doi:10.1111/j.1475-5661.2008.00293.x

Leoontidou, L. (2010). Urban social movements in 'weak civil societies': The right to the city and cosmopolitan activism in southern Europe. *Urban Studies (Edinburgh, Scotland), 47*(6), 1179–1203. doi:10.1177/0042098009360239

Letsch, C. (2013, June 3). Social media and opposition to blame for protests, says Turkish PM. *The Guardian*. Retrieved September 3, 2013, from http://www.theguardian.com/world/2013/jun/02/turkish-protesters-control-istanbul-square

Levendusky, M. (2009). *The partisan sort: How liberals became Democrats and conservatives became Republicans.* Chicago: University of Chicago Press. doi:10.7208/chicago/9780226473673.001.0001

Levendusky, M. (2013). Why do partisan media polarize viewers? *American Journal of Political Science*, *57*(3), 611–623. doi:10.1111/ajps.12008

Lev-On, A. (2011). Campaigning online: Use of the Internet by parties, candidates and voters in national and local election campaigns in Israel. *Policy & Internet*, *3*(1), 1–28. doi:10.2202/1944-2866.1045

Lewis-Beck, M. S., Jacoby, W. G., Norpoth, H., & Weisberg, H. F. (2011). *The American Voter Revisited.* Ann Arbor, MI: The University of Michigan Press.

Lilleker, D., & Koc-Michalska, K. (2014). Online Election Campaigning: Exploring Supply and Demand During the France 2012 Presidential Election. In A.Solo (Ed.), Political Campaigning in the Information Age (pp. 287-304). Hershey, PA: IGI Global.

Lilleker, D. (2006). *Key Concepts in Political Communication.* London: Sage.

Lilleker, D. G., & Jackson, N. A. (2010). Toward a more participatory style of election campaigning: The impact of Web 2.0 on the U.K. 2010 general election. *Policy & Internet*, *2*(3), 69–98. doi:10.2202/1944-2866.1064

Lilleker, D. G., & Jackson, N. A. (2011). *Political campaigning, elections and the Internet: Comparing the U.S., U.K., France and Germany.* New York: Routledge.

Lilleker, D. G., & Malagón, C. (2010). Levels of Interactivity in the 2007 French Presidential Candidates' websites. *European Journal of Communication*, *25*(1), 25–42. doi:10.1177/0267323109354231

Lippmann, W. (1927). *The Phantom Public.* New York: MacMillan.

Liu, Y., & Zhou, Y. (2011). *Social media in China: Rising Weibo in government.* Paper presented at the Digital Ecosystems and Technologies Conference (DEST). doi:10.1109/DEST.2011.5936628

Livingstone, S. (1999). New media, new audiences. *New Media & Society*, *1*(1), 59–66. doi:10.1177/1461444899001001010

Lock, A., & Harris, P. (1996). Political marketing - vive la difference. *European Journal of Marketing*, *30*(10-11), 21–31.

López García, G. (2014). *Estrategias de movilización política de los partidos para un público desmotivado: Internet y las Elecciones Europeas de 2014.* Paper presented at the III Congreso Internacional de Comunicación Política y Estrategias de Campaña 2014 de la Asociación Latinoamericana de Investigadores en Campañas Electorales (ALICE), Madrid, Spain.

Lorica, B. (2009). *Facebook is growing fast in Asia, Europe and the Middle East.* Retrieved May 13, 2010 from http://radar.oreilly.com/2009/03/facebook-is-growing-fast-in-asia-europe-middleeast.html

Lowry, D. T., & Naser, M. A. (2010). From Eisenhower to Obama: Lexical characteristics of winning versus losing presidential campaign commercials. *Journalism & Mass Communication Quarterly*, *87*(3-4), 530–547. doi:10.1177/107769901008700306

Luciani, G. (1988). Economic foundations of democracy and authoritarianism: The Arab world in comparative perspective. *Arab Studies Quarterly*, 457–475.

Lu, J., & Qiu, Y. (2013). Microblogging and Social Change in China. *Asian Perspective*, *37*(3), 305–331.

Lupia, A., & Sin, G. (2003). Which public goods are endangered?: How evolving communication technologies affect the logic of collective action. *Public Choice*, *117*(3-4), 315–331. doi:10.1023/B:PUCH.0000003735.07840.c7

MacLeod, D. (2005). *Downsizing the state: Privatization and the Limits of Neoliberal Reform in Mexico*. Pennsylvania, PA: Penn State Press.

Macnamara, J. (2008). The internet and the public sphere: The 2007 Australian e-electioneering experience. *Media International Australia*, *129*, 7–19.

Macnamara, J., & Kenning, G. (2011). E-electioneering 2010: Trends in social media use in Australian political communication. *Media International Australia*, *139*, 7–22.

Maggini, N. (2014). A turnout like in 2009 but with many "Europes" within the EU. In L. De Sio, V. Emanuele, & N. Maggini (Eds.), *The European Parliament Elections of 2014* (pp. 31–36). Rome: CISE.

Maireder, A., Ausserhofer, J., & Kittenberger, A. (2012). Mapping the Austrian Political Twittersphere. How politicians, journalists and political strategists (inter-)act on Twitter. In P. Parycek, N. Edelmann & M. Sachs (Eds.), *CeDEM12. Proceeding of the International Conference for E-Democracy and Open Government* (pp. 151-163). Krems: Edition Donau-Universität Krems.

Maireder, A., Schlögl, S., Schütz, F., Karwautz, M., & Waldheim, C. (2014). *The European Political Twittersphere*. Retrieved October, 15, 2014, from www.gfk.com/twitter

Maireder, A., & Ausserhofer, J. (2014). Political discourse on Twitter: Networking topics, objects, and people. In K. Weller, A. Bruns, J. Burgess, M. Mahrt, & C. Puschmann (Eds.), *Twitter and society* (pp. 305–319). New York: Peter Lang.

Maireder, A., & Schlögl, S. (2014). 24 hours of an #outcry: The networked publics of a socio-political debate. *European Journal of Communication*, *29*(6), 687–702. first published online onSeptember22014. doi:10.1177/0267323114545710

Malcolm, M. (2014). *China kills off discussion on Weibo after internet crackdown*. Retrieved from http://www.telegraph.co.uk/news/worldnews/asia/china/10608245/China-kills-off-discussion-on-Weibo-after-internet-crackdown.html

Mance, B. (2014). Odnosi med novinarji in politiki na twitterju: od profesionalizma do »odmevne komore«. *Javnost - The Public*, *21*(Supplement), 23–40.

Mann, T., & Orenstein, N. (2012). *It's even worse than it looks: How the American constitutional system collided with the new politics of extremism*. New York: Basic Books.

Margolis, M., & Moreno-Riano, G. (2013). The Internet and the decline of the Euro-American democracy. In P. G. Nixon, R. Rawal, & D. Mercea (Eds.), *Politics and the Internet in comparative context. Views from the cloud* (pp. 26–43). London: Routledge Taylor and Francis Group.

Margolis, M., & Resnick, D. (2000). *Politics as usual: The "Cyberspace Revolution"*. Thousand Oaks, CA: Sage.

Margolis, M., & Resnick, D. (2000). *Politics as Usual: The Cyberspace Revolution* (Vol. 6). Sage Publications.

Margolis, M., & Resnick, D. (2000). *Politics as usual: the cyberspace 'revolution*. Thousand Oaks, CA: Sage Publications.

Marková, I. (2008). Persuasion and Propaganda. One or two processes? Persuasion, propaganda and rhetoric. *Diogenes*, *217*(1), 37–51. doi:10.1177/0392192107087916

Marres, N. (2007). The issues deserve more credit: Pragmatist contributions to the study of public involvement in controversy. *Social Studies of Science*, *37*(5), 759–780. doi:10.1177/0306312706077367

Marwick, A. E., & boyd, . (2011). I tweet honestly, I tweet passionately: Twitter users, context collapse, and the imagined audience. *New Media & Society*, *13*(1), 114–133. doi:10.1177/1461444810365313

Marwick, A., & Boyd, D. (2011). To See and Be Seen: Celebrity Practice on Twitter. *Convergence*, *17*(2), 139–158.

Marx Ferree, M., Gamson, W. A., Gerhards, J., & Rucht, D. (2002). Four models of the public sphere in modern democracies. *Theory and Society*, *31*(3), 289–324. doi:10.1023/A:1016284431021

Mat, F. (2014, February 27). Turkey, the web divide. *Osservatorio balcani e caucaso*. Retrieved March 26, 2014, from http://www.balcanicaucaso.org/eng/Regions-and-countries/Turkey/Turkey-the-web-divide-148380

Mattoni, A. (2013). Repertoires of communication in social movement processes. In B. Cammaerts, A. Mattoni, & P. McCurdy (Eds.), *Mediation and protest movements* (pp. 39–56). Bristol: Intellect.

Mattoni, A., & Trerè, E. (2014). Media practices, mediation processes, and mediatization in the study of social movements. *Communication Theory*, *24*(3), 252–271. doi:10.1111/comt.12038

McAdam, D., & Jr Sewell, W. H. (2001). It's about time: Temporality in the study of contentious politics. In R. Aminzade (Ed.), *Silence and voice in the study of contentious politics*. Cambridge, UK: Cambridge University Press. doi:10.1017/CBO9780511815331.005

McAtee, A., & Wolak, J. (2011). Why people decide to participate in state politics. *Political Research Quarterly*, *64*(1), 45–58. doi:10.1177/1065912909343581

McChesney, R. (2000). *Rich Media, Poor Democracy: Communication Politics in Dubious Times*. New York: New Press.

McCombs, M. E., & Shaw, D. L. (1972). The agenda-setting function of mass media. *Public Opinion Quarterly*, *36*(2), 176–187. doi:10.1086/267990

McLuhan, M., & Barrington, N. (1972). *Take today. The executive as dropout*. New York: Harcourt Brace Jovanovich.

McParland, L. J., & Whyte, A. (2008). A thematic analysis of attributions to others for the origins and ongoing nature of pain in community pain sufferers. *Psychology Health and Medicine*, *13*(5), 610–620. doi:10.1080/13548500701842966 PMID:18942015

Meadow, R. G. (1980). *Politics as communication*. Norwood, NJ: Abalex Publishing Corporation.

Medina, R. Z., & Muñoz, C. Z. (2014). Campaigning on Twitter: Towards the "Personal Style" Campaign to Activate the Political Engagement During the 2011 Spanish General Elections. *Communicatio Socialis*, *27*(1), 83–106.

Mejias, U. (2008). *Networks and the politics of the para-nodal*. Paper presented at Politics: Web 2.0: An International Conference, Royal Holloway, Egham, UK.

Melucci, A. (1996). *Challenging codes: Collective action in the information age*. Cambridge, UK: Cambridge University Press. doi:10.1017/CBO9780511520891

Melucci, A. (2004). The process of collective identity. In H. Jonhston & B. Klandermans (Eds.), *Social movements and culture* (pp. 41–63). Minneapolis, MN: University of Minnesota Press.

Meraz, S. (2011). Using time series analysis to measure intermedia agenda-setting influence in traditional media and political blog networks. *Journalism & Mass Communication Quarterly*, *88*(1), 176–194.

Merino, M. (2001). *La participación ciudadana en la democracia*. México: Instituto Federal Electoral.

Messaris, P. (2012). Visual "literacy" in the digital age. *The Review of Communication*, *12*(2), 101–117. doi:10.1080/15358593.2011.653508

Messaris, P., & Abraham, L. (2001). The role of images in framing news stories. In S. D. Reese, O. H. Gandy, & A. E. Grant (Eds.), *Framing public life: Perspective on media and our understanding of the social world* (pp. 215–226). Mahwah, NJ: Lawrence Erlbaum Associates.

Messina, C. (2007a). Groups for Twitter; or A Proposal for Twitter Tag Channels. *FactoryCity*. Retrieved October, 15, 2014, from http://factoryjoe.com/blog/2007/08/25/groups-for-twitter-or-a-proposal-for-twitter-tag-channels/

Meyrowitz, J. (1985). *No Sense of Place. The Impact of Electronic Media on Social Behavior*. New York, Oxford: Oxford University Press.

Miller, J. (2013). *Visual framing and social networking: A content analysis of the 2012 Barack Obama and Mitt Romney Facebook pages*. (Unpublished MA Thesis). The University of Alabama.

Miller, L. R., & Brewer, J. D. (Eds.). (2003). *The A-Z of Social Research*. London: Sage.

Miotto, A. (1953). *Psicologia della Propaganda*. Florence: Editrice Universitaria.

Miriam, E., & Jonathan, K. (2013). *Edward Snowden never crossed border into Russia, says foreign minister*. Retrieved from http://www.theguardian.com/world/2013/jun/25/edward-snowden-never-crossed-russia-border

Mitchell, D.-G. (2012). It's About Time: The Lifespan of Information Effects in a Multiweek Campaign. *American Journal of Political Science*, *56*(2), 298–311. doi:10.1111/j.1540-5907.2011.00549.x

Mocanu, M., Aldea, A., & Rawal, R. (2013). Why fix it when it is not broken? Continuity and adaptation in Romanian presidential e-campaigning. In P. G. Nixon, R. Rawal, & D. Mercea (Eds.), *Politics and the Internet in comparative context. Views from the cloud* (pp. 75–95). London: Routledge Taylor and Francis Group.

Momoc, A. (2014). Social networks - Public space or political tool? Voters and candidates on Facebook during the elections for the European Parliament. In G. Horvath, R. K. Bako, & E. Biro-Kaszas (Eds.), *Ten years of Facebook* (pp. 435–456). Debrecen: Debrecen University Press.

Moraga, S. (2012, July 24). #YoSoy132 busca ser la sombra del poder en México. *ADN Político*. Retrieved from http://www.adnpolitico.com/2012/2012/07/21/el-yosoy132-busca-ser-la-sombra-del-poder-en-mexico

Moriarty, S. E., & Popovich, M. N. (1991). Newsmagazine visuals and the 1988 presidential election. *The Journalism Quarterly*, *68*(3), 371–380. doi:10.1177/107769909106800307

Morozov, E. (2011). *The net delusion: The dark side of Internet freedom*. New York: PublicAffairs.

Morozov, E. (2011). *The Net Delusion: The Dark Side of Internet Freedom*. New York: PublicAffairs.

Mossberger, K., Tolbert, C., & McNeal, R. (2007). *Digital citizenship: the Internet, society and participation*. Cambridge, MA: MIT Press.

Mossberger, K., Tolbert, C., & Stansbury, M. (2003). *Virtual inequality: beyond the digital divide*. Washington, DC: Georgetown Press.

Murdock, G. (1992). Citizens, consumers and public culture. In M. Skovmand & J. C. Schroder (Eds.), *Media Cultures. Reappraising Transnational Media* (pp. 17–41). London, New York: Routledge.

Murdock, G. (1993). Communications and the constitution of modernity. *Media Culture & Society*, *15*(4), 521–539. doi:10.1177/016344393015004002

Mutz, D. (2002). Cross cutting social networks: Testing democratic theory in practice. *The American Political Science Review*, *96*(1), 111–126. doi:10.1017/S0003055402004264

Mutz, D., & Martin, P. (2001). Facilitating Communication Across Lines of Political Difference: The Role of Mass Media. *The American Political Science Review*, *95*(1), 97–114.

National Telecommunications and Information Administration. (2014). *Exploring the digital nation: Embracing the mobile internet.* Retrieved from http://www.ntia.doc.gov/files/ntia/publications/exploring_the_digital_nation_embracing_the_mobile_internet_10162014.pdf

Negroponte, N. (1995). *Being Digital.* New York: Knopf.

Neubig, G., & Duh, K. (2013). *How Much Is Said in a Tweet? A Multilingual, Information-theoretic Perspective.* Paper presented at the AAAI Spring Symposium: Analyzing Microtext.

Neuendorf, K. A. (2002). *The Content Analysis Guidebook.* London: Sage.

Neuhaus, F., & Webmoor, T. (2012). Agile ethics for massified research and visualization. *Information Communication and Society, 15*(1), 43–65. doi:10.1080/1369118X.2011.616519

Noesselt, N. (2014). Microblogs and the Adaptation of the Chinese Party-State's Governance Strategy. *Governance: An International Journal of Policy, Administration and Institutions, 27*(3), 449–468. doi:10.1111/gove.12045

Norris, P. (2004). Political Communications. In *Encyclopedia of the Social Sciences.* Retrieved from http://www.hks.harvard.edu/fs/pnorris/Acrobat/Political%20Communications%20encyclopedia2.pdf

Norris, P. (2000). *A Virtuous Circle: Political Communication in Post-Industrial Democracies.* New York: Cambridge University Press. doi:10.1017/CBO9780511609343

Norris, P. (2002). Campaign communications. In L. LeDuc, R. G. Niemi, & P. Norris (Eds.), *Comparing democracies 2: new challenges in the study of elections and voting* (pp. 127–147). London: SAGE.

Norris, P. (2003). Preaching to the converted? Pluralism, participation and party websites. *Party Politics, 9*(1), 21–45. doi:10.1177/135406880391003

Norris, P. N. (2001). *Digital Divide, Civic Engagement, Information Poverty and the Internet Worldwide.* Cambridge, UK: Cambridge University Press. doi:10.1017/CBO9781139164887

North, R., Holsti, O. R., Zanninovich, M. G., & Zinnes, D. A. (1963). *Content analysis.* Northwestern University Press.

Notimex (2013, February 11). Afirman que movimiento "Yo Soy 132" carece de fecha de caducidad. *Crónica.* Retrieved from http://www.cronica.com.mx/notas/2012/664356.html

O'Keefe, G. J. (2015). Persuasion: Theory and Research (3rd ed.). Los Angeles, CA: Sage.

O'Keefe, G. J., & Atwood, L. E. (1981). Communication and Election Campaigns. In D. D. Nimmo & K. R. Sanders (Eds.), *Handbook of Political Communication* (pp. 329–357). Beverly Hills, CA: Sage Publications.

Oblak Črnič, T., & Amon-Prodnik, J. (2014). Samopromocijski novičarski mediji? Analiza spletnih mest slovenskih političnih akterjev. *Teorija in Praksa, 51*(6), 1321–1343.

OECD. (2001). *Understanding the digital divide.* Retrieved October 23, 2014, from http://www.oecd.org/internet/ieconomy/1888451.pdf

OECD: Selected Indicators for Greece . (n.d.). Retrieved January 27, 2015, from OECD website, http://data.oecd.org/greece.htm#profile-innovationandtechnology

Öktem, K. (2013). Why Turkey's mainstream media chose to show penguins rather than protests. *The Guardian.* Retrieved July 18, 2014, from http://www.theguardian.com/commentisfree/2013/jun/09/turkey-mainstream-media-penguins-protests

Olesen, T. (2004). The transnational Zapatista solidarity network: An infrastructure analysis. *Global Networks - A Journal of Transnational Affairs, 4*(1), 89-107.

Ovadia, S. (2009). Exploring the potential of Twitter as a research tool. *Behavioral & Social Sciences Librarian*, *28*(4), 202–205. doi:10.1080/01639260903280888

Pabst, S. (2014, May 15). *Europoliticians take on social media*. Retrieved from http://www.dw.de/euro-politicians-take-on-social-media/a-17627641

Page, R. (2012). The Linguistics of Self Branding and Micro-celebrity in Twitter: The Role of Hashtags. *Discourse and Communication*, *6*(2), 181–201. doi:10.1177/1750481312437441

Paltridge, B. (2012). *Discourse analysis: an introduction* (2nd ed.). London: Bloomsbury.

Panagopoulos, C. (2011). Timing is Everything? Primacy and Recency Effects in Voter Mobilization Campaigns. *Political Behavior*, *33*(1), 79–93. doi:10.1007/s11109-010-9125-x

Papacharissi, Z. (2002). The virtual sphere The internet as a public sphere. *New Media & Society*, *4*(1), 9–27. doi:10.1177/14614440222226244

Papacharissi, Z. (2010). *A private sphere: Democracy in a digital age*. Cambridge, MA: Polity.

Parker, G. R. (1981). Interpreting Candidate Awareness in U. S. Congressional Elections. *Legislative Studies Quarterly*, *6*(2), 219–233. doi:10.2307/439646

Parmalee, J. H., & Bichard, S. L. (2012). *Politics and the Twitter revolution. How tweets influence the relationship between political leaders and the public*. Plymouth: Lexington Books.

Parmelee, J. H. (2014). The agenda-building function of political tweets. *New Media & Society*, *16*(3), 434–450. doi:10.1177/1461444813487955

Parmelee, J. H., & Bichard, S. L. (2011). *Politics and the Twitter revolution: How tweets influence the relationship between political leaders and the public*. Lexington Books.

Paul, E. (2013). *Snowden affair blunts U.S. push for China to curb cyber theft*. Retrieved from http://www.reuters.com/article/2013/07/09/us-usa-china-cyber-idUSBRE96713220130709

Payne, J., Golden, J. L., Marlier, J., & Ratzan, S. C. (1989). Perceptions of the 1988 Presidential and Vice-Presidential Debates. *The American Behavioral Scientist*, *32*(4), 425–435. doi:10.1177/0002764289032004008

Pérez de Acha, G. (2012, September 19). La democracia de #YoSoy132. *Animal Político*. Retrieved from http://www.animalpolitico.com/blogueros-blog-invitado/2012/09/19/la-democracia-de-yosoy132/#ixzz33PD7zyBc

Perugorría, I., & Tejerina, B. (2013). Politics of the encounter: Cognition, emotions, and networks in the Spanish 15M. *Current Sociology*, *61*(4), 424–442. doi:10.1177/0011392113479743

Petrocik, J. R., Benoit, W. L., & Hansen, G. J. (2003). Issue Ownership and Presidential Campaigning, 1952-2000. *Political Science Quarterly*, *118*(4), 599–626. doi:10.1002/j.1538-165X.2003.tb00407.x

Pew Internet & American Life Project. (2013a). *72% of Online Adults are Social Networking Site Users*. Retrieved March 10, 2014, from http://www.pewinternet.org/files/oldmedia/Files/Reports/2013/PIP_Social_networking_sites_update_PDF.pdf

Pew Internet & American Life Project. (2013b). *Teens, Social Media, and Privacy*. Retrieved March 10, 2014, from http://www.pewinternet.org/2013/05/21/teens-social-media-and-privacy

Pew Research Centre. (2014). *The EU Elections on Twitter: Mixed Views about the EU and Little Passion for the Candidates*. Retrieved October 15, 2014, from http://www.journalism.org/files/2014/05/2014-05-22_The-EU-Elections-on-Twitter.pdf

Pilkington, E., & Michel, A. (2012). Obama, Facebook and the power of friendship?: The 2012 data election. *The Guardian*. Retrieved from http://www.theguardian.com/world/2012/feb/17/obama-digital-data-machine-facebook-election

Poell, T. (2009). Conceptualizing forums and blogs as public spheres. Digital Material, 239-251.

Politics, C. N. N. (2012). *America's choice: Issues*. Retrieved from http://www.cnn.com/election/2012/campaign-issues.html

Ponnam, A., & Dawra, J. (2013). Discerning product benefits through visual thematic analysis. *Journal of Product and Brand Management*, *22*(1), 30–39. doi:10.1108/10610421311298669

Poster, M. (1997). Cyberdemocracy: Internet and the public sphere. In D. Porter (Ed.), *Internet culture* (pp. 201–218). New York: Routledge.

Postill, J. (2011). Democracy in the age of viral reality. *Media/Anthropology*. Retrieved 16 March, 2013 from http://johnpostill.com/2011/11/07/democracy-in-the-age-of-viral-reality-3/

Poulakidakos, S., & Veneti, A. (forthcoming). The sentimental element in public discourse as a factor of formation of polarization in Greece. In F. Morandau & D. Stefenel (Eds.), Understanding local and global trans-formations across cultures. Research and practice in social and human sciences. Academic Press.

Poulakidakos, S. (2014). *Propaganda and Public Discourse. The presentation of the MoU by the Greek Media*. Athens: DaVinci Books.

Poulakidakos, S., & Armenakis, A. (2014). Propaganda in Greek Public Discourse. Propaganda Scales in the presentation of the Greek MoU-bailout agreement of 2010. *Revue des Sciences Politiques*, *41*, 126–140.

Pratkanis, A., & Aronson, E. (2001). *Age of Propaganda: The Everyday Use and Abuse of Persuasion*. New York: Owl Books.

Presno Linera, M. A. (2012). ¿Nos representan o no? *Anales de la Cátedra Francisco Suárez*, (46), 93-109.

Prior, M. (2007). *Post broadcast democracy*. New York: Cambridge University Press. doi:10.1017/CBO9781139878425

Psimitis, M. (2011). The Protest cycle of spring 2010 in Greece. *Social Movement Studies*, *10*(2), 191–197. doi:10.1080/14742837.2011.562365

Putnam, R. (2000). *Bowling alone: The collapse and revival of American community*. New York: Simon & Schuster. doi:10.1145/358916.361990

Putnam, R. D. (2001). *Bowling alone*. Simon and Schuster.

Qiang, X. (2011). The battle for the Chinese Internet. *Journal of Democracy*, *22*(2), 47–61. doi:10.1353/jod.2011.0020

Quintelier, E., & Theocharis, Y. (2012). Online political engagement, Facebook, and personality traits. *Social Science Computer Review*, 0894439312462802.

Radio-Television of Slovenia. (2014). *Roles of Slovenian public broadcasting services for the use of airtime for the presentation of candidate lists or candidates for MP's election in National Assembly in 13th July 2014* [in Slovenian]. Retrieved January 1, 2015, from https://www.rtvslo.si/files/novice_zavoda/pravila_-_drzavni_zbor-2014.pdf

Raine, L., Horrigan, J., & Cornfield, M. (2005, March 6). *The Internet and campaign,2004*. Retrieved from http://www.pewinternet.org/Reports/2005/The-Internet-and-Campaign-2004/1-Summary-of-Findings.aspx

Rainie, L. (2012, November 6). *Social media and young*. Retrieved from http://www.pewinternet.org/Reports/2012/Social-Vote-2012.aspx

Rainie, L., & Smith, A. (2012). *Social networking sites and politics*. Retrieved September 12, 2014 from http://www.pewinternet.org/files/old-media//Files/Reports/2012/PIP_SNS_and_politics.pdf

Raymundo, S. (2014, March 21). Twitter users mock Turkish government over attempted social media ban. *Latin Post*. Retrieved August 8, 2014, from http://www.latinpost.com/articles/9285/20140321/twitter-users-mock-turkish-government-over-attempted-social-media-ban.htm

Reif, K., & Schmitt, H. (1980). Nine Second-Order National Elections. A Conceptual Framework for the Analysis of European Election Results. *European Journal of Political Research*, *8*(1), 3–44. doi:10.1111/j.1475-6765.1980.tb00737.x

Reilly, I. (2011). "Amusing Ourselves to Death?" Social Media, Political Satire, and the 2011 Election. *Canadian Journal of Communication*, *36*(3), 503–511.

Reilly, P. (2013). Ourselves alone (but making connections): The social media strategies of Sinn Fein. In P. G. Nixon, R. Rawal, & D. Mercea (Eds.), *Politics and the Internet in comparative context. Views from the cloud* (pp. 154–169). London: Routledge Taylor and Francis Group.

Rennie, E. (2006). *Community media: A global introduction*. Oxford, UK: Rowman & Littlefield Publishers.

Rettman, A. (2014a, June 11). Turkey at 'crossroads' to authoritarian rule, Amnesty says. *EU Observer*. Retrieved July 18, 2014, from http://euobserver.com/foreign/124551

Rettman, A. (2014b, March 21). Turkey's Twitter can prompt instant EU criticism. *EU Observer*. Retrieved August 8, 2014, from http://euobserver.com/foreign/123564

Reuter, O. J., & Szakonyi, D. (2015). Online social media and political awareness in authoritarian regimes. *British Journal of Political Science*, *45*(1), 29–51. doi:10.1017/S0007123413000203

Rheingold, H. (2002). *Smart mobs*. Cambridge, MA: Perseus Books.

Riker, W. H. (1990). Heresthetic and Rhetoric in the Spatial Model. In J. M. Elenow & M. J. Hinich (Eds.), *Advances in the Spatial Theory of Voting* (pp. 46–65). Cambridge, UK: Cambridge University Press. doi:10.1017/CBO9780511896606.005

Ritter, K. W. (1980). American political rhetoric and the jeremiad tradition: Presidential nomination acceptance addresses, 1960–1976. *Communication Studies*, *31*(3), 153–171.

Rodriguez, C. (2001). *Fissures in the mediascape: An international study of citizens' media*. Hampton Press.

Rogers, E. M., & Dearing, J. W. (1988). Agenda-setting research: Where has it been, where it is going. *Communication Yearbook*, *11*, 555–594.

Ronfeldt, D., Arquilla, J., Fuller, G., & Fuller, M. (1998). *The Zapatista 'Social Netwar' in Mexico*. Santa Monica: RAND.

Rosanvallon, P. (2008). *Counter-Democracy. Politics in an Age of Distrust*. Cambridge University Press. doi:10.1017/CBO9780511755835

Rothenbuhler, E. W. (1998). *Ritual Communication. From Everyday Conversation to Mediated Ceremony*. Sage.

Russell, J. W. (2009). *Class and Race Formation in North America*. Toronto: University of Toronto Press.

Sabety, S. (2010). Graphic content: The semiotics of a YouTube uprising. In I. Y. Kamalipour (Ed.), *Media, power, and politics in the digital age: The 2009 presidential election uprising in Iran* (pp. 119–124). Roman & Littlefield Publishers.

Sader, E. (2001). Hegemonía y contra-hegemonía para otro mundo posible. In J. Seoane & E. Taddei (Eds.), *Resistencias Mundiales* [De Seattle a Porto Alegre] (pp. 23–45). Buenos Aires: CLACSO.

Salgado Andrade, E. (2013). Twitter en la campaña electoral de 2012. *Desacatos, 42*, 217–232.

Salgado, S. (2013). Online party politics: Studying the presence of some African political parties on the Internet. In P. G. Nixon, R. Rawal, & D. Mercea (Eds.), *Politics and the Internet in comparative context. Views from the cloud* (pp. 118–135). London: Routledge Taylor and Francis Group.

Salmon, C. (2010). *Storytelling. Bewitching the modern mind.* London: Verso.

Salmore, B. G., & Salmore, S. A. (1989). *Candidates, Parties, and Campaigns.* Washington, DC: Congressional Quarterly Press.

Sanderson, J. (2013). From Loving the Hero to Despising the Villain: Sports fans, Facebook and Social Identity Treats. *Mass Communication & Society, 16*(4), 487–509. doi:10.1080/15205436.2012.730650

Sandoval-Almazan, R., & Gil-Garcia, J. R. (2013, January). Cyberactivism through Social Media: Twitter, YouTube, and the Mexican Political Movement I'm Number 132. In *Proceedings of the 46th Hawaii International Conference on System Sciences (HICSS)* (pp. 1704-1713). Wailea, HI: IEEE. doi:10.1109/HICSS.2013.161

Saville-Troike, M. (2003). *The Ethnography of Communication.* Malden, MA: Blackwell Publishing. doi:10.1002/9780470758373

Scbweitzer, E. J. (2008). Innovation or normalization in e-campaigning? Structural analysis of German party Websites in the 2002 and 2005 national elections. *European Journal of Communication, 23*(4), 449–470. doi:10.1177/0267323108096994

Schill, D. (2012). The Visual image and the political image: A review of visual communication research in the field of political communication. *The Review of Communication, 12*(2), 118–142. doi:10.1080/15358593.2011.653504

Schmitt-Beck, R., & Farrell, D. M. (2002). Studying political campaigns and their effects. In D. M. Farrell & R. Schmitt-Beck (Eds.), *Do Political Campaigns Matter? Campaign Effects in Elections and Referendums* (pp. 1–21). London: Routledge. doi:10.4324/9780203166956_chapter_1

Schols, S. (2014, April 10). *A more visual EU elections?* Retrieved from http://europedecides.eu/2014/04/a-more-visual-eu-election/

Schroedel, J., Bligh, M., Merolla, J., & Gonzalez, R. (2013). Charismatic rhetoric in the 2008 presidential campaign: Commonalities and differences. *Presidential Studies Quarterly, 43*(1), 101–128. doi:10.1111/psq.12005

Schudson, M. (1998). *The Good Citizen: A History of American Public Life.* The Free Press.

Scoble, R., & Israel, S. (2006). *Naked Conversations: how blogs are changing the way businesses talk to customers.* Hoboken, NJ: John Wiley and Sons.

Sears, D., & Freedman, J. (1967). Selective exposure to information: A critical review. *Public Opinion Quarterly, 31*(2), 194–213. doi:10.1086/267513

Segerberg, A., & Bennett, W. L. (2011). Social media and the organization of collective action: Using Twitter to explore the ecologies of two climate change protests. *Communication Review, 14*(3), 197–215. doi:10.1080/10714421.2011.597250

Selwyn, N. (2004). Reconsidering political and popular understandings of the digital divide. *New Media & Society, 6*(3), 341–362. doi:10.1177/1461444804042519

Servaes, J. (1996). Participatory communication research with new social movements: A realistic utopia. In J. Servaes, T. L. Jacobson & S. A. White (Eds.), Participatory communication for social change (pp.82-108). New Delhi: Sage.

Servaes, J., & Malikhao, P. (2005). Participatory communication: The new paradigm? In O. Hemer & T. Tufte (Eds.), Media & Global change. Rethinking communication for development (pp. 91-103). Buenos Aires: Consejo Lationamericano de Ciencias Sociales.

Servaes, J. (1999). *Communication for development: One world, multiple cultures*. Cresskill, NJ: Hampton Press.

Shaheed, A. (2014). *Layers of Internet censorship in Iran*. Retrieved October 2, 2014, from http://shaheedoniran.org/english/blog/layers-of-internet-censorship-in-iran/

Shahid, A. (2010). Chinese woman, Cheng Jianping, sentenced to a year in labor camp over Twitter post. *NY Daily News*. Retrieved August 8, 2014, from http://www.nydailynews.com/news/world/chinese-woman-cheng-jianping-sentenced-year-labor-camp-twitter-post-article-1.454253

Shea, D. M. (1996). *Campaign Craft: The Strategies, Tactics, And Art of Political Campaign Management*. Westport, CT: Praeger.

Sheafer, T., & Weimann, G. (2005). Agenda building, agenda setting, priming, individual voting intentions, and the aggregate results: An analysis of four Israeli elections. *Journal of Communication*, *55*(2), 347–365. doi:10.1111/j.1460-2466.2005.tb02676.x

Shifman, L. (2012). An anatomy of a YouTube meme. *New Media & Society*, *14*(2), 187–203. doi:10.1177/1461444811412160

Shihadem M., Fominaya, C. & Cox, C. (2012). The season of revolution: the Arab spring and European mobilizations. *Interface: A Journal for and about Social Movements, 4*(1), 1-16.

Shirky, C. (2008). *Here comes everybody: How change happens when people come together*. London: Penguin.

Shirky, C. (2011). The political power of social media. *Foreign Affairs*, *90*(1), 28–41.

Sides, J. (2006). The Origins of Campaign Agendas. *British Journal of Political Science*, *36*(3), 407–436. doi:10.1017/S0007123406000226

Sides, J., Shaw, D., Grossmann, M., & Lipsitz, K. (2013). *Campaigns & elections: Rules, reality, strategy, choice*. New York City: W. W. Norton & Company.

Simiti, M. (2014, February). Rage and protest: The case of the Greek indignant movement. *Hellenic Observatory Papers on Greece and Southeast Europe*. London School of Economics and Political Science (LSE). Retrieved September 22, 2014, from: http://www.lse.ac.uk/europeanInstitute/research/hellenicObservatory/CMS%20pdf/Publications/GreeSE/GreeSE-No82.pdf

Siomkos, G. I., & Vasilakopoulou, A. (2005). *Implementation of Analysis Methods in Market Research*. Athens: Ath. Stamoulis.

Small, T. (2011). What the hashtag? A content analysis of Canadian politics of Twitter. *Information Communication and Society*, *14*(6), 872–895. doi:10.1080/1369118X.2011.554572

SMaPP Data Report. (2013). *A breakout role for Twitter? The role of social media in the Turkish protests*. Retrieved September 10, 2014 from http://smapp.nyu.edu/reports/turkey_data_report.pdf

Smith, A. (2009). *The Internet's Role in Campaign 2008, Pew Internet & American Life Project*. Retrieved September 11, 2013, from http://pewinternet.org/Reports/2009/6--The-Internets-Role-in-Campaign-2008.aspx

Smith, A., & Rainie, L. (2008). *The internet and the 2008 election', Pew Internet & American Life Project.* Retrieved September 11, 2013, from http://www.pewinternet.org/PPF/r/252/report_display.asp

Smith, A., & Rainie, L. (2008, June 15). *The Internet and the 2008 election.* Retrieved from http://www.pewinternet.org/~/media/Files/Reports/2008/PIP_2008_election.pdf

Smith, J. (2001). Globalizing resistance: The of Seattle and the future of social movements. *Mobilization: An International Journal*, *6*(1), 1–19.

Smith, R. D. (2002). *Strategic Planning for Public Relations*. Mahwah, NJ: Lawrence Erlbaum Associates.

Snow, N. (2002). *Propaganda Inc.: Selling America's culture to the world.* New York: Seven Stories Press.

Splichal, S. (2006). In search of a strong European public sphere: Some critical observations on conceptualizations of publicness and the (European) public sphere. *Media Culture & Society*, *28*(5), 695–7147. doi:10.1177/0163443706067022

Splichal, S. (2011). *Transnationalization of the Public Sphere and the Fate of the Public (Euricom Monographs).* Hampton Press.

Statham, P., & Trenz, H.-J. (2012). *The Politicization of the European Union: Media Discourse, Political Contestation and the Public Sphere*. London: Routledge.

Statista. (2014). *Penetration of selected social networks in Turkey as of 2nd quarter 2014*. Retrieved September 10, 2014, from http://www.statista.com/statistics/284503/turkey-social-network-penetration/

Stein, K., & Church, S. (2007). *Success Strategies by Candidates in Presidential Debates, 1960-2004.* Paper presented in the annual convention of National Communication Association, Chicago, IL.

Stelter, B. (2011, December 1). Camps are cleared, but '99 percent' still occupies the lexicon. *The New York Times*, p. A1.

Stemler, S. (2001). *An Introduction to Content Analysis.* ERIC Digest. ERIC Clearinghouse on Assessment and Evaluation College Park MD. Retrieved December 6, 2011, from http://www.ericdigests.org/2002-2/content.htm

Stieglitz, S. & Dang-Xuan, L. (2012). Social media and political communication: a social media analytics framework. *Soc. Netw. Anal. Min.*, published online 25 August 2012. doi: 10.1007/s13278-012-0079-3

Stieglitz, S., & Dang-Xuan, L. (2012). Social media and political communication: A social media analytics framework. In *Social Network Analysis and Mining*. Springer-Verlag. Retrieved September 11, 2014, from www.researchgate.net/publication/235632721_Social_Media_and_Political_Communication_-_A_Social_Media_Analytics_Framework/links/09e41512111a26d3f3000000

Stimson, J. A. (2004). *Tides of consent: How public opinion shapes American politics.* Cambridge, UK: Cambridge University Press. doi:10.1017/CBO9780511791024

Stoiciu, A. (2000). *Comunicarea politică – cum se vând idei şi oameni./Political communication - How to sell ideas and people*. Bucureşti: Humanitas-Libra.

Stoker, G. (2006). *Why politics matters: making democracy work.* Basingstoke, UK: Palgrave Macmillan.

Stoker, L., & Jennings, K. (2008). Of time and the development of partisan polarization. *American Journal of Political Science*, *52*(3), 619–635. doi:10.1111/j.1540-5907.2008.00333.x

Stokes, D. E. (1963). Spatial Models of Party Competition. *The American Political Science Review*, *57*(2), 368–377. doi:10.2307/1952828

Stokes, D. E. (1992). Valence Politics. In D. Kavanaugh (Ed.), *Electoral Politics* (pp. 141–164). New York: Oxford University Press.

Strömbäck, J., Maier, M., & Kaid, L. L. (2011). Political communication and election campaigns for the European Parliament. In M. Maier, J. Strömbäck, & L. L. Kaid (Eds.), *Political Communication in European Parliamentary Elections* (pp. 3–16). Aldershot, UK: Ashgate.

Strömbäck, J., Maier, M., & Kaid, L. L. (2011). Political communication and election campaigns for the European Parliament. In M. Maier, J. Strömbäck, & L. L. Kaid (Eds.), *Political communication in European Parliamentary elections* (pp. 3–16). Farnham, MD: Ashgate.

Stromer-Galley, J. (2014). *Presidential campaigning in the internet age*. Oxford, UK: Oxford University Press. doi:10.1093/acprof:oso/9780199731930.001.0001

Stroud, N. (2008). Media use and political predispositions: Revisiting the concept of selective exposure. *Political Behavior*, *30*(3), 341–366. doi:10.1007/s11109-007-9050-9

Stroud, N. (2012). *Niche news: The politics of news choice*. New York: Oxford University Press.

Subirats, J. (2012). ¿Qué democracia tenemos? ¿Qué democracia queremos? *Anales de la Cátedra Francisco Suárez*, (46), 155-180

Subirats, J. (2002). The dilemmas of an inevitable relationship: democratic innovation and the information and communication technology. In J. Jordana (Ed.), *Governing Telecommunications and the New Information Society in Europe* (pp. 228–250). Edward Elgar Publishing. doi:10.4337/9781781950463.00021

Sudulich, M. (2013). Do ethos, ideology, country and electoral strength make a diffence in cyberspace? In P. Nixon, R. Rawal & D. Tercea (Eds.), Politics and the Internet in Comparative Context: Views from the Cloud (pp. 75-94). Routledge.

Sulkin, T. (2001). Explaining Campaign Intensity. *American Politics Research*, *29*(6), 608–624. doi:10.1177/1532673X01029006004

Sunstein, C. (2002). *Republic.com*. Princeton, NJ: Princeton University Press.

Surowiecki, J. (2005). *The Wisdom of Crowds: Why the Many Are Smarter Than the Few and How Collective Wisdom Shapes Business, Economies, Societies and Nations*. Anchor Books.

Svensson, M. (2014). Voice, power and connectivity in China's microblogosphere: Digital divides on SinaWeibo. *China Information*, *28*(2), 168–188. doi:10.1177/0920203X14540082

Sweetser, K. D., Golan, G. J., & Wanta, W. (2008). Intermedia agenda setting in television, advertising, and blogs during the 2004 election. *Mass Communication & Society*, *11*(2), 197–216. doi:10.1080/15205430701590267

Sweetser, K., & Weaver Lariscy, R. (2008). Candidates make good friends: An analysis of candidates' uses of Facebook. *International Journal of Strategic Communication*, *2*(3), 175–198. doi:10.1080/15531180802178687

Tapscott, D. (2011, February 14). The debate on social media and revolutions. Reality steps in. *HuffPost*. Retrieved January 14, 2013, from http://www.huffingtonpost.com/don-tapscott/social-media-key-to-revol_b_823043.html

Tarde, G. (1989). Opinion and conversation. (J. Ruth, Trans.). Paris: Presses Universitaires de France. (Original work published 1899).

Tarrow, S. (1994). *Power in movement: Collective action, social movements and politics*. Cambridge, UK: Cambridge University Press.

Tarrow, S. (1995). Cycles of Collective Action: Between Moments of Madness and the Repertoire of Contention. In M. Traugott (Ed.), *Repertoires and Cycles of Collective Action* (pp. 89–116). Durham, NC: Duke University Press.

Tarrow, S. (1998). *Power in Movement: Social Movements and Contentious Politics*. Cambridge, UK: Cambridge University Press. doi:10.1017/CBO9780511813245

Tascón, M. & Quintana, Y. (2012). *Ciberactivismo. Las nuevas revoluciones de las multitudes conectadas*. Madrid: Los libros de la Catarata.

Taylor, P. (2004). *War and International Relations in the Information Age*. Athens: Papazisis.

Taylor, V., & Whittier, N. (2004). Analytical approaches to social movements culture: The culture of the women's movement. In H. Jonhston & B. Klandermans (Eds.), *Social movements and culture* (pp. 163–187). Minneapolis, MN: University of Minnesota Press.

Tejerina, B., Perugorría, I., Benski, T., & Langman, L. (2013). From indignation to occupation: A new wave of global mobilization. *Current Sociology*, *61*(4), 377–392. doi:10.1177/0011392113479738

Theocharis, Y., Lowe, W., van Deth, J. W., & Garcia-Albacete, G. (2015). Using Twitter to mobilize protest action: Online mobilization patterns and action repertoires in the Occupy Wall Street, Indignados, and Aganaktismenoi movements. *Information Communication and Society*, *18*(2), 202–220. doi:10.1080/1369118X.2014.948035

Theodorakopoulos, Ch. (2006). *Propaganda the Glorious*. Athens: Sideris.

Thornton, A. L. (2001). Does the Internet create democracy? *Ecquid Novi: African Journalism Studies*, *22*(2), 126–147. doi:10.1080/02560054.2001.9665885

Thussu, D. K., & Freedman, D. (2003). *War and the Media: Reporting Conflict 24/7*. London: Sage.

Tilly, C. (1978). *From mobilization to revolution*. Reading, MA: Addison-Wesley.

Tilly, Ch. (1995). *Popular Contention in Great Britain, 1758-1834*. Cambridge, MA: Harvard University Press.

Toffler, A. (1980). *La tercera ola*. Bogotá: Plaza & Janes.

Tomanić Trivundža. I. (2014). Vernakularna vizualna politična kultura: vizualni tviti v predvolilni kampanji za EP 2014. *Javnost - The Public, 21*(Supplement), 41–58.

Tong, J., & Zuo, L. (2014). Weibo communication and government legitimacy in China: A computer-assisted analysis of Weibo messages on two 'mass incidents'. *Information Communication and Society*, *17*(1), 66–85. doi:10.1080/1369118X.2013.839730

Towner, L. T., & Dulio, A. D. (2012). New Media and Political Marketing in the United States: 2012 and Beyond. *Journal of Political Marketing*, *11*(1-2), 95–119. doi:10.1080/15377857.2012.642748

Trending.gr. (n.d.). *Power by Monitor*. Retrieved April 18, 2015, from http://trending.gr/

Trenz, H.-J. (2008). Measuring the Europeanisation of Public Communication. *European Political Science*, *7*(3), 273–284. doi:10.1057/eps.2008.19

Triandafyllidou, A., Gropas, R., & Kouki, H. (Eds.). (2013). *The Greek Crisis and European Modernity*. Palgrave Macmillan. doi:10.1057/9781137276254

Trippi, J. (2004). *The revolution will not be televised: Democracy, the Internet and the overthrow of everything*. New York, NY: Harper Collins.

Tsagarousianou, R. (1998). Electronic democracy and the upblic sphere: Opportunities and challenges. In R. Tsagarousianou, D. Tambini, & C. Bryan (Eds.), *Cyberdemocracy: Technology, Cities and Civic Networks* (pp. 167–178). London: Routledge. doi:10.4324/9780203448847

Tumasjan, A., Sprenger, T. O., Sandner, P. G., & Welpe, I. M. (2010.) *Predicting elections with Twitter: What 140 characters reveal about political sentiment.* Paper presented at the Fourth International AAAI Conference on Weblogs and Social Media, Washington, DC.

Tumasjan, A., Sprenger, T. O., Sandner, P. G., & Welpe, I. M. (2011). Election Forecasts With Twitter How 140 Characters Reflect the Political Landscape. *Social Science Computer Review*, *29*(4), 402–418. doi:10.1177/0894439310386557

Tumber, H. (1993). Taming the Truth. *British Journalism Review*, *4*(1), 37–41.

Turan, I. (1986). Türkiye'de siyasal kültürün oluşumu. In E. Kalaycıoğlu & A. Y. Sarıbay (Eds.), *Türk siyasal hayatının gelişmesi* (pp. 461–487). Istanbul: Beta.

Turkey, T. (n.d.). *Website.* Retrieved October 11, 2014, from http://twiplomacy.com/info/europe/turkey/

TurkStat. (2014, August 22). *Hanehalkı bilişim teknolojileri kullanım araştırması.* Retrieved December 12, 2014, from http://www.tuik.gov.tr/PreHaberBultenleri.do?id=16198

Twitter. (n.d.). *Transparency report.* Retrieved December 23, 2014, from https://transparency.twitter.com/removal-requests/2014/jan-jun

Ulbig, S. (2002). Policies, procedures, and people: Sources of support for government. *Social Science Quarterly*, *83*(3), 789–809. doi:10.1111/1540-6237.00115

Uzun, S. (2013, December 2). Gezi parkı iddianamesinde 'Erdoğan' sansürü. *Hürriyet.* Retrieved January 20, 2015, from http://www.hurriyet.com.tr/gundem/25259300.asp

Vaccari, C. (2008). Surfing to the Elysee: The Internet in the 2007 French Elections. *French Politics*, *6*(1), 1–22. doi:10.1057/palgrave.fp.8200139

Van de Donk, W. (2000). Infocracy or infopolis? In J. Hoff, I. Horrocks, & P. Tops (Eds.), *Democratic Governance and New Technology* (pp. 138–154). London: Routledge.

van Dijck, J. (2013). *The Culture of Connectivity. A Critical History of Social Media.* Oxford, UK: Oxford University Press. doi:10.1093/acprof:oso/9780199970773.001.0001

Van Dijk, T. A. (2001). *Political discourse and ideology.* Paper presented at Jornadas del Discurso Politico, Barcelona, Spain.

Van House, N. A. (2011). Personal photography, digital technologies and the uses of the visual. *Visual Studies*, *26*(2), 125–134. doi:10.1080/1472586X.2011.571888

Van Laer, J., & Van Aelst, P. (2009). Cyber-protest and civil society: the Internet and action repertoires in social movements. In Y. Jewkes & M. Yar (Eds.), *Handbook on Internet Crime* (pp. 230–254). Portland, OR: Willan Publishing.

Van Leeuwen, T. (2007). Legitimation in discourse and communication. *Discourse & Communication*, *1*(1), 91–112. doi:10.1177/1750481307071986

Vargas Llosa, M. (1990, September 1). México es la dictadura perfecta. *El País.* Retrieved from http://elpais.com/diario/1990/09/01/cultura/652140001_850215.html

Varnelis, K. (2012). *Networked publics.* The MIT Press.

Varoufakis, Y. (2014). *The Birth of Memorandum Greece: A chronicle of the crisis.* Athens: Gutenberg.

Vatikiotis, P., & Yörük, Z. (2013, April). *Arab spring: A networked social imaginary?* Paper presented at New Media – New Politics: (post) Revolutions in Theory and Practice Conference, London, UK.

Vatikiotis, P. (2005). Communication theory and alternative media. *Westminster Papers in Communication and Culture, 2*(1), 5–29.

Vatikiotis, P. (2011). Networking activism: Implications for Greece. *Estudos em Comunicação. Communication Studies, 10*, 169–185.

Vázquez, J. J. M. (1997). *La televisión y el poder político en México*. Madrid: Diana.

Veneti, A. (2014). Campaigns, Virtual. In H. Kerric & G. J. Geoffrey (Eds.), *Encyclopedia of Social Media and Politics* (pp. 214–218). London, UK: Sage.

Veneti, A., & Karadimitriou, A. (2013). Policy and Regulation in the Media Landscape: The Greek Paradigm Concentration of Media Ownership versus the Right to Information. *Management Dynamics in the Knowledge Economy, 1*(3), 439–457.

Vergeer, M. (2013). Politics, elections and online campaigning: Past, present . . . and a peek into the future. *New Media & Society, 15*(1), 9–17. doi:10.1177/1461444812457327

Vergeer, M., Hermans, L., & Cunha, C. (2012). Web campaigning in the 2009 European Parliament elections: A cross-national comparative analysis. *New Media & Society, 15*(1), 128–148. doi:10.1177/1461444812457337

Vergeer, M., Hermans, L., & Sams, S. (2011). Online social networks and micro-blogging in political campaigning: The exploration of a new campaign tool and a new campaignstyle. *Party Politics*, 477–501.

Verschueren, P. (2012). *Picturing Afghanistan: The photography of foreign conflict*. New York: Hampton Press.

Verser, R., & Wicks, R. H. (2006). Managing voter impressions: The use of images on presidential candidate web sites during the 2000 campaign. *Journal of Communication, 56*(1), 178–197. doi:10.1111/j.1460-2466.2006.00009.x

Verstraeten, H. (1996). The Media and the Transformation of the Public Sphere A Contribution for a Critical Political Economy of the Public Sphere. *European Journal of Communication, 11*(3), 347–370. doi:10.1177/0267323196011003004

Verweij, P. (2012). Twitter links between Politicians and Journalists. *Journalism Practice*, 1-12.

Vesnic-Alujevic, L. (2011). *The Role of Internet in Political Communication: A Case Study of the 2009 European Parliament Elections*. Gent: University Press (doctoral dissertation).

Vickery, G., & Wunsch-Vincent, S. (2007). *Participative web and user-created content: Web 2.0 wikis and social networking*. OECD.

Villamil, J. (2012). *El sexenio de Televisa: conjuras del poder mediático*. México: Random House Mondadori.

Vitak, J., Zube, P., Smock, A., Carr, C. T., Ellison, N., & Lampe, C. (2011). It's complicated: Facebook users' political participation in the 2008 election. *Cyberpsychology, Behavior & Social Networking, 14*(3), 107-114. doi:10.1089/cyber.2009.0226

Vitak, J. (2012). The impact of context collapse and privacy on social network site disclosures. *Journal of Broadcasting & Electronic Media, 56*(4), 451–470. doi:10.1080/08838151.2012.732140

Vitak, J., & Ellison, N. B. (2013). 'There's a network out there you might as well tap': Exploring the benefits of and barriers to exchanging informational and support based resources on Facebook. *New Media & Society, 15*(2), 243–259. doi:10.1177/1461444812451566

Vobič, I., Maksuti, A., & Deželan, T. (2014). *Social negotiation of roles on Twitter : analysing journalists-politicians conversations before national elections.* Paper presented at Open Conference of the COST Action IS0906 "Transforming audiences, transforming societies: the future of audience research: agenda, theory and societal significance", University of Ljubljana, Slovenia, February 5-7, 2014.

Walgrave, R., & van Aelst, P. (2004). New media, new movements? The role of the internet in shaping the anti-globalization movement. In W. van de Donk, L. D. Loader, P. G. Nixon, & D. Rucht (Eds.), *Cyberprotest. New media, citizens and social movements* (pp. 97–122). London: Routledge.

Walzer, M. (1984). Liberalism and the Art of separation. *Political Theory, 12*(3), 315–330. doi:10.1177/0090591784012003001

Wang, N., She, J., & Chen, J. (2014). *How big vs dominate chinese microblog: a comparison of verified and unverified users on sina weibo.* Paper presented at the 2014 ACM Conference on Web Science. doi:10.1145/2615569.2615683

Wanta, W., & Hu, Y.-W. (1994). Time-lag differences in the agenda-setting process: An examination of five news media. *International Journal of Public Opinion Research, 6*(3), 225–240. doi:10.1093/ijpor/6.3.225

We are Social. (2014). *European Digital Landscape in 2014.* Available at: http://wearesocial.net/blog/2014/02/social-digital-mobile-europe-2014/

We are Social. (2014, July 24). *Digital landscape: Middle East, North Africa and Turkey.* Retrieved September 10, 2014 from http://wearesocial.net/tag/social-media/

We are Social. (2015). *Digital, Social and Mobile in 2015.* Available at: http://wearesocial.net/blog/2015/01/digital-social-mobile-worldwide-2015/

We Fight Censorship. (n.d.). *Wave of dismissals after Gezi Park protests.* Retrieved January 22, 2015, from http://wefightcensorship.org/censored/wave-dismissals-after-gezi-park-protestshtml.html#forbidden-content

Weaver, D., & Elliott, S. N. (1985). Who sets the agenda for the media? A study of local agenda-building. *The Journalism Quarterly, 62*(1), 87–94. doi:10.1177/107769908506200113

Webster, F. (2011). Information and democracy: the weakening of social democracy. *Media Perspectives for the 21st Century*, 21-40.

Webster, F. (2006). *Theories of the Information Society* (3rd ed.). London: Routledge.

Wei, S. (2014, December 17). Inside the firewall: Tracking the news that China blocks. *ProPublica*. Retrieved January 5, 2014, from https://projects.propublica.org/firewall/

Wellman, B. (2000). Physical place and cyberspace: The rise of networked individualism. *International Journal of Urban and Regional Research, 25*(2), 227–252. doi:10.1111/1468-2427.00309

Wessels, B. (2014). Voters' Motivations: How and Why Short-Term Factors Grow in Importance. In B. Wessels, H. Rattinger, S. Rossteutscher, & R. Schmitt-Beck (Eds.), *Voters on the Move or the Run* (pp. 238–262). Oxford, UK: Oxford University Press. doi:10.1093/acprof:oso/9780199662630.001.0001

West, D. M. (2013). *Air wars: Television advertising and social media in election campaigns, 1952-2012.* Washington, DC: CQ Press.

Williams, C., & Gulati, G. (2013). Social networks in political campaigns: Facebook and the congressional elections of 2006 and 2008. *New Media & Society, 15*(1), 52–71. doi:10.1177/1461444812457332

Wilson, C., & Dunn, A. (2011). Digital media in the Egyptian revolution: Descriptive analyses from the Tahrir data set. *International Journal of Communication*, *5*, 1248–1272.

Wlezien, C., & Erikson, R. S. (2002). The timeline of presidential election campaigns. *The Journal of Politics*, *64*(04), 969–993. doi:10.1111/1468-2508.00159

Wolfsfeld, G., Segev, E., & Sheafer, T. (2013). Social Media and the Arab Spring. Politics Comes First. *The International Journal of Press/Politics*, *18*(2), 115–137. doi:10.1177/1940161212471716

Wolfsfeld, G., Segev, E., & Sheafer, T. (2013). Social media and the Arab Spring: Politics comes first. *The International Journal of Press/Politics*, *20*(10), 1–23.

Wright, S. (2012). Politics as usual? Revolution, normalization and a new agenda for online deliberation. *New Media & Society*, *14*(2), 244–261. doi:10.1177/1461444811410679

Wu, H. D., & Coleman, R. (2009). Advancing agenda-setting theory: The comparative strength and new contingent conditions of the two levels of agenda-setting effects. *Journalism & Mass Communication Quarterly*, *86*(4), 775–789. doi:10.1177/107769900908600404

Xenos, M., & Moy, P. (2007). Direct and differential effects of the internet on political and civic engagement. *Journal of Communication*, *57*(4), 704–718. doi:10.1111/j.1460-2466.2007.00364.x

Xenos, M., Vromen, A., & Loader, B. (2014). The great equalizer? Patterns of social media use and youth political engagement in three advanced democracies. *Information Communication and Society*, *17*(2), 151–167. doi:10.1080/1369118X.2013.871318

Xiao, M. (2011). *Research Report on Chinese Microbloggers' Behavior in 2010*. Beijing: Social Sciences Academic Press.

Yetkin, M. (2014, March 21). Turkish Twitter users defy Erdogan's ban. *Hürriyet Daily News*. Retrieved March 28, 2014, from http://www.hurriyetdailynews.com/turkish-twitter-users-defy-erdogans-ban.aspx?pageID=238&nID=63899&NewsCatID=409

Youmans, W., & York, J. (2012). Social media and the activist toolkit: User agreements, corporate interests, and the information infrastructure of modern social movements. *Journal of Communication*, *62*(2), 315–329. doi:10.1111/j.1460-2466.2012.01636.x

Yu, L., Asur, S., & Huberman, B. A. (2011). *What trends in Chinese social media.* arXiv preprint arXiv:1107.3522

Yu, G. (2011). *Zhongguo shehui yuqing niandu baogao 2011* [Chinese Society Public Opinion, Annual Report 2011]. Beijing: People's Daily Press.

Yunis, H. (1996). *Taming democracy: Models of political rhetoric in classical Athens*. Cornell University Press.

Yurdakul, M. (2014, April 3). Twitter yasağı kalktı. *Milliyet*. Retrieved August 8, 2014, from http://www.milliyet.com.tr/twitter-yasagi-kalkiyor-mu /gundem/detay/1861721/default.htm

Zalewski, P. (2014, May 6). Erdoğan turns on Gulenists' "parallel state" in battle for power. *Financial Times*. Retrieved August 8, 2014, from http://www.ft.com/cms/s/0/0e7a3854-cc98-11e3-ab9900144feabdc0.html#axzz3GOGlssxv

Zaller, J. (1992). *The nature and origins of mass opinion*. New York: Cambridge University Press. doi:10.1017/CBO9780511818691

Zappavigna, M. (2014). Enacting identity in microblogging through ambient affiliation. *Discourse and Communication*, *8*(2), 209–228. doi:10.1177/1750481313510816

Zhang, W., Seltzer, T., & Bichard, S. L. (2013). Two Sides of the Coin Assessing the Influence of Social Network Site Use During the 2012 US Presidential Campaign. *Social Science Computer Review*, *31*(5), 542–551. doi:10.1177/0894439313489962

Zúñiga, H. G., Jung, N., & Valenzuela, S. (2012). Social media use for news and individuals' social capital, civic engagement and political participation. *Journal of Computer-Mediated Communication*, *17*(3), 319–336. doi:10.1111/j.1083-6101.2012.01574.x

About the Contributors

Tomaž Deželan is Associate Professor of Political Science at the Faculty of Social Sciences at the University of Ljubljana, Slovenia, and a researcher at the Centre for Political Science Research at the same faculty. He is an associate researcher at the University of Edinburgh, School of Law, where he acts as a country expert in the Citsee project. His research interests include citizenship concepts, debates and regimes, new modes of governance, parliamentary cohesion, electoral studies, youth, gender and civil society. He has authored or co-authored more than 20 peer reviewed articles in international journals and scientific volumes and 3 scientific monographs. He has experience with international research projects and networks, either as co-responsible or as a researcher. Past projects he worked on have been funded by the Slovenian research agency, European Union's FP6 framework, European Science Foundation of the European Union and various other national agencies.

Igor Vobič is Assistant Professor of Journalism Studies at the Faculty of Social Sciences at the University of Ljubljana in Slovenia, and a researcher at the Social Communication Research Centre at the same faculty. His research interests include social communication in contemporary media environment, journalism and new media articulations, and online news production. He has a member of the editorial board of the journal Medijska istraživanja/Media Research and has recently published in Journalism Studies, Journalism Practice, Journalism, Convergence and Javnost–The Public.

* * *

Lázaro M. Bacallao-Pino is a postdoctoral fellow at the National Autonomous University of Mexico (Postdoctoral Fellowship Programme, UNAM). He earned his PhD in Sociology at the University of Zaragoza in 2012. His main research interests include communication and power relationships, as well associal movements, mainlytheir communication dimension and the use of ICTs.

Camelia-Mihaela Cmeciu is an associate professor in the Department of Cultural Anthropology and Communication Studies at the Faculty of Journalism and Communication Studies, University of Bucharest, Romania and a postdoctoral researcher at the Romanian Academy (Iasi Branch). Her research interests cover semiotics, organizational and political communication, advertising discourse and linguistics. She is the author of Strategii persuasive în discursul politic (Persuasive Strategies in Political Discourse, 2005, Universitas XXI, Iaşi, Romania) and Semiotici textuale (Textual Semiotics, 2011, Institutul European, Iaşi, Romania). Her work on political discourse, social semiotics and organizational discourse appears in academic journals like Semiotica, Public Relations Review, International Journal of Humanities and Social Science, Styles of Communication and Cultural Perspectives. Journal for Literary and British Cultural Studies in Romania.

Marta Pérez Escolar is a PhD student at the Faculty of Social Sciences and Communication, Catholic University of Murcia. Her research interests focus on cyber-activism, political participation, civic engagement, activism, social demonstrations and civil protests.

Helin Alagöz Gessler holds a Ph.D in EU Politics and International Relations from the EU Institute of Marmara University in Istanbul since 2012. She worked as lecturer and researcher at universities in Istanbul and Berlin. Currently, she is working as a lecturer at the Business and Information Technology School Berlin and conducting independent research.

Justin Holmes is an assistant professor of Political Science at the University of Northern Iowa. His research focuses on how people obtain and use information to form opinions about the political world, and is particularly interested in the intersection of communication technology and the psychology of opinion formation. He has published in a number of journals including Presidential Studies Quarterly and Political Psychology.

Shaohai Jiang is a PhD student from the department of communication at Texas A&M University. He received MA in Communication and New Media from City University of Hong Kong. Before his doctoral studies, he worked as a communication officer for Oxfam Hong Kong. He has a strong interest in new media, particularly how the Internet influences political communication and health communication. Specifically, he is interested in civic engagement and social media in China. His research also deals with how Internet use can help improve people's health outcome.

Alem Maksuti is a PhD candidate at the Faculty of Social Sciences, University of Ljubljana. His dissertation examines the idiosyncrasy of Slovenian election campaigns during the democratic post-communist period. His current areas of interest concentrate on the impact of Internet technologies on the transformation of Slovenian political actors' political communication practices. His broader research interests lie in the areas of political communication, political participation, political culture, and election campaigns. He has authored/co-authored one monograph, several scientific papers, articles published in indexed journals, as well as chapters on elections and political communication in Slovenia.

Ramona McNeal is an associate professor in the Department of Political Science at the University of Northern Iowa. Her chief research interests include e-government, telehealth, campaign finance reform and telecommunications policy. She also studies the impact of technology on participation, including its relationship to voting, elections, and public opinion. She has published work in a number of journals including Journal of Information Technology & Politics, Social Science Quarterly, Policy Studies Journal, Public Administration Review, Political Research Quarterly and State Politics and Policy Quarterly. She is a co-author of Digital Citizenship: The Internet, Society and Participation (MIT Press, 2007) with Karen Mossberger and Caroline Tolbert.

Maria Francesca Murru, PhD, is a Post-Doctoral researcher at Catholic University of Milan, Faculty of Political Sciences. She is currently working as a researcher at OssCom, an academic research centre for media and communication based at the same university. Her research fields include civic participation in online public spheres, media and children.

Stamatis Poulakidakos is a Senior Research Associate and Teaching Assistant at the Department of Communication and Media Studies of the National and Kapodistrian University of Athens.

Ashik Shafi is a second year doctoral student at Department of Communication at Wayne State University. He did his masters from Texas Tech University and worked as a newspaper reporter in Bangladesh. His research areas include political discussion on the Internet, new media journalism and media in the developing world.

Pantelis Vatikiotis is an Associate Professor of Sociology of Media in the Department of Media and Communication, Faculty of Communication, at Izmir University of Economics, Turkey. He received his degree in Sociology from Panteion University of Social and Political Sciences, Athens, Greece in 1997 and he did his postgraduate studies in Media and Communication at the University of Westminster, London in 2001. He received his PhD in Media Studies (Alternative/Grassroots Media Practices) from the University of Westminster in 2004. He has taught at the: University of Westminster, University of Ioannina, Panteion University, New York College of Athens, Business College of Athens, and he has worked in media industry as programmer/scheduler for SKAI TV Channel. In 2010 he joined Izmir University of Economics where he teaches in BA and MA programs. Since 2011 he is coordinator of the 'Erasmus Program' and coordinator of the MA program 'Media and Communication'. He is member of international Sociological and Media/Communication associations. His research interests cover the areas of social theory and media, political communication and culture, political economy of media, alternative media, collective action, globalization, new media and cyberculture. His publications include several book chapters and journal articles in international academic publications on the subjects of democratization of communication, public sphere and civil society, grassroots media practices, social movements, social media, and TV programming/scheduling.

Anastasia Veneti is a Lecturer in Marketing Communications at the Media School, Bournemouth University.

Lucia Vesnic-Alujevic is an independent researcher in the field of digital communications and online politics. After obtaining her PhD from Ghent University in 2011, she has worked as a Visiting Fellow at the Centre for European Studies and a postdoctoral researcher at the European Commission's Joint Research Centre. Her research interests include political communication, new technologies, online communication and political participation.

Fred Vultee is an associate professor of journalism in the Wayne State University Department of Communication.

Index

T

U

V

www.ingramcontent.com/pod-product-compliance
Lightning Source LLC
LaVergne TN
LVHW060418300926
849162LV00006B/1463